הגדה של פסח

the Rechnitz edition

ArtScroll Mesorah Series®

הגדה של פסח

HAGGADAH
Anthology

FROM TALMUDIC AND RABBINIC LITERATURE

by Rabbi Moshe Lieber
Edited, with an Overview by
Rabbi Nosson Scherman

the Rechnitz edition

The PESACH
THE LIVING EXODUS

with commentary and anecdotes

Published by

Mesorah Publications, ltd

ARTSCROLL MESORAH SERIES®

"THE PESACH HAGGADAH ANTHOLOGY" / THE LIVING EXODUS

Published by **MESORAH PUBLICATIONS, LTD.**
4401 Second Avenue / Brooklyn, N.Y 11232 / (718) 921-9000 / Fax: (718) 680-1875
e-mail: artscroll@mesorah.com

Distributed in Israel by SIFRIATI / A. GITLER
10 Hashomer Street / Bnei Brak 51361

Distributed in Europe by J. LEHMANN HEBREW BOOKSELLERS
20 Cambridge Terrace / Gateshead, Tyne and Wear / England NE8 1RP

Distributed in Australia and New Zealand by GOLD`S BOOK & GIFT SHOP
36 William Street / Balaclava 3183, Vic., Australia

Distributed in South Africa by KOLLEL BOOKSHOP
22 Muller Street / Yeoville 2198, Johannesburg, South Africa

Printed in the United States of America by
Noble Book Press Corp.
Custom bound by Sefercraft, Inc. / 4401 Second Avenue / Brooklyn N.Y. 11232

ISBN: 0-89906-393-4

Dedicated in honor of

ר׳ יצחק צבי בן שלמה שיחי׳
רבקה בת יצחק יעקב שתחי׳

Henry and Regina Rechnitz, עמו״ש

Born in Bendzin, Poland,

they represent a generation

that literally experienced the meaning of

מעבדות לחרות, from slavery to freedom.

They were privileged to establish and raise

three generations that continue

in the paths

of their own parents

שלמה ורבקה רכניץ ז״ל
יצחק יעקב ועטא רוס ז״ל

The Rechnitz Family
Los Angeles, California

Publisher's Preface

Every year before Pesach, people always are astounded that yet more commentaries on the Haggadah are being published. "What? Another Haggadah? We haven't nearly finished the last ten or twenty or thirty!"

Nevertheless, we publish this Haggadah with pride and we have no doubt that those who study it will understand very well that it is not "just another" Haggadah. Aptly entitled "The Living Exodus," this new anthology focuses on the Exodus not merely as a celebration of a seminal event in our history, not merely as a remembrance of the glories of the past, and not even as a harbinger of the long-awaited future redemption — but as a constant reality. In the words of the Haggadah itself, "In every generation, it is one's duty to regard himself as though he personally had gone out from Egypt."

Memories are less than realities; and for the Jew, the Exodus from Egypt is a *reality*, a reality that one recalls every day and relives at the Seder.

The Egyptian exile and Exodus showed Israel that it could not exist without its Maker's intervention, that nature was but a tool in the hand of its Wielder, and that Israel's new nationhood was as much an act of creation as the *ex nihilo* creation of heaven and earth. These concepts are fundamental to our faith and mission on earth — and these concepts are the unifying threads of this exceptional commentary to the Haggadah.

Rabbi Moshe Lieber distinguished himself as an outstanding thinker and anthologizer with his much admired **Pirkei Avos Treasury.** In this remarkable work, he continues where he left off. Skillfully and sensitively he weaves together many strands of commentary, and spices them with rich sprinklings of anecdotes and parables. Rabbi Lieber expresses his admiration for **Rabbi Joseph Elias**, whose original ArtScroll Haggadah remains a very popular classic, twenty years after its first appearance. It was an invaluable source for this work, as it has undoubtedly been for many others.

This work has been dedicated by **Mr. and Mrs. Bob Rechnitz and family** of Los Angeles, in honor of their parents. These are families, all three generations of them, that have fulfilled the challenge of keeping the Exodus alive and passing on its message from generation to generation. This dedication by Mr. and Mrs. Rechnitz is a magnificent tribute to their parents and a gift to the entire Jewish community.

Rabbi Jack Simcha Cohen, a dear friend of the Rechnitz family, has inspired many people with the beauty of Torah as a living, thriving way of life and call to greatness. We are grateful for his interest.

The beautiful and imaginative page design and layout is yet another example of the unexcelled artistry of our dear friend and colleague REB SHEAH BRANDER. He continues to outdo himself, volume after volume.

We are grateful also to the many people who contributed their skills to make this work possible. Among them are: REB AVRAHAM BIDERMAN, who guided the production step by step, MRS. UDI KLEIN and TOBY HEILBRUN, who expertly typeset this book, and MRS. FAIGIE WEINBAUM and MRS. MINDY STERN, who proofread masterfully. The jacket was skillfully designed and executed by REB ELI KROEN.

We are especially grateful to the **Trustees and Governors** of the **Mesorah Heritage Foundation.** In the relatively brief existence of the Foundation, they have made a major impact on Jewish life. They have been participants in the creation of a splendid chapter in Jewish history. We look forward to many more years of productive activity in the service of Hashem, His Torah, and His people.

Rabbi Meir Zlotowitz / Rabbi Nosson Scherman

Tishrei 5758 / October 1997

AN OVERVIEW: THE LIVING HAGGADAH

◆§ An Overview /
The Living Haggadah

I. The Partnership*

כָּל בַּר נַשׁ דְּאִשְׁתָּעִי בִּיצִיאַת מִצְרַיִם וּבְהַהוּא סִפּוּר חָדֵי בְּחֶדְוָה . . .
וְהקב"ה חָדֵי בְּהַאי סִפּוּר . . . וְאָמַר לוֹן "זִילוּ וְשִׁמְעוּ סִפּוּרָא דְּשִׁבְחָא דִּילִי
. . . וְאָז מִתְוַסֵּף לוֹ חֵילָא וּגְבוּרְתָּא לְעֵילָא וְיִשְׂרָאֵל בְּהַהוּא סִפּוּרָא יָהֲבֵי
חֵילָא לְמָארֵיהוֹן

Any person who discusses the Exodus from Egypt, and rejoices with that narrative . . . the Holy One, Blessed is He, also rejoices with that narrative . . . And He says to the Heavenly company, "Go and listen to the narrative of My praise . . ." At that time His power and strength increase On High, and by means of that narrative Israel provide strength to their Master (Zohar).

Shared Roles REUBEN AND SIMEON ARE BUSINESS PARTNERS. Reuben owns the premises and the machinery. He pays all the bills and salaries and has the sole right to close down the business, should he ever become dissatisfied with its performance. But Reuben never enters the plant. That is Simeon's role. He hires, purchases, manages, and sells. Neither the customers nor the employees ever see Reuben. Most of them do not even know there is such a person.

Who is the more important partner — the one with full financial control or the one with full operational control?

Who is the more important partner — the one with full financial control or the one with full operational control? The one who is never seen but can close down operations whenever he wishes, or the one who keeps the business running?

This is the sort of "partnership" that God ordained for the universe.

In a sense, this is the sort of "partnership" that God ordained for the universe. Every part of Creation, from the tiniest microbe to the mightiest star in a distant galaxy, exists because the Creator wills it so at every moment. Every aspect of their existence depends on what God ordains for them. As we say in our daily prayers, וּבְטוּבוֹ מְחַדֵּשׁ בְּכָל יוֹם תָּמִיד מַעֲשֵׂה בְרֵאשִׁית, *In His goodness [God] renews daily, perpetually,*

---

*This section of the Overview is based on *Daas Tevunos*.

the work of Creation. The universe is not an independently functioning machine; it depends on God's constant largess for its very existence.

But there is one exception. The Sages teach: הַכֹּל בִּידֵי שָׁמַיִם חוּץ מִיִּרְאַת שָׁמַיִם, *Everything is in the hands of Heaven, except for fear of Heaven* (*Berachos* 33b). Man alone has freedom of choice. Not the animal kingdom, not even the angels — only man. Before a soul was united with a body, it, too, had no free choice; only when it came to earth was it given the ability to choose whether it would do good or evil.

Man alone has freedom of choice. Not the animal kingdom, not even the angels — only man.

God goes further. Not only does He give man independence, He also gives him the power to determine the course of the "business" that we call the universe. In the *Song of Songs*, King Solomon has God saying of Israel, אַחַת הִיא יוֹנָתִי תַמָּתִי, *Unique is she, My constant dove, My perfect one* (6:9). The *Zohar* expounds that the word תַמָּתִי, *My perfect one*, should be interpreted as if it read תְּאוֹמָתִי, *My twin*. Israel is God's "twin," as it were, because both have the power to influence the course of Creation. This is Israel's greatness.

Righteous people who observe the commandments of the Torah are God's partners, as it were, because His wisdom has ordained that the perfection of His Creation — or the opposite — should depend on how well they approach His will. The narratives of the Torah show that virtue brings reward and sin brings punishment. When Israel obeys God, it is blessed with success and happiness; when it rebels, it brings woe and suffering upon itself. That theme runs throughout Scripture, and we would do well not to be deflected from it by the details of the narrative and the beauty of the Torah's expression. The rest of the world is affected, as well. As the Sages comment, if the nations of the world had realized how much they benefited when the Temple stood and the *Kohanim* performed its service, they would have mounted guards to prevent anyone from harming it.

The narratives of the Torah show that virtue brings reward and sin brings punishment.

BEFORE THE SOUL CAME TO EARTH TO JOIN ITS BODY, it was like the angels — a spiritual being that enjoyed proximity to the Source of all holiness — but its greatness, like that of the angels, was flawed. All the spiritual beings above *enjoyed* their heavenly bliss, but none had *earned* it, because they never had to cope with the adversity and temptation that go with life on earth. The body wants physical pleasure, the soul wants spiritual growth. The body wants to obey the dictates of its senses, the soul wants to obey the dictates of the Torah. When the soul completes its task on earth, it is not what it was when it joined its bodily host. In its lifetime on earth, it had been challenged

The Soul's Challenge

and enticed incessantly in a material environment where one must search long and hard for elusive sparks of holiness. If it had succeeded in overcoming the temptations and obstacles thrown up by life, it would have earned the spiritual reward that awaits it in the World to Come. If it had failed, it would have become sullied and diminished, and would have faced punishment.

The arena for this struggle was prepared in the generations from Creation until the Torah was given. The first twenty generations failed, so that Abraham was chosen to carry the burden of God's mission to humanity (see *Avos* 5:1). Israel became a nation during the Egyptian exile, and received its Divine charge when the Torah was given at Mount Sinai. From that time onward, the essence of world history has been the story of the nation's spiritual successes and failures.

From that time onward, the essence of world history has been the story of the nation's spiritual successes and failures.

The Sages state the dictum that גָּדוֹל הַמְצֻוֶּה וְעוֹשֶׂה מִמִּי שֶׁאֵינוֹ מְצֻוֶּה וְעוֹשֶׂה, *One who is commanded [to perform a commandment] and does so is greater than one who performs it without being commanded (Kiddushin 31a).* On the surface this seems puzzling. We would have thought that one who performs a commandment voluntarily is superior to one who is instructed to do so. *Tosafos* (ibid.) explains that it is natural for people to resist when they are *ordered* to do something; recalcitrance is an all too familiar human instinct. Volunteers have no such resistance mechanism, so it is easier for them to act, and therefore their reward is not so great.

Rabbi Moshe Chaim Luzzatto explains it differently, and applies the dictum specifically to the performance of commandments, not to secular pursuits. When a human being carries out God's command, he is serving his "Partner" by injecting a Divine spark into Creation. This can happen only when the deed is done according to the Torah's prescription; only then does the act have God's imprimatur. Two people can perform the Temple's sacrificial service — one a *Kohen* and one an Israelite. Because the *Kohen's* act is a mitzvah, it has all the cosmic implications of the performance of God's will. Not only has the Israelite failed to perform a mitzvah, his act is a sin.

Two people can perform the Temple's sacrificial service. Because the Kohen's act is a mitzvah, it has cosmic implications; the Israelite failed to perform a mitzvah, his act is a sin.

The point is that only God's command confers holiness on a deed. A Jew who eats matzah and *maror* on the Seder night pours holiness into the world. Let him do the same thing on any other night of the year and he has merely eaten supper. That is why a deed performed because God commanded it is greater than one done voluntarily. The Divine command invests the act with the power to change the world in ways perceptible only to God.

This power was not given to animals. Not even to angels. Only a Jew with the potency of the Torah, the sanctity of God's command, has such awesome ability. This privilege was granted to Israel at Mount Sinai, where God charged Israel to be מַמְלֶכֶת כֹּהֲנִים וְגוֹי קָדוֹשׁ, *a kingdom of priests and a holy nation (Exodus 19:6)*. That conferred royal authority on Israel, as it were, making them God's agents in maintaining His universe by carrying out His will, as He would express it in the Torah.

This attribute, like Creation itself, is renewed constantly. The people may backslide, but their potential and responsibility is immutable, just as the Torah itself is immutable. In charging Israel before his death, Moses told the people הַיּוֹם הַזֶּה נִהְיֵיתָ לְעָם , *on this day you became a people (Deuteronomy 27:9)*. That was a constant injunction: *on **this** day. **Every** day*. No matter where he is or when it is, a Jew must view himself as if he had just been given the Torah and invested with the royal prerogative to shape the world through his behavior.

No matter where he is or when it is, a Jew must view himself as if he had just been given the Torah.

II. Power of Renewal*

ALL OF THIS MAY BE INSPIRING, but, like all constants, it tends to grow stale. People crave newness. They fail to be excited by repetition, even when the repetition is as thrilling as a partnership with God Himself. How can we drag ourselves loose from the quicksand of habit? The Haggadah tries to provide the answer.

The New Moon and Time

At the beginning of his commentary to the Torah, *Rashi*, quoting the Sages, wonders why the Torah did not begin with the first commandment to the Jewish people, the commandment for the courts to declare the New Moon. The question implies that the entire Book of *Genesis* and the first eleven chapters of *Exodus* are incidental to the mission of Israel. Of all the 613 commandments, why should that of the New Moon have had such primacy?

Of all the 613 commandments, why should that of the New Moon have had such primacy?

Sforno explains straightforwardly. Until their last few weeks in Egypt, even though the progression of the Ten Plagues prevented the Egyptians from forcing them to work, Jews were still slaves, nominally and legally. A slave owns nothing. Even his time is not his own. The commandment of the New Moon was the symbol of Israel's newfound freedom, because it gave them authority over the calendar. No longer did their taskmasters own everything — from that moment onward, Jews were masters of their own time, just as they had taken possession of their bodies. As we say in *Kiddush Levanah,* the monthly

*This section of the Overview is based on *Ohr Gedalyahu*

Sanctification of the Moon, שֶׁהֵם עֲתִידִים לְהִתְחַדֵּשׁ כְּמוֹתָהּ, *[Jews] are destined to renew themselves, like [the moon].*

In a deeper sense, not only did Israel achieve personal freedom, they were given control over time itself, because they, through their courts, declared when months would begin and thereby assumed authority over everything relating to the calendar.

The New Moon implied that God had conferred upon Israel the power of renewal.

That this new Jewish status was stated by means of the New Moon implied that God had conferred upon Israel the power of renewal. Just as the cycle of months and years always renews itself, so Israel would always be able to renew itself.

Time is a function of nature, like most things in our experience, and nature has a deadening effect. It is predictable. It is measurable. It convinces people that they have no control over their destinies. It is the opposite of rejuvenation. The Egyptian kingdom, itself, symbolized nature. One of its gods was the Nile. The land's prosperity was based on the river's "automatic" overflow. Cosmetics were invented in Egypt — and were worn by the *men*, who were virtually freed from work by the availability of slaves and the Nile's largess. There was no need to pray for rain. When Moses spoke to Pharaoh about God's command to release the Jews for only a few days of worship, the king feigned shock: "Who is HASHEM that I should heed His voice?" (*Exodus* 5:2).

Renewal

Their very first mitzvah represented the principle that Israel would always be fresh and new.

THE FIRST STEP OF THE REDEMPTION was to declare by means of the New Moon that time itself had been redeemed from the powerful grip of slothful nature. Not only would Israel assume control over the calendar, it would assimilate the lesson that it had the power of renewal; just as the moon wanes every month until it disappears completely, but always renews itself, so Israel would never be eclipsed permanently. History is filled with periods when Israel waned and seemed to be doomed, but it always returned to its former glory. So it was that their very first mitzvah represented the principle that Israel would always be fresh and new, thanks to its allegiance to, and study of, the Torah.

This seems strange, however, because the renewal of the moon is hardly a miraculous, cosmic event. The so-called "renewal" is an automatic process, and its timing can be calculated by any schoolboy, using a simple mathematical formula. If so, why do we recite the Sanctification of the Moon every month during its early phases? The *Talmidei Rabbeinu Yonah*, one of the classic early commentators, explains that the blessing is appropriate since it *seems* to the human eye to be a renewal. The answer itself requires an explanation, because, appearances to the contrary, every intelligent person still knows that the phases of the moon are the same every month, like clockwork!

The Continuum

THIS CAN BE UNDERSTOOD BASED ON A PRINCIPLE enunciated by *Maharal* (*Gevuros Hashem* ch. 46). The Torah speaks of the Three Pilgrimage Festivals as agricultural events: Pesach is the festival of spring, Shavuos the festival of the harvest, and Succos the festival when the crops are gathered in from the field, after the hot, dry summer (see *Exodus* 34:18, 22; *Deuteronomy* ch. 16). Clearly, these are hardly the sole or even the major reasons for the festivals; in fact, in the context of Israel's spiritual mission on earth, they even seem to be rather trivial. Since the Torah itself identifies the Pilgrimage Festivals as the times of redemption, of the giving of the Torah, and of the commemoration of the shelter God gave the Jewish people in the harsh Wilderness, how can they be described as agricultural celebrations?

Natural phenomena must be understood as the end result of a continuum beginning with God, Who created and renews the life of the universe constantly. The Torah was the blueprint of Creation, and just as a builder must translate a blueprint into steel, brick, and mortar, so the physical requirements of a commandment are translations of metaphysical concepts into acts and artifacts that human beings can deal with, even if they cannot understand how the prescribed deeds have efficacy.

Natural phenomena must be understood as the end result of a continuum beginning with God, Who created and renews the life of the universe constantly.

As a simple illustration, one may compare the physical fulfillment of a commandment with its philosophical underpinnings, as discussed by the classic commentators over the centuries. It is as if the commandment has a dual identity. On the one hand, the *mitzvah* with all its minutiae, as elaborated in the Oral Law and codified in the *Shulchan Aruch*, must actually be performed. On the other hand, it is replete with meaning that speaks to the mind and heart. None of this profundity, however, is a substitute for performance. Someone who absorbs all the literature about Pesach, but does not eat the requisite amount of matzah, prepared in the prescribed manner, is a sinner, plain and simple. Furthermore, even commentators who sought to provide rational explanations for the commandments, such as *Rambam, Kuzari,* and *Chinuch*, stressed that they had not plumbed God's wisdom. They attempted only rationales that might satisfy limited human intelligence.

Someone who absorbs all the literature about Pesach, but does not eat the requisite amount of matzah, is a sinner.

Similarly, there is a detailed body of halachah that regulates the ways in which children must honor their parents. In a sense, one may view these laws as outgrowths of the love people feel for their mothers and fathers, but that is not the entirety of the commandment. What are the yet higher spiritual values that underlie such love? Why did God inculcate such instinctive love into human beings? Whether or not we know the answers, they are embodied in the Divinely ordained laws of the commandment.

When the angels argued that it was sacrilegious to give the Torah to ordinary, flawed human beings (*Shabbos* 88a), they proposed to interpret the laws of the Torah, such as honor to parents and eating matzah, on their own higher level. But their argument against Moses was rejected because the Torah applied also to flesh-and-blood people, and so had to be transmitted to Israel. Thus, the earthly manifestation of a commandment may be understood as the physical embodiment of God's own wisdom, wisdom that is infinitely beyond human comprehension, but that can be manifested in the performance of the *mitzvah*.

Tangible Manifestation

The festivals are the tangible manifestations of profound spiritual truths.

IN THIS VEIN, *MAHARAL* EXPLAINS that the festivals are the tangible manifestations of profound spiritual truths. The earth begins its productive year with springtime, when the frigid land awakens from a winter of inactivity, ready to pour out its generosity to the people and animals awaiting its summer of growth. That period of productivity is nurtured by lengthening days with sunlight that caresses the growing new crop until it is ready to be harvested. Finally, there is the joyous time when summer's work is done and the finished, threshed crop is ready to be gathered into silos and homes to provide nourishment and prosperity for the long nights and dour days of winter. These three periods are cause for celebration and thanksgiving to the Creator for His blessings.

There is a higher necessity of life, one that transcends the laws of nature and agriculture — the existence of the Jewish people, without whose dedication to the Torah the universe could not exist. The Jewish nation came into being in the month of springtime, with the miracles of Pesach. The Torah commands us always to remember the day when God took Israel from Egypt (*Exodus* 13:3), because that was the key moment of the national creation. The promise of that day came to fruition on Shavuos, when Israel accepted the Torah. Shavuos has no defined calendar date — it is the fiftieth day from Pesach — because it is inextricably bound up with Pesach; without the acceptance of the Torah, Israel had no justification to be freed. Finally comes Succos, commemorating God's "ingathering" of Israel into His clouds of glory and protection. Just as a harvest is truly complete only when a farmer brings it in from the field, so God's harvest of Israel from exile was climaxed when He brought His nation into the shelter of His glory, in the form of the clouds that protected and guided it in the Wilderness.

God's harvest of Israel from exile was climaxed when He brought His nation into the shelter of His glory.

When we celebrate milestones in the earth year, we are also symbolizing more significant milestones in the cosmic year. Earth is a metaphor for heaven.

In explaining why the Torah promises material rather than spiritual rewards (see *Leviticus* ch. 26 and *Deuteronomy* ch. 28), *Sh'lah* pursues a similar line of thought. When we see a human eye, it should make us realize that God's eye sees everything. The Sages use rain and dew as metaphors for God's life-giving mercy, just as moisture and precipitation make life possible on earth. Similarly, such rewards as life, prosperity, security, fertility, and health are used as metaphors for the greater spiritual rewards in this world and surely in the World to Come.

R' TZADDOK HAKOHEN ELABORATES ON THE TEACHING of the Sages that the entire world was created for the sake of a God-fearing person (*Berachos* 6b). It means that God filled the world with phenomena that one can utilize to recognize His Presence and thereby increase one's devotion to Him. The prophet Isaiah urges us to raise our eyes to the heavens and see Who created all this (*Isaiah* 40:26). Seen with honest eyes — and especially as scientists learn more and more about the incredible vastness of space — can anyone honestly maintain that the galaxies came into being by accident, from nothing? So it is with everything around us. God gave them to man as a means of increasing his awareness and fear of God. King David sings: מָלְאָה הָאָרֶץ קִנְיָנֶךָ, *the earth is full of Your possessions* (*Psalms* 104:24). Homiletically, Chassidic masters have rendered the passage *the earth is full of ways to possess You*, i.e., we are surrounded by experiences and sights that help us "possess" knowledge of God.

To Observe and to See

As scientists learn more and more about the incredible vastness of space — can anyone honestly maintain that the galaxies came into being by accident, from nothing?

Without such aids — and, of course, the self-discipline to take advantage of them, it would be extremely difficult for man to keep God always in his consciousness. After all, His Presence is hidden. Scientific, media, and intellectual establishments deny it. Man's animal nature is hardly conducive to holiness. It is all too easy to forget that there is a God. Unless God had given us the means with which to reinforce our knowledge of His existence, it would have been unreasonable for the Torah to command such awareness. We can be commanded to perform *acts*, such as eating matzah or eating in a succah; we can be commanded to *refrain* from acts, such as eating forbidden foods or desecrating the Sabbath. But God would not simply command that we recognize His existence, without providing the tools to make such recognition possible.

God would not simply command that we recognize His existence, without providing the tools to make such recognition possible.

Therefore, the Ten Commandments begin not with a formal commandment, but a *statement*: *I am* HASHEM, *your God* (*Exodus 20:2*). How can one forge into his being the firm belief in God? The means are given in the second commandment, that it is forbidden to give recognition to other gods. *R' Tzaddok* interprets the word "gods" in its broader sense, as "powers." Man has many personal powers, such as the use of his five senses and his ability to move about, create, and accomplish. The Torah forbids man to think of these powers as independent forces that are inherently his. He should train himself to recognize that whatever he is and whatever he possesses were given him by God, and that they may be used only as God wishes.

The world around us is filled with gifts and forces — food and drink, thunder and lightning, oceans and mountains, resources that can be used for good and for ill. If they are enjoyed and used with consciousness that they were created by God, they become means to strengthen the conviction that I am HASHEM your God.

If they are enjoyed and used with consciousness that they were created by God, they become means to strengthen the conviction that I am HASHEM *your God.*

For this reason, the Sages instituted the recitation of blessings for various kinds of pleasure and for many of the natural wonders of the world. These blessings are constant reminders that God is the Creator and Giver. Conversely they taught that whoever enjoys this world without blessing the One Who gave it is guilty of misappropriating Divine property for his personal use (*Berachos* 40b). Thus, in effect, the first two of the Ten Commandments summarize the two major tenets of the Jew's existence. *I am* HASHEM — and the way for you to reinforce this statement of fact is by never taking any talent, enjoyment, force, or resource for granted. We must always acknowledge its origin (*Tzidkas HaTzaddik* 232).

Message of the Moon

The first commandment to the nation as a whole was an injection of hope.

IN EGYPT, THE COMMANDMENT OF THE NEW MOON, the first commandment to the nation as a whole, was an injection of hope that, in a sense, made the Ten Commandments possible. Jews had become the prisoners of time, of habit, of an oppression that had robbed them of the ability to be fresh and creative. Then came the new commandment. You are to take control of the calendar. You are to reclaim for yourselves the vision that enabled your forefathers to recognize the presence of God in a world where He had been overshadowed by the worship of heavenly bodies and earthly artifacts.

Until then mankind had come full circle from God's vision for the world, the vision He was to proclaim once again when He would give the Ten Commandments to Israel. Instead of recognizing that the sun was a daily reminder of god's power, and food a constant witness to His mercy, man began to worship the sun and the sheep as gods.

Five centuries before the Exodus, Abraham had turned from his father's idol factory and found God in the world. As a child, he had recognized that "The mansion cannot exist without a Master!" That was one of history's greatest examples of looking at a stale reality with fresh eyes. Abraham became a pioneer. He looked at the sun and saw its Creator. He fed travelers and exhorted them to thank the God Who created food for them. Though he remained a lonely, if respected, figure, he was able to produce an Isaac and a Jacob. The family became a nation that, despite the slavery and degradation of a 210-year exile in Egypt, still had the inner strength to respond to the call of Moses and Aaron. And when God commanded them to renew themselves, they responded by following Him faithfully into an unknown Wilderness, where they found the Mountain of God.

Abraham became a pioneer. He looked at the sun and saw its Creator.

When God commanded them to renew themselves, they responded by following Him faithfully.

THE HAGGADAH PROCLAIMS THAT EVERY JEW must consider himself as if he were one of those who left Egypt. The narrative, the matzah, the bitter herbs, the Four Cups, the *mitzvah* to recline, the declaration that the more one speaks about the Exodus, the more praiseworthy one is — all of these contribute to the personalization, to the immediacy, of the Exodus. Many communities have a variety of customs to re-enact the Exodus and elaborate on the plagues and the other miracles of the Exodus. These, too, are devices to make people feel as if they were reliving the event.

In fact, the widespread custom to discuss ingenious halachic and homiletical interpretations of the text of the Haggadah often misses the point. The Haggadah's statement that it is praiseworthy to elaborate on the Exodus is designed to make participants in the Seder bring the Exodus alive, to make it a real experience, rather than a historical commemoration. The main topic of discussion should be the miracles and how they affect us to this day.

The Haggadah's Answer

The main topic of discussion should be the miracles and how they affect us to this day.

III. Back to the Source

Meaning of Redemption

THE EXODUS IS CALLED A גְּאוּלָה, *REDEMPTION*. The Hebrew word גאל has two connotations. According to *Malbim*, it implies that the redeemer has a personal closeness to the one he is helping, and therefore a responsibility to redeem him from his predicament (*Leviticus* 25:42; *Isaiah* 35:9). In this context, God redeemed Israel from Egypt because He felt a "familial responsibility" to do so, as it were. Indeed, when God sent Moses to Egypt, He said, *My firstborn son is Israel* (*Exodus* 4:22).

The word גאל implies that the redeemed thing is being returned to its original state.

The word גאל also has another connotation. It implies that the redeemed thing, after having had its status changed, is being returned to its original state. For example, in giving the law of the Jubilee Year, when sold properties return to their original ancestral owner, the Torah states, גְּאֻלָּה תִּתְּנוּ לָאָרֶץ, *you shall provide redemption for the land* (*Leviticus* 25:24). The land had been assigned to a particular owner, who had chosen to sell it, but the Jubilee Year *redeems* it and brings it back to the one for whom it had been intended.

In light of the above, the redemption from Egypt had a dual nature: God exercised His responsibility to save the nation that was close to Him. And, in the process, He brought Israel back to its original nature, as the children of the Patriarchs and the Matriarchs.

In the process, He brought Israel back to its original nature, as the children of the Patriarchs and the Matriarchs.

The people renewed themselves by returning to the vitality of their ancestors. They had been *imprisoned* by time; now they rose up and became the *masters* of time. As the vehicle of the redemption, God chose to bring the Ten Plagues upon Egypt, thus displaying to the scoffing Pharaoh and his doubting minions that He, Hashem, was indeed the Master of nature. He made it, and He could change it, whenever it suited His plan to do so.

Maharal comments that the Pesach evening ritual is called Seder, which means Order, because miracles are not haphazard; God performs them with a preordained, thought out order. The commentators agree that, as the Torah itself makes clear, the plagues — as a group and individually — were designed to proclaim God's sovereignty unmistakably.

At the conclusion of the Exodus narrative, the Haggadah proclaims:

> *In every generation, it is one's duty to regard himself as though* **he personally** *had gone out from Egypt . . . It was not only our fathers whom the Holy One, Blessed is He, redeemed from slavery; we, too, were redeemed with them.*

The redemption continues. It is daily. Constant.

It began with the call to renewal. It plucked Israel out of its sloth of accepting what was and exhorted it to look to the heavens and see how the moon came back after having disappeared.

And what about those Jews who refused the call to see the universe as a means to remember that God was everywhere? They remained in Egypt; as the head of the household tells the Wicked Son, *"had he been there, he would not have been redeemed."* Precisely. "Redemption" implies that God is close and that the one He redeems will go back to his pristine origins — but the Wicked Son does not feel the closeness. He prefers to remain locked in the chains of habit, of public opinion, of an unwillingness to look beneath the surface, of an adamant refusal to acknowledge that there is Giver, a Creator, a Redeemer. It was not God Who rejected the Wicked Son and his ilk from redemption; it was they who rejected God. They chose to remain with the old, so they could not be renewed.

For us, the Haggadah is a living narrative of our own redemption, because the redemption from Egypt never ended. In the year 2448, it brought our ancestors back to their origins, and it has been doing the same every year since.

Rabbi Nosson Scherman

Tishrei 5758 / October 1997

The redemption continues. It is daily. Constant. It plucked Israel out of its sloth of accepting what was and exhorted it to look to the heavens and see how the moon came back after having disappeared.

For us, the Haggadah is a living narrative of our own redemption.

הגדה של פסח

The PESACH

THE LIVING EXODUS

HAGGADAH

Anthology

בְּדִיקַת חָמֵץ

The *chametz* search is initiated with the recitation of the following blessing:

בָּרוּךְ אַתָּה יהוה, אֱלֹהֵינוּ מֶלֶךְ הָעוֹלָם, אֲשֶׁר קִדְּשָׁנוּ בְּמִצְוֹתָיו, וְצִוָּנוּ עַל בִּעוּר חָמֵץ.

Upon completion of the *chametz* search, the *chametz* is wrapped well and set aside to be burned the next morning and the following declaration is made. The declaration must be understood in order to take effect; one who does not understand Aramaic text may recite it in English, Yiddish or any other language. Any *chametz* that will be used for that evening's supper or the next day's breakfast or for any other purpose prior to the final removal of *chametz* the next morning is not included in this declaration.

כָּל חֲמִירָא וַחֲמִיעָא דְּאִכָּא בִרְשׁוּתִי, דְּלָא חֲמִתֵּהּ וּדְלָא בְעַרְתֵּהּ וּדְלָא יְדַעְנָא לֵהּ, לִבָּטֵל וְלֶהֱוֵי הֶפְקֵר כְּעַפְרָא דְאַרְעָא:

◆§ The Search for *Chametz*

At nightfall of Erev Pesach, the 14th of Nissan, the search for *chametz* is held, in all places where *chametz* might have been brought during the year.[1]

The Torah requires that we remove all *chametz* from our possession before Pesach. Theoretically this requirement may be fulfilled in one of two ways — either through a declaration of renunciation of ownership of all *chametz* in our possession (*bittul*) or through physically disposing of it (*biur*). In practice both methods are em- ployed. The Sages feared that if one were to rely on *bittul* alone, the renunciation might be done without sufficient sincerity and would therefore be invalid, leaving the *chametz* in the possession of its owner. They were also concerned that if we were to keep *chametz* physically in our homes, we might forget ourselves and eat it, since we are accustomed to eating *chametz* all year round. The Sages therefore required us to search for and physically dispose of all *chametz* in our homes. Although all known *chametz* is thus removed from our possession, the declaration of renunciation is made anyway, to cover any *chametz* that may have been overlooked in the search.[2]

---

1. **Clean Money.** One must check the pockets of clothing in case *chametz* may have been put there (*Rema*, O.C. 433:11). *Shelah*, based on the concept that the search for *chametz* symbolizes an introspective spiritual stocktaking, comments that one ''searches one's pockets'' to be sure that one has no money earned through illicit means, such as dishonest business practices, chicanery or shortchanging employees or the like. Also, one should determine that any business dealings were arranged in such a way that they would involve no forbidden interest payments.

2. **In Charge of God's Agenda.** Since it is forbidden to benefit from *chametz* during Pesach, it has no value and is halachically ownerless. Nevertheless, its ostensible owner is responsible for it, and is held liable for its possession as if it were actually his. This teaches us that people must sometimes take responsibility even for things that are technically not theirs. A person who has the ability to support Torah endeavors, but fails to do so, cannot absolve himself of the responsibility by claiming that the institution or project is not his. He is considered to have actually undermined the strength of the Torah (*R' Moshe Feinstein*).

Even though one may fulfill his Biblical obligation by simply nullifying his *chametz*, nonetheless he must dispose of it physically. This teaches us that not only must one emotionally nullify the lure of sin and commit himself to a virtuous future, but he must also act to translate that commitment into reality (*Beis Avraham*).

THE SEARCH FOR CHAMETZ

The *chametz* search is initiated with the recitation of the following blessing:

Blessed are You, HASHEM, our God, King of the universe, Who has sanctified us with His commandments and commanded us concerning the removal of *chametz.*

Upon completion of the *chametz* search, the *chametz* is wrapped well and set aside to be burned the next morning and the following declaration is made. The declaration must be understood in order to take effect; one who does not understand Aramaic text may recite it in English, Yiddish or any other language. Any *chametz* that will be used for that evening's supper or the next day's breakfast or for any other purpose prior to the final removal of *chametz* the next morning is not included in this declaration.

Any *chametz* which is in my possession which I did not see, and remove, nor know about, shall be nullified and become ownerless, like the dust of the earth.

During the days before the search, the house should be thoroughly cleaned. Any *chametz* that is to be sold to a non-Jew should be put away in a safe, segregated place; *chametz* for the next morning's breakfast should likewise be set aside in a secure place.

It is customary to put ten pieces of bread throughout the house, to be found during the search. This is done in order to ensure that the person carrying out the search will truly try to find something, and not just go through the motions of looking. Another reason for this custom is that if someone would not find any *chametz* at all, he might forget in the morning to recite the required declaration, which is usually done in conjunction with the burning of the *chametz*. However, even if this custom is not observed, and one finds nothing during the search, the search and its blessing were not in vain; the commandment is to *search* for *chametz*, not to *find* it.[1]

The blessing recited before the search mentions the *disposing of chametz*; it does not speak of a search. This is because the purpose of the search for *chametz* is to dispose of any that may be found (*Mishnah Berurah* 432 §2).[2]

A candle must be used to carry out the search.

---

1. **Agents of Iniquity.** Since the search for *chametz* may be said to allude to the internal search to ferret out and dispose of all spiritual impurity, we place ten pieces of *chametz* to symbolize the ten agents of sin, as enumerated by the Sages (*Nedarim* 32b): two hands, two legs, two eyes, two ears, the sex organ and the mouth.

◆§ **Toil Rewarded.** *R' Levi Yitzchak of Berditchev* was famous as the defender of the Jewish people par excellence. Once, after the search for *chametz*, he recited the prayer some say after the blowing of the shofar: "May it be Your will that the angels who emerge from קשר"ק (an acronym for the different shofar sounds) rise up to Your holy throne and plead on our behalf." "On the eve of Pesach," explained the Berditchever, "קשר"ק stands for קֵרְצוּף, *scraping;* שְׁפְשׁוּף, *scrubbing;* רְחִיצָה, *washing;* נִקּוּי, *cleaning.* May the merit of the backbreaking toil of Jewish women to prepare for Pesach be a source of merit for all Jews!"

2. **Leaven of the Soul.** The Talmud (*Berachos* 17a) refers to the Evil Inclination as the "leaven in the dough." Just as leaven causes dough to rise, so the Evil Inclination incites man to sin. Furthermore, just as leaven sours dough, so sin leaves a negative impact on man's soul. *Alshich* suggests that the numerical value of פְּגִימָה, *imperfection*, 138, is the same as that of חָמֵץ (chametz), because sin causes flaws in the soul.

Chida's prayers after the search and the burning of the *chametz* allude to this: "May You enable us to

בִּעוּר חָמֵץ

The following declaration, which includes all *chametz* without exception, is to be made after the burning of leftover *chametz*. It should be recited in a language which one understands. When Passover begins on Saturday night, this declaration is made on Saturday morning. Any *chametz* remaining from the Saturday morning meal, is flushed down the drain before the declaration is made.

כָּל חֲמִירָא וַחֲמִיעָא דְּאִכָּא בִרְשׁוּתִי, דַּחֲזִתֵּהּ וּדְלָא חֲזִתֵּהּ, דַּחֲמִתֵּהּ וּדְלָא חֲמִתֵּהּ, דְּבִעַרְתֵּהּ וּדְלָא בִעַרְתֵּהּ, לִבָּטֵל וְלֶהֱוֵי הֶפְקֵר כְּעַפְרָא דְאַרְעָא.

עֵרוּב תַּבְשִׁילִין

It is forbidden to prepare on Yom Tov for the next day even if that day is the Sabbath. If, however, Sabbath preparations were started before Yom Tov began, they may be continued on Yom Tov. *Eruv Tavshilin* constitutes this preparation. A *matzah* and any cooked food (such as fish, meat, or an egg) are set aside on the day before Yom Tov to be used on the Sabbath and the blessing is recited followed by the declaration [made in a language understood by the one making the *Eruv*]. If the first days of Passover fall on Thursday and Friday, an *Eruv Tavshilin* must be made on Wednesday. In Eretz Yisrael, where only one day Yom Tov is in effect, the *Eruv* is omitted.

בָּרוּךְ אַתָּה יהוה אֱלֹהֵינוּ מֶלֶךְ הָעוֹלָם, אֲשֶׁר קִדְּשָׁנוּ בְּמִצְוֹתָיו, וְצִוָּנוּ עַל מִצְוַת עֵרוּב.

בַּהֲדֵין עֵרוּבָא יְהֵא שָׁרֵא לָנָא לַאֲפוּיֵי וּלְבַשּׁוּלֵי וּלְאַטְמוּנֵי וּלְאַדְלוּקֵי שְׁרָגָא וּלְתַקָּנָא וּלְמֶעְבַּד כָּל צָרְכָּנָא, מִיּוֹמָא טָבָא לְשַׁבְּתָא לָנָא וּלְכָל יִשְׂרָאֵל הַדָּרִים בָּעִיר הַזֹּאת.

seek out and discover the spiritual diseases we have contracted as a result of the insidious counsel of our Evil Inclination. Just as we have removed the *chametz* from our homes and have burned it, so, dear God, allow us always to eradicate the Evil Inclination from our midst for all the days of our life. May we merit to cleave closely to our Good Inclination. . . .''

Every person has his own area of spiritual darkness, which he must fight and eradicate. This battle is so crucial that one's Evil Inclination will allow him some degree of peripheral spiritual success, as long as he ignores the focal point of his personal spiritual battle. For example, an individual's personal flaw may be excessive greed, which, naturally, will tend to impair his spiritual growth in many ways. The Evil Inclination will allow him to advance in various areas, knowing that his basic character flaw will always be a drag on him. The disposal of *chametz* is symbolic of this idea. Just as the smallest bit of *chametz* can sour an entire batch of dough, so one's particular spiritual leaven can induce spiritual decline, if left unchecked (*Nesivos Shalom*).

BURNING THE CHAMETZ

The following declaration, which includes all *chametz* without exception, is to be made after the burning of leftover *chametz*. It should be recited in a language which one understands. When Passover begins on Saturday night, this declaration is made on Saturday morning. Any *chametz* remaining from the Saturday morning meal, is flushed down the drain before the declaration is made.

Any *chametz* which is in my possession, which I did or did not see, which I did or did not remove, shall be nullified and become ownerless, like the dust of the earth.

ERUV TAVSHILIN

It is forbidden to prepare on Yom Tov for the next day even if that day is the Sabbath. If, however, Sabbath preparations were started before Yom Tov began, they may be continued on Yom Tov. *Eruv Tavshilin* constitutes this preparation. A *matzah* and any cooked food (such as fish, meat, or an egg) are set aside on the day before Yom Tov to be used on the Sabbath and the blessing is recited followed by the declaration [made in a language understood by the one making the *Eruv*]. If the first days of Passover fall on Thursday and Friday, an *Eruv Tavshilin* must be made on Wednesday.
In Eretz Yisrael, where only one day Yom Tov is in effect, the *Eruv* is omitted.

Blessed are You, HASHEM, our God, King of the universe, Who has sanctified us with His commandments and has commanded us concerning the commandment of Eruv.

Through this Eruv may we be permitted to bake, cook, fry, insulate, kindle flame, prepare for and do anything necessary on the festival for the sake of the Sabbath — for ourselves and for all Jews who live in this city.

A flashlight is recommended for places that cannot be reached safely or effectively with a candle.[1]

After the search, the master of the house makes the *Kol Chamira* declaration, nullifying any *chametz* that might have been overlooked in the search. One who does not understand Aramaic should recite it in a language he understands.

All *chametz* that was found during the search should be put in a safe place until morning, when it will be burned, along with any *chametz* left over from breakfast. If a person has too much *chametz* to be burned easily, part of it may be destroyed by

---

1. **Spiritual Spotlight.** Man's God-given soul is the lamp that provides illumination for him to find his path through life, avoiding the falsehoods and impurities of the environment. Furthermore, just as one searches in darkness by means of a candle, so God searches man's thoughts by employing the human soul as His lamp: *A man's soul is the lamp of HASHEM, which searches the chambers of one's innards* (Proverbs 20:27). On the eve of Pesach, as we prepare for true freedom, we search every nook and cranny for *chametz* as a symbol of our personal search of even the smallest vestige of spiritual impurity (*Chochmah U'Mussar*).

הדלקת הנרות

The candles are lit and the following blessings are recited.
When Yom Tov falls on the Sabbath, the words in parentheses are added.

בָּרוּךְ אַתָּה יהוה אֱלֹהֵינוּ מֶלֶךְ הָעוֹלָם, אֲשֶׁר קִדְּשָׁנוּ בְּמִצְוֹתָיו, וְצִוָּנוּ לְהַדְלִיק נֵר שֶׁל (שַׁבָּת וְשֶׁל) יוֹם טוֹב.

Some women do not recite the following blessing now, but wait until *Kiddush*.

בָּרוּךְ אַתָּה יהוה אֱלֹהֵינוּ מֶלֶךְ הָעוֹלָם, שֶׁהֶחֱיָנוּ וְקִיְּמָנוּ וְהִגִּיעָנוּ לַזְּמַן הַזֶּה.

It is customary to recite the following prayer after the kindling.
The words in brackets are included as they apply.

יְהִי רָצוֹן לְפָנֶיךָ, יהוה אֱלֹהַי וֵאלֹהֵי אֲבוֹתַי, שֶׁתְּחוֹנֵן אוֹתִי [וְאֶת אִישִׁי, וְאֶת בָּנַי, וְאֶת בְּנוֹתַי, וְאֶת אָבִי, וְאֶת אִמִּי] וְאֶת כָּל קְרוֹבַי; וְתִתֶּן לָנוּ וּלְכָל יִשְׂרָאֵל חַיִּים טוֹבִים וַאֲרוּכִים; וְתִזְכְּרֵנוּ בְּזִכְרוֹן טוֹבָה וּבְרָכָה; וְתִפְקְדֵנוּ בִּפְקֻדַּת יְשׁוּעָה וְרַחֲמִים; וּתְבָרְכֵנוּ בְּרָכוֹת גְּדוֹלוֹת; וְתַשְׁלִים בָּתֵּינוּ; וְתַשְׁכֵּן שְׁכִינָתְךָ בֵּינֵינוּ. וְזַכֵּנִי לְגַדֵּל בָּנִים וּבְנֵי בָנִים חֲכָמִים וּנְבוֹנִים, אוֹהֲבֵי יהוה, יִרְאֵי אֱלֹהִים, אַנְשֵׁי אֱמֶת, זֶרַע קֹדֶשׁ, בַּיהוה דְּבֵקִים, וּמְאִירִים אֶת הָעוֹלָם בַּתּוֹרָה וּבְמַעֲשִׂים טוֹבִים, וּבְכָל מְלֶאכֶת עֲבוֹדַת הַבּוֹרֵא. אָנָּא שְׁמַע אֶת תְּחִנָּתִי בָּעֵת הַזֹּאת, בִּזְכוּת שָׂרָה וְרִבְקָה וְרָחֵל וְלֵאָה אִמּוֹתֵינוּ, וְהָאֵר נֵרֵנוּ שֶׁלֹּא יִכְבֶּה לְעוֹלָם וָעֶד, וְהָאֵר פָּנֶיךָ וְנִוָּשֵׁעָה. אָמֵן.

---

other means prior to the burning.

Chametz may be eaten until about 2½ hours before noon, but the exact time varies according to the place and the time of year. The elimination of *chametz* from one's possession must be completed within the next hour. After the burning, a second declaration is recited. This time, however, we nullify any and all *chametz* in our possession, even that

which was not covered by the first *Kol Chamira* (i.e., the *chametz* that had been set aside for eating or selling). This declaration thus brings about the total removal of *chametz* from our possession.

After the burning of the *chametz*, some people recite a prayer from the *AriZal*, asking, "Just as I remove *chametz* from my house and possession, so may You, HASHEM, remove the spirit of impurity from the earth, and our Evil

LIGHTING THE CANDLES

The candles are lit and the following blessings are recited. When Yom Tov falls on the Sabbath, the words in parentheses are added.

Blessed are You, HASHEM, our God, King of the universe, Who has sanctified us with His commandments and commanded us to kindle the flame of the (Sabbath and the) festival.

Some women do not recite the following blessing now, but wait until Kiddush.

Blessed are You, HASHEM, our God, King of the universe, Who has kept us alive, sustained us, and brought us to this season.

It is customary to recite the following prayer after the kindling.
The words in brackets are included as they apply.

May it be Your will, HASHEM, my God and God of my forefathers, that You show favor to me [my husband, my sons, my daughters, my father, my mother] and all my relatives; and that You grant us and all Israel a good and long life; that You remember us with a beneficent memory and blessing; that You consider us with a consideration of salvation and compassion; that You bless us with great blessings; that You make our households complete; that You cause Your Presence to dwell among us. Privilege me to raise children and grandchildren who are wise and understanding, who love HASHEM and fear God, people of truth, holy offspring, attached to HASHEM, who illuminate the world with Torah and good deeds and with every labor in the service of the Creator. Please, hear my supplication at this time, in the merit of Sarah, Rebecca, Rachel, and Leah, our mothers, and cause our light to illuminate that it be not extinguished forever, and let Your countenance shine so that we are saved. Amen.

Inclination from within us . . ."[1]

If the day before Pesach is a Sabbath, the search is performed on Thursday night (the 13th of Nissan), and the *chametz* is burnt on Friday morning, although some *chametz* will have to be left over for the Sabbath meals. At the conclusion of the morning Sabbath meal, any traces of *chametz* left from the Shabbos meals should be rinsed down the drain (see ArtScroll *Pesach* pp. 123-176 for full details of the laws of Erev Pesach which occurs on Shabbos). Following that, the declaration of nullification is recited, at the same time as it would be on a weekday Erev Pesach.

---

1. **Fighting Fire With Fire.** Sometimes we can nullify our illicit desires by viewing them as "insignificant as dust of the earth," i.e., through rational analysis of how worthless they are. But there are moments when passions are too intense to be controlled by cool reason. At such times one must divert his passion toward love of God, by concentrating on themes that will appeal to his emotions. In order to do away with the *chametz* of the soul, both tactics are required. Sometimes we must negate the significance of a temptation. At other times we can succeed only by burning the *chametz* with the fire of the love of God (*Nesivos Shalom*).

⇜§ Preparing for the Seder

Every person's share of the Final Redemption and his spiritual station at that time is a result of how he acts on the Seder night and to what extent he is able to generate spiritual striving during these special moments (*R' Aharon of Karlin*).

This is alluded to in the words of the prophet (*Micah 7:15*): *As in the days you left Egypt I will show you miracles.* The extent that we will experience God's miraculous delivery of us in days to come is directly linked to the way we celebrate the days that we left Egypt (*Imrei Emes*).

The Seder table should be completely arranged and set up during the day, so that the Seder can be started without delay. Furthermore, since the *afikoman* should be eaten before midnight it is important that we begin the Seder promptly. Nevertheless, *Kiddush* may not be recited until after nightfall, since it is also the first of the Four Cups, which must be drunk only after the night has begun.

Since the centerpiece of the Seder is the matzah and *maror* (and, in Temple times, the *pesach* offering), these, along with other symbolic items, are placed on the table in front of the leader of the Seder.

Three matzos are set before the leader of the Seder, as opposed to a regular Shabbos or Yom Tov, when only two loaves are required. (The third matzah will be broken into two pieces, as explained below, and therefore is not counted as one of the Yom Tov loaves.) Several symbolic meanings have been attached to the three matzos: They represent the entirety of the Jewish people (who are composed of כֹּהֲנִים לְוִיִם וְיִשְׂרָאֵלִים — *Kohanim*, Levites and Israelites);[1] or our three Patriarchs, whose merit helped bring about our redemption from Egypt (*HaManhig*); or the three measures of flour from which Abraham baked matzos for the three angels in *Genesis 18:5*.

According to others, the three matzos parallel the three types of matzah prescribed for the thanksgiving offering that the Torah (*Leviticus*

7:12) requires of someone who has been released from prison or has recovered from illness or traversed an ocean or desert. The Jews of the Exodus fell into every one of these categories, and our three matzos symbolize their thanksgiving offering (*Rav Sherira Gaon; Maharal*). The three matzos should be on top of one another. According to *AriZal*, they should be separated by napkins or inserted into separate compartments of the Seder plate. All the matzah used for the Seder must be מַצָּה שְׁמוּרָה, matzah made specifically for Pesach, from grain that was specially guarded against any conditions (e.g., dampness) that could cause it to become *chametz*.

Since these three matzos will undoubtedly not suffice to supply the minimum amount of matzah to all the participants of the Seder, additional matzos should be prepared. It should be recalled that on three occasions during the Seder each participant must eat a quantity of matzah that, if ground up, would equal at least the volume of an olive.

There are various opinions as to the exact size of the piece of matzah needed each time. See *The Kol Dodi Haggadah*.

Several items are arranged on top of the Seder plate. Perhaps the most important is the *maror* (bitter herb).

The Talmud mentions several kinds of vegetables suitable for use as *maror*, among them horseradish, and *chazeres*, or romaine lettuce. Lettuce has the advantage over horseradish in that the required quantity can be eaten easily; however, it is extremely difficult to cleanse it of the tiny insects that may infest it. For this reason many people use only the central stalks, and not the dark, leafy parts. Some opinions accept the use of regular iceberg lettuce or endives for *maror*.

If horseradish is used, it may not be cooked or prepared with vinegar. In order for it to retain some of its sharpness when it is eaten at the Seder, it should be kept well wrapped or sealed, and it should not be grated too long before the Seder.

---

1. **Brothers of Redemption.** *Seder HaAruch* suggests that this subdivision of the Jewish people into these three parts is noted at the Seder because it was a *Kohen* (Aaron) assisting a *Levite* (Moses) who served as God's agents to free the *Israelites*.

For this reason the grating of the horseradish is best not done on Friday when Erev Pesach is on Shabbos; instead, the horseradish should be grated just before the beginning of the Seder, employing a slight change from the normal way of grating (*Mishnah Berurah* 473 §36). Likewise, *maror* for the second Seder should be prepared just before the Seder, since day-old horseradish will very likely have lost its sharpness (*Yesod VeShoresh HaAvodah*).

Like the matzah, the quantity of *maror* to be eaten on each occasion must also be equal to an olive (see *The Kol Dodi Haggadah* for exact modern equivalents). And, as with the matzah, additional portions should be prepared, as the Seder plate will generally not hold sufficient *maror* to provide for all Seder participants.

In addition to the *maror*, the Seder plate should contain a roasted bone with some meat on it and a hard-boiled egg, representing respectively the *pesach* and *chagigah* offerings, which were eaten at the Seder in the times of the Temple. The bone representing the *pesach* sacrifice is often the shoulderbone of a lamb, while some use the neckbone or wing of a chicken. To represent the *chagigah*, we use an egg, which is a sign of mourning for the destruction of the Temple. Its round shape symbolizes the cyclical nature of life and holds out the hope for the speedy reestablishment of God's presence in the Temple.

Another food placed on the Seder plate is the חֲרוֹסֶת (*charoses*), a mixture of grated fruits mixed with red wine and spiced with cinnamon and other spices. The *charoses* mixture is of claylike color and consistency, reminiscent of the mortar used by the Jews in their forced labor. Furthermore, the cinnamon sticks represent the straw that they put into the bricks (*Mordechai*); the red wine represents the spilled blood of the Jews (*Yerushalmi Pesachim* 10:3); the apple is a re-

minder of the fact that, as the Midrash relates, the pious Jewish women went into the apple orchards, to give birth without the knowledge of the Egyptians (see *Song of Songs* 8:5), and God cared for them there (*Yalkut*). The *maror* will be dipped into the *charoses* in order to counter any possible harmful effects of the *maror's* sharpness.

Finally, the Seder plate contains *karpas* (a vegetable such as celery, parsley, radish or boiled potato — but not a vegetable that can be used for *maror*). *Karpas* is dipped into salt water and eaten right after *Kiddush*. A bowl of salt water should therefore be prepared in advance (especially if the Seder night is on a Shabbos, as it is not permitted on Shabbos to prepare salt water in quantity or in very strong concentration).[1]

There are several customs regarding the arrangement of the Seder plate. Perhaps the most prevalent practice is to follow the directions of the *AriZal*, Rabbi Yitzchak Luria (see diagram). In this

ביצה
BEITZAH

זרוע
Z'ROA

מרור
MAROR

כרפס
KARPAS

חרוסת
CHAROSES

חזרת
CHAZERES

ג' מצות
3 MATZOS

1. **Diluting the Pain.** Scripture refers both to the salting of sacrificial meat and to suffering as a בְּרִית, *covenant*. Just as salt brings out the flavor of meat, so pain provides atonement for sins (*Berachos* 5a). The analogy goes further. Too much salt makes meat inedible; likewise, too much pain debilitates a person instead of engendering spiritual catharsis. At the Seder, therefore, we dip into diluted salt water, rather than directly into salt. This symbolizes the fervent hope that our present-day exile experience should not become overwhelming, but that it should bring out the best in us (*Maor VeShamesh*).

way, the proximity of each food is determined according to the order of its use, making it unnecessary for the leader of the Seder to reach over any one item in order to obtain what is needed next. However, there are other opinions on how to arrange the Seder plate — notably that of the *Gaon of Vilna* (see diagram); also, the Gaon used only two matzos, in accordance with the

opinion of many early authorities. *Maharal* held that the salt water, too, should be placed on the Seder plate.

The Seder also calls for wine — enough to fill four cups. The cups must hold at least a *revi'is* of wine; there are various opinions as to what a *revi'is* is equivalent to in modern measurements (see *The Kol Dodi Haggadah*).

As a sign of freedom and royalty, we are required to recline on our left side when we drink the Four Cups, and while we eat matzah, *korech, afikoman* and, according to some, *karpas*. It is thus advisable that pillows be provided to facilitate proper reclining. Only men are *required* to recline, although women may also do so if they wish.

A widespread, time-honored custom calls for the leader of the Seder to wear a white *kittel* — a sign of special dignity on this solemn night when he, in a certain sense, functions like the High Priest on Yom Kippur (who wore a white linen robe), performing the Divine service to obtain forgiveness and redemption for the Jewish people. *Maharal* also notes that a white garment reflects the joyousness of the Yom Tov and the purity attained on this evening. At the same time, the *kittel* (also worn by the dead) evokes humility and prevents excessive exuberance on this joyous evening (*Taz*).

It has been further suggested that the *kittel* is reminiscent of the spiritual tenacity of our forefathers in Egypt, who did not change their distinctively Jewish attire (*B'nei Yisaschar*).[1]

1. **A Coat of Many Colors.** *Divrei Negidim* refers to the fact that white contains all the colors, yet has no color of its own. Thus, white alludes to God Who contains everything, yet is unfathomably greater than all. The Egyptian Exodus assumed no specific hue, for it was God Himself Who saved us. *Nesivos Shalom* views white as symbolic of humility; for this reason, burial shrouds are white. Since matzah — a food of utmost simplicity, with no added ingredients — alludes to the humility that is the antithesis of the haughty and blown-up *chametz*, we don white on this night.

R' Leibele Eiger finds the reason for wearing white in the teaching of the Sages that the seven weeks between Pesach and Shavuos parallel the seven-day purification period which a woman undergoes before reuniting with her husband. With the beginning of the Exodus, the Jewish people began the process of shedding the effects of the forty-nine degrees of contamination they had experienced in Egypt, so we begin tonight this very same process. At the end of seven weeks, they were worthy to receive God's most intimate expression of love, His Torah. We too look forward to reuniting, as it were, with God every year, when we will again receive the Torah on Shavuos.

Thus, just as a woman wears white during her purification process, we too don the white *kittel* tonight, to signal the commencement of our spiritual regeneration, which will reach its apex on Shavuos, when we again become one with God through the Torah.

THE ORDER OF THE SEDER — סִימָנֵי הַסֵּדֶר

קַדֵּשׁ. וּרְחַץ. כַּרְפַּס. יַחַץ. מַגִּיד. רָחְצָה.
KADDESH. URECHATZ. KARPAS. YACHATZ. MAGGID. RACHTZAH.

מוֹצִיא מַצָּה. מָרוֹר. כּוֹרֵךְ. שֻׁלְחָן עוֹרֵךְ.
MOTZI MATZAH. MAROR. KORECH. SHULCHAN ORECH.

צָפוּן. בָּרֵךְ. הַלֵּל. נִרְצָה.
TZAFUN. BARECH. HALLEL. NIRTZAH.

◆§ The Order of the Seder

There is a brief poem summarizing the order of the Seder's components. The poem is commonly called the "*Simanim*" (סִימָנִים), or "Symbols." During the course of the Seder, it is customary to announce aloud each step of the Seder, as it is described in the *Simanim*, as a reminder of the proper sequence in which the various rituals are performed, and to help avoid mistakes. But it is more than simply a matter of convenience; it also makes us aware of the profoundly significant pattern of the Seder observance and all its details.

[Some people recite the entire poem at the outset, in addition to announcing each step in its appropriate place. This is done so that the youngsters will be aware beforehand of what is to take place, and to encourage them to inquire about each new step (*Vayaged Moshe*).]

The structure of the Seder is meant to help us relive the experience of the Exodus, and every step contains deep lessons and esoteric allusions, not only as a reminder of the Exodus that was, but also as an element in the ongoing spiritual march of the Jewish people. Our Sages have taught that every Pesach brings with it the spiritual emanations of the original Exodus; it is for this sense that our prayers refer to Pesach as זְמַן חֵרוּתֵנוּ, *the time of our freedom* — every Pesach enables us to free ourselves from the encrustations of impurity that cling to our material existence. Since each Pesach adds yet another element to the totality of Jewish experience, we help prepare the pattern of the future redemption by carefully following the required sequence of steps that are prescribed for the Seder.

It is for this reason, writes *Maharal*, "Everyone should seek in awe to fulfill the directions of the Sages who arranged the observances of the Seder and the Haggadah. Let nothing appear petty in one's eyes, even if there are many things at the Seder which would appear not to matter . . . for there is nothing insignificant among them."

The rhyme given here, the most widely accepted one of several, is ascribed to *Rashi* or to Rabbi Shmuel of Falaise,[1] one of the *Baalei Tosafos*. It

---

1. **Fixed Debate.** Rabbi Shmuel was a contemporary of the author of *Sefer Mitzvos Gedolos* (*Smag*) and of Rabbeinu Yechiel of Paris. In June 1240, he and three of his colleagues participated in a public debate with the viciously anti-Semitic apostate Nicholas Donin of La Rochelle. Although they displayed great scholarship, courage and dignity in their defense of the Talmud, the official verdict against them was a foregone conclusion. A church tribunal condemned the Talmud to be burned, and shortly thereafter church agents eagerly confiscated over 1200 manuscripts of the Talmud and commentaries. More than twenty wagonloads of these sacred writings were publicly burned in Paris, one of the blackest days in medieval Jewish history. In the preprinting-press world, this dealt a terrible blow to the French Jewish community.

קדש

Kiddush should be recited and the Seder begun as soon after synagogue services as possible — however, not before nightfall. Each participant's cup should be poured by someone else to symbolize the majesty of the evening, as though each participant had a servant.

sums up the Seder in fifteen stages, which correspond to the fifteen steps that the Levites ascended to the Temple Courtyard, and which King David commemorated in writing the fifteen psalms known as שִׁירֵי הַמַּעֲלוֹת, *Songs of Ascents* (*Psalms* 120-134). On the Seder night, the anniversary of our initiation as servants of God, we seek to emulate the Levites and ascend to successively greater heights of Divine service. To advance from the first level, starting with *Kiddush*, to the fifteenth, *Nirtzah*, fourteen steps are taken. They correspond to the יָד הַגְּדוֹלָה, *the great hand* [יד has the numerical value 14], that God showed in Egypt, and to which we pray tribute at the Seder (*Maharal*). As we perform these rituals, we pray that in turn we may be privileged once again to see God's hand revealed in the world, with the coming of *Mashiach*.

Sefer HaToda'ah suggests that the fifteen steps of the Seder correspond to the fifteen acts of Divine kindness that are enumerated in *Dayeinu*. In reenacting our redemption from Egypt on this night, we once again climb the spiritual ladder that leads from physical redemption to the spiritual freedom that we experienced when God allowed us to build a Temple to atone for all our sins and to enable us to experience His Presence (the progression described in *Dayeinu*).[1]

⋙ קַדֵּשׁ וּרְחַץ — literally **sanctify** (by reciting

Kiddush) and **wash** (the hands).

Interpreted allegorically, this teaches that one should never be complacent about one's spiritual growth. Instead of being self-satisfied with his previous spiritual gains, a person must build on past successes to raise his standards. Thus קַדֵּשׁ, *sanctify yourself* — but once you have achieved a spiritual plateau do not rest on your laurels. Go on to the next step: וּרְחַץ, *wash* away your previous achievements, in the sense that you should not be enamored with the past. Instead, use it only as a springboard for continued growth and progress (*The Saraf of Magelnitza*).

According to *Yismach Yisrael*, the lesson of these two *Simanim* is one of perspective. As man ascends the ladder of spiritual progress he acquires a broader perspective on life and his mission. The greater the spirit of sanctity one assumes in life, the higher the standard he must set for himself.

Thus, on this exalted and sanctified night, when we relive the experience of the Exodus, we see with new clarity that *I am HASHEM your God Who has taken you out of the land of Egypt* (*Exodus* 20:2). From our newfound spiritual perch (קדש), therefore, it behooves us to reassess our previous lifestyle and cleanse ourselves of its impurities (רחץ). If we seize the moment to make a fresh commitment to God, He will help us bring our

---

1. **Code of Self-discovery.** *Tiferes Ish* offers a homiletical explanation for the use of *Simanim*, which can be translated as *identifying signs*. The Talmud (*Bava Metzia* 28b) teaches that to prove ownership of a lost item, a claimant must provide an identifying feature (*siman*). Man, too, under the strain of his personal spiritual exile and the travails of life, can lose the intensity of his connection to God and Judaism. On this night, the anniversary of the birth of the Jewish people, one can ''find'' himself and reclaim his Jewish identity. The Seder conducted with these fifteen *signs* helps one identify his essence and reclaim himself for God.

Beis Avraham notes that the order of the Seder is a road map for one's spiritual growth throughout the year and, in fact, for one's entire life. In this vein, many commentators offer homiletic interpretations of the *Simanim*. We will offer some during the course of this work.

KADDESH

Kiddush should be recited and the Seder begun as soon after synagogue services as possible — however, not before nightfall. Each participant's cup should be poured by someone else to symbolize the majesty of the evening, as though each participant had a servant.

wishes for self-improvement to fruition.[1]

R' Aharon of Koidanov offers an uplifting insight into the nature of this night's personal redemption. Generally, one must prepare himself for positive spiritual progress by first shedding the negative habits he has acquired along life's path. Thus, King David teaches סוּר מֵרָע וַעֲשֵׂה טוֹב, *[First] turn from evil and [then] do good* (*Psalms* 34:15). If one were to follow this course, one would first (רחץ) cleanse oneself of the iniquities of his past and only then (קדש) sanctify oneself. However, this night, like the first Pesach in Egypt, is different. Just as God took us from spiritual darkness to light without preparation on our part, so at the Seder we can make a spiritual quantum leap and strive for sanctity, even without the prerequisite purification.

◆§ Recite *Kiddush.*

Shabbos and Yom Tov meals begin with *Kiddush*. Although the blessing that constitutes *Kiddush* has already been *recited* in the evening prayers, the recitation of *Kiddush* at the meal illustrates that synagogue prayers are not enough to proclaim the sanctity of the day. Its sanctity and celebration must permeate the home, where people pursue their mundane activities (*Rabbi S. R. Hirsch*).

The *mitzvah* to recite — or hear — *Kiddush* over a cup of wine is incumbent upon men and women alike. At the Seder, this cup has double significance: In addition to serving as the cup used for *Kiddush*, it is also the first of the Four Cups that both men and women are obligated to drink.

On the Sabbath, the first paragraph of *Kiddush* (taken from *Genesis* 2:1-3) is in the nature of testimony to the fact that God completed the labor of Creation in six days and rested on the seventh. By observing the Sabbath we bear weekly testimony to God's creation of the universe. Although this paragraph has already been recited in the *Maariv* prayer (and for this reason is not included in the synagogue *Kiddush*), it was included in the *Kiddush* at home for the benefit of women and children who may not have recited the evening service. When the festivals occur on weekdays, *Kiddush* begins with the blessing over wine.

The head of the household, or another adult, recites the *Kiddush* while holding a full cup of wine (or grape juice) in his right hand. He should bear in mind that his recitation is the fulfillment of the *mitzvah* of *Kiddush* for both himself and the others who are listening. Those listening should bear in mind that their hearing is in fulfillment of the *mitzvah* of *Kiddush*, and should remain silent except when responding *Amen*. Some people have

---

1. **Make Each Day an Improvement.** *Rabbi Saadia Gaon* once told this story to his disciples:

Once, as a traveler, I spent a day at an inn, where the innkeeper treated me as he would any other guest. The next morning, the leading citizens of the town converged on the inn to greet me. When they had departed, the innkeeper approached trembling and in tears, saying, "Please, master, forgive me for not serving you properly."

"But you treated me very well. Why do you apologize?" I replied.

"I treated you as I treat all my guests. Had I only known yesterday who you were, I would have served you as befits a person of your stature!"

That, Rabbi Saadia told his students, illustrates the feelings that a Jew should have. The innkeeper was not remiss, but if he had known a day earlier what he found out a day later, he would have acted differently. In our service to God, we should feel similarly. We should never make today only an imitation of yesterday; we should strive to grow every day.

On Friday night begin here:

(וַיְהִי עֶרֶב וַיְהִי בֹקֶר)

יוֹם הַשִּׁשִּׁי: וַיְכֻלּוּ הַשָּׁמַיִם וְהָאָרֶץ וְכָל צְבָאָם. וַיְכַל אֱלֹהִים בַּיּוֹם הַשְּׁבִיעִי מְלַאכְתּוֹ אֲשֶׁר עָשָׂה, וַיִּשְׁבֹּת בַּיּוֹם הַשְּׁבִיעִי מִכָּל מְלַאכְתּוֹ אֲשֶׁר עָשָׂה. וַיְבָרֶךְ אֱלֹהִים אֶת יוֹם הַשְּׁבִיעִי וַיְקַדֵּשׁ אֹתוֹ, כִּי בוֹ שָׁבַת מִכָּל מְלַאכְתּוֹ אֲשֶׁר בָּרָא אֱלֹהִים לַעֲשׂוֹת.¹

On all nights other than Friday, begin here.

סַבְרִי מָרָנָן וְרַבָּנָן וְרַבּוֹתַי:

בָּרוּךְ אַתָּה יהוה אֱלֹהֵינוּ מֶלֶךְ הָעוֹלָם, בּוֹרֵא פְּרִי הַגָּפֶן:

---

the custom to stand during *Kiddush*. Others sit, and still others stand for the introductory paragraph (recited on the Sabbath) and then sit.

וַיְכֻלּוּ הַשָּׁמַיִם וְהָאָרֶץ — *Thus the heavens and the earth were finished.* The Talmud (*Shabbos* 119b) derives homiletically from this verse that whoever recites this passage is regarded as God's partner in Creation, because the word וַיְכֻלּוּ homiletically can be vocalized וַיְכַלּוּ, *and they* (i.e., God and everyone who acknowledges His Creation) *finished*. God's Creation would fall short of its purpose if man did not acknowledge Him as the Creator (*Maharsha*). In this sense, the Sabbath was an essential part of Creation, and not merely a cessation of God's activity, because it is an eternal reminder that God is the sole Creator, and that our task in the world is to do His will.

וְכָל צְבָאָם — *And all their array.* The word צָבָא, *array* or *legion*, refers to an organized, disciplined group acting in unison. The heavenly bodies and spiritual beings are a *legion* because they act only according to God's plan. On earth, it is the duty of Israel, by living according to the Torah, to be His earthly legion (*R' Bunam of P'shis'cha*).

וַיְכַל . . . וַיִּשְׁבֹּת — *Completed . . . and He abstained.* These two words have different connotations. He *completed* (וַיְכַל) means that the task at hand was finished, with nothing left to be done; *He abstained* (וַיִּשְׁבֹּת) implies that more was to be done, but it was set aside for another day. The Torah uses both words to teach us that even if we are still in the middle of our work when the Sabbath arrives, we should consider it completed and not think about it on the Sabbath (*Avnei Eliyahu*).[1]

---

1. **The Final Human Touch.** The Sabbath day is saturated with purpose. The Torah states that God *abstained from all His work* (Genesis 2:3), implying that the essence of the day is to commemorate cessation from work, but in the very next phrase, the Torah says *to make*, implying that accomplishment was simultaneous with rest. But there is no contradiction in this. God rested from *physical* creation, but He created the *spiritual* universe that comes into being every Sabbath. The world of the Sabbath is far above that of the six days it succeeds, but they are not separate from one another. The bridge between the mundane and the sacred, between the weekdays and the Sabbath, is man. Adam and Eve were created last, just before the Sabbath, because only man has the intelligence and wisdom to bring the holiness of the Sabbath into the activities of the workweek. Of all the creatures in the universe, only he can *create* holiness. Angels *are* holy, but they are static; they cannot improve themselves or the world. Only man can do both. The Sabbath is God's seal, and man is the one who must impress it upon God's universe; indeed, man's activities transform the universe from an apparently aimless amalgamation of matter into the mirror of God's will (*R' Nosson Scherman*).

On Friday night begin here:

(And there was evening and there was morning)

The sixth day. Thus the heavens and the earth were finished, and all their array. On the seventh day God completed His work which He had done, and He abstained on the seventh day from all His work which He had done. God blessed the seventh day and sanctified it, because on it He abstained from all His work which God created to make.[1]

On all nights other than Friday, begin here.

By your leave, my masters and teachers:

Blessed are You, HASHEM, our God, King of the universe, Who creates the fruit of the vine.

---

(1) *Genesis* 1:31-2:3.

וַיְבָרֶךְ . . . וַיְקַדֵּשׁ — *Blessed . . . and sanctified.* God *blessed* the Sabbath with abundant goodness, for on it there is a renewal of physical creative strength, and a greater capacity to reason and exercise the intellect. He *sanctified* it by not doing any work on it (*Ibn Ezra*).[1]

אֲשֶׁר בָּרָא אֱלֹהִים לַעֲשׂוֹת — *Which God created to make.* The word לַעֲשׂוֹת, *to make*, implies that there was an ongoing process of creation: The living creatures of the universe were granted the ability to *reproduce* themselves (*Radak*). Another explanation is offered by *Chasam Sofer*: People can labor long and hard to *create* something — whether it is a house, a tool or a business. Then it is up to them to *use* (לַעֲשׂוֹת) it properly. God created the world for the use of humanity; then He entrusted it to mankind. Now it is up to us to use it as He intended. Only if we do so is Creation complete.[2]

---

1. **Petty Thievery.** A certain greedy storekeeper in Radin used to close his shop late on Friday and reopen before the Sabbath had ended. The *Chafetz Chaim* said to him. "Let me tell you a story. There once was a potato farmer who carted his crop to a wholesaler. They agreed on a price per sack — but the farmer could not count; how would he know how many sacks there were? The wholesaler suggested, 'As the stevedores unload the sacks, I will give you a penny for each sack. When we are fully unloaded, I will exchange each penny for a gold coin.' The farmer agreed. As the wholesaler kept giving him pennies, the farmer couldn't resist the opportunity to put some of the pennies in his pocket. The wholesaler noticed but didn't react since every penny the farmer pocketed saved him the price of a sack.

"You know the farmer was a fool," continued the sage of Radin, "but you act the same way. God made the Sabbath the source of all blessing. According to the *Zohar*, all six days of the week receive their sustenance from the Sabbath. Thus every hour of Sabbath observance provides sustenance and financial success for six weekday hours. How foolish to 'steal' an hour of Shabbos, when in reality you are stealing from yourself!"

2. **The Divine Imprint.** *R' Elie Munk* poetically captures the spirit of man's partnership with God in imprinting the Godly seal on Creation: The process of creation lasts as long as the conflict between good and evil remains unresolved. Ethically, the world is incomplete, and mankind has the glorious privilege of being able to contribute to its perfection. Through moral conduct, man can bring about the victory of the forces of good. Thus, as the story of Creation draws to a close . . . the fate of Creation is put in man's hands. The true completion of Creation will come only when man has established the kingdom of God on earth.

בָּרוּךְ אַתָּה יהוה אֱלֹהֵינוּ מֶלֶךְ הָעוֹלָם, אֲשֶׁר בָּחַר בָּנוּ מִכָּל עָם, וְרוֹמְמָנוּ מִכָּל לָשׁוֹן, וְקִדְּשָׁנוּ בְּמִצְוֹתָיו. וַתִּתֶּן לָנוּ יהוה אֱלֹהֵינוּ בְּאַהֲבָה (שַׁבָּתוֹת לִמְנוּחָה וּ)מוֹעֲדִים לְשִׂמְחָה, חַגִּים וּזְמַנִּים לְשָׂשׂוֹן, אֶת יוֹם (הַשַּׁבָּת הַזֶּה וְאֶת יוֹם) חַג הַמַּצּוֹת הַזֶּה, זְמַן חֵרוּתֵנוּ (בְּאַהֲבָה) מִקְרָא קֹדֶשׁ, זֵכֶר לִיצִיאַת מִצְרָיִם,

---

אֲשֶׁר בָּחַר בָּנוּ — *Who has chosen us. Ramban* (*Deuteronomy* 7:8) explains that God chose Israel because He knew that its obstinate faithfulness would cause it to be unswervingly loyal to Him. It is natural for someone to choose a lover who will remain unconditionally committed no matter how great the difficulty. As the most obstinate and head-strong of all the nations (see *Beitzah* 25b), Israel can withstand all trials and tribulations.

וְרוֹמְמָנוּ מִכָּל לָשׁוֹן — *Exalted us above all tongues* (i.e., languages). Human language in general is capable of capturing sublime thoughts and complex ideas, but Israel was granted the language of the Torah, which encompasses God's own wisdom and which is uniquely suited to express concepts of holiness.

וְקִדְּשָׁנוּ בְּמִצְוֹתָיו — *And sanctified us through His commandments.* Unlike the laws of human legislatures and monarchs, which are intended merely to regulate daily life in an equitable fashion, the laws of the Torah infuse holiness into those who observe them.

מוֹעֲדִים לְשִׂמְחָה חַגִּים וּזְמַנִּים לְשָׂשׂוֹן — *Appointed times for gladness, festivals and times for joy.* [1] The term *appointed times* (or *encounters*) refers to the historic role of the festivals as times when God and Israel "encountered" one another, in Egypt and the Wilderness. The חַגִּים, *festivals,* from the word חוּג, *circle,* connotes the festivals as times of national reunion. *Times for joy* refers to the seasonal nature of the festivals, which reveals God through nature (*Rabbi S.R. Hirsch*).

The festivals, including the Sabbath, are referred to as *appointed* also because they are special days when Jews "meet," as it were, with God.[2]

חַג הַמַּצּוֹת הַזֶּה — *This . . . the Festival of Matzos.* The Torah uses this name for the festival, while we call it Pesach (Passover), referring to the day when God "passed over" our houses in Egypt. *Kedushas Levi* explains that God uses a name that praises Israel for trusting God so intensely that they left Egypt with no provisions except for a few matzos. We Jews, on the other hand, use a name that recalls our gratitude to God for saving us.

---

1. **Wellsprings of Joy.** The expression *appointed times* **for** *gladness* implies that the festivals are not only days of rejoicing, but sources of joy and inspiration for the remainder of the year (*Chidushei HaRim*). Similarly, שַׁבָּתוֹת לִמְנוּחָה, *Sabbaths* **for** *rest,* implies that the Sabbath provides blessing for the entire week (*Sfas Emes*).

2. **Meetings of Spirit.** Just as *moed* in space refers to a meeting place where men assemble for a designated purpose, so *moed* in time is a point in time that summons people to an appointed activity — in this case, spiritual growth. Thus, *moadim* are days that stand out from the rest of the year and summon us to dedicate our spiritual activities to a higher purpose. From this point of view, Sabbath and Yom Kippur are also *moadim*.

"The *moadim* interrupt the ordinary activities of our life and give us the spirit, power and consecration for the future by revivifying those ideas upon which our whole life is based, or they eradicate such evil consequences of past activity as are deadly to body and spirit and thus restore to us lost purity and the hope of blessing" (*Horeb*, Chapter 23).

Blessed are You, HASHEM, our God, King of the universe, Who has chosen us from among all nations, exalted us above all tongues, and sanctified us with His commandments. And You, HASHEM, our God, have lovingly given us (Sabbaths for rest), and appointed times for gladness, festivals and times for joy, this day of (Sabbath and this day of) the Festival of Matzos, the time of our freedom (in love), a holy convocation in memory of the Exodus from Egypt.

זְמַן חֵרוּתֵנוּ – *The time of our freedom.* The Midrash (*Shemos Rabbah* 3:12) teaches that we were freed from Egyptian bondage in anticipation of our acceptance of the Torah at Mount Sinai. The physical liberation of Pesach became complete only with the spiritual liberty we received along with the Torah on Shavuos. As the Mishnah teaches, "you can have no freer man than one who is engaged in the study of Torah" (*Avos* 6:2).[1]

מִקְרָא קֹדֶשׁ – *A holy convocation.* The festivals are days when the people are "invited," קְרוּאִים, to assemble in prayer and thanksgiving, and to celebrate with fine clothing and festive meals (*Ramban*).[2]

זֵכֶר לִיצִיאַת מִצְרָיִם – *In memory of the Exodus from Egypt.* This phrase occurs in every *Kiddush*, not only that of Pesach, which specifically cele-

---

1. **Free to Be Me.** The Torah is not a crushing and constricting yoke; it is a source of freedom that allows man to be loyal to himself and his Godly soul, to be free to live according to the internal harmony of his personality. Unless man lives as God created him to, he is a slave to his own passions, the mores of society, or the despotism of dominant or fashionable cultures (*Meiri*).

In the words of *Ibn Ezra* (*Numbers* 6:7): "All men are slavish prisoners of human passions and desires. The true king, who rightfully wears the crown of royalty, is the person who is free of the beckoning call of desire." In a letter to his son, Ramban wrote, "Subjugate your body to your soul, for of such subjugation is born freedom in this world and the next."

The word חֵרוּת, *freedom*, is related to חָרוּת, *engraved* (see *Avos* 6:2). The spirit of freedom which permeates this season must be permanently engraved upon the heart of every Jew. *Pesach* must liberate us of all mortal shackles so that we are free to be ourselves all year round (*R' Aharon of Karlin*).

⁍ **Fleeting Passion.** *Ramban* writes that the word for freedom דְּרוֹר (see *Leviticus* 25:10) is a contraction of the words דּוֹר דּוֹר, *generation* written twice. This alludes to the idea that דּוֹר הוֹלֵךְ וְדוֹר בָּא, *one generation leaves and the next generation comes*, because freedom is the product of successive generations carrying on the traditions of their forefathers.

True freedom is rooted in the realization that everything in this world is temporary, here today and gone tomorrow. To chase after one's desires is therefore foolish and futile since none of the thrills are forever. One who can elevate himself to view life from this perspective is truly free (*R' Chaim Zeitchik*).

R' S. R. Hirsch eloquently portrays this perspective on freedom: "Freedom calls upon man to recognize the Source of his freedom. Our Merciful Father has given us the gift of freedom from our burdens and cut our imprisoning chains. We must therefore link our lives with His will so that we not remain slavishly indentured to our passions and whims."

2. **True Joy.** *Rambam* (*Hilchos Yom Tov* 6:18) writes: When one eats and drinks [on the festivals] he must feed strangers, orphans, widows and other indigent and unfortunate people. One who closes his door and feasts only with his wife and children, ignoring the needs of the poor and the embittered souls, does not practice joy of *mitzvos*; rather, he experiences a gastronomic celebration.

By giving honor and distinctiveness to the day through festival foods and clothing, we focus our minds on it and thereby foster a realization of the spiritual opportunities it offers, if we utilize them properly (*HaKsav VeHaKabbalah*).

כִּי בָנוּ בָחַרְתָּ וְאוֹתָנוּ קִדַּשְׁתָּ מִכָּל הָעַמִּים, (וְשַׁבָּת) וּמוֹעֲדֵי קָדְשֶׁךָ (בְּאַהֲבָה וּבְרָצוֹן) בְּשִׂמְחָה וּבְשָׂשׂוֹן הִנְחַלְתָּנוּ. בָּרוּךְ אַתָּה יהוה, מְקַדֵּשׁ (הַשַּׁבָּת וְ)יִשְׂרָאֵל וְהַזְּמַנִּים.

On Saturday night, add the following two paragraphs:

בָּרוּךְ אַתָּה יהוה אֱלֹהֵינוּ מֶלֶךְ הָעוֹלָם, בּוֹרֵא מְאוֹרֵי הָאֵשׁ.

בָּרוּךְ אַתָּה יהוה אֱלֹהֵינוּ מֶלֶךְ הָעוֹלָם, הַמַּבְדִּיל בֵּין קֹדֶשׁ לְחוֹל, בֵּין אוֹר לְחֹשֶׁךְ, בֵּין יִשְׂרָאֵל לָעַמִּים, בֵּין יוֹם הַשְּׁבִיעִי לְשֵׁשֶׁת יְמֵי הַמַּעֲשֶׂה. בֵּין קְדֻשַּׁת שַׁבָּת לִקְדֻשַּׁת יוֹם טוֹב הִבְדַּלְתָּ, וְאֶת יוֹם הַשְּׁבִיעִי מִשֵּׁשֶׁת יְמֵי הַמַּעֲשֶׂה קִדַּשְׁתָּ, הִבְדַּלְתָּ וְקִדַּשְׁתָּ אֶת עַמְּךָ יִשְׂרָאֵל בִּקְדֻשָּׁתֶךָ. בָּרוּךְ אַתָּה יהוה, הַמַּבְדִּיל בֵּין קֹדֶשׁ לְקֹדֶשׁ.

On all nights conclude here:
One should bear in mind that this blessing applies to all observances of the Seder.
Women who recited this blessing at candle-lighting should not repeat it now.

בָּרוּךְ אַתָּה יהוה אֱלֹהֵינוּ מֶלֶךְ הָעוֹלָם, שֶׁהֶחֱיָנוּ וְקִיְּמָנוּ וְהִגִּיעָנוּ לַזְּמַן הַזֶּה.

The wine should be drunk without delay while reclining on the left side. It is preferable to drink the entire cup, but at the very least, most of the cup should be drained.

---

brates the Exodus, but also the *Kiddush* of the Sabbath and the other festivals. All are reminders of the Exodus from Egypt, because their observance began only with the birth of the Jewish people (*Avudraham*).[1]

According to *Beis Yaakov* (*Izhbitz*), the reason so many *mitzvos* are in remembrance of the Exodus is because freedom is not only a result of Torah, but a prerequisite to it. If man is a prisoner — whether of people or of nature — he fails to see the hand of God in all that happens. Since all of the *mitzvos* were given in order that we recognize God and thank

Him for creating and sustaining us (see *Ramban* to *Exodus* 13:17), one must have freedom in order not to be blinded by the natural course of events.[2]

(בְּאַהֲבָה וּבְרָצוֹן) בְּשִׂמְחָה וּבְשָׂשׂוֹן — *(In love and in favor) in gladness and in joy.* In the *Kiddush* and in the prayer liturgy the Shabbos is characterized as "given in love and favor," while the festivals are "given in gladness and in joy." *R' Tzadok HaKohen* explains: The relationship between God and His people is of a dual nature. God loves us unconditionally and constantly, regardless of our behavior. In addition to this, we gladden God when we follow

1. **Stirring of the Soul.** *Bircas Avraham* of *Slonim* offers an inspiring interpretation of the phrase מִקְרָא קֹדֶשׁ זֵכֶר לִיצִיאַת מִצְרָיִם. When man feels a call to sanctity, he often feels inadequate. His Evil Inclination whispers, "You have sunk so low that you cannot escape the shackles of impurity. You are my prisoner forever!" Therefore we are taught to remember the Exodus. Wallowing in almost fatal impurity, the Jewish people were extracted by God and elevated to great spiritual achievement. Likewise, God can help every Jew, no matter what his present spiritual station is — if only the Jew wants to hearken to the call to sanctity.

For You have chosen us and sanctified us above all peoples, (and the Sabbath) and Your holy festivals (in love and in favor), in gladness and joy have You granted us as a heritage. Blessed are You, HASHEM, Who sanctifies (the Sabbath and) Israel and the festivals.

On Saturday night, add the following two paragraphs:

Blessed are You, HASHEM, our God, King of the universe, Who creates the illumination of the fire.

Blessed are You, HASHEM, our God, King of the universe, Who distinguishes between the sacred and secular, between light and darkness, between Israel and the nations, between the seventh day and the six days of activity. You have distinguished between the holiness of the Sabbath and the holiness of a Festival, and have sanctified the seventh day above the six days of activity. You have distinguished and sanctified Your nation, Israel, with Your holiness. Blessed are You, HASHEM, Who distinguishes between holiness and holiness.

On all nights conclude here:
One should bear in mind that this blessing applies to all observances of the Seder.
Women who recited this blessing at candle-lighting should not repeat it now.

Blessed are You, HASHEM, our God, King of the universe, Who has kept us alive, sustained us and brought us to this season.

The wine should be drunk without delay while reclining on the left side. It is preferable to drink the entire cup, but at the very least, most of the cup should be drained.

His will. Thus His joy is in response to our actions, while His love is constant. The sanctity of Shabbos, which is constant and does not require the proclamation of a court, is an expression of God's constant love for us. The sanctity of the festivals, on the other hand, results from the court's declaration of the new month (and thus the festival); this is God's joyous reaction to our proclamation.

מְקַדֵּשׁ (הַשַּׁבָּת וְ)יִשְׂרָאֵל וְהַזְּמַנִּים – *Who sanctifies (the Shabbos and) Israel and the festivals.* When a festival falls on the Sabbath, the Sabbath is mentioned first, because it was sanctified at the creation of the world, long before the Jewish people were created. The festivals, however, depend on the Jewish people — represented by the Rabbinic Court — which fixes the calendar by declaring the onset of each month. Therefore the sanctity of the Jewish people is mentioned before that of the festivals (*Beitzah* 17a).

שֶׁהֶחֱיָנוּ – *Who has kept us alive.* This blessing, recited at the beginning of every new holiday or

2. **Rising Above it All.** *R' Shlomo Weinberg, the martyred Rebbe of Slonim, by homiletically relating* מִצְרַיִם, *Egypt, to* מְצָרִים, *narrow straits, interprets the phrase* זֵכֶר לִיצִיאַת מִצְרַיִם *as a reminder to leave all spiritual constriction and narrowness. Everyone has the ability to rise above all smallness and pettiness — he need only be reminded of his purpose in life and his royal status as a Jew.*

God and man are like two friends who parted ways over what one perceived to be an abuse of the relationship. If the friendship is basically fragile, the injured party may remind his former friend once or twice that he must make amends. If there is no response, the friendship will atrophy. However, close friends will remind each other incessantly, because they really want the old closeness to be restored. Likewise, God wants the Sabbath and festivals to awaken us to reestablish our relationship with Him, by transcending the narrowness of our spiritual vistas.

וּרְחַץ

The head of the household — according to many opinions, all participants in the Seder — washes his hands as if to eat bread (pouring water from a cup, twice on the right and twice on the left), but without reciting a blessing.

כַּרְפַּס

All participants take a vegetable other than *maror* and dip it into salt water. A piece smaller in volume than half an egg should be used. The following blessing is recited (with the intention that it also applies to the *maror* which will be eaten during the meal) before the vegetable is eaten. It is preferable that those who did not wash their hands at *urechatz* not touch the vegetable with their hand, but use a utensil.

בָּרוּךְ אַתָּה יהוה אֱלֹהֵינוּ מֶלֶךְ הָעוֹלָם, בּוֹרֵא פְּרִי הָאֲדָמָה.

performance of a rare *mitzvah*, speaks of three things. We praise God *Who has kept us alive* and saved us from the ravages of exile and persecution; we rejoice over the fact that He has *sustained us* by strengthening our faith in Him and our resolve to fulfill His will under all circumstances; and we thank Him for having *brought us to this season* by providing all our physical needs and granting us the wherewithal to fulfill His *mitzvos* (*Maaseh Nissim, Bircas HaShir*).[1]

וּרְחַץ — Wash the hands.[2]

This washing is in preparation for eating the *karpas* dipped in salt water, but no blessing is recited after this washing. In Temple times, however, when people were able to fully observe the laws of ritual purity, they were required to wash their hands before eating any food that had been dipped in water (or certain other liquids), and they recited a blessing, just as we do when washing the hands before eating bread.

1. **Golden Opportunity.** This blessing expresses gratitude for a Divinely given opportunity to serve God and elevate ourselves. Rabbi Berel Wein illustrates this concept with a personal anecdote (*Vintage Wein*, pp. 94-95).

"I have a close friend in the Midwest. He and I attended the same yeshivah, and now he's a highly successful investment counselor with a nationwide clientele.

"I once spoke in his town and afterwards I spent the night in his home. Naturally, we stayed up, reminiscing — until 12 o'clock at night. At that point I said I was quite tired; so I excused myself to go to bed. He said, 'All right, I've still got a few calls to make.'

"My ears perked up and I remarked, 'Calls to make! It's midnight — whom are you going to call?'

" 'You don't understand,' my friend replied. 'I have some very important information to give a number of clients — absolutely great opportunities — I'll call them tonight, and when the market opens in the morning, they'll be ready. They'll appreciate the call.'

" 'You're going to call someone at 12 or 1 o'clock in the morning to tell them that?'

" 'What, are you crazy, Berel?' he replied. 'I'm telling you, this is business. That's why they stick with me. They know I'll call them at 3 in the morning and tell them, "Hey — we can make money tomorrow!" '

"So, I sat there and thought to myself — and I think to myself often — if I could be like him . . . and if I really believed the speeches that I make, then I would call my congregants also at 1 o'clock in the morning and tell them, 'Look, I've got a great *hachnasas-kallah* (charity for brides) for you — it's available in the morning!' 'There's a *mitzvah* over here — a Jew we can help. We can save him. At the opening bell we can save him for sure.' But I'm afraid I'll wake them up and they'll be angry, so I don't call after 9:30 or 10 p.m. I look at it as a burden — and God looks at it as an opportunity."

URECHATZ

The head of the household — according to many opinions, all participants in the Seder — washes his hands as if to eat bread (pouring water from a cup, twice on the right and twice on the left), but without reciting a blessing.

KARPAS

All participants take a vegetable other than *maror* and dip it into salt water. A piece smaller in volume than half an egg should be used. The following blessing is recited (with the intention that it also applies to the *maror* which will be eaten during the meal) before the vegetable is eaten. It is preferable that those who did not wash their hands at *urechatz* not touch the vegetable with their hand, but use a utensil.

Blessed are You, HASHEM, our God, King of the universe, Who creates the fruit of the soil.

According to some opinions, this washing is not required nowadays (when we are unable to attain the high degree of ritual purity required for the Temple service), and only the leader of the Seder should wash at this point (without a blessing — see *O.C.* 158, *M.B.* §20). According to this view, the washing is a reminder of the procedure that was followed in the time of the Temple and expresses the hope that we will soon be subject to this law again, with the coming of Messiah. Moreover, it serves to arouse the curiosity of the children, like many other Seder-night practices that help to keep them awake.

Many authorities, however, hold that washing is required even nowadays whenever one eats food that has been dipped in liquid. According to them, all participants at the Seder must wash their hands before eating the *karpas.* Yet other authorities hold that although washing is generally not required nowadays, at the Seder we should be scrupulous to observe even practices that are not strictly required. They agree, therefore, that all participants should wash.[3]

כַּרְפַּס — *Karpas.*

In ancient times banquets were started by serving appetizers with a dip. This custom is still followed at the Seder, in order to provoke the children to notice and question the evening's

2. Faith in Man, Faith in God
The term רָחַץ, which in Hebrew means *to wash,* has the meaning *to trust* in Aramaic. Man can succeed at purifying himself and cleansing his soul of the filth and residue of sin only if he has firm trust that God frees those who wholeheartedly repent from the albatross of sin. Furthermore, one must profoundly believe that the tiny spark of good and Godliness in man will eventually triumph (*Zera Kodesh*).

Alternatively, first man must try to infuse his life with *sanctity* (קָדֵשׁ). If that fails, he should not despair. He must have *faith* (וּרְחַץ) that God will reward his efforts (*Divrei Sholom*).

3. Careful Reorientation
Imrei Emes suggests a reason why one should be especially scrupulous to observe halachic stringencies at the Seder. The Mishnah (*Zevachim* 2a) teaches that all sacrifices that had been offered without proper intent are valid, with the exception of the *pesach* and sin offerings. It stands to reason that when someone makes a new beginning in life, it must be sincere. The *pesach* offering was the vehicle through which we *became* the servants of God, and the sin offering is the vehicle through which a sinner reestablishes the tone of his life after having strayed. Such offerings must be performed with perfect intent; when setting the compass of his life, one must pay attention to every detail. Thus, at the Seder, which establishes *seder* (order) in a Jew's life, we assume halachic stringencies that we do not observe at other times.

יחץ

The head of the household breaks the middle matzah in two. He puts the smaller part back between the two whole matzos, and wraps up the larger part for later use as the *afikoman*. It is preferable that an amount of matzah adequate for all the participants be set aside. Some briefly place the *afikoman* portion on their shoulders, in accordance with the Biblical verse (*Exodus* 12:34) recounting that Israel left Egypt carrying their matzos on their shoulders, and say, בְּבֶהָלוּ יָצָאנוּ מִמִּצְרַיִם, ''In haste we went out of Egypt.'' The remaining matzah should be the equivalent of a *kezayis*.

oddities (*Pesachim* 114a). Thus we begin the Seder by dipping a vegetable.[1] Furthermore, eating delicacies in such a fashion is a sign of comfort and indulgence, a luxury that symbolizes Israel's "newfound" status as free men rather than persecuted slaves. This expression of "extravagance" arouses the curiosity of children.[2]

Although it is ostensibly a symbol of freedom, we dip the *karpas* in salt water, to remind us of the bitter tears of bondage (*Shelah*).[3]

Moreover, the very name of *karpas*, when it is read backwards, alludes to Egyptian slavery: ס׳

פֶּרֶךְ — *sixty [myriads of Jews] at hard labor*. The *karpas* is thus a symbol of both bondage and freedom. This explains why authorities differ regarding whether one should recline while eating it.

Rabbeinu Manoach sees an allusion in the word כַּרְפַּס to the כְּתֹנֶת פַּסִים, the multicolored fine wool tunic that Jacob made for Joseph (see *Genesis* 37:3). According to the Talmud (*Shabbos* 10b), this sign of favoritism caused Joseph's brothers to sell him to Egypt, beginning the chain of events that ultimately resulted in the Egyptian exile. Thus we allude at the beginning of the Seder to the root

1. **Premature Prominence.** *Yismach Yisrael* offers a homiletical interpretation for the significance of *karpas*. A Jew who feels that he is no better than a child in his immature, inadequate service of God is presented with the *karpas*. "Of what significance is this vegetable?" he asks. We answer, "Generally such a vegetable is consumed during or after the meal, but tonight we eat it before the meal." This represents the Seder's lesson that God grants man the ability to scale levels of spiritual growth that people normally expect to attain only after years of effort. In Egypt, God enabled our forefathers to catapult to levels far beyond their own powers. Such is the potential of the Seder, even now.

2. **Nothing out of the Ordinary.** Rabbi Tzvi Hirsch Levin, while serving as rabbi of Mannheim, enjoyed a friendly relationship with the local duke, who appreciated the rabbi's wit and wisdom. The duke once asked him, "Why is it only on Pesach that your children ask, 'Why is this night different from all other nights?' On Succos your people leave their homes to dwell in a branch-covered shanty, open to the cold wind and the dampness and rain. Shouldn't Jewish children question this at least as much as the changes on Pesach?"

R' Tzvi Hirsch cleverly replied: "On Pesach a Jewish child sees his elders reclining like carefree aristocrats. A festive aura, complete with fine food and wine, adorns the table. Unaccustomed to such a royal atmosphere in Jewish homes, the children wonder, 'Why is this night different?' On Succos, however, nothing is incongruent with the reality of Jewish existence in the exile. Bereft of home and hearth and exposed to the elements, the Jew finds himself in what seems to be his natural habitat. Hence the child finds no reason to wonder, since this night seems as foreboding and inhospitable as many other nights of our long exile."

3. **Freedom Born of Tears.** Interpreted homiletically, the dipping in salt water may allude to the fact that the freedom (symbolized by the *karpas*) came about because God heard the tearful cries of our forefathers. As the Torah teaches, *we cried to HASHEM, the God of our fathers, and HASHEM heard our voice* (*Deuteronomy* 16:7). Thus the freedom (*karpas*) is drawn from the tears (salt water).

YACHATZ

The head of the household breaks the middle matzah in two. He puts the smaller part back between the two whole matzos, and wraps up the larger part for later use as the *afikoman*. It is preferable that an amount of matzah adequate for all the participants be set aside. Some briefly place the *afikoman* portion on their shoulders, in accordance with the Biblical verse (*Exodus* 12:34) recounting that Israel left Egypt carrying their matzos on their shoulders, and say, בְּבְהִלוּ יָצָאנוּ מִמִּצְרָיִם, "In haste we went out of Egypt." The remaining matzah should be the equivalent of a *kezayis*.

---

cause of our Egyptian sojourn.[1]

We do not recite a blessing that we were "commanded to eat *karpas*," because it began as a custom, rather than a formal enactment of the Rabbis. However, since the *karpas* is not part of the meal, we recite the *haadamah* blessing. According to some authorities, one should have in mind that this blessing applies also to the *maror* that will be eaten during the meal. We eat less than a כְּזַיִת (volume of an olive) of the *karpas* so that we do not have to make a concluding blessing over it, for if we were to recite it, a new blessing might be required before eating *maror*.

יַחַץ — *Break the middle matzah.*

As we prepare to begin the narrative of the Exodus, we set the stage by showcasing the matzah. The Sages taught that the *mitzvah* to recite the story of our national freedom can be performed only "when the matzah and *maror* lie before you"

(see p. 58). As our Rabbis point out, the Biblical description of matzah as לֶחֶם עוֹנִי, *bread of affliction* (*Deuteronomy* 16:3), may also be understood as *bread of recitation* (לֶחֶם שֶׁעוֹנִין עָלָיו דְּבָרִים הַרְבֵּה — "bread over which many words are recited").

The term לֶחֶם עוֹנִי also bears the connotation of *the bread of poverty*. Thus, before reciting the Haggadah, we break the middle matzah in two, putting the smaller part back on the Seder plate, between the two whole matzos. In doing so, we follow the practice of the poverty stricken, who often eat broken fragments of bread rather than whole pieces.

The larger piece is set aside for the *afikoman*, the piece of matzah eaten at the end of the meal, which takes the place of the *pesach* offering that was eaten at the end of the meal in Temple times.[2]

---

1. **Undivided Attention.** Accordingly, we might suggest a homiletic rendering of the two *simanim*, כַּרְפַּס (*karpas*) and יַחַץ (*breaking the matzah*). Rather than showering attention and affection on our children in a disproportionate fashion, as Jacob did when he gave a tunic only to Joseph, we should divide (יַחַץ) our expressions of affection equally among our children, seeking always to accentuate the positive attributes and achievements of each child.

2. **A Little Piece of Redemption.** The larger part of the matzah, the *afikoman*, is also called צָפוּן, *the hidden part*, which alludes to the idea that the Egyptian Exodus was only the beginning of the redemptive process, but the ultimate redemption is "hidden away" until the time when all parts of human existence will fall into place and God's scheme for the universe will become apparent to all. Every Pesach that we celebrate is a small installment towards the great prize of Divine redemption that we will enjoy at the End of Days with the coming of the Messiah (*Sfas Emes*).

⊰§ **Providing for Later.** The Psalmist speaks of the great spiritual reward that awaits the righteous in the World to Come: *How abundant is Your goodness that* [צָפַנְתָּ] *You have hidden away for those who fear You* (*Psalms* 31:20). Thus, the larger piece of matzah that is put aside for the end of the meal alludes to the spiritual activities, which provide one's share in the World to Come. These activities, such as Torah study, charity, prayer and good deeds, must take up the greater part of one's time, effort and resources. It is the smaller share of a person's life that should be used for his here-and-now needs, symbolized by the smaller piece of matzah, which we eat as part of the meal (*Yismach Yisrael*).

According to *Be'eros HaMayim*, the message of יַחַץ is one of unity, brotherhood and sharing. On this night of Pesach, when we yearn for the final redemption, we are taught to view ourselves as only a part,

---

מַגִּיד

The Seder plate (if it contains the matzos) or the matzos are lifted for all to see as the head of the household begins with the following brief explanation of the proceedings. One should, at this point, declare his intent to fulfill the *mitzvah* to retell the story of our Exodus from Egypt. The Haggadah is to be recited with reverence, and thus is not recited while reclining.

הָא לַחְמָא עַנְיָא דִּי אֲכָלוּ אַבְהָתָנָא בְּאַרְעָא דְמִצְרָיִם.

Just as Temple offerings were brought from the best of one's livestock, so the larger of the two halves of the matzah is left for the *afikoman.*

The top matzah is not broken because the *hamotzi,* the first blessing at the beginning of the meal, should be recited over *whole* matzos. The second blessing mentions the commandment of *matzah,* the "bread of poverty," which is symbolized by the broken piece. Therefore, the matzos are arranged in the order of the blessings, with the unbroken matzah on top.

Many explanations have been offered for the custom of wrapping up the *afikoman* and hiding it away, often under a pillow: It is to protect the *afikoman* (in keeping with the obligation to *safeguard the matzos — Exodus* 12:17); to insure that it should not be mixed up with other matzos; and not to "shame" the matzah, so to speak, since it will be set aside and not used until the very end of the meal.

Futhermore, the hiding of the *afikoman* stimulates the children's attention and keeps them awake by encouraging them to try to find it and "steal" it. This custom is another of the devices designed to keep young children interested and awake.

According to *Rokeach,* by wrapping up the *afikoman* we reenact the way in which the Jews carried their dough out of Egypt (*Exodus* 12:34). This is also the reason for the custom of some families to put the *afikoman* on one's shoulder, for the Torah says that when the Jews left Egypt they carried the leftover matzos on their shoulders (*Exodus* 12:34); they cherished the *mitzvah* too much to let their animals carry them (*Mechilta*).[1] There is a custom among some Sephardic Jews for the leader of the Seder to walk with the matzah on his shoulder and to carry on a dialogue with the children. They ask him what he has and where he is going and so on, and he responds that he is leaving Egypt. These customs are designed to help us "relive" the Exodus.

Maharshal and *Mateh Moshe* suggest that the *afikoman* is hidden under pillows in commemoration of the leftover dough that the Jews bound up in their garments when they left Egypt (see *Exodus* 12:34).

מַגִּיד — *Reciting the Haggadah.*

As is obvious from the next several passages, the "Haggadah" refers not only to the actual story of the Exodus, but also to stimuli that recall the event, and proof that the Torah commands us to tell about it.

---

incomplete without our fellows. We break the matzah in half and take the smaller part, symbolic of the humble realization that we need our fellow Jew to act as our complementary second half. We leave the larger half for the hidden *afikoman*, which represents the ultimate redemption that will come about as a result of the love that we demonstrate when we make do with less in order to provide for our brothers.

1. **Squandered Opportunity.** The *Chidushei HaRim* once visited his mother and was shocked to see the aristocratic and righteous woman gathering straw in the field. "Mother, why are you gathering straw?" he asked. "We are gathering straw to provide mattresses for a poor couple who are to be married," she replied. "But mother, let me hire a non-Jewish farm hand to perform such a menial task!" She replied: "What?! Should I give away my *mitzvah* to a non-Jew?"

MAGGID

The Seder plate (if it contains the matzos) or the matzos are lifted for all to see as the head of the household begins with the following brief explanation of the proceedings. One should, at this point, declare his intent to fulfill the *mitzvah* to retell the story of our Exodus from Egypt. The Haggadah is to be recited with reverence, and thus is not recited while reclining.

This is the bread of affliction that our fathers ate in the land of

הָא לַחְמָא עַנְיָא – *This is the bread of affliction.*

We now focus on the matzah in order to provide a frame of reference for the Haggadah. According to *Kol Bo*, this declaration is offered as an explanation to the children for our having broken the matzah in half: This is the bread of poverty that our forefathers ate in the land of Egypt. Like poor men, our forefathers ate bread of poverty. In reliving the Exodus we, too, eat a broken piece of matzah.

The Torah stresses the connection between matzah and remembering the Exodus; it stresses that . . . *you shall eat matzos . . . so that you will remember the day of your departure from the land of Egypt all the days of your life (Deuteronomy 16:3).* Therefore, we keep the matzah uncovered throughout the recitation of the Haggadah. Whenever we lift our cups, however, we cover the matzah, in order not to "shame" it, so to speak, while it is being ignored in favor of the wine (see *O.C.* 473:7 and *M.B.* §78).

Although the Haggadah must be recited at a time when the *pesach* offering, matzah and *maror* lie before us (p.58), we begin the narrative here by referring exclusively to the matzah. In fact, this passage emphasizing matzah is not found in the earliest Haggadahs; it was composed after the destruction of the Second Temple and the beginning of the exile, which explains why it ends with a prayer for redemption (*HaShir VeHaShevach*; see *Rambam*). This would explain why only matzah is mentioned here: Without the Temple, we cannot fulfill the Biblical commandments of the *pesach* offering and *maror*, since the Scriptural commandment to eat *maror* applies only when there is a *pesach* offering. (Nowadays, *maror* is a Rabbinic obligation.) Consequently, matzah is left as the most important obligation of the evening.

As noted above, matzah is *the bread over which many words are recited,*[1] and it symbolizes both bondage and freedom. Our forefathers ate matzah when they departed Egypt so hastily that there was no time for the dough to rise; thus it symbolizes freedom. Before that, it served as food for the enslaved Jews, so it also conveys a message of bondage (*Ramban* to *Deuteronomy* 16:2). The broken piece of matzah symbolizes its slavery aspect, the bread of affliction and poverty. It was a common food of slaves because it was easy to prepare and very filling.

According to *Maharal*, לֶחֶם עוֹנִי (in Aramaic לַחְמָא עַנְיָא) should be rendered *poor bread.* Not embellished by juice, eggs or the like, matzah is composed of the bare minimum of ingredients: flour and water. Like a poor man who has only the bare necessities of life, matzah has no additives. (Egg matzah, on the other hand, is referred to as מַצָּה עֲשִׁירָה, "wealthy" matzah.) Paradoxically, such poverty reflects a truly meaningful freedom. Possessions can enhance the quality of life only as long as one does not consider them to be necessities. When they change from being desirable to indispensable, they become encumbrances rather than comforts; one becomes a prisoner of his perceived needs — far from the free man he thought he was. Thus, matzah — the most simple,

---

1. **Catalyst of Praise.** The word עָנִי has the same numerical value as קוֹל, *sound* or *voice*. The matzah elicits the "voice of Jacob" (*Genesis* 27:22), which praises God for all that He does for His people.

poor bread — is the symbol of true freedom.[1]

By its nature, matzah triggers a recollection of the events in Egypt, and helps us project ourselves into the situation of our forefathers — so that we can better feel the relief and joy of the deliverance. This, after all, is the goal of the Seder.

According to *Abarbanel, Malbim* and others, the entire הָא לַחְמָא עַנְיָא paragraph is essentially an invitation to the poor. Thus, we commence by announcing that tonight we are all eating *poor bread,* so that the poor will feel no shame in accepting our invitation. Tonight we are equal, all of us the children of freed slaves, eating the food of slaves.

According to *Maaseh Nissim,* this declaration was instituted after the destruction of the Second Temple in response to the claim that in exile there is no legitimate cause to celebrate that we were freed from Egyptian bondage. To this we reply that having once been freed, we are confident that we will soon be freed again. Thus the celebration of the past is in reality also a rejoicing over the future. We eat the bread of affliction as a reminder of the redemption in our past and are thus encouraged that our future portends even greater salvation. We conclude that while this year we are here in the bitter exile we are sure that next year we will be in the Land of Israel; while this year we are bent by the burden of servitude, we hope that next year we will walk upright, our heads held high as free men.

There are various reasons why this declaration is in Aramaic: Aramaic was the prevalent tongue among Jews at the time it was composed (*Ritva*). Since this is a call to guests on the part of the householder, it is issued in the common language (*Maharal*). As we relive the Exodus and express our yearning for the ultimate redemption, we fear that the angels might claim that we are undeserving, just as they did in Egypt. Thus we speak in Aramaic, a tongue unfamiliar to angels (see *Shabbos* 10b) (*Avudraham*).

---

1. **Free to Escape.** If the lesson of the matzah is that man should pare his needs to a minimum and learn to forego the pleasures of the world, why does God not ask us to subsist on this simple fare all year round? Why is a week of self-control and simplicity sufficient?

The Alter of Novardok explained with a parable. A policeman was escorting a prisoner on the way to his trial. Afraid that the defendant might escape, the guard attached the prisoner to himself by means of handcuffs, locking one cuff on his own right arm and the other cuff on the prisoner's left arm. As they walked through the street, passersby looked scornfully at the prisoner.

The prisoner could not bear the silent stares of condemnation and shouted: "Don't look at me that way! It is not the policeman who leads me, but *I* who lead *him*. Don't think I am chained to him; he is chained to me!"

A wise man was not fooled. He replied to the indignant prisoner, "Let us see you escape from your 'captor' and we will know who is the captive."

Likewise, explained the Alter, there is nothing wrong with enjoying some of the good things of life. Nevertheless, the Mishnah (*Avos* 6:1) teaches that the way of Torah is "eat bread dipped in salt and drink water in measure." It all depends on whether one merely partakes of the world's pleasures or whether he becomes their prisoner.

The litmus test to determine if man is the prisoner of his passions or whether he controls them is whether he can unlock the chains of desire at will and still be content. If he *must* have his wants and cannot escape their shackles, then he is truly their prisoner.

God allows us to indulge ourselves to some extent, symbolized by the leavened bread we eat all year long. On Pesach, we are given the opportunity to escape and show that we are not hopelessly chained to our every whim. We eat the poor, unleavened bread as a sign of escape, thus showing that we are in control of our lives. Then we may resume eating regular bread and enjoy life without the fear of becoming enmeshed in the mundane. Thus, through eating matzah, the poor bread, we break the shackles of servitude on the Festival of Freedom.

Egypt. All who are hungry, let them come and eat. All who are needy, let them come and celebrate the Pesach Festival! Now, we are here;

כָּל דִּכְפִין יֵיתֵי וְיֵכוֹל — *All who are hungry, let them come and eat.*

An invitation to guests is proper on all festivals (see *Rambam Hil. Yom Tov* 6:18), but it is particularly appropriate on Pesach.[1] Various explanations are given. Among them are:

☐ If this were literally an invitation to guests, it should have been made during the day or in the synagogue, not in the privacy of our own homes, after the Seder is already underway. Rather, this passage is a further illustration of why matzah is the "bread of poverty." In Temple times guests could not be invited while the Seder was in progress, because the *pesach* offering could be shared only with prearranged participants. That we are now, at the Seder, still permitted to invite guests to join our meal is because, in our spiritual poverty, we have no *pesach* offering. Thus our call to guests is to emphasize that we are in exile.[2]

☐ Pesach recalls not only God's kindness to the Jewish people, but also the kindness that Jews extend to their fellow Jews (*Shelah*). Our Sages tell

1. Many allegorical interpretations have been offered for the invitation offered here and for the הָא לַחְמָא עַנְיָא paragraph in general:

◆§ **Growing With Zest.** A person can eat only as much as his appetite allows. This is doubly true in spiritual matters, for spiritual advancement requires desire. Thus on this night, when a great spiritual feast awaits us, we are enjoined to work up an appetite for growth of the soul: *All who are hungry come and eat* (*Imrei Emes*).

On this night God is ready to grant greater spiritual gifts than we have earned with our actions. Just as He redeemed His undeserving people on that night in Egypt, so He is ready to grant us לֶחֶם עֹנִי, *bread of [spiritual] poverty*, implying that we will receive more than we have earned. Thus, even undeserving people can satisfy their spiritual hunger on this night (*Nesivos Shalom*).

◆§ **Passport out of Poverty.** We preface our remarks with a declaration that the matzah was the bread of affliction that we ate in Egypt. Almost drowning in the sea (יָם) of spiritual constriction and narrowness (מֵצַר), we were able to be cured of the nearly fatal effects of the 49 degrees of impurity by means of the matzah, which the *Zohar* calls מֵיכְלָא דְאַסְוָותָא, *the food of [spiritual] healing*. Likewise, today when we partake of the matzah, its spiritually therapeutic power reasserts itself, curing us of all those things that stand in the way of our freedom from spiritual poverty. We invite all who need spiritual renewal to come and partake of the matzah, the cure for our spiritual maladies (*Yismach Yisrael*).

2. **The Unfortunate Come First.** This may be the reason for the institution of מָעוֹת חִטִּים, *money for wheat*, i.e., the customary collection of funds before Pesach for matzos and other needs of the poor. And it also explains why such special emphasis is placed on inviting needy guests for Pesach.

Communal leaders throughout the generations took special care to meet the needs of the impoverished — even more than their own needs.

Rabbi Shmuel Mohilever was very involved in helping Jews who had been drafted into the anti-Semitic Russian army. He arranged for a kosher kitchen to supply their needs and would invite many of them to his home for Sabbaths and Festivals.

Once, before Pesach, the community head came to him and said, "*Rebbe*, we're suffering from a bad drought this year. Prices have been going up by the day and people simply cannot afford to pay the costs involved in buying the Pesach needs of the soldiers."

R' Shmuel said, "Let us assemble the rabbinical court and permit the use of *kitniyos* (legumes forbidden on Pesach according to Ashkenazic custom) this year."

"*Rebbe*," said the man, "you have taken a load off my shoulders. I was trying to see how we could feed the soldiers during Pesach, but now that you have permitted the use of *kitniyos* I can rest easier."

"Jewish soldiers?" said R' Shmuel in indignation. "That I will not allow. You, I and all the members of the community will eat *kitniyos* this Pesach. But as far as the soldiers are concerned, we must feed them only the best, just as in any other year."

לְשָׁנָה הַבָּאָה בְּאַרְעָא דְיִשְׂרָאֵל. הָשַׁתָּא עַבְדֵי, לְשָׁנָה הַבָּאָה בְּנֵי חוֹרִין.

us that the Jews merited redemption from Egypt because no Jew ever informed on another to the Egyptian authorities, no matter how cruel the persecution and how lowly the spiritual state of Israel. To the contrary, they made a covenant among themselves to preserve whatever they had learned from the Patriarchs and to render kindness to each other (*Tanna DeVei Eliyahu*). In turn, they merited that the wellsprings of Divine kindness were opened to them, leading to their redemption. Furthermore, the blind faith with which Jews followed God into the uncharted and parched desert after the Exodus is described by the prophet as *"the kindness of your youth"* (*Jeremiah* 2:2). It was in the merit of this "kindness" to God that He mirrored our behavior and redeemed us from Egypt. Although we had no merit to justify such salvation, He showed unmitigated kindness and freed us.

As we relive that special moment we invite *all* people to join our celebration and share with them our bountiful blessing. Thus we begin our Seder with an act of benevolence.

כָּל דִּצְרִיךְ יֵיתֵי וְיִפְסַח – *All who are in need, let them come and celebrate the Pesach festival*. We do not translate וְיִפְסַח as "let him come and partake of the *pesach* sacrifice," for today we have no *pesach* sacrifice, and even in Temple times, as mentioned above, only prearranged guests could eat of it. The term וְיִפְסַח may, however, perhaps refer to the eating of the *afikoman* which nowadays takes the place of the *pesach* sacrifice (*Ravan*). However, the most likely understanding of the word is that it is simply an invitation to "celebrate the Pesach festival" with us — paralleling the preceding phrase, וְיֵכוֹל, "let him come and eat."[1]

According to *Avudraham*, the duplicate invitation addresses itself first to the poor man's general needs: *All who are hungry, let them come and eat*. But beyond this, the special needs of Pesach (wine, matzos, etc.) create an extra burden upon the poor. We therefore invite them to join us for Pesach (וְיִפְסַח) without worrying about the extra expenses.[2]

---

1. **Spiritual Propellant.** This invitation can be understood allegorically. Man's life is an ongoing battle between the temporal and the spiritual. One who constantly craves (דִּכְפִין) to satisfy his base desires is invited to partake of the matzah which, according to the *Zohar*, is food for faith.

After he has subdued his burning physical passions, an insatiable hunger for true spiritual growth awakens in him. Often he feels stifled, unable to attain the level of spirituality that he truly perceives as his spiritual inheritance. Thus the Haggadah teaches כָּל דִּצְרִיךְ — whoever feels a need to propel himself to greater spiritual attainments, יֵיתֵי — let him come on this special night, וְיִפְסַח — and skip (as in "to skip" or "pass over"), ascending to new spiritual plateaus. On the night of Pesach, all fifty gates of purity are open to every Jew. He only needs to open his lips in sincere prayer and God will grant him spiritual salvation. This is alluded to in the words of the Haggadah: כָּל דִּצְרִיךְ, Whoever needs any of the fifty gates of spiritual purity (כל = 50), יֵיתֵי וְיִפְסַח, *Let him come and let his mouth speak* (פֶּה סָח = the mouth speaks) and pray to God. On this special night God will certainly grant him his heart's desire. Just as God heard the cries of the Jews in Egypt as they yearned to be free of Pharaoh and free to be true servants of God, so every year God listens to our cries as we yearn for true spiritual liberty (*Yismach Yisrael*).

2. **Twin Sustenance.** The twin invitations can also be taken as offers of both physical and spiritual sustenance to the needy. Our exile today, like that in Egypt, is marked by both material and spiritual impoverishment. We therefore offer aid for both — providing first for material needs (וְיֵכוֹל), and then for spiritual ones (וְיִפְסַח) — as our father Abraham did for his guests. And we pray that we ourselves may thereby become worthy of redemption in both body and soul.

In a similar vein, it has been suggested that the "bread of poverty" before us should be a source of encouragement in our exile. We are threatened by physical extinction and by ideological assimilation. We

next year may we be in the Land of Israel! Now, we are slaves; next year may we be free men!

הַשַׁתָּא הָכָא . . . הַשַׁתָּא עַבְדֵי — *Now, we are here . . . Now, we are slaves.* We pray for a twofold redemption: Not only do we yearn for our Holy Land, we want to be free — that is, to have freedom as defined by the Sages: "No one is truly free unless he occupies himself with Torah" (*Avos* 6:2). The implication is that one can be in the Holy Land and yet not be free — or that even if Jews cannot have *Eretz Yisrael*, they should at least be able to attain

freedom of the spirit, wherever they may be (*Rabbi Elazar Fleckeles*).

At present, we might have complete civil rights in the material sense, but we may still be called slaves in the spiritual sense — in bondage to erroneous ideas, or serving God only out of fear and awe (like a servant) rather than out of love (like a son) (*Tiferes Shlomo*).[1]

What is the relevance of this prayer for redemp-

therefore invite those who are fearful of these twin threats to come and celebrate with us; they will realize that God saved us from these same dangers in Egypt. And we too will attain a twofold redemption, physical and spiritual (*HaShir VeHaShevach*).

1. **Matzah — the Great Equalizer.** *Binah Leltim* explains the flow of ideas in this paragraph as follows. The declaration that matzah is the poor man's bread which our forefathers ate in Egypt serves as an introduction to the invitation we extend to the needy to join us at our Seder table. The shame and loneliness they feel over having to depend on us for their needs instead of enjoying their own Seder weighs heavily on their hearts. It is to these unfortunates that we say, "Our forefathers also ate the bread of poverty long ago in Egypt when they too had nothing and no place to call their own. Ultimately, God redeemed them and raised them from their sorry situation. Realize, dear brothers, that you too may now feel yourselves at a low point. This year you are here, seated at our table rather than at your own; however, next year you will, please God, be free men."

⋙ **Caring — Road Map for Glory.** Another explanation for the appropriateness of the prayer for redemption at this point is given by *Simchas HaRegel*. The prophet Isaiah tells us that righteousness and charity are the keys to the Final Redemption. *Zion shall be redeemed with justice and her returnees with righteousness* (*Isaiah* 1:27). As we begin our Seder on this night of redemption, we invite our less fortunate brothers to join us. This spirit of caring prompts us to express our dreams and hopes for the full realization of the Great Redemption. *Now we are here, next year in the Land of Israel; now we are slaves, next year we shall be free men.*

Jeremiah mourned that גָּלְתָה יְהוּדָה מֵעוֹנִי, *Judah* (the Jewish people) *went into exile because of poverty* (*Lamentations* 1:3) — the word עוֹנִי can be taken as meaning "poverty" as well as being a reference to the matzah, the bread of poverty. The Sages saw in this verse an allusion that our exile was due to our neglect of matzah as well as to our disregard of the needs of the poor. These transgressions highlighted Israel's failure to do its duty both toward God and toward fellow Jews. As we lift the matzah and welcome the poor to our table, we pray that as a consequence we may merit a speedy redemption (*Chasam Sofer*).

⋙ **Awaiting Payday.** *The Dubno Maggid* illustrates the relevance of the prayer for redemption with one of his characteristic parables: A poor man who became very wealthy adopted an opulent lifestyle. With a huge mansion, the finest cuisine and wines, servants to wait on his every whim, and elegant clothing, he enjoyed the best this world has to offer. Fearful of becoming totally caught up in his extravagance and afraid that he would forget to thank God for his prosperity, he adopted a custom of finishing every meal with a small bit of hard bread dipped in salt, to remind himself of his humble roots.

Eventually his fortunes turned and he was forced to become an itinerant beggar. Once he came to the home of a wealthy man with whom he had done much business in better times. The old friend was saddened by the depths to which his former business associate had fallen, and invited the fallen magnate to partake of a lavish meal. At the end of the meal, the now destitute man asked his host for a piece of hard bread and salt. The wealthy man was surprised at the request and the beggar explained his custom to

The Seder plate is removed and the second of the four cups of wine is poured.
The youngest present asks the reasons for the unusual proceedings of the evening.

מַה נִּשְׁתַּנָּה הַלַּיְלָה הַזֶּה מִכָּל הַלֵּילוֹת?

tion to the invitation to the poor? According to *Abarbanel,* the statement *Now, we are here* comes in anticipation of a question one might ask upon hearing the invitation to *come in and make Pesach*: How can one bring the *pesach* offering outside of the Temple in Jerusalem? In response we say, *Now, we are here;* we cannot bring the actual offering, but we will commemorate it with the *afikoman*. We pray, however, that *next year we will be in the Land of Israel,* with the rebuilt Temple, where the offering can be brought. We go on to explain that we are not celebrating Pesach in Jerusalem because *now, we are slaves,* but we hope that *next year we will be free men,* who will be able to perform the *mitzvah* as it was meant to be performed.

The phrase לְשָׁנָה הַבָּאָה, *next year,* was formulated in Hebrew rather than Aramaic, in order not to give offense to foreign rulers who might view it as a call to rebellion (*Kol Bo* and *Rokeach*).

מַה נִּשְׁתַּנָּה — *Why is this night different from all other nights?* One of the unique features of the Seder is its question-and-answer format. Although the Exodus from Egypt must be recalled every single day (*Deuteronomy* 16:3), that command-

ment may be fulfilled by a mere mention of the event, or (according to some opinions) even simply by mentally remembering the events. The special *mitzvah* of the Seder night, however, entails a full telling of the story, specifically within the framework of questions and answers.

Why the need for questions? The Sages based this formula on the model found in Scripture: *And it shall be when your son will ask you at some future time, "What is this?" you shall say to him. . .* (*Exodus* 13:14).

Ksav Sofer notes the pedagogical principle that learning is best understood and longest remembered if it engages the interest and curiosity of the student. He who is driven to inquire after solutions to problems will succeed best. On the night of Pesach, we strive to inculcate in ourselves, and especially in our impressionable children, a firm belief in God Who brought about the Exodus and demonstrated thereby that only He is Master of the universe. In order to instill this lesson and leave a lasting impression, we seek to excite the children so that they will seek answers and reasons, and thereby we hope to insure that the lessons of the evening will have a lasting effect on them.[1]

always end a meal with bread and salt in order to remember the time when he was poor.

The host laughed sadly. "My dear friend, when you were wealthy I could appreciate such an admirable custom. However, now you *are* a poor beggar again; why do you need to *remember* your days of poverty by eating the fare of the impoverished?"

Replied the guest: "You are mistaken — when I was wealthy I invested 10,000 gold coins with someone. Even though I seem to have lost everything, in truth I still have that investment. The banker with whom I invested has been phenomenally successful and it is only a matter of time until the investment period is up. Then I will reap huge profits and be rich again."

When we left Egypt we acquired great spiritual wealth. Even though we are now back in exile, our loyalty to God has been an investment that has yielded great spiritual profit. A great redemption is in store for us. In truth we are fantastically wealthy, waiting patiently for the time to come. Thus we remember the poverty of Egypt as we await the spiritual wealth of the Great Redemption.

1. **Intergenerational Links.** It is especially important to pass on the message of Pesach to our children because the assurance of our national continuity lies within the family unit. If parents can inspire their children to turn to their elders for the inherited wisdom of our people — *Ask your father and he will relate it to you. . .* (*Deuteronomy* 32:7); *Hear, my child, the discipline of your father . . .* (*Proverbs* 1:8) — then we can hope that "in every generation a person will see himself as having gone out of Egypt" and will take to

The Seder plate is removed and the second of the four cups of wine is poured.
The youngest present asks the reasons for the unusual proceedings of the evening.

Why is this night different from all other nights?

The Mishnah lists specific questions about four specific aspects of the Seder: Matzah, *maror*, the *pesach* offering and the two dippings. After the destruction of the Temple, the question about the offering was replaced by the one concerning reclining.[1]

The commentators are divided over whether one must ask *these* four questions or whether any questions relating to the Seder will suffice. *Malbim* (based on *Tosafos*, *Pesachim* 115b) submits that these questions are required, in addition to any other inquiries of the children that are generated by the changes from the regular pattern of Yom Tov meals.[2]

This text was designated as a format for children who lack the intellectual capacity to devise their

heart the lessons of that great event. We generate this interest among our children by arousing them to question the incongruities of the night.

On the other hand, failure to train our youth leads to national disaster. The Torah reading of Tishah B'Av (*Deuteronomy* 4:25) speaks of the harm that results from a failure to maintain the freshness and excitement of a constant renewal of faith, of no longer aspiring to a deeper Jewish consciousness. Parents forget — and let their children forget — about Israel's Divine mission. That may be why our Sages point out an inner connection between the Seder night and Tishah B'Av (which always fall on the same day of the week in any given year): In connection with the destruction of the Temple, we have to grieve that *He filled me with bitterness; sated me with wormwood* (*Lamentations* 3:15). From this we may infer that if we are too comfortable in our host nations to feel the yearning for spiritual freedom, as symbolized by the bitter herbs of the Seder, we may well experience the sort of bitterness our forefathers felt at the Temple's destruction.

1. **Princes in the King's Palace.** *Shir Ma'on* explains that in Temple times, reclining was not an anomaly, since people always reclined when eating sacrificial meat. Furthermore, distinguished people always reclined whenever they ate. Nowadays, however, when people normally do not recline during meals, this is conduct that arouses questions.

2. **Children of God.** The Mishnah (*Pesachim* 116a) introduces the four questions with the phrase וְכָאן הַבֵּן שׁוֹאֵל, *At this point the child asks.* R' Aharon of Karlin interpreted homiletically that every Jew, as a child of our Father in Heaven, may come on the Seder night and make requests of God.

R' Gedaliah Schorr elaborates: God redeemed the Jewish people from Egypt by extricating them in an instant from the forty-nine levels of spiritual impurity to which they had descended. At that moment they were exposed to the full forty-nine degrees of holiness to which a human being can aspire. However, that spiritual edification was granted them בִּשְׁאֵלָה, as a *loan* — only momentarily were the people exposed to that glimpse of a Jew's spiritual potential; then it was taken away. Having seen the top of the spiritual ladder, they would have to climb it by dint of their own efforts. In his personal spiritual journey, every Jew undergoes this same process. In order that he be inspired to take the necessary strides toward spiritual growth, God grants extraordinary success to his initial steps. That is a Heavenly gift so that he will then exert the effort to *earn* spiritual progress in his life. Then, he must have the courage to wage the fight, and the confidence to believe in his own eventual success.

The *Maggid of Mezritch* compared this to a person who was in a dark forest in search of a castle. He was lost and without hope of ever finding his destination, when a lightning bolt suddenly lit up the entire landscape. For one fleeting moment he saw the beautiful castle at a distance. Even though the lightning was gone as quickly as it came and he was again plunged into darkness, the traveler renewed his efforts to reach the castle. Having seen it for but a moment, he was ready to do whatever would be necessary to reach it.

On the night of Pesach, every Jew is God's firstborn child. Just as at the time of the Exodus we "borrowed" from God the great experience of spiritual exaltation in order that we could then make the necessary effort to earn and deserve it, so we may now borrow from God whatever degree of inspiration we need in order to overcome our spiritual shortcomings and become truly spiritually free.

שֶׁבְּכָל הַלֵּילוֹת אָנוּ אוֹכְלִין חָמֵץ וּמַצָּה,
הַלַּיְלָה הַזֶּה – כֻּלּוֹ מַצָּה.

שֶׁבְּכָל הַלֵּילוֹת אָנוּ אוֹכְלִין שְׁאָר יְרָקוֹת,
הַלַּיְלָה הַזֶּה – מָרוֹר.

שֶׁבְּכָל הַלֵּילוֹת אֵין אָנוּ מַטְבִּילִין אֲפִילוּ פַּעַם אֶחָת,
הַלַּיְלָה הַזֶּה – שְׁתֵּי פְעָמִים.

own penetrating questions. However, our Sages teach that even two scholars who conduct the Seder together should ask these questions of one another as an introduction to the narration of the Exodus.

The four subjects of the questions encapsulate the entire story of the Egyptian bondage and Exodus. The humble matzah and the bitter *maror* are symbolic of the enslavement, while the dippings and reclining, which emulate the conduct of wealthy aristocrats, are overt symbols of the salvation and freedom. Rather than waiting for the entire drama to unfold with the detailed account of the Haggadah, we allude to the story in capsule form through the four questions.[1]

According to *Abarbanel*, the uniqueness of these particular four questions caused the Sages to include them in the text of the Haggadah. They focus on the internal inconsistencies we exhibit on this night. We dip many times during the meal, a practice of the aristocracy, yet we also eat matzah, the bread of slaves. The mixed signals of reclining (demonstrating freedom) and the bitter herbs (connoting bondage) arouse bewilderment in

young and old alike, as freedom and bondage intermingle on this night.[2]

Others suggest that these four question were chosen in order to demonstrate that the Biblical commandments of the evening (matzah, *maror*) and the Rabbinic ones (dipping, reclining) are equally important.

Aruch HaShulchan differs from the conventional translation that renders מַה as *why*. He points out that the word for "why" is לָמָּה, and not מַה. Instead he interprets מַה as an exclamation: *How different and wondrous is this night from other nights!* The Seder is the forum to discuss and analyze these ideas and the inspiring feelings they engender.

חָמֵץ וּמַצָּה הַלַּיְלָה הַזֶּה כֻּלּוֹ מַצָּה – *[We may eat] chametz and matzah, but on this night — only matzah.* The term *only* is not meant to exclude all other foods. It refers only to the two kinds of bread, leavened and unleavened. On other festival nights, when we are obligated to partake of bread as part of the festive meal, we may eat both *chametz* and matzah; on the Seder night we may eat only matzah (*Machzor Vitry*).

1. **The Torah's Allusion to the Four Questions.** *Beis Avraham* notes that the words of the Biblical verse וְהָיָה כִּי יִשְׁאָלְךָ בִנְךָ מָחָר, *It will be when your son asks you at some future time* (*Exodus* 13:14), are the *gematria* equivalent — 737 — of מַצָּה וּמָרוֹר וּטְבִילָה וַהֲסֵיבָה, *matzah, maror, dipping and reclining*, the subjects chosen for the child's questions at the Seder.

2. **Light up the Night.** The questions are introduced by the phrase, "Why is this *night* different . . .," because the revelation of God's presence figuratively lit up the night, providing a clear perspective on life and God's Presence in all that we experience. This revelation made the night itself different from ordinary nights. Usually commandments are not assigned exclusively to nighttime; and we never say *Hallel* at night. However, this night when Hashem revealed Himself in Egypt was lit up like day (*Psalms* 139:12), and therefore it is actually called day (*Exodus* 13:8). This is why Scripture (*Numbers* 8:17) refers to the night when the Egyptian firstborn died as "the *day* in which I smote all the firstborn" (*Sfas Emes*).

1. **On all other nights** we may eat *chametz* and matzah,
but on this night — only matzah.
2. **On all other nights** we eat many vegetables,
but on this night — we eat *maror*.
3. **On all other nights** we do not dip even once,
but on this night — twice.

Earlier we explained that matzah is symbolic of the Exodus. We now question why matzah must be the exclusive type of bread permitted; let us eat a bit of matzah as a remembrance of bygone days, but then let us switch over to rich man's bread (*Chasam Sofer*).

R' Shmuel of Amsterdam explains that this question alludes to the thanksgiving offering that is brought by someone who is released from prison (see *Berachos* 54b), an offering that includes breads of both matzah and *chametz* (*Leviticus* 7:12). On this night, however, the thanksgiving and gratitude we offer God is accompanied only by matzah.

שְׁאָר יְרָקוֹת הַלַּיְלָה הַזֶּה מָרוֹר — *We eat many vegetables, but on this night — we eat maror.* Unlike most nights when we eat sweet vegetables to enhance the taste of our food, tonight we eat bitter herbs (*Avudraham*). On all other nights each person eats whatever vegetables he enjoys, cooked or raw. Tonight we eat bitter and sharp vegetables, which do not taste particularly good when eaten alone, and in order to taste their full bitterness, we eat them raw.

Even when we eat horseradish or the like on other nights, it is as a condiment to enhance the taste of other food. Tonight we eat the bitter herb itself — in order to taste the bitterness (*Rokeach*).

While wealthy people generally begin a meal with appetizers and tasty hoers d'oeuvres in order to arouse the appetite, tonight we will begin our meal with bitter herbs.

אֵין אָנוּ מַטְבִּילִין אֲפִילוּ פַּעַם אֶחָת — *We do not dip even once.* It is true that on other nights, too, we may occasionally dip vegetables, but only as *part* of the meal; however, tonight we do so *prior* to eating the meal (*Avudraham*).

הַלַּיְלָה הַזֶּה שְׁתֵּי פְעָמִים — *But on this night — twice.* We have already dipped the *karpas* in salt water and later we will dip the *maror* in *charoses* (*Rashbam, Pesachim* 116a). Although the second dipping has not yet taken place, the questioner sees the *maror* and *charoses* on the Seder plate and presumably knows how they will be eaten. Knowing their purpose, he now probes and asks about both dippings (*Seder HaAruch*).[1]

1. **Dispersion Caused by Unity.** *Ben Ish Chai* comments that the two dippings symbolize two events associated with Pesach — one that precipitated Jacob's descent to the Egyptian exile and another that was related to the Exodus. The first dipping recalls how Joseph's brothers dipped his tunic into the blood of a goat after they sold him, and brought the blood-soaked tunic to Jacob to convince him that Joseph had been killed by a wild animal. This hatred of their own brother started the chain of events that ended in Israel's enslavement in Egypt.

The second dipping recalls the *pesach* offering in Egypt, which was the prelude to the redemption. On the afternoon before the Exodus, the Jewish people slaughtered the *pesach* offering. They were commanded to dip a bundle of hyssop into the blood of the offering and apply it to their doorposts and lintels, as protection against the Plague of the Firstborn (*Exodus* 12:21-24). The hyssop tied into a bundle symbolized the unity of the Jewish people — and it was a precondition for them to leave Egypt.

According to the Midrash, the Jewish people in Egypt did not slander or gossip about one another during their exile, and they were thus able to rectify the sin of Joseph's brothers, which had brought them to Egypt in the first place. By doing the same in our time we can hope to leave the current exile as well (*Rabbi Mattisyahu Solomon*).

שֶׁבְּכָל הַלֵּילוֹת אָנוּ אוֹכְלִין בֵּין יוֹשְׁבִין וּבֵין מְסֻבִּין, הַלַּיְלָה הַזֶּה – כֻּלָּנוּ מְסֻבִּין.

The Seder plate is returned. The matzos are kept uncovered as the Haggadah is recited in unison. The Haggadah should be translated, if necessary, and the story of the Exodus should be amplified upon.

עֲבָדִים הָיִינוּ לְפַרְעֹה בְּמִצְרָיִם, וַיּוֹצִיאֵנוּ יהוה אֱלֹהֵינוּ

אָנוּ אוֹכְלִין בֵּין יוֹשְׁבִין וּבֵין מְסֻבִּין הַלַּיְלָה הַזֶּה כֻּלָּנוּ מְסֻבִּין — *We eat either sitting or reclining, but on this night — we all recline.* All the foods that are eaten or drunk as signs of freedom are consumed while reclining, as a sign of freedom. (For the exact occasions when one must recline and who must recline, see *O.C.* 472.)

As noted above, this question is not mentioned in the Mishnah, since the prevalent custom in those days was to eat in a reclining position all year round. In those days the fourth question was why the *pesach* offering may be eaten only roasted.[1]

עֲבָדִים הָיִינוּ לְפַרְעֹה בְּמִצְרָיִם — *We were slaves to Pharaoh in Egypt.* This passage, based on *Deuteronomy* 6:21, is the Torah's answer to the

1. **Endless Exile.** The author of *Kli Yakar* interprets the *Mah Nishtanah* homiletically as a reference to the exile, which is symbolized by the term *"this night"*:

Why is this exile different from all other exiles of our history? Why is this exile seemingly endless, while the previous periods of exile and subjugation were of limited duration? There are four reasons, which are alluded to in the four contrasts that are now detailed in the *Mah Nishtanah*:

(a) The word חָמֵץ, *leaven*, alludes to strife, for yeast causes dough to ferment and become agitated, which, in turn, makes it rise. On the other hand, matzah — simple flour and water in their humble, pristine state — represents peace and harmony. In earlier times, while there may have been a certain degree of discord and rivalry among Jews, there was also, at the same time, a considerable degree of harmony and internal peace. In the current exile, however, there is a tragic abundance of almost constant strife. The matzah can symbolize this unfortunate condition, as well, because euphemistically the word matzah can mean strife, in the same way that a blind man is delicately called a סַגֵּי נְהוֹר, *one with abundant "light."* Until we are at peace with one another, we cannot expect God to ease our plight among the nations. Thus, we sadly proclaim, our life once contained both harmony and strife — but now, we are entirely filled with strife!

(b) In other exiles, we were not beset by such single-minded pursuit of material wealth and luxury. We sought any vegetables, i.e. simple, unpretentious living. But in the current exile we have descended to an excessive craving for *maror*, a bitter passion for excess and luxury.

(c) In other exiles, we did not provoke gluttonous cravings by dipping our foods into exotic sauces, i.e., we did not seek ways to excite our senses. But in this exile, we allow ourselves to "double dip," i.e., we ravenously pursue physical pleasures.

(d) In times past, we were sometimes arrogant, as symbolized by haughty reclining in a position of comfortable disregard, and sometimes we sat in simple humility. In this exile, however, we are constantly reclining, i.e., we have grown arrogant, convinced that our *own* wealth, wisdom and strength are responsible for whatever successes we have attained (*Olelos Ephraim*).

❧ **Freedom From Need.** Even a pauper must recline on this night and conduct himself as a fully free person (see *Pesachim* 99b). When the Israelites left Egypt in haste, they took no food for the journey; they went into a barren desert with faith that God would provide for them. This poverty in no way diminished their sense of freedom; if anything, the dependence on God only enhanced the spirit of liberation (*HaSeder HaAruch*).

4. On all other nights we eat either sitting or reclining, but on this night — we all recline.

The Seder plate is returned. The matzos are kept uncovered as the Haggadah is recited in unison. The Haggadah should be translated, if necessary, and the story of the Exodus should be amplified upon.

We were slaves to Pharaoh in Egypt, but HASHEM our God took us

question of the wise son (see p. 48). It is a brief summary of the events of the Exodus from Egypt, and is therefore cited here in response to the four questions.[1]

In describing ourselves as former slaves who were liberated by God, we acknowledge that as such we owe Him our total allegiance. This explains why we are obligated to perform all the commandments and carry out all the customs mentioned in the four questions, whether or not we understand them. They were ordained or sanctioned by God, to Whom we are beholden for having freed us from Egyptian bondage (*Maaseh Nissim*).

The father's words also provide an explanation of the particular observances mentioned by the child, for, as noted above, two of them symbolize freedom and two symbolize slavery. Now the father says that we began this night as slaves and ended it as free people, and therefore our conduct at the Seder alludes to both conditions. Thus, even

now, while still in exile, we act in the spirit of free men (*Avudraham*).[2] According to *Shibbolei HaLeket*, this sentence explains only the dipping and reclining, which are indicative of freedom; the matzah and *maror* will be explained later in the passage *Rabban Gamliel* (p. 132).

This passage is laden with subtle implications: We were slaves *to Pharaoh*, a merciless dictator who showed no sympathy; and the place of our bondage was *in Egypt*, a harsh country from which escape was impossible. Thus, our ancestors could never have freed themselves in the natural order of events. In fact, as slaves, we had been totally broken by our masters. They represented brute force at its worst, and sought to rob us of the last shreds of our humanity. At that point, God took us out of Egypt. In overthrowing Egypt and turning a horde of slaves into a nation, He demonstrated that even the most powerful empires are impotent before Him. Thus we owe Him our full allegiance (see *Ramban* to *Deuteronomy* 6:21).

---

1. **Creating the Chain.** When answering the questions, the father summarizes the story and tells his children that when they will have families of their own, they, in turn, should pass on to their children this tradition of faith and freedom. This is alluded to in the verse וְהִגַּדְתָּ לְבִנְךָ בַּיּוֹם הַהוּא לֵאמֹר, *You shall tell your son on that day, saying* (*Exodus* 13:8). The word לֵאמֹר (*saying*) literally means "to say," implying that you should tell *your* children *to say* the story of the Exodus to theirs — so that the tradition remains unbroken (*Haflaah*).

2. **Majestic Prince.** Even in exile, Jews celebrate the freedom we were granted on this night. As R' Moshe of Kobrin said: The greatest sin a Jew can commit is to forget that he is royalty, the son of the King, because to do so will remove him from his personal pedestal and lead to continuously escalating sins. When God released us from Egypt we were born as a nation, His firstborn son. Tonight, on the anniversary of that cosmic event, we relive the moment and resolve to be worthy of the majesty implied by that title.

◄§ **Freedom-minded.** Freedom is a state of mind. One can be physically oppressed yet still maintain one's human dignity and personal sense of identity. On the other hand, one may enjoy prosperity and freedom, but be slavishly indentured to his own desires and passions and the whims of society. Is one who feels compelled to dress according to the dictates of fashion or to live only in trendy neighborhoods truly free? Is not the person secure enough to opt for a life of simplicity and spirituality truly liberated? At the Seder, as we reexperience the hand of God breaking all shackles, we may aspire to a release from all our personal houses of bondage.

מִשָּׁם בְּיָד חֲזָקָה וּבִזְרֹעַ נְטוּיָה. וְאִלּוּ לֹא הוֹצִיא הַקָּדוֹשׁ בָּרוּךְ הוּא אֶת אֲבוֹתֵינוּ מִמִּצְרַיִם, הֲרֵי אָנוּ וּבָנֵינוּ וּבְנֵי בָנֵינוּ

Geulas Avraham notes that the words עֲבָדִים הָיִינוּ (which we have translated as "we were slaves") can also have the connotation "We *became* slaves," seemingly suggesting that we made slaves of ourselves. Why doesn't the Haggadah say more simply "Pharaoh enslaved us"? Furthermore, why does the Haggadah have to say "We were slaves *to Pharaoh* in Egypt"? Wouldn't it have been sufficient to say "We were slaves in Egypt"? It thus appears, he concludes, that the Haggadah here is alluding to the words of the Talmud (*Sotah* 11a):

Why does the Torah say *and they put taskmasters over "him"* (*Exodus* 1:11)? Should it not have said: "And they put over *them* taskmasters"? They said in the school of Rabbi Elazar ben Rabbi Shimon, "This teaches us that they brought a model of a brick and hung it from the neck of Pharaoh. [Thus, it was as if Pharaoh himself had to submit to a taskmaster.] If any Jew would say, 'I am too delicate [to perform hard manual labor],' the Egyptians would say to him, 'Are you more delicate than Pharaoh?' "

This is why the Haggadah tells us "We became slaves unto Pharaoh," and stresses the connection to the person of Pharaoh, for of their own volition the Jews dedicated their labor to the sovereign.[1]

וַיּוֹצִיאֵנוּ ה' אֱלֹהֵינוּ מִשָּׁם — *But HASHEM our God took us out from there.* Only the Appellation *Hashem* (י־ה־ו־ה) occurs in the verse in *Deuteronomy* (6:23) upon which this passage is based; the Haggadah adds the Name אֱלֹהִים, *our God. Sfas Emes* explains

this anomaly as follows. The Torah uses only the name *Hashem*, which denotes God's attribute of kindness and mercy, because it wants us to emphasize to our children God's kindness in redeeming us. The Haggadah, however, adds אֱלֹהֵינוּ, the Name denoting God's attribute of strict judgment, to show that we also appreciate His sternness in putting us into bondage in the first place, for our suffering ultimately led to our momentous liberation and made it such a monumental event. This reflects the spirit of the Sages' instruction that, in reciting the Haggadah, מַתְחִיל בִּגְנוּת וּמְסַיֵּם בְּשֶׁבַח, *one starts with the shameful part and ends with the praise* (*Pesachim* 116a). Salvation is always more treasured when it is contrasted with the deprivation that preceded it, and our appreciation of the liberation is heightened through this method of presentation of events.[2]

According to the *Vilna Gaon* the term אֱלֹהֵינוּ is added in order to provide three terms to parallel the three expressions at the beginning of the passage. We were (1) *slaves* (2) *to Pharaoh* (who was a harsh ruler) (3) *in Egypt* — a harsh land. Correspondingly, (1) *HASHEM . . . took us out* of slavery. Through His great miracles, God showed conclusively that He is the only deity. (2) *Our God* — God freed us from slavery and subjugation to any power but Him. "Our God" implies that now He is our sole Master. (3) *Out from there* is a reference to the oppressive land of Egypt.

בְּיָד חֲזָקָה וּבִזְרֹעַ נְטוּיָה — *With a strong hand and an outstretched arm.* On an elementary level the term

1. **Pathetic Pandering.** Many Jews suffer from a slavish need to ingratiate themselves to their host culture, a dangerous obsession rooted in insecurity. People who feel like strangers tend to hope that the "master" will like them more and treat them better if they are properly servile. Historically, however, this ploy has backfired, and the bewildered Jew has been showered with abuse and contempt. The freedom granted us on Pesach allows us the psychological freedom to be proud of who we are.

2. **Spiritually Buoyed.** Homiletically, it has been said that the narrative of the Haggadah has a purifying power, alluded to in this formula of remembering the shame before recounting the glory. Even if one comes to the Seder night with a shameful and inglorious spiritual past, he can rise above it. Let him throw himself intellectually and emotionally into the spirit of the night and focus on the message of the story — then he will emerge from the Seder evening a vastly elevated person (*Yismach Yisrael*).

out from there with a strong hand and an outstretched arm. Had not the Holy One, Blessed is He, taken our fathers out from Egypt, then we, our children and our children's children would

---

strong hand refers to the power and intensity with which the plagues were delivered while *outstretched arm* expresses the fact that they extended over a period of time, rather than being a freak phenomenon that occurred for a fleeting moment (*Maharal*).

Malbim views the two terms as mirroring the physical and psychological aspects of redemption. It was God's *strong hand* that physically overpowered the Egyptians and took the Jews out of Egypt. However, it was also necessary to "take Egypt out of the Jews." They were so enamored by the grandeur of Egypt and its culture that God found it necessary to free them with a dazzling display of His might. The *outstretched arm* made it clear that the redemption was not a confluence of political factors or accidents of nature, but rather the Divine intervention of God. This outstretched arm drew the Jews away from the paganism of Egypt and brought them to a full recognition of the Most Powerful.[1]

Netziv offers another explanation of the term *strong hand*. As slaves of Pharaoh many Jews served in the halls of government and the royal court. Freed of physical toil, they were in many ways even more beholden to the Egyptians and enmeshed in their charms. These people didn't really want to leave Egypt and had to be removed forcefully by God's *strong hand*.

Furthermore, the concentration of all Jews in one land (Egypt) could have theoretically facilitated a large-scale annihilation of the entire people at the hands of the Egyptians.[2] To prevent this, God subdued the Egyptians with a *strong hand*.

וְאִלּוּ לֹא הוֹצִיא הַקָּדוֹשׁ בָּרוּךְ הוּא אֶת אֲבוֹתֵינוּ — *Had not the Holy One, Blessed is He, taken our fathers out.* It is unlikely that without the Exodus

---

⇥§ **Bootstrap Redemption.** The formula of beginning the Haggadah with our shameful origins is more than a device to appreciate the redemption more fully. It is an essential feature of the liberation process. Only after realizing how far one has fallen will man be moved to call out to God to save him. In Egypt, it was only when the people cried out in anguish over their servitude that God dispatched Moses to redeem them. Until then, they had accepted their servitude as their unavoidable lot, which they had no choice but to bear. God awaits man's prayers, so that He can respond and help him (*Chidushei HaRim*). As R' Avraham of Slonim said, "The greatest foe of spiritual growth is complacency."

God chose us as His nation while we were at our lowest spiritual level, in order to emphasize that our chosenness did not result from righteousness, but rather as an expression of His intrinsic and unconditional love for the children of the Patriarchs and Matriarchs. Such love will always exist, as the Sages taught: "Any love that depends on a specific cause, when that cause is gone, the love is gone; but if it does not depend on a specific cause, it will never cease" (*Avos* 5:19) (*Nesivos Shalom*).

1. **Mutual Destiny.** *Maaseh Nissim* suggests that the reason God brought about the Exodus with such an overpowering display of might was to provide Moses with grounds to plead on behalf of the Jewish people when they worshiped the Golden Calf. Moses prayed, *Why should Egypt say the following: With evil intent did He take them out to kill them in the mountains and to annihilate them from the face of the earth?* (*Exodus* 32:12). According to *Ramban*, Moses argued that since the Exodus included a remarkable display of God's attribute of mercy on behalf of Israel and His attribute of judgment against Egypt, it would be a grave desecration of His honor to let Israel's enemies claim that He later replaced mercy with harsh judgment. Had Pharaoh released them on his own volition, however, this plea would not have been possible. Thus the strong hand with which God extracted His People provided them later with a mitigating plea.

2. **Protectively Dispersed.** The Talmud (*Pesachim* 87b) teaches that it is an act of God's kindness and mercy that He spreads us in exile among many nations. Were we all in one place, our enemies could, God forbid, effect a "Final Solution to the Jewish problem."

מְשֻׁעְבָּדִים הָיִינוּ לְפַרְעֹה בְּמִצְרָיִם. וַאֲפִילוּ כֻּלָּנוּ חֲכָמִים, כֻּלָּנוּ
נְבוֹנִים, כֻּלָּנוּ זְקֵנִים, כֻּלָּנוּ יוֹדְעִים אֶת הַתּוֹרָה, מִצְוָה עָלֵינוּ

the Jewish people would still be slaves in Egypt, after the passing of more than thirty centuries. However, they would have fallen to the fiftieth level of impurity, from which there is no return, and they would have become completely assimilated into the Egyptian nation.[1] It should be noted that the Haggadah does not say that we would still be *slaves* (עֲבָדִים) to the Egyptians, but rather that we would be *enslaved* (מְשֻׁעְבָּדִים), or *subordinated*, to them and their culture.

Furthermore, even if the Jews had somehow found their way out of Egypt through natural political developments, we would nevertheless be מְשֻׁעְבָּדִים — in the sense of *beholden* — to the Egyptians who agreed to grant us independence, or perhaps *under the domination* (מְשֻׁעְבָּדִים) of the false notion that our independence had been brought about by our own might and skill,[2] failing to recognize the hand of God that is the true shaper of history (*Michtav MeEliyahu*).[3]

1. **Distantly Cold.** Had that generation not left Egypt, their children, who were even further removed from the Patriarchs and the twelve tribes, would never have been able to withstand the spiritually fatal impurity of Egypt. Thus all the later generations would have been irreversibly assimilated into the Egyptian melting pot (see commentary to וְהִיא שֶׁעָמְדָה) (*Sfas Emes*).

2. **Hidden Faces.** *Ramban* (based on *Deuteronomy* 31:18) describes the process of the Final Redemption as occurring in two stages. Initially God will hide His countenance from His people because of their sins. Eventually they will realize that they suffered because they did not allow God to be a real presence in their lives. But even after repenting, the Jews will seek their salvation through political forces and alliances. Consequently, God will still withhold His mercy — until Israel acknowledges Him as the only source of salvation.

This false illusion of alternative sources of success has plagued us throughout our history. As a community we believe in God, but we rely on governments and various stratagems to bring Jewish salvation. God responds in kind to our lack of faith, by turning His countenance away from us. Thus, His apparent uninvolvement in Jewish history is a mirror image of our own behavior toward Him.

At the time of the Balfour Declaration, many Jews thought that their problems would be solved by the mighty British Empire. However, they were soon disappointed when the British first tilted away from the Jews, and then — just when the danger to Europe's Jews was becoming undeniable — they drastically limited and then virtually halted Jewish immigration to *Eretz Yisrael*. Later, Jews fantasized that the international community of nations, embodied in the United Nations, would be the source of Jewish salvation, and their hopes were dashed yet again. Again and again, Jews have relied on the nations of the world to be their savior, only to be disillusioned.

By personally redeeming us from Egypt, God set the tone so that we might realize that only He is our real savior.

3. **Eternal Redemption.** God's direct involvement is the ultimate reason why the Exodus, once and for all, freed us from enslavement for all time. God *alone does great wonders, for His kindness endures forever* (*Psalms* 136:4); *Sfas Emes* interprets this verse to mean that God's kindness endures forever when *He* is the One Who has performed the *great wonder*. Anything done by human beings, however, is transitory by its very nature and passes with time, because human beings and their deeds are limited. Even Divine help can be of limited duration if it was sent through intermediaries, miraculous though the deliverance might have been. Thus, even after the miracle of Purim, we still remained subjects of Ahasuerus and his successors (*Megillah* 14a), for God saved us indirectly, through the efforts of His servants, Mordechai and Esther.

In Egypt, however, when God Himself took one nation from the midst of another, with signs and miracles, contrary to every rule of nature and history, He created a new phenomenon, a people belonging to Him — and this act can never be undone. In the same way, the fall of the Egyptians was a phenomenon

still be subservient to Pharaoh in Egypt. Even if we were all men of wisdom, understanding, experience and knowledge of the Torah, upon us it would still be an obligation to

וַאֲפִילוּ כֻּלָּנוּ חֲכָמִים — *Even if we were all men of wisdom.* The Haggadah now defines the parameters of the obligation of retelling the story of the Exodus. This obligation applies to all Jews, no matter how educated or experienced they may be.

Avudraham defines the different types of scholars mentioned here as: *men of wisdom,* in knowing the ways in which God directs human affairs; of *understanding* the deep wisdom underlying the *mitzvos*; and *of experience,* having reviewed this story many times in past years.

According to *Abarbanel,* these three terms for scholars correspond to their ability to comprehend three benefits. *Even if we were all men of wisdom,* i.e., people who understand the forces of the cosmos and could appreciate the supernatural dimensions of God's relationship with Israel; even if *we were all men of understanding,* i.e., well versed in human hierarchies and could appreciate the stature acquired by the Jewish people at the time of the Exodus; and even if *we were all men of*

knowledge of the Torah and could properly appreciate the exquisite perfection of what we received at Mount Sinai — *upon us it would still be an obligation to tell about the Exodus from Egypt,* the source of all of these blessings.

Great intellectual achievement does not absolve one from fulfilling the Biblical obligation to retell the story of the Exodus. Since it was an act of God, one can never fully exhaust its infinite depths of meaning; God *performs great deeds that cannot be fathomed (Job 5:9).* With each new insight we discover new avenues of thought to pursue.[1]

Alternatively, this teaches us that an intellectual understanding of the events of the Exodus is not sufficient. The Seder night is dedicated to inculcating deep and vibrant faith in God and His constant involvement in history. Even if we intellectually know the entire Torah, its message of faith will not penetrate our hearts unless we verbalize these eternal truths.[2]

Everyone has his own particular emotional perception of events, which he alone feels. By discussing the

of everlasting impact. Thus, at the Sea of Reeds Moses told the Jews that *never again will you see the Egyptians as you have seen them today (Exodus 14:13).*

It is true that in the course of history mankind has turned its back on God time and again; the Jewish people, too, has fallen short of its assigned task, and that is why we have gone through exile after exile. But never have we returned to the abject state of slavery in which we found ourselves in Egypt. No matter how difficult the exile, we retained our sense of national unity, based on our knowledge of God and Torah. Our redemption from Pharaoh's rule and acceptance of the Torah have left their eternal mark on us, so that we have remained forever free in our innermost and essential self *(Maharal).*

1. **A Child at Heart.** *Even if we were all men of wisdom, etc.* Much of the Seder ritual is to arouse the questions of children and help them understand its message. This is suitable for children, but how can such techniques work for educated and sophisticated adults? *R' Eliyahu Dessler* contends that while the mind may be wise, the heart is a simple and naive child. When the message of freedom is spoken on a simple but heartfelt level, it reaches the heart.

2. **Faith Talk.** *R' Avraham of Slonim* suggests a homiletic allusion to the principle that faith is acquired by constant verbalization. The Psalmist says, *I believed because I spoke (Psalms 116:10);* it is not the mind, but the heart and emotions that are the seat of one's faith. Verbal expression of the eternal certitudes of faith help them penetrate to the deepest recesses of our conscious and subconscious.

In this vein he homiletically interpreted the verse *Faith is forgotten; it is detached from their mouths (Jeremiah 7:28).* Faith became a lost art because people stopped talking about it. (This may be why many have the custom of reciting the Thirteen Principles of Faith (אֲנִי מַאֲמִין) every day after the morning prayers.)

לְסַפֵּר בִּיצִיאַת מִצְרַיִם. וְכָל הַמַּרְבֶּה לְסַפֵּר בִּיצִיאַת מִצְרַיִם, הֲרֵי זֶה מְשֻׁבָּח.

מַעֲשֶׂה בְּרַבִּי אֱלִיעֶזֶר וְרַבִּי יְהוֹשֻׁעַ וְרַבִּי אֶלְעָזָר בֶּן עֲזַרְיָה וְרַבִּי עֲקִיבָא וְרַבִּי טַרְפוֹן שֶׁהָיוּ מְסֻבִּין בִּבְנֵי בְרַק, וְהָיוּ מְסַפְּרִים בִּיצִיאַת מִצְרַיִם כָּל אוֹתוֹ

Exodus with others, one can share his personal perception with them and simultaneously share their experience of the Exodus (*Beis Avraham*). *Yismach Yisrael* suggests that even scholarly and informed people should discuss the Exodus in a fashion that makes it accessible to those not quite as intellectually astute. (Furthermore, even the sophisticated scholar does well to inculcate himself with a simple, straightforward faith in God. Thus, even he should retell the story of the Exodus and garner its message.)

According to *Maharal* and *Malbim*, we relate the great miracles of the Exodus on this night not merely to repeat God's praises, but rather to express our continuing gratitude to Him for everything He did. We would be remiss, and even ungrateful, if we did not thank Him for His unending beneficence. Neither our inability to fully express our debt of gratitude nor our intellectual awareness of the debt absolve us from giving it verbal expression to the best of our ability.

וְכָל הַמַּרְבֶּה לְסַפֵּר — *The more one tells.* [1] The term "the more" can be interpreted in two ways: either that more time be devoted to the discussion, or that the narrative be related at greater length and depth.

Kolbo and others explain that one is encouraged to continue talking about the Exodus even after he

has recited the basic facts outlined in the Haggadah; or that he continues the discussion even after the Seder (*Kolbo*).[2]

Rambam (*Hilchos Chametz U'Matzah* 7:4) asserts that the duty to elaborate upon the story of the Exodus applies particularly to the exegetical analysis of the verses of *An Aramean tried to destroy my father* (p. 70). See also ibid. 7:1, however.

Netziv contends that the Haggadah refers to the time allotted to the narrative. Although the time frame for this commandment is the same as that of eating matzah — until midnight, or, according to some, until daybreak — we are now told that this is the *minimum* time allotment. Going beyond that minimum, however, is permitted, and even encouraged.

הֲרֵי זֶה מְשֻׁבָּח — *The more he is praiseworthy.* Normally the Sages frown upon lengthy or elaborate expressions of praise of God, lest someone create the impression that he has exhausted the full description of God's glory (*Megillah* 18b). The Sages compare this to someone who, upon seeing a royal treasure house filled with millions of gold coins, praises the king as the possessor of thousands of silver coins. This "praise" is in reality an insult, for it falls short both in quality and quantity. Likewise, any praise of Hashem must vastly under-

1. **Polished Diamonds.** *R' Aharon of Karlin* rendered the word לְסַפֵּר as "shine" (as in אֶבֶן סַפִּיר, *sapphire*). Thus, one who seeks brilliant clarity in areas of faith and commitment can achieve this through the discussions of this night. Furthermore, on this night one can attain his own potential and let the luster of his soul shine forth. As the *Rebbe of Lechovitch* said, "A Jew is like a diamond rolling around in the mud. Pick it up, wash off the dirt and you see its natural luster." Tonight, inspired by the events in Egypt when God lifted His people out of the spiritual slime of Egypt, every Jew can be elevated and made to shine.

2. **Wake Up!** One should not hold too much of a discussion *before* the meal, so that the children will not doze off before being taught about *pesach*, matzah and *maror* (*Rashbam*).

tell about the Exodus from Egypt. The more one tells about the Exodus, the more he is praiseworthy.

It happened that Rabbi Eliezer, Rabbi Yehoshua, Rabbi Elazar ben Azaryah, Rabbi Akiva and Rabbi Tarfon were reclining (at the Seder) in Bnei Brak. They discussed the Exodus from Egypt all that

state the reality. Hence we are enjoined to keep to the standard praises formulated by the Men of the Great Assembly. An exception to this rule, however, is made for someone who has personally experienced God's salvation; he may praise God without constraint, for such an outpouring of copious, spontaneous praise is indeed the proper way of showing one's gratitude (*Maharal*). We, who are enjoined to see ourselves as direct, actual beneficiaries of the Exodus (see p. 140), are thus encouraged to enlarge upon the story of the Exodus and to praise God in every possible way (*Divrei Shaul*).

In a homiletical vein, the word מְשֻׁבָּח may also be translated according to a meaning that it often bears in Mishnaic Hebrew — *improved*. The more one talks about the Exodus the more he improves himself as a person, for he internalizes within himself the great lessons imparted by the story of the Exodus. Someone who speaks at length of the Exodus indicates that he is a person of refinement (*R' Shlomo Kluger*).[1]

מַעֲשֶׂה – *It happened.* The Haggadah now seeks to bolster its assertion that everyone must tell the miraculous story of our national birth. The fact that scholars of the caliber of R' Eliezer, R' Yehoshua, R'

Elazar ben Azaryah and R' Akiva did so proves that even if *we were all men of knowledge of the Torah*, we would still have to fulfill this commandment. The fact that they engaged in this commandment all night reflects the idea that *whoever tells about it at length is praiseworthy* (*Vilna Gaon, Abarbanel* et al.).

Maharal suggests that these great scholars were so caught up in their discussions that they lost track of time and stayed up all night. Had they been aware of the lateness of the hour, they certainly would have recessed, in order to sleep in fulfillment of the Biblical precept to rejoice on the festival (*Deuteronomy* 16:14).

According to *Abarbanel*, the all-night discussion of the Exodus was itself a reenactment of the Exodus and a fulfillment of the obligation to make oneself appear as though he had personally come out of Egypt. Between the service of the *pesach* offering, with its concomitant commandments, and the preparations for their departure, the Children of Israel were awake all night on the night of the original Pesach. The Sages' endeavor to commemorate this aspect of the Exodus and their engrossment in its discussion was itself an expression of festive rejoicing.

1. **Enduring Wealth.** *Divrei Shaul* explains this with a parable. A poor, ignorant man experienced a turn of fortune and became very wealthy. With his newfound riches he was able to hire tutors who taught him all the different areas of human knowledge. Before long he became an accomplished scholar and a true man of letters. Unfortunately, his fortunes took a downward turn and he eventually lost all his money, becoming a pauper again. Nonetheless, he continued to celebrate the anniversary of the day he had become wealthy, much to the amazement of his neighbors. The man explained: "True, I have lost all my money, but the knowledge I was able to acquire thanks to my wealth remains with me. Thus I celebrate the benefits my money brought me."

Jews celebrate the Exodus from Egypt even at times when we do not have physical freedom. Though we are in exile, we praise God for the Egyptian Exodus, for we benefit continuously from the spiritual treasures that we received as a result of our liberation from Egypt.

It is a mark of distinction that we continue to speak at length of the Exodus, for this indicates that we are spiritually sophisticated enough to realize that we still possess its most important fruits.

הַלַּיְלָה. עַד שֶׁבָּאוּ תַלְמִידֵיהֶם וְאָמְרוּ לָהֶם, רַבּוֹתֵינוּ הִגִּיעַ זְמַן קְרִיאַת שְׁמַע שֶׁל שַׁחֲרִית.

אָמַר רַבִּי אֶלְעָזָר בֶּן עֲזַרְיָה, הֲרֵי אֲנִי כְּבֶן שִׁבְעִים שָׁנָה, וְלֹא זָכִיתִי שֶׁתֵּאָמֵר יְצִיאַת מִצְרַיִם בַּלֵּילוֹת, עַד שֶׁדְּרָשָׁהּ בֶּן זוֹמָא, שֶׁנֶּאֱמַר, לְמַעַן תִּזְכֹּר אֶת יוֹם צֵאתְךָ מֵאֶרֶץ מִצְרַיִם כֹּל יְמֵי חַיֶּיךָ.[1] יְמֵי חַיֶּיךָ

הִגִּיעַ זְמַן קְרִיאַת שְׁמַע שֶׁל שַׁחֲרִית — *It is [daybreak] time for the reading of the morning Shema.* The commentators see a deeper, allegorical significance in the disciples' words. The *Shema's* central theme is acceptance of God's sovereignty. The disciples were implying that despite the grim political situation and tyrannical Roman oppression, the disciples were so moved by their rabbis' enthusiastic discussion of the Exodus and the exalted spiritual status that this event bestowed upon the Jews, that they found themselves capable of truly and wholeheartedly accepting upon themselves the majesty of God.

אָמַר רַבִּי אֶלְעָזָר בֶּן עֲזַרְיָה הֲרֵי אֲנִי כְּבֶן שִׁבְעִים שָׁנָה — *R' Elazar ben Azaryah said: I am like a 70-year-old man.* This statement [quoted from the Mishnah (*Berachos* 1:5)] concerns the recitation of the *Shema*. The third passage of the morning *Shema* (*Numbers* 15:37-41) includes mention of the Exodus, in fulfillment of the commandment to recall the Exodus every day of our lives (*Deuteronomy* 16:3). The majority of the Sages held that this commandment does not apply at night; hence the third passage of the *Shema* need not be recited at night. R' Elazar ben Azaryah, however, held that the passage must be recited even at night.[1]

While R' Elazar's statement did not refer to the duty of retelling the story of the Exodus at the Seder, it is included in the Haggadah because it underlines the centrality of the redemption from Egypt. In the words of *Sefer HaChinuch* (21): "The Exodus is a pillar and fundamental principle of our Torah and our faith." Thus, after offering the episode in Bnei Brak as proof of the great obligation to discuss the Exodus, the Haggadah follows with R' Elazar's view as evidence of the all-encompassing nature of the theme of the Exodus (*Maharal, Abarbanel*).

According to *Maaseh Nissim* and *Aruch HaShulchan*, this paragraph actually has an indirect bearing on the Seder night: If we are commanded to mention the Exodus *every* night, it follows that the special obligation on the night of Pesach must go beyond mere mention, requiring a complete and thorough discussion of the Exodus.

הֲרֵי אֲנִי כְּבֶן שִׁבְעִים שָׁנָה — *I am like a 70-year-old man.* Rabbi Elazar ben Azaryah did not say he was actually 70 years old, but rather that he was *like* a 70-year-old. The Talmud explains this expression: After Rabban Gamliel was deposed as *Nasi* (head of the Sanhedrin), the 18-year-old R' Elazar was chosen to be his successor. He hesitated to accept the nomination, fearing that he would not command sufficient respect on account of his youth,

---

1. **Light in the Midst of Darkness.** Homiletically, this teaches us that even in the dark, foreboding "night" of exile, when we are under the oppressive hands of the nations and barely feel the benefits of the Exodus, we still must keep the memory of our freedom in our hearts and on our lips. Only through faith in God as our Redeemer can we keep alive our hopes for the ultimate Redemption. As long as we remember who we are and how God liberated us from the spiritually stifling atmosphere of Egypt, we can survive the physical and spiritual oppression of any situation.

night, until their students came and said to them: "Our teachers, it is [daybreak] time for the reading of the morning Shema."

Rabbi Elazar ben Azaryah said: "I am like a 70-year-old man, but I could not succeed in having the Exodus from Egypt mentioned every night, until Ben Zoma expounded it: It says: 'So that you will remember the day of your departure from the land of Egypt all the days of your life.'[1] 'The days of your life' indicates

_____

(1) *Deuteronomy* 16:3.

_____

whereupon his beard miraculously grew several rows of white hairs, giving him the appearance of a 70-year-old (*Berachos* 27b).[1] Despite his newfound august visage, R' Elazar says that he was not successful in persuading his colleagues of the correctness of his opinion until Ben Zoma presented a Scriptural basis for the law. According to *Rambam* (*Mishnah Commentary*), the premature white hairs were a result of R' Elazar's ceaseless toil at Torah study. Although he exerted 70 years worth

of toil in 18, and despite his constant exposure to high-caliber scholars, he had never been able to find a proper source for his opinion, until Ben Zoma expounded on the verse. Hence, וְלֹא זָכִיתִי might be rendered as, "*I did not (personally) merit the clarity of knowing a source for my opinion,*" rather than, "*I did not merit to have the law follow my opinion.*"[2]

כָּל יְמֵי חַיֶּיךָ — *All the days of your life.* [3] Were the verse to read simply "*the days*" of your life, one would have been obligated to remember the

_____

Zecher LePesach suggests that the position of the Sages, who obligate one to mention the Exodus even during the Messianic Age, may also serve as proof that even the greatest scholars must retell the story at the Seder. In spite of the prophecy of universal knowledge in Messianic times, *like the water that covers the sea* (Isaiah 11:9), we will still be obligated to remember the source of our liberty. Likewise, in spite of his towering intellect and deep understanding, even the greatest scholar must tell the story and engage in inculcating faith into his children and himself.

1. **Existential Interpretation.** R' Elazar ben Azaryah experienced firsthand the miraculous power of God to take someone who is unfit for a particular station and overnight make him spiritually fit. Thus he, more than others, sensed the importance of remembering the Exodus at night, for the Exodus, too, was a demonstration of an overnight transformation. Homiletically, this calls for us, even when experiencing the spiritual darkness symbolized by night, to firmly believe that just as God removed a nation from the depths of spiritual impurity and raised it in a moment to the spiritual pinnacle of sanctity, so He may save us from spiritual despair and elevate us to true freedom and joy (*R' Baruch Klein*).

2. **Yielding to Youth.** *Malbim*, in a novel interpretation, submits that the source verse was suggested by R' Elazar ben Azaryah himself. Nonetheless, the other Sages were reluctant to accept and rule according to the opinion of such a young man. It was only when they heard the words of Ben Zoma (*Avos* 4:1), *Who is truly wise? One who learns from every man*, that they agreed to follow the opinion of their younger colleague.

3. **Passion Rekindled.** With repetition and the passage of time, one often loses his excitement over the opportunity to serve God, and his relationship with God becomes stale. With the passage of time what was once viewed as a special chance to spend time with the King declines to habitual performance of a religious ritual. Only by reawakening and reliving the original encounter can we recapture and retain the freshness and excitement of that first moment. Therefore we are commanded to remember the Exodus, the moment when we first became, as a nation, servants of God. Thus we hope to reawaken the great love that existed between us and God at that moment — a love that should permeate all the days of our lives (*Shem MiShmuel*).

הַיָּמִים, כֹּל יְמֵי חַיֶּיךָ הַלֵּילוֹת. וַחֲכָמִים אוֹמְרִים, יְמֵי חַיֶּיךָ הָעוֹלָם הַזֶּה, כֹּל יְמֵי חַיֶּיךָ לְהָבִיא לִימוֹת הַמָּשִׁיחַ.

בָּרוּךְ הַמָּקוֹם, בָּרוּךְ הוּא. בָּרוּךְ שֶׁנָּתַן תּוֹרָה לְעַמּוֹ יִשְׂרָאֵל,

Exodus only at some time during the daylight hours, just as one must perform the *mitzvah* of *lulav* or *shofar* only by day. The inclusive word כֹּל, *all*, extends the obligation to some additional time period. According to Ben Zoma, *all* implies an obligation to remember the Exodus at night, as well as by day (see *Shaagas Aryeh* 12). The Sages contend that the inclusive term *all* teaches that the obligation to remember the Egyptian Exodus will continue even in the Messianic Era.[1]

The Vilna Gaon sees the point of contention as revolving around the definition of the word *all*. "All" can be understood in two ways. It can mean "the entire," or it can mean "every." To the Sages, "all the days of your life" connotes "*every* day," even the days of the Era of *Mashiach*. To Ben Zoma, it connotes "*the entire* day," that is, both parts of the day — daytime and nighttime.

Malbim views the dispute as related to the proper emphasis in the phrase "the days of your life." According to Ben Zoma, it means the *daytimes* of your life. Thus *all* extends the commandment to the nighttimes. The Sages interpret the word *the days* as the various *time spans* of your life. *All* extends the commandment to a different period of life, namely

the Messianic Age.

בָּרוּךְ הַמָּקוֹם — *Blessed is the Omnipresent.* The preceding passages demonstrated the importance of recalling the Exodus and showed that this duty is incumbent on all Jews, from the simple to the scholarly. Having explained the *who* and *how much* of the commandment, the Haggadah now shows *how* this is to be done. It notes that there are four places in the Torah where we are commanded to tell the Exodus story to our children, and explains that each of the passages is addressed to a different type of child.

According to Abarbanel, this introduction (בָּרוּךְ הַמָּקוֹם) precedes the discussion of the four proto-type children, because that discussion demonstrates Hashem's concern that the delight of the Torah be accessible to every Jew. By supplying four different answers to the same question, the Torah goes to great lengths to assure that every individual will find an answer befitting him. Thus, it is proper that we praise and bless Hashem for this display of kindness, for the most precious of Hashem's gifts to man is the knowledge of His Torah.

Furthermore, this discussion of the four sons shows us the richness and universality of the Torah.

---

1. **Exodus — Roots of the Future.** *Rambam* (*Hil. Melachim* 11,12) teaches that all commandments of the Torah will still apply during the Messianic Age. Why, then, might one suppose that this *mitzvah* should be suspended during the times of the Messiah?

R' Yehoshua Leib Diskin explained: The great miracles that will accompany the Messianic Age will far outshine the miracles that God wrought in conjunction with the Exodus (see *Berachos* 12b). Hence, in our excitement and jubilation over the more recent miraculous events, we might find it difficult to be emotionally moved by the events of our ancient liberation. Thus we are commanded always to remember those days — even after the coming of the Messiah — for it was then, during the Egyptian Exodus, that we were born as a nation, fit to receive the Torah and spiritually imbued for a Messianic world.

The term לְהָבִיא לִימוֹת הַמָּשִׁיחַ, lit., *to bring to the days of the Messiah* is also given a homiletical interpretation. It is our deep-seated faith in God expressed in remembering the Exodus and in our fervent hope for His Redemption that will actually cause the Messianic Age to arrive. As the *Midrash* says: "In reward for their hopes alone do they deserve to be redeemed" (*Yalkut, Tehillim* 736). All of man's hopes, dreams and even actions should be focused on bringing about the ultimate redemption. *"All the days of your life"* — to bring the days of the Mashiach (*Beis Avraham*).

the days. 'All the days of your life' indicates the nights. The other Sages say, 'the days of your life' indicates the world in its present state. 'All the days of your life' includes the days of *Mashiach.*"

Blessed is the Omnipresent; blessed is He. Blessed is the One Who has given the Torah to His people Israel;

Every individual, whatever his situation in life, can find in the Torah a message particularly meaningful to him. This sets it apart from the words of man, which contain a limited number of messages, of negligible value to those not attuned to them.

We refer to God as הַמָּקוֹם, which literally means *the Place.* The *Midrash* (*Bereishis Rabbah* 78:10) explains, הוּא מְקוֹמוֹ שֶׁל עוֹלָם וְאֵין הָעוֹלָם מְקוֹמוֹ, *He is the Place of the universe, and the universe is not His place.* God is not limited or encompassed by space; rather, He encompasses everything, and therefore is present everywhere (see *Ibn Ezra*, Introduction to *Esther*).[1]

בָּרוּךְ הוּא — *Blessed is He.* The phrase בָּרוּךְ הוּא, *Blessed is He,* has been explained as a response to the leader of the Seder. The original custom was for him to intone, בָּרוּךְ הַמָּקוֹם, *Blessed is the Om-* nipresent, and the participants would respond in unison, בָּרוּךְ הוּא, *Blessed is He.* The leader of the Seder would then declare *Blessed is the Giver of the Torah,* and again the response would be, *Blessed is He* (*Malbim*). The response may be understood as "even without us praising and blessing Him, *God is intrinsically blessed*" (*Rashbatz*).

According to *Kol Bo*, the four expressions of praise correspond to the four sons. We acknowledge God's kindness in granting us the blessing of children, though raising them properly is often fraught with great difficulty. We continue by thanking God for the wisdom of the Torah which provides us with guidelines and insight to help us raise each kind of child properly (*R' Joseph Elias*).[2]

בָּרוּךְ שֶׁנָּתַן תּוֹרָה לְעַמּוֹ יִשְׂרָאֵל — *Blessed is the One Who has given the Torah to His people Israel.* The

---

1. **Transcendently Immanent.** *R' Yehudah HaLevi* poetically captures the paradox of God being simultaneously immanent and transcendent.

אַיֵּה אֶמְצָאֲךָ הֲלֹא אַתָּה טָמִיר וְנֶעְלָם   וְאַיֵּה לֹא אֶמְצָאֲךָ כְּבוֹדְךָ מָלֵא עוֹלָם

Where can I find You; You are hidden and inscrutable.
Where can I not find You; Your glory fills the world!

According to *Ritva*, it was the giving of the Torah to Israel that provided man with the key to revealing the Godly light in all of existence. Hence, we thank God for giving us the Torah, for through it we may discover the "place" where He may be found.

2. **Redeeming the Unredeemable.** The Torah (*Exodus* 12:25-27) relates that upon being informed that their children will ask, "What is this service to you?" the Jews in Egypt bowed in gratitude to God. *Rashi* explains that this was an expression of thanks for having heard that they would merit to have future offspring. But since the question quoted in this verse is identified as that of the wicked son (as the Haggadah will shortly show), why were they so thankful? *R' Tzadok HaKohen* submits that to parents, every child should be seen as a blessing and a challenge. Even the rebellious, wicked child must be nurtured patiently. Eventually, with God's help, the rebellion may be quelled and the child may be turned to good. Parents have no right to shirk responsibility for their children, no matter how difficult and stressful child-rearing may be.

Imrei Emes suggests that the unstated message of this verse is that through Torah even the most wicked of sons is spiritually redeemable. The spark of Godliness in every Jew can never be totally destroyed. While the wicked son may not have deserved to join in the Exodus, now that Israel has the Torah, it can provide even him with spiritual regeneration.

בָּרוּךְ הוּא. כְּנֶגֶד אַרְבָּעָה בָנִים דִּבְּרָה תוֹרָה: אֶחָד חָכָם,
וְאֶחָד רָשָׁע, וְאֶחָד תָּם, וְאֶחָד שֶׁאֵינוֹ יוֹדֵעַ לִשְׁאוֹל.

essence of Israel is its connection to the Torah. The main reason why the Jews were liberated from Egypt was in order that they accept the Torah at Sinai (*Sefer HaChinuch* 306). This is reflected in the words of God when He charged Moses with the mission of taking the Israelites out of Egypt: *When you take the people out of Egypt you will serve God on this mountain* (*Exodus* 3:12). The *Midrash* (*Shemos Rabbah* 6:6) explains that it was in the merit of the future revelation, when the Jews would accept the Torah at Mount Sinai, that God redeemed them from Egypt. Thus, before we begin providing each type of child with his own tailor-made approach to the Exodus and its lessons we emphasize the goal of it all — the acceptance of the Torah (*HaSeder HaAruch*).[1]

כְּנֶגֶד אַרְבָּעָה בָנִים דִּבְּרָה תוֹרָה — *Concerning four sons does the Torah speak.* On the day marking the

birth of our nation we are particularly concerned to safeguard our national continuity by passing on our sacred legacy to our children (*R' Hirsch*).[2] This dedication to pass on our traditions to the next generation may also be seen as a repudiation of Pharaoh, who made numerous attempts to sever the connection between Jewish parents and children — through the murder of newborn boys, the interring of babies in the walls of Pithom and Raamses, interrupting Jewish family life (see p. 93), and trying to keep the children from leaving Egypt with their parents to worship God [*Exodus* 10:8-11] (*Toldos Moshe*).[3]

As mentioned above, the fact that the Torah presents four different ways for fathers to teach their children about the Exodus prompts the *Mechilta* (quoted here by the Haggadah) to interpret each dialogue (or, in one case, a monologue)

1. **Freedom for Commitment.** The numerical value of the words יְצִיאַת מִצְרַיִם, *the Egyptian Exodus* (891), is equal to that of נַעֲשֶׂה וְנִשְׁמַע, *we will do and we will listen*. The Jews were freed from bondage so that they might unconditionally commit themselves at Mount Sinai to God and His Torah.

2. **The Unbroken Chain.** With the Exodus marking the creation of the Jewish people, and Pesach its birthday, the Seder night is the national night of Judaism, an affirmation of national continuity — which has its natural roots in the family. Hence, every year, a father has to speak anew to his children, to make them fully aware of their beginnings, and to add them as new links to the unbroken chain of our national tradition. The child is made to experience the happenings of Pesach with stark immediacy — for in retelling what has been passed down through the generations, the father is no purveyor of a legend, but the witness to historical truth and national experience. "He does not speak to his children as an individual, weak and mortal, but as a representative of the nation, demanding from them the loyalty to be expected . . ." (*R' Isaac Breuer*).

3. **Newborn Fathers.** With the birth of "My firstborn son, Israel," God makes His first appearance as אָבִינוּ, "our Father." At the Seder, man emulates God, by passing on the parental heritage of belief and commitment to his own children. Thus, on this night we address our words to our children, seeking to free them of ignorance or worse, just as God showed His care for His children and freed them from servitude.

The Mishnah teaches that on the night of Pesach each father should instruct his son according to the child's intelligence (*Pesachim* 116a). According to *Yismach Yisrael*, "the father" homiletically refers to our Father in Heaven. Every Jew is a child to God, who wants to know God and how to please Him. However, with our limited understanding and intelligence, we don't always perceive what He wants from us. We therefore ask that on this night our Father teach us, each according to his intelligence. "Enlighten us so that all of our words of Torah and prayer will be imbued with spiritual light so that we can please You, and You will derive pleasure from all that we say and do. Allow us all to be a source of pride to You."

blessed is He. Concerning four sons does the Torah speak: A **wise** one, a **wicked** one, a **simple** one, and one **who is unable to ask.**

---

as a reference to a specific type of child.[1]

אֶחָד חָכָם וְאֶחָד רָשָׁע — *A wise one, a wicked one.* The word אֶחָד may also be rendered *whether*; i.e., the Torah speaks to every child, no matter what his abilities or interests, whether he is wise or wicked, simple or unable to ask (see *Bava Kamma* 45b).[2]

According to *Shibbolei HaLeket*, the fourfold blessing of God in the introductory paragraph of בָּרוּךְ הַמָּקוֹם, *Blessed is the Omnipresent*, corresponds directly to the four sons. The "Omnipresent" symbolizes the wicked son, for even he has a "*place*" in God's world and can find it through repentance.[3] The child who is unable to ask is related to the wicked son, in the sense that both are uninvolved, one by design and the other by default. Thus he is mirrored in the phrase *Blessed is He.* The next phrase, *Blessed is the One Who has given the Torah to His people Israel*, mirrors the wise son, for it is the Torah that makes someone truly wise,[4] as Moses said, *For [the Torah] is your wisdom and discernment in the eyes of the peoples* (Deuteronomy 4:6). The repetition of *Blessed is He* refers to the naive son. He is related to the wise

---

1. **Like Student, Like Son.** The Torah commands all who can to teach Torah to students (*Rambam, Hilchos Talmud Torah* 1:3). This imperative is expressed in parental terms: וְשִׁנַּנְתָּם לְבָנֶיךָ, *You shall teach them thoroughly to your children* (Deuteronomy 6:7). The Sages likens students to children (see *Rashi* ad loc.).

R' Shlomo Freifeld suggested that the Torah equates students to children in order that we never write off anyone with the judgment that he lacks the intellectual ability or curiosity to succeed. Just as he will make whatever efforts necessary, whatever the cost in time or money, in order to help his own children succeed, so he must be uncompromisingly dedicated to his students.

2. **Complex Man.** Man is a mixture of refinement and crudeness, of proper, ethical conduct and base selfishness and even cruelty. We are mistaken to think of good as the absence of bad; the two usually coexist in the same person at the same time. One can be wise and righteous and yet be hounded by inner wickedness that gnaws at his conscience and attempts to dominate his inner self. Likewise, one's tendencies to negativity do not have exclusive control of him; one's intrinsic good is no less vibrant an ingredient in his makeup (*R' Chaim Shmulevitz*).

This is the homiletic message of the four sons — there is really only one (אֶחָד) son, who is wise, and yet that same one is also wicked. The word אֶחָד (gematria = 13), multiplied by the four sons, equals 52, the gematria equivalent of בֵּן, *son*. All four sons are in reality different aspects of the same son, who often suffers from "spiritual schizophrenia."

3. **God — Refuge for the Displaced.** The term הַמָּקוֹם is emphasized when visiting the sick (see *Shabbos* 12b); when comforting mourners we say הַמָּקוֹם יְנַחֵם אֶתְכֶם, *May the Omnipresent comfort you*, and on behalf of our brethren who are delivered into distress and captivity we offer the prayer הַמָּקוֹם יְרַחֵם עֲלֵיהֶם, *May the Omnipresent have mercy on them.* God is the repository of the universe. Even those who feel displaced, either physically or emotionally, may take solace and strength from the fact that He always has a place for them, that He is their immediate Companion, the All-Embracing One Who envelops all (*R' Yosef Dov Soloveitchik*).

4. **Six Doctorates.** R' Chaim Heller once called a young lady, who had recently been granted a master's degree, to suggest a marriage partner for her. The young man was an intellectual phenomenon, a dazzling Talmudic genius who knew little in the way of secular knowledge. "I have a young man for you who has six doctorates," R' Chaim told her. "Isn't mastery of *Nezikin* (the mishnaic order about monetary laws) a doctorate? Even one who masters *Bava Basra* (a large Talmudic tractate) alone is deserving of a doctorate. This young genius has mastered all six sections of the Talmud and deserves at least six doctorates!" R' Chaim concluded. They eventually married and produced a family famed for its Torah scholarship.

חָכָם מָה הוּא אוֹמֵר? מָה הָעֵדֹת וְהַחֻקִּים וְהַמִּשְׁפָּטִים אֲשֶׁר צִוָּה יהוה אֱלֹהֵינוּ אֶתְכֶם?[1] וְאַף אַתָּה אֱמָר לוֹ כְּהִלְכוֹת הַפֶּסַח, אֵין מַפְטִירִין אַחַר הַפֶּסַח אֲפִיקוֹמָן.

son, for he, too, would like to be wise and informed; he simply lacks the ability to be so.[1]

חָכָם מָה הוּא אוֹמֵר — *The wise son — what does he say?* The Haggadah now asks, "Which of the questions mentioned in the Torah is that of the wise son?" (*Iyun Tefillah*).[2]

According to R' Shlomo Alkabetz, the term חָכָם does not designate intellectual prowess; rather, it refers to one who is scrupulous in his fulfillment of *mitzvos* (see *Deuteronomy* 4:6). Thus the רָשָׁע, who disdains any commitment to God, is the direct antithesis of the חָכָם.[3]

מָה הָעֵדֹת — *What are the testimonies?* The wisdom of this son is seen in his ability to discern between the different types of *mitzvos* — testimonies, decrees and ordinances. In the context of the Seder, "testimonies" are laws (such as the eating of matzah, *maror*, etc.) that "testify" to historical events; "decrees" are statutes whose rationales are not readily understood, such as the rule against breaking a bone of the *pesach* offering;[4] and "ordinances" are laws that regulate our relations with other people, such as the Torah's ordinance that an

---

1. **Generational Breakdown.** *Malbim* views the four sons as representative of a historical pattern in the decline of Torah observance. The first generation of alienation, the wise one, follows the *mitzvos* of the Torah, yet questions why all different types of *mitzvos* are necessary, voicing skepticism to its children. Unwilling to submit unqualifiedly to the will of God as did their pious fathers, they want to know the meaning of every aspect of the ritual. The child of the next generation, the wicked son, sees no need to observe his father's "ancient and outdated" practices. "What is the purpose of all that *you* do?" he snickers. "Why should I perform rituals that even you yourself feel are futile?" he asks his father.

As to be expected, the wicked son offers his own child no Jewish education or exposure to vibrant Judaism, and the youngster grows up bereft of his spiritual heritage. Only on Pesach when the family visits grandparents for the Seder does he see a fleeting display of Torah and *mitzvos*. Unfamiliar with these strange practices he asks, "What is this?" He is the simple son.

The most tragic of all is the next generation, the simple son's child. He does not even have the opportunity to visit with an observant grandfather and at least once a year taste the beauty of real Judaism. He grows up in total ignorance, completely uninformed and unable to participate at all (*Malbim to Exodus* 13:14).

2. **Verbally Defined.** The way one speaks is indicative of his essential character. The Talmud (*Pesachim* 3b) relates that two students who studied under Rav were both expressing their feelings of fatigue after having studied a particularly difficult Talmudic topic. One said, "The topic made me feel like a tired swine," while the other compared himself to a fatigued lamb. Rav severely censured the first student for speaking in such a degrading manner. Thus, we might homiletically render: חָכָם, *What identifies someone as a wise man?* מָה הוּא אוֹמֵר, *What he says.* So, too, the wicked son. He is recognizable by the manner in which he expresses himself (*R' Baruch of Mezhibezh*).

3. **No Questions Asked.** According to *the Chafetz Chaim* the first son is called the חָכָם, *wise one*, rather than the seemingly more appropriate "righteous son," the term that would best contrast him with the wicked son. The reason is that a genuinely righteous person serves God with accepting simplicity, and feels no urge to ask questions.

4. **The Rewards of Obedience.** The wise son's request for an explanation of the חֻקִּים, *decrees*, is seemingly misplaced, since a חֹק, by definition, is a law whose reason is not known. *Sfas Emes* explains: While initially God does not teach us the reason for a חֹק, one who follows God's will even without understanding is eventually granted the enlightenment to penetrate the meaning of even these *mitzvos*. As King David teaches, סוֹד ה' לִירֵאָיו, *The secret of Hashem [is revealed] to those who fear Him* (*Psalms* 25:14).

The wise son — what does he say? "What are the testimonies, decrees and ordinances which HASHEM, our God, has commanded you?"[1] And you should also tell him the laws of Pesach: that one may not eat dessert after the final taste of the *pesach* offering.

_____

(1) *Deuteronomy* 6:20.

_____

uncircumcised person may not partake from the *pesach* offering (*Rashi*).

Although the Haggadah criticizes the wicked son for addressing the Jewish people as "you," as if to remove himself from the congregation (see below), the wise son uses the word *you* to address the older people who, unlike himself, had personally participated in the Exodus. By saying *Hashem, our God*, the wise son clearly indicates that he views himself as subservient to God's will (*Machzor Vitry*). Furthermore, he does not refer to the *mitzvos* as עֲבוֹדָה, *labor*, a term the wicked son employs pejoratively, as if serving God were an onerous burden (*Shibbolei HaLeket*; see *Yerushalmi*, *Pesachim* 10:4). The wise son clearly sees Divine service as a pleasurable opportunity and a privilege.

וְאַף אַתָּה אֱמָר לוֹ כְּהִלְכוֹת הַפֶּסַח — *And you should also tell him the laws of Pesach.*[1] The Torah's response to the question of the חָכָם is עֲבָדִים הָיִינוּ, *we were slaves to Pharaoh in Egypt, and HASHEM took us out from there. . . And he commanded us to perform all these decrees . . .* (*Deuteronomy* 6:21-25). Earlier the Haggadah paraphrased this verse as

a general answer to the four questions. Here, however, the Haggadah does not quote this passage in response to the wise son; instead it tells the father to instruct his son about the laws of Pesach, and specifies only the rule that nothing may be eaten after the *afikoman*. Why does the Haggadah veer from the response supplied by the Torah itself [see chart, p. 56], and why does it substitute this peculiar answer?

According to *Abarbanel*, *Malbim*, et al., when the Haggadah says, *also tell him the laws of Pesach*, it does not mean that we should omit the Torah's answer to his question; on the contrary, we should surely give him that answer. However, since the wise son's question indicates that he seeks clarity and understanding regarding the commandments of Pesach, we must go beyond the Torah's basic answer of the Torah and teach him all the detailed laws, down to the last set of Pesach laws in the Mishnah tractate *Pesachim*: *it is forbidden to eat anything after the Pesach offering* [which is symbolized by the *afikoman*].[2] Thus, the passage might be rendered "and you should also tell him the laws of Pesach [in their entirety], *until* the law regarding not

_____

1. **Laws — Bearer of the Message.** This response indicates that a discussion of the *laws* of Pesach qualifies as fulfillment of the obligation to discuss the Exodus (*Beis HaLevi*).

2. **Retaining the Effect.** In asking about all the different types of *mitzvos*, the wise son seeks to discover the common thread that expresses their essential message. We reply that the taste of the *pesach* must remain in his mouth. The main goal of the commandments is that God remain an ever-present reality in our lives, not merely an idea relegated to the "religion compartment" of our mind and life.

⋖§ **A Reminder of Good Times.** *Zichron Kedoshim* elaborates, in a similar vein. The wise son wants to know why the Torah needs to reiterate so often that we must follow the commandments. Shouldn't the sheer joy of following the will of God be sufficient motivation? We reply by citing the Mishnah that teaches about the time after the eating of the *pesach* sacrifice; homiletically this refers to the exile experience, when the *pesach* cannot be offered. Not always do we sense the beauty of the Torah life. In times of spiritual darkness we need to be reminded of the sweet taste of serving God. Thus, the Torah offers repeated reminders to keep its way of life so that the taste of its freedom will always remain in our mouths.

רָשָׁע מָה הוּא אוֹמֵר? מָה הָעֲבֹדָה הַזֹּאת לָכֶם?[1] לָכֶם וְלֹא לוֹ, וּלְפִי שֶׁהוֹצִיא אֶת עַצְמוֹ מִן הַכְּלָל, כָּפַר בְּעִקָּר

eating any dessert after eating the *pesach* offering."

Maharal notes that the Torah's answer to the wise son concludes: HASHEM *commanded us to perform **all** these decrees to fear* HASHEM *our God, for our good all the days* (Deuteronomy 6:24). Thus, the Torah itself alludes that a discussion of all the laws of Pesach is an appropriate response to the wise son.

The words אֵין מַפְטִירִין mean *one should not conclude* with a dessert after eating the *pesach* offering. Similarly, the Torah reading of the Sabbath and festivals concludes with the *Haftarah*, an additional reading from the Prophets, which is a "dessert," so to speak (*Avudraham*).

אֲפִיקוֹמָן — *A dessert*. *Afikoman* is a Greek word meaning *dessert* (see *Tosafos R' Akiva Eiger*). It has also been explained as a contraction of the Aramaic words אַפִּיקוּ מִינֵי מְתִיקָה, *bring on the sweets* (*Rashbam*); normally, after the main course of a festive meal people would ask for some sweet type of dessert. Thus, the Mishnah quoted here teaches that after partaking of the *pesach* offering one may not issue a call for dessert, so that the taste of the *pesach* offering should remain in one's mouth as

long as possible.

In current usage the term *afikoman* has been borrowed to designate the final piece of matzah eaten as "dessert" at the end of the Seder meal.

רָשָׁע מָה הוּא אוֹמֵר — *What does the wicked son say?* This father-son dialogue is taken from *Exodus* 12:26. The Haggadah assigns this question to a wicked son, because his choice of the word *to you* shows that he removes himself from participation in the commandments. There must be some other indication of wickedness than this in the verse, however, for the wise son also uses the word "you" in his question (see above)! *Chukas HaPesach* notes that the verse here introduces this son's "question" as כִּי יֹאמְרוּ אֲלֵיכֶם בְּנֵיכֶם — *when your sons will **say** to you* (Exodus 12:26) — they are making a *statement*, rather than seeking an answer to a question.[1]

In introducing the question of the wise son, the Torah speaks in the singular, *your son*, for all truth is one and indivisible. The question of the wicked son, however, is introduced in the plural, *your sons*, because there are as many different ways of deserting the truth as there are sinners (*Rabbi M. Lehmann*).[2]

1. **Unquestioning Compliance.** It is noteworthy that the questions of the wise and righteous sons are described in the Torah as being asked *tomorrow*. The righteous son never questions whether or not he should fulfill the commandments; he fulfills them today — and only afterwards seeks enlightenment about their deeper meaning so that he may appreciate their profundity and significance. Not so the wicked son. His question might be rephrased as, "Give me a good reason why I should do what the Torah asks of me." His question is asked today, not tomorrow, because he is in reality not ready to act with faith (*She'eiris Menachem*).

2. **Looking for Answers, Looking for Questions.** *Meshech Chochmah* notes that only the question of the רָשָׁע lacks the term לֵאמֹר, *saying*. According to *Sifre* (*Va'eschanan*), לֵאמֹר in the context of a question means "provide an answer." But the רָשָׁע seeks no answers — he knows his answer even before he asks the question.

In a similar vein, *Pachad Yitzchak* explains why the Haggadah uses the same verse in answer to both the wicked son and the son who does know how to ask. Both ask no questions, and hence do not need replies. We merely teach both of them the story of the Exodus and emphasize whatever points we think will spiritually arouse them.

⦿§ **Looking for Answers.** The wise son raises his questions in private, and reverently questions his elders in search of truth and enlightenment. Hence his question is couched in terms of a singular questioner. Wicked people, however, in their zeal to ridicule the Torah and those who are loyal to it, air their scornful questions publicly, seeking to spread their heresy wherever possible. Thus their statement-question becomes a public matter, placed in the mouths of many "children" (*Maskil LeEisan*).

The wicked son — what does he say? "Of what purpose is this service to you?"[1] "To you," thereby excluding himself. Since he excludes himself from the group he denies everything.

(1) *Exodus* 12:26.

By saying "Of what purpose is this service to *you*?" the wicked son is, as the Haggadah puts it, "excluding himself from the community." He implies that God's commandments are neither binding nor beneficial; rather they are irrelevant.[1] Therefore his question must be understood as a sarcastic statement of derision: "What is the burden that you impose upon us every year?" (*Yerushalmi, Pesachim* 10:4). He does not necessarily negate the importance of the Exodus, but he rejects — as so many Jews in later generations did as well — the necessity of observing rituals to arrive at the desired spiritual and mental goals (*R' Shlomo Kluger*).

וּלְפִי שֶׁהוֹצִיא אֶת עַצְמוֹ מִן הַכְּלָל כָּפַר בְּעִקָּר – *Since he excludes himself from the group he denies everything.* The question clearly indicates that he excludes himself from the community of God's servants, and that attitude ultimately leads to denial of God Himself. Negation of the Divine origin of the commandments is, in effect, a rejection of God's word (*Machzor Vitry*).

Rambam (*Hil. Teshuvah* 3:11) writes that one who consciously separates himself from the Jewish community and does not share in its troubles or triumphs is considered a heretic who has no share in the World to Come. Even if he transgressed no particular sin by his actions or beliefs, his decision to sever his ties with the nation becomes a fact, and like a severed limb, the spiritual life-giving blood of Jewish nationhood does not reach him.

The very act of separating oneself from the Jewish people is a form of separation from God; for we are linked to Him through the common unity of all Jewish souls, and through our common historical heritage. Furthermore, since the Jewish people serve as witnesses to God's existence, both through following His will and by its miraculous survival, cutting one's ties is tantamount to refus-

1. **Sincere Interest.** *R' Reuven Rabinowitz* offered the following parable to explain the difference between the wise and wicked sons. A store owner hired a clerk to assist him in managing the store and sales. The new employee was a great boon to the business, assiduously memorizing the different types of merchandise and the price of each item, serving customers cheerfully and climbing up and down the ladder all day, bringing people whatever they wanted to consider. Eventually the owner's son grew up and was brought into the business. The young man worked as hard as the clerk. After hours, after the clerk had gone home, the son would pepper his father with questions about the business. "What makes this item better? Why is this one cheaper?" The son wanted to know every detail. Finally, exasperated, the father lost his patience. "Why so many questions? The clerk has been working here for years, but he never asked me about quality or the pricing schedule. Why do you pester me so much?"

The son replied, "What kind of comparison is that? He is a mere worker; he wants to do a good job but has no real interest in the success of the business. For him the main thing is his paycheck. My role is different. As your son, I want to do whatever I can to make your business successful and profitable. That is why I ask so many questions."

The wicked son is like the clerk. Even if he keeps the *mitzvos* he is only in it for the reward, the "paycheck." Basically, he sees it as a tiresome burden. "Of what purpose is this service to you?"

Not so the wise son. A loyal son of his Father, he asks many questions about the different types of *mitzvos*, all so that he may yield more spiritual profit on behalf of his Father Whom he loves and to Whom he feels so deeply indebted. "What are the testimonies, etc.?"

וְאַף אַתָּה הַקְהֵה אֶת שִׁנָּיו וֶאֱמָר לוֹ, בַּעֲבוּר זֶה עָשָׂה יהוה לִי בְּצֵאתִי מִמִּצְרָיִם.¹ לִי וְלֹא לוֹ, אִלּוּ הָיָה שָׁם לֹא הָיָה נִגְאָל.

תָּם מָה הוּא אוֹמֵר? מַה זֹּאת? וְאָמַרְתָּ אֵלָיו, בְּחֹזֶק יָד הוֹצִיאָנוּ יהוה מִמִּצְרַיִם מִבֵּית עֲבָדִים.²

---

ing to bear witness for God.[1]

וְאַף אַתָּה הַקְהֵה אֶת שִׁנָּיו — *You too should blunt his teeth.* [2] Once again the Haggadah provides an answer different from the Biblical one. In the Torah the wicked son's question is answered thus: *And you shall say, "It is a pesach offering for HASHEM, Who passed over the houses of the Children of Israel, when He struck Egypt and saved our houses"* (*Exodus* 12:27).

Actually, as *Ritva* points out, there is a strong connection between the answers of the Torah and the Haggadah, for the basic message of the Torah's reply is that the *pesach* offering is brought for Hashem, and is closed to nonbelievers. Hashem spared those people in Egypt who followed His instructions, "passing over the houses of the

Children of Israel" when He saw the sacrificial blood on the doorposts.

Instead of simply quoting the Torah's response verbatim, the Haggadah tells us the underlying message of that response, in a direct and blunt manner: If you had been there, you would not have been redeemed. This thought is actually expressed most clearly in the Torah's answer to the son who does not know how to ask. He is told, *for the sake of my fulfilling these laws* (pesach, matzah and maror), *God did this for me, and redeemed me from Egypt;* — *if you had been there, you would not have been redeemed.* You would have died in the three days of darkness, as did other Jews who did not deserve redemption (*Shibbolei HaLeket*),[3] or perhaps you would have disappeared through assimilation into

---

1. **Nationally Anonymous.** Heresy is a direct result of a refusal to share in the national mission of the Jewish people. The wicked son begins by rejecting the responsibilities incumbent upon a Jew; only afterwards does he fabricate the "ideology" necessary to justify his carefree lifestyle (*R' Isser Zalman Meltzer*).

2. **Useless Teeth.** It is appropriate to blunt the teeth of the wicked son. He demands to know how there can be a connection between Divine service [עֲבוֹדָה] and personal, physical enjoyment [לָכֶם, *what belongs to you*]. Looking at the Seder, he says, "Drinking wine, eating matzah, a sumptuous festive meal — what do these have to do with service of God?"

We answer that everything God gave man was meant to be a tool in His service. Teeth are made in order to help man eat, the better to serve God. Hence we blunt his teeth and, pointing to the matzah, we tell him, "Do you really think God created you with teeth only in order to eat, drink and be merry? It was in order to perform *mitzvos*, such as eating matzah, that God took us out of Egypt! If you are uninterested in these things, you have no proper use for your teeth!" (*Kozhnitzer Maggid*).

3. **The Sustainable Spirit.** The answer to the pessimism of the wicked son is to remind him that we left Egypt fortified with a belief in God and His ability to transform us from slaves into a holy people. We followed God out into an unsown land symbolic of our spiritual emptiness. It was due to our faith in ourselves and in God as One Who "plants righteousness and sprouts salvation" that we had the courage to leave the familiar and thus comfortable Egypt.

We thus tell the wicked son: "It was because of this that God provided for me when I left Egypt." With the same faith, we still obey His will. Had our ancestors had your attitude of despair, they would have lacked the courage to leave Egypt and would not have been redeemed. Like our forefathers in Egypt, we

You too should blunt his teeth and tell him: "It is because of this that HASHEM did so for me when I went out of Egypt."[1] "For me," but not for him — had he been there, he would not have been redeemed.

The simple son — what does he say? "What is this?" And you shall say to him: "HASHEM took us out of Egypt, from the house of bondage, by strength of hand."[2]

---

(1) *Exodus* 13:8. (2) 13:14.

Egyptian society long before the hour of redemption, or remained behind in perpetual slavery.

תָּם — *The simple son.* The Haggadah now introduces the third prototype son to whom we must provide answers and guidance.

The word תָּם carries several shades of meaning. According to *Machzor Vitry, Kol Bo,* et al., he lacks the sophistication to frame his questions clearly and intellectually. He speaks in generalities and simply expresses his wonderment at everything that is going on, seeking to be enlightened as to its nature and meaning. Unlike the wicked son, however, he is sincere in wanting to learn and does not question in a contentious fashion (see *Rashi, Exodus* 13:14).

According to the *Vilna Gaon,* the תָּם (related to תָּמִים, *complete*) possesses a moral wholesomeness in his attitude toward God and his duties toward Him. Thus, he is the antithesis of the wicked son. *Rashi* (*Genesis* 25:27) defines a תָּם as one who lacks the duplicity to deceive people. He says what he thinks and enjoys a morally refreshing naivete.

The question of this son — *What is this?* — appears in the Torah with regard to the commandment of the sanctification of the firstborn (*Exodus* 13:14), yet the Haggadah construes it as referring to Pesach. *Abarbanel* explains: In *Exodus* 13:2, God commanded Moses: "Sanctify to Me every firstborn, the first issue of every womb among the Children of Israel, of man and beast; it is Mine." Rather than immediately conveying this to the people, Moses launched into a lengthy introduction enjoining the Jews to remember the Exodus, reviewing the prohibition against eating *chametz* on Pesach, stressing the command to eat matzah and introducing the commandment of *tefillin.* By doing so, Moses meant to imply that the plague of the firstborn, which is commemorated by the sanctification of the firstborn, is itself part of the broader theme of commemoration of the Exodus.[1] Moses therefore introduced this *mitzvah* by listing other commandments that share its basic motif to stress the centrality of this idea to the Jewish faith. Thus when the son asks, *What is this?,* he refers not merely to the sanctification of the firstborn, but to the whole idea of commemorating the Exodus and all of its concomitant *mitzvos.*

מַה זֹּאת — *What is this?* His question is simple and straightforward — "What is this?" Unlearned in the symbols of the Seder, he expresses a straightforward desire to be informed.

---

must only take the first step and follow our Godly instincts into the wasteland of our latent strengths. With faith that better days are coming, we in fact will be blessed with permanent success at our spiritual development (*Yismach Yisrael*).

1. **Homage to Our Creator.** We are commanded to offer the first of all our possessions to God. Whether through our sons, our livestock, the *challah* (first bit of dough) or the *bikkurim* (first fruits), we express the eternal truth that God created all and that we are beholden to Him for all that we have. We were taught this lesson when God miraculously annulled all the laws of nature in order that Egypt — and, more importantly, Israel — realize that *there is none like Me in all the world* (*Exodus* 9:14) and *so that you shall know that the earth [and all it contains] is* HASHEM'S (ibid. 29).

וְשֶׁאֵינוֹ יוֹדֵעַ לִשְׁאוֹל, אַתְּ פְּתַח לוֹ. שֶׁנֶּאֱמַר, וְהִגַּדְתָּ לְבִנְךָ בַּיּוֹם הַהוּא לֵאמֹר, בַּעֲבוּר זֶה עָשָׂה יהוה

According to *Kli Yakar*, the timing of this question shows that the simple son seeks answers, rather than a legitimization not to live according to the Torah. He asks his question *tomorrow*, after having redeemed his firstborn. Only on the morrow, having faithfully done his duty, does he question in earnest, "I have been loyal to the Torah, now please explain to me the significance of what I have done." Likewise, his questions about the Seder ritual are asked with a true desire to know, rather than to challenge and question.

וְאָמַרְתָּ אֵלָיו — *And you shall say to him.* We answer his simple question in a general manner, by invoking the words of Scripture: *With a strong hand HASHEM removed us from Egypt.* In a dazzling display of might, God removed us from being enslaved to mortal men and inculcated in us the faith to follow Him and serve Him.[1]

We reassure the תָּם by reminding him that God intervened in Egypt "with a strong hand" to make us His people; that intervention is the assurance of our survival, throughout all future periods of exile and persecution (*Rabbi M. Lehmann*).[2]

מִמִּצְרַיִם מִבֵּית עֲבָדִים — *From Egypt, from the house*

of bondage. The redemption was spiritual and physical. Not only were we freed from the *house of physical* bondage, but we also were cleansed of any spiritual residue from having been exposed to the lure of the culture and immorality of *Egypt*. [3]

וְשֶׁאֵינוֹ יוֹדֵעַ לִשְׁאוֹל — *As for the son who is unable to ask.* The fourth type of child lacks either the intellect or motivation to question his elders about the Exodus and, more generally, about his spiritual heritage. The child who is still too immature to search for truth must be inspired to ask questions — therefore, *you must open conversation with him.* *Shelah* suggests that this son is in certain ways worse than the wicked son. Severed from all connection to the authentic sources of Torah and Judaism and its practitioners, he has no lifeline from which to draw spiritual sustenance. He is so apathetic about the needs of his soul that he feels no urge to ask questions. His silence does not come from insufficient intellect; rather it represents apathy regarding the needs of his soul and spirit. The

---

1. **Curing Spiritual Schizophrenia.** We sometimes suffer from "spiritual schizophrenia." When in the synagogue or the study hall, in the company of righteous and upstanding people, we desire the spiritually uplifting pursuit of Torah study or prayer, but when we return to our homes or businesses we may lapse into our more base concerns. We ask, *What is this?* The key to resolve this personal dilemma is to remember that God removed us from Egypt with a "strong hand," implying that strong conviction and consistency are the necessary ingredients to remain on an unswerving course of spiritual growth (*Zichron Kadosh*).

◆§ **A Moving Experience.** The simple son suffers from spiritual apathy; nothing moves him. The word תָּם contains the same letters as מֵת (dead), for apathy is spiritually fatal. The only answer for him is to shake himself free from his complacent indifference. We tell him of the strong hand with which God removed us from Egypt and hope that he too will be able to rouse himself from his spiritual slumber (*Nesivos Shalom*).

2. **Awaiting Your Cry.** On a more personal level, the simple uninitiate must be reassured that no matter how far he strayed from the Godly path or how deeply he finds himself enmeshed in sin, God only awaits for him to cry out for help and He will extricate him from his spiritual bondage. Just as God showed His strong arm and removed an undeserving people from the throes of almost fatal impurity, so God can and will save us from being overwhelmed by the forces of negativity in society and in man (*R' Tzadok HaKohen*).

3. **Strengthened, Not Subdued.** Egypt served as the womb that carried the nation of Israel during its spiritual gestation (see *Deuteronomy* 4:34). We survived exposure to the impurity of Egypt without signs of spiritual damage. Thus, we left not only the house of bondage — we even left behind the influence of Egypt. It is to this challenge that we must always rise in whatever exile we find ourselves. We must be strengthened by the experience of having retained strong Jewish identity while under spiritual siege, and constantly renew the effort to insure that we are not drawn into the cultural milieu of our host nation.

As for **the son who is unable to ask,** you must open conversation with him, as it is stated: "And you shall tell your son on that day, saying, 'It is because of this that HASHEM did so

wicked son asks brazenly, but at least he opens lines of communication. This son is content with his spiritual wilderness.[1]

אַתְּ פְּתַח לוֹ – *You must open conversation with him.* Open the doors of inquiry for this son who is unable or uninspired to speak for himself (*Malbim*). Provide him with the stimuli to want to question what he sees (*Shibbolei HaLeket, Avudraham*). This educational process is best started by focusing his attention on the concrete visual symbols of *pesach,* matzah and *maror.*

The term אַתְּ is the female form of the word *you.* Seemingly אַתָּה, the male form, would be more appropriate and in line with the usage in regard to the other sons. Many explanations have been advanced: A son who cannot or does not want to ask questions is often the result of having not received a proper education. Since teaching a child Torah is a paternal (rather than a maternal) obligation, the Haggadah refers to the child's father with the female term, as an allusion that the father was remiss in properly educating the child (*Seder HaAruch*).

Generally paternal guidance is offered with a firm hand and a hard and demanding tone, while maternal help is usually offered more tenderly. The child who has drifted far from his sources and heritage needs to be embraced with motherly love in order to bring him spiritually back home. Thus, אַתְּ פְּתַח לוֹ — it is with the feminine touch that we will succeed in saving this type of son for our nation.[2]

Torah Temimah finds in this word a homiletical allusion that parents should provide a thorough education for the uninitiated. Do not be satisfied with a simple explanation of the symbols of the Seder. Instead, teach this child step by step, "from A to Z," all that he is able to comprehend and absorb about the Exodus and faith in God. Thus, אַתְּ פְּתַח לוֹ — "open up for him from *Aleph* (the first letter of the Hebrew alphabet) to *Tav* (the last letter)," giving him the full picture of our history, heritage and faith.

שֶׁנֶּאֱמַר וְהִגַּדְתָּ לְבִנְךָ בַּיּוֹם הַהוּא לֵאמֹר – *As it is stated: "And you will tell your son on that day, saying."*[3] This is the only Biblical verse speaking of retelling

1. **Signposts Along Life's Path.** This child does not want to consult older people. He refuses to understand the truth so poetically captured by the *Chazon Ish*: "Man goes through life like one hopelessly lost in the thick overgrown forest with neither a trail nor even a footpath. If not for the help of those who once passed through and who, by designating mental signposts along the way, can serve as the eyes of the young, the footsteps of the youngsters would slip on the thorns and thistles strewn along life's path as it traverses the mountains and valleys spread across the land of living" (*Collected Letters* I:55).

We must impress upon him that the basis of our Torah is the chain of tradition and transmission from generation to generation. It is because of this quality of intergenerational communication that God saved us from Egypt.

2. **Tough but Tender.** Effective education demands a blend of encouragement and confidence-building coupled with the harsh realities of life. On one hand we want to be gentle with our young, but on the other hand we do them an injustice if we allow them to grow up in a fantasy world where everything they do is unconditionally acceptable.

The verse cited by Haggadah alludes to this synthesis of tough and tender: וְהִגַּדְתָּ, *and you shall tell,* mirrors the hard approach, as the Sages interpret this expression to mean that we must address them with words that are "hard like sinews" [גִּידִין] (see *Rashi* to Exodus 19:3). On the other hand this must be tempered with לֵאמֹר, *saying* (the verb implying gentle speech — see *Rashi* ibid.), in a way that allows gentle concern to be conveyed to the child all the while (see *Tiferes Shlomo*).

3. *The Steipler Gaon* suggests a *gematria* allusion to this verse being a reference to the son who is unable to ask: וְהִגַּדְתָּ לְבִנְךָ בַּיּוֹם הַהוּא לֵאמֹר equals לָזֶה שֶׁאֵינוֹ יוֹדֵעַ לִשְׁאוֹל, *to this one (son) who is unable to ask* (866).

לִי בְּצֵאתִי מִמִּצְרָיִם.[1]

יָכוֹל מֵרֹאשׁ חֹדֶשׁ, תַּלְמוּד לוֹמַר בַּיּוֹם הַהוּא. אִי

the Exodus to children that is not preceded by a question. Thus it clearly refers to the child who is unable to ask (*Torah Temimah*).[1]

The verse goes on to state that it was in order to fulfill the *mitzvos* of matzah and *maror* that God redeemed us. This son more than others needs these physical props in order to generate his interest and participation. Thus it is this verse that the Torah prescribes in addressing him.[2]

The basic attitudes of the four sons described by the

SON	TORAH'S QUESTION	TORAH'S ANSWER	HAGGADAH'S ANSWER
Wise	If your child asks you tomorrow, saying, "What are the testimonies, decrees and ordinances which HASHEM, our God, has commanded you?" (*Deut*. 6:20).	You shall say to your child, "We were slaves in Egypt and HASHEM, our God, took us out of Egypt with a strong hand" (*Deut*. 6:21).	Instruct him in the laws of Pesach, that one may not eat anything after eating the *pesach* offering.
Wicked	And it shall be when your children say to you, "Of what purpose is this service to you?" (*Exodus* 12:26).	You shall say, "It is the *pesach* feast offering to HASHEM Who passed over the houses of the Children of Israel in Egypt, etc." (*Exodus* 12:27).	You must blunt his teeth and tell him, "It is because of this that HASHEM acted on my behalf when I went out of Egypt."
Simple	And it shall be when your son will ask you at some future time, "What is this?" (*Exodus* 13:14).	You shall say to him, "With a strong hand HASHEM took us out of Egypt" (*Exodus* 13:14).	Same as the Torah's.
Uninformed	No question.	And you shall tell your son on that day, saying, "It was because of this that Hashem acted on my behalf when I went out of Egypt."	Same as the Torah's.

1. **Breaking the Silence.** This passage of the Haggadah is interpreted in a homiletic vein by *R' Moshe of Kobrin*. Each of us comes to the Seder seeking to emerge from our own emotional imprisonment so that we may earnestly turn to God in prayer. We hope to bare our hearts of our innermost desire to be close to Him, and yet we find ourselves unable to ask of Him what we truly seek. We are like the son who is unable to ask. We implore our Father to take the initiative, "You open us up. Smash the locks that seal our hearts, so that we may turn to You in prayer."

In every Jew is a soul that yearns to be close to its Source, as King David said, *But as for me, God's nearness is my good* (Psalms 73:28). In the course of time this focal point of spiritual light becomes dimmed as layers upon layers of spiritual callousness envelop our hearts and emotions. Trapped inside is a stifled soul unable to ask for its most profound wish. Tonight we beg of God that He remove the impediments that imprison our true will. The gates of heaven (from א to ת) are open only to someone who knows that he doesn't know how to ask (*R' Chaim of Sanz*).

2. **Self-Expression.** The Torah teaches that we should tell our children and grandchildren of the great miracles that Hashem did in the process of taking us out of Egypt *so that you may know that I am HASHEM* (Exodus 10:2). Seemingly "so that *they* may know" would have been more appropriate.

R' Yehoshua of Belz explained: In order to tell our children about God and to inculcate them with faith, we ourselves must know, clearly and unequivocally, that *I am HASHEM*. Only if we are excited and animated as we relate the Exodus story will we succeed in penetrating the heart and conscience of every child.

for me when I went out of Egypt.'"[1]

One might think [that the obligation to discuss the Exodus commences] with the first day of the month of Nissan, but the Torah says: "You shall tell your son on that day." But the ex-

---

(1) *Exodus* 13:8.

Torah still exist today. The wise son is eager to learn about the various commandments of the Torah; he is the Torah scholar. It is from such scholars that the simple, unlearned Jew seeks inspiration and instruction. The wicked son, on the other hand, shows his contempt for the Torah and its teachers; he seeks to decide for himself what should or should not be done. Such people stand out as examples for the uninquisitive son to follow — he is the Jew who does not seek spiritual enrichment, but self-indulgence and permissiveness. As deniers of the importance of the Torah and of any spiritual relationship to God, such people show that they have no connection to the redemption from Egypt — and "if they had been there they would not have been redeemed" (based on *Malbim*).[1]

יָכוֹל מֵרֹאשׁ חֹדֶשׁ — *One might think [that the obligation to discuss the Exodus commences] with the first of the month.* This passage elaborates on the verse which we just quoted in response to the "son who is unable to ask," and seeks to define the exact meaning of *that day.* It is included here so that after

explaining *how* and to *whom* the story of the Exodus should be retold, it will now give us a time frame and tell us *when* it is to be recounted (*Rashbam*).

The Haggadah quotes the *Mechilta* regarding the exact time when one may fulfill the Biblical command of recounting the Exodus.

One might have thought that the time for recounting the story of the Exodus starts at the beginning of the month of Nissan, for the process of redemption began on the first day of the month, with God's instructions to Moses concerning the *pesach* offering (see *Exodus* 12:1-20) (*Rashbam*). In fact, because Moses started instructing the Jews about the laws of Pesach on that day, we are enjoined every year to study these laws from this day on (*Tosefta, Megillah* 3:2) (*Ritva*). Moreover, the Torah commands וְעָבַדְתָּ אֶת הָעֲבוֹדָה הַזֹּאת בַּחֹדֶשׁ הַזֶּה, *you shall perform this service in this month (Exodus 13:5)*[2] —

---

1. **A Four-sided Equation.** According to *Sfas Emes* each of the four sons focuses on a different aspect of the Exodus and its commemoration. The wise son wants to know God's *purpose* in instituting the Pesach observances, and he is told that they were ordained in order to inculcate within us certain lofty principles that apply to us today as in the past. The simple son asks *what happened,* and is told the story of the redemption. The wicked son wants to know what gain there is in performing these rituals, and he is told that if he is concerned only with material gain, he indeed has no share in the Pesach observances. And the fourth son looks on in uninspired silence. He sees the triumph of evil in the world, and the celebration of deliverance seems hollow to him in such a context. To him we declare that by observing the Pesach rituals we will bring in the future redemption.

These four attitudes and their respective replies are reflected as well in the Seder's four cups of wine. The first cup is drunk at *Kiddush,* which speaks of God's purpose in creating the world and choosing Israel as His nation. The second cup is for *Maggid,* which retells the story of the Exodus. *Bircas HaMazon,* the third cup, praises God for the benefit we derive from His world if we use it in His service. And *Hallel,* the fourth cup, speaks of the final redemption.

2. **Service Initiation.** Even though all commandments are Godly service, the generic term *service* is employed here specifically to describe the *pesach* offering. R' Yitzchak Hutner suggests a halachic analogy. One of the modes of acquisition [*kinyan*] by which a master may acquire title to a servant is by having the servant perform some service on his behalf. The very act of service is what makes the servant into a servant. In contrast to other commandments, which are performed by people who are *already* servants of God, the *pesach* offering was the initiation rite through which we *became* God's servants. Hence it is called an intrinsic *"service."*

בַּיּוֹם הַהוּא, יָכוֹל מִבְּעוֹד יוֹם, תַּלְמוּד לוֹמַר בַּעֲבוּר זֶה. בַּעֲבוּר זֶה לֹא אָמַרְתִּי אֶלָּא בְּשָׁעָה שֶׁיֵּשׁ מַצָּה וּמָרוֹר מֻנָּחִים לְפָנֶיךָ.

---

which certainly might have been taken as an indication that the discussion of the Exodus should start at the beginning of the month (*Machzor Vitry, Malbim*).[1]

R' Moshe Feinstein submits that Rosh Chodesh is a significant time to begin recounting the miracles since it was on that day that God promised that He would redeem His people on the fifteenth day of Nissan. Unlike mortal man who may or may not honor his promises, God's word is as good as done. Hence, in essence the redemption was a *fait accompli* on Rosh Chodesh; it was only the mere passage of time that had to occur.[2]

Netziv suggests that the Torah indicates that the month of Nissan is in itself a contributing factor in our freedom and a propitious time to inculcate principles of faith and to strengthen one's commitment to Divine service. *You shall observe the Festival of Matzos . . . for in the month of the spring [Nissan] you went forth from Egypt (Exodus 34:18).* Thus, one might entertain the idea that discussion of the story of the Exodus is already appropriate from Rosh Chodesh.[3]

יָכוֹל מִבְּעוֹד יוֹם — *Could be understood to mean only during the daytime.* Granted that *that day* means that the verbal transmission of the Exodus does not begin before Pesach, we might still assume that the Haggadah should be recited on the afternoon before Pesach, since that was the time when the *pesach* offering was brought (*Kol Bo, Machzor Vitry*) and the time which the Torah refers to as *the*

---

1. **Totally Unprepared.** Just as one must prepare for the Sabbath both physically and spiritually, so one must prepare for Pesach. In Egypt, Moses prepared the people for the cataclysmic events as early as Rosh Chodesh, when he instructed them about the *pesach* offering. On the day before the start of the holiday, the offering was brought, in preparation for the special sanctity that was to come at night.

Bircas Avraham (*Slonim*) offers a homiletic rendering based on this idea. One might think that the unique spiritual experience and the light of faith that Pesach brings with it is available only to those who prepared for it properly *from Rosh Chodesh*. Therefore we are taught that even if one prepared only *on that day* it is sufficient. However, it is seemingly necessary to at least prepare oneself spiritually on the afternoon before Pesach. That is when one must destroy all the *chametz* of the heart, and bring the *pesach* offering, in order to usher in the holy day of Pesach. But we are taught that even with no preparation whatsoever, we may be raised in a split second to a spiritual peak. At the Seder, when we are surrounded with matzah and *maror*, we are able to shake all those things that spiritually confine us and we can achieve true liberty.

2. **Delivered Promises.** *Rashi* (*Exodus 6:3*) notes that the Four-letter Name of God (יְ-הֹ-וָ-ה) represents God as the One Who carries out His pledges. *R' Yitzchak Hutner* explained that the Four-letter Name connotes two manifestations of God: (1) He is מְהַוֶּה כָּל הַנִּמְצָאִים, *He brought everything into existence;* and (2) He is הָיָה הֹוֶה וְיִהְיֶה, *He is, was and will be,* i.e., God is timeless and eternal.

Man cannot be sure that he will fulfill his promises, because a greater force may prevent him from doing so, and he may not live long enough. God, however, having created all, is in full control of everything; nothing can impede Him from doing as He pleases. And because He is eternal, He will always be here to keep His word.

3. **At the Head.** The New Year is called Rosh Hashanah, literally "the head of the year," since like the head in a human organism, it controls and encapsulates the entire year. Likewise the sanctity of a month is basically contained in its first day. One blessed with sensitivity to sanctity is able to feel the "difference in the air" already beginning from Rosh Chodesh. Thus we might consider beginning the Pesach narration from Rosh Chodesh (*R' Tzadok HaKohen*).

pression "on that day" could be understood to mean only during the daytime; therefore the Torah adds: "It is because of this [that HASHEM did so for me when I went out of Egypt]." "Because of this" could not be said except at the time when matzah and *maror* lie before you.

---

appointed time of your departure from Egypt (see *Deuteronomy* 16:6) (*Rashi*). Furthermore, we might interpret "that *day*" as indicating that this is a *daytime mitzvah.*

בַּעֲבוּר זֶה לֹא אָמַרְתִּי אֶלָּא בְּשָׁעָה שֶׁיֵּשׁ מַצָּה וּמָרוֹר מֻנָּחִים לְפָנֶיךָ — *"Because of this" could not be said except at the time when matzah and maror lie before you.* Here the Torah specifically indicates that the time for recounting the story of the Exodus, although referred to as "that *day*," is actually in the evening, when *pesach*, matzah and *maror* lie before us;[1] it is only then that we can point to them and declare that we were redeemed בַּעֲבוּר זֶה, *on account of these things* (*Rashi*). Apparently, then, the term "day" can also refer to nighttime. Similarly, when the Torah speaks of the first *days* of Creation, it refers to the night as well as the day. The Torah also refers to the night when the Egyptian firstborn were killed as *the day I struck every firstborn . . .* (*Numbers* 3:13).[2] The goal of the

Exodus was to enable us to fulfill God's will as free men. Thus the retelling of the story of our national liberation only assumes meaning in the context of the *mitzvos* of the night, for only when we are surrounded by these *mitzvos* does our freedom have eternal meaning.

Mishnah Berurah (218 §7) interprets this passage in light of the *halachah* that one who sees the place where a miracle occurred to his ancestors should recite the blessing "Who performed miracles for our forefathers in this place" (*Berachos* 54a). Likewise, one must praise God when he sees the matzah and *maror*, which are reminiscent of the great miracles that occurred to us in Egypt. Thus, on the Seder night when we relive the experience of our national birth, we undergo a personal sensation of freedom. As we look at the matzah and *maror* we remember the great miracles that happened to us at this time and recite the Haggadah with praise and thanksgiving in our heart.

---

1. **Bittersweet Living.** The Haggadah is recited when both the matzah and the *maror* are in front of us to symbolize that not only the events that are clearly liberating (represented by the matzah) are part of God's plan to free man, but even the *maror* of life — experiences that are bitter and painful — are part of the process of freedom (*Sfas Emes*). One who speaks at length regarding the Exodus, including not only the great miracles, but even the terrible ordeal of the exile and bondage, is praiseworthy for he understands that even the *maror* is in reality part of redemption.

R' Shlomo Kluger offered an analogy. Two craftsmen were hired to produce vessels. One was given fine raw materials while the other was granted substandard materials. Nonetheless, they both produced magnificent articles. Of course the one who made maximum use of inferior materials deserves greater praise than his counterpart. Likewise, one who can find the clarity of perspective to praise God even for the *maror* of life is certainly deserving of praise.

2. **Hands On.** There is no better way to educate children than to let them see us doing what we ask of them; lessons that are reinforced by personal example strike deep roots in the hearts and minds of impressionable youngsters. Thus we are taught to speak to our children at the time when matzah and *maror* are present.

R' Nochum Mordechai Perlow of Novominsk once advised a young father: "If you want your children to study Torah, let them observe you learning. While study in a *shul* or a *beis midrash* is admirable, it is worthwhile to study at home occasionally so that the children have a live example of our hopes for them."

מִתְּחִלָּה, עוֹבְדֵי עֲבוֹדָה זָרָה הָיוּ אֲבוֹתֵינוּ, וְעַכְשָׁו קֵרְבָנוּ הַמָּקוֹם לַעֲבוֹדָתוֹ. שֶׁנֶּאֱמַר, וַיֹּאמֶר

מִתְּחִלָּה – *Initially.* The Mishnah (*Pesachim* 116a) teaches that the Haggadah should follow the formula of מַתְחִיל בִּגְנוּת וּמְסַיֵּים בְּשֶׁבַח, *One should begin [the discussion] with the disgrace [of our people] and conclude with the glory,* [1] but the Sages of the Talmud disagree regarding which "disgrace" is meant. It records a controversy about the proper historical starting point for discussing the Exodus. Shmuel interprets this directive as a call to begin with a discussion of our *physical* enslavement and the subsequent liberation from bondage. According to him, the narrative begins with the physical enslavement. Rav, on the other hand, maintains that the primary disgrace, which serves as the backdrop to our eventual greatness, refers to the *spiritual* paucity of our early history, when our ancestors worshipped idols.

Our Haggadah incorporates both opinions — we first answer our children עֲבָדִים הָיִינוּ, *we were slaves in Egypt;* then we go back and tell them מִתְּחִלָּה עוֹבְדֵי עֲבוֹדָה זָרָה הָיוּ אֲבוֹתֵינוּ, *Initially our fathers were idol worshippers* at the dawn of our history. *Ritva* suggests that this duality is not because we are trying to satisfy both opposing opinions. Rather, he asserts, Rav and Shmuel agreed that *both* versions should be mentioned; they disagreed only about which of the two passages should be recited first.[2] According to *Ritva*, we follow Shmuel's opinion by recalling our physical bondage first, and then our former spiritual imperfection.[3]

The term *our fathers* (in the plural) includes Terah and Nahor, but not Abraham, who recognized Hashem from a very young age (*Ritva*, see *Nedarim*

1. **Ultimate Destination.** Homiletically, this implies that every Jew, no matter what his spiritual point of embarkation on the Seder night, can become uplifted to a praiseworthy peak of fulfillment (*Alexander Rebbe*).

2. **Furnace Forged.** Rav and Shmuel deal with two different aspects of our historical experience. From a purely material perspective, we should recall the physical enslavement and deliverance; but when viewed from this perspective, our gratitude to God is somewhat tempered by the realization that it was He Himself Who brought the Egyptian servitude upon us in the first place. Seen from a broader, spiritual perspective, however, this difficulty fades away, because our ancestors were once idolaters, a profound and destructive form of spiritual imperfection, that could be negated only through the purifying "furnace" of Egypt. It was only by experiencing this ordeal and the subsequent miraculous delivery from it that we were able to achieve spiritual heights and become the bearers of God's message in the world (*Tosefos Rid*).

Modern Relics. During the Haskalah (Enlightenment) movement, many Jews became freethinkers and considered themselves to be "progressive" by discarding traditional practices. One of these *maskilim* met the Rebbe of Tchortkov, and chided him as to why traditional Jews insist on embracing ancient practices and refuse to accept modernism.

The Rebbe replied, "You have reversed the facts. The Haggadah states otherwise; that you are the ancients and we are the moderns. Originally, our early ancestors were idolaters and freethinkers who indulged every desire and temptation by inventing gods that would tell them what they wished to hear. We are the moderns, who have accepted upon ourselves the rule of Divinely ordained morals and ethics. All you have done is to go back to the behavior of precivilized mankind."

3. **Physical — Key to the Spiritual.** Shmuel sees the physical aspect of exile as no less significant than the spiritual, for physical safety and proper living conditions are integral elements of spiritual growth. As *Rambam* (*Hilchos Teshuvah* 9:1) explains, the Torah's promises are assurances that we will be provided with the conditions necessary to serve God if we in fact show that we seek to do His will (*HaSeder HaAruch*).

Initially our fathers were idol worshippers, and now the Omnipresent has brought us close to His service, as it is stated:

32a). *Rambam*'s opinion, however, is that Abraham was an idolater until he was 40 years old, and only then recognized Hashem. According to this, he too is included in the words "our fathers" (*HaGriz*).

Although chronologically we should begin with the story of Terach, the father of Abraham, we nonetheless begin with the slavery, which happened centuries later, because it answers in capsule form the questions posed in the *Mah Nishtanah*, by explaining the juxtaposition of bondage and liberation. Thus, the opening paragraphs of the narrative present a concise account of the Exodus as the reply to the children, containing all the essential elements of the story: (a) the original servitude and lowliness of our people (עֲבָדִים הָיִינוּ); (b) their liberation (...וַיּוֹצִיאֵנוּ ה'); (c) the obligation to consider ourselves as having personally experienced the Exodus (...הֲרֵי אָנוּ וּבָנֵינוּ); and even (d) the mention of *pesach*, matzah and *maror* (...בְּשָׁעָה שֶׁיֵּשׁ). After the basic requirements of telling the story of the Exodus have been fulfilled, we now set out to follow the dictum: *The more one tells about the Exodus, the more he is praiseworthy* (*Orchos Chaim, Kol Bo*).

Furthermore, since עֲבָדִים הָיִינוּ is the Torah's answer to the question of the wise son, it is the most appropriate response to the questions of the chil-

dren. In order to grasp the wider spiritual significance of the Exodus we then expand our discussion with the theme of our ancestral history of idolatry (*Avudraham*).

Rabbeinu Manoach explains that Rav (who holds that the Haggadah should begin with the idolatry of the ancients) also bases himself on the Torah's reply to the wise son, except that he focuses on a different phrase in that answer: *and God commanded us to perform all these laws to fear* HASHEM, *our God* (*Deuteronomy* 6:21). From these words Rav understands that the Torah does not want us to dwell only on our physical bondage and redemption, but on our spiritual elevation from idolatry.

וְעַכְשָׁו קֵרְבָנוּ הַמָּקוֹם לַעֲבוֹדָתוֹ — *And now the Omnipresent has brought us close to His service.* [1] We begin with the disreputable beginnings of the nation in order to fully appreciate the redemption and be able to properly express our appreciation for all God has done for us. One can rejoice fully only when one remembers the pain that preceded his joy (*Meiri*).

It is only by contrasting where we *are* with where we *were* that we can truly appreciate our freedom. We therefore paint the entire spectrum of our national experience, from idolatry to Sinai and finally to wholehearted service of God in His Temple (*Malbim*).[2]

---

1. **Square One.** Now the Omnipresent brought us near to His service — "now" is whenever a Jew is inspired to commit himself to God and Torah. Let him say to himself, "The past is gone — from now on I will begin to come closer to God" (*Beis Avraham*).

2. **Constant Beginnings.** After successfully enticing someone to sin, the Evil Inclination seeks to induce despair of ever repenting. The Haggadah teaches us not to fall prey to such pessimism. Our forefathers were originally idolaters — the worst of all sins — yet God still brought them near to His service. Certainly we, no matter what we have done in the past, can repent and bring ourselves close to serve God.

When a manual laborer comes home from work, he showers, although he knows that tomorrow he will again become filthy in the course of his work. Likewise, inspired by our forefathers, we seek to repent and mend our ways, even though we know that we may weaken and sin again — but we plead with Hashem that He grant us the strength to remain clean and pure forever (*Beis Avraham*).

≈ **Spiritual Immunity.** According to *Maharal*, the Jewish nation possesses a special talent to turn impurity to purity and to rechannel the forces of evil into something positive. Thus we recount the inglorious beginnings of the nation since it was this very status that they transformed into a force for good. Likewise, their exposure to the decadence of Egyptian culture enabled them to achieve great levels of sanctity as they became disgusted with the spiritual impurity of the land.

יְהוֹשֻׁעַ אֶל כָּל הָעָם, כֹּה אָמַר יהוה אֱלֹהֵי יִשְׂרָאֵל, בְּעֵבֶר
הַנָּהָר יָשְׁבוּ אֲבוֹתֵיכֶם מֵעוֹלָם, תֶּרַח אֲבִי אַבְרָהָם וַאֲבִי נָחוֹר,
וַיַּעַבְדוּ אֱלֹהִים אֲחֵרִים. וָאֶקַּח אֶת אֲבִיכֶם אֶת אַבְרָהָם
מֵעֵבֶר הַנָּהָר, וָאוֹלֵךְ אוֹתוֹ בְּכָל אֶרֶץ כְּנָעַן, וָאַרְבֶּה אֶת זַרְעוֹ,
וָאֶתֶּן לוֹ אֶת יִצְחָק. וָאֶתֵּן לְיִצְחָק אֶת יַעֲקֹב וְאֶת עֵשָׂו, וָאֶתֵּן

According to *Maharsha* (*Pesachim* 116a), we remember our ignoble beginnings in order that joy in our new-found status not induce feelings of arrogance. (A similar reason is offered by *Taz* for wearing the *kittel* [also worn by the dead] at the Seder. We seek to evoke a certain sense of humility, to prevent excessive exuberance and frivolity on this joyous evening.)

Ksav Sofer adds that the more we realize how far we had sunk before God freed us, the greater will be our appreciation for His salvation. Like a father who saves his rebellious child despite the pain he has caused him, God saved us from Egypt even though we came from idolaters and had to some extent reverted back to their practices instead of faithfully carrying on the faith of the Patriarchs. Thus, by highlighting our ignoble beginnings, we emphasize the greatness of God's miracles and the intensity of His love for us.

The Sages also enjoined us to employ the formula of beginning with ignominy as a backdrop to praise in order to assure us that God does not fault man for the "baggage" of his past if he earnestly sets out in a new direction. By charting a new course for himself and his descendants, Abraham merited the great gift of the Land of Israel as an eternal inheritance, even though he came from the household of Terah. [1] Likewise, no man need be burdened with the sins of his ancestors; if he repents, God will be good to him no matter who his antecedents were (*Kol Bo*).[2]

שֶׁנֶּאֱמַר — *As it is stated.* We offer a short synopsis of the history from the time when our forefathers were idolaters until Jacob and his children went down to Egypt. This thumbnail sketch is taken from *Joshua* rather than the detailed accounts in *Genesis* and *Exodus*, for the sake of brevity (*Malbim*). Alternatively, since one of the great lessons of this night is an appreciation of Hashem as the source of all goodness and kindness, we quote the words of *Joshua*, which provide clear evidence of His benevolence toward our forefathers. Originally Abraham was neither a wealthy landowner nor a believer in God, nor did he have children. All these gifts were granted him by God, as evidenced by the words of *Joshua* (*Abarbanel* — see below).

---

1. **Evaporated Past.** The *Midrash* teaches that Abraham, when he finally came to recognize God, was haunted by his checkered past. In an expression of self-doubt he wondered, "What will be of the many years I practiced idolatry?" (See *Rambam, Hilchos Avodah Zarah* 1:3 and *Raavad* ad loc.) God consoled him, saying, לְךָ טַל יַלְדֻתֶךָ, *You retain the dewlike freshness of your youth* (*Psalms* 110:3), for just as dew evaporates quickly so had Abraham's sins evaporated without leaving the slightest trace on his soul.

2. **The Gift of Closeness.** Until Abraham, humanity was steeped in vanity and foolishness, with no one recognizing the need to serve the true God. Even the righteous Shem and Eber had no eager children and few disciples; their surroundings were permeated with idolatry and wickedness. But now Hashem has brought us close to Him. Even Abraham, for all his righteousness, was brought closer to God only as an act of Divine mercy. God endowed him with a purity of heart so that he might seek out the true Master of the Universe. Thus we thank God for having offered us a closeness far beyond what is justified by our deeds (*R' Eliyahu Kitov*).

"And Joshua said to all of the people, So says HASHEM the God of Israel, Of old, your forefathers dwelt beyond the river — Terah, the father of Abraham and the father of Nahor, and they worshiped other gods. And I took your father Abraham from beyond the river, and I led him throughout all the Land of Canaan, and I multiplied his seed, and I gave Isaac unto him, and I gave Jacob and Esau unto Isaac, and I gave

---

בְּעֵבֶר הַנָּהָר יָשְׁבוּ אֲבוֹתֵיכֶם מֵעוֹלָם – *Of old, your forefathers dwelt beyond the river.* Terah and all the descendants of Shem lived in Babylonia, far away from the Land of Canaan which was on the other side of the Euphrates. Then God led Abraham through the length and breadth of the land as an act of acquisition, thus rendering him the eternal owner of the land (*Abarbanel*).

וַיַּעַבְדוּ אֱלֹהִים אֲחֵרִים – *And they worshiped other gods.* Coming from such stock it would only be natural for Abraham to follow in the footsteps of his father and older brother. Terah's two sons, Abraham and Nahor, developed differently. Terah did not educate them to serve one God; Abraham alone discovered this truth as a result of his realization that a world so complex must have a Master. He had both the insight to recognize the Creator while still a child and the strength of character to resist the prevailing cultural environment, even when he had to risk his life. Therefore Abraham merited to become the founder of the Jewish people, and set into motion a process that ultimately led to the redemption from Egypt, the giving of the Torah and the building of the Temple.

His rejection of idolatry qualified him to receive the land as his inheritance. The Torah (*Leviticus* 18:24; see *Ramban*'s commentary ad loc.) tells us that the holiness of the land demands higher standards of conduct. Like a prince with a delicate constitution who disgorges spoiled food, the land cannot abide sins of idolatry in its midst; it will spew out its inhabitants. This is so because *Eretz Yisrael* is *the land that HASHEM seeks out; His eyes are always upon it (Deuteronomy* 11:12). While God assigns the guardianship of other lands and peoples to other heavenly forces, *Eretz Yisrael* is God's

own province. Thus idolatry in *Eretz Yisrael* constitutes a rebellion against the King in His own palace. Only someone like Abraham who rejected the paganism of his forefathers could be granted ownership of the Royal palace (*Acharis LeShalom*).

וָאוֹלֵךְ אוֹתוֹ בְּכָל אֶרֶץ כְּנַעַן – *And I led him throughout all the Land of Canaan.* A gardener who sees a fruit tree planted in a dry and rocky field will replant it in fertile soil. Likewise, God saw the great spiritual potential of Abraham and uprooted him from his birthplace so that he could flourish spiritually in the Holy Land, where the Divine Presence resides and where prophecy is accessible. There Abraham would grow into the founder of the Jewish nation (*Malbim* to *Joshua* 24:3).

According to *Ramban* (*Genesis* 12:6), Abraham was commanded to walk through the length and breadth of the land in order that it be easier for his children to capture it from the Canaanites when they would enter the land in the days of Joshua.

וָאַרְבֶּה אֶת זַרְעוֹ – *And I multiplied his seed.* This "multiplication" refers to the fact that Abraham had two sons, Isaac and Ishmael; one a paragon of virtue (Isaac), the other a wild man who would become an untamed brigand, a hated plunderer and a warrior. This phenomenon repeated itself when Isaac was blessed with two sons of diametrically opposed temperaments and spiritual hue — Jacob and Esau.

Why are Ishmael and Esau mentioned in this context, which seems to be a description of the greatness of the Patriarchs? Ishmael and Esau played an indirect role in the spiritual purification process that produced the nation of Israel. Any possible negative aspects of Abraham's kindness — which manifests itself in self-indulgence and

לַעֲשׂוֹ אֶת הַר שֵׂעִיר לָרֶשֶׁת אוֹתוֹ, וְיַעֲקֹב וּבָנָיו יָרְדוּ מִצְרָיִם.[1]

בָּרוּךְ שׁוֹמֵר הַבְטָחָתוֹ לְיִשְׂרָאֵל, בָּרוּךְ הוּא.

---

hedonism — was incorporated into Ishmael, so that Isaac inherited his father's character traits only in their most pristine form. Likewise, the strict justice of Isaac was passed on to Jacob in an unadulterated form — which manifests itself in cruelty, bloodshed and lack of mercy — with the dross of this character trait becoming the genetic heritage of Esau. Thus, only the purest forms of Abraham's *chessed* (kindness) and Isaac's *din* (strict justice) were blended in Jacob. This spiritual winnowing process produced the Jewish people. Hence, all of Abraham's children (even Ishmael) were part of the process.

Alternatively, while Abraham had only one son who absorbed his values and carried out his heritage — Isaac — the verse refers to the multiplication of Abraham's descendants throughout the generations.

Rashi (*Joshua* ad loc.), based on *Yerushalmi* (*Pesachim* 10:5), interprets the term וָאַרֶב (which lacks a concluding ה in the Biblical text) in the sense of רִיב, *contention*. God "contended" with Abraham (and Sarah) and put him through many tests before granting him Isaac.

Abraham and Sarah were incapable of having children without God's miraculous intervention. The same was true of Isaac and Rebecca, and of Rachel.[1] This was not a coincidence; the Divine intercession that was required to produce the children of the Patriarchs made manifest the fact that these people represented a totally new

beginning and bore no hereditary contamination through their idolatrous ancestors, whom they repudiated. As *Maharal* declares: "Just as God created a fully formed world at the outset of Creation, so He created His people not through natural evolutionary processes in the normal manner in which all nations are brought into existence, but rather miraculously, in defiance of all the rules of nature and principles of history."

וָאֶתֵּן לְיִצְחָק אֶת יַעֲקֹב וְאֶת עֵשָׂו — *And I gave Jacob and Esau unto Isaac.* Jacob and Esau were born as twins to indicate that though they shared the same background, it was their individual choices in life that determined who they were and how they lived. Jacob chose the path of righteousness, while Esau came to epitomize evil incarnate (*Ritva*).

וָאֶתֵּן לְעֵשָׂו אֶת הַר שֵׂעִיר — *And I gave unto Esau Mount Seir.* Esau was to have no share in the legacy of Abraham; instead he would be the archrival and antagonist of his twin brother Jacob. Mount Seir was given to Esau as a gift to be temporarily occupied until the Messianic age when the Jewish nation will conquer and occupy it (*Chayei Adam* — see *Rashi* to *Genesis* 33:14). At that time, *The rescuers will ascend Mount Zion in order to judge the mountain of Esau* (*Ovadiah* 1:21).

Joshua mentioned the diversion of Esau to the Mountain of Seir because it is one of God's kindnesses to Israel that He separated Esau, so that he not influence Jacob. In exchange for his share,

---

1. **Miraculous Birth.** The birth of the Jewish people was miraculous in the extreme. Sarah, a woman who was infertile even in her youth, gave birth to a son at the age of 90. From its very inception, the Jewish people and its survival transcend the rules of nature. No Jew should therefore ever despair of being helped from Above and being saved, no matter how insurmountable a situation he faces. "Even if a sharp sword is stretched across one's neck, let him not despair of Divine mercy" (*Berachos* 10a).

Thus the prophet exhorts us, "Look to Abraham your forefather and to Sarah who bore you" (*Isaiah* 51:2). That is, look to Abraham and Sarah who had good reason to despair of ever having children, yet God miraculously granted them Isaac. Likewise, no matter how bleak your situation may seem, remember that God can miraculously provide salvation (*R' Tzadok HaKohen*).

unto Esau Mount Seir to inherit, but Jacob and his sons went down to Egypt."[1]

Blessed is He Who keeps His promise to Israel; blessed is He!

---

(1) *Joshua* 24:2-4.

Esau was ready to forgo any claim to a share of *Eretz Yisrael* (*Vilna Gaon, Shem MiShmuel*).

וְיַעֲקֹב וּבָנָיו יָרְדוּ — *But Jacob and his sons went down to Egypt.* The three Patriarchs laid the cornerstone of the Jewish people, each one making his own particular contribution. Yet, before their descendants could assume their crucial place in world history, one more step was necessary — they had to undergo the bitter process of exile to be purged of the last residue of their pagan past. Furthermore, our Sages teach that the gifts of Torah, *Eretz Yisrael* and the World to Come cannot be acquired without experiencing some suffering (*Berachos* 5a). Thus, in order to receive these gifts, Israel had to experience the painful exile of Egypt.[1]

Rashi (*Genesis* 36:7) makes clear that the gift of *Eretz Yisrael* could only be acquired by paying the price of suffering through the Egyptian exile. The promise of *To your descendants I have given this land* (*Genesis* 15:18) is contingent on the fulfillment of *your offspring shall be aliens in a land not their own* (ibid. 13). Thus, when Esau left to Mount Seir before the exile to Egypt he forfeited any claims to the land.

בָּרוּךְ שׁוֹמֵר הַבְטָחָתוֹ לְיִשְׂרָאֵל — *Blessed is He Who keeps His promise to Israel.* A "blessing" is in order when someone does something he did not have to do. To bless Hashem, Who is the epitome of truth and justice, for merely keeping His word would seem to be inappropriate. Could the Judge of the entire world possibly have done otherwise? Rather, the emphasis here is on *Israel*. Having issued His promise to Abraham, He could have fulfilled His word through Ishmael, the children of Keturah, born to Abraham in his old age, or through Esau. Instead He *kept His promise to Israel,* and fulfilled His word through Jacob and his descendants. It is for this that we are eternally grateful and bless Him (*Abarbanel*).

This passage, one of the few non-Midrashic, non-Talmudic parts of the Haggadah, was inserted into the text during the Gaonic period (c. 680 to 980 C.E.), when the Haggadah underwent its final editing. In it we thank God for His direction of our destinies and the formation of our spiritual constitution.

This passage follows the previous one, in which the paths of Esau and Jacob are described, in order to assure us of the ultimate ascendancy of Jacob. Let one not be blinded by the contrast between Esau's tranquility and Jacob's exile. The initial pain and suffering was a necessary means to achieve the eventual goodness that God promised His people. While initially painful, it was to lead to a good life unimaginable for Esau and his cohorts (*Chayei Adam*). Thus we praise God as One Who keeps His promises. Even when we do not see this

---

1. **Egypt: A Purification Process.** The Talmud teaches that God gave Jews three special gifts: Torah, *Eretz Yisrael* and the World to Come, all of which could be acquired only by means of suffering (*Berachos* 5a). *Maharal* explains that man is a synthesis of body and soul. Each of these elements seeks the controlling interest in the person. The greater the share of the soul, the less that of the body. Physical pain diminishes the vitality and power of the corporeal, allowing the soul to become ascendant. In order to merit the spiritual gifts of Torah, *Eretz Yisrael* and the World to Come, one must himself become a spiritual being, which is accomplished through subduing his physical side.

Thus, the Egyptian exile was not meant as punishment for a sin, as evidenced by the fact that God told Abraham about it long before it happened. Rather, the terrible ordeal was meant to purify us and make us fitting receptacles for God's Torah and land (*Nesivos Shalom*).

שֶׁהַקָּדוֹשׁ בָּרוּךְ הוּא חִשַּׁב אֶת הַקֵּץ, לַעֲשׂוֹת כְּמָה
שֶׁאָמַר לְאַבְרָהָם אָבִינוּ בִּבְרִית בֵּין הַבְּתָרִים, שֶׁנֶּאֱמַר,
וַיֹּאמֶר לְאַבְרָם, יָדֹעַ תֵּדַע כִּי גֵר יִהְיֶה זַרְעֲךָ בְּאֶרֶץ

immediately, we bless Him out of a deep and abiding faith that He keeps His promises — sometimes sooner and sometimes later.[1]

The term שׁוֹמֵר may also be rendered as *anxiously awaits* (see *Genesis* 37:11). God not only keeps His promise, He also anxiously awaits the opportunity to save His children (*Siach Yitzchak*). Sometimes God waits for us; if only we raise our voices in prayer He will immediately respond.

שֶׁהַקָּדוֹשׁ בָּרוּךְ הוּא חִשַּׁב אֶת הַקֵּץ — *For the Holy One, Blessed is He, calculated the end [of the bondage].* Although God told Abraham that his children would be aliens in a land not their own for 400 years, God reckoned the extraordinary severity of their subjugation to be tantamount to the full 400 years mentioned in the prophecy to Abraham. In reality they spent 210 years in actual exile, 116 years of servitude and 86 years of hard labor (see *Megillah* 9a). But translating qualitative suffering into quantifiable time equivalents is the exclusive province of God. Thus God says, "For I have

known of its sufferings" (*Exodus* 3:7). Only God could calculate the extent of their suffering and expedite their redemption accordingly.

The numerical value of קֵץ, *end,* is 190, for God subtracted 190 years from the projected 400 years, leaving 210 years of actual exile (*Shibbolei HaLeket*).

Divrei Shaul suggests that the severe pain inflicted by the Egyptians helped hasten the redemption, since it caused the Jews to emit a heartfelt cry of prayer that God heard and responded to by redeeming them.

We thank God not only for keeping His promise to redeem us, but also for setting limits on the severity of the bondage and for letting it unfold in stages. The Egyptian bondage entailed not only a vast degree of physical suffering but, even more significantly, it carried within itself the potential for profound or even fatal spiritual danger. God saved us from it all by carefully orchestrating the stages of exile.[2]

1. **Roundabout Redemption.** The *Midrash* makes a cryptic comment. The Torah teaches that God took the Jews out of Egypt and sent them on a circuitous path through the Sinai desert in order to avoid confrontation with the warlike Philistines: וַיַּסֵּב אֱלֹהִים אֶת הָעָם, *So God turned the people* (*Exodus* 13:18). From here, says the Midrash, we learn that even the poorest man must recline on the night of Pesach. (The word for reclining, יַסֵּב, is from the same root as וַיַּסֵּב, *turn.*) Seemingly, this is nothing more than a play on words.

R' Yosef Dov Soloveitchik explained: God took Jews on a roundabout path that seemed to lead to aimless wandering, not freedom. Nonetheless, it eventually became clear that only in this fashion could true freedom be achieved. Had they been attacked by the Philistines they would have returned to Egypt. Thus God took them on a long journey filled with frustrations and setbacks. They followed God in all these wanderings out of a sense of faith that God keeps His promises and would ultimately lead them to eternal freedom. Likewise, on a personal level, we tell the poor man to recline while eating on this night, as if he is already free. Though he wallows in poverty, he is truly free. What seems like a circuitous route is in reality a road to redemption.

2. **Divine Vaccine.** *Sfas Emes* suggests the analogy of a vaccination. In creating a vaccine to inoculate against a disease, one must induce a strain of the disease into the system. If the strain is too strong, it may prove harmful or even fatal to the patient. On the other hand, too weak a dose will not force the immune system to produce antibodies to combat the real disease. Thus it is necessary to calibrate the vaccine to exactly the proper potency so that exposure to the strain will foster immunity.

The Jewish nation in Egypt was like a fetus in its mother's womb. It was there that exposure to the forty-nine degrees of impurity served to inoculate them against being overwhelmed by any later exposure

For the Holy One, Blessed is He, calculated the end [of the bondage] in order to do as He said to our father Abraham at the Covenant Between the Parts, as it is stated: "He said to Abram, 'Know with certainty that your offspring will be aliens in a land

---

בִּי גֵר יִהְיֶה זַרְעֲךָ — *That your offspring will be aliens.* In the Covenant Between the Parts (*Genesis* 15), God foretold three forms of adversity that would face Abraham's descendants: (a) They would be strangers; (b) they would be in servitude; (c) they would be oppressed and tormented. According to *R' S.R. Hirsch,* the first stage, גֵרוּת, began with the birth of Isaac: Although he and his descendants lived in the Land of Israel, the Canaanite natives regarded them as aliens. [According to some historians, Canaan was technically a part of the Greater Egyptian Empire, which would account for the Torah's statement that the Jews dwelt *in Egypt* for 430 years (*Exodus* 12:40).]

During this Canaanite exile, the Patriarchs implanted the virtues that characterized their way of

life into their descendants. It was only then that Jacob and his sons were ready to descend to Egypt, to become "strangers in an alien land" in the fullest sense of the words.

The deterioration of their condition accelerated when *the eyes of the Jews were dulled by the burden of the bondage* (*Rashi* to *Genesis* 47:28). This refers to the general discomfort the Jews felt in their relationship with their host nation long before the physical enslavement. Slavery, the second stage foretold at the Covenant Between the Parts, began only with the death of Levi, 116 years before the Exodus. When Miriam[1] was born, 86 years before the Exodus, the third phase of the prophecy began. It was characterized by עֱנוּי, *harsh oppression* — including torture and murder.

---

to spiritual "disease." God in His mercy calibrated exactly how much impurity they could stand and for how long. Forty-nine degrees of tumah were survivable; fifty would have been fatal. Furthermore, remaining exposed to such contamination for so long a time could deal a spiritual death blow. Thus הקב"ה, חִשֵּׁב אֶת הַקֵּץ, *the Holy One, Blessed is He, calculated the end,* the exact point at which to end the exile and yet leave His people fortified with spiritual "antibodies."

Thus the Haggadah continues וְהִיא שֶׁעָמְדָה לַאֲבוֹתֵינוּ: This spiritual inoculation against impurity and immorality protected us in all our exile experiences throughout the generations. Many enemies, both physical and spiritual, have risen against us, yet the spiritual mettle we acquired in the "furnace of Egypt" has withstood the test of time. With the strength born of resistance to perversions, we have survived it all.

⊷§ **Emerging From Immersion.** For the Jews to reject all that Egypt stood for, it was necessary that they first be immersed in the Egyptian world. Thus they were awed by its culture and power, and were influenced by its way of life; and, in due course, they sank to the very lowest level short of actual assimilation into the Egyptian morass. This is the nature of a smelting furnace — a substance thrown into it necessarily loses its form and consistency — and sometimes it can dissolve and disappear.

To forestall this, and to make sure that the Jews would survive their bondage, its scope was carefully limited by Divine wisdom. This was made very clear when God announced the impending exile to Abraham. In the first place, the Biblical account, which is here quoted by the Haggadah, stresses that their exile was to last 400 years; it was not meant to go on until such time as the Jews would earn their redemption by their own merits. After all, that moment might never have come (*R' Joseph Elias*).

We too in our present exile are assured that we will not disappear as a nation. The cancer of assimilation may destroy great parts of the nation, but we will survive and achieve redemption.

2. **Initial Bitterness.** According to *Rashi* (*Songs of Songs* 2:13), the name Miriam is related to מַר, *bitter,* for upon her birth the Jews began to taste the bitterest stage of the exile.

לֹא לָהֶם, וַעֲבָדוּם וְעִנּוּ אֹתָם, אַרְבַּע מֵאוֹת שָׁנָה. וְגַם אֶת הַגּוֹי אֲשֶׁר יַעֲבֹדוּ דָּן אָנֹכִי, וְאַחֲרֵי כֵן יֵצְאוּ בִּרְכֻשׁ גָּדוֹל.[1]

The matzos are covered and the cups lifted as the following paragraph is proclaimed joyously. Upon its conclusion, the cups are put down and the matzos are uncovered.

וְהִיא שֶׁעָמְדָה לַאֲבוֹתֵינוּ וְלָנוּ, שֶׁלֹּא אֶחָד בִּלְבָד

וְגַם אֶת הַגּוֹי אֲשֶׁר יַעֲבֹדוּ דָּן אָנֹכִי – *I will also judge the nation that they will serve.* The Egyptians were eventually punished for their cruel treatment of the Jews.[1] Even though, ostensibly, they were carrying out God's will, they were punished because their cruelty went far beyond any reasonable bounds (see *Raavad, Hilchos Teshuvah* 6:5 and *Ramban, Exodus* 18:11). *Ramban* suggests further that one is absolved of punishment for carrying out God's will only when he does so out of a pure motivation to serve God. But if one does so out of brutish personal considerations, he deserves to be punished.

See *Ramban* to *Genesis* 15:13 for a historical exposition of this principle.

According to *Rambam* (ibid.), since the Biblical prophecy did not specify who was to be the antagonist of the Jews, the Egyptians were faulted for volunteering their services. (See *Ramban* to *Genesis* 15:13 for objections to this position.)

וְאַחֲרֵי כֵן יֵצְאוּ בִּרְכֻשׁ גָּדוֹל – *And afterwards they will go out with great possessions.* God promised Abraham that when his children finally left the exile of Egypt, they would go with great wealth. In fact, before the Jews left Egypt, God asked Moses to "please" have them request valuables from their Egyptian neighbors (*Exodus* 11:2), in order that the soul of Abraham would have no grievance against God for having meticulously carried out the half of the prophecy calling for his offspring to be oppressed, but not fulfilling His promise that they would leave captivity with great wealth. To forestall

such a complaint, God pleaded, as it were, that Moses prevail upon the Jews to request valuables from the Egyptians (*Rashi* to *Exodus* 11:2).

According to many commentators, the promised "wealth" was the spiritual elevation that enabled Israel to experience God's revelation at the splitting of the Sea, the giving of the Torah at Sinai and the eventual rendezvous with God's Presence in the Tabernacle and later in the Temple.

Others understood this in a literal sense. God provided them with their physical needs and with the wherewithal to be free of pursuing a living so that they might spend their time and efforts tending to their spiritual growth. *Mei Marom* suggests that this wealth was provided them in order that they be fit for prophecy and the prophetic experience at the Sea of Reeds. In the words of the Sages, "Prophecy comes only to one great in wisdom, strength and wealth" (*Shabbos* 92a).

Wealth also gives one a sense of self-esteem. Having been slaves for so long it was necessary to free them of their slave mentality. Thus God had them leave Egypt as a wealthy and respectable people (*R' Yosef Dov Soloveitchik*).

Before reciting the next paragraph we cover the matzos and raise our cups, based on the *Yerushalmi* (quoted in *Tur O.C.* 271), which teaches that the bread on the table must be covered during *Kiddush.* The reason is that in the hierarchy of blessings, the *hamotzi* over bread takes precedence over the *hagafen* for wine. Therefore, it would be "embarrassing" to the bread, as it were, for it to be exposed while it is being bypassed as *Kiddush* is

1. **Atomic Promises.** With the words דָּן אָנֹכִי, *I will judge,* God promised Abraham to punish the nation that would oppress his offspring. On the basis of this two-word promise, He unleashed an unheralded barrage of miracles during the Exodus. Can we even imagine the scope of the miracles that will accompany the Final Redemption, which God portrayed so vividly in the words of many prophets? (*R' Saadia Gaon*).

not their own, they will serve them and they will oppress them for four hundred years; but I will also judge the nation that they will serve, and afterwards they will go out with great possessions.'"[1]

The matzos are covered and the cups lifted as the following paragraph is proclaimed joyously. Upon its conclusion, the cups are put down and the matzos are uncovered.

It is this that has stood firm by our fathers and us. For it was not

---

(1) *Genesis* 15:13-14.

---

recited over the wine. Consequently the bread is covered as an act of delicacy when the wine is given prominence. Similarly, when the cup of wine is raised during the recitation of the Haggadah, the matzos should be covered. [See *O.C.* 473 and *Magen Avraham* §27 in the name of *Shelah*, *M.B.* §73.]

The raising of the cup of wine at this time is alluded to in the verse *I will raise the cup of salvations and will invoke the Name of Hashem* (*Psalms* 116:13). When invoking the Name of God in praise over our salvation, we raise our cups (*Leket Yosher*, citing *Rokeach*). *Maharal* elaborates further: The four cups of wine correspond to the four expressions of redemption. The second cup (the one lifted at this point) alludes to the second of these expressions, וְהִצַּלְתִּי, *I will rescue* you from their service (*Exodus* 6:6). As we thank God for saving us from

our enemies generation after generation, we raise our cups in joy and thanksgiving for having been spared.

Some hold (rather than raise) the cup. They contend that וְהִיא שֶׁעָמְדָה is recited as a statement of fact rather than as a song of praise, so that the verse regarding *raising the cup of salvation* is inapplicable (*Aruch HaShulchan, Minchas Elazar*).

וְהִיא שֶׁעָמְדָה — *It is this that has stood firm.* The promise He made to our fathers at the Covenant Between the Parts, that He would be with us always, has stood firm for our forefathers and for us. According to the *Midrash* (*Bereishis Rabbah* 44:22), when God promised Abraham that He would exact retribution from the Egyptians and eventually free his offspring from bondage, the promise included salvation from all future exiles as well.[1] God assured Abraham that *and also the*

---

1. **Eternal Nation.** The *Midrash* interprets the verse *a deep sleep fell on Abraham and behold — a dread! Great darkness fell upon him* (*Genesis* 15:12) as an allusion to Israel's progressively intensifying subjugations under the Four Kingdoms: *Dread* represented Babylonia; *darkness* was Media-Persia; *great darkness* was Greece (i.e., the Syrian-Greeks of Antiochus, who persecuted Israel in the times of the Chanukah story); and *fell upon him* was the crushing present exile initiated by Rome. All of them ruled Israel in *Eretz Yisrael*; Babylonia destroyed the First Temple and Rome the Second, and the others dominated the land during parts of the Second Temple era. Thus, God warned Abraham that Israel might be subjugated and/or exiled by these four powers — but this was to happen only if Israel were to sin (*Ramban*).

However, even when Israel sins, it remains God's people and is assured of its *national* survival. This assurance was reiterated at the conclusion of the *Tochachah*, admonition (*Leviticus* 26), with which God warned the Jewish people if they would fail to live up to their obligations. At the conclusion of a series of the increasingly severe and appalling punishments that are intended to influence the people to repent, God comforts His exiled and tormented children: *But despite all of this, while they will be in the land of their enemies, I will not be revolted by them nor will I reject them to obliterate them, to annul My covenant with them — for I am HASHEM, their God* (ibid. 26:44). Let us never think that the atrocities of exile prove that we are, God forbid, no longer His Chosen People. Even in exile we are still His beloved children whom He will eventually redeem.

עָמַד עָלֵינוּ לְכַלּוֹתֵנוּ. אֶלָּא שֶׁבְּכָל דּוֹר וָדוֹר עוֹמְדִים עָלֵינוּ לְכַלּוֹתֵנוּ, וְהַקָּדוֹשׁ בָּרוּךְ הוּא מַצִּילֵנוּ מִיָּדָם.

nation that they shall serve I shall judge (Genesis 15:14). The word *also* indicates that, like the Egyptians, the Four Kingdoms — i.e., all the nations that persecute Israel throughout its history — will not escape punishment. While the Jewish people will survive, their oppressors will be paid back for their cruelty (*Rashi* ad loc.). This Divine assurance served our fathers in good stead during the terrible times of subjugation to Babylonia, Persia and Greece, and which has been our lifesaver in the darkest days of our tragic existence in the present exile (*Shibbolei HaLeket, Maharal*).[1]

In every generation there are enemies who would exterminate us. It is only because of the promise that He made to Abraham that God rescues us from their hands (even if we truly deserve punishment) and pun-

ishes them (*Abarbanel, Avudraham*).

According to *Netziv*, וְהִיא refers not to God's promise of salvation and protection, but to Israel's exile status of strangers and sojourners, for this quality allows us to survive the spiritual ravages of exposure to foreign and often degenerate cultures. God's promise to Abraham that his "offspring would be aliens in a land not their own" was the greatest insurance against assimilation. Israel's refusal to allow its personal and national identity to be obliterated in the melting pots of exile has proven to be its most successful survival tactic. A Jew should never feel completely at home or at ease; wherever he is, he must sense that he is not truly in his home. This perception saved us from disappearance.[2]

1. **Out of the Ashes.** What but a Divine promise could have worked the miracle of the rebirth of the Jewish people out of the embers of Hitler's furnace?

The *Klausenberger Rebbe* related: "Languishing in a Nazi slave labor camp, I was approached by a professor, who asked me derisively: 'So, what have you to say about the lot of the Jews?'

" 'It will be good,' I answered. I then explained, 'I am not a prophet. Rather, my conviction is based on historic fact. Notice,' I pointed out to him, 'how many nations have resolved to annihilate the Jewish people. Consider how many millions of Jews have already perished, in sanctification of God's Name, at the hands of mighty empires and nationalities — empires and nationalities of which there remain no living trace today. The Jewish people continue to exist, their many persecutions and travails notwithstanding. There are today sizable families, who trace their ancestry to a particular grandfather, who had perished some generations earlier in sanctification of God's Name, even as his executioners and their commanders have fallen into total oblivion. Although I cannot tell you what will happen to me, personally, I am nevertheless certain that the Jewish People as a whole will survive and will witness the downfall of their adversaries. I can guarantee this, based on thousands of years of Jewish history, persisting to this very day.' Lowering his head, the professor conceded the point to me."

According to the *Vilna Gaon*, the blessings recited in conjunction with the *Shema* contain an allusion to the protective power of God's unconditional love for Israel. In the morning blessing (in *Nusach Ashkenaz*) we speak of אַהֲבָה רַבָּה, God's *great love*. In the evening blessing we speak of אַהֲבַת עוֹלָם, God's *eternal love*. Daytime, which symbolizes clarity, represents periods of redemption when Israel is worthy of Hashem's great love. Evening, a time of shadows and darkness, is symbolic of the exile when, removed from a sense of God's presence, we do not deserve His great love. Then we speak of "eternal" love, for in such periods we enjoy His love not in our own merit, but because of the eternal promise he made to our forefathers. Thus, it is His promise that sheds light upon us throughout the long night of exile.

2. **Persecution — Survival Insurance.** *R' Marcus Lehmann* captures the sentiment: It is this very persecution which is the guarantor of Jewish eternity. Often in our history, the cordiality of a host has tempted us to assimilate and abandon our sense of apartness. Then, anti-Semitic hatred has reminded us that we are indeed unique; we may forget it temporarily, but our enemies will always remind us that we are Jews. Thus, it is the underlying enmity of our enemies that *has stood* to protect us.

one alone who rose against us to annihilate us. Rather in every generation there are those who rise against us to annihilate us. But the Holy One, Blessed is He, saves us from their hand.

Maaseh Nissim sees yet another aspect of the exile experience as the element of our salvation. That God redeemed us from Egypt before we were totally swallowed up in its impurity offers hope that God does not abandon Israel. The thought that God seeks to sustain us through our difficult existence in exile provides us with the strength and courage to persevere.

In sum, God's promise to Abraham and His Divine Presence are always with us and protect us from our enemies (*Iyun Tefillah*). Furthermore, He will never allow our enemies to fully unite against us (*Sfas Emes*)[1] nor would He allow them to go beyond the stage of "merely" oppressing us and succeed in totally annihilating us (*Ohr Yesharim*).

Abarbanel views the word וְהִיא as a numerical acronym for key ingredients of Jewish survival. Thus the ו refers to the *Six* Orders of the Mishnah, the foundation of the Oral Law; the ה to the *Five* Books of Moses, the basic text of the Written Torah; the י to the *Ten* Commandments which encapsulate the general principles of all the *mitzvos*; and the א to the *One* and Only Lawgiver. The Torah and our loyalty to it and to its Giver have stood by us.

שֶׁלֹּא אֶחָד בִּלְבָד עָמַד עָלֵינוּ לְכַלּוֹתֵנוּ — *For it was not one alone who rose against us to annihilate us.* During all of our exile, we have been threatened by physical and spiritual enemies and God has saved us from them (*Rokeach*). This, too, was a result of God's promise to Abraham. Abraham was called *Ivri* (Hebrew), because all the world stood on one bank (*ever*) of the "river" (בְּעֵבֶר אֶחָד) and he stood on the other bank (עֵבֶר אַחֵר). In response to this courageous resolve to follow God's law even at the cost of such isolation, God created, in the Egyptian smelting furnace, a people who would be different; they would be God's people. It is this insistence on being different and maintaining a higher moral and ethical standard that elicits such venomous hatred on the part of the nations of the world.[2] Our

---

The ability of Jews to withstand the plague of assimilation is alluded to in the Covenant Between the Parts. While the heifers, goats and rams were divided, the bird remained whole (see *Genesis* 15:9-10 and *Rashi* ad loc.). This symbolizes that while other nations lose their special identity when they mingle with different peoples, we will survive forever with our national identity and heritage intact. Just as in Egypt we retained our identity, never changing our distinctly Jewish language, names and modes of dress, so it was our sense of separatism in all our wanderings that helped us retain our specialness.

This ability to remain separate from our host environment is alluded to by our raising of the cups when reciting this passage. The decree to forbid wine touched by gentiles (see *Shabbos* 17b and *Yoreh Deah* 123:1) was intended to prevent intermarriage by forestalling fraternization between Jews and gentiles. Thus the very wine in our cups protected us spiritually from our enemies. We offer praise to the wine itself, symbolic of our separatist posture while in exile among the nations. We are different and must never forget it!

1. **All His Eggs in Many Baskets.** God has done us a great favor by dispersing us among many nations. Had we been all in one place we would have been more vulnerable to physical extinction (*Pesachim* 87b and *Rashi* ad loc.).

2. **Prophetic Enemy.** *R' Moshe Sherer* writes: Sometimes a single piece of paper can capture the theme of an entire era. Years ago, the famed Holocaust researcher and spokesman of the generation of survivors, Reb Moshe Prager ע"ה, presented me with an amazing document, the likes of which one does not find in Holocaust museums; for some reason, apparently, it has not been deemed museum worthy. Unfortunately, the museum curators do not understand. I carry it with me in my wallet, so it should always be with me, as a constant reminder of a unique insight.

This document transmits a memorandum dispatched by I.A. Eckhardt ש"ימ, from the Chief of the German Occupation Power. It is an order, dated October 25, 1940, from *das Reichssicherheitshauptamt* — the Central Office of the German Security Forces — to the Nazi district governors in occupied Poland,

צֵא וּלְמַד מַה בִּקֵּשׁ לָבָן הָאֲרַמִּי לַעֲשׂוֹת לְיַעֲקֹב

unique, unnatural origin and unusual nature has brought us enemies[1] in every generation (*Rabbi A. Wolf*).

While innumerable enemies have risen against us we are confident that none of them can prevail, since God is still with us. Thus, homiletically we might render the passage שֶׁלֹּא אֶחָד עָמַד עָלֵינוּ בִּלְבָד, *for the One and Only has not turned against us*, and for this reason we rejoice in His salvation (*R' Baruch of Mezhibezh*).

אֶלָּא שֶׁבְּכָל דּוֹר וָדוֹר עוֹמְדִים עָלֵינוּ לְכַלּוֹתֵנוּ — *Rather in every generation there are those who rise against us to annihilate us.*

In every generation Providence arranges that someone arises who seeks to fatally harm us. God does this so that He will be able to save us from them and thus demonstrate that we are His special people over whom He constantly

watches (*Avudraham*).[2]

Geulas Avraham suggests that the Haggadah's mention of adversaries other than Pharaoh is in order to show that God's promise to Abraham was ongoing and not limited to one particular historical occurrence. For this reason, the Haggadah spoke earlier of the fact that God *keeps* (present tense) His promise. As adversaries continually rise against us throughout history, God provides us with ongoing redemption, and He uses this concern with Jews as a means to display His control of human destiny. This itself is an indication of His intense love for His people. Were the Exodus to have been a one-time episode, God's omnipotence may have been long forgotten by the nations of the world. By allowing them to rise up against His people and then thwarting them, He reiterates to

---

instructing them not to grant exit visas to *Ostjuden* (Jews from Eastern Europe). The reason behind this order is clearly spelled out: the fear that because of their *"Orthodoxen einstellung"* (Orthodoxy), these *Ostjuden* would provide *"die Rabbiner und Talmudlehrer"* (the rabbis and teachers of Talmud), who would create *"die geistige Erneuerung"* (the spiritual regeneration) of the Jews in America and throughout the world.

Obviously the Germans realized that they would not succeed in fulfilling their dream of physically exterminating all the Jews. But they did deem it possible to *spiritually* annihilate all Jews throughout the world who would evade their net of destruction. King David expressed such schemes with the words *Let us destroy them from being a nation so that the Jewish name will no longer be remembered* (*Psalms* 83:5).

1. **Joy Born of Adversity.** Just as fine wine is made by aggressively smashing grapes, so does the vine of Israel (see *Chullin* 92a) yield its finest spiritual wine as a result of the constant threat of oppression by their enemies. As the Sages taught, "The removal of Ahaseurus' signet ring [to confer imperial powers upon Haman, to issue his decree of annihilation] was more effective than all the prophets and prophetesses who prophesied to Israel" (*Megillah* 14a). None of the prophets was as successful in motivating the Jewish people to repentance as was the threat of destruction by Haman, for it bespoke the great hatred Ahasuerus harbored toward them and inspired them to wholehearted contrition (see *Maharsha* ad loc.).

Thus we raise our cup of wine as a symbol of the hearty taste of true repentance which saved us and which was a result of the threats of our enemies (*Chodesh HaAviv*).

❧ **Emotional Unification.** *Sfas Emes* suggests that it is unity among Jews that has proven to be the key to our survival in exile. Thus he homiletically renders שֶׁלֹּא אֶחָד בִּלְבָד, *it is only the not being as one*, עָמַד עָלֵינוּ, *that has risen up against us to destroy us*.

2. **Installment Plan.** Even when God finds it necessary to bring pain and punishment upon Jews, He does so in small installments so that the pain never becomes overwhelming. It is for this reason that *in every generation* some nation or individual arises against the Jews. Rather than having one nation arise that could deliver one overpowering and crippling blow, God arranges that foes arise in every generation, thus dissipating the intensity of the hardship so that we can survive it. This is God's way of softening the blow of exile, by parceling out the pain over many generations; it has preserved our forefathers and us (*Yismach Yisrael*).

the nations of the world that there is none like Him in the midst of the earth (*Maasei Hashem*).

וְהַקָּדוֹשׁ בָּרוּךְ הוּא מַצִּילֵנוּ מִיָּדָם — *But the Holy One, Blessed is He, saves us from their hand.* Even when our salvation appears to be a result of natural causes or of human endeavor, it is God's intervention that is the cause of our salvation (*Malbim*).[1]

Often we are granted God's salvation through the very enemies who rise against us. God demonstrates His love for us by employing them as the means to provide us with the help we need. Thus מַצִּילֵנוּ מִיָּדָם might be rendered as *God saves us through* (not *from*) *their hands*. Pharaoh's oppression cleansed and purified the Jews so that they were ready for the great gift of the Torah. Similarly, Haman unwittingly set the stage for his own downfall when he convinced Ahasuerus to have Vashti killed, thus paving the way for Esther's ascent to the throne. Haman then built the gallows for Mordechai, but God had them built for Haman himself. Furthermore, the signet ring which Ahasuerus gave to Haman in order to seal the fate of the Jews in fact served as the catalyst that propelled the Jews to repent (*Megillah* 14a). These are but a few examples of how the diabolical plans of the enemies of God and Israel are boomeranged against them, resulting in their own downfall (*Acharis LeShalom*).

צֵא וּלְמַד — *Go out and ascertain.* The Haggadah has suggested that the 190 years (beginning from the birth of Isaac) that preceded the actual bondage of Egypt were counted as part of the total 400 years during which *your offspring will be an alien* (*Genesis* 15:13). *Go out and ascertain* from Laban that this is indeed so, for during those years Jacob and his

family faced the threat of imminent death. During a time so fraught with peril, Jacob could not be considered at home in his land. When he said to Esau, *I sojourned* [גַּרְתִּי] *with Laban* (*Genesis* 32:5), he surely meant that the decree of *your offspring will be an alien* [גֵּר] was fulfilled through him. Similarly, Abraham referred to this point when he said, "*I am an alien* [גֵּר] *and a resident with you*" (*Genesis* 23:4), as did God when He said to Isaac, "*Sojourn* [גּוּר] *in this land*" (*Genesis* 26:3). Hence, the 190 years of the sojourning of all of our forefathers are part of the fulfillment of *your offspring will be an alien* (*Geulas Avraham*).

The term *Go out and ascertain* carries the connotation of "investigate thoroughly and draw the proper conclusions" (see *Tosafos Yom Tov* to *Avos* 2:9 based on *Song of Songs* 3:11). This is given as a charge and instruction as we begin the heart of the Haggadah text, the elucidation of the Scriptural portion of אֲרַמִּי אֹבֵד אָבִי, *An Aramean tried to destroy my forefather. Rambam* states: "It is a positive commandment to recount the miraculous events that occurred to our ancestors in Egypt. All who expand their discussion of these events are deemed praiseworthy.....One should elucidate the Biblical portion of *An Aramean tried to destroy my forefather* from the beginning until he finishes that Biblical portion. Anyone who adds and expands on the elucidation *of this portion* is considered worthy of praise" (*Hil. Chametz U'Matzah* 7:1-4). Thus, merely reading these or other appropriate verses from the Torah is insufficient in fulfilling the special *mitzvah* of this night — to retell the story of our liberation and national genesis. We must *elucidate* it, by fleshing out the details of this portion based on the tradition of the Sages as explained in the Oral Torah.

---

1. **From Death's Grip.** *R' Klonymus Kalman of Piacezna* spent the years of the Holocaust in the Warsaw Ghetto. Every Shabbos and Yom Tov he would gather with Jews and speak words of Torah seeking to comfort and strengthen them. On Pesach 1941 he taught the following: "Not only does God save us countless times from falling into the hands of our enemies, but even when their grip is *already* around our necks and we are already in their hands we need not despair. God even saves us *from their hand* (מַצִּילֵנוּ מִיָּדָם)."

אָבִינוּ, שֶׁפַּרְעֹה לֹא גָזַר אֶלָּא עַל הַזְּכָרִים, וְלָבָן בִּקֵּשׁ לַעֲקוֹר אֶת הַכֹּל. שֶׁנֶּאֱמַר:

אֲרַמִּי אֹבֵד אָבִי, וַיֵּרֶד מִצְרַיְמָה וַיָּגָר שָׁם בִּמְתֵי מְעָט, וַיְהִי שָׁם לְגוֹי, גָּדוֹל עָצוּם וָרָב.[1]

Homiletically, *Acharis LeShalom* interprets this as a call to the scholar that if he wants to fully appreciate the underhanded trickery of Laban, he must *go out* of the study hall (where life is sincere and honest) and encounter the "real" world of deceit and deception.[1]

שֶׁפַּרְעֹה לֹא גָזַר אֶלָּא עַל הַזְּכָרִים — *For Pharaoh decreed against only the males.* The deliverance from Laban's hand was even more remarkable, because he posed a far greater danger than that posed by Pharaoh, for Laban was ready to murder Jacob and his family, whereas Pharaoh wanted merely to enslave the Jews.

This statement seems strange in the narrative of the Egyptian persecution. Why should we minimize the intensity of Pharaoh's brutality, all for the sake of building up the evil of Laban, who is not even a major figure in the Haggadah's discussion? We must thus understand this as a continuation of the previous paragraph, an illustration of how "in every generation they rise up to destroy us and God saves us from their hand" (*Shibbolei HaLeket*).

Jacob fled to Laban's home to escape the physical threat of Esau, only to, so to speak, "go from the frying pan into the fire" of the spiritual threat of Laban. Nevertheless God protected him; he built his family and fortune, and ultimately left with great wealth. Similarly, the Jews went to Egypt to escape the threat of famine, and there in the moral cesspool of Egypt they evolved into a nation, to whom He gave the Torah, His greatest treasure. It shows furthermore that God protects us from those who seek to harm us even when we are unaware of the danger, as was the case in Laban's pursuit of Jacob (*Genesis* 31:24) (*Vilna Gaon, R' Yechezkel Levenstein*).[2]

R' Chaim Soloveitchik comments that Laban's plan for the total eradication of the Jewish people was beyond the realm of possibility, for Abraham was promised after the *Akeidah* that his children could never be totally decimated (see *Ramban* to *Genesis* 22:16-17). However, Pharaoh's plan to kill only the males could theoretically have been accomplished, for it would not entail the disappearance of the Jewish people. Had the surviving Jewish women married Egyptians or other gentiles, the children of the union would be halachically Jewish (see *Yevamos* 23a and *Rashi* ad loc.), thus providing for Jewish continuity. (See, however, *Ramban* to *Leviticus* 24:10.) Nonetheless, God in His mercy thwarted Pharaoh's evil design.[3]

---

1. **In God We Trust.** Generally we are enjoined to judge people favorably (*Avos* 1:6). Here we are taught that deceitful evildoers like Laban are an exception to this rule. *Go out*, i.e., depart, from the general rule *and ascertain* the full depths of his evil. As the Talmud (*Megillah* 13b) teaches, citing *Psalms* 18:27 — *With the pure you act purely; and with the crooked you act perversely* — while it is never permitted to lie or steal one must protect himself against connivers and liars. When Rachel asked Jacob for his justification in acting deceitfully toward Laban, he quoted this verse. When others try to deceive them, even the righteous may counter in kind. Jacob said, "I am his brother and equal in deceit [when necessary]."

The *Chafetz Chaim* once remarked: "The Torah teaches תָּמִים תִּהְיֶה עִם ה' אֱלֹהֶיךָ, *You shall be whole-hearted with Hashem, your God* (*Deuteronomy* 18:13). With God you must be naive and trusting, but when dealing with people you must protect your interests!"

2. **Parallel Pursuit.** The *Vilna Gaon* notes further that both the Jews who left Egypt and Jacob were pursued by those who had been reluctant to free them. Both were miraculously saved.

3. **Saving Royalty.** While Jewishness is determined by maternal descent, it is the paternal line that determines whether one is a *Kohen* or Levite. Likewise, a Jewish king must be a descendant of halachically

Jacob, our father! For Pharaoh decreed only against the males, Laban attempted to uproot everything, as it is stated:

An Aramean tried to destroy my forefather. Then he descended to Egypt, and sojourned there, with few people; and there he became a nation — great, mighty and numerous.[1]

---

(1) *Deuteronomy* 26:5.

Some commentators maintain that Laban did not wish to *kill* Jacob and his family, but to force them to return with him to Aram, and bring them into his sphere of influence — and *this* is what the Haggadah refers to as *to uproot everything* (*Chayei Adam*).[1]

Laban was the very personification of dishonesty. Thus, Jacob found it necessary after his escape to tell Esau that גַּרְתִּי עִם לָבָן, *I dwelt with Laban* (*Genesis* 32:5), which the Midrash interprets as תַּרְיַ"ג מִצְוֹת שָׁמַרְתִּי, *I observed the 613 Commandments* [despite the adverse conditions] (גַּרְתִּי has the numerical value of תַּרְיַ"ג, 613). (*Rashi*, from *Pesikta Zuta*). Although Jacob and his wives had the fortitude to resist the corruption of Laban's household, his children would almost certainly have assimilated and adopted his way of life, preventing the emergence of a Jewish people altogether.

In a sense Pharaoh's cruel infanticide posed a lesser threat than Laban did. The Sages state a general principle that קָשֶׁה הַמַּחֲטִיאוֹ יוֹתֵר מִן הַהוֹרְגוֹ, *he who makes somebody sin is worse than he who kills him*, for the latter deprives him only of his earthly life, while the former divests him also of life in the World to Come.

The Haggadah compares Laban to Pharaoh since both hated Jews for no apparent reason. Esau, on the other hand, felt that Jacob had robbed him of his birthright and thus felt justified in his hatred [Thus, we speak of Pharaoh's edict against the Jewish males rather than his pursuit of the escaping Jews, for at the Sea, although he sought their total annihilation, he had a reason — as retribution for their failure to return.] (*Maharal*).

שֶׁנֶּאֱמַר אֲרַמִּי אֹבֵד אָבִי — *As it is stated, "An Aramean tried to destroy my forefather."* This passage from *Deuteronomy* 26:5 summarizes our descent to Egypt, the harrowing experience of the exile and bondage, and the eventual Exodus. The opening phrase is understood by the Sages as referring to Laban the *Aramean* (see *Targum Onkelos* to *Deuteronomy* 26:5), who tried to deceive Jacob at every turn and finally pursued him with the intention of killing him. As Laban said to him when he finally caught him in pursuit, *"It is in my power to do you all harm"* (*Genesis* 31:29). Only because God came to Jacob's defense and warned Laban not to dare harm him did Laban desist (*Ritva*).

Laban is identified as "an Aramean" because the term is generically used as a euphemism for an idolater (see *Megillah* 25a, *Sanhedrin* 81b and *Rambam, Hil. Issurei Biah* 12:5). Since Laban is the first idolater specifically identified as such in Scripture (when Rachel stole his idols), he is given the appellation of "Aramean" (*Simchas Yaavetz*).

Other commentators interpret אֹבֵד to mean "wandering" rather than "would destroy." They identify the אֲרַמִּי as either Abraham, who wandered from the land of Aram to Canaan (*Rashbam*), or

---

pure parents. Hence, had Pharaoh's edict succeeded, the Jewish people would continue to exist, but the institutions of *Kohanim*, Levites and royalty would cease. Thus, for ignoring Pharaoh's instructions and, in their deep-felt fear of God, saving the Jewish males, the Jewish midwives were rewarded with descendants who were *Kohanim*, Levites and kings (see *Rashi* to *Exodus* 1:21) (*R' D. Soloveitchik*).

1. **Whitewash.** The Evil Inclination employs various tactics in his campaign to ensnare us. Sometimes it panders to our baser instincts. Other times it tries to convince us that the forbidden is in reality a *mitzvah*. The first tactic is, according to *R' Mendel of Rimanov*, known as Pharaoh (anagram of פֶּה רַע, *an evil mouth*), while the second insidious approach is known as Laban (לָבָן, *white*), since it seeks to whitewash evil and disguise it as good.

וַיֵּרֶד מִצְרַיְמָה – אָנוּס עַל פִּי הַדִּבּוּר.
וַיָּגָר שָׁם – מְלַמֵּד שֶׁלֹּא יָרַד יַעֲקֹב אָבִינוּ
לְהִשְׁתַּקֵּעַ בְּמִצְרַיִם, אֶלָּא לָגוּר שָׁם. שֶׁנֶּאֱמַר, וַיֹּאמְרוּ

Jacob (*Ibn Ezra*). Some understand אֹבֵד to mean "tried to destroy," as the Haggadah does, but take the *Aramean* to be Balaam (*Shelah*, based on *Targum Yonason* to *Numbers* 22:5), who advised Pharaoh to kill the Jewish baby boys. The Haggadah, however, follows the Midrashic opinion of *Sifre* that the reference is to Laban.

The portion of *bikkurim* [first fruits] was chosen as the springboard text for our discussion of the Exodus because the theme of the Seder is to offer thanks to God for bringing our nation into being and sustaining it. Thus the "*Bikkurim* Declaration," a moving paean of gratitude to God for His eternal role as the Guide of Jewish history, is very apropos (see *Rashi* to *Deuteronomy* 26:3). Furthermore, the gift of *bikkurim*, one's first fruits and the symbol of man's creative ability, reflects man's recognition that all that he has, including his ability to be productive, is God given. In retelling the Exodus story, we focus on its eternal message that "Hashem's is the earth and all that it contains."

וַיֵּרֶד מִצְרַיְמָה – *Then he descended to Egypt.* What is the connection between Laban's ill treatment of Jacob and his descent to Egypt more than 30 years later? According to *Rashi* (ad loc.), וַיֵּרֶד מִצְרַיְמָה is an independent clause, meaning that in *addition* to the threat of Laban, we were exposed to others who sought our destruction, physical or spiritual. Egypt was a prime example of such a situation.

Jacob's stay with Laban helped prepare Jews for the trials and temptations of the exile, and it also convinced Jacob not to go back to him when famine struck the Land of Canaan, so that the Divine decree that Abraham's children would be aliens could not be fulfilled in Aram (although food was available there). Thus Jacob and his children went to Egypt (*Maasei Hashem*).

Mahari Bei Rav sees yet another reason to consider Laban the cause for our descent to Egypt. His trickery in exchanging Leah for Rachel as

Jacob's first wife laid the foundation for the bickering among Jacob's sons. The ultimate result was the sale of Joseph and the migration of Jacob's family to Egypt.

The Haggadah now elucidates the portion of the Torah that was to be recited by farmers when they brought the first fruits of their land (בִּכּוּרִים, *bikkurim*) to the Temple. It is a declaration of God's kindness to us in bringing our nation into existence with the Exodus from Egypt and the conquest of the Land of Israel. The first four verses of this "*Bikkurim* Declaration" (מִקְרָא בִּכּוּרִים) are a terse recapitulation of Israel's genesis. The first verse speaks of the travails of Jacob and his descent to Egypt; the second describes the Egyptians' persecution; the third depicts our prayers to God and His response; and the fourth describes the miraculous liberation from Egypt. These four verses (*Deuteronomy* 26:5-8) are expounded upon by the Midrash (*Sifre*) in great detail, and these verses, with their midrashic interpretation, form the backbone of the Haggadah text, which begins here.

Malbim offers insight into the structure of this elucidation. Some points of the story are explicitly stated in this declaration, while others are implied by language that alludes to other verses in the Torah. Furthermore, either through juxtaposition of ideas or by restating seemingly repetitious ideas in different words, this short recitation encapsulates the entire story of the descent to Egypt and the Exodus as told at length in the Books of *Genesis* and *Exodus*.

וַיֵּרֶד מִצְרַיְמָה – אָנוּס עַל פִּי הַדִּבּוּר – *Then he descended to Egypt — forced by the word [of God].* Jacob did not go down to Egypt willingly; it was the Divine decree that Abraham's children would be aliens in a land not their own that "compelled" him to do so (*Lekach Tov*). Furthermore, by bringing the famine in Canaan, God forced Jacob's

Then he descended to Egypt — forced by the word [of God]. **He sojourned there** — this teaches us that our father Jacob did not descend to Egypt to settle, but only to sojourn temporarily, as it is stated: "And they (the sons of Jacob) said

---

family to travel to Egypt (*Abarbanel* and *Chayei Adam*; see *Sforno* to *Genesis* 45:28).

The term וַיֵּרֶד, *he descended* (rather than וַיֵּלֶךְ, *he went*, or וַיֵּצֵא, *he left to go*), is indicative of having gone under duress (*Machzor Vitry*).

Jacob intended merely to see his beloved son Joseph once again and then return to the task of settling and building up the Land of Canaan. In fact, the Sages teach that Jacob was hesitant and afraid to leave the Holy Land (see *Rashi* to *Genesis* 46:3). It was only after he had already embarked upon his journey that Hashem informed him that the Divine plan for the Jewish people required a prolonged stay in Egypt. God therefore reassured him: *Do not be afraid to go down to Egypt.*

Chayei Adam suggests that Jacob was *forced by the word* of Abraham, not the word of God, for the Talmud (*Nedarim* 32a) teaches that the Egyptian exile was a consequence of Abraham's request for a sign from God that his children would inherit the land. The question *Whereby shall I know that I am to inherit it?* (*Genesis* 15:8) was a shortcoming in Abraham's faith, which required that his children be purified in the smelting furnace of Egypt. Thus Jacob went down to Egypt *forced by the [questioning] word* of Abraham.

Maggid Tzedek views *the word* as referring to the evil reports that Joseph told Jacob regarding Joseph's brothers (see *Genesis* 37:2). This caused the brothers to hate him and eventually sell him into slavery. Thus, an irreversible chain of events for Abraham's descendants was set into action (see also *Sfas Emes*).

Malbim notes that this line (וַיֵּרֶד מִצְרַיְמָה, אָנוּס עַל פִּי הַדִּבּוּר) does not appear in the *Sifre* as does the rest of the exegesis quoted in the Haggadah (nor is it found in Rambam's Haggadah). He views it is a mere statement of historical fact by the author of the Haggadah.

The descent to Egypt due to God's decree is one more illustration of the subtle guiding hand of God which shapes events to occur in ways that benefit

His people. The Talmud asserts that Jacob should have been dragged to Egypt in iron chains, as are most exiles, but his merit spared him this degradation. Instead, the exile was imposed upon him gently, by his love of Joseph and historical circumstances (see *Shabbos* 89b). Hence, Jacob was forced down to Egypt by the word of God rather than by the cruel methods employed by human captors (*Vilna Gaon*).

Maharal offers a perspective on the seminal place of the Exodus in history and in the formation of the Jewish nation. Had Jacob's descent to Egypt been an act of free choice, the later liberation could have been considered an event that "just happened" to occur. But the birth of God's chosen people was of such cosmic significance that it could not be perceived to be the product of chance and whim. God forced Jacob to go to Egypt so that the nation that emerged from that spiritual crucible be formed by the hand of God, not by human decisions.

וַיָּגָר שָׁם – מְלַמֵּד שֶׁלֹּא יָרַד יַעֲקֹב אָבִינוּ לְהִשְׁתַּקֵּעַ בְּמִצְרַיִם — *And sojourned there — this teaches us that our father Jacob did not descend to Egypt to settle.* The term וַיָּגָר comes from the same root as גֵּר, *stranger*. While ostensibly the verse describes the limited period that Jacob *lived* in Egypt, it is interpreted here more pointedly as focusing on Jacob's *intentions* in going there. If this passage were referring to the long time span that Jacob and his family actually lived in Egypt, the term וַיֵּשֶׁב שָׁם, *and he dwelt there*, which indicates a protracted residence, should have been used. *And he sojourned* [וַיָּגָר] connotes transience, which applies to what Jacob *intended* rather than to what *actually* happened (*Abarbanel*).

Malbim derives from the word order of the verse that the phrase *and he sojourned* refers to Jacob's intent, rather than to the actual duration of the Jewish settlement. Had the verse read *he descended to Egypt with a*

אֶל פַּרְעֹה, לָגוּר בָּאָרֶץ בָּאנוּ, כִּי אֵין מִרְעֶה לַצֹּאן אֲשֶׁר לַעֲבָדֶיךָ, כִּי כָבֵד הָרָעָב בְּאֶרֶץ כְּנָעַן, וְעַתָּה יֵשְׁבוּ נָא עֲבָדֶיךָ בְּאֶרֶץ גֹּשֶׁן.[1]

בִּמְתֵי מְעָט – כְּמָה שֶׁנֶּאֱמַר, בְּשִׁבְעִים נֶפֶשׁ

---

family few in number and sojourned there, the last phrase might be interpreted as referring to the ongoing condition of Jacob's family while in Egypt. However, since the phrase שָׁם וַיָּגָר, *he sojourned there*, is inserted before בִּמְתֵי מְעָט, *with few people*, *Sifre* interprets it as reflective of the stranger's mindset with which Jacob and his family went to Egypt.

Though they could expect to be treated royally in Egypt, and were in fact treated so until Joseph's death, they nevertheless left *Eretz Yisrael* reluctantly and always regarded themselves as strangers (*Chida*).[1]

Jacob did not go to Egypt לְהִשְׁתַּקֵּעַ (*to settle*, lit., *to submerge himself*). By avoiding immersion in the culture and social mores of the land, he and his descendants were able to avoid being spiritually engulfed in its impurity and immorality (*Yalkut Tov*). Jacob's concern not to form an attachment with Egyptian society extended to his deathbed wish that he be buried in *Eretz Yisrael*. He wanted to serve as a link to *Eretz Yisrael* so that the following generations would always remember where their real home was (*R' S.R. Hirsch*).

The *Vilna Gaon* notes that it was a Divine kindness that influenced Jacob to go to Egypt with the intention that it was to be on a temporary basis. Had he intended to settle permanently, his descen-

dants would not been worthy of redemption.

שֶׁנֶּאֱמַר וַיֹּאמְרוּ אֶל פַּרְעֹה – *As it is stated: "And they said to Pharaoh . . ."* The Haggadah now sets out to prove that וַיָּגָר שָׁם is indicative of an intent to dwell temporarily. The supporting verse (cited from *Genesis* 47:4) proves that in the context of Jacob's descent to Egypt the word וַיָּגָר indeed means *to sojourn* temporarily. When Pharaoh asked Joseph's brothers their occupation they responded by telling him that they were shepherds: *"We have come to sojourn [לָגוּר] in the land since there is no grazing for your servants' flocks, for the famine is severe in the Land of Canaan."* They requested permission to live temporarily in Goshen, a grazing area, only until the famine in Canaan would pass. Thus, the cited verse complements the elucidation and clarifies it beyond any doubt; without the supporting verse the point would be incomplete (*Malbim, Machzor Vitry, Maaseh Nissim*).

This statement represents the nation's resolve that its true home is *Eretz Yisrael*. The brothers stated emphatically to Pharaoh that they would remain in Egypt only until God would permit them to return where they belonged (*R' Nosson Scherman*).

---

1. **Rude Awakening.** It was only later, the *Midrash* tells us, that they sought to assimilate and be as Egyptian as the Egyptians. According to the *Midrash,* in a crude attempt to imitate their Egyptian hosts, many Jews stopped practicing circumcision after Joseph died. This only elicited the wrath of the Egyptians and increased their hatred for the Jews.

This phenomenon repeats itself in every generation. Whenever we seek to assimilate and be like our non-Jewish neighbors, we are met with scorn and even violence. The non-Jew resents our attempt to be like him and resoundingly reminds us of who we are and whom we had better remain (*Netziv*).

R' Elchonon Wasserman commented that it is no fluke of history that Germany, where assimilationist tendencies were most rampant, was the cradle of the Holocaust. The slogan "Be a Jew in your home and a man outside" was given a most bloody response, as we were reminded that we are Jews wherever we go.

to Pharaoh: 'We have come to sojourn in this land because there is no pasture for the flocks of your servants, because the famine is severe in the Land of Canaan. And now, please let your servants dwell in the Land of Goshen.' "[1]

With few people — as it is stated: With seventy persons,

---

(1) *Genesis* 47:4.

כִּי אֵין מִרְעֶה — *For there is no pasture.* Why did Jacob's sons claim to have come to Egypt in search of pasture? After all, was there not a famine in Egypt, too? *Ramban* (ad loc.) suggests that some vegetation grew despite the famine; but in Canaan the starving inhabitants would eat it themselves, whereas in Egypt real food could be bought. Another possibility is that Egypt had some grass because its land was irrigated from the Nile, while Canaan was dependent on rain for water (*Ritva*; see *Deuteronomy* 11:10).

Joseph wanted to guarantee that his family would live in Goshen, where they would live apart from the corrupting influence of Egyptian society. *Chidushei HaRim* remarks that Joseph was establishing a pattern for his successors to follow in every generation: Do not seek the grace of gentile rulers; neither emulate their ways nor mingle with them socially. Knowing that Pharaoh would wish to recruit officials and courtiers from the talented and successful family that had produced his viceroy, Joseph counseled his brothers on how to respond to the king: They should be truthful, but in a way that would deter Pharaoh from developing an association with them. Knowing that the animal-worshiping Egyptians abhorred shepherds, Joseph had them introduce themselves as herdsmen. Thus, Pharaoh would shun them and let them settle in the relative isolation of Goshen.

R' Yosef Dov Soloveitchik views the description of their occupation as a spiritual survival tactic. Shepherds are basically nomads who never develop emotional ties to the place they reside. Whenever they finish grazing in one place they have no emotional difficulties in picking up and leaving for another. Not so those who are involved in agriculture; they tend to bond with the land and find separation from the "motherland" very painful. Thus, the brothers chose to be shepherds in order to retain an alien mindset during their sojourn in Egypt.

בִּמְתֵי מְעָט — *With few people.* [1] The supporting verse from *Deuteronomy* 10:22 is cited to quantify the term "few" and is brought as historical reinforcement rather than to prove a point (*Malbim*). [2]

The seventy people who went down to Egypt were the nucleus of a nation that in due course would occupy a central place in the history of the

---

1. **Low Profile.** It would seem more appropriate for the order of the verse to be different: "And he descended to Egypt with few people, and he sojourned there," since Jacob descended to Egypt with few souls, and only afterward lived there as a foreigner. Thus the verse teaches us a cardinal rule of survival in exile. Even when Jews enjoy financial success it is imperative that they maintain an understated lifestyle. Ostentatious displays of wealth or highhanded political power can often backfire, arousing the jealousy and wrath of our host nations. Thus, we are taught that when Jacob descended to Egypt he sojourned there בִּמְתֵי מְעָט, with a humble and diminished lifestyle (*Imrei Emes*).

2. **It's in the Script.** *Chidushei HaRim* explains the phrase כְּמָה שֶׁנֶּאֱמַר [lit. *as it is stated*] to mean that whatever happens to Israel is according to what is said in the Torah or as a reflection of the guiding hand of God's Providence. Let no one imagine that anything that occurred to Jews in Egypt or any exile was coincidental, the result of God's abandonment. Jewish history is the direct result of a Divine edict כְּמָה שֶׁנֶּאֱמַר, "in accordance with what was stated."

יָרְדוּ אֲבֹתֶיךָ מִצְרָיְמָה, וְעַתָּה שָׂמְךָ יהוה אֱלֹהֶיךָ כְּכוֹכְבֵי הַשָּׁמַיִם לָרֹב.[1]

וַיְהִי שָׁם לְגוֹי – מְלַמֵּד שֶׁהָיוּ יִשְׂרָאֵל מְצֻיָּנִים שָׁם.

---

world and its seventy nations.[1] The Sages suggested an analogy of "a sheep among seventy wolves" that survives due to God's personal involvement in their existence. Thus, their number at the time foreshadowed their future role as a counterpoint to the other nations of the world. Therefore, the Torah teaches: *He set the borders of the peoples according to the numbers of the Children of Israel* (*Deuteronomy* 32:8).[2]

The Haggadah cites *Deuteronomy* 10:22 rather than the more explicit verse in *Genesis* 46:27: *All the persons coming with Jacob . . . were seventy.* *Maaseh Nissim* suggests two reasons for this. Firstly, the verse in *Genesis* does not clearly refer to the time when Jacob came to Egypt, and it might be misconstrued as referring to the size of the Jewish people *after* having settled in Egypt. However, *Deuteronomy* indicates clearly that the small number was at the time of *descent*, and that later they multiplied in a miraculous and disproportionate fashion. Alternatively, the number seventy is not intrinsically a small number; only in contrast to a large multitude, such as the number of stars,[3] is

---

1. **Souls Encoded.** The Sages teach that there are seventy aspects to the Torah (*Bamidbar Rabbah* 13:15), and that the Torah was given in seventy languages (*Sotah* 32a). Correspondingly the Jewish nation, as guardian of the Torah, began with seventy souls.

R' Tzadok HaKohen (*Tzidkas HaTzaddik* 196) offers perspective on the relationship between the Torah and its bearers. The Godly soul in every Jew is unfathomable; God gave us the Torah in order that we may penetrate the depths of our souls. Since the Torah is Godly intelligence, one may be able to perceive the Godliness in himself through developing his mind and emotions to function in a Godly manner. Torah, then, is an explication of the Divine wisdom that is otherwise beyond human comprehension. Only with God's intelligence can we understand Godliness.

Thus, the seventy aspects of Torah and the seventy languages in which it was given are a mirror of its function — the unraveling of the mysteries of the seventy souls of the Jewish nation. The nation — whose nucleus was formed of seventy prototype souls — received the formula for self-discovery, the Torah, which was given in seventy languages and bearing seventy aspects.

For this reason, R' Tzadok explains, love for a fellow Jew is, in a fashion, of greater import than love of Torah. Love of a fellow Jew is really love for Torah in its most primary form.

2. **God's Nation.** Each of the seventy nations has its own historical role to play; in the same way, within the ranks of the Jewish people, each of the seventy souls of Jacob's family was destined to make a unique contribution to the future course of history (*R' Joseph Elias*).

The connotation of this parallelism between the number of Jews and the number of nations is that when the nations at large forfeited their opportunity to be the bearers of God's mission for humanity, He substituted Israel for them and made the number of Jewish families parallel to the number of primary national groups. This illustrates that God ordered history in consonance with the needs of Israel, for if Jews were to carry out God's designs for history, the conditions of human experience should enable them to do so. Thus, the Torah refers to Israel as *His people* — God's portion on earth (*R' Nosson Scherman*).

3. **Shining Star.** While in its simplest sense the analogy to stars is meant to convey the vast multitude of descendants that were born to those original seventy souls, the comparison has other aspects. Within the larger harmony of the galaxies, God *calls each star by name* (*Isaiah* 40:26), assigning to each its own specific function in the universe; in the same way, each Jew has to be aware that "for my sake the world was created" and that he has his own individual role to play, for which he must accept the full responsibility. Furthermore, stars appear to man to be small and insignificant due to their distance, while

your forefathers descended to Egypt, and now HASHEM, your God, has made you numerous as the stars of heaven."[1]

And he became there a nation — this teaches that the Jews were distinctive there.

---

(1) *Deuteronomy* 10:22.

---

seventy of small significance. Thus, the Haggadah quotes a verse that shows the historical development of the nation from a nucleus of seventy souls into a people as numerous as the stars.[1]

The total of seventy souls consisted of the following: Sixty-six people set out on the journey from Canaan to Egypt — Leah's thirty-two descendants, Zilpah's sixteen, Rachel's eleven and Bilhah's seven — and Joseph and his two sons were awaiting them in Egypt, for a total of sixty-nine. The seventieth soul, the Sages teach, was Yocheved, who was born just as they entered Egypt (see *Genesis* 46:8-27, and *Rashi*).

There are other views of who the seventieth soul was: Jacob himself is counted among the group, as implied by the expression *Jacob and his children* (*Ibn Ezra*). Or, the *Shechinah* (Divine Presence) was the seventieth, for God joined their group, as it were, in fulfillment of His promise to Jacob: *I shall descend with you* (*Genesis* 46:4).

וַיְהִי שָׁם לְגוֹי – מְלַמֵּד שֶׁהָיוּ יִשְׂרָאֵל מְצֻיָּנִים שָׁם — *And he became there a nation — this teaches that the Jews were distinctive there.* The word שָׁם, *there,* appears twice in the verse; the second שָׁם seems superfluous, since it is obvious that Jacob's family was *there*. It is on this basis that the Haggadah

concludes that the Jews in Egypt were praised for preserving their identity by not changing their language or their way of life. It was a type of greatness that could only have come about *there*, by maintaining their sacred identity even in a non-Jewish society (*Malbim, Geulas Avraham*).

According to *Netziv* (based on the *Vilna Gaon*), it is the term גּוֹי, *nation*, that connotes a distinct national identity. This is based on the verse in *Genesis* 10:20 that describes the sons of Ham *by their families, by their languages, in their lands,* בְּגוֹיֵהֶם — *by their nationalities* (*Genesis* 10:20). That verse lists four characteristics which distinguish nations. Families, languages, and lands are self-explanatory. Nationalities refers to the customs that are peculiar to distinct nationalities. The verse quoted here by the Haggadah says that the Jews became a גּוֹי, a distinct "national entity" distinguishable by a unique pattern of behavior — adherence to the commandments of God.

This national identity evolved in the crucible of Egypt, where the Jews strove against all odds to preserve their identity against the onslaught of Egyptian culture and against the emotionally draining and debilitating bondage.

In what way were the Jews *distinctive*? *Avudraham, Ritva* quoting *Rashi*, and *Shibbolei*

---

in truth most of them are even more luminous than the sun. Likewise, the nations of the world, so emotionally and spiritually removed from the Jewish people, have little appreciation or perception for the spiritual light that emanates from the luminous soul of Israel.

1. **United Animosity.** The verse speaks of seventy *souls*, yet the word נֶפֶשׁ, *person*, or *soul*, is in the singular; while in the case of Esau's children, the Torah uses the plural form: נַפְשׁוֹת בֵּיתוֹ, *the persons in his family* (*Genesis* 36:6). The souls of the Jewish people are like one unit, joined in their collective closeness to God; whenever Jews affirm their bond with God, they are a single spiritual organism. Conversely, it is only in unity that "one nation on earth" can bond with the One God. Thus, their faith in God's help united them in Egypt, to the point where there were no traitors or informers among them, and this made possible their deliverance; likewise, when they came to Mount Sinai, they were united *like one man, with one heart* (*Exodus* 17:2, *Rashi*), and thus were ready to receive the Torah.

גָּדוֹל עָצוּם – כְּמָה שֶׁנֶּאֱמַר, וּבְנֵי יִשְׂרָאֵל פָּרוּ וַיִּשְׁרְצוּ וַיִּרְבּוּ וַיַּעַצְמוּ בִּמְאֹד מְאֹד, וַתִּמָּלֵא הָאָרֶץ אֹתָם.[1]

וָרָב – כְּמָה שֶׁנֶּאֱמַר, רְבָבָה כְּצֶמַח הַשָּׂדֶה נְתַתִּיךְ, וַתִּרְבִּי וַתִּגְדְּלִי וַתָּבֹאִי בַּעֲדִי עֲדָיִים, שָׁדַיִם נָכֹנוּ וּשְׂעָרֵךְ צִמֵּחַ, וְאַתְּ

HaLeket suggest that they lived together in a close-knit community, which helped them strengthen each other; *Machzor Vitry* points to their extraordinary fruitfulness. Thus מְצֻיָּנִים might be rendered as *outstanding*.

Most commentators, however, explain the distinctiveness of the Jews in terms of the well-known tradition outlined in the *Mechilta* — that the Jews remained distinct from the Egyptians by keeping their ancestral language and names and by not adopting Egyptian immorality, and harbored no informers in their midst. *Kol Bo* adds that they also retained their distinct identity by not changing their mode of attire.[1]

Furthermore, even in the hardest moments of their bondage, the Jews clung to each other. *Tanna DeVei Eliyahu* teaches that "the Jews in Egypt assembled and made a covenant that they would deal kindly with one another, remember God's covenant with Abraham, Isaac and Jacob, serve their Father in Heaven alone, and retain their ancestral language and not speak the language of Egypt."[2]

Many versions have the text וַיְהִי שָׁם לְגוֹי גָּדוֹל, *They became there a great nation.* (That is, they include the word גָּדוֹל, *great*.) Outstandingly great, they were of sufficient spiritual stature to avoid being drawn after the prevalent mores of their surroundings (*Orchos Chaim*).

1. **Distinctly Jewish.** Our Sages emphasize that the Jews remained distinct in their clothes, their names and their language. This may not necessarily mean that they wore specific Jewish garb or only spoke Hebrew. Perhaps their distinctiveness lay in the fact that, unlike the Egyptians, they only spoke modest attire; when they talked, "the Name of God was regularly on their lips"; and they did not give their children the names of Egyptian deities (*R' Joseph Elias*).

Maor VaShemesh writes that it is inconceivable that the Jews did not learn the Egyptian language or speak it in many of their affairs. Nor does the term לְשׁוֹן הַקֹּדֶשׁ, *the holy tongue*, refer to Hebrew *per se*. Rather, the holiness of speech depends on how successfully one does not profane his tongue through foul and obscene language, and how much he sanctifies it through using his power of intelligent speech for Torah, prayer and the performance of the commandments. In this sense, the Jews in Egypt did not change the quality and sanctity of their speech, regardless of the language they may have spoken.

Jewish identity is not only expressed in externals; it is an internalization of distinctly Jewish values and instincts and the pride in being a Jew that allows one to unashamedly be different than the alien surroundings.

2. **At the Brink.** The Jews' steadfast refusal to give up their identity and their determination to maintain the bonds of brotherhood and the traditions of their fathers seem to conflict with the statement of our Sages that they had sunk to the forty-ninth level of impurity, and were in imminent danger of descending to the fiftieth level, the point of no return. The solution to this difficulty may be explained as follows.

It should be understand that there are many facets to human behavior, that people can be strong and good in some ways, yet weak and vulnerable in others. The Jews were fully exposed to Egyptian civilization, without the benefit of the Torah and its commandments, which protected their future descendants from total assimilation. Because of this, their way of thinking was inevitably influenced and distorted by their environment, and they were dragged down to increasingly lower levels of impurity. Nevertheless, they remained loyal to their inherited ways of life and moral standards, and because of this they were able to survive as a people (*Rabbi Aharon Kotler*).

Great, mighty — as it says: And the Children of Israel were fruitful, increased greatly, multiplied and became very very mighty; and the land became filled with them.[1]

And numerous — as it is stated: I made you as numerous as the plants of the field; you grew and developed, and became charming, beautiful of figure; your hair grown long; but you

---

(1) *Exodus* 1:7.

גָּדוֹל עָצוּם – *Great, mighty.* Great in quantity, yet mighty. Although Jewish mothers had multiple births — even miraculously giving birth to six children at once — the children were all healthy and strong. This was unusual, since children of multiple births are often weaker, and often die shortly after birth (*Abarbanel, Chayei Adam*).

According to *Shibbolei HaLeket*, "great" refers to the people's tall stature, and "mighty" refers to their extraordinary fertility.

וּבְנֵי יִשְׂרָאֵל פָּרוּ – *And the Children of Israel were fruitful . . .* The six expressions in the verse allude to the supernatural fertility of the Jewish women in Egypt, where as many as six children were born at one gestation (*Daas Zekeinim*; see *Shemos Rabbah* 1:8).

This phenomenon was a result of the Divine assurance that the more the Egyptians tormented the Jews, the more the Jewish population would increase (see *Exodus* 1:2). This explains why the censuses of the Book of *Numbers* show that the Levites were extraordinarily fewer in number than the other tribes. This was because the Levites were not enslaved in Egypt, and so were not threatened with decimation; therefore, God did not intervene to increase their numbers (*Ramban* to *Numbers* 3:14)

The Torah begins the account of the Egyptian affliction with this account of the Jews' extraordinary fertility, because each newborn child incited the Egyptians to hate the people more and more (*HaShir VeHaShevach*).

וַתִּמָּלֵא הָאָרֶץ אֹתָם – *And the land became filled with them.* The Jews were originally ensconced in Goshen, and the Egyptians felt claustrophobic when Jews started settling throughout Egypt. *Yalkut Shimoni* (*Exodus* 1:7) explains the expres-

sion "the land became filled with them" by commenting that the Jews would crowd into Egypt's public places of entertainment, thereby further stimulating the hatred of their hosts. It is interesting to note that the Levites, who remained separate from the Egyptians, did not undergo the persecution and slavery that befell their fellow Jews (see *Sforno* ad loc.).

וָרָב – *And numerous.* The term does not merely denote great numbers; the great *size* of the nation was already stressed with the words *great, mighty* mentioned earlier. Rather, it means continuous growth, constantly getting bigger and better (*Tosafos Rid*). *Abarbanel* renders וָרָב as *and formidable.* Considering the terrible strain under which the Jews lived, one might expect their children to have been physically, intellectually and emotionally underdeveloped, a result of insufficient care and nurture. Nonetheless, the Jewish people in Egypt were *formidable.* The children grew up perfectly developed in all respects, despite having not received proper parental care.

כְּמָה שֶׁנֶּאֱמַר רְבָבָה כְּצֶמַח הַשָּׂדֶה – *As it is stated: I made you as numerous as the plants of the field.* The young grew up in Egypt totally unattended, much like plants of the field that grow wild, never nurtured or tended to. Like wild vegetation, which is often more lush and beautiful than the handiwork of an artist or crops grown through careful nurturing, the generations of Jews who grew up in Egypt untended by their weary parents nevertheless assumed dazzling moral, ethical and spiritual beauty (*Abarbanel*). Furthermore, the more grass is cut the more it grows, and so the Jewish people, through God's blessing, became more numerous in

עֵרֹם וְעֶרְיָה; וָאֶעֱבֹר עָלַיִךְ וָאֶרְאֵךְ מִתְבּוֹסֶסֶת בְּדָמָיִךְ, וָאֹמַר לָךְ, בְּדָמַיִךְ חֲיִי, וָאֹמַר לָךְ, בְּדָמַיִךְ חֲיִי.[1]

וַיָּרֵעוּ אֹתָנוּ הַמִּצְרִים, וַיְעַנּוּנוּ, וַיִּתְּנוּ עָלֵינוּ עֲבֹדָה קָשָׁה.[2]

---

response to the Egyptian oppression (*Ritva, Avudraham*).[1]

וְאַתְּ עֵרֹם וְעֶרְיָה – *But you were naked and bare.* This verse is taken from the Book of *Ezekiel*, where the prophet metaphorically depicts the nascent Jewish nation in Egypt as an abandoned baby girl who was adopted and cared for by God. When the baby came of age, God saw that she was *naked and bare*, and He clothed her. The meaning of the parable is that the Jewish people in Egypt were bare of the commandments by which they might

merit redemption. The merit of the Patriarchs [זְכוּת אָבוֹת] and God's covenant with them meant that He would, in due course, deliver them from bondage, but they still needed *mitzvos* by means of which to show their readiness for redemption. Therefore, God gave them two commandments: the *pesach* offering and circumcision. The two commandments are alluded to in the words בְּדָמַיִךְ חֲיִי, repeated twice, which means *through your [two] bloods you shall live*, i.e., the blood of the offering and the blood of circumcision. [2]

---

1. **Stripped of Success.** God grants us success, but hopes that it will not lead us to become pompous and arrogant. If this does indeed occur, then all our accomplishments are for naught, and God may decide to take back everything He has allowed us to attain. *R' Moshe of Kobrin* saw a homiletic allusion to this in this verse from *Ezekiel*: רְבָבָה, even when you became great, כְּצֶמַח הַשָּׂדֶה, remain humble and lowly like the grass in the field, which becomes more bent over the higher it grows. However, if וַתִּרְבִּי וַתִּגְדְּלִי, you become great and haughty, then וְאַתְּ עֵרֹם וְעֶרְיָה, you actually are naked, stripped of all moral stature and without any redeeming value.

2. **Rites of Passage.** Since it was through these two bloods that the Jewish nation came to life, one who abstains from performing them may therefore have severed one's connection to the nation. It is for this reason that they are the only two positive commandments in the Torah whose deliberate disregard is punishable by *kares*, the excision of one's soul from its spiritual connection to its people. (Generally *kares* is the punishment for transgressing some of the most fundamental *prohibitions* in the Torah.)

One who is unwilling to reenact the initiation rite which allowed us to successfully leave the Egyptian womb, in effect spiritually aborts himself (*Bnei Yissaschar*).

◆§ **Isolation for Survival.** This verse compares the state of the Jewish people at the time of the Exodus to that of a newborn infant still dirty with the blood of the afterbirth. Unwashed, the infant is esthetically displeasing. Likewise, the Jews in Egypt suffered from spiritual filthiness. The verse then concludes, "I said to you, 'by your blood you shall live'; I said to you, 'by your blood you shall live.' " *Rashi* (ad loc.) explains, "Even as detestable as you are, you will not spiritually expire."

Seemingly, this contradicts the Talmudic interpretation (*Kereisos* 9a, see *Rashi* ad loc.) which views this as a reference to the blood of circumcision and the blood of the *pesach* offering, the two *mitzvos* through which Jews merited salvation.

Beis HaLevi explains: Circumcision is a physical sign of demarcation between Jews and non-Jews. The slaughter of the *pesach* offering was also a clear statement that we Jews are different and reject the pagan deities of the Egyptians. In the eyes of the Egyptians these two *mitzvos* signified that Jews view themselves as different. In their view, this isolationism was what makes Jews ugly. However, in truth it is this "ugliness" that saved us from becoming totally assimilated. Thus, the bloods which made us ugly are in reality the bloods that saved us.

In every generation it is those things which are patently Jewish that make us detestable in the eyes of our non-Jewish neighbors. These very things are our guarantor against the disaster of spiritual suicide.

were naked and bare. And I passed over you and saw you down-trodden in your blood and I said to you: 'Through your blood shall you live!' And I said to you: 'Through your blood shall you live!' "[1]

The Egyptians did evil to us and afflicted us; and imposed hard labor upon us.[2]

(1) *Ezekiel* 16:7,6. (2) *Deuteronomy* 26:6.

וַיָּרֵעוּ אֹתָנוּ הַמִּצְרִים – *The Egyptians did evil to us.* Having explained the first verse of the *Bikkurim* Declaration, which described the descent of the House of Jacob to Egypt and their subsequent growth and development into a full-fledged nation, the Haggadah now quotes in full the second verse, which describes the Egyptian attempts to suppress their growth. This is followed by a phrase-by-phrase analysis.

The rendering of וַיָּרֵעוּ as "*did evil*" is somewhat problematic, because the supporting verse cited does not speak of ill treatment at all; rather, it describes the desire of the Egyptians to devise a scheme to do away with the perceived threat posed by the Jews. Thus, *Rashi, Ritva* and others suggest rendering the phrase as *the Egyptians treated us worse* than did our earlier enemies such as Esau. Pharaoh felt that Esau had made a mistake in waiting for Isaac to die before taking revenge on Jacob. By the time Isaac died, Jacob's family was too big to be decimated in one blow. Pharaoh was committed not to make the same mistake.[1]

Abarbanel, Rashbatz and others render this phrase *the Egyptians considered us evil* — i.e., they viewed us as a threat to the stability of their land and society. The verse cited to illustrate this is appropriate, as it shows that the Egyptians considered the Jews a treacherous people.

In a homiletical rendering, *Chasam Sofer* interprets וַיָּרֵעוּ as being related to רֵעוּת, *friendship.* The Talmud tells us that initially the Egyptians used a cunning scheme to impose slavery upon the Jews. On a certain day, Pharaoh proclaimed a national day of voluntary labor, in which everyone in the country was to take part. In order to set an example, Pharaoh himself started making bricks, and the Jews, eager to prove their loyalty, participated in the effort with enthusiasm. At the end of the day Pharaoh appointed taskmasters to record the number of bricks made by the Jews on that day, and then he imposed an obligation upon them to repeat their performance every day thereafter.

Thus, through their initial demonstration of friendship towards the Jews, the Egyptians led them to believe that they were brothers who would jointly bear the national burden. In this manner they lulled the Jews into slowly but surely surrendering their independence.[2]

1. **Incomplete Purging.** The purification process which is the result of hard, backbreaking work was cut short when God redeemed the Jews after 210 years, rather than the 400 years foretold to Abraham. According to *Chasam Sofer*, it was because they were not completely purified that the Jews became involved with the Golden Calf. Thus וַיָּרֵעוּ might be translated as "the Egyptians *made us bad*" (not allowing us to be completely cleansed) through the merciless hard work that speeded the liberation.

2. **Terminal Friendship.** Literally, וַיָּרֵעוּ לָנוּ means "they did bad to us" (see *Numbers* 20:15). But here the Torah writes וַיָּרֵעוּ אֹתָנוּ, the Egyptians *made us bad*. According to many commentators this teaches that the Egyptians viewed us as bad people who might eventually revolt and overthrow their Egyptian rulers. In order to abort the revolution before it even started, they placed heavy work upon the Jews.

In a more homiletic view *R' Shlomo Alkabetz* interprets the phrase as "*they made us bad*." The influence of Egyptian culture and mores left a spiritually negative impact on us. The Egyptians understood that assimilation is the key to Jewish destruction.

Others suggest rendering וַיָּרֵעוּ as *they befriended*. The sweet talk of brotherly love and friendship with our foreign masters is the kiss of death for the Jews.

וַיָּרֵעוּ אֹתָנוּ הַמִּצְרִים — כְּמָה שֶׁנֶּאֱמַר, הָבָה נִתְחַכְּמָה
לוֹ, פֶּן יִרְבֶּה, וְהָיָה כִּי תִקְרֶאנָה מִלְחָמָה, וְנוֹסַף גַּם הוּא עַל
שֹׂנְאֵינוּ, וְנִלְחַם בָּנוּ, וְעָלָה מִן הָאָרֶץ.[1]
וַיְעַנּוּנוּ — כְּמָה שֶׁנֶּאֱמַר, וַיָּשִׂימוּ עָלָיו שָׂרֵי מִסִּים,

---

Eitz Chaim justifies the standard translation of וַיָּרֵעוּ as *did evil*, based on *Talmud Yerushalmi (Peah 1:1)*, which explains that when the nations of the world plan to do evil, God considers the mere intent as if it had actually been carried out. *Avudraham* explains that this is because only God's intervention prevents the execution of these plans, so that the potential perpetrators cannot be excused for not carrying out their plans. At any rate, according to this principle, the evil *schemes* of the Egyptians are considered by God as actual mistreatment.

Ramban comments that Pharaoh's goal was not slave labor, but the extermination of Israel, because he considered the Jews to be a threat in the event of an invasion. He could not say so openly because his people would not have accepted so monstrous a crime, and he needed their consent and cooperation. Therefore, he proceeded in steps:[1] first, slavery in the form of a labor tax; then, ordering the midwives to kill male babies secretly; then, having the Egyptians throw Jewish babies into the river and, finally, sending soldiers to search all Jewish homes for hidden infants.[2]

◆§ **Bringing Out the Worst.** *R' Moshe of Kobrin* adduces a homiletical interpretation of *Exodus* 1:14, וַיְמָרֲרוּ אֶת חַיֵּיהֶם בַּעֲבוֹדָה קָשָׁה בְּחֹמֶר וּבִלְבֵנִים, as follows: The Egyptians brought out the worst in us. They caused us to claim that עֲבוֹדָה, the *service* of God, is קָשָׁה, too *difficult* for us. Sometimes this complaint assumed the form of a claim that we were so deeply enmeshed in *physicality* (בְּחֹמֶר) that we could never truly attain spiritual freedom, while at other times it entailed the claim that we all are *lily white* (בִּלְבֵנִים, related to לָבָן, *white*) with nothing about us needing correction.

Finally, *Shaarei Aharon* offers a historical insight based on this verse. In good times people do not begrudge others the best. See *Rashi* to *Genesis* 41:2, who interprets the symbolism of the fat, nice-looking cows in the dream of Pharaoh: "During times of plenty, people appear cheerful ('nice looking') to each other with everybody happy over his friend's success and prosperity." However, bad times tend to bring out an ugliness among people. In his admonition to the people, Moses said, *The man among you who is tender and very delicate will turn selfish against his brother and the wife of his bosom and against the remaining children that he has let survive (Deuteronomy 28:54)*. The Torah goes on to describe unfathomable cruelty and inhumanity, for terrible conditions bring out the worst in people. Thus, by treating us badly, the Egyptians also turned us into bad people.

1. **Devilishly Inhuman.** Such a formula is well known to us from the tyrants and villains of recent times. The infamous Nuremburg Laws were the first step towards a Final Solution of the "Jewish problem." By dehumanizing the Jew and painting him in devilish strokes, the enemy was able to swing world opinion towards tacit acceptance of the cruelest policies against the Jews. Once they can show how we do not deserve even the most basic of human rights, it is but a short way to the cruelest oppressions.

2. **If It Hurts, Scream!** The Sages taught that three people participated in a conference with Pharaoh regarding the plan to kill the Jewish babies: Balaam, Job and Jethro. Balaam, who proposed the idea, was eventually killed; Job, who remained silent and did not protest the cruelty of the plan, was destined to undergo unbearable pain; Jethro, who couldn't bear to be an accomplice to such cruelty, ran away. As a reward he merited to have descendants who were members of the Sanhedrin (*Sotah* 11a).

The *Brisker Rav* explained why Job was punished. Job thought that since, in any event, Pharaoh would not listen, it was futile to protest. In truth, however, one cannot remain silent in the face of cruelty and injustice, whether one's protest will help or not. A decent person must feel so upset by such horrors that he cries out.

The Egyptians did evil to us — as it is stated: Let us deal cunningly with it lest it multiply and, if we happen to be at war, it may join our enemies and fight against us and then leave the country.[1]

And afflicted us — as it is stated: They set taskmasters over

---

(1) *Exodus* 1:10.

Malbim submits that the supporting text cited shows that the Egyptian oppression of the Jews was in fact a paranoid reaction to the increase in Jewish population. Thus, the second verse, which describes the Egyptians' cruel reaction, flows directly from the first verse which depicts the growth of the Jews. Afraid of a Jewish rebellion and takeover of their land, the Egyptians sought to quash the potential for such an uprising by oppressing the Jews.[1]

The phrase נִתְחַכְּמָה לוֹ is usually translated as *let us deal cunningly **with it*** (the Jewish people), but it can also be translated *with **Him***, referring to God. Our Sages (*Sotah* 11a), taking the word in this sense, explain that the Egyptians tried to "outsmart" God by oppressing the Jews in a way that would be immune to Divine retribution. Pharaoh knew that God punishes sinners in a way that corresponds to their sin (מִדָּה כְּנֶגֶד מִדָּה). He thus calculated that he would be safe in drowning

Jewish infants, for God had sworn in the days of Noah never again to bring a flood to destroy mankind. Pharaoh's mistake, however, was that the oath applied only to a *total* annihilation of mankind, not to an individual person or nation; the Egyptians met their fate by drowning in the Sea of Reeds.

וַיְעַנּוּנוּ — *And afflicted us*. The word עִנּוּי refers to abuse inflicted solely in order to inflict pain, not to mistreatment that is oriented toward a goal. Thus, the support verse cited teaches that Pharaoh appointed taskmasters over the Jews in order to afflict them with their burdens. The sole purpose of the labor was to inflict unbearable suffering on the people. [Furthermore, they hoped that the backbreaking labor would help curtail Israel's high birth rate (*Ibn Ezra*).] The primary goal of the Egyptians was not the building projects; their main aim was to oppress and decimate the

It was this lesson that Job was taught by being punished with physical pain. Pain elicits shouts of agony even though the person, in his saner moments, realizes that the screaming really doesn't help. Nonetheless, if it hurts, one screams. Decent people may never allow themselves to become so desensitized that they become emotionally impervious to injustice; even if it won't help, one must cry out.

Much of the world's silence during Hitler's reign of terror and blood was rooted in hatred of Jews; people were not pained enough to register a complaint.

1. **Cunningly Enslaved.** The Egyptians were frightened that the Jews were becoming too numerous, too strong. They might overwhelm the natives — but they were also too useful to be permitted to leave the country. It was the first instance in history of what has become the familiar pattern of anti-Semitism: The Jews are too dangerous to keep and they are too important to lose. So Pharaoh proposed a solution. He would harness the Jews by enslaving them, so that the state could benefit from their talents without fear that they would destroy the country. As for gratitude for Joseph's leadership and the legacy of prosperity that he had left the nation, that problem, too, was solved. A "new" Pharaoh came to the fore who *did not know of Joseph*. Either it was literally a new king, or an existing monarch with new policies, who found it convenient to ignore Joseph's monumental contributions to the country (*Sotah* 11a), probably on the grounds that whatever the Jew Joseph had done for Egypt was ancient history and no longer mattered. This "what-have-you-done-for-me-lately" kind of anti-Semitism is another familiar phenomenon of Jewish history (*Rabbi Nosson Scherman*).

לְמַעַן עַנֹּתוֹ בְּסִבְלֹתָם, וַיִּבֶן עָרֵי מִסְכְּנוֹת לְפַרְעֹה, אֶת פִּתֹם וְאֶת רַעַמְסֵס.[1]

וַיִּתְּנוּ עָלֵינוּ עֲבֹדָה קָשָׁה — כְּמָה שֶׁנֶּאֱמַר, וַיַּעֲבִדוּ מִצְרַיִם אֶת בְּנֵי יִשְׂרָאֵל בְּפָרֶךְ.[2]

וַנִּצְעַק אֶל יהוה אֱלֹהֵי אֲבֹתֵינוּ, וַיִּשְׁמַע יהוה אֶת קֹלֵנוּ, וַיַּרְא אֶת עָנְיֵנוּ, וְאֶת עֲמָלֵנוּ, וְאֶת לַחֲצֵנוּ.[3]

Jews by conscripting them for forced labor (*Yalkut Me'am Loez*). This is evident from the poor conditions in which the Jews were kept, which is counterproductive to maintaining a healthy and motivated work force, and also by the fact that the sites chosen for the cities of Pithom and Raamses were too marshy to support large buildings, as the Sages point out, thus forcing the construction work to be repeated endlessly to little apparent purpose (*Sotah* 11a).

The term שָׂרֵי מִסִּים, *taskmasters*, literally means *tax collectors*. According to *Iyun Tefillah*, the Egyptian monarch instructed his tax collectors to allow the Jewish tax liability to grow by not collecting from them. Eventually it became so overwhelming that the Jews had no way to pay it except by enlisting as a slave labor force for the king.[1]

וַיִּתְּנוּ עָלֵינוּ עֲבֹדָה קָשָׁה — *And they imposed hard labor upon us.* This refers to labor which does not require physical exertion, but is nonetheless difficult because it is labor one is not used to; for example, assigning men to do women's work and vice versa. This is alluded to by the word in the supporting verse בְּפָרֶךְ, "with crushing harshness," which is composed of the words פֶּה רַךְ, *soft* mouth, i.e., labor that one can be easily persuaded to perform because it appears soft and easy (*Vilna Gaon*).

As the Jews increased, Egypt's attitude changed from fear to hatred, with the result that the forced labor was intended less to be productive than to break them in body and spirit; everything was designed to be בְּפָרֶךְ, *with crushing hardness.* The word בְּפָרֶךְ carries many connotations: The Sages see it as illustrating the increasing severity of the Jews' enslavement. At first they were talked into voluntary labor (בְּפֶה רַךְ, *with soft talk*) and ultimately they were ground under (נִפְרַךְ) by the hardships imposed on them (*Rashi* to *Sotah* 11b).

The Egyptians devised novel ways of making life miserable for the Jews. They made them sleep over at their workplaces, separated from their families, asserting that this would increase their work efficiency. Accordingly *Rashbatz* notes the relationship between בְּפָרֶךְ and פָּרֹכֶת, *a separating curtain.*

Tosafos HaRosh infers this from the verse in *Leviticus* (25:46) that forbids one to subjugate his servant with oppressive labor [בְּפָרֶךְ]. The Sages interpret this as forbidding the master to force his servant to leave his wife and cohabit with a maidservant, as a means to produce new slaves for the master.

Yalkut Shimoni relates that the women would, however, steal out to the fields at night to take care of their exhausted husbands, bringing them water and food and much-needed moral support, reminding them that the redemption was sure to come soon. In this way the women were able to preserve family life and maintain the spirit of the

---

1. *Mesillas Yesharim* (Chapter 2) asserts that Pharaoh's plan was analogous to the strategy of the Evil Inclination. If man can be kept harried by an overwhelming work load he will never have the time or peace of mind to focus on his goals in life and on whether he is headed along the proper path.

On this night, as we reexperience our freedom from Pharaoh, we can refocus our attention on giving our lives direction and meaning.

them in order to oppress them with their burdens; and they built Pithom and Raamses as treasure cities for Pharaoh.[1]

And they imposed hard labor upon us — as it is stated: The Egyptians subjugated the Children of Israel with hard labor.[2]

And we cried out to HASHEM, the God of our fathers; and HASHEM heard our voice, and saw our affliction, our burden and our oppression.[3]

(1) *Exodus* 1:11. (2) 1:13. (3) *Deuteronomy* 26:7.

people. As the Sages declare: "The deliverance of our forefathers from Egypt was due to the righteous women of that generation" (*Sotah* 11b).

וַנִּצְעַק — *And we cried out.* The third verse of the *Bikkurim* Declaration describes the heartrending cries of the Jews in Egypt and their prayers to God. God heard their prayers and, empathetically involved with their distress, He hearkened to their entreaties.

Although the 400-year exile (decreed at the Covenant Between the Parts) had not been completed, the Jews felt it proper to pray for an early redemption based on two factors: (a) The large amount of people, the result of the inordinate population explosion, produced a number of man-hours of work equivalent to 400 years. (b) The intensity of the oppression and the physically crushing work were the qualitative equivalent of 400 years of normal toil and oppression. Thus, this verse is a continuation of the previous verses. Since we became a great and populous nation that could produce 400 years of work in 210 years, and since the Egyptians afflicted us and imposed hard labor upon us, therefore we felt justified in calling out to God to save us after only 210 years in Egypt (*HaShir VeHaShevach*).

Ramban (*Exodus* 2:25 and 12:42) explains that although, as a result of the extreme oppression, the time for redemption had come, nonetheless the Jews lacked any redeeming merit. As the prophet describes it, *But they disobeyed Me and refused to listen to Me . . . they did not abandon the idolatries of Egypt. I thought to pour out My anger upon them . . . . However I acted for My Name's*

sake, that it should not be profaned in the eyes of the nations (*Ezekiel* 20:8-9).

The nation of oppressed people was not ready for this historic moment. The reception accorded by the slaves to the message of deliverance was not as joyous as might be expected, for the condition God attached to their liberation — namely, abandoning all vestiges of Egypt's idolatrous culture — seemed too difficult to them. God could have legitimately poured out His wrath upon them and been done with them, but He decided otherwise. His aim to elevate this people to become His nation was the overriding factor. In the midst of a demoralized world, one nation was to emerge that would serve as the bearers of God's Name and will, and thus proclaim the true destiny of mankind (see commentary of *R' Joseph Breuer* to *Ezekiel* ibid.).

The Midrash tells us that five things brought about the redemption of our forefathers from Egypt: (1) their pain and suffering; (2) prayer; (3) the merit of the Patriarchs; (4) repentance and (5) the arrival of the appointed time. Likewise, we will be redeemed from our present long and bitter exile in merit of these five things (*Yalkut Tehillim* 110 §465; see also *Yerushalmi, Taanis* 1:1).

Avnei Nezer notes that the verse describes their cries as directed toward the God of *their fathers* yet the response came as Hashem heard *their* voices. This reflects the teaching of the Talmud that one who bases his prayers on the merit of others is answered in his own merit while one who prays based on his own merits is answered in the merit of others (*Berachos* 10b). Thus, the Jews prayed to the God of their fathers, begging to be redeemed in merit of the loyalty that their forefathers showed God. God responded by answering their prayers in their own merit.

The Haggadah now elucidates the verse, explaining and expanding upon each phrase.

וַנִּצְעַק אֶל יהוה אֱלֹהֵי אֲבֹתֵינוּ – כְּמָה שֶׁנֶּאֱמַר, וַיְהִי בַיָּמִים הָרַבִּים הָהֵם, וַיָּמָת מֶלֶךְ מִצְרַיִם, וַיֵּאָנְחוּ בְנֵי יִשְׂרָאֵל מִן הָעֲבֹדָה, וַיִּזְעָקוּ, וַתַּעַל שַׁוְעָתָם אֶל הָאֱלֹהִים מִן הָעֲבֹדָה.[1]

וַנִּצְעַק אֶל ה׳ אֱלֹהֵי אֲבֹתֵינוּ כְּמָה שֶׁנֶּאֱמַר וַיְהִי בַיָּמִים הָרַבִּים הָהֵם – *We cried out to HASHEM, the God of our fathers, as it is stated: And it happened in the course of those many days.*

The verse speaks of "those many days," for even a few days of trouble and pain seem like many (*Ritva*).[1] Time spent in suffering always seems much longer than time spent in happiness. Thus, the unremitting hardship in Egypt made it seem as though the days were many and endless (*Ramban*). Furthermore, the exile that was supposed to last 400 years was considered by God to be "condensed" into the 210 years of intense toil that the Jews underwent. Thus, in God's eyes, the 210 years were considered as "many days" (*HaSeder HaAruch*).

Ramban (*Exodus* 2:23) submits that the "many days" were the approximately 60 years of Moses' personal exile from when he fled Egypt as a young man until his return to free God's people.

וַיָּמָת מֶלֶךְ מִצְרַיִם וַיֵּאָנְחוּ בְנֵי יִשְׂרָאֵל – *The king of Egypt died; and the Children of Israel groaned.* The bondage in Egypt was so crushing that the enslaved were afraid even to complain about the inhuman conditions under which they lived. Only upon the death of Pharaoh could the Jews, under the guise of mourning the king's death, express their pain and emit a heartrending cry. Only they knew the true source of their cry — the backbreaking work and subhuman servitude. The Egyptians were sure that the Jews were responding to the tragic death of the monarch, yet their cry was understood by God, Who knows the secrets of every man's heart, as a pleaful prayer to be saved from their terrible oppression (*Malbim*; see also *Kli Yakar* to *Exodus* 2:23).

Ramban (ad loc.) suggests that upon Pharaoh's death the Jews feared that the new Pharaoh would be even worse than the old one. Thus they cried out to God to save them from the new tyrant.[2]

1. **Poised Prayers.** The Torah does not state that *after* many days they cried out to God, but *"in the course of those many days."* Jews prayed all the time. Throughout the darkest days of the Egyptian purgatory, Jews never stopped praying that God save them. All of these prayers were gathered together awaiting an answer. Finally, at the moment when the gates of heaven opened, all of those prayers ascended to God Who heard them and extended His mercy to His nation (*Chidushei HaRim*).

Baal Shem Tov offers an interpretation along similar lines to a Talmudic teaching regarding the exalted level of prayer. Every heartfelt prayer uttered by man has an impact. Sometimes its effect is felt immediately while at other times it may take years until the prayer accomplishes its desired goal. Thus, every prayer ascends to heaven. Some prayers work immediately, while others await the opportune moment when the heavenly gates open and the prayer is allowed to enter.

Unknowing people often disdain the power of their prayers when they do not see immediate results. They fail to realize that the prayer may be kept in abeyance for the right time. Thus the Talmud describes prayer as something which "stands at the supreme heights of the world and [yet] is disdained by people" (*Berachos* 6b).

2. **The Stirrings of the Soul.** One may often prefer a familiar purgatory to an unknown paradise. One can become so accustomed to misery that he is no longer aware of just how bad life has become. This was the exact situation of the Jews in Egypt. They were so emotionally submerged in the toil and the resultant degradation of human dignity that they didn't even realize the ravaging spiritual effects of the exile and how

We cried out to HASHEM, the God of our fathers — as it stated: And it happened in the course of those many days that the king of Egypt died; and the Children of Israel groaned because of the servitude and cried; and their moaning rose up to God from the labor.[1]

---

(1) *Exodus* 2:23.

Chizkuni views the prayers of the Jews as a reaction to their disappointment and dashed hopes for an improvement of conditions under the new king. When the old king died and they realized that nothing would change, they groaned under the hopelessness of their situation and called out to God. Also, during the lifetime of the Pharaoh who had instituted the oppression of the Jews, there was always the possibility that he might change his attitude; upon his death, however, his decrees became enshrined as the official, established national policy (*Rabbi S.R. Hirsch*).

According to *Rashi* and *Ritva*, the cry was because the new king instituted a policy of coercing the Jews to participate in the idol worship of the Egyptians, a policy not pursued by earlier kings out of respect for Joseph and his contribution to national survival during the famine.

According to the *Midrash* (*Shemos Rabbah* 1:41), the death of Pharaoh of this verse is meant in an allegorical sense; he did not actually die, but became afflicted with צָרַעַת, a skin disease with leprosy-like symptoms. (The Sages teach that a person with this disease is considered dead in a sense, for he must live by himself and is excluded from all human contact.) Pharaoh's doctors, the *Midrash* continues, prescribed that he bathe in blood, and Jewish children were murdered for this purpose. This is why Pharaoh's "death"

triggered such an outburst of grief among the Jews.

Generally the Torah does not refer to a person by his title when it speaks of his death, for אֵין שִׁלְטוֹן בְּיוֹם הַמָּוֶת, *there is no sovereignty on the day of death* (see *Bereishis Rabbah* 96:3). The fact that the Torah does indeed refer to Pharaoh here as "the king of Egypt" is possibly a support for the *Midrash's* interpretation that he did not really die (*Vilna Gaon, Malbim*).

וַתַּעַל שַׁוְעָתָם אֶל הָאֱלֹהִים מִן הָעֲבוֹדָה — *And their moaning rose up to God from the labor.* There is no more perfect prayer in the eyes of God than one uttered out of the sense of hopelessness associated with terrible trouble and pain. Thus, as Jews cried out to God He accepted their prayer which they offered "from the labor" (*Rabbeinu Bachya, Exodus* ibid.). Their outcry was not born of anger at their lot, nor did it in any way smack of dissatisfaction with God's treatment of them; rather, it was the result of heartfelt repentance. They appealed to the God of their fathers to save them in their merit (*Abarbanel*).

Maaseh Nissim and *Ohr HaChaim* (to *Exodus* ibid.) disagree. The cry emitted by the Jews was not one of prayer directed to God, or of repentance; it was merely an instinctive, primitive shout elicited by the searing pain of the hard work. Nonetheless, God was aroused by His pained children and was moved to respond with mercy. Their entreaties penetrated in spite of not being

removed they had become from God. Only when the monarch of Egypt died did the first stirrings of redemption awaken them to realize the spiritual damage the exile had inflicted upon their souls. Only then, when the exile became unbearable for them, did they cry out to God. This is alluded to in God's promise to the Jews. *I will take you out from under the burden of Egypt* (*Exodus* 6:6). Only when they felt Egypt to be an unbearable burden were they ready to be redeemed (*Chidushei HaRim*).

וַיִּשְׁמַע יהוה אֶת קֹלֵנוּ – כְּמָה שֶׁנֶּאֱמַר, וַיִּשְׁמַע אֱלֹהִים אֶת נַאֲקָתָם, וַיִּזְכֹּר אֱלֹהִים אֶת בְּרִיתוֹ אֶת אַבְרָהָם, אֶת יִצְחָק, וְאֶת יַעֲקֹב.[1]

וַיַּרְא אֶת עָנְיֵנוּ – זוֹ פְּרִישׁוּת דֶּרֶךְ אֶרֶץ, כְּמָה שֶׁנֶּאֱמַר, וַיַּרְא אֱלֹהִים אֶת בְּנֵי יִשְׂרָאֵל, וַיֵּדַע אֱלֹהִים.[2]

---

the result of the purest of motivations[1] (see also *Sforno, Exodus* ibid.). Their prayers were ungraceful and plainly the cry of the uncouth menial laborer who is inarticulate and unable to express himself clearly to God. Nonetheless, his primitive expression of pain rouses God to take pity on him and save him (*Haamek Davar*).

וַיִּשְׁמַע ה' אֶת קֹלֵנוּ כְּמָה שֶׁנֶּאֱמַר וכו' — *And Hashem heard our voice, as it is stated, etc.* It was not their prayers that God heard; it was their raised voices and the painful cry that stormed the gates of Heaven. One should always cry out from the depths of his heart when praying to God. Hence the Torah here teaches us to raise our voices in prayer as did our forefathers in Egypt.[2]

וַיִּזְכֹּר אֱלֹהִים אֶת בְּרִיתוֹ — *And God remembered His covenant.* Although the Jews may not have been deserving of redemption by dint of their own merit, their cries evoked memories of who their forefathers were and the covenant that God had made with them (*Kol Bo*, et al.).

A covenant creates a relationship that is unconditional and not contingent on the behavior of any of the parties.

Thus, even when Jews are not deserving of God's intervention, He still is bound by the covenant with the Patriarchs. Although the *merit* of the Patriarchs is at times insufficient to earn God's salvation for their offspring, the *covenant* is by definition inviolable (see *Shabbos* 55a, *Tosafos* ad loc. s.v. ושמואל and *Ramban, Genesis* 6:18).

Seemingly, the first phrase of the support text (*Exodus* 2:24) that tells of God hearing their groan is sufficient evidence of the facts indicated in the verse from the *Bikkurim* Declaration. Why is it necessary to quote the rest of the verse, which speaks of God remembering the Patriarchal covenant? *Maaseh Nissim* explains: The memory of the forefathers' covenant is also part of the evidence — evidence that the Jews cried out to the God of their forefathers and thus were able to summon their merit and the covenant that God made with them.

וַיַּרְא אֶת עָנְיֵנוּ — *And saw our affliction.* The verse continues to describe the reaction of God to the enslavement of the Jews. Besides focusing on their prayers, God took note of their suffering. *Maasei Nissim* comments that in the face of

---

1. **Paternal Arousal.** A father whose son finds himself in deep trouble would certainly prefer that his son turn to him in his hour of distress and ask for his help. However, even if the son merely cries over the pain he feels, the cries will be sufficient to arouse the father's compassion. Likewise, although God would hope that we turn to Him in prayer during our hour of need, He is still compassionate when we merely cry out from the pain of the immediate crisis.

2. **Tones of Betrayal.** Isaac defined the distinctive character of Jews when he said הַקֹּל קוֹל יַעֲקֹב, *the voice is the voice of Jacob* (*Genesis* 27:22). While Esau and his compatriots live by the sword, the Jew knows that his prayer — "his voice" — is the most effective weapon in his arsenal. Although Jews might have been so influenced by Egyptian culture that they seemed to have totally assimilated, their voices raised in prayer belied their true identity. No disguise can mute their true self, for the voice is that of Jacob. God heard their voice and He knew that it was His children calling out for help.

HASHEM heard our voice — as it is stated: God heard their groaning, and God remembered His covenant with Abraham, with Isaac and with Jacob.[1]

And saw our affliction — that is the disruption of family life, as it is stated: And God saw the Children of Israel, and God knew.[2]

---

(1) *Exodus* 2:24. (2) 2:25.

---

the Heavenly decree that they would be aliens in a foreign land for four hundred years, their prayers might not have been accepted. However, the extreme ill treatment at the hands of the Egyptians (which was not included in the decree) hastened the redemption. Thus, we describe the different facets of Egypt's oppressive and excessive cruelty.

זוֹ פְּרִישׁוּת דֶּרֶךְ אֶרֶץ — *That is the disruption of family life*. In order to curtail the Jewish population explosion, the disruption of their family life was a primary objective of the Egyptians. For this reason they forbade the men to return home at the end of the workday (*Avudraham*, *Rashbam*, *Machzor Vitry*). Even when they did occasionally join their families, they were totally exhausted from the heavy work burdens imposed on them (*Ritva*).

Furthermore, many Jews decided on their own to separate from their wives, for they did not wish to bring children into the world only to see them murdered at Pharaoh's hand (*Rashbam*, based on *Sotah* 11b).

In doing so they followed the example of Moses' father Amram, who was a great spiritual leader at the time. He divorced his wife Yocheved for the reason just mentioned, but his daughter Miriam reproached him, arguing that such a decision was even harsher than Pharaoh's, for Pharaoh wanted to kill only the boys,

while Amram's conduct would lead to no offspring whatsoever. Her father conceded to her reasoning and remarried Yocheved, after which Moses was born (*Sotah* 12a).

The Egyptians psychologically forced the Jews to abstain from normal family life. In their misery and despair Jews saw no reason to engage in normal marital relations. Why bring another generation into a wretched and cruel world? (*Abarbanel*). God took note of this distress and thus hastened to free His children.[1]

כְּמָה שֶׁנֶּאֱמַר וַיַּרְא אֱלֹהִים אֶת בְּנֵי יִשְׂרָאֵל וַיֵּדַע אֱלֹהִים — *As it is stated: And God saw the Children of Israel and God knew*. This indicates that the verse refers to something only God could know — abstinence from normal marital life (*Vilna Gaon* et al.). The supporting verse must therefore be rendered as: God saw the private tribulations of His people; things that only He could know, and He gave the Jewish people the desire to procreate despite the bleak prospects of their descendants to survive the tyranny of Egypt.[2]

The verb *to know* has the connotation of marital relations, as in the verse *And Adam knew Eve his wife and she conceived* (*Genesis* 4:1).

According to *Ibn Ezra* the two verbs *saw* and *knew* (or *took note*) refer to two types of oppression. God saw the *visible* afflictions that all people can see and even took note of those *silent* mea-

---

1. **Courageous Survivors.** R' Yosef Friedenson relates that in the D.P. camps after World War II he and his wife, as one of the few married couples, served as surrogate parents to accompany brides and grooms down the aisle to be married. It was the courage of these young people, many of whom had no surviving relatives, which brought a new generation of deeply committed Jews to the world.

2. **Heroic Women.** The Midrash teaches that Jewish women would go out to the fields, dressed attractively in order to encourage their husbands not to yield to the tyranny of Pharaoh who tired them out so that they would refrain from bringing families to the world.

וְאֶת עֲמָלֵנוּ – אֵלּוּ הַבָּנִים, כְּמָה שֶׁנֶּאֱמַר, כָּל הַבֵּן הַיִּלּוֹד הַיְאֹרָה תַּשְׁלִיכֻהוּ, וְכָל הַבַּת תְּחַיּוּן.[1]

וְאֶת לַחֲצֵנוּ – זוֹ הַדְּחַק, כְּמָה שֶׁנֶּאֱמַר, וְגַם רָאִיתִי אֶת הַלַּחַץ אֲשֶׁר מִצְרַיִם לֹחֲצִים אֹתָם.[2]

---

sures with which the Egyptians embittered the lives of the Jews.[1] *Rashi* renders וַיֵּדַע אֱלֹהִים as *and God empathized* with their plight — God closely identified with them and their pain and, in a sense of immediacy, paid attention to their situation. God no longer ignored their misery; He knew of their pain and focused on seeking to remedy it.[2]

1. **Leadership Qualities.** The verse following this one begins וּמֹשֶׁה, *and Moses . . .* (*Exodus* 3:1). Not only did God know everything His children were undergoing, but Moses did also. *Divrei Shmuel* homiletically views this as an allusion to the ability of true Jewish leaders to deeply sense the pain and travail of the people. Emulating God, the truly righteous know the pain of their flock and live it no less than the people themselves.

Thus empathy with the downtrodden masses and a profound, but not condescending, sensitivity to the plight of individuals is the true litmus test of Jewish leadership. The Talmud relates that the great *Nasi* (president of the Sanhedrin) Rabban Gamliel went to the home of R' Yehoshua in order to apologize for having asserted his authority as *Nasi* in a manner that was insulting to R' Yehoshua. As Rabban Gamliel approached the home of his colleague and noticed that the walls of the house were soot black, he said to R' Yehoshua, "From the walls of your home it is apparent that you are a blacksmith." R' Yehoshua replied, "Woe to the generation that has you as its leader, for you are unaware of the travails of its scholars in their efforts to earn a living!" (*Berachos* 28a).

Jewish leaders must stand spiritually above the crowd yet they must be intimately involved in the most mundane details of their charges. R' Yaakov Kamenetsky was such a Torah leader. By nature, he loved people and that trait served him well as a *rav* in the town of Tzitevian. His predecessor, Rabbi Aharon Burstein, who had gone on to become the *rav* of the much larger city of Tavrig, once returned to Tzitevian for a visit. After *davening* one morning, he watched as his successor approached one of his congregants and asked him what he was thinking about.

"About my cow," was the response.

"Is there something wrong with your cow?" Reb Yaakov asked, his voice tinged with concern.

After witnessing this exchange, and how Reb Yaakov listened patiently to a full account of the cow's woes, the Tavriger Rav commented that he had never been able to immerse himself in such mundane conversations while he had been in Tzitevian. That, Reb Yaakov added when recounting this incident, was why the Tavriger Rav, who was a great man, was better suited to being *rav* of a large community than a rural village.

2. **Anesthetized Patient.** Once a deathly ill young man needed an operation. It held out the only promise for recovery, yet it was fraught with danger. His mother gave vent to her fears while discussing the operation with the doctors: "I know you must amputate my son's leg, yet I am petrified of the powerful anesthesia you must use. Who can guarantee that my son will awaken from it?"

The anesthesiologist sought to calm her fears. "We have special compounds to resuscitate our patients. These compounds are so powerful that they can almost resurrect the dead. We know exactly how much anesthesia to administer so that we can successfully bring him back to consciousness."

Jews in exile are the patients who must undergo the painful surgical scalpel of exile in order to regain their spiritual health. God, the Merciful Surgeon, takes efforts to administer an exact dose of spiritual and emotional "anesthesia" so that we not realize the full extent of the pain which is entailed in the life-saving operation.

Only God knows the extent of the pain necessary in order to successfully perform the operation. He is able in His mercy to deaden our pain and allow us to survive the surgery, so that when we awaken at the

And our burden — that means the children, as it is stated: Every son that is born you shall cast into the river, but every daughter you shall let live.[1]

And our oppression — that means pressure, as it is stated: I have also seen how the Egyptians are oppressing them.[2]

---

(1) *Exodus* 1:22. (2) 3:9.

וְאֶת עֲמָלֵנוּ – אֵלוּ הַבָּנִים – *And our* burden — *that means the children.* Pharaoh saw that his attempt to control the Jewish population by forcing abstinence from marital relations had failed. He then came up with the idea of solving the Jewish problem by murdering the Jewish infants. This is alluded to by "And our burden," for in this case, the Jewish parents had already undergone some of the burden of raising children by the time their sons were taken from them (*Geulas Avraham*).

A person toils incessantly, pouring all of his time, energy and resources into raising his children properly and inculcating them with Torah knowledge and values and proper, ethical conduct. Even his efforts to amass wealth is only for his children (*Ritva*, *Shibbolei HaLeket* et al.).

Malbim notes that the term עָמָל denotes effort that one expends out of self-motivation and for personal gain, but which does not meet with success. People toiled to successfully raise children only to see them thrown into the river.[1]

The Haggadah quotes the end of the verse *but every daughter you shall let live* — although it would seem to be a mitigation of the wickedness of Pharaoh — to emphasize that even this was part of Pharaoh's diabolical plan to contain and destroy the nation. The Egyptian wanted to secure the remaining Jewish women for their own immoral purposes (see *Shemos Rabbah* 1:22). In fact this was an even more insidious decree than the instruction to drown the males. Physical decimation is not nearly as terrible as spiritual annihilation (*Ritva*).

וְאֶת לַחֲצֵנוּ זוֹ הַדְּחַק – *And our oppression — that means pressure.* The "pressure" that is referred to here is the cruel treatment which the Egyptians showed to their Jewish slaves.

The Egyptians kept the Jews working at a frenzied pace, constantly increasing the work quotas (*Rashbatz*). According to *Malbim* and *R' Bachya*, the word דְּחַק might be rendered as *overcrowding.* In spite of the population explosion in the Jewish community, the Egyptians kept them in the overcrowded ghetto of Goshen.

According to *Ritva*, however, the *pressure* that the Haggadah mentions here is a reference to the Egyptian attempts to convert the Jews to their

---

end of the long night of exile we will have fully reattained our spiritual health.

God saw the Children of Israel as they underwent the painful but life-giving process of exile in Egypt. In His infinite mercy, He administered spiritual "anesthesia" so that they never realized the full extent of the pain. Yet *God, the Master Surgeon, knew.*

1. **Desirable Burden.** Even after the supporting verse is quoted, how does the Haggadah know that "burden" refers to children? R' Shlomo Zalman Auerbach points out that the word עָמָל is always used when describing a duty which is wearying, but very much desired. An example is עֲמַל הַתּוֹרָה, the duty of "exerting oneself for the study of Torah," which, for all its incessant difficulty, is a most precious and desired pursuit. Such is also the case with children; despite all the hardships that were involved in bringing them to life in Pharaoh's Egypt, everyone longed for them intensely.

A young father once visited with R' Yaakov Kamenetsky who inquired how the young man was faring. "Fine, thank God," he replied, "but my children keep me up at night." He then groaned, "Oy, the pain of raising children (צַעַר גִּדּוּל בָּנִים).." R' Yaakov replied, "That is not pain, that is גִּדּוּל בָּנִים — normal raising of children. May God save us all from the *real* pain of raising children!"

וַיּוֹצִאֵנוּ יהוה מִמִּצְרַיִם בְּיָד חֲזָקָה, וּבִזְרֹעַ נְטוּיָה, וּבְמֹרָא גָּדֹל, וּבְאֹתוֹת וּבְמֹפְתִים.[1] וַיּוֹצִאֵנוּ יהוה מִמִּצְרַיִם – לֹא עַל יְדֵי מַלְאָךְ, וְלֹא

pagan way of life. When they saw that they could not stem the *physical* growth of the Jewish people through decimation, they decided to apply pressure on the Jews to assimilate.

R' Moshe Sternbuch submits that the Jewish soul, by its very nature free (see *Maharal* to *Avos* 6:2), found servitude to a mortal master emotionally confining.

The term לַחַץ can refer to either physical brutality or emotional strain and mental cruelty. The Haggadah thus makes the point that it refers to *pressure*, the psychological strain of the incessant stress of labor rather than its physical manifestation. This is a private suffering that only God could truly fathom (*Abarbanel*).

The three items listed in this verse (*affliction, burden* and *oppression*) are not merely restatements of the three expressions (*did evil to us, afflicted us* and *imposed hard labor upon us*) mentioned in the previous verse of the *Bikkurim* Declaration. The first verse refers to the indignities heaped upon the Jews publicly while the second verse focuses on those private tribulations about which only God knew.

Alternatively, we might say that the common feature of *affliction, burden* and *oppressions* — which the Haggadah interprets respectively as *disruption of family life*, *the children,* and pressure — is not so much the private nature of the suffering they connote, as the fact that they were forms of mental

and emotional anguish as opposed to the physical rigor referred to in the preceding verse (*Abarbanel*).

Chanukas HaTorah, in a brilliant interpretation, explains these three items as an allusion to the three reasons why God legitimately reduced the time the Jews spent in Egypt from 400 years to 210 years. *Our distress* refers to the fact that the Egyptians interrupted normal family life by forcing the Jewish men to remain working in the fields at night. Since they worked at night as well they were able to complete 400 years of normal (daytime) work in less time.

Furthermore, God saw *our travail,* namely the sons born to us in Egypt. The increased work force that resulted from the extraordinary reproduction rate among the Jews was able to do 400 years of work in much less time, thus providing God with the ability to free them earlier.

Thirdly, *the oppression* and the inhuman work quotas and conditions increased the qualitative degree of oppression, thus allowing God to decrease the amount of time it was necessary for Jews to remain in Egypt.

וַיּוֹצִאֵנוּ **וכו׳** — *And* HASHEM *brought us out . . .* This, the fourth and final verse of the *Bikkurim* Declaration, describes the scope of God's miraculous deliverance of the Jews. As before, the Haggadah quotes the verse in its entirety and then offers a word-by-word interpretation.[1]

---

1. **Glory Revealed.** The present-day Jew deeply senses the catastrophe of the Nazi era and the death of six million of our people. He feels with the physical suffering of Russian Jewry in the past and the even more debilitating present-day spiritual brutality that often seem irreparable. Compared to these contemporary happenings, the long-ago bondage of our people in Egypt does not really touch his emotions. Yet on the Seder night we realize that Egypt subjugated our entire people for several generations with dehumanizing slave labor and calculated brutality, breakup of families, murder of children, crushing of any opposition — with no end in sight to all the suffering. When we let our mind dwell on the full dimensions of the tragedy, we can begin to see the Egyptian exile as the heart-wrenching archetype of all later Jewish suffering — and the miraculous redemption as an extraordinary and overwhelming revelation of God in His world (*R' Joseph Elias*).

And HASHEM brought us out of Egypt with a strong hand and with an outstretched arm, with great awe, with signs and with wonders.[1]

And HASHEM brought us out of Egypt — not through an angel,

(1) *Deuteronomy* 26:8.

לֹא עַל יְדֵי מַלְאָךְ — *Not through an angel.* The killing of the firstborn, which was the climax of the events leading up to the Exodus, occurred at midnight following the fourteenth day of Nissan. At that moment Israel was freed — not through any organized uprising or through a charismatic leader or through some natural catastrophe or social upheaval, but by God Himself, Who administered one decisive, crippling blow against Egypt.

Malbim sees the textual allusion to this in the seemingly repetitious use of the word *Hashem* in these verses. Since the previous verse had already spoken of our outcry and God's attentiveness to our plea, this verse could have said simply "and *He* brought us out." By repeating Hashem's Name, it stresses that God Himself took us out of Egypt. In contrast to many instances where God does His bidding through various types of angels, agents and intermediate causes, here He acted alone in bringing about the death of the Egyptian first-born.[1]

מַלְאָכִים are angels who are created for specific tasks. When they complete their missions, they cease to exist, only to be recreated for another task as the need arises. שְׂרָפִים, *seraphim* (from the word שָׂרַף, meaning *enflamed*), carry the Heavenly fire as they surround the Heavenly throne. שָׁלִיחַ, *messenger*, connotes a Divinely appointed guiding force invested with the ability to act independently on behalf of the One Who dispatched it. Specifically, *the* messenger refers to the Heavenly forces given the task of protecting the Jewish people (*Ritva*).

Ramban (*Exodus* 12:13) suggests that *seraphim* are called by that name because they are the "firepower" of God to exact retribution from His enemies.

Many reasons have been advanced as to why God deemed it necessary to be the direct cause of the death of the firstborn. The Talmud (*Bava Metzia* 61b) teaches that only God Himself has the ability to differentiate and know which children are truly firstborn.

If a stillbirth or a miscarriage preceded the birth of a particular child, a subsequently born child would not have the status of a firstborn. Furthermore, unlike the firstborn status among Jews, which is halachically determined by whether the child is פֶּטֶר רֶחֶם, the *first issue of the womb*, in Egypt even firstborn of fathers died in the plague. Thus, only God could determine the paternity of any given child (see *Rashi* ad loc.).

Even a Jewish firstborn who found himself in an Egyptian home at midnight was saved. Likewise, an Egyptian firstborn met death that night even if he was in the home of a Jew. An angel was unequal to such a tasks.

According to the *Zohar* (*Bereishis* 117a), the overwhelming spiritual impurity of Egypt was of such intensity that no angel could risk exposure to it. Only God Himself, Who is immutable and immune to the effects of even the greatest degree of impurity, could pass through Egypt and decimate its firstborn.

R' Bachya suggests a different approach to explain why the plague of the firstborn had to be administered directly by God Himself. If punishment of the Egyptians had been brought about through the usual agents of Divine justice, the Jews, too, would have been punished for their sins,

---

1. **Serene Silence.** The Talmud (*Bava Kamma* 60b) teaches that the barking or wailing of dogs is a sign that the Angel of Death is present in the city. Since the death of the Egyptian firstborn was an act of God Himself, not the Angel of Death, there was no such barking, as the Torah says, *And for all the Children of Israel no dog shall whet its tongue* (*Exodus* 11:7). The Torah is telling us, in effect, that while the Egyptians will react to the split-second death of their firstborn with unprecedented shrieks, no dog shall whet its tongue to bark or howl against them — they will enjoy complete tranquility (*R' David Feinstein*).

עַל יְדֵי שָׂרָף, וְלֹא עַל יְדֵי שָׁלִיחַ, אֶלָּא הַקָּדוֹשׁ בָּרוּךְ הוּא בִּכְבוֹדוֹ וּבְעַצְמוֹ. שֶׁנֶּאֱמַר, וְעָבַרְתִּי בְאֶרֶץ מִצְרַיִם בַּלַּיְלָה הַזֶּה, וְהִכֵּיתִי כָל בְּכוֹר בְּאֶרֶץ מִצְרַיִם מֵאָדָם וְעַד בְּהֵמָה, וּבְכָל אֱלֹהֵי מִצְרַיִם אֶעֱשֶׂה שְׁפָטִים, אֲנִי יהוה.[1]

וְעָבַרְתִּי בְאֶרֶץ מִצְרַיִם בַּלַּיְלָה הַזֶּה – אֲנִי וְלֹא מַלְאָךְ. וְהִכֵּיתִי כָל בְּכוֹר בְּאֶרֶץ מִצְרַיִם – אֲנִי וְלֹא שָׂרָף. וּבְכָל אֱלֹהֵי מִצְרַיִם אֶעֱשֶׂה שְׁפָטִים – אֲנִי וְלֹא הַשָּׁלִיחַ. אֲנִי יהוה – אֲנִי הוּא, וְלֹא אַחֵר.

because they did not have the merits to be worthy of redemption.[1] Indeed, the Sages tell us that when the Sea of Reeds was split, the angels protested before God that the Jews should be treated no differently than the Egyptians. Therefore, God Himself inflicted the plague upon the firstborn, and, because of the covenant with the Patriarchs, He skipped over the Jewish houses, wherever the blood of the *pesach* offering was on the doorposts as a sign that the inhabitants acknowledged Hashem.

Sfas Emes elaborates: In order to differentiate between the Jews and the Egyptians, the Jews needed a saving grace. None of the myriad angels was able to find such a redeeming quality for the Jewish firstborn. Only God Himself, Who endowed the Jewish people with a Godly soul, could perceive its remaining trace upon His people. Hence, only God could save them.

Ohr HaChaim views God's personal intervention as indicative of His great love for His nation, "My firstborn son Israel" (*Exodus* 4:22).

Maharal captures the motif: From the foundation of Israel as a nation, God's relationship to it was direct and personal, without an intermediary. Thus, when it was time to seal His covenant with His people by freeing them from the land of their enslavement, God did not delegate the task. Furthermore, the birth of Israel occurred at the strike of midnight on that very special night. Simultaneous with the mass death of the Egyptian firstborn, there emerged a new nation — God's firstborn people of Israel. Since birth is one of the three "keys" that God grants to no one (*Taanis* 2a), only He could be the midwife, as it were, for the emergent nation.

Finally, we might better understand God's direct involvement against the backdrop of the purpose of the

1. **Redeeming the Unredeemable.** Lacking any merits of their own, the Jewish people did not deserve to be redeemed; only an outpouring of Divine mercy could make them God's nation. Throughout history, only God could provide the "unredeemable" with ways to return to Him. King Menashe (*II Chronicles* 33:12-13), whose wickedness was such that repentance should have been inpossible, was enabled to repent because, in the simile of the Sages, "God dug a tunnel under His Throne of Glory for Menashe to return."

Likewise, every Jew, no matter how many barriers he has erected between himself and God, can "leapfrog" all the impediments and, with God's personal intervention, can savor the taste of being truly free (*Yismach Yisrael*).

not through a *seraph,* not through a messenger, but the Holy One, Blessed is He, in His glory, Himself, as it is stated: I will pass through the land of Egypt on that night; I will slay all the firstborn in the land of Egypt from man to beast; and upon all the gods of Egypt will I execute judgments; I, HASHEM.[1]

I will pass through the land of Egypt on that night — I and no angel; I will slay all the firstborn in the land of Egypt — I and no *seraph*; And upon all the gods of Egypt will I execute judgments — I and no messenger; I, HASHEM — it is I and no other.

---

(1) *Exodus* 12:2.

Exodus. Egypt's pagan world questioned God's mastery over nature and human destiny. They negated or questioned such basic articles of faith as God's creation of the world, His involvement in human affairs and His ability to control the natural world. For Jews to achieve true freedom, they had to become God's people by accepting His overlordship unconditionally, and they would then be under His personal care and protection. In order to bring this about, God had to crush all pagan forces in a manner that left no doubt as to Who the real Power is. There could be no place to even imagine that the redemption was the result of accidents or aberrations within nature. Although everything that occurs is the work of Divine Providence, it is brought about by Divine messengers within the normal framework that we call "nature." Miracles — such as the first nine plagues — are breaks in this pattern and show that God is the Master of nature and history. Even the effect of miracles, however, is limited when they are brought about by Divine agents, which are themselves limited. The spiritual blindness and impurity of Egypt was so intense that only God's self-revelation could make the necessary impact (*Haflaah*).

Although the Torah states that God sent a "messenger," i.e., Moses, to take the Jews out of Egypt (*Numbers* 20:16), this messenger was but God's tool in the process. We might compare this to a tailor who makes a suit. Certainly it is the person, not the sewing machine, who makes the garment. Thus, Moses' role in the Exodus was simply that of being God's instrument.

Tosafos Rid views Moses' role as that of a spokesman sent to relate to Pharaoh that God,

in His glory, Himself, would redeem the Jews. The redemption itself could not be done by Moses, but *the Holy One, Blessed is He, in His glory, Himself.*

Although it was the All-knowing Himself Who passed over the land, it was necessary to place blood on the doorposts — not because God needed the blood to inform Him that the house was inhabited by Jews, but to call attention to the two bloods (the *pesach* offering and circumcision) in whose merit the Jews were redeemed (*Abarbanel*).

שֶׁנֶּאֱמַר — *As it is stated.* Though the verse in the *Bikkurim* Declaration states that God brought us out of Egypt, it does not say explicitly that God used no intermediary for either the Exodus or for slaying the Egyptian firstborn. Thus it is necessary to cite a complementary verse from *Exodus* as proof that neither an angel, a *seraph* nor a messenger was involved. For this reason the Haggadah cites the verse in Exodus with the introductory שֶׁנֶּאֱמַר, for unlike earlier citations, which were meant to serve as historical reinforcement for the text of the *Bikkurim* Declaration, here the citation is used to prove the point of the explication of the *Bikkurim* verse (*Malbim*). Ramban (*Exodus* 12:12) points out that since the verse consisted of words related to the Children of Israel by Moses, the more correct form would be "and *God* will pass over Egypt." The use of the first person — "and *I* will pass through" — indicates

בְּיָד חֲזָקָה – זוֹ הַדֶּבֶר, כְּמָה שֶׁנֶּאֱמַר, הִנֵּה יַד יהוה הוֹיָה בְּמִקְנְךָ אֲשֶׁר בַּשָּׂדֶה, בַּסּוּסִים בַּחֲמֹרִים בַּגְּמַלִּים בַּבָּקָר וּבַצֹּאן, דֶּבֶר כָּבֵד מְאֹד.[1]

וּבִזְרֹעַ נְטוּיָה – זוֹ הַחֶרֶב, כְּמָה שֶׁנֶּאֱמַר, וְחַרְבּוֹ שְׁלוּפָה בְּיָדוֹ, נְטוּיָה עַל יְרוּשָׁלָיִם.[2]

וּבְמֹרָא גָּדֹל – זוֹ גִּלּוּי שְׁכִינָה, כְּמָה שֶׁנֶּאֱמַר, אוֹ הֲנִסָּה אֱלֹהִים לָבוֹא לָקַחַת לוֹ גוֹי מִקֶּרֶב גּוֹי, בְּמַסֹּת, בְּאֹתֹת,

that it was God Himself Who did so.[1]

The exact time of midnight changes from place to place according to its latitude and longitude. Thus, in a large country such as Egypt, had all the firstborn died simultaneously, all the deaths could not have occurred exactly at their own midnight. God went from place to place within Egypt slaying the firstborn in each place according to *its* midnight (*R' Yehoshua Leib Diskin*).

בְּיָד חֲזָקָה זוֹ הַדֶּבֶר – *With a strong hand — refers to the pestilence.* Pestilence was only one of the ten plagues; why is it singled out? According to the Midrash (*Shemos Rabbah* 10:2), each of the ten plagues was accompanied by pestilence (*Orchos Chaim, Kol Bo, Shibbolei HaLeket*). This would explain why the Haggadah identifies the "strong hand" that brought about the Exodus as pestilence.

Many commentators note that the pestilence is referred to as Hashem's *hand* because it was the fifth plague and, since each plague was administered through one of God's fingers, as it were (see *Exodus* 8:15), this plague showed God's complete hand.[2] In contrast, the Haggadah sees "the out-

---

1. **Biased Oversight.** The *Chozeh of Lublin* interprets וְעָבַרְתִּי, *and I passed over*, in the sense of ignoring something. In order to save the Jewish people it was necessary for God to ignore, as it were, the claims of the Heavenly angels that the Jews were no more deserving of being saved than the Egyptians. There was no tangible proof to refute that argument; God redeemed them because of His faith in the Jewish people and His confidence that their Divine soul would ultimately triumph. Thus He figuratively "passed over" the incriminating faults of the Jews.

An important lesson may be learned from this. One might do well in his dealings with others — or even with his own children — to occasionally turn a blind eye to their shortcomings and concentrate instead on doing whatever is necessary to spiritually enrich them.

◆§ **Temporarily Unemployed.** If it was God Himself Who smote the Egyptian firstborn, why does the Torah speak of the "Destroyer" (מַשְׁחִית) being "denied admittance" to Jewish homes? The *Vilna Gaon* takes this term to mean the Angel of Death. On a normal night he would have claimed a number of victims among the large Jewish population; but if any Jews whatsoever had died on the night of Pesach, the Egyptians would have contended that the Jews, too, had been affected by the plague. Therefore, the Angel of Death was forbidden to smite even those Jews who should have died a natural death on that night.

2. **Indestructible Might.** *Torah Temimah* offers an explanation of why pestilence in particular is a manifestation of God's *strong hand*. When King David sinned by counting the nation (*II Samuel* 24), the prophet Gad came to him and, in the Name of God, offered him a choice of punishments: The people would be stricken either with pestilence or hunger or military defeat. David replied, *Let us fall into the hand of Hashem, for His mercies are abundant; but let me not fall into human hands* (ibid. 24:14). The Talmud explains David's choice. He said: If I choose hunger, people will claim that I rely on my wealth to save me from the ravages of hunger. Likewise, if I submit to the punishment of war, people might believe that I am

With a strong hand — refers to the pestilence, as it is stated: *Behold, the hand of* HASHEM *shall strike your cattle which are in the field, the horses, the donkeys, the camels, the herds, and the flocks — a very severe pestilence.*[1]

And with an outstretched arm — refers to the sword, as it is stated: *His drawn sword in his hand, outstretched over Jerusalem.*[2]

And with great awe — alludes to the revelation of the *Shechinah*, as it is stated: *Or has any god ever attempted to take unto himself a nation from the midst of another nation by trials, miraculous*

---

(1) *Exodus* 9:3. (2) *I Chronicles* 21:16.

---

stretched *arm* of Hashem" as a reference to the slaying of the firstborn, since it marked the climax of the plagues and had the greatest impact (*Maaseh Nissim*).

According to *Netziv* and *Aruch HaShulchan*, this pestilence is not the fifth plague; rather, it refers to a similar phenomenon that affected Jews who were so firmly rooted in Egyptian society and culture that they were unable to muster the courage to leave. The Sages teach that during the three days of intense darkness, four fifths of the Jews — those who lacked the requisite faith in God to merit redemption — were decimated. It was God's strong hand of pestilence that accomplished the task.

The prophet *Ezekiel* (20:33-34) also speaks of the strong hand of God turning against Jews: *As I live, says God, if I will not rule over them with a strong hand, an outstretched arm and an outpouring of wrath.*

וּבִזְרֹעַ נְטוּיָה – *And with an outstretched arm.* The supporting verse quoted here speaks of an *outstretched sword*; the Haggadah therefore concludes that the "outstretched arm" of God also refers to the wielding of a sword. Yet the Torah does not mention swords in connection with the Exodus. According to *Ritva*, "the sword" is a general metaphor for Divine retribution and vengeance.

God keeps His metaphorical sword unsheathed ready to avenge the oppression of any Jew.[1]

Others view "the sword" as a reference to the slaying of the firstborn. The Midrash (*Yalkut Shimoni, Exodus* 136) recounts that when the plague of the firstborn was first announced it precipitated a bitter civil war; when the firstborn heard of their impending fate they took up arms to force the government to free the Jews and thereby avert the evil decree. According to some commentators, the verse in *Psalms* (136:10) that God *struck the Egyptians through their firstborn* (and not "struck the Egyptian firstborn") refers to this battle, in which many Egyptians were killed (*Kolbo*).

וּבְמֹרָא גָּדֹל זוֹ גִּלּוּי שְׁכִינָה — *With great awe — alludes to the revelation of the Shechinah [Divine Presence].* The Exodus entailed not only the removal of the Jews from bondage; it was a miraculous exhibition of God's involvement in human affairs and destiny. God showed, step by step, through the ten plagues, that He is not merely a theological concept; He is a constant Presence on earth involved in man's everyday life. Even the Egyptian sorcerers were forced to concede that the plagues were *the finger of God* (*Exodus* 8:15), and Moses predicted them before they came and even

---

counting on my military prowess. However, all people are equally vulnerable to pestilence, and I, along with the entire populace, have nothing to rely on but the hand of Hashem.

1. **Sword of Vengeance.** The word חֶרֶב, *sword,* has the numerical value of 210, an allusion that the Egyptians were punished by God's sword of vengeance for the 210 years of Jewish exile (*Pe'er Aharon*).

וּבְמוֹפְתִים, וּבְמִלְחָמָה, וּבְיָד חֲזָקָה, וּבִזְרוֹעַ נְטוּיָה, וּבְמוֹרָאִים גְּדֹלִים, כְּכֹל אֲשֶׁר עָשָׂה לָכֶם יהוה אֱלֹהֵיכֶם

specified an exact time when they would end (ibid. 8:25).

This revelation of the Divine Presence induced great terror, for when God reveals His glory, people are overawed and become frightened (*Ritva, Avudraham*).[1]

Rashi and *Machzor Vitry* (based on *Onkelos* ad loc.) render the phrase *with great visibility* (from the root רָאָה, *to see*). In Egypt, God showcased His majesty, and, in an awe-inspiring spectacle, showed all of mankind that He rules uncontested over heaven and earth as Judge and Controlling Force, with unlimited ability to thwart all the laws of nature at will (see *Malbim*).[2]

The revelation of God's Presence occurred in stages. Even in the spiritual swampland of Egypt, God revealed Himself to Moses and Aaron. On the night of the redemption an even more intense revelation occurred when God Himself, as it were, passed through Egypt to slay its firstborn (*Ritva*). An even more awesome display of the *Shechinah* occurred at the splitting of the Sea of Reeds. In the

words of our Sages (*Mechilta* to *Exodus* 15:2), "Even a lowly maidservant saw things at the Sea that Ezekiel and the greatest prophets did not merit to envision." So clear was the manifestation of Godliness to the Jews at the Sea that even the humblest person could literally point with his finger and say, "This is my God" (*Rashi* to *Exodus* ibid.; *Avudraham*).

The revelation of the *Shechinah* occurred for the benefit of the Jews, not merely to impress the Egyptians and other nations with God's awesome power. Sunken as they were in the spiritual morass of Egypt's pagan culture, the Jews had to sever their ties to it. The appearance of the Divine Presence began to draw the Jews toward the pristine purity of sanctity according to the Torah. By showing the powerlessness of the pagan deities, God was able to draw His people toward Him (*Malbim*).[3]

Shelah offers the novel opinion that the *great awe* fell upon the Jews. When God revealed His Presence on the night He slayed the firstborn, the

---

1. **Divine Entrance Pass.** Even God's quiet, inconspicuous involvement in history can evince a fear of Heaven. When the hidden miracles of the Purim story unfolded fully the *Megillah* relates that many of the people of the land became Jews, "for the fear of the Jews had fallen upon them" (*Esther* 8:16). *Rema*, in his *Megillah* commentary *M'chir Yayin*, interprets the phrase פַּחַד הַיְּהוּדִים not as *the fear of the Jews*, but rather as *the Jewish fear* — fear of Heaven.

The revelation of God's Presence and fear of Him are reciprocal. The clear vision of His Presence in our lives induces in us a reverence for Him and His word. Simultaneously, through deep-rooted fear of God one is able to discern His involvement even when to others it is not apparent. As the *Kotzker Rebbe* replied to a young *chassid* who remarked that God is to be found everywhere, "No, no! Only where He is allowed to enter!" Our reverence for God is His key to enter our lives.

2. **Self-Destructing Deities.** *Rashi* teaches that when the Divine Presence revealed itself in Egypt all the Egyptian deities self-destructed. Those of wood crumbled, and those of metal melted. *R' Itzele of Volozhin* compares this to schoolchildren who are involved in mischief while their teacher is out of the room. All of a sudden, in the heat of the ruckus, the teacher returns. The children stop dead in their tracks and hide their faces in shame, embarrassed that the teacher discovered them to be nothing more than immature juveniles.

Likewise, until God revealed Himself, the deities projected an image of powerfulness and were treated as forces of significance. Subject to the shadow of the true God, they self-destructed and were revealed to all as the insignificant and powerless frauds that they really are (*R' Elisha Sandler*).

3. **Spiritual Periscope.** Homiletically, we might relate מֹרָא to מַרְאֶה, *a mirror*. Just as one may employ a mirror to view something that is hidden around a corner, so too great supernatural miracles serve as a mirror

signs and wonders, by war and with a strong hand and outstretched arm and by awesome revelations, as all that HASHEM your God did

Jews were fearful of being included in the wave of death. Since they had no merit that might distinguish them from their Egyptian neighbors, what was to provide them with saving grace? God saved them because He knew that buried deep within them was a spark of Godliness that could never be extinguished. Over the next seven weeks, this spark would grow into the flaming Godliness that was revealed at Mount Sinai.

כְּמָה שֶׁנֶּאֱמַר אוֹ הֲנִסָּה — *As it is stated: "or has any god ever attempted."* No god was ever able to remove one nation from the midst of another as God removed Israel from Egypt (*Rashi*). The *Midrash* (*Shocher Tov* 107) compares the liberation from Egypt to the delivery of a young animal from its mother's womb. The process is painful for the unborn animal, which is still a part of its mother. Similarly, the Jews enjoyed an almost symbiotic relationship with the Egyptians. Having developed as a nation within the incubator of Egypt, they absorbed much of its values, so much so that our Sages teach that the words *a nation from the midst of another nation* allude to the complaint of the angels that Israel did not deserve to be redeemed since "*both these (Israel) and these (the Egyptians) are idolaters*" (*Midrash Tanchuma* 15:5).

בְּמַסֹּת בְּאֹתֹת וּבְמוֹפְתִים וּבְמִלְחָמָה — *By trials, miraculous signs and wonders, by war.* This pro-cess of "removing the Egypt from Israel" was accomplished through various forms of miracles and feats, all of which revealed the Divine Presence. God showed His supremacy over all powers through *trials*, by defying Pharaoh to test him.

See *Exodus* 8:5 and Rashi ad loc.: "Make a request that you feel I cannot fulfill, and if you are right you will be able to claim that I failed the test! Tell me the moment when you want the frog infestation to end!"

The *signs* were the means by which Moses proved that God had sent him to free the nation.

Moses was shown three miraculous signs that he was commanded to perform for the Jews in order to prove his legitimacy. The inanimate staff in his hand would become a snake, his arm would wither with leprosy-like *tzaraas*, and the Nile, an Egyptian deity, would turn into blood (See *Exodus* 4:2-3).

The *wonders* — i.e. the plagues — were one more link in the series of revelations of God's hand, intended to exorcise the last vestiges of paganism from the Jews. Through the *war* He waged with the Egyptians at the Sea of Reeds, God finally brought the Jews to full faith in him. It was there that the Jews reached the spiritual plane of "belief in God and His servant Moses" (*Exodus* 14:31).[1]

וּבְיָד חֲזָקָה וּבִזְרוֹעַ נְטוּיָה וּבְמוֹרָאִים גְּדֹלִים כְּכֹל אֲשֶׁר עָשָׂה לָכֶם ה' אֱלֹהֵיכֶם בְּמִצְרַיִם לְעֵינֶיךָ — *And with a strong hand and outstretched arm and by awe-some revelations, as all that HASHEM your God did*

allowing one to see the camouflaged hand of God which controls nature. As *Ramban* states in his manifesto of faith, "It is from the great and famous miracles that one comes to realize regarding even hidden (recurrent) miracles that everything is miraculous; there is nothing 'natural' about these things at all — they are all truly miracles."

1. **Slow Reorientation.** The series of plagues and miracles that accompanied the Exodus could not have been replaced by one fatal blow delivered to the Egyptians by God. In order for the Jews to change their orientation and become fully committed servants of God it was necessary, by means of the many, constant miracles, to totally wean them from idolatry. This could only be accomplished through the cumulative effect of a series of miracles which showed God's absolute mastery of the world.

This principle applies not only for world outlooks; good character traits can also be developed only through constant repetitive action. Even if they are done on a small scale, many good deeds have a more far-reaching effect on one's character and emotional orientation than one great deed, no matter how grandiose in scale (*Rambam*).

בְּמִצְרַיִם לְעֵינֶיךָ.[1]

וּבְאֹתוֹת – זֶה הַמַּטֶּה, כְּמָה שֶׁנֶּאֱמַר, וְאֶת הַמַּטֶּה הַזֶּה תִּקַּח בְּיָדֶךָ, אֲשֶׁר תַּעֲשֶׂה בּוֹ אֶת הָאֹתֹת.[2]

וּבְמֹפְתִים – זֶה הַדָּם, כְּמָה שֶׁנֶּאֱמַר, וְנָתַתִּי מוֹפְתִים בַּשָּׁמַיִם וּבָאָרֶץ –

As each of the words דָּם, "blood," אֵשׁ, "fire," and עָשָׁן, "smoke," is said, a bit of wine is removed from the cup, with the finger or by pouring.

דָּם וָאֵשׁ וְתִימְרוֹת עָשָׁן.[3]

---

for you in Egypt, before your eyes. The *strong hand* refers to the triumphal manner in which the Jews left Egypt. They left with banners, song and celebration, indicating that they had no plan to return to slavery (*Ibn Ezra, Ramban*).[1] The *outstretched arm*, according to *Ibn Ezra*, alludes to the pillars of cloud and fire that accompanied and protected the Jews. *Sforno* interprets the *outstretched arm* figuratively as a warning to the Egyptians that God was ready to strike again if they did not free the Jews.[2]

All these miracles were performed *for you in Egypt*, i.e. for the benefit of Jews who needed to cut the umbilical cord attaching them to Egypt. God accomplished this by performing all of these feats *before your eyes*, so that you could witness first-hand all these manifestations of His power and therefore abandon all ties to Egypt (*Malbim*).

וּבְאֹתוֹת זֶה הַמַּטֶּה — *And with signs refers to [the*

miracles performed with] the staff.* The staff, which Moses used to implement many of the miracles, was created by God at twilight of the sixth day of Creation (see *Avos* 5:8), and it was passed on through the generations, from Adam to Noah, to the Patriarchs, and so on until it came to Moses (*Pirkei DeRabbi Eliezer*, Ch.50). This indicates that the Exodus and the birth of the Jewish nation were part of God's plan from the beginning of Creation.

Midrash Tanchuma relates that the rod was made of sapphire stone. On it were inscribed the ineffable Four-letter Name of God and the initials of the Ten Plagues — דְּצַ"ךְ עֲדַ"שׁ בְּאַחַ"ב — which were the *signs* that Moses was commanded to perform with the staff. It was this staff that he turned into a snake at the court of Pharaoh. When the Egyptian magicians duplicated his feat, their snakes were swallowed up by his staff.[3]

וּבְמֹפְתִים זֶה הַדָּם — *With wonders — alludes to the*

---

1. **Under His Own Power.** *Sfas Emes* and others interpret the *strong hand* figuratively as referring to the fact that God redeemed us even though we lacked merit. When man acts according to the will of God he adds strength to God, so to speak, by providing Him with a legitimate reason to bestow His beneficence on man. When man lacks merit and God nonetheless decides to act kindly to man, He does so on His own strength and power, as it were. Thus, when God freed the undeserving Jews from Egypt he did so with His own *strong hand.*

2. **Eternal Extension.** *Sfas Emes* views the *outstretched arm* as an allusion to the lasting effect of the Exodus. God's arm, figuratively stretched out to free His children from Egypt, remains extended throughout history ready to act on behalf of His children in subduing their enemies.

3. **Serpent Undone.** The *Zohar* explains that Moses' staff was turned into a snake to serve as a reminder of Adam's sin (*Genesis* 3); the snake represents the יֵצֶר הָרָע, the Evil Inclination, from which all evil emanates when one succumbs to it. When Moses turned the snake back into a staff, he thereby served a warning to Pharaoh that, as God's messenger, he would subdue the forces of evil.

for you in Egypt, before your eyes?[1]

With signs — refers to [the miracles performed with] the staff, as it is stated: Take this staff in your hand, that you may perform miraculous signs with it.[2]

With wonders — alludes to the blood, as it is stated: I will show wonders in the heavens and on the earth:

As each of the words דָּם, "blood," אֵשׁ, "fire," and עָשָׁן, "smoke," is said, a bit of wine is removed from the cup, with the finger or by pouring.

Blood, fire and columns of smoke."[3]

---

(1) *Deuteronomy* 4:34. (2) *Exodus* 4:17. (3) *Joel* 3:3.

---

blood. According to the *Vilna Gaon*, this "blood" refers to the miracle of transforming a bit of water into blood that Moshe performed before the Jews, not to the plague of blood that is included among the signs.

Ritva and others, however, do view this as a reference to the plague of blood. According to *Rashba*, אוֹת, *sign*, refers to any supernatural occurrence, while מוֹפֵת, *wonder*, is one that has a powerful effect — either positive or negative — on others. Thus the plague of blood was the first wonder, being the first supernatural phenomenon performed by Moses that adversely affected the Egyptians.

Shibbolei HaLeket cites the *Midrash*, that if during the plague of blood, a Jew and an Egyptian were to drink simultaneously from the same cup of water, the water would change to blood for the Egyptian but not for the Jew. This is why the Haggadah considers the plague of blood to be the archetypical *wonder*.

HaShir VeHaShevach views the *blood* of this passage as speaking of the blood of the *pesach* sacrifice and circumcision, which served as identifying signs, setting the Jews apart from their gentile neighbors.

The support verse cited appears in *Joel* as part of the scenario of the redemption in the End of Days. After the great revelation of the knowledge of God that will occur in Messianic times, mankind will be exposed to supernatural phenomena that will show God's mastery of the world. The verse is cited here merely to show that the term מוֹפֵת, *wonder*, is used to refer to the manifestation of blood (*Malbim*).

It is appropriate to infer the scope of the plagues in Egypt from those promised by God in Messianic times, because the prophets promise that God will show us miracles in the end of days just as He did when we left Egypt (*Micah* 7:15).

דָּם וָאֵשׁ וְתִמְרוֹת עָשָׁן — *Blood, fire and columns of smoke.* When reciting the words דָּם, וָאֵשׁ, וְתִמְרוֹת עָשָׁן it is customary to remove three drops of wine from our cups, either with a finger or by tilting the cup. The procedure is repeated when mentioning each of the ten plagues,[1] and again for דְּצַ"ךְ עֲדַ"שׁ בְּאַחַ"ב, for a total of sixteen times (see *Rema* O.C. 473 1:4).

The method used for removing the wine may depend on the interpretation of the custom. If it is meant to be a reminder of how *the finger of God* (*Exodus* 8:15) brought the plagues, we should use our finger (*Darkei Moshe*). *Abarbanel*, however,

---

1. **Human Empathy.** Although the verse cited is not a description of events that occurred in Egypt, we nonetheless remove wine when mentioning these three. This is due to the fact that *blood, fire and columns of smoke* all allude to events which were in their own way as painful to the Egyptians as the ten plagues. When the Egyptians witnessed the sheep, which was their deity, slaughtered in cold blood and they saw it being roasted over the fire with columns of smoke rising, it was an unbearable sight for them. Thus, here also we spill off some wine (*HaShir VeHaShevach*).

דָּבָר אַחֵר – בְּיָד חֲזָקָה, שְׁתַּיִם. וּבִזְרֹעַ נְטוּיָה, שְׁתַּיִם.
וּבְמֹרָא גָּדֹל, שְׁתַּיִם. וּבְאֹתוֹת, שְׁתַּיִם.
וּבְמֹפְתִים, שְׁתַּיִם.

אֵלּוּ עֶשֶׂר מַכּוֹת שֶׁהֵבִיא הַקָּדוֹשׁ בָּרוּךְ הוּא עַל הַמִּצְרִים
בְּמִצְרַיִם, וְאֵלּוּ הֵן:

explains that we remove wine because *you should not rejoice when your enemy falls (Proverbs 24:17).*[1] Our joy is incomplete since it came at the expense of human suffering. When the angels sought to sing God's praises at the Sea of Reeds when the Egyptians were drowned, God declared, "My handiwork is drowning in the sea and you seek to sing?!"(*Megillah 10b*). According to this explanation, it is appropriate to *pour* wine from the cup.

Maharil explains that our wine cup symbolizes happiness, and we want to avert from ourselves the sort of punishment that was meted out to our enemies. We therefore symbolically remove the wine from our cup as if to pray that our cup in life will remain purely one of joy, without pain or travail. According to this interpretation, as well, it would be appropriate to *pour* wine from our cups.

According to *Be'er Miriam*, the few drops are symbolic of the cup of punishment which God will force our enemies to drink in the Messianic age. This echoes the *Talmud Yerushalmi (Pesachim 10:1),* which teaches that the four cups of the

Seder correspond to the four cups of punishment which the prophets foresee for those nations who oppress the Jewish people.

דָּבָר אַחֵר – *Another explanation.* This explanation does not contradict the previous one; it might be viewed as complementary. The language of the verse, which employs double or plural terms, indicates that each of the five phrases alludes to two items, for a total of ten. We therefore interpret it as an allusion to the ten plagues (*Malbim*).

The phrases *"strong hand," "outstretched arm"* and *"great awe"* each refer to two plagues, because they are composed of two words, each word standing for a plague. In the case of the first two of these phrases it may also be said that the expressions *"strong hand"* and *"outstretched arm"* are suggestive of repeated, continuous action, and are therefore seen as representing more than one plague each. *"Signs"* and *"wonders,"* being in the plural, clearly refer to two plagues each (*Kol Bo, Shibbolei HaLeket*).

Maaseh Hashem elaborates: According to the earlier interpretation, only three of the ten plagues are alluded to in the verse from the *Bikkurim*

1. **No Gloating.** We should not rejoice when our enemy falls. In connection with the observance of Pesach the Torah therefore emphasizes the memory of our *liberation* from slavery rather than the *downfall* of the Egyptians. This explains why the Jews were already told in Egypt that the seventh day of Pesach was to be a holiday — even though they only observed one day of Pesach in that first year. If the commandment concerning the seventh day had been given only after their liberation, they would have considered that day as a celebration of the drowning of the Egyptians in the Sea, which occurred on that day (*Meshech Chochmah*).

In connection with Succos, the Torah commands us three times to be joyful; but with reference to Pesach, rejoicing is not even mentioned once. The obligation to rejoice on Pesach is only inferred as a derivative from the other holidays. This is for the same reason — because the Egyptians died on Pesach. Similarly, we find that we recite *Hallel* all the seven days of Succos; but on Pesach we only recite it on the first day of *Yom Tov* (*Yalkut*).

Another explanation of the preceding verse: [Each phrase represents two plagues], hence: **strong hand** — two; **outstretched arm** — two; **great awe** — two; **signs** — two; **wonders** — two.

These are the ten plagues which the Holy One, Blessed is He, brought upon the Egyptians in Egypt, namely:

Declaration (pestilence, slaying of the firstborn and blood). While not dismissing that approach, now the Haggadah finds Scriptural allusion to all ten plagues. *Aruch HaShulchan* adds that according to the original interpretation, the other seven plagues are alluded to only under the generic heading *the signs*. Here we seek to spell out an explicit source for each plague.

אֵלּוּ עֶשֶׂר מַכּוֹת שֶׁהֵבִיא הַקָּדוֹשׁ בָּרוּךְ הוּא עַל הַמִּצְרִים בְּמִצְרָיִם — *These are the ten plagues which the Holy One, Blessed is He, brought upon the Egyptians in Egypt.* The ten plagues were brought not only to punish the Egyptians for their excessive cruelty toward the Jews, but even more so to prove conclusively that *I am God in the midst of the land (Exodus 8:18).* Although God's abode is in Heaven, He is intimately involved in human affairs here on earth (see *Rashi* ad loc.).

These ten plagues are a central point of discussion at the Seder. *Yesod VeShoresh HaAvodah* writes that when explaining the Haggadah to his family, one should elaborate upon the effects of each plague on the Egyptians. The Talmud and *Midrash* go into great detail about each individual plague.

Rather than crippling the Egyptians with one fatal blow, the Divine plan provided for a gradually escalating process with the climactic liberation occurring with the slaying of Egypt's firstborn.

Why was this the case? The gradual sequence of plagues gave the Egyptians ample opportunity to reconsider their ways and repent of the evils they were perpetrating against the Jews, before Divine punishment would be unleashed against them in full.

Rambam (Hil. Teshuvah 6:3) addresses the problem that *God hardened Pharaoh's heart* for the last five plagues, depriving him of the ability to set the Jews free. This is in apparent contradiction of the cardinal principle of free choice; how was it proper for Pharaoh, in effect, to be forced to sin? *Rambam* explains that Pharaoh had shown through his attitude during the course of the first five plagues, when the Torah tells us that "Pharaoh's heart became hard (of his own doing)," that he no longer deserved the privilege of free choice. His fate had effectively been sealed as a result of his own repeated obstinacy. God then proceeded to harden his heart for the next five plagues. When someone's lack of free choice and the inability to repent is self-induced, a result of his earlier sins and freely chosen obstinance, he is culpable for what he does even after losing his autonomy.[1]

Midrash Tanchuma points out that the order of the ten plagues paralleled the strategy employed by an army in laying siege to a city. The plague of blood corresponded to the poisoning of the

---

1. **Losing Choice.** This may be compared to a person who indulges in some habit-forming act until he becomes addicted to it. Although he eventually becomes truly incapable of doing otherwise, he is nevertheless responsible for his actions, because he became addicted by choice.

This process can occur on the positive side as well. One may so consistently make proper choices that he will eventually be rewarded by achieving total nullification of any influence from his Evil Inclination. Nonetheless, since he brought himself to such a position he is rewarded even for the good he does after his loss of free choice (see *Tosafos* to *Bava Basra* 17a s.v. שלשה לא שלטה).

As each of the plagues is mentioned, a bit of wine is removed from the cup.
The same is done at each word of Rabbi Yehudah's mnemonic.

דָּם. צְפַרְדֵּעַ. כִּנִּים. עָרוֹב. דֶּבֶר. שְׁחִין. בָּרָד. אַרְבֶּה. חֹשֶׁךְ. מַכַּת בְּכוֹרוֹת.

---

besieged city's drinking water; the frogs, to trumpeters whose blasts would strike fear into the hearts of the inhabitants; the lice, to arrows shot into the city, and so on.

In addition, the *Midrash* shows how each plague was a punishment for a particular offense that the Egyptians committed against the Jews: The Egyptians made the Jews water-carriers, and so their river was turned to *blood*; they forced them to load cargo for them, and the *frogs* destroyed it; they made them sweep the streets, and so their dust turned to *lice*; they compelled the Jews to tend to their children, so God sent *wild animals* that devoured the children. The Egyptians made them cattle-herders, so a *pestilence* killed their herds. The Egyptians forced the Jews to prepare baths for them, and so they developed *boils* which made it impossible for them to bathe. The Egyptians used Jewish labor for stonecutting, for which God sent *hailstones* against them. The Jews were forced to tend the Egyptian farms, so *locusts* consumed all that grew. The Egyptians sought to deprive the Jews of their freedom by keeping them prisoner, and were therefore shackled by the plague of thick *darkness*; their murderous designs upon the Jews brought upon themselves the *killing of the firstborn*; and their drowning of Jewish children in the Nile was requited by their own deaths in the Sea of Reeds (*Tanchuma*).

Maaseh Nissim points out an enlightening aspect of the significance of *ten* plagues. They can be perceived as a parallel to the עֲשָׂרָה מַאֲמָרוֹת, the ten Divine pronouncements that brought the world into existence (*Avos* 5:1). The redemption of the Jews from Egypt would thus appear to be a counterpart to the creation of the world. The process of Creation showed God as the Master of nature; the Exodus showed Him as the Ruler of history, bending the laws of nature to His purposes. God created the world in ten utterances in order to give increased reward to the righteous, whose lifestyles justify the creation of the entire cosmos (see *Pirkei Avos Treasury* p.299). Thus the ten pronouncements of Creation are symbolized by the Ten Commandments. The evil, who wreak havoc on God's world by flouting His will as represented by the Ten Commandments, incur great punishment. Thus Pharaoh, who audaciously declared, "I do not know HASHEM," (*Exodus* 5:2) and denied Him as the Creator, was rudely awakened to the existence and domination of the One Who Created the world with ten utterances. Subjected to the ten plagues, Pharaoh woke up too late to the reality that "I am God Who took you out of Egypt."

Maharal points out that the ten pronouncements created the *world*, while the ten plagues brought about the creation of the *Jewish people*, whose existence and spiritual mission is the *raison d'etre* of all of existence.[1]

אֵלּוּ עֶשֶׂר מַכּוֹת שֶׁהֵבִיא הַקָּדוֹשׁ בָּרוּךְ הוּא עַל הַמִּצְרִים בְּמִצְרַיִם וְאֵלּוּ הֵן — *These are the ten plagues that the Holy One, Blessed is He, brought upon the Egyptians in Egypt.* According to the *Zohar* (2:29, 2:36), the ten plagues were both punishment for the Egyptians and spiritual therapy for the Jews. With every plague the faith of the Jews in God and Moses as His agent was strengthened. Furthermore, every plague weakened the spiritual sway that the deep impurity of Egypt held over the Jews.

---

1. **The Corrected Edition.** In a sense, the creation of the Jewish nation was the re-creation of man. Much like the second edition of a book, which comes to correct the mistakes that crept into the first edition, the Jewish people were created to rectify the mistakes of the ten generations from Adam to Noah, and again in the ten generations from Noah to Abraham.

As each of the plagues is mentioned, a bit of wine is removed from the cup.
The same is done at each word of Rabbi Yehudah's mnemonic.

1. Blood 2. Frogs 3. Lice 4. Wild Beasts
5. Pestilence 6. Boils 7. Hail 8. Locusts
9. Darkness 10. Plague of the Firstborn.

Thus, as Egypt was subdued, Jews emerged from spiritual impurity as their innate holiness came to the fore.

דָּם — *Blood.* God commanded Moses to meet Pharaoh on Pharaoh's daily visit to the Nile. Because he had declared himself a deity who had no need to perform normal bodily functions, he would go to the River every morning to relieve himself unobserved (*Midrash*). As Pharaoh was doing so, Moses performed the miracle of turning all the water into blood so that Pharaoh would see it happen with his own eyes.

The *Midrash* (*Shemos Rabbah* 9:9) tells us that the Jews became wealthy as a result of the plague of blood. When a Jew and an Egyptian would drink water from the same barrel, the Egyptian's cup would be filled with blood while the Jew's cup would contain water. Frustrated, the Egyptian would ask the Jew to share his water, but to no avail — as soon as the Jew poured his water into the Egyptian's cup it would turn to blood. Even if they simultaneously drank from the same vessel, the water would remain water only for the Jew; for the Egyptian, it would be blood. Only if the Egyptian *bought* the water from the Jew would it remain water.[1]

צְפַרְדֵּעַ — *Frogs* [lit. *Frog*]. The term appears in the singular and might better be rendered as *the frog-infestation* (*Rashi*). According to one opinion in the Talmud, at first only one frog emerged from the River, but as the Egyptians struck it, it split into swarms and swarms of frogs, which inundated the land (see *Sanhedrin* 67b).[2] The frogs crawled into every imaginable place, even penetrating the ovens in Egyptian homes. The Talmud expounds upon the experience of Chananiah, Mishael and Azariah, who were given a choice by Nebuchadnezzar to either bow to an idol or be thrown into a fiery furnace (*Daniel* 3). They chose to die in order to sanctify God's Name, and based their decision on the frogs, who willingly cast themselves into the burning Egyptian ovens in order that the Egyptians see the hand of God (*Pesachim* 53b). *Maharsha* sees this as a call for us to show self-sacrifice in our service of God, and to go against our natural inclinations. Even though frogs instinctively avoid heat, these frogs willingly went into the ovens. Likewise, we must counter our ingrained habits in order to do God's will.[3] There is nothing more pleasing to God than to see us subdue our nature for His sake.

When Moses asked Pharaoh to request a particu-

---

1. **Blood Money.** The word דָּמִים means both *money* and *blood*. For the Egyptians it was blood, but for the Jews it was money.

2. **Blind Anger.** Anger and frustration are blinding. Even when one sees the obviously negative results of these emotions he continues to pursue his course. Although the Egyptians saw that striking the frog was self-defeating they obstinately continued to do so. Our Sages (*Sifri, Mattos*) captured the sentiment: "Once a person is gripped by anger he is led to error" (*Steipler Gaon*).

3. **Seize the Opportunity.** Each frog could have very well allowed other frogs the privilege of entering the furnace by choosing for itself different parts of the Egyptian houses to infest. Nonetheless, they willfully assumed the heroic role in order to sanctify God's Name. Likewise, we should view the opportunity to do something difficult for God's sake as a privilege to be cherished, and not as a burden to be avoided where possible (*R' Yonason Eibeschutz*).

Those who are asked to strain themselves to contribute to charity or to help others should cherish the special opportunity Providence has brought to their doorstep.

lar time for the end of this plague, Pharaoh was sure that the plague was about to end in any case, and that Moses would expect him to beg for an immediate cessation of the plague. Thinking he would expose Moses as a fraud, Pharaoh asked him to pray that the plague should end the *next* day (*Exodus* 8:6). So vain and stubborn was Pharaoh that he was willing to endure additional pain as long as it might make the messenger of God look foolish.

כִּנִּים — *Lice.* The third plague entailed a total infestation of lice, with all the dust of the Egyptian earth turning into lice.

The plagues of blood and lice were not brought on directly by the hand of Moses, because both the Nile and the dust of the land had served him and it would have been ungrateful for him to smite them. When Moses was an infant, his mother had placed him in a basket by the River, and when he was forced to kill an Egyptian torturer, he concealed the body in the dust of the land (*Rashi*).[1]

Unable to reproduce the plague of lice, Pharaoh's sorcerers were forced to concede that Moses and Aaron performed their feats not with magic, but as agents of God. Though they had to acknowledge that the plague was of Divine origin, the magicians attempted to minimize it. By calling

it only a *finger of God* (*Exodus* 8:15) they implied that it was inconsequential. Thus Pharaoh's resolve was bolstered, and when the plagues ceased he again stubbornly refused to allow the Jews to leave.

עָרוֹב — *Wild beasts* [lit. *mixture*], a swarm of every imaginable type of aggressive wild beast, snake and scorpion attacked the Egyptians. Instead of being restrained by their natural fear of humans, the animals were Divinely incited to attack people (*Malbim*).[2] The animals stripped trees, destroyed crops and even devoured Egyptian babies (*Midrash Lekach Tov*). The plague was so pervasive that not only were animals roaming freely throughout the land, pillaging wherever they went, but even the very ground of Egypt teemed with snakes and subterranean creatures. This was done in order to instill fear in the Egyptians so that they could not feel secure even behind locked doors (*Sforno*).

This plague was the beginning of the second set of three plagues, which was sent by God to prove His intimate involvement in all the details of earthly events (see below). Thus the Torah stresses that these three plagues did not affect the Jewish people, which demonstrated that God controlled all minutiae of earthly happenings. Although the first three plagues also did not affect Jews, the

---

1. **Unmeaning Benefactor.** Similarly, with the plague of blood, Moses was not the one who struck the water of the Nile, which had provided his escape from detection as an infant. One must express gratitude for favors he receives even if the benefactor was unaware or did not intend to show kindness to the beneficiary. As the Talmud teaches: Do not throw a stone into the well you drank from (*Bava Kamma* 92b). For this reason Moses was forbidden to smite either the water or the earth (two inanimate objects) since he had benefited from them. Likewise, the Sages taught that the Biblical dictum regarding the disposal of the flesh of an animal torn in the field (טְרֵפָה), that it be *thrown to the dogs* (*Exodus* 22:30), is meant as an expression of gratitude: God does not let any good deed go unrewarded, and therefore He commanded that we show our appreciation to the dogs for their silence, which provided the contrast between our tranquility and the Egyptian pandemonium during the slaying of the firstborn (*Exodus* 11:7). We do this by throwing them the meat which is forbidden to us (*Rashi to Exodus* 22:30).

Since any good or favor that man receives was ultimately mandated by God, with the benefactor nothing more than God's agent, we must acknowledge the favor of even an inanimate or unthinking benefactor. "One who is ungracious regarding his friend's favors is as if he was ungracious toward God" (*Midrash HaGadol Shemos* 1:8).

2. **Follow the Frogs.** The Talmud (*Sanhedrin* 38a) explains that man was created on the last day of Creation in order to temper his arrogance. If one becomes the victim of self-obsession we tell him, "The fly preceded you in Creation."

Thus Pharaoh who imprudently asked, "Who is God that I should listen to Him?" (*Exodus* 5:2), was shown that even the frogs, grasshoppers, lice and wild beasts recognize the imperative of following His directives (*R' Meir Chodosh*).

Torah does not mention that factor, because their primary purpose was to establish the undeniable existence of *Hashem* (see *Exodus* 8:19).

דֶּבֶר — *Pestilence.* The fifth plague was an epidemic that decimated great portions of the Egyptian livestock, but miraculously did not affect the livestock of the Jews.

Even old and feeble Jewish animals stayed alive in order to distinguish clearly between Jewish and Egyptian livestock (see *Exodus* 9:4) (*R' Yehoshua Leib Diskin*).

Since the Egyptians worshiped animals and detested sheepherders, they kept their flocks outside the main cities and concentrated most of them in Goshen, where they mingled with the Jewish livestock. Thus, the survival of Jewish animals — which shared the pasture, water and air of Egyptian livestock — was an undeniable miracle (*Ramban*).

Nonetheless, Pharaoh became stubborn, obstinately not allowing the Jews to leave. Unlike earlier plagues that continued for a period of several days, the epidemic of pestilence did not continue because the animals died almost immediately. Once his livestock was dead, Pharaoh had no motivation to relent and release the people. Hence his ingrained wickedness reasserted itself (*Sforno*).

שְׁחִין — *Boils.* God commanded Moses to throw furnace soot up into the air. It miraculously spread over the entire land of Egypt and induced boils which erupted into blisters (*Rashi, Ramban*). With this plague a new phenomenon began. Pharaoh's personal stubbornness was broken and he would have freed the people. The wizards who had strengthened his resolve were now incapacitated by the boils and were unable to give him the confidence to ignore God's demand (see *Ramban* to *Exodus* 9:12). God therefore strengthened his heart so that he not repent and be absolved of all punishment, even for his earlier sins.

Rambam writes: "It is possible for a person to commit such a great sin, or so many sins, that justice before the Judge of Truth provides. . . that repentance be foreclosed from him and that he not be permitted the right to repent from his wickedness, so that he will die and be lost because of the sin that he committed. . . . Therefore it is written in the Torah *and I shall strengthen the heart of Pharaoh*, for at first he sinned of his own accord and did evil to the people of Israel who dwelled in his land. . . consequently, justice provided that repentance be denied him so that he would be punished for his sin"[1] (*Hil. Teshuvah* 6:3).

Alternatively, *Ramban* suggests that during the last five plagues God did not *force* Pharaoh's reaction. Rather Pharaoh was someone whose activities are inhibited by great pain, but if his doctor were to administer a powerful painkiller, he would be able to resume his normal activities. Certainly the decision to do so would be his alone; the doctor merely makes it possible for him to make the choice. Likewise God strengthened Pharaoh's heart so that he might endure the pain; then it was up to him to make a rational, uncoerced decision whether to free the Jews or not.

בָּרָד — *Hail.* The third series of plagues began with hailstones, which miraculously fell together with fire. This was a compounded miracle since (a) fire usually rises, and does not shoot downwards, (b) fire and water are opposites, but here, to serve God, fire and water made peace with each other

---

1. **Irreversible Effects.** God punished Pharaoh even for those sins which he committed after losing his free choice. Since he was the direct cause of losing the opportunity to repent, his claim of acting under duress rings hollow.

Tosafos (*Bava Basra* 17 s.v. שלשה שלא) offers an example of this phenomenon in its positive manifestation. The Talmud (ibid.) says that there were people in history over whom the Evil Inclination held no sway. "If so," questions *Tosafos*, "how did they receive reward for their actions, since they had no choice but to do good?"

Tosafos replies that initially these people had an Evil Inclination; however, by dint of their own efforts they were rewarded that it became totally nullified and powerless. Since this situation was a result of their own herculean efforts, they were even rewarded for the good they did after they no longer had real free choice.

and functioned in unison (*Rashi*).[1] In a thunderous storm, God unleashed these hailstones, destroying the Egyptian flax and barley crops.

The Torah describes this plague as being sent against the hardness of Pharaoh's heart which had prevented him from obeying God up to that point. God would show conclusively that He is unmatched by any power (see *Exodus* 9:14) by having fire and water, which naturally cannot coexist, do so for His sake. He instilled in them their natural tendencies in the first place, and would at will suspend these characteristics.

אַרְבֶּה — *Locusts.* The eighth plague was a locust-swarm so pervasive as to totally block out any vision of the earth (*Exodus* 10:5). The locusts infiltrated all the Egyptians' homes, beginning with Pharaoh's palace and ending with the hovels of the peasantry. Pharaoh felt the effects of the plague first, because he was the most responsible for the persecution of the Jews.

These locusts devoured all the grass and vegetation that remained after the plague of hail: *No greenery remained on the trees or the grass of the field in the entire land of Egypt* (ibid. 10:15). The scope of this invasion of locusts was unprecedented and never again reproduced in human history (ibid. 10:14).

In response to Pharaoh's request for forgiveness God changed the east wind, which had brought the locusts, to a west wind, which blew them away, with none remaining. However, since Pharaoh's "repentance" was insincere — he wanted only to be rid of the plague — God strengthened his resolve to not allow the Jews to leave.

חֹשֶׁךְ — *Darkness.* The ninth plague was a darkness that was much more than the mere absence of light. *Ramban* explains that it was an opaque, foglike condition that extinguished all flames, so that the Egyptians could not even use lamps. He cites *Ibn Ezra* that it may have been a very dense fog, like that which sometimes closes in over the ocean, and it was so dark that the Egyptians could not even keep track of the days.

The darkness during the day was darker than that of a normal night, and at night it became even more intense. After the first three days of the plague, the darkness entered a new stage; it was so thick that the Egyptians could not even move (*Rashi*). In all Jewish dwellings, however, there was light.

There were two reasons for the plague of darkness: (a) Among the Jews, there were people who did not deserve to be freed (because they were so assimilated into Egyptian culture that there was no hope for them to return to the covenant of Israel) and who were to die. God provided the darkness so that the Egyptians would not see the Jews die and claim that the plagues affected Jews and Egyptians alike; (b) the darkness provided an opportunity for the Jews to circulate in the Egyptian homes to determine the location of valuables that they would later ask to borrow (*Rashi*). Later, when the Egyptians realized that the Jews had been in their homes and had the opportunity to loot at will, but had not done so, Israel earned esteem in the eyes of the Egyptians (*Mechilta,* 12:36).

מַכַּת בְּכוֹרוֹת — *Plague of the Firstborn.* Unlike the previous nine, the Haggadah (based on *Exodus* 12:29) refers to this as *the plague* of the firstborn. While all other plagues are called by the name of the agent God used to punish the Egyptians, the firstborn were the *victims* of this plague, not its perpetrator. Therefore it is called the "plague" of the firstborn (*Malbim*).

According to the *Midrash* (*Shocher Tov* 136), the Egyptian firstborn themselves revolted against Pharaoh when they heard of their own imminent

1. **Peacemakers.** Even people with seemingly irreconcilable differences must heed the lesson of the hail and put their quarrels aside in order to unite in brotherhood to serve God. The Chassidic masters in a homiletical interpretation explain קָשָׁה עָלַי פְּרֵדַתְכֶם (see *Rashi* to *Leviticus* 23:36) — which is correctly translated as "it is hard from me to part from you" — as "The separation between you is unbearable for Me." Nothing pains a father more than dissension among his children. What difference does it make if we are right or wrong in our personal quarrels? The pain we cause our Father should force us to reconsider and find a way to make up even with those people with whom we share a "fire and water" relationship.

death and Pharaoh's refusal to yield to God. In a riotous bloodbath, the firstborn killed many Egyptians (see *Psalms* 136:10).

The killing of the firstborn represented the climax of the retribution visited upon Egypt. Moses announced it in his first confrontation with Pharaoh (*Exodus* 4:22-23): *So said HASHEM: My firstborn son is Israel . . . but you have refused to let him go; behold, I shall kill your firstborn son.* God alone carried this out, at the exact moment of midnight on the fifteenth of Nissan. As the firstborn of the Egyptians were dying, God's firstborn son Israel was "born" and came into being as a nation.

Moses himself, however, did not say that the plague would occur *exactly* at midnight, but at *about* midnight (*Exodus* 11:4), because Pharaoh's astronomers might miscalculate the time and think that the moment of the plague was somewhat before or after midnight. If so, they would claim that Moses was a charlatan for predicting the wrong time (*Rashi* to *Exodus* 11:4).[1]

R' Bachya adds that since the third plague, when the magicians were forced to admit that God was at work in Egypt, their belief in Moses' veracity had been reinforced as the plagues progressed. Now, if Moses were to "err" in predicting the exact time of the last plague, the Egyptian wise men would retroactively lose faith in Moses.

Every firstborn in Egypt died at the predicted moment. Pharaoh (himself a firstborn) was spared, so that he could tell all the world about God's greatness. The native Egyptian firstborn died because they had persecuted the Jews; those of the captives died because they also made use of Jewish slave labor, or so that they would not be able to claim that their idols had come to their defense. The plague struck down not only those who were known to be firstborn, but also the eldest children of men who lived with women other than their wives. In a country as licentious as Egypt, this meant that a given household could have had many firstborn, whose paternity was known only to God. In addition, if there was no firstborn in a house, the oldest member of the household died. Thus the Torah tells us that *there was not a house where there was no corpse* (*Rashi* to *Exodus* 12:30). However, among the Jews not one firstborn died on that night. Even if someone was supposed to have died of natural causes on that night his death was postponed in order to show a clear demarcation between the Jews and the Egyptians.

Various *Midrashim* and commentators point out that the plagues struck מִדָּה כְּנֶגֶד מִדָּה, *measure for measure,* in corresponding and symmetrical retribution for the suffering of the Jews. God smote the Egyptians with ten plagues as Divine response to ten evil decrees that they promulgated against the Jews. In the future God will likewise punish measure for measure the nations who oppress his people (*Bamidbar Rabbah* 10:12).

The Egyptians forced Jews to serve as water-carriers and were punished by having their water turn into **blood** (*Tanchuma, Bo*). Furthermore, God brought the plague of blood in response to the shedding of Jewish blood and the drowning of Jewish children in the Nile (*Abarbanel*).

The Egyptian taskmasters would awaken Jews early in the morning to begin another day of backbreaking toil by rapping on their windows, causing a jolting and upsetting noise. Thus, God repaid them by bringing frogs with their croaking sound. Furthermore, God brought the frogs as a reminder of the screaming and pleading of Jewish

---

1. **Discrediting the Credible.** Moses' reticence to pinpoint the moment when the plague would occur out of fear of the cynical skepticism of the Egyptians offers insight into a less than savory aspect of human nature. Although the firstborn were dying all around them, the astrologers would snatch at a straw to discredit Moses. This sort of perverse attitude has corrupted human behavior throughout history. Such is the nature of the wicked; their belief in God is so fragile that they will discard it with the slightest excuse (*R' Nosson Scherman*).

Likewise, we are often quick to discredit our leaders when they tell us things we would rather not hear. We cynically impute all kinds of personal bias and agenda as the motive for their advice born of concern. אֱמוּנַת חֲכָמִים, trust in our wise and righteous leaders, is one of the cardinal lessons of the Exodus. When the Jews experienced the splitting of the Sea of Reeds, the Torah tells us *They had faith in HASHEM and in Moses, His servant* (*Exodus* 14:31).

parents who saw the Egyptians drag their children away. Just as their screams continued to ring in the ears of the Egyptians as they coldly ignored the heartrending cries, so the frogs came forth from the river, their annoying sound ringing in the ears of the Egyptians.

As janitors and cleaning personnel for the Egyptians, the Jews were forced to sweep homes, public thoroughfares and roads. In retribution, God turned all the dust into **lice** leaving the Jews with nothing to sweep (*Yalkut Shimoni Va'eira* 182). Alternatively, the Egyptians deprived the Jews of water to cleanse themselves from dirt and perspiration after a day of toil. As a result of such unsanitary conditions the Jews suffered from vermin; God responded to the Egyptians' cruelty with a plague of lice (*Midrash Lekach Tov*).

The swarm of wild beasts was God's way to punish the Egyptians for sending the Jews afield to bring back animals for the pleasure and amusement of the Egyptians (*Yalkut*). Just as the Egyptians made peace with each other in order to oppress the Jews, so God caused wild beasts, which by nature are aggressively competitive, to join forces against the Egyptians. Finally, the heinous crime of snatching Jewish children from their mothers was paid back in kind when the wild beasts indiscriminately attacked Egyptian homes, devouring all children in their path (*Abarbanel*).

By sending Jews to faraway places to tend the Egyptian sheep and cattle they succeeded in disrupting normal Jewish family life. God said, "I will provide them with a 'shepherd' who will really 'take care' of their sheep." He brought **pestilence** among the Egyptian cattle, thus making their care a moot issue (*Shemos Rabbah* 11). According to *Abarbanel*, the Egyptians used Jews instead of animals as beasts of burden. Since they showed that they did not need their animals, God decimated them with pestilence.

The **boils** that God brought upon the Egyptians made them physically repulsive to their wives. This was Divine vengeance for their efforts to upset marital life among Jews through their oppressive work regimen.

As gardeners for the Egyptians, the Jews were forced to plant and tend to their gardens, vineyards, orchards and trees. God thus brought **hailstones** against them, which destroyed the trees and fruit (*Shemos Rabbah* 12).

As punishment for robbing Jews of the produce of their fields, the Egyptian fields were stripped bare by the **locusts** (*Abarbanel*). Furthermore, lest the Egyptians benefit from the agricultural labor the Jews performed on their behalf, God brought the locusts to devour it all (*Yalkut Shimoni, Va'eira* 182).

Imprisoned in the hermetically sealed Egyptian house of bondage, Jews felt themselves as if in a dark and deep cellar with no hope of ever escaping. The hopelessness of their situation was not lost on God Who gave the Egyptians "a taste of their own medicine," imprisoning them in a darkness from which no one could rise from his place (*Tanchuma*; see *Exodus* 10:22).

The final plague, **the slaying of the firstborn,** was in retribution for the Egyptian decree to kill the male children (*Yalkut*). The wicked attempt of the Egyptians to abort the spiritual birth of God's firstborn, Israel, resulted in the destruction of their own firstborn (*Abarbanel*).

רַבִּי יְהוּדָה הָיָה נוֹתֵן בָּהֶם סִמָּנִים — *Rabbi Yehudah abbreviated them by their Hebrew initials.* Why did R' Yehudah find it necessary to coin a memory aid for the ten plagues? *Ritva* and *Machzor Vitry* suggest that he sought to teach the plagues in a concise form so that they and their order could be remembered easily. This is in the spirit of the Talmudic dictum "Let one always teach his student in the most concise manner" (*Pesachim* 3b).[1]

R' Yehudah would use abbreviations to express even halachic ideas. The *Mishnah* (*Menachos* 96a) quotes his mnemonics regarding the laws of the two breads offered on Shavuos and the showbread placed on the Table in the Temple.

Rabbi Judah abbreviated them by their Hebrew initials:
D'tzach, Adash, B'achab.

According to the *Vilna Gaon*, R' Yehudah held that the names of the plagues were etched into Moses' staff in this abbreviated form.

This contradicts other opinions that the names were fully written out on the staff (see *Shemos Rabbah*).

Shibbolei HaLeket, quoting R' Yehudah HaChasid, suggests that the abbreviation comes to teach that the order of the plagues listed in the Torah is chronologically correct. This was necessary since in two places in *Psalms* (78:43-51 and 105:28-36) a different order is implied for the plagues than that given in the Torah. Therefore, R' Yehudah stressed that the order of appearance in the Torah is indeed the correct chronological order.

Sometimes things are listed in the Torah in a particular order that is based on considerations other than chronology. This principle is known as אֵין מוּקְדָם וּמְאוּחָר בַּתּוֹרָה, meaning that no chronological conclusion may be drawn from something written earlier or later in the Torah.

According to *R' S.R. Hirsch*, R' Yehudah's opinion is in contradistinction to "another explanation" cited earlier, which grouped the plagues in five groups of two plagues each; R' Yehudah groups them in *three* — and not five — groups. He points out that the first plague in each group (*blood*, *wild beasts* and *hail*) humbled the Egyptians to the point where they felt the insecure existence of strangers (גֵרוּת) in their own land. The second plague in each group (*frogs*, *pestilence* and *locusts*) deprived them of their possessions and their sense of superiority, reducing them to lowly submission (עַבְדוּת). And the third plague in each group (*lice*, *boils* and *darkness*) imposed actual physical suffering (עִנּוּי) upon them. This arrangement of the plagues served as retribution for the Egyptians' oppression of the Jews, which had taken these same three forms, as God had foretold Abraham: *They will be aliens* (גֵּר) in a land not their own. They will enslave them (וַעֲבָדוּם) and oppress them (וְעִנּוּ אֹתָם). After the three sets of three plagues, their punishment reached its climax with the tenth plague, the slaying of the firstborn.

Ritva suggests that each group of plagues came to teach the cynical Pharaoh — and the rest of the world — one of the three fundamental principles of belief in God. The first set of plagues was intended to establish the existence of God the Creator; these three plagues were introduced by the warning *you shall know that I am Hashem* (*Exodus* 7:17), countering Pharaoh's audacious declaration (ibid. 5:2): *"I do not know Hashem!"* This first series of plagues achieved its purpose when, at their end, Pharaoh's magicians were forced to admit, *It is a finger of God* (ibid. 8:15). The second group was to demonstrate God's guiding hand in the everyday affairs of man; here the introduction is *you will know that I am God in the midst of the land* (ibid. 8:18). The third group was to show the truth of prophecy; in connection with this group the Torah specifies those *who did not take God's word to heart* (ibid. 9:21).

Within each group of three plagues, only the first two were preceded by warnings to Pharaoh. When he ignored them, the two plagues became "witnesses" that established the intended point, as noted above. The third plague in each series was not preceded by a warning; since the point had been made and proven, the third plague came as a

---

1. **A Question of Interpretation.** During the Middle Ages the Church, with the support of the government, would frequently force the Jews and their leaders to participate in religious debates, often facing off against priests or apostates. At one such debate a priest suggested that דְּצַ"ךְ alludes to the Jewish "custom" of using Christian blood for an ingredient in the matzos and stands for דָּם צְרִיכִים כּוּלָנוּ, *We all need blood.* Before he could continue, one of the rabbis interjected. "My colleague is correct. These words are abbreviations. However, in his ignorance he doesn't know what they stand for. דְּצַ"ךְ means דּוֹבְרִים צוֹרְרֵינוּ כָּזָב, our enemies speak falsehood, בַּאַחַ"ב alludes to בְּנֵי, עֲלִילַת דַּם שֶׁקֶר, *the blood libel is false,* עַדַ"שׁ means אַבְרָהָם חָלִילָה זֹאת, *God forbid the children of Abraham would do such a thing."*

The cups are refilled. The wine that was removed is not used.

רַבִּי יוֹסֵי הַגְּלִילִי אוֹמֵר: מִנַּיִן אַתָּה אוֹמֵר שֶׁלָּקוּ
הַמִּצְרִים בְּמִצְרַיִם עֶשֶׂר מַכּוֹת, וְעַל הַיָּם לָקוּ
חֲמִשִּׁים מַכּוֹת? בְּמִצְרַיִם מָה הוּא אוֹמֵר, וַיֹּאמְרוּ הַחַרְטֻמִּם
אֶל פַּרְעֹה, אֶצְבַּע אֱלֹהִים הוּא.[1] וְעַל הַיָּם מָה הוּא אוֹמֵר,
וַיַּרְא יִשְׂרָאֵל אֶת הַיָּד הַגְּדֹלָה אֲשֶׁר עָשָׂה יְהוָה בְּמִצְרַיִם,

punishment to Pharaoh and his people for not heeding the message of the previous two plagues (*Malbim*).

R' Bachya notes that the first warning of each set was delivered at the River and the second warning was in the royal palace, because those were the symbols of Pharaoh's arrogance. He regarded himself as the master of the River, which was the source of agricultural life in arid Egypt, and when he was buffeted by a plague, his resistance would be stiffened by the palace, the seat of his power. Therefore, God chose those two places to proclaim Pharaoh's downfall and show him that he was powerless to defy the Divine will.

רַבִּי יוֹסֵי הַגְּלִילִי — *R' Yose the Galilean.* In a continuation of the detailed exposition of the scope of the plagues, the Haggadah now quotes three opinions regarding the contrast between the plagues inflicted on the Egyptians while in Egypt with those they suffered at the Sea of Reeds.[1]

R' Yose compares the expressions used to describe the Divine retribution that occurred in Egypt with the terms used to portray God's punishment of the Egyptians at the Sea. The ten plagues that struck them in Egypt are each called, metaphorically, the *finger of God*, while the punishment in-

flicted upon the Egyptians at the sea are called God's *great hand*. Since a hand contains five fingers it follows that we may assume that the Egyptians' suffering at the sea was five times as great as what they endured in Egypt — fifty plagues.

The *Mishnah* (*Avos* 5:5) states that God brought *ten* plagues upon the Egyptians at the Sea, not fifty. This would seem to contradict our passage in the Haggadah, which is based on the *Mechilta*. The opinions quoted here clearly indicate that five times as many plagues occurred at the Sea as in Egypt. *Rashbatz* indeed views this as a point of disagreement between the two Tannaitic sources. *Rambam* (*Avos* ad loc.) suggests that while there were more than ten plagues at the Sea, they were all of the same ten *categories* as those that occurred in Egypt, meaning that they were offshoots and different aspects of the ten primary afflictions known as the Ten Plagues.

While the phrase "finger of God" appears only in the context of the plague of lice, it does not refer to that plague alone. The sorcerers who used the phrase had been able to duplicate the previous plagues of blood and frogs, but they were unable to duplicate the plague of lice. At this point they realized that Moses and Aaron had brought about the earlier plagues through miraculous means rather than sorcery, and they said that it — that is, the broad phenomenon of the plagues rather than the particular plague of lice — is the

1. **All-Powerful.** *Maharal* explains the redemption of the Jews as a two-stage process. Man is susceptible to harm both from other human beings and from the forces of nature; God redeemed Israel from both sources. Pharaoh and the mighty Egyptian empire were defeated during the Exodus, thus exhibiting that no human power can stand up against God. The splitting of the Sea proved beyond a shadow of a doubt that the Creator has full control of His world and can change the "immutable" laws of nature on behalf of His people.

The Midrash Tanchuma (*Va'eira* 5) points out that Pharaoh said, מִי ה׳, *who is Hashem?* (*Exodus* 5:2), and he received his answer at the Sea when he and his army were struck by fifty plagues (מִי = 50).

Rabbi Yosi the Galilean says: "How does one derive that the Egyptians were struck with ten plagues in Egypt, but with fifty plagues at the Sea? Concerning the plagues in Egypt the Torah states: The sorcerers said to Pharaoh: 'It is the finger of God.'[1] However, of those at the Sea, the Torah relates: 'And Israel saw the great hand which HASHEM laid upon the Egyptians,

---

(1) *Exodus* 8:15.

---

finger of God (Abarbanel).

According to *Aruch HaShulchan*, the greater number of plagues at the Sea was in response to the arrogant defiance of the Egyptians. After experiencing the miraculous events of the Exodus they should have surrendered to God's will. Instead, in a display of contemptuous insolence, they sought to recapture the escaping Jews and force them back to Egypt.[1]

וַיַּרְא יִשְׂרָאֵל אֶת הַיָּד הַגְּדֹלָה — *And Israel saw the great hand.* The verse speaks of three stages: (a) They saw; (b) they feared Hashem; (c) they believed in God and Moses His servant; one stage led to the next. As eyewitnesses to the openlydisplayed hand of God, they achieved a heightened level of fear of God. As a result of this reverence, their faith was transformed from a vague idea into a vibrant, almost tangible, reality (*Lev Eliyahu*).[2]

Ksav Sofer suggests that the splitting of the Sea was a potent catalyst of belief than the Exodus itself, since it was at the Sea that the symmetry of God's justice was revealed. Since the Egyptians decreed that all Jewish males be thrown into the Nile they were, in a display of poetic justice, drowned in the Sea. This retribution "measure for measure" strengthened Jewish faith in God.[3]

---

1. **Safe Haven.** *Vayaged Moshe* offers a reason why there were fewer plagues in Egypt than at the Sea. Since Egypt was our home, we must feel a sense of gratitude toward the Egyptian nation. Although they were far from being genial hosts, it would have been improper for them to suffer the full extent of God's wrath in their own land. The Torah similarly commands us *you shall not reject an Egyptian, for you were a sojourner in his land* (Deuteronomy 23:8). At the Sea, however, they had no such meritorious protection and were smitten with the full hand of God.

2. **The Faith Reflex.** Faith is often more indomitable than even personal witness. People can sometimes block out things that they have seen, but the power of faith is such that its truth constantly reasserts itself. Faith transforms truth into a powerful reality. Thus, the Torah teaches that even after the Jews witnessed the miraculous events of the Exodus and the splitting of the Sea, they ascended to an even more elevated plateau — that of faith: *And Israel saw the great hand . . . and they had faith* (Exodus 14:31).

A follower of the Kotzker Rebbe told him about another *rebbe* who claimed to actually *see* the *Ushpizin* (the seven Biblical saints who, according to the *Zohar*, visit us in spirit in the *succah*). Replied the Kotzker: "I don't see them, but I *believe* they come to my *succah*. And that is even greater."

The folk-saying has it that "seeing is believing." In fact, believing is even more.

3. **Faith in Self-Potential.** The Sages teach that at the Sea even the lowliest maidservant witnessed a Divine revelation greater than that revealed to the prophets (see *Rashi* to *Exodus* 15:2). When the Jews saw this, they realized the potential of every Jew for spiritual greatness; every Jew could be as righteous as Moses (see *Rambam, Hilchos Teshuvah* 5:2). Hence, they saw God's great hand and they believed in Him and in [their potential to be like] Moses (*Kedushas Levi*).

R' Tzadok HaKohen gives this idea expression: Just as one must believe in God, so must he believe in his own potential and that God is intimately concerned with him and rejoices over every manifestation of his Godly soul and its effect on his life (*Tzidkas HaTzaddik* 154).

וַיִּירְאוּ הָעָם אֶת יהוה, וַיַּאֲמִינוּ בַּיהוה וּבְמֹשֶׁה עַבְדּוֹ.[1] כַּמָּה לָקוּ בָּאֶצְבַּע? עֶשֶׂר מַכּוֹת. אֱמוֹר מֵעַתָּה, בְּמִצְרַיִם לָקוּ עֶשֶׂר מַכּוֹת, וְעַל הַיָּם לָקוּ חֲמִשִּׁים מַכּוֹת.

רַבִּי אֱלִיעֶזֶר אוֹמֵר. מִנַּיִן שֶׁכָּל מַכָּה וּמַכָּה שֶׁהֵבִיא הַקָּדוֹשׁ בָּרוּךְ הוּא עַל הַמִּצְרִים

The principle of "measure for measure" means that God treats people exactly in accordance with their own deeds, both for the good and for the bad, although the fairness of His judgment is not always apparent to us. At the Sea, however, His justice was so clearly calibrated to the crime that every Jew attained the level of prophecy and understood God's ways. Even Jethro, who was not himself part of the miracle, was able to understand it clearly enough to declare the supremacy of God. Thus he said: *Now I know that HASHEM is greater than all the gods, for in the very matter which [the Egyptians] had conspired [He brought punishment] upon them* (Exodus 18:11) (*R' Nosson Scherman*).[1]

According to one opinion in the Talmud (*Zevachim* 116a), it was the splitting of the Sea that caused Jethro to join the Jewish people. Similarly the inhabitants of Canaan told the spies that *we heard how God dried up the waters of the Sea of Reeds. . . and our hearts melted*. We remember this seminal historical event every day in our prayers, in order to constantly strengthen the flame of faith that was ignited in the Jewish national subconscious at that time (*Chidushei HaRim*).[2]

רַבִּי אֱלִיעֶזֶר אוֹמֵר – *R' Eliezer says.* R' Eliezer accepts the axiom of R' Yose that the ratio of one to five exists between the *finger of God* in Egypt and his great hand at the Sea. However, he views the plagues in Egypt as having been comprised of four elements, based on the verse in *Psalms* (78:49). Thus, R' Eliezer interprets *His fierce anger* as a general description of the Ten Plagues, each of which was fourfold in nature: *wrath, fury, trouble and a band of emissaries of evil*. R' Akiva understands that each plague contained *five* parts — with *fierce anger*, representing the fifth (*Akeidas Yitzchak*).

R' S. R. Hirsch identifies the root of עֶבְרָה as לַעֲבֹר, *to overstep* certain boundaries, alluding to an

---

1. **Spiritual Alarm Clock.** Punishment is not merely punitive; its main purpose is to arouse people to repent. Thus God punishes "measure for measure"; the form of punishment will make people realize what they must correct. Furthermore, the exactness of the retribution does not allow us to foolishly conclude that what happened is a mere coincidence.

2. **Look, No Hands!.** If witnessing great miracles so fortifies faith, why does God not perform such open wonders more frequently? *Ramban* (Exodus 13:16) suggests that one must be on a sufficiently high spiritual level to witness such evidence of God's intervention. *R' Archik Bakst* offered a different approach, by way of a parable. When a child begins to walk, his parent holds on to him so that he does not fall and hurt himself or, even worse, lose his confidence that he can, in fact, walk. However, once the child grows and matures, the father lets go since now the child can walk on his own.

The newborn nation of Israel needed to be emotionally supported by God until they would mature and grow into a solid, implacable faith. Thus, their national birth was accomplished through great miracles. Once they received the Torah at Mount Sinai, however, the message of faith is imbibed through study of God's Torah and fulfillment of His commandments. Able to stand and walk by themselves, the Jewish people no longer needs miracles. King David captured the sentiment when he said, *Open my eyes and I will behold wondrous things in Your Torah* (Psalms 119:18).

and the people feared HASHEM and they believed in HASHEM and in His servant Moses.'[1] How many plagues did they receive with the finger? Ten! Then conclude that if they suffered ten plagues in Egypt [where they were struck with a finger], they must have been made to suffer fifty plagues at the Sea [where they were struck with a whole hand]."

Rabbi Eliezer says: "How does one derive that every plague that the Holy One, Blessed is He, inflicted upon the Egyptians

_____

(1) *Exodus* 14:31.

anger of such intensity that it defies containment. וַעַם implies *directed* Divine wrath, which strikes a specific target visibly and directly.

Incensed over the cruel mistreatment of His children, God could not contain His anger, as it were, at their tormentors. He therefore took vengeance and visibly struck the Egyptians.

The plagues were like a delegation of evil messengers. By means of their punitive power, they served as God's messenger to convey a lesson to the Egyptians (*Radak*).

Why were the Sages so interested in amplifying the number of plagues visited upon the Egyptians? For one thing, they wanted to show the huge range of miracles that God showered upon us during the Exodus from Egypt, thus increasing our awareness of the extent to which we must be grateful to Him. (This is the theme of the following paragraph, דַּיֵּנוּ, as well.)

The *Vilna Gaon* suggests another reason for the Sages' attempts to assign ever larger numbers of plagues to the Egyptian downfall. It is in order to increase the import of a corresponding promise issued by God to the Jews: *If you heed the voice of HASHEM, your God, and do what is proper in His eyes, and listen to His commandments and guard His statutes, all the diseases I inflicted on Egypt I will not inflict on you, for I am HASHEM, your healer* (*Exodus* 15:26; see also *Deuteronomy* 7:15). The more disasters that befell Egypt, the greater God's guarantee of protection to the Jewish people if they obey His word.[1]

R' Yechezkel Levenstein submits that the great amounts of plagues brought upon Egypt indicate God's great love for His people. The more precious a child is to its father, the greater the father's wrath towards anyone who dares harm him. The Sages sought to clarify the scope of the plagues as a barometer of God's love for His people.

Furthermore, the promise of the future redemption is expressed by the prophet (*Micah* 7:15) in terms of the Egyptian Exodus: *As in the days when you left Egypt I will show you wonders.* Thus, our attempts to clarify the parameters of the miraculous Egyptian Exodus serve as a source of hope and strength as we await the ultimate redemption, which will parallel those wonders.

1. **Therapeutic Pain.** Even when God brings suffering upon Israel, His intention is *never* to destroy them, as He did Egypt. Rather, God is Israel's Healer, and even exile and suffering are meant only to purge them of sin and influence them to repent. The immediacy of our pain often does not allow us to see the therapeutic value of God's actions. Like a patient who only feels the pain, we often wonder why God allows us to undergo such physical and emotional distress.

The Torah in this verse promises that if we truly fulfill God's will, we will realize that even when He forces us to swallow a bitter pill, He is our Healer (*R' Tzadok HaKohen*).

בְּמִצְרַיִם הָיְתָה שֶׁל אַרְבַּע מַכּוֹת? שֶׁנֶּאֱמַר, יְשַׁלַּח בָּם חֲרוֹן אַפּוֹ – עֶבְרָה, וָזַעַם, וְצָרָה, מִשְׁלַחַת מַלְאֲכֵי רָעִים.[1] עֶבְרָה, אַחַת. וָזַעַם, שְׁתַּיִם. וְצָרָה, שָׁלֹשׁ. מִשְׁלַחַת מַלְאֲכֵי רָעִים, אַרְבַּע. אֱמוֹר מֵעַתָּה, בְּמִצְרַיִם לָקוּ אַרְבָּעִים מַכּוֹת, וְעַל הַיָּם לָקוּ מָאתַיִם מַכּוֹת.

רַבִּי עֲקִיבָא אוֹמֵר. מִנַּיִן שֶׁכָּל מַכָּה וּמַכָּה שֶׁהֵבִיא הַקָּדוֹשׁ בָּרוּךְ הוּא עַל הַמִּצְרִים בְּמִצְרַיִם הָיְתָה שֶׁל חָמֵשׁ מַכּוֹת? שֶׁנֶּאֱמַר, יְשַׁלַּח בָּם חֲרוֹן אַפּוֹ, עֶבְרָה, וָזַעַם, וְצָרָה, מִשְׁלַחַת מַלְאֲכֵי רָעִים.[1] חֲרוֹן אַפּוֹ, אַחַת. עֶבְרָה, שְׁתַּיִם. וָזַעַם, שָׁלֹשׁ. וְצָרָה, אַרְבַּע. מִשְׁלַחַת מַלְאֲכֵי רָעִים, חָמֵשׁ. אֱמוֹר מֵעַתָּה, בְּמִצְרַיִם לָקוּ חֲמִשִּׁים מַכּוֹת, וְעַל הַיָּם לָקוּ חֲמִשִּׁים וּמָאתַיִם מַכּוֹת.

כַּמָּה מַעֲלוֹת טוֹבוֹת לַמָּקוֹם עָלֵינוּ.

כַּמָּה מַעֲלוֹת טוֹבוֹת לַמָּקוֹם עָלֵינוּ — *How many levels of goodness has the Omnipresent One provided us!* According to *Abarbanel*, this poem was composed by R' Akiva in order to delineate as much as humanly possible the scope of the beneficences that God showered upon us in the course of our redemption from Egypt. It, as well as the immediately preceding discussion regarding the plagues in Egypt and those at the Sea, are omitted in the Haggadah text of the *Rambam's Yad HaChazakah*. According to his son *R' Avraham,* he did recite them at his own Seder, yet he omitted them from his version of the Haggadah because they are not an integral part of the Haggadah. *Abarbanel* suggests that this is so since these passages speak mainly about miracles and events that occurred *after* the Jews left Egypt.

R' Yosef Dov Soloveitchik bases the omission on the *Rambam's* codification of the commandment to relate the story of the Exodus: "It is a Biblically mandated positive commandment to relate the miracles and wondrous events that occurred to our forefathers *in Egypt* on the night of the fifteenth of Nissan" (*Hilchos Chametz U'Matzah* 7:1). This would seem to exclude a discussion of the events at the Sea of Reeds or thereafter. However, *Rambam* (*Sefer HaMitzvos*, Positive Command 157) writes that the commandment includes a general discussion of how God avenged our degradation from our oppressors, which implies that our miraculous deliverance at the Sea may also be considered germane to the night's discussion.

Nonetheless, we include the subsequent steps in our Haggadah and thank and praise God for all of His favors, including splitting the Sea, giving us the Torah, granting us the gift of His land and the building of the Temple. In truth these favors are the ultimate expression of redemption, as the Torah states: *I took them out of the land of Egypt in order to dwell in their midst; I am HASHEM*

in Egypt was equal to four plagues? As it says, 'He sent upon them His fierce anger: wrath, fury, and trouble, a band of emissaries of evil.'[1] [Since each plague in Egypt consisted of] (1) wrath, (2) fury, (3) trouble and (4) a band of emissaries of evil, therefore conclude that in Egypt they were struck by forty plagues and at the Sea by two hundred!"

Rabbi Akiva says: "How does one derive that each plague that the Holy One, Blessed is He, inflicted upon the Egyptians in Egypt was equal to five plagues? As it says, 'He sent upon them His fierce anger: wrath, fury, trouble, and a band of emissaries of evil.'[1] [Since each plague in Egypt consisted of] (1) fierce anger, (2) wrath, (3) fury, (4) trouble and (5) a band of emissaries of evil, therefore conclude that in Egypt they were struck by fifty plagues and at the Sea by two hundred and fifty!"

How many levels of goodness has the Omnipresent One provided us!

---

(1) *Psalms* 78:49.

---

their God (*Exodus* 29:46).[1]

After depicting the plagues visited upon the Egyptians we continue by spelling out all the great acts of kindness that God did for us, which were an expression of His great affection for us (*Shibbolei HaLeket*).[2]

Malbim views this poetic delineation of God's beneficence as a prelude to the praise of God we offer in the paragraph that begins: "Therefore it is our duty to thank, to praise, etc.," which introduces the *Hallel*.

Malbim explains that the Haggadah is recited in fulfillment of the verse *And you shall tell your son, saying, "It is for this that God did to me when I left Egypt"* (*Exodus*

---

1. **Reattained Pinnacle.** *Ramban* (Introduction to *Exodus*) gives expression to the ultimate definition of freedom and redemption: "For the exile was not over until the time that they would return to their place [natural habitat] and to the spiritual station of their forefathers." He explains that the redemption from Egypt did not end with the Jews' physical departure from the land of enslavement, nor was it complete even with the giving of the Ten Commandments, though the Revelation at Sinai was the stated goal of the Exodus (see *Exodus* 3:12). The Exodus achieved its ultimate purpose only when the Jews gave the experience at Sinai a permanent home by building the Tabernacle, thus regaining the spiritual heights they had temporarily achieved at the Giving of the Torah. The Tabernacle, and later the Temple in Jerusalem, were intended to be the central rallying point of the nation and the place to which every Jew would — through the vehicle of offerings — come to elevate himself spiritually and create a close relationship with God.

2. **Vicarious Joy.** We refer to the fifteen favors God granted us as being לַמָּקוֹם עָלֵינוּ, literally **to** *the Omnipresent upon us*. The term מֵהַמָּקוֹם עָלֵינוּ, **from** *the Omnipresent*, would seem more accurate.

The greatest joy a father experiences is when he witnesses the success of his children. Similarly, God rejoices when our behavior enables Him to bestow favors upon the Jewish people. Thus we now list a long series of favors that God *received* when we were the beneficiaries of His kindness! (*Kedushas Levi*).

13:8). The text follows the pattern of this verse. Thus the retelling of the story of our national birth is encapsulated in the words "you shall tell your son," while our extended praise, included in the *Dayeinu* poem, is alluded to in the word "saying," indicative of verbosity. This is then followed by Rabban Gamliel's exposition of the three commandments of the evening (*pesach*, matzah and *maror*) alluded to with the words *it is for this*, a reference to the precepts of the night. Finally we give expression to the sentiment *that God did for me* when we speak of the obligation in each generation to sense the Exodus as a personal experience. Only then, having to the best of our abilities evoked the full extent of God's beneficence, are we ready to offer praise and thanksgiving to Him.

The word מַעֲלוֹת is understood by *Abarbanel* as favors that are granted purely as signs of love and affection, and not in order to fill a need.

Malbim suggests that מַעֲלוֹת is employed in the sense of לְעַלֵּה, *to extol.* Each one of the enumerated favors is in itself sufficient cause to extol God's goodness.

In *Maharal's* view, מַעֲלוֹת means *steps*. The poem describes a spiritual progression which began with the Exodus and raised us step by step to the ultimate goal of the intimate relationship with God that was attained in the Temple. There, appearing before the Divine Presence, we were able to find constant spiritual rejuvenation and inspiration.

The climb to this spiritual peak is described here in fifteen steps represented by fifteen acts of Divine Kindness. *Ritva* sees an allusion to God's

Name יָ־הּ (*gematria* 15), while *Avudraham* views the fifteen steps as mirroring the fifteen Songs of Ascent composed by King David (*Psalms* 120-134), which correspond to the fifteen steps in the Temple, leading from the Women's Courtyard to the Courtyard of Israelites. During the *Beis HaSho'eivah* celebration on Succos, the Levites stood on those steps singing praises of God (see *Succah* 51b). The Seder, too, is conducted with fifteen steps, which are mentioned in the *Kadesh URechatz* song (see p. 11). See Haggadah *Geulas Avraham* for an exposition of how each of King David's psalms corresponds to one of the fifteen steps enumerated here.

God is referred to here as מָקוֹם, *Omnipresent*, since the fifteen favors cited here are indicative of God's constant presence and involvement in the lives of His children (*Netziv*).[1]

אֵלּוּ הוֹצִיאָנוּ מִמִּצְרַיִם וְלֹא עָשָׂה בָהֶם שְׁפָטִים — *Had He brought us out of Egypt, but not executed judgments against them it would have sufficed us* [to praise and thank Him].

The term דַּיֵּנוּ should not be understood as "that would have sufficed, and that some of the other favors were truly unnecessary." Can one fathom a Jewish people without Torah, or without the eternal gift of *Eretz Yisrael*? Rather, דַּיֵּנוּ should be rendered as *it would have been sufficient cause to praise God* (*Malbim*).[2]

---

1. **Full Moon.** The *Vilna Gaon* notes that from Abraham (to whom God foretold the exile and the redemption) until King Solomon, who built the Temple, there were fifteen generations. The fifteen-step process that culminated in the apex of our national destiny began with Abraham and ended fifteen generations later with King Solomon. Much like the moon, which is full on the fifteenth of the month, reflecting as much as possible the brilliance of the sun, so the Temple was the most powerful medium to shed the light of Godliness in the world. Noting that the Exodus occurred on the fifteenth of Nissan, *Olelos Ephraim* comments that just as the moon is then at its greatest intensity, so the newborn nation of Israel became the greatest among the nations as the mirror of the Divine light of God and Godliness.

2. **Linked Destiny.** Why is the punishment of the Egyptians listed as one of the favors God did for *us*? The dazzling display of God's powers made it crystal clear to all that He was the Redeemer. Thus, when the Jews committed the grievous sin of the Golden Calf, Moses was able to plead that God not destroy His people so that Egypt would not say that *"He took them out in order to kill them in the desert mountains and decimate them from the face of the earth"* (*Exodus* 32:12). Thus the judgments God inflicted on the Egyptians were a favor for the Jews in the sense that through these judgments the Jews could beg a stay of

Had He brought us out of Egypt,
but not executed judgments against the Egyptians,
it would have sufficed us.

The first of the fifteen favors for which we thank Hashem is the redemption from Egypt. Although this occurred chronologically after He inflicted judgments (the ten Plagues) upon the Egyptians, we mention it first since these plagues and punishments are only meaningful in the context of the subsequent redemption (*Abarbanel*).

Chukas HaPesach suggests that the *judgments* referred to are the plagues that descended upon the Egyptians at the Sea. [The two opinions, of *Abarbanel* and *Chukas HaPesach*, seem to mirror the argument regarding God's promise to Abraham that eventually He would judge the nation that oppressed his people (*Genesis* 15:44). According to *Rashi* (ibid.) this refers to the Ten plagues, while according to *Yonasan ben Uziel* it denotes the 250 plagues inflicted on the Egyptians at the Sea of Reeds.]

Even without all of the accompanying wonders, the Exodus was a life-saving miracle. As explained above, the Jews were in many ways no different from their Egyptian hosts, mired in the depths of spiritual impurity and almost without redeeming merit. God extracted them from the life-threatening "womb" of Egypt before their inception as a nation would have been aborted (*Shibolei HaLeket*). God not only redeemed them, but also severely punished their tormentors. In this way the Jews were granted a glimpse of His awesome powers and came away from the experience with a strengthened belief in Him (*Sforno*).[1]

Rashba comments that *it would have been a sufficient [fulfillment of God's obligations towards us]*, i.e., any one of these many favors would have been more than we deserve. How fortunate we are to have received so many benefits from him![2] (*Ritva*).

Although God had promised to judge our tormentors, we must thank Him for doing so since He could have punished only some of the Egyptians execution on the grounds that their death might cause a desecration of God's Name (*Maaseh Nissim*).

The *Vilna Gaon* (in *Aderes Eliyahu*) explains the allegory of *Deuteronomy* 32:11, that God acted toward the Jews in Egypt as an eagle awakens its young — first tapping on the nest lightly and slowly arousing them from their slumber. Likewise, the Jews in Egypt suffered from spiritual slumber, lulled into a complacent sleep by the spiritual impurity of Egyptian culture and by the debilitating conditions under which they lived. When Hashem wanted to wake them He "tapped on the nest" with the Ten Plagues and revealed His Divine Presence to His people in small increments. Finally, after the plagues, they were able to see His light. Thus, the plagues were a favor for the Jews in that they served as a spiritual "wake-up call" to rouse them to their destiny — to be the servants of God.

1. **Even Only One.** According to the *Alter of Kelm*, each of these fifteen Divine favors is sufficient to bring one to a vibrant faith in God. Just as Jethro was drawn to belief in God when he saw the symmetrical justice of God's drowning the Egyptians in retribution for throwing Jewish babies into the Nile (see *Rashi to Exodus* 18:11), so it would have sufficed to strengthen our faith if God had performed only one of the myriad favors He did for us.

2. **Reluctant Recipients.** Aware of his own inadequacies and how far his service of God falls short of where it should be, one feels that he will never be able to sufficiently thank God for all that He does. We express this sentiment in the *Nishmas* prayer: *Were our mouth as full of song as the sea, and our tongue as full of joyous song as its multitude of waves, and our lips as full of praise as the breadth of the heavens, and our eyes as brilliant as the sun and the moon, and our hands as outspread as eagles of the sky and our feet as swift as hinds — we still could not thank You sufficiently. . . and bless Your Name for even one of the thousand thousands and myriad myriads of favors that You performed for our ancestors and for us.*

In spite of this frustration we must resign ourselves to the will of the Beneficent God and accept His favors knowing full well that we will never be able to thank Him properly.

אִלּוּ עָשָׂה בָהֶם שְׁפָטִים וְלֹא עָשָׂה בֵאלֹהֵיהֶם דַּיֵּנוּ.

אִלּוּ עָשָׂה בֵאלֹהֵיהֶם וְלֹא הָרַג אֶת בְּכוֹרֵיהֶם דַּיֵּנוּ.

אִלּוּ הָרַג אֶת בְּכוֹרֵיהֶם וְלֹא נָתַן לָנוּ אֶת מָמוֹנָם דַּיֵּנוּ.

אִלּוּ נָתַן לָנוּ אֶת מָמוֹנָם וְלֹא קָרַע לָנוּ אֶת הַיָּם דַּיֵּנוּ.

---

rather than all of them (*Rashbam, Kol Bo, Avudraham*). *Zeroa Yemin* submits that since God in His mercy freed us before the set time, He might have forgone judging the Egyptians. Nonetheless, He did not spare them His wrath over their excessive zeal in oppressing His children.

וְלֹא עָשָׂה בֵאלֹהֵיהֶם — *But not upon their gods.* The wooden idols of the Egyptians rotted and the metal ones melted in the face of God's revelation, when He Himself passed through Egypt, slaying all the Egyptian firstborn (*Rashi* to *Exodus* 12:12).

Angels, too, are referred to as אֱלֹהִים; hence, this term can be taken as a reference to them. The heavenly forces that guide and protect the destiny of Egypt were struck in this plague, so that Egypt would be completely defenseless (*Ramban* ad loc.).

This was a favor for the Jews, because the destruction of the Egyptian gods proved that God in His love for Israel had intervened to save Israel (*Kol Bo*). Moreover, this destruction of the forces of evil served as a harbinger and example of the ultimate and total decimation of evil that will characterize the Messianic Age, as the prophet promised: *As in the days when you left Egypt I will show it wonders* (*Micah* 7:15). Everything that occurred then was symbolic of what will occur in the Final Redemption (*Maaseh Nissim*).

וְלֹא הָרַג אֶת בְּכוֹרֵיהֶם — *But not slain their firstborn.* On the night of the fifteenth of Nissan, God carried out the plague of the firstborn. Every firstborn in the land of Egypt was slain. Since the Torah does not speak only of *Egyptian* firstborn, it implies that the plague struck even the firstborn of foreigners who were *in the land of Egypt*. From *Psalms* 136:10, the Sages derive that even Egyp-

tian firstborn who were out of the country died (*Rashi*).

Even if God had not destroyed their firstborn but had only stripped them of any delusions regarding the power of their idols, it would have been sufficient cause to praise and thank God.

וְלֹא נָתַן לָנוּ אֶת מָמוֹנָם — *But not given us their wealth.* When God told Abraham of the exile his children would undergo, He promised him: *and afterwards they shall leave with great wealth* (*Genesis* 15:14). God asked Moses to make a special effort to prevail upon the Jews to request valuables from their Egyptian neighbors, because if they did not do so, the soul of Abraham would complain that God carried out in full measure the prophecy that his offspring would be oppressed, but not the accompanying promise that the Jews would leave their captivity with great wealth. To forestall this, God pleaded, as it were, with Moses to prevail upon the Jews to request valuables from the Egyptians (*Rashi* to *Exodus* 11:2).

Since during the plague of darkness the Jews were able to ascertain the location of the Egyptian wealth, the Egyptians could not deny its existence. Hence the Jews were successful in acquiring the wealth of their enemies.

The Talmud teaches that the Jews emptied Egypt of its wealth, leaving it as empty as deep water that is without fish (*Berachos* 9b). The Egyptians could not be exempted from paying reparations for the material wrongs done to victims of theft and plunder or for the wages of their erstwhile slaves. Using this argument, Geviha ben Pesisa claimed reparations from the Egyptians for the Jews, whom they had stripped of their rights and possessions (*Sanhedrin* 91a; see *Munk, Bereishis*).

Furthermore, at the Sea of Reeds Israel received even greater wealth as spoils of war. The Israelites had no need for the riches of Egypt during their

Had He executed judgments against them,
    but not upon their gods,   it would have sufficed us.
Had He executed judgments against their gods,
    but not slain their firstborn,   it would have sufficed us.
Had He slain their firstborn,
    but not given us their wealth,   it would have sufficed us.
Had He given us their wealth,
    but not split the Sea for us,   it would have sufficed us.

---

forty years in the desert. Hashem supplied them with the heavenly manna and the water from the Well of Miriam. Their clothes and shoes did not wear out.[1] It was given to them only so that they could emerge as a nation with all the prerequisites needed to dedicate themselves to God's service. They were granted great wealth at a time when they had no material needs so that they might realize that the true function of wealth is as a tool for the discharge of one's earthly mission and not as a means to attain creature comforts (*Zekan Aharon*).[2]

וְלֹא קָרַע לָנוּ אֶת הַיָּם — *But not split the Sea for us.* On the night of the seventh day of Pesach the Egyptians caught up to the escaping Jews. Caught between the pursuing Egyptians and the Sea, the Jews were terrified. God commanded Moses to stretch out his hand and cause the Sea to split.

According to *R' Bachya* and *Sforno*, the Sea split as soon as Moses stretched out his hand; then the east wind dried the seabed so that the Jews could walk across in comfort.

The Jews had to prove their faith by plunging into the water before it split. Nachshon ben Aminadav, later the leader of the tribe of Judah, was the first to obey Moses' command; he walked forward until the water was up to his nose — then the Sea split (*Shemos Rabbah* 21:9).

The episode at the Sea occurred so that Jews could openly witness the glory of God as He demonstrated conclusively, both to them and to the world at large, that He is Master of all. When the wicked are punished, God is glorified. Thus the Sages (*Mechilta Beshalach*) teach that a simple maidservant witnessed a revelation of God's glory at the Sea that even the great prophet Ezekiel never experienced.

---

1. **Money Well Spent.** The riches of Egypt served the Jews well at a later date. They used those riches as ransom when threatened by Shishak, king of Egypt (see *I Kings* 14:25-26), and Zerach, the king of Kush (see *Pesachim* 119a). King David alluded to this future ransom, saying, *A song of ascents, by David. Had not HASHEM been with us. . . when men rose up against us, then they would have swallowed us alive. . . . Blessed is HASHEM, Who did not present us as prey for their teeth (Psalms* 124:1-6). They consumed our riches, and spared us.

2. **Not for the Price of Money.** There are many instances in life when all the material wealth in the world is worthless. One suffering from an incurable disease would pay all the money in the world to treat his malady, but he will not be able to buy life. Likewise, one may be blessed with seemingly endless resources and yet not be able to "buy" *nachas* from his children.

The Jewish people learned this lesson when they left Egypt and the sea with enormous riches, yet just a short while later they came to Marah and could not drink the bitter waters there. Close to death by thirst, their money was useless in procuring drinkable water. Only when Moses prayed and God instructed him to throw a branch into the water did it turn sweet.

Had God slain the firstborn and not given us their riches it would have been enough, for money *cannot* buy everything! (*Chochmah U'Mussar*).

אִלּוּ קָרַע לָנוּ אֶת הַיָּם

וְלֹא הֶעֱבִירָנוּ בְתוֹכוֹ בֶּחָרָבָה דַּיֵּנוּ.

אִלּוּ הֶעֱבִירָנוּ בְתוֹכוֹ בֶּחָרָבָה

וְלֹא שִׁקַּע צָרֵינוּ בְּתוֹכוֹ דַּיֵּנוּ.

אִלּוּ שִׁקַּע צָרֵינוּ בְּתוֹכוֹ

וְלֹא סִפֵּק צָרְכֵּנוּ בַּמִּדְבָּר אַרְבָּעִים שָׁנָה דַּיֵּנוּ.

אִלּוּ סִפֵּק צָרְכֵּנוּ בַּמִּדְבָּר אַרְבָּעִים שָׁנָה

וְלֹא הֶאֱכִילָנוּ אֶת הַמָּן דַּיֵּנוּ.

וְלֹא הֶעֱבִירָנוּ בְתוֹכוֹ בֶּחָרָבָה — *But not led us through it on dry land.* The path that the Jews took through the Sea did not lead them across it from one bank to the other. They traveled in a bow-shaped arc and emerged on the same bank from which they entered (see *Tosafos, Arachin* 15a; *Rambam* to *Avos* 5:4). Why then did Hashem take them through the Sea? First, to lure the Egyptians into the Sea to give them their just due. Second, to demonstrate His greatness by performing miracles. While Hashem could have split the Sea and let the Jews cross the muddy seabed, this would have been an arduous trek. Instead, He brought a strong east wind to blow throughout the night, to dry the seabed and make it easy to walk on. At the same time, He leveled the seabed, flattening its hills and filling its canyons. It is with regard to this manifestation of Hashem's concern for the welfare of His people that we say *it would have sufficed* (*Abarbanel, Aruch HaShulchan*).

וְלֹא שִׁקַּע צָרֵינוּ בְּתוֹכוֹ — *But not drowned our oppressors in it.* In a historic demonstration of how human beings can refuse to see the truth, the Egyptian survivors of the ten plagues refused to realize that a sea that had never before split had been manipulated by God to save His people. The pillars of fire and cloud made no impression on them; they saw what they wanted to see and believed what they wanted to believe. So they saw a vulnerable nation of slaves, *their* slaves, and they

plunged after them into the newly vacated seabed. Then, *Hashem looked down* [a term that implies anger] *at the camp of Egypt* (*Exodus* 14:24) and poured out His wrath. The Egyptian debacle began with an incredible, confounding meteorological phenomenon, and then the hardened seabed turned hot and muddy. As the Psalmist expressed it: *Clouds streamed water, heavens sounded forth, even your arrows* [*of lightning*] *sounded forth. The rumbling of your thunder was in the rolling wind, lightning bolts lit the world, the earth trembled and roared* (*Psalms* 77:18-19).

Finally, when the entire Egyptian force was in the Sea, the walls of congealed water collapsed upon them and Egypt as a world power exited the stage of history. Thus not only in a physical sense but even in a metaphysical sense the guardian angel of Egypt was destroyed along with his nation (*R' Nosson Scherman*).

God could have very well allowed the Jews to pass through the Sea and then prevented the Egyptians from pursuing them (*Rashbam*). Instead He allowed Pharaoh to realize that the Jews were not coming back, and strengthened his heart so as to overcome his terror at standing in their way. God coaxed Pharaoh into such insanity in order to remove the influence of the Egyptian culture from the Jews.

וְלֹא סִפֵּק צָרְכֵּנוּ בַּמִּדְבָּר אַרְבָּעִים שָׁנָה — *But not provided for our needs in the desert for forty years.*

Had He split the Sea for us,
   but not led us through it on dry land,
                                    it would have sufficed us.

Had He let us through it on dry land,
   but not drowned our oppressors in it,
                                    it would have sufficed us.

Had He drowned our oppressors in it,
   but not provided for our needs in the desert for forty years,
                                    it would have sufficed us.

Had He provided for our needs in the desert for forty years,
   but not fed us the manna,   it would have sufficed us.

Though they had money to purchase food from the nations whose borders they passed and were able to have meat from the animals they took with them, God's generosity made all this unnecessary (*Avudraham, Rashbam, Kol Bo*). Had God taken them through Philistine territory, they might have found "natural" sources of food there (*Shibbolei HaLeket*). Nonetheless, God provided His people with all their needs during their forty-year sojourn in the desert. Food, drink, clothes, shelter, even shoes that didn't wear out were all miraculously provided to them allowing them to lead a worry-free life dedicated to the service of God.[1]

וְלֹא הֶאֱכִילָנוּ אֶת הַמָּן — *But not fed us the manna.* Rather than miraculously providing us with natural bread in an arid desert where nothing could grow, God gave us the supernatural manna which our Sages call "the food of angels" (*Yoma* 75b). It was of a totally spiritual nature; one did not need to expend any effort in preparing it and yet it had whatever taste one wished it to have.[2]

There were eight miraculous aspects of the manna. (1) It was created out of thin air. (2) It was a miracle that lasted for forty years, the longest of any of the miracles mentioned in Scripture. (3) No matter how much manna one gathered, he ended

---

1. **Caring Father.** *Netziv* sees this as a lesson in survival for the long, foreboding exile. When God decreed in the wake of the debacle of the spies (*Numbers* 14) that Jews would spend forty years in the desert, the people must have been sure they could not survive, yet God provided for them at every step. Likewise, let us be strengthened as we go through the exile and never despair of survival. Our loving Father in Heaven will always take care of us.

2. **Angel Food.** One's food has a profound spiritual effect. The Sages teach that consumption of non-kosher food deadens one's spiritual capacities and denies him the full opportunity to attain sanctity. For this reason *Rema* (*Yoreh Deah* 81:7) cautions that even small children, who bear no halachic responsibility for their actions, should still be prevented from eating forbidden foods, lest their spiritual potential be impaired. *Sefer HaChinuch* notes that the harm caused by non-kosher food is not physical, but rather it impedes the heart from attaining the higher values of the soul.

In this light we may understand the spiritual gain of having received the *manna* as our food. As a result of being nurtured on the food of angels, the Jews were able to attain a level of purity that prepared them to receive the Torah. Having imbibed angelic food, human beings were able to declare נַעֲשֶׂה וְנִשְׁמַע, *we will do and we will obey.* According to the Talmud (*Shabbos* 88a), this unquestionable submissiveness to God's will is typical of angels.

Accordingly, *Mechilta* (*Beshalach* 17) teaches that the Torah was specifically given to the generation that ate manna (based on *Maaseh Nissim*).

אִלּוּ הֶאֱכִילָנוּ אֶת הַמָּן וְלֹא נָתַן לָנוּ אֶת הַשַּׁבָּת דַּיֵּנוּ.

אִלּוּ נָתַן לָנוּ אֶת הַשַּׁבָּת וְלֹא קֵרְבָנוּ לִפְנֵי הַר סִינַי דַּיֵּנוּ.

אִלּוּ קֵרְבָנוּ לִפְנֵי הַר סִינַי וְלֹא נָתַן לָנוּ אֶת הַתּוֹרָה דַּיֵּנוּ.

אִלּוּ נָתַן לָנוּ אֶת הַתּוֹרָה
וְלֹא הִכְנִיסָנוּ לְאֶרֶץ יִשְׂרָאֵל דַּיֵּנוּ.

up with the same quantity — one *omer*. (4) If any of it was left over until morning, it became rotten and wormy. (5) On Friday, however, the leftover manna remained fresh for the Sabbath. (6) It did not come down on the Sabbath. (7) It stopped coming down when they reached inhabited land. (8) A jar of it was stored in the Tabernacle (and later the Temple) and lasted for generations (*Abarbanel*).

וְלֹא נָתַן לָנוּ אֶת הַשַּׁבָּת — *But not given us the Sabbath.* The Talmud describes the Sabbath as a special gift that God took from His treasure house to give to His people (*Shabbos* 10b). Not only did God provide us with spiritual manna, He even allowed us the Sabbath, which is a sample taste of the World to Come (*Shibbolei HaLeket*).

The gift of the Sabbath is listed separately from and before the gift of Torah, because Jews were commanded regarding it at Marah before the Revelation at Sinai (*Machzor Vitry*).[1]

וְלֹא קֵרְבָנוּ לִפְנֵי הַר סִינַי — *But not brought us near Him at Mount Sinai.* Were God to have given us the entire Torah, as He gave us the Sabbath, at Marah — namely, through Moses rather than directly — it would have been an awesome favor. Instead, in His great love for us, he brought us to Mount Sinai and

allowed us to hear the Ten Commandments directly from Him (*Aruch HaShulchan*).

אִלּוּ קֵרְבָנוּ לִפְנֵי הַר סִינַי וְלֹא נָתַן לָנוּ אֶת הַתּוֹרָה דַּיֵּנוּ — *Had He brought us before Mount Sinai, but not given us the Torah, it would have sufficed us.* The Sinaitic Revelation has a value that goes beyond the specific content of what God taught us at that historical moment. The Sages taught that at Sinai the Jewish nation was purged of the spiritual impurity which mankind suffered since the time of Adam's sin. This was in and of itself a significant spiritual milestone (*Avudraham, Machzor Vitry, Alshich*). *Rashbatz* adds that the awesomeness of the Sinai episode with its thunder and lightning and powerful shofar blasts instilled in the Jewish people a palpable fear of Heaven, *for in order to elevate you has God come, so that awe of Him shall be upon your faces so that you shall not sin* (*Exodus* 20:17). This fear of Heaven and sense of being ashamed to flout God's will became an integral part of the Jewish psyche. The Sages say of one who lacks a healthy sense of shame that his forefathers were probably not present at Mount Sinai (see *Nedarim* 20a).[2] Furthermore, it was at Sinai that God opened the heavens above and the nether regions

1. **A Taste of Shabbos.** Jews received the gift of the Sabbath before Sinai so that they would experience the "extra soul" (heightened spiritual sensitivity) of the day and thus develop an appetite for receiving the Torah, which embodies this elevated spirituality (*Siduro Shel Shabbos*). This is the import of what we say in our Sabbath prayers: *Those who taste it merit life.* One who truly experiences the Sabbath will be ignited with a passion for Torah, the true essence of life.

2. **Spiritual Thermos.** According to R' Yerucham Levovitz (*Mashgiach* of the Mirrer Yeshivah), the purpose of our receiving the Torah was in order that we maintain the level of reverence for God and spirituality that we attained as a nation at Sinai. Much like a thermos bottle that maintains the heat of boiling water, so our spiritual level was brought to boil at Sinai — we now must learn and practice Torah to keep our souls figuratively "piping hot."

Had He fed us the manna, but not given us the Sabbath,
it would have sufficed us.

Had He given us the Sabbath,
but not brought us near Him at Mount Sinai,
it would have sufficed us.

Had He brought us before Mount Sinai,
but not given us the Torah,   it would have sufficed us.

Had He given us the Torah,
but not brought us into the Land of Israel,
it would have sufficed us.

---

below so that it would be clear to every Jew that there is only the One God (*Rashi* to *Deuteronomy* 4:35). *Abarbanel* suggests that we might have been given a minimal amount of commandments at Sinai, yet God gave us the Torah with its full complement of commandments and ways to come close to Him.[1]

Ksav Sofer and *R' Shimon of Amshinov* offer a novel interpretation. At Sinai the Jews achieved an almost unparalleled sense of unity and brotherly love among themselves. The Sages (see *Rashi* to *Exodus* 19:2) teach that they were like one man with one united heart. In reaching this spiritual pinnacle they captured the message of the Torah, for, as Hillel told a potential proselyte who wanted to learn the entire Torah at once, "Whatever is hateful to you, do not do to your neighbor; this is the essence of Torah — all the rest is commentary." Thus, even if God had not spelled out the details of Torah we would have been able, by our united presence at Mount Sinai, to absorb the essential message of Torah.[2]

The key phrase, according to *Aruch HaShulchan*, is "not given *us* the Torah." Had God given us only the Written Law, it would have remained a closed book without the oral tradition. Therefore He implanted within His people the principles, ability and wisdom to interpret the nuances of the Written Text and apply its words to life situations as they unfold. In this sense the Oral Law is likened to a tree that is *implanted . . . within us*. Just as a tree, once planted, has the capacity to grow and produce fruit and the seeds for more trees, so the Oral Law enables those who study it to elucidate the Written Law and produce ever more wisdom and applications, all emanating from the same roots.

וְלֹא הִכְנִיסָנוּ לְאֶרֶץ יִשְׂרָאֵל — *But not brought us into the Land of Israel.* Had God given us the Torah without the gift of His Land we might have fulfilled the commandments dependent on the Land

---

1. **Almost Unlimited Opportunities.** "R' Chananiah ben Akashiah says: The Holy One, Blessed is He, wished to confer merit upon Israel; therefore He gave them Torah and *mitzvos* in abundance" (*Makkos* 22b).

God gave us much Torah and many *mitzvos* so that we could have the means to achieve perfection and go beyond the grasp of evil (*Meiri*).

Alternatively, the "abundance" refers to the fact that Israel would receive much reward for the performance of the commandments. God gave us many opportunities to merit this reward by issuing commandments about most life-situations; man is thus never left without a *mitzvah* opportunity (*Yarim Moshe*).

2. **Sinaitic Modesty.** Humility is the key to Torah. Moses, the most humble of all men, was the fitting conduit to bring the Torah to the Jewish people. The Talmud (*Megillah* 29a) defines the choice of Mount Sinai as the venue for giving the Torah as related to its lowly stature, symbolizing humility.

Had God but brought us there, we would have absorbed its message of modesty, thus enabling us to perceive the light of Torah (*R' Moshe Leib of Sassov*).

אִלּוּ הִכְנִיסָנוּ לְאֶרֶץ יִשְׂרָאֵל
וְלֹא בָנָה לָנוּ אֶת בֵּית הַבְּחִירָה דַּיֵּנוּ.

עַל אַחַת כַּמָּה, וְכַמָּה טוֹבָה כְפוּלָה וּמְכֻפֶּלֶת לַמָּקוֹם עָלֵינוּ. שֶׁהוֹצִיאָנוּ מִמִּצְרַיִם, וְעָשָׂה בָהֶם שְׁפָטִים, וְעָשָׂה בֵאלֹהֵיהֶם, וְהָרַג אֶת בְּכוֹרֵיהֶם, וְנָתַן לָנוּ אֶת מָמוֹנָם, וְקָרַע לָנוּ אֶת הַיָּם, וְהֶעֱבִירָנוּ בְתוֹכוֹ בֶּחָרָבָה, וְשִׁקַּע צָרֵינוּ בְּתוֹכוֹ, וְסִפֵּק צָרְכֵּנוּ בַּמִּדְבָּר אַרְבָּעִים שָׁנָה, וְהֶאֱכִילָנוּ אֶת הַמָּן, וְנָתַן לָנוּ אֶת הַשַּׁבָּת, וְקֵרְבָנוּ לִפְנֵי הַר סִינַי, וְנָתַן לָנוּ אֶת הַתּוֹרָה, וְהִכְנִיסָנוּ לְאֶרֶץ יִשְׂרָאֵל, וּבָנָה לָנוּ אֶת בֵּית הַבְּחִירָה, לְכַפֵּר עַל כָּל עֲוֹנוֹתֵינוּ.

---

vicariously, by means of study. Just as one who studies the laws regarding sacrifices is deemed to have offered the sacrifice (see *Menachos* 110a), so it is with all *mitzvos*: Studying the laws of a *mitzvah* is, to some extent, its fulfillment (*Kol Dodi*). According to *Ramban*, there is a dimension to fulfilling commandments in *Eretz Yisrael* (even *mitzvos* that are not dependent on the Land) that is inaccessible outside the Land (see *Ramban* to *Leviticus* 18:26).[1] *Eretz Yisrael* is the land where the "eyes" of Hashem always rest (see *Deuteronomy* 11:12). Though God oversees the entire world, His principal attention is focused on the Land. Thus, bringing us to *Eretz Yisrael* gave us yet another opportunity to connect to Him, as we experience His constant love and care (*Netziv*). Furthermore, even though one can study Torah anywhere, the Sages teach that "there is no Torah like the Torah of *Eretz Yisrael*" (*Sifre, Ekev*). Had God given us the Torah and not brought us to *Eretz Yisrael*, we might have learned and understood it Torah, but not on the level that is attainable only in *Eretz Yisrael*. [2]

This is evidenced by the fact that the Great Sanhedrin, the Supreme religious court of Israel, could be constituted only in *Eretz Yisrael*.

וְלֹא בָנָה לָנוּ אֶת בֵּית הַבְּחִירָה — *But not built the Temple for us.* The final favor God granted His People was the building of the *Beis HaMikdash*, which gave the Divine Presence a permanent home. Both the Tabernacle in the Wilderness and later the Temple in Jerusalem served as places for Jews to gain atonement for their sins and to spiritually recharge their energies. The Midrash (*Bamidbar Rabbah* 21:19) states that the morning sacrifice atoned for sins committed during the previous

---

15. **Transitory Temples.** The Talmud (*Megillah* 29a) teaches that in the Messianic Age God will move all synagogues and houses of study from the lands of exile to the Land of Israel. *Chasam Sofer* infers from this that synagogues and houses of study, even those in the Diaspora, are sanctified with the level of sanctification of *Eretz Yisrael*. Accordingly we might interpret this stich of the Haggadah as, "even had we only received the Torah and not been brought to *Eretz Yisrael*, we could recreate its sanctity by studying Torah in exile."

16. **Soul Breath.** R' Yehudah HaLevi in his famous elegy צִיּוֹן הֲלֹא תִשְׁאֲלִי (*Kinnos of Tishah B'Av*) refers to Eretz Yisrael as חַיֵּי נְשָׁמוֹת אֲוִיר אַרְצֵךְ, *the atmosphere of Your Land is the life of souls*. The added spiritual dimension of *Eretz Yisrael* adds immeasurably to one's ability to actualize the potential of his soul.

Had he brought us into the Land of Israel,
　　but not built the Temple for us,　　　it would have sufficed us.

Thus, how much more so should we be grateful to the Omnipresent a double and compounded favor that the Omnipresent has in store for us: He brought us out of Egypt; executed judgments upon them and against their gods; slew their firstborn; gave us their wealth; split the Sea for us; led us through it on dry land; drowned our oppressors in it; provided for our needs in the desert for forty years; fed us the manna; gave us the Sabbath; brought us before Mount Sinai; gave us the Torah; brought us to the Land of Israel; and built us the Temple to atone for all our sins.

---

night, while the daytime offering cleansed one of any sins done during the day. Thus no one ever lay down to sleep at night with the albatross of sin around his neck. Had God only brought us into the Land and not built us a Temple, the Land itself might have brought atonement, as *Sifre* (see *Deuteronomy* 32:43) teaches, those who live in the Holy Land are assured the opportunity of forgiveness by virtue of the quality that this Land has to be an instrument of forgiveness, an "Altar of earth" (see *Exodus* 29:21).

עַל אַחַת כַּמָּה וְכַמָּה — *Thus, how much more so. . .* Having listed all the fifteen favors which God granted us, we now acknowledge that since each of them is in itself sufficient cause to praise God, certainly the compound effect of all fifteen obligates us to show a tremendous outpouring of gratitude (*Malbim*).

The aggregate effect of many spiritual favors produces a spiritual level greater than the sum total of the individual favors. Hence our obligation to be thankful

increases exponentially with each of the favors (*Aruch HaShulchan*).

According to *Maasei Nissim*, the favors that God granted us were meant as a harbinger of the great and miraculous redemption that awaits us with the coming of the Messiah. Thus the fifteen favors are טוֹבָה כְפוּלָה וּמְכֻפֶּלֶת, *a double and compounded favor* לַמָּקוֹם עָלֵינוּ —, *that the Omnipresent has in store for us.*

וּבָנָה לָנוּ אֶת בֵּית הַבְּחִירָה לְכַפֵּר עַל כָּל עֲוֹנוֹתֵינוּ — *And built us the Temple to atone for all our sins.* Although God had granted us a Tabernacle in the Wilderness, it was a special favor that we were able to build a more permanent abode for His Presence, in Jerusalem.

In allowing the enemy to destroy the Temple, the Midrash tells us, God vented His wrath over the sins of His people on sticks and stones rather than destroying the sinners. Thus, the Temple provided God with a vehicle to atone for all of our sins (*Yaavetz*).[1]

---

1. **Uprighting the Fallen.** If a person slips and falls while walking on a dark night, it is inappropriate to blame him for his predicament. However, one who falls in broad daylight might legitimately be derided, because he should have been careful to watch where he was going. The same idea may be applied on a spiritual plane. After being granted the Torah, the ultimate source of spiritual illumination, after being allowed to breathe the enlightening and inspiring air of *Eretz Yisrael*, after being given the opportunity to create a venue where God's Presence is always accessible — we are like people who bask in the warmth and light of the midday sun. For us to rebel and ignore the will of God despite all this should be considered an unpardonable crime — nevertheless, God in His infinite kindness, allowed us *to build the Temple to atone for all our sins* (*Yismach Yisrael*).

רַבָּן גַּמְלִיאֵל הָיָה אוֹמֵר. כָּל שֶׁלֹּא אָמַר שְׁלֹשָׁה דְבָרִים אֵלּוּ בַּפֶּסַח, לֹא יָצָא יְדֵי חוֹבָתוֹ, וְאֵלּוּ הֵן,

פֶּסַח. מַצָּה. וּמָרוֹר.

Sin creates a barrier between man and God, obstructing man's ability to see the reality of God's Presence and His constant involvement in man's life. Only when man is freed of the albatross of sin is his spiritual vision restored. In the words of King David, *For with You is forgiveness, that You may be feared* (Psalms 130:4). While the fifteen favors listed here provide man with clear faith in God and His Providence, the presence of sin in one's life may distort his perception of this reality. Thus God provided us with the Temple where, through the sacrificial offerings, we could attain forgiveness and thus regain our spiritual "eyes."[1]

רַבָּן גַּמְלִיאֵל הָיָה אוֹמֵר — *Rabban Gamliel used to say.* Rashbatz identifies the author of this statement as Rabban Gamliel II, who succeeded R' Yochanan ben Zakkai as the *Nasi* (president of the Sanhedrin), at Yavneh. The phrase "the *pesach* offering that our ancestors ate *at the time when the Temple was standing*" clearly indicates that this law was taught after the destruction of the Temple, but the first Rabban Gamliel lived before the destruction.

Chida suggests that this phrase was a later addition to the Haggadah text, since it does not appear in the Mishnah's version. (See *Rambam, Hil. Chametz U'Matzah* 7:5 and *Rambam*, Haggadah text.) Accordingly, this may be the ruling of Rabban Gamliel I, who lived during the Temple era, but the wording was formulated after the destruction.

The term הָיָה אוֹמֵר carries the connotation of *was wont to say.* Rabban Gamliel would reiterate this point every year at his Seder, and we are enjoined to follow in his footsteps (*Maasei Hashem,* see *Rav* to *Avos* 1:2).

כָּל שֶׁלֹּא אָמַר שְׁלֹשָׁה דְבָרִים אֵלּוּ בַּפֶּסַח לֹא יָצָא יְדֵי חוֹבָתוֹ — *Whoever has not explained the following three things on Pesach has not fulfilled his duty.* One must explain and elucidate the meaning and reasons for these three commandments in order to fulfill his obligation to tell about the Exodus at the Seder (*Rashbam* to *Pesachim* 116a). This is a minimal obligation, even for those who, due to ignorance, are unable to read the Haggadah. Whoever does have the ability to do so must of course recite the entire text of the Haggadah (*Chukas HaPesach* quoting *Baal HaMinhagos*). According to *Ran* (*Pesachim* ibid.), the discussion of these three *mitzvos* is necessary in order to *properly* fulfill one's obligation; however, one fulfills the basic of the Seder even without it.

At this point the framework of the Haggadah's story comes full circle. It began with concrete actions — the breaking of the matzah, the noting of four unusual actions in the Four Questions, and so on — and then went on to the narrative. Now that the whole story of the Exodus has been told, the Haggadah closes its discussion by returning to explain the concrete actions mandated by the Torah on this night — the eating of the *pesach* offering, matzah and *maror*.

The commentators disagree regarding *which* obligation is not fulfilled without these words of explanation. Most commentators (*Meiri, Raavan*, et al.) view this as referring to the obligation to retell the story of the Exodus.

---

1. **Breaking the Barrier.** When a person commits a sin he has not merely become guilty in a legal sense; he has also erected a barrier between himself and God. This obstruction makes the sinner less aware of God's Presence and diminishes his awe of the Master of the Universe. Hence, when God forgives the sinner, He does more than wipe away his guilt. Divine pardon means that the barriers that separated the sinner from God are removed. Then the penitent is blessed with a new awareness of God, so that he can fear Him with heightened intensity (*Noam Megadim*).

Rabban Gamliel used to say: Whoever has not explained the following three things on Pesach has not fulfilled his duty, namely:

Pesach — the Passover Offering;
Matzah — the Unleavened Bread;
Maror — the Bitter Herbs.

According to many opinions, these explanations are the conclusion of our answer to the Four Questions. We answer the first question by explaining the significance of matzah, the second question by shedding light on the import of *maror*, and we provide enlightenment regarding the expressions of freedom (dipping and reclining) that we practice this night by expounding on the meaning of the *pesach* offering and the miraculous historic events that it alludes to.

A different approach is taken by *Orchos Chaim, Avudraham* and others. They explain that Rabban Gamliel teaches that the commandments of *pesach*, matzah and *maror* themselves that are not properly fulfilled without explaining their respective symbolic significance.

Generally, when performing a *mitzvah*, one need merely be aware that with his action he is fulfilling the will of God, and he need not concentrate on the meaning or purpose of the commandment. Here, however, the Torah states specifically: *You shall say it is a pesach offering to* HASHEM, *Who passed over the houses of the Children of Israel in Egypt, but He saved our households* (*Exodus* 12:27). Thus, the offering and its adjunct *mitzvos* (matzah and *maror* — see *Numbers* 9:11) must be explained as part of their fulfillment.

Malbim offers another approach. The requirement to have *pesach*, matzah and *maror* before us during the Haggadah is conveyed to us by the verse בַּעֲבוּר זֶה עָשָׂה ה׳ לִי, *Because of this,* HASHEM *did for me* (*Exodus* 13:8). The expression בַּעֲבוּר זֶה, *because of* **this,** would seem to indicate that not only are we to have the *pesach*, matzah and *maror* before us, but we have to explain their symbolism as well.[1]

פֶּסַח מַצָּה וּמָרוֹר — *Pesach, matzah and maror.* These three commandments seem to be out of chronological order, since the events commemorated by *maror* (bitter oppression) preceded those commemorated by *pesach* (protection from the plague of the firstborn) and matzah (liberation). In terms of their order of consumption, as well, *pesach* should have been mentioned last, for the *pesach* lamb was always eaten at the end of the meal. Why, then, is it mentioned first here?

Abarbanel answers that Rabban Gamliel is fol-

---

1. **Quantifying the Spirit.** The Seder is built around the commandments that marked that first Pesach night in Egypt — the *pesach* offering, matzah and *maror*. It would have been possible to envision a celebration based only on a recital of events; however, הָאָדָם נִפְעָל כְּפִי פְּעוּלוֹתָיו, *a man is molded according to his actions,* rather than by ideas, philosophical speculation and ideology (*Sefer HaChinuch*). For Pesach to be meaningful, therefore, there must be concrete action. In turn, it is through his readiness to act that the Jew "earns" his liberation. Now as then, therefore, these practical commandments form the center of Pesach observance.

Furthermore, as the Mishnah teaches, "Anyone whose good deeds exceed his wisdom will see his wisdom endure" (*Avos* 3:12). Only if one's learning results in increased good deeds is his wisdom of eternal value. For this reason, Judaism has been described as a faith that expresses itself in action.

The *mitzvah* of tefillin is symbolic of this concept. One places the tefillin first on the hand and then on the head; and when he removes them, the tefillin on the hand remain in place until those of the head are taken off. Thus, the head tefillin, representing wisdom, are never worn without the hand tefillin, representing action. Ideas and wisdom are most valuable if they are accompanied by action.

פֶּסַח שֶׁהָיוּ אֲבוֹתֵינוּ אוֹכְלִים בִּזְמַן שֶׁבֵּית הַמִּקְדָּשׁ הָיָה קַיָּם, עַל שׁוּם מָה? עַל שׁוּם שֶׁפָּסַח הַקָּדוֹשׁ בָּרוּךְ הוּא עַל בָּתֵּי אֲבוֹתֵינוּ בְּמִצְרָיִם. שֶׁנֶּאֱמַר, וַאֲמַרְתֶּם, זֶבַח פֶּסַח הוּא לַיהוה, אֲשֶׁר פָּסַח עַל בָּתֵּי בְנֵי יִשְׂרָאֵל בְּמִצְרַיִם בְּנָגְפּוֹ אֶת מִצְרַיִם, וְאֶת בָּתֵּינוּ הִצִּיל, וַיִּקֹּד הָעָם וַיִּשְׁתַּחֲווּ.[1]

lowing the order of the Torah in *Exodus* 12:8, which mentions the three commandments in this order. Furthermore, the *pesach* offering is of greater halachic significance than the other two *mitzvos*, as evidenced by the fact that it is one of the only two positive commandments in the Torah whose transgression incurs the punishment of *kares*, i.e, spiritual excision and premature death (the other such commandment is circumcision).[1]

Maharal explains that matzah is mentioned before *maror* because it is a Biblically commanded precept even in the absence of the Temple, when the *pesach* offering cannot be brought. Regarding *maror*, however, the Torah commands that it be eaten together with the *pesach* offering; nowadays, therefore, the obligation to eat *maror* is of Rabbinic origin (see *Pesachim* 115a).

In a homiletic vein, this order comes to teach that even after one's situation improves he should never forget the bitterness and pain of days gone by. Only through remembering one's terrible or-deal of the past is one assured of constantly thanking God for His deliverance (*Maayanah Shel Torah*). Furthermore, it is only out of a perspective of freedom that one can fully appreciate the ramifications of having been released from the misery of his former existence. Only then can one realize how indebted he is to his Redeemer (*Beis HaLevi*). Finally, according to *Sfas Emes*, the order (*maror* after matzah) enlightens us to the realization that, viewed in retrospect, the bitterness itself was part of the redemption process. During the exile and enslavement, the physical and spiritual misery seemed to be nothing more than senseless oppression on the part of the cruel Egyptians. In hindsight, our forefathers understood that it was just this bitter atmosphere that caused them to cry out to God to help us regain our spiritual identity. Thus, we speak first of the matzah, for it is only in the context of the newfound freedom that we recognize the oppression signified by the *maror* is also an ingredient in the liberation.[2]

1. **Initiation Rites.** The commentators note that the blood of the *pesach* offering and the blood of circumcision served as the merit to bring about the redemption, and hence the birth, of the Jewish nation. Anyone who willingly refrains from these two rites of passage, therefore, severs his connection to His people by incurring the *kares* penalty, which the Torah refers to as "being cut off from one's people."

2. **Light From Dark.** R' Yonah (*Shaarei Teshuvah* 2:5) speaks of the special loftiness born of spiritual downtroddenness. It is fitting for one who truly trusts in God to hope, in the gloom of his anguish, that his darkness will result in a corresponding light, as it is written, *Do not rejoice over me, my enemy; though I fell, I will rise! Though I sit in the darkness, HASHEM is a light unto me!* (Micah 7:8). Our Sages commented: "If I had not fallen, I would never have risen; if I had not dwelled in darkness, He would have never been a light for me" (*Midrash Tehillim,* Psalm 22).

Noting the rule that "the reward [for a *mitzvah*] is in proportion to the exertion" (*Avos* 5:26), R' Yisrael Salanter comments that one who commits transgressions that could be easily avoided deserves a more severe punishment than one who is ensnared by a powerful desire to sin. Conversely, a *mitzvah* performed under trying conditions is of much greater significance than one performed when optimal conditions exist. The terrible ordeal of the Egyptian exile created a situation in which even the few and imperfect virtues and

Pesach — Why did our ancestors eat the *pesach* offering at the time when the Temple was standing? Because the Holy One, Blessed is He, passed over the houses of our fathers in Egypt, as it is stated: "You shall say: It is a *pesach* offering for HASHEM, Who passed over the houses of the Children of Israel in Egypt when He struck the Egyptians, and spared our houses." And [upon hearing this] the people bowed down and prostrated themselves."[1]

---

(1) *Exodus* 12:27.

פֶּסַח וכו׳ עַל שׁוּם מָה — *Why ... the "pesach" offering?* Since this discussion is part of the *mitzvah* of relating the story of our national birth — which the Torah expresses in the form of a child questioning his parent — we express it in question-and-answer form (*R' Yitzchak Hutner*).

Although we no longer are able to bring the *pesach* offering, we mention it in the Haggadah as an implied prayer that we be granted the Messianic restoration of the Temple rites (*Chodesh HaAviv*). Furthermore, by discussing the *pesach* we may be considered, in some fashion, to have offered it, in the spirit of the prophecy *Let our lips be a substitute for bulls* (*Hosea* 14:2).

עַל שׁוּם שֶׁפָּסַח הַקָּדוֹשׁ בָּרוּךְ הוּא עַל בָּתֵּי אֲבוֹתֵינוּ בְּמִצְרָיִם — *Because the Holy One, Blessed is He, passed over the houses of our fathers in Egypt.* At the fateful moment of midnight, when God passed through Egypt slaying the Egyptian firstborn, He simultaneously freed Israel and brought it into existence as a nation. As we say in the morning *Shacharis* prayer, "All their firstborn You slew, but Your firstborn (i.e., Israel) You redeemed."

Rashi (*Exodus* 12:27) offers two possible translations of פָּסַח: either *passed over* or *pitied*.

The freedom was both spiritual — being severed from the spiritually impure womb of Egyptian culture, morals and values — and physical —

being saved from the deathblow dealt the Egyptian firstborn. The blood of the *pesach* offering was spread on the doorposts of Jewish homes as a sign of their faith in God and as a statement renouncing any belief at all in the pagan gods of Egypt, of which the sheep, an Egyptian idol, was the prime example. In response to this show of faith and allegiance, God performed the miracle of skipping over Jewish homes during that terrifying night. Thus, every *pesach* offering, reminiscent of the original one sacrificed in Egypt, reminds us of the degree of faith we attained and its miraculous results (*Maasei Nissim*).

The *pesach* offering, which triggered the final stage of our Exodus, bears the message of Israel's new freedom and dignity. This new status is reflected in the fact that they were not permitted to eat it in the manner of poor, starving slaves who would break its bones or boil its meat to get every last bit of marrow or taste out of it (see *Exodus* 12:9,46), or save it up for another day, or take it with them wherever they went (*Sefer HaChinuch*).

וְאֶת בָּתֵּינוּ הִצִּיל — *And spared our houses.* Why does the Torah demand such a great acknowledgment of gratitude to God for having "passed over our houses"? After all, the Jews were not the target of the plague in the first place; it was intended to be a punishment for the Egyptians' wickedness

---

mitzvos that the Jews were able to accomplish were of inestimable value, as the Torah says, *Their moaning rose up to God from the labor* (*Exodus* 2:23).

For this reason we eat *maror* after matzah, since the *maror* of our existence was inseparable from the freedom symbolized by matzah.

The middle *matzah* is lifted and displayed while the following paragraph is recited.

מַצָּה זוֹ שֶׁאָנוּ אוֹכְלִים, עַל שׁוּם מָה? עַל שׁוּם שֶׁלֹּא הִסְפִּיק בְּצֵקָם שֶׁל אֲבוֹתֵינוּ לְהַחֲמִיץ, עַד

---

and obstinacy. The answer to this may perhaps lie in the fact that, as our Sages point out, God also reached into the homes of the Jews to kill those Egyptian firstborn who tried to seek refuge there; yet, at the same time, no Jews were affected by the plague, even though they had not yet purified themselves from the contamination of Egyptian influence. This situation indeed marked a miraculous salvation! (*Baruch She'amar*).

The Haggadah quotes this verse to its end, which describes the reaction of the Jews to the news of their imminent freedom. They bowed in gratitude for the news that they would soon be liberated. Furthermore, according to *Rashi*, they thanked God for the reiterated promise regarding being given the Land of Israel and the news that they would merit future generations of children.[1]

Mechilta views the gratitude as a response to the fact that the Egyptians did not become aware of (and hence could not rejoice over) the death, during the three days of intense darkness, of those Jews who lacked full faith in the redemption.

Alternatively, the end of the verse is quoted to teach that the account of the Exodus and its

accompanying miracles must elicit an outpouring of joy and praise to God. Jethro, who heard everything that God had done to Moses and to Israel, rejoiced over all the good that Hashem had done for Israel, that He had rescued them from Egypt [see *Exodus* 18:1 and 18:9] (*Mechilta, Shemos* 12:26).

מַצָּה זוֹ שֶׁאָנוּ אוֹכְלִים — *We eat this unleavened bread.* As we recite the words *this matzah*, we raise the broken piece of matzah for all to see (*Rema, O.C.* 473:7). According to *Malbim*, this demonstrativeness echoes the verse that teaches that we must mention these three items while reciting the Haggadah: *And you shall tell your son on that day saying, "It is because of this that Hashem acted on my behalf when I left Egypt"* (*Exodus* 13:8). The Jewish parent declares to his children that the nation was redeemed only *because of this*, i.e., the commandments of *pesach*, matzah and *maror*. Thus we speak of *this* matzah that we eat.

Since in our day we cannot bring any offerings, it is forbidden to raise the shank bone while speaking of the *pesach* offering, since that would give the impression that one has in fact sanctified this meat as a *pesach*

---

1. **Rising to the Challenge.** As *Rashi* notes, the Jews bowed in gratitude for the news that they would have children — even though the child described in this verse is the wicked son. To parents, every child is a blessing and a challenge. It is up to them to cope with his rebellion and influence him to do good. This view of child-rearing — as a challenge that one must rise to with relish — is poignantly expressed in a diary entry of R' Yitzchak Hutner upon the birth of his daughter:

"When our friends came to wish me *mazal tov* upon your birth, some of them made me the butt of their humor, thinking to themselves that I was probably disappointed that the child granted us was a daughter, rather than a son. For posterity I note my answer to them: Every child given to parents is a challenge and a test for them. If the parents are successful in inculcating the child's heart with the sanctity of true Jewish living, we may say that they have passed the test. Since we are well aware that to guide a daughter along our holy path is a far more difficult task than to raise a son in the way of Torah, to the marriage canopy and to good deeds, it therefore follows that the birth of a daughter presents parents with a much more severe test than does the birth of a son. Thus I told them, 'I am happy that I was granted the more difficult and challenging of the two situations.' "

The entry ends with a request from father to daughter: "I ask that my words always be etched in your memory."

Matzah — Why do we eat this unleavened bread? Because the dough of our fathers did not have time to become leavened

---

offering (*Tur* based on *Pesachim* 116b; see *O.C.* 473:7 *M.B.* §72). We therefore speak of "the *pesach* offering that our fathers ate in Temple times" rather than "*this* pesach offering."

Abarbanel views the term *this* as differentiating between the matzah eaten by our forefathers in Egypt from the present obligation to eat matzah (see below).

Rabban Gamliel seems to be saying that the reason we eat matzah on the Seder night is because at the time of the Exodus the Jews had no time to wait for their dough to rise.[1] But in fact they were commanded two weeks before the Exodus to eat matzah with the *pesach* offering (*Exodus* 12:8), which was consumed the night *before* the Exodus occurred. It is clear, therefore, that they ate matzah that first year solely because of the Divine commandment to do so.[2] Rabban Gamliel, however, explains *why* this commandment was given: Since God knew that the liberation from Egypt would come suddenly and hurriedly, and, to symbolize this important facet of their redemption, He told the Jews in advance to eat matzah on *Pesach* night (*Shibbolei HaLeket*;

1. **Beyond Time.** The spiritual level that Jews achieved at the Exodus was so exalted that they transcended all natural limitations, even becoming free of the strictures of time. This power to transcend even time found expression in the haste with which they left Egypt and ate the *pesach* offering. By not allowing sufficient time for the dough to rise, God indicated that His people are not bound or limited by time. Thus *chametz*, which needs time in order to rise, is emblematic of an existence controlled by time and nature, while matzah, which is baked quickly without any delay, represents the supernatural existence of God's people.

The Sages (*Mechilta*) derive the obligation to perform commandments with alacrity from the verse וּשְׁמַרְתֶּם אֶת הַמַּצּוֹת, *you shall safeguard the matzos* (*Exodus* 12:17). The letters מצות may also be pronounced מִצְוֹת, *commandments*. By performing *mitzvos* without undue delay, we show clearly that *mitzvos* and the search for spirituality is a timeless pursuit of a level of existence that is unfettered by physical limitations (*Maharal*).

R' Yitzchak Hutner explains *Maharal* to mean that the attribute of alacrity with respect to *mitzvah* performance is a manifestation of the soul's yearning to free itself from the shackles of time, in an effort to return to its spiritual roots, a domain that transcends time. Such yearning, Rabbi Hutner continues, applies only to Israel, and is more than a simple expression of a desire to get the job at hand done quickly. It is part and parcel of the attribute of eternity that pertains only to Israel — the attribute that came into being as a result of the Exodus. Thus it is fitting that we derive the importance of alacrity vis-a-vis the *mitzvos* from the commandment to "safeguard the matzos," since this command was given at the moment when Israel's connection with eternity was established.

2. **Obedience — the Key to Understanding.** We eat matzah, as we perform all commandments, not because we are aware of the underlying reason, but simply in order to obey the will of God. Only after committing ourselves to such unconditional obedience do we seek reasons and rationales for the Torah's commandments so that, to the best of our ability, we may try to fathom God's will and thus engender an excitement and passion about fulfilling it. Thus we do not ask, "Why do we eat the matzah?" Rather, we state an immutable fact — "This matzah that we eat" — and only then do we ask, "Why do we do so?" In this sense we echo the attitude of Israel at Sinai, when the people said first נַעֲשֶׂה, *we will do*, and only afterwards וְנִשְׁמָע, *we will listen* (or *understand*), to hear the reasons. Once we have made the commitment, however, we are enjoined to explore the meaning of each *mitzvah*. As *Rambam* states: "It is proper for one to contemplate the meaning of the laws of the Torah to understand them as best as humanly possible" (*Hilchos Me'ilah* 8:8).

שֶׁנִּגְלָה עֲלֵיהֶם מֶלֶךְ מַלְכֵי הַמְּלָכִים הַקָּדוֹשׁ בָּרוּךְ הוּא
וּגְאָלָם. שֶׁנֶּאֱמַר, וַיֹּאפוּ אֶת הַבָּצֵק אֲשֶׁר הוֹצִיאוּ מִמִּצְרַיִם
עֻגֹת מַצּוֹת כִּי לֹא חָמֵץ, כִּי גֹרְשׁוּ מִמִּצְרַיִם, וְלֹא יָכְלוּ
לְהִתְמַהְמֵהַּ, וְגַם צֵדָה לֹא עָשׂוּ לָהֶם.¹

Avudraham in the name of *R' Yosef Kimchi*). The verse quoted here simply describes the historical fact that the moment of freedom came so suddenly that the Jews did not even have enough time to bake matzah for the journey, and they simply took along their raw dough on their backs.

According to *Abarbanel*, Rabban Gamliel means to resolve a contradiction. When the *mitzvah* of eating matzah first appears in the Torah, before the actual Exodus from Egypt, the phrase used is (*Exodus* 12:8): *and matzos — with bitter herbs they shall eat [the pesach offering]*. The linkage of matzos with *maror* indicates that both were intended to commemorate bondage. On the other hand, when the commandment is repeated, it appears it was intended to commemorate the speed of the redemption, as it says (*Deuteronomy* 16:3): *seven days you shall eat matzos . . . because you departed from the land of Egypt in haste.* Rabban Gamliel resolves this contradiction by proposing that the two verses refer to two different periods. The first verse, which gives the reason for eating matzah as a commemoration of bondage, applies to the Pesach that the Jews celebrated just before they left Egypt. The second verse gives the reason for the performance of the mitzvah by *future* generations. This is why Rabban Gamliel says **this** matzah that **we** eat, with the stress on *this* and *we*, in contradistinction to the matzah that our ancestors ate in Egypt, which was eaten for a different reason.[1]

Malbim suggests that this reason impresses upon us that the main element of our redemption was to provide spiritual salvation. Had Israel remained but a second longer in the spiritual impurity of Egypt, the nation would have become too hopelessly assimilated to have emerged as a *kingdom of priests and a holy nation* (*Exodus* 19:6). In order for Israel to receive the Torah and dedicate themselves to leading the world toward an understanding and acceptance of the Godly mission, they had to remove themselves from the temptations and urges that drag human beings down from the spiritual level to which they should aspire. Thus, the speed with which they left Egypt was integral to their spiritual salvation. It is this speedy spiritual salvation that we commemorate with the matzah.[2]

---

1. **A Stage for the Divine Drama.** "God looked into the Torah and created the world" (*Bereishis Rabbah* 1:2) is the Midrashic expression of the truism that human history is the result of God building His world according to the blueprint of Torah, rather than the laws of Torah being a result of human history. We do not eat matzah because the dough of the Jews did not rise. Just the opposite; the dough did not rise because God's will, as expressed in the Torah, calls for matzahs to be eaten. Thus, the reason cited here is in reality nothing more than the means by which God accomplished His goal (*Beis HaLevi*). The Torah's commands do not commemorate human events; human affairs create the conditions for a realization of the Divine Plan.

2. **Growing Against the Odds.** The commentators note that God had to remove the Jews from Egypt quickly, in order that they not be irretrievably sunken in the morass of the fifty degrees of Egyptian impurity.

Divrei Shmuel questions the premise. Why did God find it necessary to subject them to such life-threatening spiritual contamination and then free them in the split second before they succumbed to its fatal effects? Would it not have been better for them never to have been exposed to such *tumah*? He before the King of kings, the Holy One, Blessed is He, revealed Himself to them and redeemed them, as it is stated: "They baked the dough which they had brought out of Egypt into unleavened bread, for it had not fermented, because they were driven out of Egypt and could not delay; nor had they prepared any provisions for themselves."[1]

---

(1) *Exodus* 12:39.

עַד שֶׁנִּגְלָה עֲלֵיהֶם . . . הַקָּדוֹש בָּרוּך הוּא – *Before the Holy One, Blessed is He, revealed Himself to them.* Where does Rabban Gamliel find this revelation in his supporting verse? It is alluded to in the apparent redundancy of *They were driven from Egypt and could not linger* — if they were driven, it is obvious that they could not linger. From this we derive that the Holy One, Blessed is He, revealed

Himself; in addition to being driven away by the Egyptians, the Jews could not bear to linger in Egypt because of the unquenchable longing for God's Presence instilled in them by His revelation.[11]

They knew that He would reveal Himself to them in the Wilderness, and would not delay their departure even for as long as it would take to

---

explains with an analogy: A seed planted in the ground will not sprout until it is *almost* completely disintegrated. Any lesser degree of breakdown will not allow for growth. On the other hand, total disintegration would destroy all potential for life. The seed must be brought to the edge of destruction for new life to be able to flourish.

Likewise, before the new nation of Israel was born, the spiritual germination process had to become complete. By exposing the soul of the nation to the ravaging effects of full-blown spiritual impurity, God totally broke down the seed from which the new and spiritually strengthened nation would flourish. The Jewish nation was forged in the crucible of such intense spiritual ferment so that it could flourish into the great tree which yields succulent fruit for its Master.

Life often subjects people to seemingly unbearable difficulties. The Egyptian experience teaches that true growth results from spiritual adversity.

1. **Seizing the Moment.** The Egyptian exile was not only a historical episode, it is an experience faced by every person in every generation. Mired in passion and sin, one may feel imprisoned in his personal house of bondage. The spiritual constriction of unrelenting desires for all sorts of spiritual ugliness often feels like an inescapable prison (מִצְרַיִם, *Egypt,* is related to the word מֵצַר, *narrow strait*).

God, in His infinite mercy, may arouse man to at least *try* to escape from his spiritual lethargy. At the very moment that God causes a spiritual rumbling in his soul, man must drop everything; there may be no looking back, for even a moment's hesitation can be fatal. One cannot afford to plan his escape calmly — it may never happen; instead one must seize the opportunity to attain spiritual freedom. Even considerations of what one must do in order to earn a living are secondary — of what value is prosperity if one is spiritually dead? The Jews left Egypt in a hurry, for at the critical moment, they chose spiritual freedom. This is the message of matzah. At the moment that God revealed Himself we left quickly, unwilling to remain in the spiritual impurity of Egypt for even a moment. Just as one under attack by murderers or wild beasts cannot afford to worry about something as mundane as food, so one caught in the throes of sin can ill afford to fret over something as temporal as physical sustenance (*Likutei Halachos*).

Man's initiation into God's service must be pursued with alacrity, just as the *pesach* offering in Egypt had to be eaten quickly. Therefore, at the very moment one is inspired to do so, one must sever one's tenacious ties to lusts and passions. Inspiration is fleeting and can easily become dissipated; one must take advantage of it while he can. Afterwards, one may follow the spirit of the post-Exodus *pesach* offerings, which are eaten slowly, and proceed step by step in his spiritual growth (*Tzidkas HaTzaddik* 1).

The *maror* is lifted and displayed while the following paragraph is recited.

מָרוֹר זֶה שֶׁאָנוּ אוֹכְלִים, עַל שׁוּם מָה? עַל שׁוּם שֶׁמֵּרְרוּ הַמִּצְרִים אֶת חַיֵּי אֲבוֹתֵינוּ בְּמִצְרָיִם. שֶׁנֶּאֱמַר, וַיְמָרְרוּ אֶת חַיֵּיהֶם, בַּעֲבֹדָה קָשָׁה, בְּחֹמֶר וּבִלְבֵנִים, וּבְכָל עֲבֹדָה בַּשָּׂדֶה, אֵת כָּל עֲבֹדָתָם אֲשֶׁר עָבְדוּ בָהֶם בְּפָרֶךְ.[1]

בְּכָל דּוֹר וָדוֹר חַיָּב אָדָם לִרְאוֹת אֶת עַצְמוֹ כְּאִלּוּ

---

prepare provisions (*Geulas Avraham*).

Since the prohibition of eating *chametz* for seven days did not apply on the first Pesach (see *Pesachim* 28b; see however *Ramban* to *Exodus* ibid.), the Jews could have prepared regular bread for their journey. Nonetheless, they did not do so. They carried out dough on their backs, and baked it in the broiling sun (see *Targum Yonason* to *Exodus* 12:39). In commemoration of those unleavened cakes, we were commanded to refrain from *chametz* and to eat matzah for a full seven days (*Shibbolei HaLeket*).

מָרוֹר זֶה שֶׁאָנוּ אוֹכְלִים עַל שׁוּם מָה — *Maror — Why do we eat this bitter herb?* The verse sheds light on the symbolism of bitterness (*Malbim*). The *real* reason we eat it — as in the performance of all commandments — is that God commanded it.

As free men we look back at the terrible ordeal of the Egyptian house of bondage and thank God for releasing us from it. However we eat the *maror* only after the matzah, the symbol of freedom, as if to say that even after becoming free, we do not cast away all the bitterness of life. Rather we emphasize that our joy over freedom is not because we were freed *from* the bitterness of exile, but because we were freed to become servants of God — even though it may often be in bitter circumstances (*Maasei Nissim*).

Furthermore, the extreme bitterness of the Egyptian sojourn is one of the reasons that the 400 promised years of exile were reduced to 210. Thus, the *maror*, too, is a symbol of freedom (*Birchas HaShir*).

According to the *Vilna Gaon*, the above comment is alluded to in the cantillation (*trop*) of the phrase cited here: וַיְמָרְרוּ אֶת חַיֵּיהֶם, *they embittered their lives*. The

cantillation notes are קַדְמָא וְאַזְלָא, which may be translated as *they went out early* [as a result of the bitter oppression]. The numerical value of the words קַדְמָא וְאַזְלָא equals 190, the amount of years deducted from the 400-year sentence as a result of the excessive bitterness (*Pe'er Aharon*).

בְּכָל דּוֹר וָדוֹר חַיָּב אָדָם לִרְאוֹת אֶת עַצְמוֹ כְּאִלּוּ הוּא יָצָא מִמִּצְרַיִם — *In every generation it is one's duty to regard himself as though he personally had gone out from Egypt.* At all times, whether it is a period when the Jews reside peacefully in *Eretz Yisrael* and do not suffer the travails of exile, or we are displaced and tormented, we must feel with a sense of immediacy the freedom of having left Egypt and all it represents.

According to *Malbim*, this obligation reflects the historical reality expressed earlier in the Haggadah (p. 34) that had God not redeemed us from Egypt, "we, our children and grandchildren would all have remained enslaved to Pharaoh in Egypt." *Maharal* rejects this understanding, for if this were so, the obligation to sense the redemption as a personal experience should apply equally to Purim, when Israel was saved from slaughter, or to any of the many deliverances throughout our long and stressful history (see also *Maasei Nissim*).

Maharal explains that the redemption from Egypt did not affect only the *individuals* who were present in Egypt at that time. Rather, God freed the Jews *as a nation* from their spiritually constricting ties to Egypt and everything it stood for. In freeing us, God infused our nation with an indelible sense of spiritual royalty. Thus, the Talmud

The *maror* is lifted and displayed while the following paragraph is recited.

Maror — Why do we eat this bitter herb? Because the Egyptians embittered the lives of our fathers in Egypt, as it is stated: "They embittered their lives with hard labor, with mortar and bricks, and with all manner of labor in the field: Whatever service they made them perform was with hard labor."[1]

In every generation it is one's duty to regard himself as though

_____

(1) *Exodus* 1:14.

teaches that even while in exile all Jews have the status of royalty (*Shabbos* 111a). Despite our physical exile, we reassert the reality that we are intrinsically free, that we are children of the King. This remains the unique and permanent legacy of the Exodus.

The deliverance from Pharaoh's servitude gave us חֵרוּת עוֹלָם, *everlasting freedom*. Unlike the Jews in Egypt, we have the Torah, which allows us to unlock the storehouse of true freedom with which God endowed us on this night of the Exodus (see *Abarbanel*).

The *mitzvos* of the Seder are relatively easy to perform — one can embellish the Exodus narrative, eat the required quantities of matzah and *maror*, and drink the four cups of wine with relative ease. But for a person to be wise and sensitive enough to feel as though he himself had been rescued from Egypt — that is exceedingly difficult (*Moadim U'Zmanim*).[1]

By performing the *mitzvos* of the Seder — by eating the matzah reminiscent of the speedy redemption we experienced, by tasting the bitter *maror* and conjuring up the image of the physical and emotional cruelty we underwent in Egypt, by reliving the severance of ties from idolatry and decadence symbolized by the *pesach* offering — we are able to see ourselves as if we personally emerged from Egypt. This allows us to accomplish the main purpose of the Seder. Just as our forefathers came to accept God as their King when they left the sovereignty of Pharaoh to enter His, so must we utilize the experiences of the Seder and all it represents to proclaim our own redemption from

1. **A Royal State of Mind.** Though it is not easy for every Jew to feel the experience of the Exodus personally at the Seder, it can be accomplished. Our imaginations are very creative, as evidenced by how vividly we can dream in our sleep, and even when we are awake. Our ingenious minds can create three-dimensional scenes in rich colors, and we can see ourselves fully participating in these scenes. Being familiar with the story of the Exodus, one should meditate and create the various scenes in his mind. He should see himself in the straw pits, clearing the straw, mixing it with mud and baking it into bricks in the tropical sun. He should hear the scolding of the Egyptian taskmasters and feel the lashes of their whips on his back. He should then visualize the various plagues and the panic of the Egyptians. Then he should see himself as part of the throng leaving Egypt, following Moses into the barren desert. Finally, he should be standing at the edge of the Sea of Reeds as it splits open.

Appreciating the Exodus in a personal manner in every generation is mandatory. The sweet taste of liberty cannot be appreciated as long as oppression is only an abstraction. The acceptance of the omnipotence of God is incomplete unless one has seen the many miracles with one's own eyes.

The Seder ritual facilitates this experience. We eat the matzah, the bread which the slaves were given to satiate their hunger. We taste the bitterness of the *maror*. We explain in great detail every step of the Exodus. Now one must close one's eyes and relive the Exodus oneself, for only then can we fully appreciate its greatness, and only then can we properly acknowledge our gratitude to God (*R' A. J. Twersky*).

הוּא יָצָא מִמִּצְרָיִם. שֶׁנֶּאֱמַר, וְהִגַּדְתָּ לְבִנְךָ בַּיּוֹם הַהוּא לֵאמֹר, בַּעֲבוּר זֶה עָשָׂה יהוה לִי, בְּצֵאתִי מִמִּצְרָיִם.¹ לֹא אֶת אֲבוֹתֵינוּ בִּלְבַד גָּאַל הַקָּדוֹשׁ בָּרוּךְ הוּא, אֶלָּא אַף אֹתָנוּ גָּאַל עִמָּהֶם. שֶׁנֶּאֱמַר, וְאוֹתָנוּ הוֹצִיא מִשָּׁם, לְמַעַן הָבִיא אֹתָנוּ לָתֶת לָנוּ אֶת הָאָרֶץ אֲשֶׁר נִשְׁבַּע לַאֲבֹתֵינוּ.²

---

the yoke of the transitory and accept upon ourselves עוֹל מַלְכוּת שָׁמַיִם , *the yoke of the Heavenly Kingdom* (*R' Yeruchom Levovitz*).[1]

The purpose of this personal identification with the liberation, according to *Netziv*, is in the spirit of the Talmudic dictum that everyone should feel that the entire world was created for his sake (*Sanhedrin* 37a), meaning that man can live in a way that justifies the creation of the entire cosmos. This notion can inspire one to undreamt-of spiritual heights. Likewise, the personal aura of redemption one experiences may propel him to even

---

1. **All-Inclusive Covenant.** Just as those who left Egypt did so with the understanding that they were going to receive the Torah, so must each individual in every generation make a renewed commitment to accept the Torah. *He redeemed us,* too — He took the Children of Israel out of Egypt so that they should commit themselves to Torah for all times. Here, the Haggadah reiterates the message of the Torah regarding the oath Moses administered to the Jews before he died. *Not with you alone do I seal this covenant and this imprecation, but with whoever is here, standing with us today before Hashem, our God, and with whoever is not here with us today* (Deuteronomy 29:13-14). Thus, the covenant was binding even on unborn generations, for parents and children are like trees and fruit; future generations are contained, in a sense, in the parents who will give birth to them, and they are bound by the parental covenant. Alternatively, all Jewish *souls* were present at this covenant, just as they were at Sinai when the Torah was given. Only the *bodies* were not yet born (*R' Bachya*).

Rabbi Shimon Schwab once offered an example to express this concept. When he was nine years old in Frankfurt, he contracted whooping cough, which causes shortness of breath and violent coughing spells. At the time, the standard treatment was to have the patient inhale hot vapors from the spout of a kerosene-heated kettle.

As young Shimon bent over the pot, it tipped over, and the scalding hot water, along with some kerosene, poured over his left arm, burning him badly and painfully. After what seemed an eternity, a doctor arrived. He spread ointments and salves on the raw surface of the burned arm, and eventually the sharp pain subsided. However, his arm remained discolored for a full year until the skin regenerated and returned to its natural color.

More than half a century later, Rabbi Schwab recalled the incident and said, pointing to his left arm, "If I tell you today that this is the arm that was burned, I am telling the truth. Yet in actuality, not one cell that existed in my arm then is in my body today. Cells have a relatively short life span, and new ones are born to take their place. Cells constantly regenerate themselves, so that, in a sense, this is a brand-new arm. Nevertheless, it is fair to say that this arm I am showing you now, although it is three times the size it was then, is the same one that I burned as a youngster."

Rabbi Schwab used this episode to illustrate the words of the Haggadah. "The Haggadah instructs us: בְּכָל דּוֹר וָדוֹר חַיָּב אָדָם לִרְאוֹת אֶת עַצְמוֹ כְּאִלּוּ הוּא יָצָא מִמִּצְרָיִם, *In every generation it is one's duty to regard himself personally as though he had gone out from Egypt.* How can I view myself that way? I wasn't there, my father wasn't there, my grandfather wasn't there. Yet in a sense we *were* all there, because the generations that actually left Egypt reproduced and recreated themselves until our very day. And so, as we look at ourselves today, we — the offspring of that generation — can say that we indeed left Egypt."

he personally had gone out from Egypt, as it is stated: "And you shall tell your son on that day, saying, 'It is because of this that HASHEM did for "me" when I went out of Egypt.'"[1] It was not only our fathers whom the Holy One, Blessed is He, redeemed from slavery; we, too, were redeemed with them, as it is stated: "He brought 'us' out from there so that He might take us to the land which He had promised to our fathers."[2]

_____

(1) *Exodus* 13:8. (2) *Deuteronomy* 6:23.

greater heights of commitment to God and His Torah, the very essence and primary purpose of the Exodus.

Rambam has a different version of the text: חַיָּב אָדָם לְהַרְאוֹת אֶת עַצְמוֹ, *it is one's duty to portray himself* as if he had left Egypt בְּעַצְמוֹ עַתָּה, *himself, now* (*Hil. Chametz U'Matzah* 7:6). *Chida* explains: One must be demonstrative and physically display his excitement over having left Egypt, as if the event just occurred. It is not enough to feel this in one's heart; he must give expression to his enthusiasm. In this way his household will notice his joyful activity and demeanor and become caught up themselves in the spirit of freedom. Thus they too will experience it as a living and present reality, rather than as an ancient historical event.[1]

Maasei Hashem sees in the words *In every generation* an allusion to the constant sense of redemption from the recurrent threats that occur throughout Jewish history. As we said earlier in the evening, "in every generation they rise against us to annihilate us. But the Holy One, Blessed is He, rescues us from their hand." Thus, every Jew actually tastes a bit of the physical freedom which our forefathers experienced so long ago.

שֶׁנֶּאֱמַר — *As it is stated.* This verse, addressed to the Jews who were about to enter the land forty years after the Exodus, speaks of telling their sons בַּיּוֹם הַהוּא, *on that day*, i.e., in the distant future, that "in the merit of my fulfilling the commandments of Pesach — namely matzah, *maror* and the *pesach* offering — God caused the redemption for me (עָשָׂה ה' לִי), not only for my ancestors" (*Maharsha*).

לֹא אֶת אֲבוֹתֵינוּ בִּלְבָד — *It was not only our fathers.* According to most commentators, this continues and explains the previous statement. Since the redemption included us as well as our ancestors, we should view ourselves as having personally left Egypt.

Maharal elaborates: God redeemed Israel as a nation, thereby causing us as well as our forefathers to be free men. We should therefore focus on the personal liberty we gained on this night.

The Haggadah cites two different verses (*Exodus* 13:8 and *Deuteronomy* 6:23) to show that the Torah expects even people in future generations to consider themselves as having personally experienced the Exodus. *Malbim* explains that both verses are needed to bolster the point. The obligation to retell the Exodus as if it were a personal experience is derived from the verse in *Exodus*, *You shall tell your son etc.* HASHEM *did for* **me,** implying that the commandment refers to those who could speak from personal experience. The

1. **Reflexive Praise.** *R' Hai Gaon* (quoted by *Maharal*) suggests that this sensation of personal redemption explains why we do not recite a blessing over the recitation of *Hallel* at the Seder, as we do when we recite it during holiday services. The blessing states that God sanctified us with His commandments and instructed us to recite *Hallel*. Tonight, however, we do not recite Hallel as an *obligation* to offer thanks for a past event; tonight we praise and thank God out of a sense of *personal gratitude*, for an ongoing redemption. Thus the blessing is out of place.

The matzos are covered and the cup is lifted and held until it is to be drunk. According to some customs, however, the cup is put down after the following paragraph, in which case the matzos should once more be uncovered. If this custom is followed, the matzos are to be covered and the cup raised again upon reaching the blessing אֲשֶׁר גְּאָלָנוּ, Who has redeemed us (p. 156). Some declare their intent to fulfill their obligation to drink the second of the four cups of wine.

לְפִיכָךְ אֲנַחְנוּ חַיָּבִים לְהוֹדוֹת, לְהַלֵּל, לְשַׁבֵּחַ, לְפָאֵר, לְרוֹמֵם, לְהַדֵּר, לְבָרֵךְ, לְעַלֵּה, וּלְקַלֵּס, לְמִי שֶׁעָשָׂה

verse in *Deuteronomy* — "And He took **us** out of there etc." — shows that this obligation is incumbent on *all* generations of Jews. Every Jew, in every generation, should see himself as if he took part in the Exodus.

The paragraph begins by speaking of ourselves *as if* we were freed from Egypt, and later in the paragraph we state categorically that we were *in fact* liberated along with our ancestors. We must *imagine* that we were *physically* released from Egypt since we are *in fact* beneficiaries of the *spiritual* freedom which God granted His nation in its entirety at that time.

Sfas Emes resolves this seeming contradiction by pointing to the faith to define reality. As a result of deep-seated faith that God seeks to free all Jews we merit to truly attain spiritual liberation.

We raise our cups at this point to signal the beginning of our recitation of *Hallel* and songs of praise to God. As the Sages taught, "Song [such as *Hallel*] should be recited over wine" [*Berachos* 35a] (*Kol Bo, Tur*, et al.).

One sings praises and songs of thanksgiving for a personal experience of God's beneficence and salvation, not for that of a friend. After verbalizing our belief that we ourselves were redeemed on this night we raise our cups to indicate that it is שִׁירָה —

a song of praise — that we will now sing, for the salvation is our own.[1]

לְפִיכָךְ — *Therefore.* The commentators offer a variety of interpretations to explain the connective word *therefore. Rashbam, Avudraham* and others view it as related to our personal sense of experiencing the Exodus. Since we, like our ancestors, were freed, *therefore* we offer songs of praise as they did.[2]

Sfas Emes notes the Talmudic teaching that forbids excessive praising of God, for it is impossible to fully express His praise (see *Berachos* 33b), and by expressing some praise explicitly, one implies that other praises do not apply to God. This prohibition, however, is applicable only to someone who views God's wondrous deliverance as a spectator. One who actually experiences God's salvation firsthand, however, must praise God simply out of a sense of gratitude. In such a case, one legitimately expresses his appreciation according to his personal understanding of what God did for him. Since we experience the Exodus on a personal level, we are entitled to express our subjective gratitude even with praise that, on an objective level, may be flawed.

The *Hallel* we offer on the night of Pesach is unlike the *Hallel* recited in the morning prayers. That *Hallel* is an expression of joy at the festival's

---

1. **A Toast to "Natural" Miracles.** *Aruch HaShulchan* explains the symbolism of the cup-raising at this juncture. The Hebrew words for cup (כּוֹס), the Name of God (אֱלֹהִים) and nature (הַטֶּבַע) all have the numerical value of 86. We raise our cups and praise God not only for the great miracles He wrought in Egypt, but also for the hidden miracles He performs each day. "Nature" is merely a pseudonym of God (see *Ramban, Exodus* 13:16).

2. **A Thesaurus of Praise.** *Midrash Tanchuma* (*Yisro* 3) interprets the verse "and the Children of Israel were going out with an upraised arm" (*Exodus* 14:8) as portraying a contrast to the Egyptians who cursed and blasphemed God and His people as they chased them at the Sea, while the Jews exalted and praised God with songs of exultation. Just as the Jews then thanked God with a multitude of different expressions, so too we employ a multiplicity of terms and feebly attempt to give expression to our feelings of gratitude to Him for granting us personal redemption (*Ritva*).

The matzos are covered and the cup is lifted and held until it is to be drunk. According to some customs, however, the cup is put down after the following paragraph, in which case the matzos should once more be uncovered. If this custom is followed, the matzos are to be covered and the cup raised again upon reaching the blessing אֲשֶׁר גְּאָלָנוּ, Who has redeemed us (p. 156). Some declare their intent to fulfill their obligation to drink the second of the four cups of wine.

Therefore it is our duty to thank, praise, pay tribute, glorify, exalt, honor, bless, extol and acclaim Him Who performed

arrival, while the *Hallel* of the Seder is offered in thanksgiving for the miracles of the Exodus. Only one who personally experienced a miracle is enjoined to say *Hallel* for it. Thus, we state here that the Exodus is our own personal miracle and therefore we are obligated to offer praise as personal gratitude (*Beis HaLevi*).

Malbim suggests that *therefore* is the logical conclusion of the *Dayeinu* prayer's listing of all God's great acts of kindness. Any one of these gifts would have been sufficient to require infinite expression of gratitude on our part. How much more grateful must we be that He has given us *all* of these precious gifts! *Therefore* we are eternally indebted to Him and obligated to offer all forms of praise and thanks to Him. Furthermore, this declaration serves as an introduction to the first part of *Hallel,* in which we praise Hashem for having elevated us from the profound spiritual impurity of Egypt to our present royal status as His nation and children. This is the *Hallel* that we refer to as the "new song" of praise that we sing to Him.

The Talmud states an axiom that *Hallel* is not recited over a miracle that occurred outside *Eretz Yisrael*, which is a reason why *Hallel* is not recited on Purim (*Megillah* 14a). *Maharsha* (*Arachin* 10b) explains (based on *Ramban* to *Leviticus* 18:25) that this is because in the Diaspora God generally administers the affairs of the world (including miracles) through intermediaries, while the Land of Israel merits God's personal attention and involvement. Thus, to recite *Hallel* for a miracle that occurred in the Diaspora might be inadvertently interpreted as praise of God's intermediaries rather than of Him.

The great miracles of the Exodus are different. Although they occurred outside the Land of Israel, they must still be commemorated with Hallel, since they were performed by God, Himself. This is the thrust of our declaration. Since it was You, God, Who personally dealt Egypt the final deathblow when You personally slew their firstborn and thus freed Your firstborn son, therefore it behooves us to thank, praise, laud, etc. the One Who [personally] performed all these miracles — even though they occurred outside the land (*MiBnai David*).

לְהוֹדוֹת לְהַלֵּל — *To thank, praise.* These nine expressions of praise correspond to the first nine plagues, and the general call to praise God with *a new song* corresponds to the slaying of the firstborn, which finally liberated the Jews from their oppressors. Thus, we summarize our salvation, providing praise for each step of the process.

According to *Orchos Chaim*, this paragraph stands in place of the blessing usually recited prior to *Hallel*. *Sefer HaManhig* views it as a substitute for the blessing שֶׁעָשָׂה נִסִּים לַאֲבוֹתֵינוּ (recited on Purim and Chanukah) which praises God as the One Who performed miracles for our fathers.

These ten expressions mirror the ten expressions used in the Book of *Psalms* to praise God (see *Pesachim* 117a).[1]

Throughout the first nine plagues we remained enslaved to Pharaoh; only with the tenth plague were we finally free. Thus, like Purim, when we

1. **Our Natural Lexicon.** *Rambam* said of King David, the author of *Psalms*, that "his heart was the heart of all of Israel" (*Hilchos Melachim* 3:6). From that heart emanated all the praise of the entire people of Israel, about whom God says: *this people that I fashioned for Myself that they might declare My praise* (*Isaiah* 43:21). On this night of our national birth, we muster the full gamut of praise found in our national lexicon to thank God for our very existence. We employ ten expressions, reminiscent of the heartfelt song of King David.

לַאֲבוֹתֵֽינוּ וְלָֽנוּ אֶת כָּל הַנִּסִּים הָאֵֽלוּ, הוֹצִיאָֽנוּ מֵעַבְדוּת לְחֵרוּת, מִיָּגוֹן לְשִׂמְחָה, וּמֵאֵֽבֶל לְיוֹם טוֹב, וּמֵאֲפֵלָה לְאוֹר גָּדוֹל, וּמִשִּׁעְבּוּד לִגְאֻלָּה, וְנֹאמַר לְפָנָיו שִׁירָה חֲדָשָׁה, הַלְלוּיָהּ.

---

refrain from reciting *Hallel* because "we are still slaves of Ahasuerus" (*Megillah* 14a), we do not recite *Hallel* until the tenth expression, corresponding to the final plague. Only then do we issue the call to song. Having finally left the servitude of Pharaoh and become the servants of God, we cry out, "Praise Hashem! Praise, O servants of Hashem. Praise the name of Hashem" (*Vilna Gaon*).

הוֹצִיאָֽנוּ מֵעַבְדוּת לְחֵרוּת — *He brought us forth from slavery to freedom.* This refers to the Exodus. *From grief to joy* refers to the rescue of Israel at the splitting of the Sea of Reeds. *Mourning* refers to the aftermath of the sin of the Golden Calf, when the people learned that an angel, rather than the direct Presence of Hashem, would lead them into the Land of Israel as the Torah states: *The people heard this bad tiding, and they mourned* (*Exodus* 33:4). *Festivity* refers to the Yom Kippur after the affair of the Golden Calf, when God forgave the people and Moses brought down the second set of Tablets. As the Talmud states: "Israel never had festivals as great as Yom Kippur . . ." (*Taanis* 26b). And God took us from *the darkness* of the Wilderness to the *great light* of the Land of Israel and from *servitude* to foreign nations in the days of the Judges, to *redemption* in the days of Kings David and Solomon (*Vilna Gaon*).[1]

Maasei Nissim offers a slightly different, broader historical perspective on these expressions of praise. God removed us from the *slavery* of Egypt, granting us *freedom.* He took us through the *grief* of the Babylonian exile and the destruction of the First Temple to the *joy* of its rebuilding. Furthermore, He carried us and allowed us to survive the *mourning* precipitated by the threat of annihilation in the days of Haman and to merit the *salvation* and *reprieve* which is commemorated by the joyous festivities of Purim. The thick spiritual *darkness* that enveloped the Jewish people in the Syrian-Greek exile, as a result of the anti-Torah decrees of the time, was suddenly turned to a *great light* as God granted the Hasmoneans a miraculous military victory and allowed them to rededicate the Temple with the *light* of the miraculous kindling of the *Menorah*, which we commemorate with Chanukah. The final redemption, when God will take us from *servitude* to *redemption*, will come about with the arrival of the Messiah.

וְנֹאמַר לְפָנָיו שִׁירָה חֲדָשָׁה — *We shall recite a new song before Him.* The meaning of this statement is unclear. The term "new song" is always used in Scripture to indicate an outburst of praise to God upon the occasion of some miraculous revelation of His glory. Is this then a prayer that we witness the Messianic redemption and thereupon break

---

1. **The Five Stages.** These five expressions and their historical parallels are mirrored in the famous five expressions of redemption of *Exodus* 6:6-8. *I shall take you out* (וְהוֹצֵאתִי) alludes to the Egyptian Exodus. *I shall rescue you* (וְהִצַּלְתִּי) corresponds to God's saving us from the death we might have met at the Sea of Reeds had He not intervened on our behalf. *I shall redeem you* (וְגָאַלְתִּי) recalls the spiritually redemptive quality of repentance and atonement, which is the essence of Yom Kippur. *I shall take you* (וְלָקַחְתִּי) finds expression in our leaving the foreboding existence in the desert and being granted the spiritually enlightened Land of Israel. The spiritual serenity that we achieved in Solomonic times with the building of the Temple was the fulfillment of God's promise *I shall bring you* (וְהֵבֵאתִי) to the land and the Temple.

all these miracles for our fathers and for us. He brought us forth from slavery to freedom, from grief to joy, from mourning to festivity, from darkness to great light, and from servitude to redemption. We shall recite a new song before Him! Halleluyah!

out into songs of praise?

The Sages (in *Mechilta*) note that the song of praise to be sung in the days of the final, Messianic redemption is always referred to as שִׁיר, *song*, in the masculine form, while all the others songs sung until that time are referred to by the feminine form שִׁירָה. *Tosafos* (*Pesachim* 116b) explains that until the coming of the Messiah, which will signal the end of Jewish pain and troubles, our song is always muted, to a degree. Just as a woman's joy in childbirth is tinged with the anxiety of its concurrent pain, so every period of deliverance short of the complete Messianic redemption is tinged with apprehension of the suffering that constantly recurs in exile. Our joy is incomplete, for new troubles always follow.

Thus, the feminine gender of the words שִׁירָה חֲדָשָׁה mentioned here seemingly indicates that it cannot refer to the song of the Messianic redemption of the future. Many commentators therefore interpret it is a reference to the Exodus and to the praise we offered God at *that* time. According to these opinions, then, we should pronounce the word וְנֶאֱמַר, *it was recited*, rather than וְנֹאמַר, *we shall recite* (see *Derishah* 473).

Nevertheless, our version (וְנֹאמַר, *we **shall** recite*,

in the future tense) may be understood to mean, "we will now recite *Hallel*," which, according to *Pesachim* 117a, was recited at the Exodus from Egypt, but now we *shall* recite with the "*new*" dimension of gratitude born of our sense that we ourselves were liberated on this night.[1]

We now recite the first part of *Hallel*, which speaks of the Egyptian redemption and continues the theme of the Haggadah. Then the meal will conclude the theme of the Exodus, with the eating of the *pesach* offering — or its present-day symbolic equivalent, the *afikoman*. The rest of *Hallel*, recited later, revolves around the theme of the Final Redemption. Offered as supplication and praise for that great era of the future, those psalms are recited after the meal. At that point, we implore God to parlay this partial redemption into the ultimate and complete Messianic dream (*Levush, Pri Megadim*).

Chodesh HaAviv suggests that the first part of *Hallel* is symbolic of the praise that the Jews offered God while they were still enslaved in Egypt, while the *Hallel* recited after the meal reflects the praise they offered after the Exodus. This shows the great faith the Jews had in God's promise to recite them. His mere promise, even before He

1. **An Old/New Melody.** *Rashi* comments on the verse *And Aaron did so* (Numbers 8:3), that Aaron obeyed God's command without altering His instructions. Seemingly, such simple obedience does not deserve special praise; it should be obvious that Aaron would scrupulously follow God's command!

The answer is that Aaron was able to perform the same physical act every day and yet always approach it with a spirit of freshness, constantly imbuing it with new meaning. An old melody can be a new song if we endow it with new spiritual coloratura.

An alternative explanation for the future tense is supplied by *Kav HaYashar* (90). He teaches that one who focuses on God's manifold favors and expresses gratitude to Him will merit ever-increasing kindness from Heaven. After we have joyously recited the Haggadah and recounted all that God did and still does for us, God responds by figuratively spreading His wings over us to protect us from all danger and to provide all our needs, even in miraculous ways. Thus, וְנֹאמַר may be interpreted as meaning: Just as we have praised God for all He did in the past, so may we be blessed with continued Divine blessing, so that we always have reason to sing Him a new song of gratitude and thanksgiving.

הַלְלוּיָהּ הַלְלוּ עַבְדֵי יהוה, הַלְלוּ אֶת שֵׁם יהוה.
יְהִי שֵׁם יהוה מְבֹרָךְ, מֵעַתָּה וְעַד עוֹלָם.

fulfilled it, elicited their praise and gratitude. Even in the midst of their misery they were sure that the hand of God was busy bringing about circumstances and means to extricate them.[1]

הַלְלוּיָהּ — *Halleluyah* [lit. *Praised is Hashem*]. *Psalms* 113-118 are called הַלֵּל הַמִּצְרִי (*The Egyptian Hallel*), in contradistinction to Psalm 136, which is referred to as הַלֵּל הַגָּדוֹל (*The Great Hallel*). The Talmud (*Pesachim* 118) explains that the Egyptian *Hallel* surpasses the Great *Hallel*, because it speaks of essential articles of Jewish belief: The Exodus from Egypt, the Splitting of the Sea, the Sinaitic Revelation, the Resurrection of the Dead and the cataclysmic Ultimate Redemption and the Messianic Age.

The Talmud (*Pesachim* 117a) cites numerous opinions concerning the authorship of *Hallel*: Moses and Israel recited it after being saved from the Egyptians at the Sea of Reeds; Joshua composed it after defeating the kings of Canaan; Hezekiah, after defeating Sennacherib; Chananyah, Mishael and Azariah, after emerging unscathed from the furnace where Nebuchadnezzar had cast them. Others suggest that Mordechai and Esther recited *Hallel* to celebrate the defeat of Haman, while yet others are of the opinion that the prophets of Israel composed *Hallel* for the people to recite for every great event and in every period of danger upon realizing salvation. They will also recite *Hallel* at the time of the Final Redemption. The Talmud also cites an opinion that David composed *Hallel*.

It is possible that these opinions do not contradict one another. The basic framework for *Hallel* was established by the early prophets, and it was expanded upon by successive generations, in response to historic occasions when God's salvation elicited an outpouring of praise. The final

1. **Why Wait?** *Rashi* in *Psalms* explains: The righteous are so supremely confident of God's salvation that they praise Him for it, before it actually happens. *With praises I call unto HASHEM, and I am saved from my enemies* (*Psalms* 18:4) — this was an expression of David's confidence in God's power and will to save him; David praised God even before his victory.

R' Mordechai Chaim of Slonim once hosted a *Kiddush* on the Shabbos *before* he was scheduled to undergo an operation. Close chassidim asked why he did so. Replied R' Mordechai: When I come out of the hospital after the operation is successful, I will certainly make a *Kiddush* in order to publicly thank God for His kindness. I am so confident that God will help me that I don't want to wait until afterwards. Why not thank God already?"

Thus we recite *Hallel* after the meal to express our confidence in God's salvation. As *Shelah* puts it: The righteous declare their praise of God for His salvation as soon as He promises it. This is an expression of their powerful faith in God's word and their realization that since nothing and nobody can stand in His way, it is as good as done.

This idea is also expressed in the *Ribbon Kol HaOlamim* prayer recited on Friday night before *Kiddush*: "I thank You, God, for all the kindnesses You have done for me, and for those You are yet to do for me in the future."

The chassidic master *Reb Baruch of Mezhibozh* was once reciting this prayer when he paused at this phrase, and reflected, "Why should I thank God now for future favors? Why do I not just wait and express my gratitude for them when they occur?"

Reb Baruch'l then said, "I know why! It may be that certain kindnesses may occur in a fashion that they will not appear to me to be favors. In fact, they may be delivered in an unpleasant fashion, and I will not know to thank God for these favors. That is why I must thank Him in advance."

The rabbi then began to weep. "How tragic that my intelligence is so limited that God will be doing kindnesses for me, yet I will not appreciate them when they happen!"

Halleluyah! Praise, you servants of HASHEM, praise the Name of HASHEM! Blessed be the Name of HASHEM from now and forever.

redaction of *Hallel* in its present form, however, was done by King David (*Teshuvah MeAhavah* Vol. II responsa 264).

According to *Yalkut Shimoni* (*Exodus* 210), the Jews sang *Hallel* after God smote the firstborn of the Egyptians. In the middle of the night, Pharaoh was aroused by the cries of anguish that burst from every house, for no home was spared from this plague of death. He ran through the streets in search of Moses and Aaron (for he wanted the Jews to leave Egypt immediately). When Moses and Aaron sent word to Pharaoh that they would not leave until the next morning, Pharaoh pleaded, "I beg you to leave now; if something is not done immediately, all of Egypt will be destroyed!" Moses and Aaron replied, "If you want the plague to cease, you must issue an official proclamation of emancipation for the Jews."

At this Pharaoh shouted, "In the past you were my slaves, but now you are free men! You are on your own, you are servants of God, so you must *give praise, you servants of Hashem*!" Thus, in effect, Pharaoh declared that the Jews should recite *Hallel.*

On the Seder night, when we view ourselves as having been personally redeemed, we echo the praise of God that was voiced at the Exodus. As a sign of our new-found status as free men we recite *Hallel* while sitting, in contrast to the normal practice of standing (*Maharam of Rottenburg, Shibbolei HaLeket*).[1]

As mentioned above, we divide *Hallel* into two sections. The first two psalms, which speak of the Egyptian Exodus, are recited before the meal and before the *mitzvos* associated with the Exodus, while the rest of the *Hallel,* whose theme is the future redemption, is recited later (*Abarbanel, Levush* and *Pri Megadim* O.C 486).

God's essence is unfathomable; our awareness of Him is limited to the way we perceive Him as interacting with this world. Thus we can praise God only in a partial fashion. This reality is reflected in the fact that we call for praise of יָה, the partial Name of God (*Abarbanel*).

הַלְלוּ עַבְדֵי ה' — *Praise, you servants of Hashem.* Upon being liberated, the Jews were transformed from being slaves of Pharaoh into being servants of God, for from then on they showed allegiance to no one but Him.

As committed servants of God we are called upon to render our service and offer our contribution to the advancement and realization of His purposes on earth (*R' S. R. Hirsch*). This we do in word, by singing His praises, and in deed, by serving as ambassadors of good will on His behalf. By living an upright Torah life and conducting ourselves with sterling ethical and moral standards, our very life bespeaks the existence of the Supreme God.[2]

Radak explains *servants of Hashem* as referring particularly to the pious individuals who recognize God's awesomeness and have the ability to truly praise Him. Not everyone has the right to praise God; it is the privilege of His servants. King David

---

1. **On a Clear Night You Can See Forever.** Normally *Hallel* is recited only by day, but this night is different. Daylight is symbolic of times when we clearly see God's kindness and react with a song of His praises; night conjures an image of fear and uncertainty, in which faith rather than jubilation is more appropriate. The night of Pesach, however, is unique, because God "lit up the night like day" (*Psalms* 139:12), by revealing the light of His awesome power and control of the entire cosmos. On this night that turned to day, *Hallel* is entirely appropriate.

2. **Joyous Servitude.** While most servants find their servitude emotionally depressing and constantly seek means to escape their bondage, we rejoice in our servitude to God. Just as our forefathers rushed blindly after Him, following Him into a barren wilderness, so do we seek ways to accept the yoke of His sovereignty joyously and to make our connection to Him ever closer. The great joy of Pesach is not over our physical freedom as much as over the liberty of spirit that allows us to be His servants (*Sfas Emes*).

מִמִּזְרַח שֶׁמֶשׁ עַד מְבוֹאוֹ, מְהֻלָּל שֵׁם יהוה. רָם עַל כָּל גּוֹיִם יהוה, עַל הַשָּׁמַיִם כְּבוֹדוֹ. מִי כַּיהוה אֱלֹהֵינוּ, הַמַּגְבִּיהִי לָשָׁבֶת. הַמַּשְׁפִּילִי לִרְאוֹת, בַּשָּׁמַיִם וּבָאָרֶץ. מְקִימִי מֵעָפָר דָּל, מֵאַשְׁפֹּת יָרִים אֶבְיוֹן. לְהוֹשִׁיבִי

dismisses the value of praise from the wicked with the words *But to the wicked, God said, "To what purpose do you recount My decrees?"* (*Psalms* 50:16).[1]

הַלְלוּ אֶת שֵׁם ה׳ — *Praise the Name of* HASHEM. The major purpose of the plagues and miracles of the Exodus was to display to the world that there is only one God. The most intense recognition of this truth occurred among the Egyptians, such as Pharaoh, who initially ignored Moses and scorned God with the insolent statement *Who is* HASHEM *that I should heed His voice?* (*Exodus* 5:2). In response to the liberation they could no longer deny His power, for, as God proclaimed, *And Egypt shall know that*

I am HASHEM (ibid. 7:5).[2]

מִמִּזְרַח שֶׁמֶשׁ עַד מְבוֹאוֹ מְהֻלָּל שֵׁם ה׳ — *From the rising of the sun to its setting, Hashem's Name is praised.* We are enjoined to publicize the praise of God from East to West, in every corner of the earth.

When the Jews left Egypt, the wonders that God wrought for their sake amazed the entire world. At that time, praise for God was heard even from idolaters in the furthest corners of the earth. Similarly, the wonders of the future redemption from exile will evoke praise from all the people of the earth (*R' A.C. Feuer*).[3]

According to *Abarbanel* and the *Vilna Gaon*, these first verses address the questions of "who,

1. **The Praise of the Righteous.** This idea is reflected in Psalm 33:1, which we recite in our Sabbath prayers לַיְשָׁרִים נָאוָה תְהִלָּה — *for the upright, praise is fitting*. When one's rhetoric is not consistent with one's lifestyle, the song of praise is off key and unpleasing. Only praise of God that is accompanied by a life of righteousness and morality is a pleasing symphony to God. The higher the spiritual level of the person, the more meaningful the manner in which he praises God. R' Shraga Feivel Mendlowitz noted this upward progression in the *Nusach Sefard* version of Sabbath prayer beginning שׁוֹכֵן עַד, *He Who abides forever*: While the *upright* exalt God with their *mouth*, the *righteous* use articulated *words*. The *devout* use their *tongue*, implying praise which emanates from a deeper source within oneself. The *holy* person praises God with his very essence (קֶרֶב, literally, *inner being*).

In reality, only one who is not indentured to his passions and is not imprisoned by flaws of character can possess the spiritual vision to truly see the hand of God. It is from such pristine purity that one is able to perceive Godliness in everything that crosses his path. Thus, it is only the true servants of God who can praise Him (*R' Simchah Zissel of Kelm*).

2. **Saved for Himself.** We pray three times a day that God *bring a Redeemer for His Name's sake, with love* (first blessing of *Shemoneh Esrei*). As much as God seeks to save us for our sake and out of His love for us, He equally wants to redeem us so that we may bring about the realization of His will in this world. Thus, we praise Him as His servants out of gratitude for our freedom, and also praise His Name, for it is due to His will that He saved and continues to save us (*Maharal*).

3. **Unconditional Praise.** Sunrise is symbolic of good times and rising expectations, while sunset symbolizes disappointment and decline. Both the Jewish nation as a whole and each individual member have experienced these two emotional poles. Nevertheless, whatever we undergo, whether God seems to smile to us or to frown — מְהֻלָּל שֵׁם ה׳, *praised be the Name of* HASHEM. Always confident that His ways are just, we bless Him for all of life's manifestations. It is this equal presence of mind in the face of all the highs and lows of life that we speak of here (*R' A.C. Feuer*).

From the rising of the sun to its setting, HASHEM's Name is praised. High above all nations is HASHEM, above the heavens is His glory. Who is like HASHEM, our God, Who is enthroned on high, yet deigns to look upon the heavens and earth? He raises the impoverished from the dust, from the trash heaps He lifts the destitute — to seat them

---

when and where," regarding the praise of God. *The servants of God* should praise God from *now*, the time of the Exodus, when God revealed His absolute mastery of every aspect of existence, *and forever*. The arena for this praise is *from the rising of the sun to its setting*, for to the eyes of the enlightened, God is present everywhere.

רָם עַל כָּל גּוֹיִם ה׳ עַל הַשָּׁמַיִם כְּבוֹדוֹ — *High above all nations is* HASHEM, *above the heavens is His glory*. Although all the peoples may attempt to praise and exalt God, no one can truly grasp His *glory*, for it is *above* and beyond the comprehension of the *heavens* and the celestial legions. They, too, attempt to sing of God's wonders, but fail to exhaust His infinite praises (*Radak*). According to *Abarbanel* and others, the verse provides the non-Jewish perspective on God, as being so far above this world as to be totally uninvolved in human affairs. At best, the nations recognize His glory as being above the heavens, but they do not concede to Him any role in their earthly affairs — these they pursue in whatever way their desires and ambitions move them. Jews, however, understand that although He is enthroned on high, He looks down upon the earth, governs our destinies and demands our loyalty. Pharaoh did not understand this; he asked: *Who is* HASHEM *that I should listen to His voice?* (Exodus 5:2). The fall of his empire and the triumph of his erstwhile slaves provided the answer. Thus we proclaim, *Who is like* HASHEM *our God, Who is enthroned on high — Who deigns to look upon the heavens and the earth?* While other nations acknowledge God as Creator of the world, they claim that His awesome stature keeps Him aloof from direct contact with man or knowledge and involvement in his affairs. They profess that He is so exalted that His glory is only *above* the Heavens. We, however, know that He involves Himself with all of mankind, down to the lowest indigent or the most despair-ridden barren woman.[1] We thus praise Him not only for what He has done for us but for the hope we place in His ability to suddenly reverse even the most desperate situations, just as He did in Egypt.

הַמַּשְׁפִּילִי לִרְאוֹת בַּשָּׁמַיִם וּבָאָרֶץ — *Yet deigns to look upon the heavens and earth*. When compared to God's unfathomable greatness, even involvement in the affairs of the *heavens* entails lowering Himself, as it were. Nevertheless, in His infinite kindness toward man, God lowers His Presence to become intimately involved in man's life, just as He is involved in the affairs of Heaven (*Vilna Gaon*).[2]

מְקִימִי מֵעָפָר דָּל מֵאַשְׁפֹּת יָרִים אֶבְיוֹן — *He raises the impoverished from the dust, from the trash heaps He*

---

1. **Personal Project.** According to *Malbim*, the contrast painted here is not merely one of perception but reflects an actual principle, as explained by *Ramban* (*Leviticus* 18:25). While God ordains the destiny of all nations, He controls them through intermediaries and heavenly hosts. Thus, the Sages speak of the angel of Esau, etc. However, the destiny of God's nation, the people of Israel, is directly controlled by God Himself. Consequently, to the nations He is in Heaven, totally removed from direct contact with them, while to us He is our God, fully present in our most mundane affairs.

2. **A Mirror of Involvement.** God acts as our mirror image; as we act toward Him, so He reacts toward us. When we ignore His Presence and figuratively turn our faces and attention from Him, He responds by withdrawing high *above the heavens*, turning His face, as it were, from us. When we welcome His proximity and make the effort to have Him enter our lives and become an integral part of them, He responds by lovingly involving Himself in every facet of our lives.

עִם נְדִיבִים, עִם נְדִיבֵי עַמּוֹ. מוֹשִׁיבִי עֲקֶרֶת הַבַּיִת, אֵם הַבָּנִים שְׂמֵחָה, הַלְלוּיָהּ.[1]

בְּצֵאת יִשְׂרָאֵל מִמִּצְרָיִם, בֵּית יַעֲקֹב מֵעַם לֹעֵז. הָיְתָה יְהוּדָה לְקָדְשׁוֹ, יִשְׂרָאֵל מַמְשְׁלוֹתָיו. הַיָּם רָאָה וַיָּנֹס,

---

lifts the destitute. Human fate is so totally in the hands of God that one's situation can in a moment be dramatically and totally altered. Anyone who suffers, whether from physical deprivation or the emotional pain of feeling powerless, may look directly to God for a change for the better in his unhappy lot. The דָּל, *impoverished* person, who suffers from unfortunate circumstances will be raised up by God and lifted out of his abject poverty. Likewise the אֶבְיוֹן, *destitute* person, who is even more pathetic than the impoverished, can hope to be saved. In need of everything, a destitute person scours the trash heap in order to salvage whatever he can.[1]

R' Hirsch equates trash heaps with the dung pile where people deposit everything they deem to be worthless. A destitute person may be viewed by society as an unproductive parasite; he may be shunted aside, like human refuse. However, in

God's scheme he may very well be elevated to prominence. Thus, if he relies on God, even he can be elevated.

לְהוֹשִׁיבִי עִם נְדִיבִים עִם נְדִיבֵי עַמּוֹ — *To seat them with the nobles, with the nobles of His people.* God does not merely lift the poor and needy out of degradation; He also elevates them to the highest ranks of nobility and they enter the aristocracy of God's chosen nation (*Radak*). The *Vilna Gaon* renders these verses as a progression. If someone's spiritual poverty is such that he cannot feel spiritually productive by fulfilling the positive commandments, he is granted Divine assistance to lift himself up by his bootstraps. Even one who is hungry for everything, including forbidden pleasures, and suffers the indigence of wallowing in spiritual dumping grounds can be uplifted by God. One need not remain a prisoner of his past. Through heartfelt repentance one can recreate himself and be ele-

---

1. **Upward Mobility.** Man often becomes accepting of abject spiritual poverty; sometimes he even begins to enjoy the familiar comfort of the spiritual "trash heap" and feels no urge whatsoever to upgrade the level of his spiritual life. Even such a person can be granted enlightenment as God lifts him from groveling in spiritual waste (*Tzuf Amarim*).

The definition of a *trash heap* is relative. To a hungry pauper, a garbage dump is a source of food, and he feels no shame scavenging there. A very wealthy person may be embarrassed to shop in even a thrift shop, much less scrounge for food in dung hills. The higher one rises on the economic ladder, the loftier are his ideas of what is beneath his station, and he will become disdainful of his everyday practices of the past. So it is spiritually, as well. When a person elevates himself to a higher spiritual level, he is shocked at the activities that he once did routinely. "How could I ever have allowed myself to be so degraded?" he will wonder. Such were the results of the Exodus. After Israel left Egypt, they looked back at their past and realized that, in comparison with their new aspirations, they had been living in trash heaps (*Sfas Emes*).

On the night of Pesach the nation of Israel, the royal children of God, came into existence. Elevated to such a spiritual pinnacle, we are expected to abandon the spiritual trash heap and maintain a standard of behavior that befits royalty. *R' Abraham of Slonim* offered a homiletic interpretation of the words of King Solomon that conveys this sentiment. מוּסַר ה' בְּנִי אַל תִּמְאָס, *My child, do not despise God's discipline* (Proverbs 3:11). How does God chastise us to help us direct our lives? He says, "You are *My child*, a royal prince! אַל תִּמְאָס, *do not make yourself despicable*, by staining yourself with the filth of sin. Conduct yourself in keeping with your royal descent and thus protect the honor of the King."

with the nobles, with the nobles of His people. He transforms the barren wife into a glad mother of children. Halleluyah![1]

When Israel went forth from Egypt, Jacob's household from a people of alien tongue, Judah became His sanctuary, Israel His dominions. The Sea saw and fled; the

---

(1) *Psalms* 113.

---

vated to undreamt-of heights.

מוֹשִׁיבִי עֲקֶרֶת הַבַּיִת אֵם הַבָּנִים שְׂמֵחָה הַלְלוּיָהּ — *He transforms the barren wife into a glad mother of children. Halleluyah!* The Creator's complete control over nature is vividly demonstrated when He suddenly transforms *the barren wife* into a mother (*Radak*).

Rashi suggests that we interpret this verse as a reference to Israel in exile, in the spirit of *Isaiah 54:1, Sing out, O barren one who did not give birth,* where desolate Jerusalem is depicted as an unfertile woman, empty and barren of her populace. In the future, Zion and Jerusalem will be teeming with inhabitants and the celebration in the city will resemble a joyful homecoming, as *Isaiah 66:8* foretells: *as Zion went through her labor and birth to her children* [who will return from the four corners of the earth].[1]

בְּצֵאת יִשְׂרָאֵל מִמִּצְרָיִם בֵּית יַעֲקֹב מֵעַם לֹעֵז — *When Israel went forth from Egypt, Jacob's household from a people of alien tongue.* This chapter of *Psalms* describes God's Providence, as manifested in the Exodus. It portrays how Israel achieved the level of nobility described earlier. As a result of

Israel's tremendous self-sacrifice and unquestioning loyalty at the Sea of Reeds, the people were lifted from the spiritual abyss to the pinnacle of the Sinaitic revelation.

The *Vilna Gaon* renders עַם לֹעֵז as a *slanderous nation: When Israel* (the men) *went forth from Egypt, Jacob's household* (the women) *from a slanderous nation. . .* The Jewish women were targets of Egyptian slander regarding their moral stature, but those virtuous women were exonerated, for the Torah attests that, with only one exception, they were uncontaminated by the men of Egypt (see *Vayikra Rabbah* 32:5).

Radak views מֵעַם לֹעֵז as indicative of the care Jews took in their manner of speech. Both the women, who did not mingle with the Egyptians (*Ibn Yachya*), and the tribe of Levi (*Alshich*), which was not enslaved, spoke only the Holy Tongue. Even the Jews who were forced to communicate in Egyptian did so only under duress. Among themselves they spoke only the Holy Tongue and regarded Egyptian as a foreign language.[2]

הָיְתָה יְהוּדָה לְקָדְשׁוֹ — *Judah became His sanctuary.* The Jews were afraid to approach the Sea of Reeds

---

1. **Rekindled Romance.** R' Yehudah HaLevi describes the rekindled "romance" between God and His people in his liturgical poem *Yom LeYabashah: Betroth her again and drive her out no more; let her sunlight rise and let the shadows [of exile] flee.* The climax of this reestablished love will occur when *Eretz Yisrael,* our Mother Land, which spiritually nurtures and sustains her children, will rejoice as her sons return to their boundaries (see *Jeremiah* 31:16).

A barren woman always fears rejection by her husband or, even worse, divorce. Once God grants her children, she feels more secure and hence happier in her home. We await the time when God will reestablish us in our homeland, like a mother surrounded by her children.

2. **Foreign Tongue.** Moses initially refused to be God's representative to Pharaoh, with the excuse that he was tongue tied (*Exodus* 4:10). *Rashbam* (ad loc.) explains that Moses was *not* suffering from a physiological speech impediment, but that he found his speech impaired when he spoke the Egyptian language.

The *Rogatchover Gaon* points out that Moses should have been quite comfortable and fluent in the

---

הַיַּרְדֵּן יִסֹּב לְאָחוֹר. הֶהָרִים רָקְדוּ כְאֵילִים, גְּבָעוֹת כִּבְנֵי צֹאן. מַה לְּךָ הַיָּם כִּי תָנוּס, הַיַּרְדֵּן תִּסֹּב לְאָחוֹר. הֶהָרִים

until Nahshon ben Aminadav, the leader of the tribe of Judah, jumped into the threatening waters. Buoyed by his display of unbridled faith, the members of his own tribe followed him in. They, in turn, were followed by the rest of the Jewish people (see *Sotah* 37a and *Bamidbar Rabbah* 13:7). Thus, by demonstrating such perfect faith in God's word, the tribe of Judah sanctified His Name among His people (*Rashi, Radak, Abarbanel*).

Maharal explains that as a result of Judah's devotion to Him (which foreshadowed the Jewish nation's bridelike, blind loyalty in following God out to the desert), God entered into an intimate relationship with Israel, with Him as the bridegroom, as it were, and Israel as the bride. The term קָדְשׁוֹ, *His sanctuary*, may homiletically be rendered *His marriage partner*, just as the word קִדּוּשִׁין, which literally means *sanctification*, is also used for *betrothal*. Since Judah is personified as the bride, the feminine form הָיְתָה is used here.

יִשְׂרָאֵל מַמְשְׁלוֹתָיו – *Israel His dominions.* Ibn Yachya renders *His governors*; i.e., as a result of its outstanding leadership qualities at the Sea, the tribe of Judah was singled out to be the progenitor of the Jewish royal family, which ruled Israel.

According to the *Vilna Gaon* the reference here is to the power of the Jewish people to assume mastery over the forces of nature.[1] When Judah, followed by all of Israel, overcame fear and submitted to the mastery of God, they in turn were granted mastery over nature.

Radak renders מַמְשְׁלוֹתָיו as *His governed ones.* The final stage of severing Egyptian dominion over the Jews occurred at the Sea. Thenceforth they were under the total sovereignty of God Who later proclaimed at Mount Sinai, *And you shall be for Me a Kingdom of priests and a holy nation* (see *Exodus* 19:6). No longer subject to the morally injurious influence of Egypt, the Jewish nation was ready to rise to the call of sanctity.[2]

Egyptian language, because he had spoken it ever since his infancy in Pharaoh's palace. Nevertheless, this language made Moses fall silent, for it reflected the depravity of the Egyptian people. As a holy man of the spirit, Moses could not communicate in a language devoted to lust and gratification of the flesh. His tongue could speak freely only in the Holy Tongue, the language of the Jewish soul.

1. **Parenting Classes.** The ability to control nature includes our power to request supernatural salvation from God. The Talmud recounts God as saying, "I rule over mankind — who rules over Me? The righteous!" (*Moed Katan* 16). The *Kozhnitzer Maggid* saw an allusion to this in the words of the prophet וְכָל בָּנַיִךְ לִמּוּדֵי ה', *And all your children will be students of HASHEM* (*Isaiah* 54:13). He renders לִמּוּדֵי ה' homiletically as *teachers of Hashem*. The righteous of Israel, so to speak, teach God how to act towards His children.

2. **Ode to Identity.** According to the *Midrash* (*Vayikra Rabbah* 32:5), Israel merited redemption from Egypt because: לֹא שִׁנּוּ אֶת שְׁמָם, *they did not change their names;* לֹא שִׁנּוּ אֶת לְשׁוֹנָם, *they did not change their tongue* (they continued to speak in the Holy Tongue — see above); שֶׁהָיוּ גְדוּרִים בָּעֲרָיוֹת, *they restrained themselves against immorality;* and שֶׁלֹּא הָיוּ בֵּינֵיהֶם דֵּלָטוֹרִין, *there were no talebearers among them* (to act as informers for the Egyptian rulers). *Chasam Sofer* sees an allusion to these merits in the first two verses of this psalm. *When Israel went forth* indicates that they always remained "Israel," retaining their Jewish names; *from a people of alien tongue* teaches that even after 210 years the Egyptian language was still an alien tongue to the Jews. *Judah became His sanctuary* alludes to the holiness of the Jews who practiced restraint against sexual immorality, a precondition to sanctity (see *Vayikra Rabbah* 24:6). Finally, even while under the brutal oppression of the Egyptians, the Jews maintained a sense of independence and brotherhood with each other; not one Jew was ready to be a turncoat and report against a fellow Jew. This admirable merit is conveyed in the words *Israel His dominions*, i.e., despite Egypt's power, the Jews remained loyal to God, and so were not disloyal to each other.

Jordan turned backward. The mountains skipped like rams, the hills like young lambs. What ails you, O Sea, that you flee? O Jordan, that you turn backward? O mountains,

---

הַיָּם רָאָה וַיָּנֹס — *The Sea saw and fled.* The Sea of Reeds miraculously split (*fled*) to allow the Jews to pass through and escape their Egyptian pursuers. When Moses lifted his staff and stretched out his hand over the Sea, it split (see *Exodus* 14:16 and 14:21). Thus, it was the staff with God's great Name engraved on it that the Sea "saw" (*Midrash Hallel*).

According to a familiar Midrashic interpretation (*Bereishis Rabbah* 87:10), the Sea saw the אֲרוֹן שֶׁל יוֹסֵף, *the casket of Joseph.* God then said: Let the Sea flee from before the one about whom it is written, *But he left his garment in her hand, and he fled (וַיָּנֹס) and went outside* (*Genesis* 39:12).

When Moses lifted his staff the waters were reluctant to halt their normal flow; they maintained that they were obliged to obey the natural law under which God had placed them. "From where shall we take the strength to break the immutable laws of nature?" they argued. But Joseph's coffin reminded them of how that righteous man had transcended his nature to resist being seduced by Potiphar's wife (*Genesis* 39:13). The Sea concluded that if a frail human being could control his nature, overcome the seemingly insurmountable force of evil and flee from sin, then it, too, could restrain its natural flow and flee for the sake of Israel (*Tiferes Shlomo*).

According to yet another Midrash it was the sight of the Jews following Nahshon into the Sea that caused it to split. Up to their noses in water, they demonstrated such complete faith in God that the Sea was forced to yield.[1]

הַיַּרְדֵּן יִסֹּב לְאָחוֹר — *The Jordan turned backward.* According to *Rashi* (*Exodus* 14:21), this too was part of the miracle of the splitting of the Sea, for all the bodies of water in the world — including the Jordan — miraculously parted at that time.

Malbim, however, comments that this describes a miracle that occurred when Joshua led the people into the land (see *Joshua 3:16*). Like the Sea of Reeds forty years before, the Jordan River parted, but the splitting of the river differed from the splitting of the Sea. The Sea was a flat, relatively placid body of water, and God sent a wind to push back the water from the seabed, to form two walls; thus, the Sea seemed to "flee" in all directions before these gusts. In the case of the Jordan, in contrast, God held back its flow, so that the water piled up into a wall, on only one side. Therefore, the Psalmist here uses the term יִסֹּב, *turned backward*, to indicate that the current was reversed from its usual path.

הֶהָרִים רָקְדוּ כְאֵילִים גְּבָעוֹת כִּבְנֵי צֹאן — *The mountains skipped like rams, the hills like young lambs.* While the Jews were physically freed from Egypt at the Sea, the residue of negative spiritual influence remained with them. Having been exposed to the forty-nine degrees of spiritual impurity, they had to undergo the spiritual cleansing period of the forty-nine days of *Sefirah*. Finally they received the Torah and were purged of the last vestiges of Egypt's spiritual contamination. At Sinai all the mountains sought to be the venue of the Revelation. Like proud creatures who prance about, displaying their beauty and height, each was figuratively arguing that it should be the mountain where God will give the Torah (*Psalms* 68:17).

According to *Rashi* (*Psalms* 29:6), the mountains and trees around Sinai all shook and trembled in awe before the Divine Presence that descended amid thunder, lightning and shofar blasts. The Psalmist employs the metaphor of skipping and dancing to capture the image.

Steep, sharp-edged mountains are described as *rams*,

---

1. **Lesson at Sea.** One may derive spiritual inspiration from the Sea of Reeds. If the Sea — an inanimate creation with no hope of being rewarded for fulfilling God's will — subjugates itself to God, certainly human beings, who possess a Godly soul and who are assured of great reward for following His will, should yield to Divine demands and expectations (*Yismach Yisrael*).

תָּרְקְדוּ כְאֵילִים, גְּבָעוֹת כִּבְנֵי צֹאן. מִלְּפְנֵי אָדוֹן חוּלִי אָרֶץ, מִלְּפְנֵי אֱלוֹהַּ יַעֲקֹב. הַהֹפְכִי הַצּוּר אֲגַם מָיִם, חַלָּמִישׁ לְמַעְיְנוֹ מָיִם.[1]

The cup is lifted and the matzos covered during the recitation of this blessing.

בָּרוּךְ אַתָּה יהוה אֱלֹהֵינוּ מֶלֶךְ הָעוֹלָם, אֲשֶׁר גְּאָלָנוּ וְגָאַל אֶת אֲבוֹתֵינוּ מִמִּצְרַיִם, וְהִגִּיעָנוּ הַלַּיְלָה הַזֶּה לֶאֱכָל

---

which are large and sharp horned; hills, which are low and shaped in soft curves and ridges, are compared to young lambs, which are small and tender (*Malbim*).

מַה לְּךָ הַיָּם כִּי תָנוּס — *What ails you, O sea, that you flee?* The Psalmist captures the sense of awe and bewilderment that seized mankind. Poetically, he asks each of them what it is that elicits such a dramatic reaction from them. To the Sea he says, "What cataclysmic happening caused you to split so miraculously?" To the mountains he says, "What caused you to prance with such vigor?"

מִלִּפְנֵי אָדוֹן חוּלִי אָרֶץ — *Before the Lord's Presence, did I, the earth, tremble.* This translation follows *Radak* who relates חוּלִי to the term חִיל וּרְעָדָה, meaning *trembling*.

The *earth*, which includes both the mountains and the seas, answers the question posed in the preceding verses: The mountains shook and the seas split because that was the will of God who is *the Lord* and Master over all.

Rashi and *Malbim* interpret חוּלִי as being related to מְחוֹלֵל, *the Creator*. All of creation fears the Master Who is the Originator of all existence.

The Midrash teaches that when Moses saw that the Sea had split, he laughed and danced for joy. He asked, "Sea, why do you flee?"

The Sea replied, "Before you ask me, why don't you ask the mountains why they skip?"

Moses then put this query to the mountains, who responded, "Before you inquire of us, why don't you ask the entire earth why it shook and jumped out of place?"

Moses then questioned the earth, which replied, "Rest assured that it was not because of Moses son of Amram that we convulsed! It was *before the Lord* alone that the earth trembled."

מִלְּפְנֵי אֱלוֹהַ יַעֲקֹב — *Before the presence of the God of Jacob.* The natural phenomena responded and explained that their reaction was in order that the God of Jacob save His people. As the Sages taught regarding the Splitting of the Sea, "The Sea fulfilled its original stipulation, for its creation was conditional upon its splitting for the sake of the Jewish people." All of nature was created for the sake of the nation of Israel, as the Sages expound on the first word of the Torah: בְּרֵאשִׁית, because of the things that are called רֵאשִׁית, *beginning* or *first*, God created heaven and earth. One of those "firsts" is Israel (see *Rashi* to *Genesis* 1:1). Thus, the forces of nature explained that they reacted to the Exodus with such alacrity because of God's — and nature's — special relationship with Israel (*Shemos Rabbah* 21:6).

הַהֹפְכִי הַצּוּר אֲגַם מָיִם — *Who turns the rock into a pond of water.* This refers to the incident described in *Exodus* 17:6. When the Jews thirsted for water in the Wilderness, God instructed Moses, *you shall smite the rock and water shall come out of it so that the people may drink*, which shows that nature bends itself totally to conform to the will of its Originator (*Radak*). Thus, the Sea explains why it split by citing the action of the rock (*Ibn Ezra*).

Alternatively, the phrase might be translated as *Who turns a pond of water* into a rock, referring to what happened when Israel crossed the Sea. At that time, God performed a double miracle. First, He transformed the pool of water into solid rock and dry land, so that Israel could walk through the Sea. When the Jews became thirsty during the crossing, God instructed them to strike the frozen

that you skip like rams? O hills, like young lambs? Before the Lord's Presence, did I, the earth tremble, before the presence of the God of Jacob, Who turns the rock into a pond of water, the flint into a flowing fountain.[1]

The cup is lifted and the matzos covered during the recitation of this blessing.

Blessed are You, HASHEM, our God, King of the universe, Who has redeemed us and redeemed our ancestors from Egypt, and enabled us to reach this night that we may eat

_____

(1) *Psalms* 114.

_____

walls of water. Miraculously, the walls, which had been like *flint,* turned into deliciously sweet springs of water, which refreshed the Jews and their cattle (*Yalkut Me'am Loez, Beshalach*).

Abarbanel explains: Nature is totally malleable in the hands of God. Just as He made the water hard as rock when He split the Sea, so He turned a rock into drinking water for the Jews in the desert.[1]

אֲשֶׁר גְּאָלָנוּ וְגָאַל אֶת אֲבוֹתֵינוּ — *Who has redeemed us and redeemed our ancestors.* This blessing, known as the *Blessing of Redemption* (see *Rashbam* to *Pesachim* 116b), concludes the *Maggid* (narrative) portion of the Seder. According to many opinions it is this blessing which constitutes the מְסַיֵּם בְּשֶׁבַח, *conclude with glory,* the Talmudic requirement of how one should conclude the Exodus narrative (see *Pesachim* 116a).

The blessing's primary theme is to offer thanks for our redemption from Egypt, which we will shortly commemorate by eating matzah and *maror.* For this reason the conclusion of the blessing is expressed in past tense — thanking God as the One Who גָּאַל יִשְׂרָאֵל, *redeemed Israel* —

although the blessing also includes a prayer for the ultimate redemption, at which time we will be able to bring the *pesach* offering once again.[2]

The insertion of this addition follows the opinion of Rabbi Akiva (*Pesachim* 116b). According to *Rambam* (*Chametz U'Matzah* 8:5), *Shibolei HaLeket* and others, R' Akiva expanded the blessing to include this request for the return of the Temple (see *Responsa Rivevos Efraim* 4:113 §9).

We speak of the redemption in personal terms since, if God had not taken our forefathers out of Egypt, we would still be enslaved, possibly physically, and certainly spiritually (*Avudraham*). This mirrors our earlier statement that not only did He redeem our ancestors, but He redeemed us with them (*Malbim*).

Unlike the earlier passage (לְפִיכָךְ) where we spoke of God as having performed miracles for our fathers and for us, here we reverse the order and mention *our* redemption before that of our fathers. *Chasam Sofer* and *Aruch HaShulchan* explain: Earlier, when recounting the historical events, we speak first of our fathers since they experienced the miracles firsthand. Here, however, when offering our song of gratitude, our own sentiments

_____

1. **Pouring Heart.** Homiletically, the rock refers to man's heart, which is frequently hardened like stone and insensitive to the call of God, which echoes in his soul (*Yismach Yisrael*). In but a moment God can soften our heart, turning it into a flowing fountain as we pour it out in prayer. We need only to will it and it can happen.

2. **Redeeming Faith.** In our daily prayers we conclude the blessing after the *Shema* (which deals with the Exodus) with גָּאַל יִשְׂרָאֵל, in past tense. Only in *Shemoneh Esrei* do we speak of God as גּוֹאֵל יִשְׂרָאֵל, the (constant) *Redeemer of Israel.* R' Hirsch explains: Only after we have set forth our faith in God as our Redeemer (as evidenced in the Egyptian Exodus) may we begin *Shemoneh Esrei* and request ongoing personal and national redemption.

בּוֹ מַצָּה וּמָרוֹר. כֵּן יהוה אֱלֹהֵינוּ וֵאלֹהֵי אֲבוֹתֵינוּ, יַגִּיעֵנוּ
לְמוֹעֲדִים וְלִרְגָלִים אֲחֵרִים הַבָּאִים לִקְרָאתֵנוּ לְשָׁלוֹם,
שְׂמֵחִים בְּבִנְיַן עִירֶךָ וְשָׂשִׂים בַּעֲבוֹדָתֶךָ, וְנֹאכַל שָׁם מִן הַזְּבָחִים
וּמִן הַפְּסָחִים – on Saturday night substitute [מִן הַפְּסָחִים וּמִן הַזְּבָחִים

---

come first.[1]

לֶאֱכָל בּוֹ מַצָּה וּמָרוֹר — *That we may eat on it matzah and maror.* We thank God for having freed us and for giving us the opportunity to commemorate His kindness by fulfilling His *mitzvos* and eating matzah and *maror.* It is not the pleasure of living *per se* for which we are grateful, but the opportunity life affords us to serve God by performing His commandments (*Malbim*).[2]

The term *and enabled us to reach* is reminiscent of the term in the שֶׁהֶחֱיָנוּ blessing, which thanks God for having given us life and preserved us long enough to perform the commandments associated with a new season or festival. Indeed, according to *Rokeach* (371) and *Avudraham*, this phrase is in place of the שֶׁהֶחֱיָנוּ blessing over the *mitzvos* of matzah and *maror.* Som versions of the Haggadah

reflect this and have a text which reads לַלַּיְלָה הַזֶּה, *to this night* (see *Rambam, Frankel* edition, *Chametz U'Matzah* 8:5), which resembles the formula of the שֶׁהֶחֱיָנוּ blessing even more closely.

כֵּן. . . יַגִּיעֵנוּ לְמוֹעֲדִים וְלִרְגָלִים אֲחֵרִים — *So. . .bring us also to future festivals and holidays.* *Festivals* refers to Rosh Hashanah and Yom Kippur, while *holidays* refers to Pesach, Shavuos and Succos, when Jews were commanded, in Temple times, to travel to Jerusalem and celebrate there (*Abarbanel*). We pray for the Final Redemption when we will be able to celebrate joyously, free of the fear of oppression that accompanies our existence in exile. Just as we have successfully conducted this Seder in commemoration of past redemption, so may we joyously celebrate future redemptions (*Maharal*).[3]

---

1. **Linked to the Past.** Throughout our prayers we refer to God as אֱלֹהֵינוּ וֵאלֹהֵי אֲבוֹתֵינוּ, *Our God and the God of our forefathers*. First we call Him *our* God because we are obligated to serve Him and know Him to the limit of *our* capacity. But there is much about His ways that we cannot understand. In response to such mysteries we proclaim that He is *the God of our forefathers,* and we have faith in the tradition they transmitted (*Dover Shalom*).

On the other hand, one must take care to develop a vibrant personal relationship with God, and not merely interact with Him as a familial tradition. In the Song at the Sea, Moses said first, *"This is my God."* Only then did he say *"the God of my father"* (*Exodus* 15:2). First a Jew should develop faith in God based on his own experiences of God's beneficence and only then relate it to his legacy of faith from his forefathers (*Ohr HaChaim*).

2. **Living for God.** The Jewish nation owes its existence purely to its allegiance to God's commandments. Life is only meaningful as a venue in which to do His will. An 80 year old once visited *R' Avraham of Kalisk* and complained that he was sick of living. "I'm 80 years old already, and I have had enough. I can't do anything worthwhile any more, anyway," said the despondent man. The *Rebbe* replied: "Foolish one! It is worthwhile to live a full 80 years just for the opportunity to put on *tefillin* once — even if someone does it out of habit and with little intent!"

3. **Unmerited Redemption.** Our prayer here, in which we ask God to allow us to celebrate future holidays as liberated, free people with the Messianic rebuilding of Jerusalem, echoes our prayer when we bless the new month. "He Who performed miracles for our forefathers and redeemed them from slavery to freedom — may He redeem us soon." Even if we do not deserve to be redeemed from our present exile, let us be like our forefathers in Egypt who, sunken in the spiritual impurity of the land, were not deserving of God's deliverance. As in the days when we left Egypt, let God once again show us miracles and redeem us soon — even if we don't truly deserve it (*R' Tzadok HaKohen*).

on it matzah and *maror*. So, HASHEM, our God and God of our fathers, bring us also to future festivals and holidays in peace, gladdened in the rebuilding of Your city and joyful at Your service. There we shall eat of the offerings and *pesach* sacrifices (on Saturday night substituite: of the *pesach* sacrifices and offerings)

According to *Chukas HaPesach*, we implore God here to give us continued opportunities to fulfill His will. Just as we have been privileged to observe the *mitzvos* of matzah and *maror*, so may we observe the commandments of all the festivals in their appointed times.[1]

שְׂמֵחִים בְּבִנְיַן עִירֶךְ וְשָׂשִׂים בַּעֲבוֹדָתֶךְ — *Gladdened in the rebuilding of Your city, and joyful at Your service.* The terms שִׂמְחָה, *gladness,* and שָׂשׂוֹן, *joy,* connote different types of happiness. The commentators offer different approaches to define the terms: According to *Eitz Chaim,* שִׂמְחָה, *gladness,* refers to external public expressions of joy while שָׂשׂוֹן is indicative of inner happiness. Hence the rebuilding of Jerusalem, which will signal the external manifestation of redemption, will elicit *gladness,* while the renewed vigor with which we will pursue the true goal of serving God will call out an inner, emotional joyousness.[2]

Malbim offers a variation on this theme, defining שִׂמְחָה, *gladness,* as happiness that may be short

term, while שָׂשׂוֹן refers to *lasting joy.* If so, this phrase may imply that while we will celebrate the rebuilding of the Temple, only by serving God through performance of the commandments can we assure that the joy will be permanent.

As holy as the city of Jerusalem is, it is only a tool whereby we can have the proper conditions to serve God. The happiness over a rebuilt Jerusalem is mundane and of little value unless it is suffused with a spirit of Godliness and a heightened commitment to Divine Service. Thus, while we will be happy over the physical joy of a renewed Jerusalem, we will spiritually exult with the expanded avenues for serving Him (*Netziv*).

וְנֹאכַל שָׁם מִן הַזְּבָחִים וּמִן הַפְּסָחִים — *There we shall eat of the offerings and pesach sacrifices.* The term *offerings* refers to the *chagigah,* the festival offering, that was required on all three pilgrimage festivals: Pesach, Shavuos and Succos. The *chagigah* is mentioned before the *pesach* offering because it was to be eaten first at the Seder, in

---

1. **Past and Future.** Whenever we thank God for past favors we continue our prayer with a request that He continue to show us His beneficence in the future. מוֹדָה עַל הֶעָבָר וְצוֹעֵק עַל הֶעָתִיד, *We express gratitude for the past and cry out in prayer regarding the future. Tur* (*Genesis* 29:35) explains Leah's temporary interruption from childbearing after the birth of Judah as a punishment for the fact that, although she thanked God for having been granted more than her fair share of children (see *Genesis* ibid.), she did not pray for the future as well.

According to R' Yonah (*Berachos* 4b), the requests one makes for the future reflect the strength of the faith in God one has developed as a result of perceiving His hand in the past. Thus, it is because we believe in God's all-encompassing power as evidenced in the Exodus that we trust in Him as the only One Who can help in the future; in recognition of past redemption we ask for future salvation (see *Sefer HaChinuch* 606). Furthermore, one's faith may serve as the catalyst for God to be beneficent in the future. Thus, after thanking Him for the freedom He granted us in Egypt, we use that faith as the foundation of our prayer for the ultimate liberty (*HaSeder HaAruch*).

2. **Self-satisfaction.** We speak of happiness over rebuilding the city of Jerusalem rather than over erecting the Third Temple. This reflects the psychological truth that a person prefers a small amount of something he produced himself to a large gift from someone else (*Bava Metzia* 38a). We will find greater happiness in the rebuilding of the city, which will be the result of our own efforts, than in the new Temple which will be built by God's hands [see *Rosh Hashanah* 30a] (*Shiras HaGeulah*).

אֲשֶׁר יַגִּיעַ דָּמָם עַל קִיר מִזְבַּחֲךָ לְרָצוֹן. וְנוֹדֶה לְךָ שִׁיר חָדָשׁ עַל גְּאֻלָּתֵנוּ וְעַל פְּדוּת נַפְשֵׁנוּ. בָּרוּךְ אַתָּה יהוה, גָּאַל יִשְׂרָאֵל.

בָּרוּךְ אַתָּה יהוה אֱלֹהֵינוּ מֶלֶךְ הָעוֹלָם, בּוֹרֵא פְּרִי הַגָּפֶן.

The second cup is drunk while leaning on the left side —
preferably the entire cup, but at least most of it.

---

compliance with the requirement that the *pesach* be eaten when one is no longer hungry (*Pesachim* 119b, see *Tosafos* ad loc. s.v. ונאמר). The reason the *pesach* was to be eaten last was so that its taste would linger in our mouths, and also in order to ensure that, our appetites already having been somewhat sated, we would not be likely to break its bones (which is forbidden by the Torah) out of hunger (*Yerushalmi, Pesachim* 6:4).

According to *Maharil* and *Mahari Weil* (see *Shaar HaTziun* 473 §80), when Pesach eve falls on a Sabbath, the order of this phrase should be changed to read מִן הַפְּסָחִים וּמִן הַזְּבָחִים, *of the pesach sacrifices and (chagigah) offerings.* The reason for the change is that a *chagigah* may not be slaughtered on the Sabbath. In such years, only the *pesach* was eaten at the Seder, and the *chagigah* was delayed until the Intermediate Days; consequently, the order of the blessing should reflect this change. The consensus of commentators, however, oppose this alteration, ruling that the format of the Sages must not be tampered with. They maintain that since this blessing is a prayer for the restoration of the Temple in time for *next year's* Pesach, there is no need to invert the order, because Pesach eve will not necessarily fall on the Sabbath next year (see *Responsa Knesses Yechezkel* cited in *Shaar HaTziun* ibid.).

אֲשֶׁר יַגִּיעַ דָּמָם עַל קִיר מִזְבַּחֲךָ לְרָצוֹן — *Whose blood will reach the wall of Your Altar for gracious acceptance.* Only when the blood of an offering has been placed on the Altar is the service valid, and only then may its flesh be eaten. Thus, this portion of the service is essential both to the validity of the offering and to the owner's ability to fulfill the commandment of eating it.

In a homiletical interpretation, *R' Reuven Margolios* explains that the blood of sin offerings is smeared on the corners at the top of the Altar, while the blood of all other types of offerings — elevation offerings, peace offerings, etc. — is poured on the wall of the Altar. As we beseech God to rebuild the Temple, we pray for a revelation of God's spirit and a revolutionary increase in knowledge of Him. This will be accompanied by the removal of all impurity from the world, leaving humanity sinless. At that time there will no longer be any need for sin offerings. Thus we ask God to redeem us again so that we need only offerings whose blood is poured on the *wall* of the Altar — and we will have no need for sin offerings whose blood is smeared on the corners. This is the type of offering which is graciously accepted (לְרָצוֹן) before God.[1]

---

1. **Graceful Sacrifice.** Throughout the generations, even when there was no Temple, the Jewish people never ceased to offer "sacrifices" to God. How much Jewish blood was spilled on the altar of history in order to sanctify God's Name? But while God cherishes every drop of blood shed for His sake, this is not the sort of service that truly pleases Him [לְרָצוֹן]. In the words of the Talmud, "When Jews are in pain, the Divine Presence articulates its empathy saying, so to speak, 'I am burdened by My head; I am burdened by My hand' " (*Sanhedrin* 46a). We pray for an end to all atrocities committed against Jews and an end to Jewish pain, so that the only blood brought on the Altar will be that which is graciously acceptable to God (*Chasam Sofer*).

whose blood will reach the wall of Your Altar for gracious acceptance. We shall then sing a new song of praise to You for our redemption and the liberation of our souls. Blessed are You, HASHEM, Who has redeemed Israel.

Blessed are You, HASHEM, our God, King of the universe, Who creates the fruit of the vine.

The second cup is drunk while leaning on the left side —
preferably the entire cup, but at least most of it.

וְנוֹדֶה לְךָ שִׁיר חָדָשׁ — *We shall then sing a new song of praise to You.* As noted earlier (page 146, s.v. וְנֹאמַר לְפָנָיו שִׁירָה חֲדָשָׁה, *and we will recite a new song before you*), all songs of praise are expressed in the feminine form [שִׁירָה], except for the song at the Final Redemption — the one referred to here — which is expressed in the masculine form, שִׁיר. The Midrash (*Shemos Rabbah* 23) explains that the joy of a woman who gives birth is tinged with fear of the pain she will suffer if she gives birth again. Similarly, past redemptions were always dampened by the thoughts of subsequent exile. However, the Final Redemption will be complete, in no way diminished by fear of recurring exile.

עַל גְּאֻלָּתֵנוּ וְעַל פְּדוּת נַפְשֵׁנוּ — *For our redemption and for the liberation of our souls.* The dual terms allude to different aspects of freedom. According to *Kol Bo, Avudraham,* etc., we will thank God for *our redemption* in the future and simultaneously we will remember *the liberation of our souls* that occurred in Egypt.

This follows the opinion of the Sages (*Berachos* 12b, quoted earlier in the Haggadah) that we will be obligated to recall the Egyptian Exodus even in the Messianic Age.

Malbim views both phrases as referring to the Great Redemption. *For our redemption* refers to the physical freedom we will achieve in the future, while *the liberation of our souls* reflects the spiritual liberty we will then enjoy. *R' Chaim Brisker* comments that both phrases refer to the Egyptian saga. Not only were we extricated from Egypt's physical domination, but we also were emotionally liberated from the slavish mentality we had developed there. We thank God for both elements of our freedom.

גָּאַל יִשְׂרָאֵל — *Who has redeemed Israel.* The Talmud explains גָּאַל יִשְׂרָאֵל in the past tense as referring to the Egyptian Exodus, while גּוֹאֵל יִשְׂרָאֵל in the present tense, which is used in the *Shemoneh Esrei*, alludes to ongoing redemptions. Accordingly, *Malbim* explains that this blessing thanks God for our freedom from Egypt (although this paragraph also includes a plea for future deliverance as well), because in that liberation lies the key to our ultimate freedom. As the prophet promised, *As in the days that you left*

≈§ **Taste of a Sinless World.** *Ramban* (*Numbers* 28:2) notes that among all additional offerings (*Mussaf*), only that of the Sabbath does not include a sin offering. The Sabbath, which is a microcosm of the World to Come, reflects a time when we will enjoy a sinless world.

Based on this, *R' Yitzchak Hutner* explains the text of the Sabbath *Mussaf Shemoneh Esrei:* "You commanded us, Hashem, our God, to offer on it (i.e., the Sabbath) the Sabbath *mussaf* offering כָּרָאוּי, *properly.*" The term *properly* does not mean "following the proper procedure" or "offering it in a timely fashion"; this goes without saying. Rather the word should be rendered *as it should be.* God's ultimate goal is that we bring about a sinless world. He commanded us to bring the Sabbath *Mussaf* offering in a fashion that reflects the world *as it should be.*

רָחְצָה

The hands are washed for matzah and the following blessing is recited. It is preferable to bring water and a basin to the head of the household at the Seder table.
Before washing, it is vital that one insure that there is adequate *matzah shemurah* for each of the participants. Some declare their intent to perform the commandment to eat matzah according to the laws of the Torah as codified by the Sages.

בָּרוּךְ אַתָּה יהוה אֱלֹהֵינוּ מֶלֶךְ הָעוֹלָם, אֲשֶׁר קִדְּשָׁנוּ בְּמִצְוֹתָיו, וְצִוָּנוּ עַל נְטִילַת יָדָיִם.

מוֹצִיא

The following two blessings are recited over matzah; the first is recited over matzah as food, and the second for the special *mitzvah* of eating matzah on the night of Pesach. [The latter blessing is to be made with the intention that it also apply to the *korech*, "sandwich," and the *afikoman*.] The head of the household raises all the matzos on the Seder plate and recites the following blessings:

בָּרוּךְ אַתָּה יהוה אֱלֹהֵינוּ מֶלֶךְ הָעוֹלָם, הַמּוֹצִיא לֶחֶם מִן הָאָרֶץ.

Those who use three matzos put down the bottom matzah at this point.

Egypt I shall show you miracles (Micah 7:15).[1]

רָחְצָה — *Washing the Hands.* In preparation for eating matzah we now ritually wash our hands. Although we already washed our hands prior to

eating the *karpas*, we must wash again, since it is assumed that we were not attentive to the ritual cleanliness of our hands during the long interim since they were washed. Theoretically, if one is sure he did not touch anything dirty he may rely on

1. **Repeat Performance.** The verse seems to indicate that the miracles of the Final Redemption will be similar to those of the Exodus. This would seem to contradict many sources that portray the Messianic Age as infinitely more wondrous than the Egyptian episode.

R' Levi Yitzchak of Berditchev offered a parable: A destitute man won a lottery worth $1 million. Suddenly freed of his crushing poverty, he was ecstatic and could find no words to express his joy. A year later he again won $1 million lottery — but since was already a millionaire, he did not reach the same degree of happiness that the first million had brought him. In order to repeat the joy of the initial prize, he would need to win a much more substantial sum.

So too, explained the *Berditchever*, when Jews were freed from Egypt under such miraculous circumstances, it brought them to the heights of true joy. In one moment they went spiritually from rags to riches. In the future redemption God will shower us with such a dazzling display of miracles that we will be able to reexperience, relative to our present spiritual and emotional state, the same level of indescribable happiness that we experienced in the days that we left the slavery of Egypt. Thus, the verse cited here means that the joy of the future will equal that of Egypt, but in order to achieve it, the miracles will have to be far greater.

RACHTZAH

The hands are washed for matzah and the following blessing is recited. It is preferable to bring water and a basin to the head of the household at the Seder table.
Before washing, it is vital that one insure that there is adequate *matzah shemurah* for each of the participants. Some declare their intent to perform the commandment to eat matzah according to the laws of the Torah as codified by the Sages.

Blessed are You, HASHEM, our God, King of the universe, Who has sanctified us with His commandments, and has commanded us concerning the washing of the hands.

MOTZI

The following two blessings are recited over matzah; the first is recited over matzah as food, and the second for the special *mitzvah* of eating matzah on the night of Passover. [The latter blessing is to be made with the intention that it also apply to the "sandwich," and the *afikoman*.] The head of the household raises all the matzos on the Seder plate and recites the following blessing:

Blessed are You, HASHEM, our God, King of the universe, Who brings forth bread from the earth.

Those who use three matzos put down the bottom matzah at this point.

---

his original washing, but the custom is to wash one's hands again in any case (see *HaSeder HaAruch* 75:4).[1]

Likutei Maharich sees an allusion to this in the *Simanim*. The first washing of the hands, which is obligatory under all circumstances, is called וּרְחַץ in the

imperative — *"Wash the hands!"* This washing, which under certain circumstances may theoretically be dispensed with, is called רָחְצָה in the noun form, *"washing of the hands."*

מוֹצִיא — *Say Hamotzi (blessing over bread).* On Sabbaths and festivals this blessing is always

---

1. **Focused Disinterest.** The Talmud derives the obligation to wash one's hands before a meal from the word וְהִתְקַדִּשְׁתֶּם, *you are to sanctify yourselves* (Leviticus 11:44 — see Berachos 53b). The washing is a form of self-sanctification, for one symbolically "washes his hands" of any personal or animalistic desire in eating; instead one consecrates and dedicates this seemingly mundane, almost animalistic act, to the service of God. The hand washing is reminiscent of the ceremony of the decapitated calf (עֶגְלָה עֲרוּפָה Deuteronomy 21:6), during which the elders of the city nearest the scene of an unsolved murder proclaim that they were innocent of any involvement in the death. They wash their hands over the calf and declare, "Our hands have not spilled this blood" (ibid. v. 7). The sanctification of hands before eating implies a similar declaration about the food: "We will partake of this food in order to serve God, but we want no involvement in the base instincts associated with this physical activity" (R' Tzadok HaKohen).

This dichotomous involvement-disinvolvement is necessary in social relationships as well. The Talmud (Shabbos 14a) teaches that King Solomon instituted two Rabbinic enactments: *eruvin* (the process by which several private properties are halachically merged together to permit carrying from one to another on the Sabbath) and *netilas yadayim* (ritual washing of the hands). R' Mendel of Kotzk explained homiletically: King Solomon, the wisest of men, successfully struck the balance in social interaction. One must be able to mix and mingle with all types of people (*eruvin*, lit., "mixing"), while simultaneously washing away all negative influences (*netilas yadayim*) that might accompany such social ties. One should be neither a lone sheep nor a blind follower of the herd.

מַצָּה

בָּרוּךְ אַתָּה יהוה אֱלֹהֵינוּ מֶלֶךְ הָעוֹלָם, אֲשֶׁר קִדְּשָׁנוּ בְּמִצְוֹתָיו, וְצִוָּנוּ עַל אֲכִילַת מַצָּה.

Each participant is required to eat an amount of matzah equal in volume to an egg. Since it is usually impossible to provide a sufficient amount of matzah from the two matzos for all members of the household, other matzos should be available at the head of the table from which to complete the required amounts. However, each participant should receive a piece from each of the top two matzos. The matzos are to be eaten while reclining on the left side and without delay; they should not be dipped in salt.

recited over two whole loaves of bread.[1] Therefore we have two unbroken matzos before us on the Seder plate. The third, broken matzah, representing the "bread of poverty," is the subject of the next blessing, concerning the commandment to eat matzah. On the Seder night, unlike any other Shabbos or *Yom Tov* meal, a broken matzah is most appropriate for the *Hamotzi* blessing, and *Hamotzi* is thus recited over all three matzos. (In fact, there is an opinion that calls for just two matzos, like other *Yom Tov* meals — one whole and one broken.)

It is interesting to note that although the *Borei pri ha'adamah* blessing recited over the *karpas* was not included in the *Simanim*, the *Hamotzi* blessing over the matzah is. *Seder HaAruch* submits that the blessing over *karpas* is not noted in the *Simanim* because there is nothing specifically "*Pesach*-like" about it. The *Hamotzi* recited tonight, however, is unique in a way that is particularly related to the Seder night, because only on this night is the blessing recited over a broken matzah, representing the bread of affliction that symbolizes this night.

מַצָּה — *Recite the blessing for the matzah and eat it.* After reciting the *Hamotzi* blessing, we now con-

tinue with the blessing of עַל אֲכִילַת מַצָּה, the blessing for eating the matzah. This blessing is a בִּרְכַּת הַמִּצְוָה, a blessing that refers to a commandment that is about to be performed. According to most authorities, this blessing refers specifically to the broken matzah — the "poor bread." Some, however, are of the opinion that it should be recited over a whole matzah (see *Tur O.C.* 475). *Mishnah Berurah* (475 §2 and *Biur Halachah* s.v. ויברך) suggests holding all three matzos in hand, so that the *Hamotzi* will refer to the top and bottom matzos, both of which are whole. Then, the bottom matzah is put down, so that one is holding both the top whole matzah and the broken one while reciting the second blessing, thus accommodating all opinions.

In accordance with the rule תָּדִיר וְשֶׁאֵינוֹ תָּדִיר תָּדִיר קוֹדֶם, which assigns precedence to blessings or *mitzvos* that come more frequently (see *Pesachim* 114a), one recites *Hamotzi* before the blessing for the *mitzvah* (*Sefer HaAsufos*). Ordinarily, we would recite the blessing שֶׁהֶחֱיָנוּ, thanking God Who *has kept us alive to this time,* which applies to a commandment that is performed seasonally, but is

---

1. **Constant Reminders.** All of man's experiences and everything he comes in contact with should remind him of God. *R' Mordechai Yosef of Izhbitza* homiletically interpreted the words מָלְאָה הָאָרֶץ קִנְיָנֶךָ, *the world is full of Your possessions* (or *acquisitions*), as teaching that the world is full of opportunities for man to "acquire" God, as it were, making Him a vibrant reality in one's life.

Thus *R' Tzadok HaKohen* explains that we recite a blessing before partaking of food not only in order to thank God for granting the pleasure of eating, but also so that we realize that our senses, which provide us with the ability to enjoy things, are but a reminder that God created us.

MATZAH

Blessed are You, HASHEM, our God, King of the universe, Who has sanctified us with His commandments, and has commanded us concerning the eating of the matzah.

Each participant is required to eat an amount of matzah equal in volume to an egg. Since it is usually impossible to provide a sufficient amount of matzah from the two matzos for all members of the household, other matzos should be available at the head of the table from which to complete the required amounts. However, each participant should receive a piece from each of the top two matzos. The matzos are to be eaten while reclining on the left side and without delay; they should not be dipped in salt.

not needed here since we have already recited that blessing in the *Kiddush*, and that recitation covered all the observances of the evening. Moreover, *Avudraham* points out that, at the conclusion of *Maggid*, we specifically thanked God "for having enabled us to reach this night to eat matzah and *maror*." This is the same thought and is similar to the wording of שֶׁהֶחֱיָנוּ, and there is therefore no need to recite the blessing at this point.

Of all the Biblically mandated commandments that are fulfilled by eating, the commandment to eat matzah at the Seder is the only one that remains with us now, in the absence of the Temple. We cannot perform the *mitzvah* of eating the *pesach* offering or any of the other offerings. *Terumah*, *maaser sheini* and similar commandments are not applicable. Only once a year is a Jew granted the opportunity to fulfill a Biblical *mitzvah* by eating — with matzah. How careful must we be at such an auspicious moment! (*Chasam Sofer*).

Unlike commandments that entail external actions, matzah enters one's body and sanctifies its inner parts. The *Zohar* refers to matzah as מֵיכְלָא דְאַסְוָתָא, *food of healing*, for it serves as a remedy for spiritual maladies.[1]

The commentators offer many shades of meaning to this concept. The Talmud (*Berachos* 17a) refers allegorically to man's Evil Inclination as the "yeast in the dough." Yeast, which causes dough to rise, symbolizes the power of evil to seduce man and induce in him an arrogance resulting in brazen transgression of God's will.[2] One can sin only

---

1. **Internal Medicine.** The *succah* surrounds man and spiritually heals him, much like an external bandage, while the matzah enters one's system, curing one's spiritual maladies like an internal medicine (*R' Naftali of Ropschitz*).

The Torah homiletically alludes to the necessity for preparation in order to properly eat the matzah, מַצּוֹת תֵּאָכֵל בְּמָקוֹם קָדֹשׁ, *It shall be eaten unleavened in a holy place* (*Leviticus* 6:9). The place into which one will place the matzah — one's mouth and innards — must be sanctified and made into a fitting receptacle for such sanctified fare.

2. **Food for Humility.** The word מַצָּה (*unleavened*) shares two of the same letters with the word חָמֵץ (*leavened*). The difference between the two is that מַצָּה has a ה, while חָמֵץ is spelled with a ח. The ה, whose left leg is broken in the middle, is symbolic of the contrite and broken heart of the humble. But when one senses himself complete like the left leg of the ח, he has spiritually soured, like leavened dough (*Zichron Kadosh*).

When one recognizes God's infinite awesomeness, he realizes how insignificant and puny he really is; in God's Presence, haughtiness is ludicrous. The matzah alludes to this idea. When God revealed His Divine Presence in Egypt to liberate the Jews, even the dough could not rise and become inflated. Thus we say, מַצָּה זוֹ . . . עַל שׁוּם מָה (see p. 136), which the *Baal HaTanya* renders homiletically as *this matzah is to teach that one must always see himself as* מָה, "What am I?"

מָרוֹר

The head of the household gives a half-egg volume of the *maror*, dipped into *charoses*, to each participant. The following blessing is recited with the intention that it also apply to the *maror* of the "sandwich." The *maror* is eaten without reclining, and without delay.

בָּרוּךְ אַתָּה יהוה אֱלֹהֵינוּ מֶלֶךְ הָעוֹלָם, אֲשֶׁר קִדְּשָׁנוּ בְּמִצְוֹתָיו, וְצִוָּנוּ עַל אֲכִילַת מָרוֹר.

when his inflated ego allows him to feel arrogantly that he has as much right as God to decide what to do or not do. Matzah, made of simple flour and water, is symbolic of simplicity and the humility never to view oneself in an inflated fashion. Thus, matzah is the cure for the spiritual malaise with which the Evil Inclination seeks to infect people (*R' Tzadok HaKohen*).[1]

Furthermore, the matzah contains only the most essential ingredients, with no other additives for

1. **Spiritual Nutrition.** Man is deeply affected by what he eats. This is in fact a significant factor in understanding the laws of *kashrus*. Just as someone who is constantly exposed to loud music and harsh noise slowly and imperceptibly suffers a loss of his ability to hear fine sounds and detect subtle modulations, so too a Jew's consumption of nonkosher food deadens his spiritual capacities and desensitizes him to the full opportunities to become holy. Worst of all, it renders him incapable of even perceiving his loss.

This idea of "spiritual nutrition" is likewise true in a positive sense. Eating matzah, the poor bread, induces humility and a sense of spiritual poverty in all who partake of it. The Hebrew word for bread (לֶחֶם) is related to that for war (מִלְחָמָה): Sustenance is a subject of contention and conflicts, and often requires self-assertion. The matzah is different; it serves as an antidote, because it conveys humility and subordination to God.

When the Jews left Egypt they ate matzah and thus developed the humility necessary to be able to receive the Torah at Mt. Sinai, a low mountain that symbolizes humility. Having partaken of matzah, the lowly and simple bread, they were ready to be taught the Torah at humble Sinai, by Moses, the humblest of men. Today, as well, we eat matzah on Pesach, infusing ourselves with the humility necessary to receive the Torah on Shavuos (*R' Tzadok HaKohen*).

◆§ **Sighting the Enemy:** The word מַצָּה also carries the connotation of *argument* and *altercation* (see *Isaiah* 58:4 and *Proverbs* 13:10), since it gives one the spiritual strength to battle and hopefully overcome his most potent adversary — his Evil Persuader. The matzah cures one of the blinding grip of sin and allows man to realize that the enemy is on the attack. While mired in sin, one does not realize the spiritual severity of his predicament. Only after repenting and realizing what he had done is one aroused to throw himself full force into the great battle of life.

Based on this idea, *R' Shlomo Freifeld* explained an anomaly in the Torah's report of the sale of Joseph by his brothers. When Joseph, as Egyptian ruler, demanded that his brothers bring Benjamin to him, they began to feel pangs of guilt. *Then they said to one another, "Indeed, we are guilty concerning our brother, inasmuch as we saw his heartfelt anguish when he pleaded with us and we paid no heed"* (*Genesis* 42:21). *Ramban* (ad loc.) wonders why this report of Joseph's pleadings is not to be found in the initial account of the episode. *R' Freifeld* explained: In the heat of sin, man is so captivated by the force of evil that he sees no legitimate counterargument. Only when they were overcome by therapeutic guilt and spiritually began to disengage themselves from the hold of the Evil Inclination did the brothers realize that Joseph had begged for mercy all during their sale of him. At the time, they had been so spiritually deaf that they heard nothing.

When one partakes of matzah it cures the soul of the spiritual blemishes that are the result of sin. Cured of spiritual maladies, one is able to recognize the enemy and join the battle. In the words of the prophet (*Hosea* 7:1): *When I would have healed Israel, the iniquity of Ephraim would be revealed* (*Chodesh HaAviv*).

MAROR

The head of the household gives a half-egg volume of the maror, *dipped into* charoses, *to each participant. The following blessing is recited with the intention that it also apply to the* maror *of the "sandwich." The* maror *is eaten without reclining, and without delay.*

Blessed are You, HASHEM, our God, King of the universe, Who has sanctified us with His commandments, and has commanded us concerning the eating of *maror.*

enrichment. Thus, matzah teaches us to avoid the blandishments of the Evil Inclination, which constantly seeks to arouse our drive for pleasures, both permitted and otherwise (*R' Leibel Eiger*).[1]

The *Zohar* (2:183b and 41:1 in *Raya Mehemna*) also refers to matzah as מֵיכְלָא דִּמְהֵימְנוּתָא, *the bread of faith.* As a tangible symbol of the Egyptian exile and Exodus, the matzah reminds us of all the great miracles that God performed on our behalf when He redeemed us from Egypt. Merely speaking about the events is insufficient; we must employ tangible symbols and concrete actions in reinforcing our own faith in these timeless truths. As the *Sefer HaChinuch* teaches, "A man is molded by his actions, for the heart is drawn in the direction set by one's actions."

Meshech Chochmah (*Exodus* 12:19) elaborates:

When the Jews left Egypt they prepared no provisions for their journey into the Wilderness. In their hasty departure from Egypt they expressed their deep faith that God would provide for their needs. Rather than complaining to Moses, "How can we go blindly to the desert; what will we eat?" they followed God loyally, like a young bride who lovingly trusts her husband (see *Jeremiah* 2:2). As we eat matzah on the night of Pesach, we reassert our faithful commitment to God and our firm belief that He will always provide for us.

מָרוֹר — *Recite the blessing over the maror and eat it.* The mitzvah to eat *maror* is Biblically linked to the eating of the *pesach* offering: *With matzos and bitter herbs shall he eat [the pesach lamb]* (*Numbers*

1. **Bread of Freedom.** The Torah makes its home only among those who understand that one cannot serve two masters, that one who becomes dependent on creature comforts will find it difficult to live without them, and that they will usually be purchased at the expense of time that would otherwise have been devoted to Torah study and the pursuit of good deeds. As a wise man once said, "Many people have the attitude that they want to learn the entire Talmud in one night — and they want to sleep, as well."

When one eats matzah, the simple unadorned bread of poverty, he symbolizes his own spiritual wealth. Satisfied with his lot in life, he is indentured to nothing but God and His Torah, but in reality he is free, because he is following the call of his innermost essence, the Godly soul with which he is endowed (*R' Tzadok HaKohen*).

According to *R' Simchah Zisel of Kelm*, God took the Jews out of Egypt without preparing provisions for the way in order to show them that the purpose of their new freedom was not so that they might enjoy the "good life." Rather, He freed them from the slavish search for all the desires our hearts fantasize that we must have. Unfettered by the worries of how to attain the physical and fiscal comfort which always seems just a step out of reach, they learned that true pleasure is linked to spiritual success.

⊷ **A Means to an End.** The first instance of eating matzah mentioned in the Torah is when the angels came to visit Abraham to convey the good news that Isaac would be born (*Genesis* 18:6). According to the Sages, that visit took place on Pesach, and Abraham served them matzos (see *Bereishis Rabbah* 48:13 and *Tosafos, Rosh Hashanah* 11a, s.v. אלא). The angels did not eat it in the literal sense; they only *appeared* to eat. Thus, matzah teaches us the proper approach to food, that eating should never become a purely physical process. Like that of the angels, our real sustenance should be spiritual, with physical eating only a means to sustain our bodies. One must eat in order to live, not live in order to eat (*Toras Emes*).

כּוֹרֵךְ

The bottom (thus far unbroken) matzah is now taken. From it, with the addition of other matzos, each participant receives a half-egg volume of matzah with an equal volume portion of *maror* (dipped into *charoses* which is shaken off). The following paragraph is recited and the "sandwich" is eaten while reclining.

זֵכֶר לְמִקְדָּשׁ כְּהִלֵּל. כֵּן עָשָׂה הִלֵּל בִּזְמַן שֶׁבֵּית הַמִּקְדָּשׁ

9:11). Nowadays, when we can no longer bring the *pesach* offering, this *mitzvah* is mandated under Rabbinic law, as a commemoration of the rite practiced in the Temple (*Pesachim* 120a).

As mentioned earlier in the Haggadah, we eat *maror* in order to remember the bitterness which we suffered at the hands of the Egyptians. This suffering actually had a redeeming quality to it. Firstly, it was due to the excess oppression on the part of the Egyptians that God deemed the 210 years spent in Egypt as the qualitative equivalent of the 400 years of exile foretold to Abraham. Thus the excessive bitterness suffered by the Jews was in fact advantageous, since it hastened the redemption (*Tiferes Yisrael*). Furthermore, it was the vitriolic hatred of the Egyptians who bitterly oppressed the Jews that caused them to retain their identity under all conditions. Thus it was a

blessing in disguise (*Sfas Emes*).[1]

We fulfill the *mitzvah* of *maror* only after matzah, following the order given in the verse cited above. Furthermore, we give precedence to the matzah, because it remains a Biblical command, even after the destruction of the Temple.

Before eating the *maror*, we dip it into *charoses*. According to the Talmud (*Pesachim* 116a), this food is reminiscent of the mortar from which Jews had to fashion bricks for the construction of Pithom and Rameses.

According to the Midrash (*Shemos Rabbah* 1) masonry work is the most backbreaking of all. *Charoses* thus symbolizes the most tedious burden borne by our forefathers in Egypt (*Maharal*). The *Talmud Yerushalmi* (*Pesachim* 10:3) submits that the wine added to the *charoses* mixture conjures the image of the blood of the innocent children[2] whom the Egyptians killed by

---

1. **Bittersweet Promises.** The bitter existence of the Jews is described as *maror*. The Talmud suggests that just as *maror* (horseradish) begins as a soft plant but eventually turns very hard, so the Jews originally were seduced by the soft talk of the Egyptians and the promises of material reward but eventually became subject to hard, backbreaking toil.

Talmud Yerushalmi (*Pesachim* 2:5) extends the analogy. The Egyptian exile was initially sweet and only later turned bitter. This initial sweetness is itself part of the bitterness of exile. Constantly we are lulled into submission by promises of equality and rights as full-fledged citizens. Eventually our patrons renege on their promises and revert back to their traditional anti-Semitic ways. Disappointed and frustrated by the broken promises, the entire experience is bitter. Thus, even the initial friendship is a sugar-coated, but bitter, pill.

2. **Innocent Blood.** After he was arrested in the fall of 1944 and transferred to a camp at Sered, Slovakia, *R' Michoel Ber Weissmandl* managed to leave the camp and return for a short time to Bratislava (Pressburg), where he immediately turned to the Slovakian Papal Nuncio to apprise him of the renewal of the expulsions. Rabbi Weissmandl presented himself as the Rabbi of Nitra and the Chief Rabbi of Slovakia. He told the Nuncio that he had just escaped from Sered, where 20,000 Jews had been gathered to be sent to their death, and begged him to intervene with President Tiso to annul the expulsions. The Nuncio reacted with indifference and said that he and President Tiso were not able to deal with secular matters on Sunday, which is a Christian holy day. Rabbi Weissmandl pleaded with him that the innocent blood of thousands of children was at stake, to which the Papal Nuncio angrily replied: "There is no such thing as the innocent blood of Jewish children! All Jewish blood is guilty, and the Jews must die because that is their punishment."

KORECH

The bottom (thus far unbroken) matzah is now taken. From it, with the addition of other matzos, each participant receives a half-egg volume of matzah with an equal volume portion of *maror* (dipped into *charoses* which is shaken off). The following paragraph is recited and the "sandwich" is eaten while reclining.

In remembrance of the Temple we do as Hillel did in Temple

placing them in the pyramids in place of bricks that the Jews failed to produce. According to one Talmudic opinion (*Pesachim* 114a), the *charoses* does not have any symbolic purpose, but is used merely as an antidote for the bitterness of the *maror*. In order that it not remove the bitter taste of the *maror* altogether, however, we shake off the *charoses* before eating the *maror*. (Similarly, the Talmud rules that the *maror* may not be swallowed whole, without chewing (*Pesachim* 115b), for it is imperative to fully taste its bitter flavor.[1])

Even according to the first view, that *charoses* is eaten to recall the Egyptian bondage and it is thus a Rabbinic commandment to have it on the Seder plate, no blessing is pronounced over it, because it is not a separate duty, but part of the obligation to eat *maror* (*Avudraham*).[2]

כּוֹרֵךְ — *Eat the sandwich of matzah and maror.* We now take the bottom unbroken matzah and utilize it for the "sandwich" of matzah and *maror*. Since it will usually not be big enough to provide adequate portions for all Seder participants, additional matzos should be used to supplement the pieces of the third matzah that they receive.

Disagreeing with the other Sages of his day, Hillel held the view that the three Torah obligations — the *pesach* offering, matzah and *maror* — must all be eaten at one time rather than one after the other.

In the absence of a *pesach* offering, since the destruction of the Temple, eating *maror* is not Biblically required either, since the Torah's com-

---

1. **Swallowing a Bitter Pill.** Some people are willing to serve God as long as life is sweet. However, when they feel the bitter taste of setbacks and calamity, they often lose their appetite for serving Him. Thus, we are taught that we must chew the *maror* and symbolically experience fully its taste. Any lesser degree of commitment to God is not enough (*Binas Yisrael*). Likewise, in interpersonal relationships one must be ready to bear the sharp and bitter taste of disappointment. One who wants friends only for the good times will never have any lasting and meaningful relationships.

Beis Yaakov (*Izhbitz*) also addresses the importance the *halachah* attaches to tasting the *maror*. The worst type of exile is when Jews feel that the diaspora is a paradise. Under such circumstances it is imperative that we realize how truly bitter the situation really is. Thus, if one swallows the *maror* he does not fulfill his obligation. It is necessary that we realize that even if the exile is physically and financially comfortable, from a spiritual standpoint it is extremely bitter.

A chassidic *rebbe* once commented to Rabbi Berel Wein tongue-in-cheek as they studied Talmud together in Rabbi Wein's backyard in Miami, Florida: "If Jews must suffer exile, Miami is not a bad place to do so."

It is to fortify ourselves against seriously adopting this attitude that we eat the *maror* to remind ourselves that *any* exile is bitter.

2. **Bitter Enough.** One of the vegetables that may be used for *maror* is חֲזֶרֶת, *romaine lettuce*. Its Hebrew name is related to חָזַר, *to return*. Often the bitterness of life's experiences causes people to reflect on the direction their life is taking and helps bring about a return to God. *R' Moshe Feinstein* offers a perspective on this:

The *Mishnah Pesachim* (39a) lists five species that can be used as *maror*. The first one on the list, *chazeres* (romaine lettuce), is the preferred species to use for this *mitzvah*; the last species in that list, *maror*, which is a less preferred species, has an exceptionally bitter taste. One would have expected the order of preference to be reversed, but it is not. There is a lesson in this for us. *Maror* is the symbol of Jewish suffering, and calls

---

הָיָה קַיָּם. הָיָה כּוֹרֵךְ (פֶּסַח) מַצָּה וּמָרוֹר וְאוֹכֵל בְּיַחַד. לְקַיֵּם מַה שֶׁנֶּאֱמַר, עַל מַצּוֹת וּמְרֹרִים יֹאכְלֻהוּ.[1]

mandment describes *maror* as something that must be eaten with the offering; if there is no offering there need be no *maror.* It is eaten nowadays as a Rabbinical requirement only. Matzah, on the other hand, is a Biblical duty (*In the evening you shall eat matzos* — *Exodus* 12:18), irrespective of whether the *pesach* offering is brought. Therefore, even Hillel would agree that nowadays matzah (a Biblical obligation) and *maror* (a Rabbinic obligation) should be eaten separately. (See, however, *Shulchan Aruch HaRav* 475:17.) However, to preserve a reminder of Hillel's practice during the time of the Temple, we now eat matzah and *maror* together, although we have already eaten them separately.[1]

Since the sandwich contains *maror,* it must be dipped into *charoses,* for either of the two reasons given above — either to neutralize the excessive bitterness of the *maror,* or in order to serve as a reminder of the mortar used by the Jewish slaves.

According to some opinions, however, the "sandwich" should *not* be dipped into *charoses.* The bitterness of the *maror,* they maintain, is neutralized just as well by the matzah, and as far as the symbolic value of the *charoses,* this has already been demonstrated when we dipped maror into it before. Furthermore, if we were to dip the "sandwich" into *charoses,* our Seder would feature *three* dippings, whereas the sources always speak of *two* (*Raviah*). *Taz*, however, rejects this point, arguing that the dipping of the *maror* and of the "sandwich" are counted as one dipping, as they are both done for the same purpose.

The verse quoted here (from *Numbers* 9:11) as the basis for Hillel's practice does not speak about the regular *pesach* offering, but about פֶּסַח שֵׁנִי, the *Second Pesach,* observed thirty days later by people who were unable to bring the *pesach* offering at the proper time (see ibid.). Although the point could have been made just as well with a similar verse (*Exodus* 12:8) that deals with the regular *pesach* offering, Hillel may have quoted this verse because it is clearer than the other one,

to mind the suffering of the Jews in Egypt. But we must remember that all suffering ultimately comes from God and has a purpose. God presents us with difficulties when we lapse, to prod us back to the correct path. These difficulties can assume many forms. The *Gemara* (*Arachin* 16b) states that even putting one's hand into his pocket and pulling out the wrong object — a mere momentary inconvenience — is an example of "suffering." God does not wish to cause us pain; His sole intent in punishing us is to make us recognize our shortcomings so that we can overcome them. The form and intensity of suffering necessary to accomplish this depends on us. If a person who misplaces his keys realizes that God wants him to take stock of his actions, the "suffering" has accomplished its purpose. If, however, he does not heed these signals, he will be reminded (God forbid) by something more severe, until he heeds the message.

Therefore, the mild *chazeres* is the preferred type of *maror.* We must keep in mind that *maror* does not necessarily have to be bitter. It is only after time, when the message of the *maror* is continually ignored, that the bitter taste must emerge.

1. **Paying for Ignorance.** During Temple times, the *maror* was definitely eaten with the *pesach* offering, so that our current practice of eating *maror* a second time is because we do not have the Temple. This explains the comment of the Midrash (*Eichah Rabbasi* 3:15) on the verse, *He made me sated with maror, He fed me with bitter roots* (*Lamentations* 3:15): The Midrash expounds, *He made me sated with maror* on Pesach, *He fed me bitter roots* on Tishah B'Av. Due to the bitter destruction that occurred on Tishah B'Av, we must eat *maror* twice, and become sated from it on Pesach (*R' Yonasan Eibschitz*).

Along similar lines, *R' Joseph Elias* submits that complacency in exile, when we fail to learn the lesson of its bitterness, will prolong the exile and cause us to suffer the bitterness of a Temple that still lies in ruins.

times: He would combine [*pesach* offering,] matzah and *maror* in a sandwich and eat them together, to fulfill that which is written, "With matzos and *maror* they shall eat it."[1]

(1) *Numbers* 9:11.

---

which says: *They shall eat the meat on this night, roasted on fire, and matzos; with maror they shall eat it.*

This verse makes a distinction between matzah and *maror*, to teach that on the Seder night, we must eat matzah even if we have no *pesach* offering, while *maror* need not be eaten without a *pesach* offering (*Reshash*). As a result, this verse does not show clearly that when we do have the offering, it should be eaten together with matzah and *maror*. Hence, Hillel quoted a verse that makes this quite clear.

R' Yehoshua of Belz offered a more homiletic explanation for Hillel's choice of a source text. The verse regarding the Second Pesach alludes to our fervent hope that though we sit here in exile on the night of Pesach, having been unable to bring the offering, God will grant us the speedy rebuilding of the Temple so that we may yet be able to bring the second *pesach* offering this very year. (See *Raviah*

to *Pesachim* 115a and *Moadim U'Zmanim* 3:250.)

פֶּסַח מַצָּה וּמָרוֹר — *Pesach offering, matzah and maror.* This version reflects exactly Hillel's practice (*Taz*). However, some authorities suggest that we should not mention the *pesach* offering, since we are unable to follow Hillel's example and include the offering in our sandwich (*Chok Yaakov*).

Alshich suggests two explanations for the symbolism of *korech*, the sandwich. Even after one is free he must not forget the terrible ordeal from which God saved him. Thus we wrap the *maror*, symbol of bitterness, inside the matzah, the symbol of freedom.[1]

Alternatively, the matzah alludes to one's Good Inclination, while the *maror* refers to the evil and bitterness that lurks in man. We must encase our negative impulses and redirect them towards good. Thus we wrap the *maror* in matzah, not to cosmetically cover our spiritual flaws, but to transform them into a force for the good.[2]

---

1. **Past Reminders.** A wealthy Jew was once searching for a promising scholar to wed to his daughter. After a long search he made his choice, a young man from a poor home. The wealthy man spared no expense to clothe his future son-in-law in the finest clothes, but he kept the old rags. Fearful that someone else might come and pluck the young man away from him, the father-in-law had a very simple wedding feast prepared so that the wedding could be held immediately. At the wedding the father-in-law took out the old clothes. The son-in-law understood why: Whenever he might forget his humble beginnings, the old clothes would remind him to be grateful to his father-in-law for having raised him out of poverty. The son-in-law therefore took a piece of food from the simple wedding banquet and put it aside so that he would also always remember how badly his father-in-law wanted him.

Likewise, the *maror* reminds us how thankful we must be to God for having saved us from bitter slavery. The matzah, symbolic of food prepared in a rush, indicates the love God displayed to us by hurriedly saving us from the fiftieth degree of impurity.

We put the matzah and *maror* together to show that God's love for us, as symbolized by matzah, is eternally linked with our response when we praise Him for saving us from the bitter *maror* of life (*R' Yehoshua of Belz*).

2. **Enwrapped in Exile.** The bitter oppression of the exile helped us retain our separate identity and values. Thus we wrap the *maror* in matzah to show that salvation is often a combination of freedom and searing pain (*Sfas Emes*). Our true freedom is achieved only when, through the pain of exile, we are purged of our spiritual imperfections. The Egyptian exile was the crucible which purified our souls so that we might receive the Torah. Thus, we link the *maror* and matzah and eat them in a sandwich.

שֻׁלְחָן עוֹרֵךְ

The meal should be eaten in a combination of joy and solemnity, for the meal, too, is a part of the Seder service. While it is desirable that *zemiros* and discussion of the laws and events of Passover be part of the meal, extraneous conversation should be avoided. It should be remembered that the *afikoman* must be eaten while there is still some appetite for it. In fact, if one is so sated that he must literally force himself to eat it, he is not credited with the performance of the *mitzvah* of *afikoman*. Therefore, it is unwise to eat more than a moderate amount during the meal.

שֻׁלְחָן עוֹרֵךְ — *Eating a Festive Meal.* The meal on this Seder night is included in the *Simanim*, a clear indication that it is not merely a fulfillment of the obligations of שִׂמְחַת יוֹם טוֹב and עֹנֶג יוֹם טוֹב (*enjoying and rejoicing on the holiday*) but rather is intrinsically related to the Seder and its themes. *Tosafos* (*Avodah Zarah* 5b, s.v. ערב יו״ט) submits that the Seder meal celebrates our redemption from slavery to freedom.[1]

According to *Netziv* and *Tiferes Shlomo*, the meal, which comes in the middle of *Hallel*, is itself a part of *Hallel*, an extension of our praise of God.

Following *Abarbanel*, that the first part of *Hallel* praises God for the Exodus, while the rest of it refers to the future redemption, we might suggest that the festive meal celebrates the Exodus. Having praised God for His kindness in the past, we will then go on to praise Him for the redemption that we know will come in the future.

Orchos Chaim writes: "It is proper that one discard all worries and distress, and eat the Seder meal joyously." One should eat at a leisurely pace in the fashion of free men and royalty (*Seder HaYom*). However, the joyous atmosphere must be blended with a sense of the solemnity of the moment (*Shelah*).[2]

One must take care to finish the meal in time to eat the *afikoman* before midnight. *Rambam* (*Chametz U'Matzah* 7:7) writes: "When one feasts on this night, all his eating and drinking should be done while reclining in the fashion of free men." If one finds sitting more comfortable he may do so. Only when eating matzah and drinking four cups is reclining a must (*O.C.* 472:7 M.B. §23).

---

1. **Human Altar.** A table becomes a Godly altar if one is careful to infuse one's eating with sanctity. But the letters of the word שֻׁלְחָן, *table*, can be rearranged to spell לְנָחָשׁ, *into a snake*. If one allows the feast to become a mere gastronomic celebration, the table is like a venomous snake, symbolic of Satan, who seeks to indict man as an unworthy sinner. Thus we express the hope that the letters of our שֻׁלְחָן will always be עָרוּךְ, *arranged* properly, never allowing them to be transformed into our adversary (*Avodas Yisrael*).

2. **Joyously Jewish.** The Midrash contrasts Jewish and gentile celebrations: If the nations of the world are granted holidays, they spend them by eating and drinking in a spirit of frivolity and senseless merriment. They use the time to attend theaters, stadiums and places of entertainment and thrills, enraging God by their behavior and crass speech. Not so the holy nation of Israel; they eat and drink, and in their joyousness they begin to praise His holy Torah. They enter their synagogues and study halls in order to offer prayers of thanksgiving for the past and entreaties for the future.

   R' Avraham of Sochatchov (author of the *Avnei Nezer*) would not allow his disciples to celebrate the Seder with him. Once a *chassid*, anxious to be at the *Rebbe's* table, asked for an explanation. The *Avnei Nezer* replied: A Jew must feel free, relaxed and joyous at the Seder. In the company of his *rebbe*, a real *chassid* is under too much strain and anxiety to have that feeling.

SHULCHAN ORECH

The meal should be eaten in a combination of joy and solemnity, for the meal, too, is a part of the Seder service. While it is desirable that *zemiros* and discussion of the laws and events of Passover be part of the meal, extraneous conversation should be avoided. It should be remembered that the *afikoman* must be eaten while there is still some appetite for it. In fact, if one is so sated that he must literally force himself to eat it, he is not credited with the performance of the *mitzvah* of *afikoman*. Therefore, it is unwise to eat more than a moderate amount during the meal.

Since we cannot bring the *pesach* offering nowadays, some people have the custom of reading the chapters of *Mishnah Pesachim* that discuss the laws of the *pesach* offering (*Siddur Yaavetz, Kaf HaChaim*).

It is customary to begin the meal with a hard-boiled egg. *Rema* (*O.C.* 476:2) offers two reasons for the custom. It is a sign of mourning for the destroyed Temple and our resultant inability to bring the *pesach* offering, since eggs are associated with mourning (see *O.C.* 552:5 and ArtScroll *Mourning in Halachah* p. 168). Furthermore, since the first day of Pesach always occurs on the same day of the week as Tishah B'Av, this evokes a sense of mourning for the destroyed Temple.[1]

The *Vilna Gaon* (*Maaseh Rav* 191) objects to any expression of mourning on *Yom Tov*. According to him, the egg is eaten to commemorate the *chagigah* offering brought on Pesach. Accordingly, one should eat the egg of the Seder plate, which commemorates the *chagigah* (*Mishnah Berurah* 476 §11).

According to *Kol Bo*, the word בֵּיעָא, Aramaic for *egg*, can also be rendered as desired. We eat the egg as a symbol of God's great desire to free His people from Pharaoh, so that they might be God's servants.[2]

1. **Mourners' Meal.** During Temple times, the main course of the meal was the meat of the *chagigah* and *pesach* offerings (see *Pesachim* 114a and *Rambam, Chametz U'Matzah* 8:7). Thus we show signs of mourning for the loss of the Temple.

According to R' Yehoshua, the Final Redemption will occur in the month of Nissan (*Rosh Hashanah* 11a). The arrival of Pesach without the appearance of the Messiah is itself cause for mourning (*Mor U'Ketziah*).

2. **Hardened People.** According to *R' Meir Shapiro* the egg is a symbol of Jewish steadfastness and strength. Unlike other foods, eggs get harder the longer they are boiled. Thus they symbolize the Jewish people who grew stronger and more numerous in response to the steadily increasing oppression of the Egyptians (see *Exodus* 1:12). Historically, as well, Jews become greater and stronger in a spiritual sense as a result of oppression. Forced by the hostile nations of the world to identify ourselves as Jews, we have no choice but to reassert our self-identity.

⋖§ **The Makings of Greatness.** *R' Leibel Eiger* comments that an egg contains all the elements necessary to develop into a live chick, provided the mother hen sits on it and keeps it constantly warm. Likewise, on the night of Pesach, the Jewish nation is reborn. God imbues the soul of every Jew with all the elements necessary for his spiritual growth. It is up to man only to give his soul constant attention, to "sit" on it and maintain its warm connection to God. One who does so will merit that by the time Shavuos comes, seven weeks later, he will be spiritually "hatched," as a live and vibrant Jew.

צָפוּן

From the *afikoman* matzah (and from additional matzos to make up the required amount), a half-egg volume portion — according to some, a full egg's volume portion — is given to each participant. It should be eaten before midnight, while reclining, without delay, and uninterruptedly. Nothing may be eaten or drunk after the *afikoman* (with the exception of water and the like) except for the last two Seder cups of wine.

צָפוּן — *Eat the Afikoman.* The word צָפוּן, which means *hidden away*, designates this stage of the Seder when we eat the *afikoman*, which was broken from the middle matzah at *yachatz* and hidden away, to be eaten now.[1]

Afikoman is a Greek word connoting dessert. *Rashbam* interprets the words as a contraction — אַפִּיקוּ, *bring out*, מָן [sweet] *things*. (See *Seder HaAruch* 97:1 for alternative explanations.) Since the Seder meal must conclude with matzah and no ordinary "dessert" may be eaten after it, the matzah eaten came to be called *afikoman* (*Shiltei HaGibborim*).

Levush suggests that the name expresses the joy with which Jews fulfill *mitzvos*. To us, this plain piece of matzah is as sweet as the delicacies usually eaten for dessert.

There are two opinions offered to explain why the Sages instituted the rule to eat this piece of matzah (*afikoman*) at the end of the meal. *Rashi* and *Rashbam* (*Pesachim* 119b) explain that originally the matzah, *maror* and *pesach* offering were eaten together (in accordance with the view of Hillel, mentioned above, p. 169). This had to be done at the end of the meal, since the *pesach*

offering was eaten after one was somewhat sated. However, *Rosh* points out that if this is so, *maror* should be eaten along with the *afikoman*.

Rosh himself rejects this opinion, because the commemoration of Hillel's "sandwich" has already been observed at the beginning of the meal. He holds that the *afikoman* is eaten in commemoration of the *pesach* offering.

Our custom follows both of these opinions — we eat two portions of matzah, one to commemorate the *pesach* offering and one to commemorate the matzah that was eaten along with it. We do not eat *maror* again at this point, however, because *maror* is only a Rabbinic requirement, so we are not so stringent as to require yet another portion of *maror* to be eaten (*Bach*).

Since the *afikoman* commemorates the *pesach* offering, we should eat it before midnight, following the opinion of R' Elazar ben Azariah, who requires that the *pesach* offering be eaten before midnight (*Pesachim* 120b).[2]

Two reasons are given for the requirement that the *pesach* offering was to be consumed toward the end of the meal. According to the *Talmud Yerushalmi*, it is a Rabbinical enactment estab-

---

1. **Stored Away for Later.** The word צָפוּן also alludes to the World to Come, where God has infinite storehouses of reward "stored away" for His loyal children and servants (see *Psalms* 31:20). We now eat the remaining larger half of the matzah to symbolize our recognition that the greater part of one's resources, talents and energies should be committed to cultivating one's share in the world God has stored for us (*Yismach Yisrael*).

2. **Early Admission.** Although the actual redemption did not occur until midnight (see *Exodus* 12:29-32), the Jews were commanded to slaughter the *pesach* offering in the afternoon and to eat it at the beginning of the night. Likewise, the *afikoman* is eaten *before* midnight. A Jew believes so firmly in God's promise of salvation that he can thank Him for His salvation even before it actually occurs. Similarly we fulfill the commandments of the night before midnight and seek to inject our hearts with a dose of firm faith that God will again keep His promise and redeem us as speedily as He did then (*Chodesh HaAviv*).

TZAFUN

From the *afikoman* matzah (and from additional matzos to make up the required amount), a half-egg volume portion — according to some, a full egg's volume portion — is given to each participant. It should be eaten before midnight, while reclining, without delay, and uninterruptedly. Nothing may be eaten or drunk after the *afikoman* (with the exception of water and the like) except for the last two Seder cups of wine.

lished in order to avoid breaking the offering's bones (a Biblical prohibition — see *Exodus* 12:46) because of a ravenous appetite. *Rashbam* (*Pesachim* 119b), however, comments that all sacrificial meat should be eaten when someone is somewhat sated, for then he will eat in a dignified, regal way, rather than like a starving pauper or an uncouth glutton.

Neither of these reasons, however, would apply to the *afikoman*; why, then, does the Talmud insist that this piece of matzah be the very last thing eaten at the Seder? Both *Rashbam* and *Tosafos* explain that as a demonstration of our love and appreciation of the *mitzvos*, we allow the taste of the *afikoman* to linger in our mouths as long as possible.[1]

Sefer HaMaor suggests that since the "Great

Hallel" that is recited later in the Seder and which was chanted when the *pesach* was offered, speaks of God as *the One Who provides food for all people* (*Psalms* 136:25), it was only proper that the *pesach* offering be eaten on a full stomach. This applies equally to the *afikoman*.

Ahavas Shalom suggests a more homiletic interpretation of this requirement. One always has an appetite for a tasty dessert (*Eruvin* 82b), even when fully sated. Thus, as an expression of our enjoyment in fulfilling *mitzvos*, we eat the *afikoman* while full, as if it were a delectable dessert.[2]

According to *Sfas Emes* we eat matzah as the last bit of food to symbolize that we should be satisfied with everything God does, even if it seems as incomprehensible as a bland and tasteless matzah.

1. **Abiding Faith.** The Exodus with all its miracles came to inculcate in the hearts and minds of Jews a deep and abiding faith in God. Faith is the ability to recall an image of the past or a vision of the future when the reality is not present. Faith allows us to hold onto and bring back the taste of having experienced God's loving Providence even at times when His care and concern are not apparent. Thus, at the end of the Seder, as we stop to take stock of our new and profound sense that God is prepared to upset all the forces of nature on our behalf, we eat the matzah, the food of faith, and leave its taste in our mouths.

2. **Pure Pleasure.** A Jew must consider his attitude toward life. He can be like a stevedore, or like someone enjoying a delicious meal. If a wagon driver is hired to transport a heavy load, he is not interested in the work; he only wants the money. If a passerby were to ask him, "Why are you carrying such a heavy load?" he would certainly answer, "In order to earn my pay." If somebody were to offer him the money without doing the work, he would be thrilled.

However, if someone enjoying a delectable meal is asked, "Why are you eating that?" the answer would be obvious. He is not being paid to eat; he does it for pleasure.

On every festival we are commanded to divide our time into two halves. Half our time and energies should be spent in personal enjoyment of the *Yom Tov* (חֶצְיוֹ לָכֶם) and the other half in prayer, study and the overt service of God (חֶצְיוֹ לַה').

One of the great chassidic masters was overheard to remark at the end of the prayer service, "Fine, we have fulfilled the חֶצְיוֹ לָכֶם, the half of the day that should be devoted to *our* enjoyment. Now, how are we ready to dedicate our *Yom Tov* feast to the service of God, to fulfill the חֶצְיוֹ לַה'?"

בָּרֵךְ

The third cup is poured and *Bircas HaMazon* (Grace After Meals) is recited.
According to some customs, the Cup of Elijah is poured at this point.

שִׁיר הַמַּעֲלוֹת, בְּשׁוּב יהוה אֶת שִׁיבַת צִיּוֹן, הָיִינוּ כְּחֹלְמִים. אָז יִמָּלֵא שְׂחוֹק פִּינוּ וּלְשׁוֹנֵנוּ רִנָּה, אָז יֹאמְרוּ בַגּוֹיִם, הִגְדִּיל יהוה לַעֲשׂוֹת עִם אֵלֶּה.

בָּרֵךְ — *Recite the Bircas HaMazon.* It is customary to recite Psalm 137 (*By the Rivers of Babylon*) before *Bircas HaMazon,* on ordinary weekdays. That psalm, which describes the descent of the Jews into exile, is meant to keep the memory of the Temple destruction fresh in our minds even when our bodies are sated and we feel comfortable in exile (*Zohar, Terumah*). However, on the Sabbath and Festivals (and, according to many opinions, on any day when *Tachanun* is not recited — see *M.B.* 1 §11), it is improper to intrude on the joy of the day with mention of the Temple's destruction (*Eishel Avraham* ibid. 5). On these holy and festive days that afford Jews a glimpse of their future elevation and glory, it is appropriate that they instead recite Psalm 126, which describes the exultation of the Final Redemption, when God will return the captivity of Zion (*Shelah*).

שִׁיר הַמַּעֲלוֹת — *A song of ascents.* These words introduce each of fifteen psalms (120-134; Psalm 121 contains a slight variant). The *ascents* refer to the fifteen steps leading up to the Inner Courtyard of the Temple. During Succos, when water was brought to the Temple for the festival's special service, groups of Levites would stand on the steps singing, with musical accompaniment, each of these fifteen psalms, as the procession went up the steps (*Succah* 51b).

As pointed out by the commentators, many psalms can be understood only as prophetic references to events that did not occur until long after David's death. Thus, this psalm is written as though it were said by the exiles in Babylon.

בְּשׁוּב ה' אֶת שִׁיבַת צִיּוֹן — *When HASHEM will return the captivity of Zion.* The translation follows *Rashi,* who interprets the verse as speaking of the time when God will *return the captivity of Zion,* i.e., the exiled captive nation that was displaced from Zion to Babylon.

Meiri interprets אֶת as *with*: God will return *with* the Jews, because His greatness was ignored and forgotten by the nations while the Jews were downtrodden. When Israel, His representative on earth, returns to its majesty, it will be an occasion of בְּשׁוּב ה', *God's return,* for He will figuratively return with His people to the consciousness of all nations. Furthermore, in an expression of empathy for the pain His children suffer while in exile, God Himself figuratively suffers exile along with them. Hence when Israel returns to Zion and a rebuilt Temple, His Presence will also be restored to its proper place.

הָיִינוּ כְּחֹלְמִים — *We will have been like dreamers.* When the long-awaited *return* to Zion finally comes to pass, the recollection of the past oppression of the exile will swiftly fade away and seem like a bad dream (*Radak*).[1]

---

1. **A Bad Dream.** In the future, we will all be like one awakened from a dream. Sometimes a dream is so remarkably vivid that we begin to think of it as reality. Only when we wake up do we realize that it was nothing more than a technicolor fantasy. When the Final Redemption arrives we will realize that our sense of being distant from God and our perceptions of all the evil that occurred to us was nothing more than a

BARECH

The third cup is poured and *Bircas HaMazon* (Grace After Meals) is recited.
According to some customs, the Cup of Elijah is poured at this point.

A song of ascents. When HASHEM will return the captivity of Zion, we will have been like dreamers. Then our mouth will be filled with laughter, and our tongue with glad song. Then they will declare among the nations: HASHEM has done great things with these.

Alternatively, the splendor of the *return to Zion* will seem like an impossible dream come true (*Sforno*).[1]

R' Tzadok HaKohen elaborates on the dream metaphor: Just as one's dream is fantasy when compared to his perception of reality, so our present understanding of ourselves and of God and of His ways will pale in contrast to the heightened understanding we will be granted in Days to Come.

R' S. R. Hirsch explained that the dreamer is out of touch with reality and is oblivious to the world around him. Similarly, while Israel barely survives in exile, it fails to comprehend the profound influence it exercises upon the gentile nations in whose midst it dwells. Only after the termination of the exile will Israel awaken from its nightmarish dream and recognize the true extent of its accomplishments.

אָז יִמָּלֵא שְׂחוֹק פִּינוּ — *Then our mouth will be filled with laughter.* The unexpected turn of events will elicit unrestrained joy. We will explode with laughter and glad song over our newfound change of fortune (*R' S. R. Hirsch*). Not a taint of sadness will ruin our complete happiness (*Sforno*).

אָז יֹאמְרוּ בַגּוֹיִם הִגְדִּיל ה׳ לַעֲשׂוֹת עִם אֵלֶּה — *Then they will declare among the nations, "Hashem has done great things with these."* The nations who had derided us will be dumbfounded by our sudden success, because they had always deemed us unworthy of anything but scorn. It will be so clear that it was God alone Who caused Israel's meteoric ascent that even these gentiles will admit, *Hashem has done great things with these* (see *Radak; Sforno*).[2]

---

dreamlike fantasy. In reality we were always close to God and everything He did was part of His plan for our benefit (*R' Tzadok HaKohen*).

1. **Courage to Dream.** Despite a bitter and seemingly endless exile, Jews never stop dreaming of their ultimate redemption. The deeper a dreamer's sleep, the more vivid the dream; if the sleeper is undisturbed by outside distractions, he will be more profoundly affected by the intensity of his dream. Similarly, when the Jews in exile shunned the alien influences of the surrounding nations, they faithfully preserved their dream of redemption. However, those Jews who were lured by the false promises of gentile culture and "enlightenment" were awakened from their dreams and swiftly abandoned their yearning for authentic redemption by the hand of God and His Messiah (*R' A. C. Feuer*).

2. **The Major Event.** When God reveals His kindness and salvation, there are two reasons for man to rejoice. The minor reason is the improvement of his situation; the major cause for celebration is the increased awareness of God that results from His intervention. Thus, the Psalmist teaches that regarding the return of the captives of Zion, the immediate benefit of the Final Redemption, we will be like dreamers who experience joy in a state of fantasy. However, the real cause of full and authentic rejoicing will be the worldwide recognition of God that will result when He saves His people (*R' Akiva Eiger*).

הִגְדִּיל יהוה לַעֲשׂוֹת עִמָּנוּ, הָיִינוּ שְׂמֵחִים. שׁוּבָה יהוה אֶת שְׁבִיתֵנוּ, כַּאֲפִיקִים בַּנֶּגֶב. הַזֹּרְעִים בְּדִמְעָה בְּרִנָּה יִקְצֹרוּ. הָלוֹךְ יֵלֵךְ וּבָכֹה נֹשֵׂא מֶשֶׁךְ הַזָּרַע, בֹּא יָבֹא בְרִנָּה, נֹשֵׂא אֲלֻמֹּתָיו.[1]

תְּהִלַּת יהוה יְדַבֶּר פִּי, וִיבָרֵךְ כָּל בָּשָׂר שֵׁם קָדְשׁוֹ לְעוֹלָם וָעֶד.[2] וַאֲנַחְנוּ נְבָרֵךְ יָהּ, מֵעַתָּה וְעַד עוֹלָם, הַלְלוּיָהּ.[3] הוֹדוּ לַיהוה כִּי טוֹב, כִּי לְעוֹלָם חַסְדּוֹ.[4] מִי יְמַלֵּל גְּבוּרוֹת יהוה, יַשְׁמִיעַ כָּל תְּהִלָּתוֹ.[5]

הִגְדִּיל ה׳ לַעֲשׂוֹת עִמָּנוּ הָיִינוּ שְׂמֵחִים — *Hashem has done great things with us, and we rejoiced.* Good fortune will not corrupt us; nor will success make us arrogant. The Jews will always attribute their fortune to God's assistance. Indeed, the very knowledge that God favors and loves us enhances our mirth immeasurably and causes us to fill our mouths with laughter (*Radak*).

Unlike the nations that will be surprised that lowly, exiled Israel has suddenly and unexpectedly been raised up by God, we are aware that God has *always done great things with us* — even during the long nights of exile. As *Chovos HaLevavos* says, "Our survival among the nations is as great a miracle as the Exodus from Egypt."

Always confident of eventual salvation, we *rejoiced* even when there was little reason for happiness (*Malbim*).[1]

כַּאֲפִיקִים בַּנֶּגֶב — *Like the springs in the desert.* Just as water turns a seemingly barren desert into a flourishing garden, so will we be transformed and gladdened by God's deliverance from our exile (*Rashi*).

One who plants in a dry land always wonders how his crops will be able to flourish. If springs come unexpectedly to water them, he is overwhelmed with joy. Such will be our joy at the redemption that will follow so much despair (*Radak*).

הַזֹּרְעִים בְּדִמְעָה — *Those who sow in tears.* The Psalmist compares those whose primary concern is with the study of Torah and performance of the commandments to farmers. The wasteland of the exile is like a parched desert. Those who toil to implant *mitzvah* observance and Torah study in the Jewish community are like struggling farmers. The tears which they shed as they labor provide the moisture to water the crops (*Radak; Ibn Ezra*).

It is Israel's mission to sow God's seeds by implanting spirituality, morality and integrity in a hostile world. The process of nurturing the seeds until they are ready for harvest can be agonizing and frustrating, but the achievement of ultimate success brings incomparable joy. The seeds of Israel's mission may become drenched in tears of unbearable suffering, but the crop, the eventual

---

1. **Just a Matter of Time.** The poor man who holds the winning lottery ticket rejoices ecstatically. To the bystander who still sees him in his hovel with its empty cupboards, the joy seems insane. However, the lucky ticket holder knows that it is only a matter of time until he goes to cash in the ticket; then his life style will be radically altered. So, too, Jews rejoice out of faith that God's salvation is certain; it is only a matter of time.

HASHEM has done great things with us, and we rejoiced. Restore our captives, HASHEM, like the springs in the desert. Those who sow in tears shall reap in joy. Though the farmer bears the measure of seed to the field in tears, he will return in exultation, a bearer of his sheaves.[1]

May my mouth declare the praise of HASHEM and may all flesh bless His Holy Name forever.[2] We will bless HASHEM from this time and forever. Halleluyah![3] Give thanks to God for He is good, His kindness endures forever.[4] Who can express the mighty acts of HASHEM? Who can declare all His praise?[5]

(1) *Psalms* 126. (2) 145:21. (3) 115:18. (4) 118:1. (5) 106:2.

harvest of homage to righteousness and truth, will be reaped in joy (*R' S. R. Hirsch*).[1]

בָּא יָבֹא בְרִנָּה נֹשֵׂא אֲלֻמֹּתָיו — *He will return in exultation, a bearer of his sheaves.* In exile, Israel is the downtrodden bearer of innumerable taxes, restrictions and badges of shame. But the day of redemption will arrive when Israel will reap the harvest of its labors. Then, instead of shame, Israel will bear rich sheaves of success (*Radak*).

בְּרְכַּת הַמָּזוֹן — *Grace After Meals.* Generally, using a cup of wine over which to recite *Bircas HaMazon* is an optional enhancement of the *mitzvah*. Tonight, however, we are required to do so, as this consti-

tutes the third cup of the Seder. One should make an effort to have at least three adult males present at the Seder so that it can be prefaced with the special praise of God that is reserved for *Zimun*, the invitation to the group to join together to thank God for providing their meal.[2]

It is customary that the master of the house leads the *Bircas HaMazon* by convening the *Zimun*. This is based on the Talmud's paraphrase of (*Proverbs* 22:9): *The gracious one should bless* (*Sotah* 22:9). Since the master of the house graciously invited, "Whoever is hungry — let him come and eat," he is the person to offer blessings.

1. **Joy Born of Tears.** Great chassidic masters read the verse differently: Those who sow with tears of joy (הַזֹּרְעִים בְּדִמְעָה בְּרִנָּה) will eventually reap (יִקְצֹרוּ). The key to spiritual success is to never allow adversity to spiritually paralyze us. We must turn the tears into joy, viewing life's difficulties as a propellant to greatness.

2. **Communal Peace.** "A few who perform a commandment are not comparable to a multitude performing a commandment" (*Rashi* to *Leviticus* 26:8). This means that when many people unite to do God's will, each individual among the group reaches a far higher level than he would have had he acted alone, no matter how meritoriously (*Chafetz Chaim*). A commandment done by an individual cannot be compared to one performed by a group.

R' S. R. Hirsch offers yet another perspective on the communal blessing: Hunger, more than any other craving, can turn people into self-centered creatures battling all others for survival. The very word לֶחֶם, *bread*, is related to מִלְחָמָה, *war*. It is likely that for this reason the Sages instituted this element of a communal blessing of God for having provided us with food. By proclaiming that the entire group has only God to thank for its sustenance, we remember that our neighbor is not a competitor to be feared, fought and defeated. Rather, we are all guests at God's table and His beneficence is sufficient for us all.

If three or more males, aged thirteen or older, participated in the meal, the leader is required to formally invite the others to join him in the recitation of Grace After Meals. Following is the 'zimun,' or formal invitation.

The leader begins:

רַבּוֹתַי נְבָרֵךְ.

The group responds:

יְהִי שֵׁם יהוה מְבֹרָךְ מֵעַתָּה וְעַד עוֹלָם.[1]

The leader continues [if ten men join the zimun, the words in parentheses are included]:

יְהִי שֵׁם יהוה מְבֹרָךְ מֵעַתָּה וְעַד עוֹלָם.[1]

בִּרְשׁוּת מָרָנָן וְרַבָּנָן וְרַבּוֹתַי, נְבָרֵךְ (אֱלֹהֵינוּ) שֶׁאָכַלְנוּ מִשֶּׁלּוֹ.

The group responds:

בָּרוּךְ (אֱלֹהֵינוּ) שֶׁאָכַלְנוּ מִשֶּׁלּוֹ וּבְטוּבוֹ חָיִינוּ.

The leader continues:

בָּרוּךְ (אֱלֹהֵינוּ) שֶׁאָכַלְנוּ מִשֶּׁלּוֹ וּבְטוּבוֹ חָיִינוּ.

The following line is recited if ten men join the zimun.

בָּרוּךְ הוּא וּבָרוּךְ שְׁמוֹ.

בָּרוּךְ אַתָּה יהוה אֱלֹהֵינוּ מֶלֶךְ הָעוֹלָם, הַזָּן אֶת הָעוֹלָם כֻּלּוֹ, בְּטוּבוֹ, בְּחֵן בְּחֶסֶד וּבְרַחֲמִים, הוּא נוֹתֵן לֶחֶם לְכָל בָּשָׂר, כִּי לְעוֹלָם חַסְדּוֹ.[1] וּבְטוּבוֹ הַגָּדוֹל,

---

נְבָרֵךְ אֱלֹהֵינוּ — *Let us bless our God.* In the blessing for the study of Torah we begin בָּרְכוּ אֶת ה׳, *Bless* HASHEM, i.e., the Name signifying God's mercy; whereas in thanking Him for nourishment we use the Name אֱלֹהֵינוּ, *our God,* signifying His strict judgment. Why the difference? *Tosafos Yom Tov* (Berachos 7:3) explains that food is given as an act of Divine justice. It would be unjust for God to create living things without providing their elementary needs. The Torah, however, is God's Divine, unfathomable wisdom. For Him to share it with mortal man is an act of boundless mercy.

בִּרְכַּת הַזָּן / **The Blessing for Nourishment**

The first blessing of *Bircas HaMazon* was composed by Moses in gratitude for the manna with which God sustained Israel daily in the Wilderness (*Berachos* 48b). For that reason it precedes נוֹדֶה, the Blessing for the Land, even though it might seem

more logical to thank God first for the land that produced the food (*Bayis Chadash*).

This first blessing in its entirety speaks of God in the third person. The next two blessings, i.e., נוֹדֶה לְּךָ and רַחֵם, are in second person, while the fourth and last blessing of *Bircas HaMazon,* הַטּוֹב וְהַמֵּטִיב, goes back to third person. *Mateh Yehudah* explains the apparent discrepancy by use of a Talmudic parable: A bride is shy and modest in the presence of her groom before they are married. After the marriage, she becomes friendly and familiar. If they are divorced, she once again becomes shy in his company (*Yoma* 54a). The blessings of *Bircas HaMazon* reflect these modes of behavior. The first blessing was composed by Moses before the Jews entered the land. Then we were yet too "shy" to speak "directly" to God. The next two blessings were composed in *Eretz Yisrael,* when Jews felt "at

ZIMUN/INVITATION

If three or more males, aged thirteen or older, participated in the meal, the leader is required to formally invite the others to join him in the recitation of Grace After Meals. Following is the 'zimun,' or formal invitation.

The leader begins:

Gentlemen, let us bless.

The group responds:

Blessed is the name of HASHEM from this moment and forever![1]

The leader continues [if ten men join the zimun, the words in parentheses are included]:

Blessed is the name of HASHEM from this moment and forever![1] With the permission of the distinguished people present, let us bless [our God], for we have eaten from what is His.

The group responds:

Blessed is He [our God] of Whose we have eaten and through Whose goodness we live.

The leader continues:

Blessed is He [our God] of Whose we have eaten and through Whose goodness we live.

The following line is recited if ten men join the zimun.

Blessed is He and blessed is His Name.

Blessed are You, HASHEM, our God, King of the Universe, Who nourishes the entire world; in His goodness, with grace, with lovingkindness, and with mercy. He gives nourishment to all flesh, for His lovingkindness is eternal.[2] And through His great

---

(1) *Psalms* 113:2. (2) 136:25.

---

home" with God. The final blessing was instituted after our sins caused us to be spurned and exiled by God; we no longer have the audacity to be as familiar with Him as we once were.[1]

בְּטוּבוֹ בְּחֵן בְּחֶסֶד וּבְרַחֲמִים — *In His goodness, with grace, with lovingkindness and with mercy.* His goodness is an all-inclusive term which is subdi-

vided into *grace, lovingkindness* and *mercy.*

הוּא נֹתֵן לֶחֶם לְכָל בָּשָׂר — *He gives nourishment to all flesh.* God's compassion is universal to *all* flesh, including animal life and undeserving people.

וּבְטוּבוֹ הַגָּדוֹל — *And through His great goodness.* That God provides sustenance for all kinds of people despite their shortcomings is evidence of His

---

1. **Return to the Source.** A disciple of the *Chidushei HaRim* once visited the Kotzker Rebbe. Upon his return, the *Chidushei HaRim* asked him to relate something he had heard from the Kotzker. Replied the *chassid*: The Kotzker wondered how it is possible that a Jew is not spiritually metamorphosed by reciting *Bircas HaMazon.* Was not that the tool employed by our forefather Abraham to bring people close to God? [Abraham would feed wayfarers and guests and then ask them to thank and bless the One Who provided for them.]

The *Chidushei HaRim* stopped for a moment and replied: "I wonder how eating itself does not bring one to an awareness of God! Does not the prophet say, *An ox knows his owner and a donkey his master's trough, but My people do not know. . .*" (Isaiah 1:3)?

תָּמִיד לֹא חָסַר לָנוּ, וְאַל יֶחְסַר לָנוּ מָזוֹן לְעוֹלָם וָעֶד. בַּעֲבוּר שְׁמוֹ הַגָּדוֹל, כִּי הוּא אֵל זָן וּמְפַרְנֵס לַכֹּל, וּמֵטִיב לַכֹּל, וּמֵכִין מָזוֹן לְכָל בְּרִיּוֹתָיו אֲשֶׁר בָּרָא. בָּרוּךְ אַתָּה יהוה, הַזָּן אֶת הַכֹּל. (אָמֵן. —Others)

נוֹדֶה לְךָ יהוה אֱלֹהֵינוּ, עַל שֶׁהִנְחַלְתָּ לַאֲבוֹתֵינוּ אֶרֶץ חֶמְדָּה טוֹבָה וּרְחָבָה. וְעַל שֶׁהוֹצֵאתָנוּ יהוה אֱלֹהֵינוּ מֵאֶרֶץ מִצְרַיִם, וּפְדִיתָנוּ מִבֵּית עֲבָדִים, וְעַל בְּרִיתְךָ שֶׁחָתַמְתָּ בִּבְשָׂרֵנוּ, וְעַל תּוֹרָתְךָ שֶׁלִּמַּדְתָּנוּ, וְעַל חֻקֶּיךָ שֶׁהוֹדַעְתָּנוּ, וְעַל חַיִּים חֵן וָחֶסֶד שֶׁחוֹנַנְתָּנוּ, וְעַל אֲכִילַת מָזוֹן שָׁאַתָּה זָן וּמְפַרְנֵס אוֹתָנוּ תָּמִיד, בְּכָל יוֹם וּבְכָל עֵת וּבְכָל שָׁעָה.

וְעַל הַכֹּל יהוה אֱלֹהֵינוּ אֲנַחְנוּ מוֹדִים לָךְ, וּמְבָרְכִים אוֹתָךְ, יִתְבָּרַךְ שִׁמְךָ בְּפִי כָּל חַי תָּמִיד לְעוֹלָם וָעֶד. כַּכָּתוּב, וְאָכַלְתָּ וְשָׂבָעְתָּ, וּבֵרַכְתָּ אֶת יהוה אֱלֹהֶיךָ, עַל הָאָרֶץ הַטֹּבָה אֲשֶׁר נָתַן לָךְ.[1] בָּרוּךְ אַתָּה יהוה, עַל הָאָרֶץ וְעַל הַמָּזוֹן. (אָמֵן. —Others)

"great" goodness. Indeed, no human being can claim to be so meritorious that he has earned *all* of God's goodness to him.

זָן . . . מְפַרְנֵס . . . מֵטִיב — *Nourishes. . . sustains. . . benefits.* זָן, *nourishes,* refers to food. מְפַרְנֵס, *sustains,* refers to clothing. מֵטִיב, *does good,* refers to shelter. Thus, in conjunction, the three phrases enumerate all the basic needs of life that are provided by God (*Eitz Yosef*).

וּמֵכִין מָזוֹן — *And He prepares food.* He anticipates the need for food and prepares it for His creatures in advance (*Iyun Tefillah*).

נוֹדֶה / The Blessing for the Land

The second blessing, beginning נוֹדֶה לְךָ, *We thank You,* is known as בִּרְכַּת הָאָרֶץ, the *Blessing for the Land*, and was composed by Joshua (*Berachos* 48a). The requirement to include thanks for the land in *Bircas HaMazon,* however, is ordained by the Torah (*Deuteronomy* 8:10) according to most commentators; Joshua merely formulated its text. He saw how desirous Moses was to be permitted entry into *Eretz Yisrael,* and how anxious the Patriarchs were to be buried in it. Therefore, when he was privileged to enter it, he composed this blessing (*Shibbolei HaLeket*).

goodness, nourishment was never lacking to us, and may it never be lacking to us forever. For the sake of His Great Name, because He is the God who nourishes and sustains all, and benefits all and He prepares food for all of His creatures which He created. Blessed are You, HASHEM, Who nourishes all.

(Others — Amen.)

We thank You, HASHEM, our God, because you have given to our forefathers as a heritage a desirable, good and spacious land; and because You removed us, HASHEM, our God, from the land of Egypt, and You redeemed us from the house of bondage; for Your covenant which You sealed in our flesh; for Your Torah which You taught us and for Your statutes which You made known to us; for life, grace, and lovingkindness which You granted us; and for the provision of food with which You nourish and sustain us constantly, in every day, in every season, and in every hour.

For all [of these], HASHEM, our God, we thank You and bless You. May Your name be blessed continuously by the mouth of all the living. As it is written, "And you shall eat and be satisfied, and bless HASHEM, your God, for the good land which He gave you."[1] Blessed are You, HASHEM, for the land and for the food.

(Others — Amen.)

---

(1) *Deuteronomy* 8:10.

וְעַל שֶׁהוֹצֵאתָנוּ — *And because You removed us.* The Exodus is described as our *personal* experience because, as the Haggadah proclaims (*Pesachim* 116b): "In every generation a person must consider himself as if he had left Egypt" (*Mateh Yehudah*).

וּפְדִיתָנוּ מִבֵּית עֲבָדִים — *And You redeemed us from the house of bondage.* Egypt was called a *house of bondage* (following *Deuteronomy* 7:8) because no slave could ever escape successfully (*Eitz Yosef*).

This description of Egypt may allude to a second concept of redemption. First, there was the physical removal from political subservience to Egypt. That, however, would have been insufficient had Israel retained either the heathen culture of that land with its enslavement to sensual desires or the slavish mentality ingrained in them over the course of bondage; hence the redemption from the *house of bondage* (*R' Y.Z. Soloveitchik*).

וְעַל תּוֹרָתְךָ שֶׁלִּמַּדְתָּנוּ. . . וְעַל אֲכִילַת מָזוֹן — *For Your Torah which You taught us. . . and for the provision of food.* First we thank God for His Torah and then for food, for of what value is eating if not in order to give us the strength to study and practice His Torah? (*R' Elya Lopian*).

וְעַל הַכֹּל — *For all [of these]*, i.e., we thank You for all of the gifts enumerated above. In a homiletic vein *R' Baruch of Mezhibuzh* renders וְעַל הַכֹּל as "and *above* all." The greatest kindness You show us, above all others, is the opportunity to *thank You and bless You.*

רַחֵם (נָא) יהוה אֱלֹהֵינוּ עַל יִשְׂרָאֵל עַמֶּךָ, וְעַל יְרוּשָׁלַיִם עִירֶךָ, וְעַל צִיּוֹן מִשְׁכַּן כְּבוֹדֶךָ, וְעַל מַלְכוּת בֵּית דָּוִד מְשִׁיחֶךָ, וְעַל הַבַּיִת הַגָּדוֹל וְהַקָּדוֹשׁ שֶׁנִּקְרָא שִׁמְךָ עָלָיו. אֱלֹהֵינוּ אָבִינוּ רְעֵנוּ זוּנֵנוּ פַּרְנְסֵנוּ וְכַלְכְּלֵנוּ וְהַרְוִיחֵנוּ, וְהַרְוַח לָנוּ יהוה אֱלֹהֵינוּ מְהֵרָה מִכָּל צָרוֹתֵינוּ. וְנָא אַל תַּצְרִיכֵנוּ יהוה אֱלֹהֵינוּ, לֹא לִידֵי מַתְּנַת בָּשָׂר וָדָם, וְלֹא לִידֵי הַלְוָאָתָם, כִּי אִם לְיָדְךָ הַמְּלֵאָה הַפְּתוּחָה הַקְּדוֹשָׁה וְהָרְחָבָה, שֶׁלֹּא נֵבוֹשׁ וְלֹא נִכָּלֵם לְעוֹלָם וָעֶד.

On the Sabbath add the following paragraph.

רְצֵה וְהַחֲלִיצֵנוּ יהוה אֱלֹהֵינוּ בְּמִצְוֹתֶיךָ, וּבְמִצְוַת יוֹם הַשְּׁבִיעִי הַשַּׁבָּת הַגָּדוֹל וְהַקָּדוֹשׁ הַזֶּה, כִּי יוֹם זֶה גָּדוֹל וְקָדוֹשׁ הוּא לְפָנֶיךָ, לִשְׁבָּת בּוֹ וְלָנוּחַ בּוֹ בְּאַהֲבָה כְּמִצְוַת רְצוֹנֶךָ, וּבִרְצוֹנְךָ הָנִיחַ לָנוּ יהוה אֱלֹהֵינוּ, שֶׁלֹּא תְהֵא צָרָה וְיָגוֹן וַאֲנָחָה בְּיוֹם מְנוּחָתֵנוּ, וְהַרְאֵנוּ יהוה אֱלֹהֵינוּ בְּנֶחָמַת צִיּוֹן עִירֶךָ, וּבְבִנְיַן יְרוּשָׁלַיִם עִיר קָדְשֶׁךָ, כִּי אַתָּה הוּא בַּעַל הַיְשׁוּעוֹת וּבַעַל הַנֶּחָמוֹת.

רַחֵם / **The Blessing for Jerusalem**

The third blessing, *Rebuilder of Jerusalem,* is required by the Torah, and its text was composed in stages, by David and Solomon. David, who conquered Jerusalem, made reference to *Israel, Your people,* and *Jerusalem, Your city.* Solomon, following his construction of the Temple, added, *Your great and holy House* (*Berachos* 48b). Their blessing was a prayer that God continue the tranquility of the land. Following the destruction and exile, a prayer for the return of the land, the Temple and the Davidic dynasty was added. Before Joshua's conquest of the land, however, the blessing took yet another form: a request for God's mercy upon the nation (*Aruch HaShulchan*).

רְעֵנוּ — *Tend us.* Provide us with the absolute necessities of life, i.e., bread and water (*Eitz Yosef*).

זוּנֵנוּ — *Nourish us.* Give additional food such as fruits and vegetables — foods that are important but not indispensable (ibid.).

פַּרְנְסֵנוּ — *Sustain us.* Give us clothing and shelter (ibid.).

וְכַלְכְּלֵנוּ — *And support us.* Make the provision of

Have mercy, (we beg you) HASHEM, our God, on Israel Your people, on Jerusalem, Your city, on Zion the resting place of Your Glory, on the monarchy of the house of David, Your anointed, and on the great and holy House upon which Your name is called. Our God, our Father — tend us, nourish us, sustain us, and support us, and relieve us; HASHEM, our God, grant us speedy relief from all our troubles. Please, HASHEM, our God, make us not needful of the gifts of human hands nor of their loans but only of Your Hand that is full, open, holy, and generous, that we not feel inner shame or be humiliated for ever and ever.

On the Sabbath add the following paragraph.

May it please You, HASHEM, our God — give us rest through Your commandments and through the commandment of the seventh day, this great and holy Sabbath. For this day is great and holy before You to rest on it and be content on it in love, as ordained by Your will. May it be Your will, HASHEM, our God, that there be no distress, grief, or lament on this day of our contentment. And show us, HASHEM, our God, the consolation of Zion, Your city, and the rebuilding of Jerusalem, city of Your holiness, for You are the Master of salvations and Master of consolations.

---

our needs steady and secure rather than sporadic and worrisome (ibid.).

וְהַרְוִיחֵנוּ — *And relieve us.* Spare us the need to scrimp and budget; allow our needs to be provided generously and abundantly (ibid.).

וְהַרְוַח לָנוּ . . . מִכָּל צָרוֹתֵינוּ — *And grant us relief . . . from all our troubles,* i.e., from all physical and spiritual woes (*Olas Tamid*).

וְנָא אַל תַּצְרִיכֵנוּ . . . לֹא לִידֵי מַתְּנַת בָּשָׂר וָדָם — *Please. . . make us not needful of the gifts of human hands.* I.e., do not make us dependent upon others.

This is also a plea that our faith in God not

be undermined by dependence upon others. God's beneficence is decreed from above and is delivered through such agents — human or natural — as He designates. The firm believer knows that God's blessing will come inevitably without requiring him to beg for favors. However, if one feels compelled by need to seek the help of others, his faith can become eroded. This is a prayer that God not put us to such a test (*Olas Tamid*).

שֶׁלֹּא נֵבוֹשׁ וְלֹא נִכָּלֵם — *That we not feel inner shame or be humiliated.* בּוּשָׁה refers to *shame* that results from pangs of conscience, while כְּלִמָּה refers to *humiliation* caused by others (*Malbim*).

אֱלֹהֵ֫ינוּ וֵאלֹהֵי אֲבוֹתֵ֫ינוּ, יַעֲלֶה, וְיָבֹא, וְיַגִּ֫יעַ, וְיֵרָאֶה, וְיֵרָצֶה, וְיִשָּׁמַע, וְיִפָּקֵד, וְיִזָּכֵר זִכְרוֹנֵ֫נוּ וּפִקְדוֹנֵ֫נוּ, וְזִכְרוֹן אֲבוֹתֵ֫ינוּ, וְזִכְרוֹן מָשִׁ֫יחַ בֶּן דָּוִד עַבְדֶּ֫ךָ, וְזִכְרוֹן יְרוּשָׁלַ֫יִם עִיר קָדְשֶׁ֫ךָ, וְזִכְרוֹן כָּל עַמְּךָ בֵּית יִשְׂרָאֵל לְפָנֶ֫יךָ, לִפְלֵיטָה לְטוֹבָה לְחֵן וּלְחֶ֫סֶד וּלְרַחֲמִים, לְחַיִּים וּלְשָׁלוֹם בְּיוֹם חַג הַמַּצּוֹת הַזֶּה. זָכְרֵ֫נוּ יְהֹוָה אֱלֹהֵ֫ינוּ בּוֹ לְטוֹבָה, וּפָקְדֵ֫נוּ בוֹ לִבְרָכָה, וְהוֹשִׁיעֵ֫נוּ בוֹ לְחַיִּים. וּבִדְבַר יְשׁוּעָה וְרַחֲמִים, חוּס וְחָנֵּ֫נוּ וְרַחֵם עָלֵ֫ינוּ וְהוֹשִׁיעֵ֫נוּ, כִּי אֵלֶ֫יךָ עֵינֵ֫ינוּ, כִּי אֵל (מֶ֫לֶךְ) חַנּוּן וְרַחוּם אָֽתָּה.[1]

וּבְנֵה יְרוּשָׁלַ֫יִם עִיר הַקֹּ֫דֶשׁ בִּמְהֵרָה בְיָמֵ֫ינוּ. בָּרוּךְ אַתָּה יְהֹוָה, בּוֹנֵה (בְּרַחֲמָיו) יְרוּשָׁלָ֫יִם. אָמֵן. (Others – אָמֵן.)

בָּרוּךְ אַתָּה יְהֹוָה אֱלֹהֵ֫ינוּ מֶ֫לֶךְ הָעוֹלָם, הָאֵל אָבִ֫ינוּ מַלְכֵּ֫נוּ אַדִּירֵ֫נוּ בּוֹרְאֵ֫נוּ גּוֹאֲלֵ֫נוּ יוֹצְרֵ֫נוּ קְדוֹשֵׁ֫נוּ קְדוֹשׁ יַעֲקֹב, רוֹעֵ֫נוּ רוֹעֵה יִשְׂרָאֵל, הַמֶּ֫לֶךְ הַטּוֹב וְהַמֵּטִיב לַכֹּל, שֶׁבְּכָל יוֹם וָיוֹם הוּא הֵטִיב, הוּא מֵטִיב, הוּא יֵיטִיב לָ֫נוּ. הוּא גְמָלָ֫נוּ הוּא גוֹמְלֵ֫נוּ הוּא יִגְמְלֵ֫נוּ לָעַד, לְחֵן וּלְחֶ֫סֶד

יַעֲלֶה וְיָבֹא... – *May . . . rise, come . . .* This prayer begins with eight words (יַעֲלֶה, יָבֹא, יַגִּיעַ, etc.) that express the same general idea: that God recall our remembrance with favor. The *Vilna Gaon* (comm. to Laws of *Rosh Chodesh*, quoted by *Eitz Yosef* and *Ishei Yisrael*) gives a lengthy, esoteric explanation of these eight words. He comments that Israel's sins caused God's Presence to withdraw from earth and remain beyond the "seven heavens" which are, in reality, seven levels of holiness separating man from God. In *Ya'aleh VeYavo*, we pray that our remembrance rise through the seven layers and then be found worthy of the eighth elevation — that they be brought directly to God.

בּוֹנֵה (בְּרַחֲמָיו) יְרוּשָׁלַיִם – *Who (in His mercy) rebuilds Jerusalem.* The present tense indicates that God rebuilds Jerusalem every day. Whenever a Jew does a good deed, he assists in this Divine task. Some add a brick, while others might lay a whole row. When enough Jews perform enough *mitzvos*, Jerusalem will finally be completely rebuilt (*R' Naftali of Ropschitz*).

הַטוֹב וְהַמֵטִיב / The Blessing for God's Goodness

The following blessing, הַטּוֹב וְהַמֵּטִיב, *Who is Good and Who does good,* was composed by the court of Rabban Gamliel in Yavneh, as an expression of

Our God and God of our fathers, may there rise, come, reach, be noted, be favored, be heard, be considered, and remembered before You — the remembrance and consideration of ourselves, the remembrance of our fathers; the remembrance of Messiah, son of David, Your servant; the remembrance of Jerusalem, Your holy city; and the remembrance of Your entire people, the House of Israel — for deliverance, for well-being, for grace, for lovingkindness and for mercy, for life and for peace on this day of the Festival of Matzos. Remember us on it, HASHEM, our God, for goodness, consider us on it for blessing, and help us on it for (good) life. Concerning salvation and mercy, have pity, show grace to us and be merciful upon us and help us. For our eyes are turned to You; for You are the Almighty, gracious, and generous (King).[1]

Rebuild Jerusalem, the Holy City, soon in our days. Blessed are You, HASHEM, Who (in His mercy) rebuilds Jerusalem. Amen.

(Others — Amen.)

Blessed are You, HASHEM, our God, King of the universe, the Almighty, our Father, our King, our Sovereign, our Creator, our Redeemer, our Maker, our Holy One, Holy One of Jacob our Shepherd, the Shepherd of Israel, the King Who is good and Who does good. For every single day He did good, does good, and will do good to us. He was bountiful with us, and will forever be bountiful with us — with grace and with lovingkindness,

(1) Cf. *Nechemiah* 9:31.

gratitude to God for preserving the bodies of the victims of the Roman massacre at Betar, and for eventually allowing them to be brought to burial (*Berachos* 48b).[1]

1. **Exile Lesson.** In the Court of Yavneh, the generation that witnessed the massacre at Betar responded: "He did good, does good and will do good for us." There is suffering in the world, there is punishment, but there is never abandonment. Betar is destroyed, but the hand of God is seen within the awful concealment. Miracles occur amidst the ruins, and the corpses are preserved. Surrounded by death and destruction, cast out of His presence, miles from the Temple and Jerusalem, man — tortured, bleeding and staggering — encounters God.

R' Nachman of Breslov taught: "There are times when a person experiences an extreme digression in his service of God. He may fall into places which are loathsome and disgusting. It will appear to him that God cannot be found in those places, and suddenly he exclaims: 'Where is the place of His glory?' By this, the individual's descent can be transformed into a great ascent" (*Likutei Maharan* 2:12).

וּלְרַחֲמִים וּלְרֶוַח הַצָּלָה וְהַצְלָחָה, בְּרָכָה וִישׁוּעָה נֶחָמָה פַרְנָסָה וְכַלְכָּלָה וְרַחֲמִים וְחַיִּים וְשָׁלוֹם וְכָל טוֹב, וּמִכָּל טוּב לְעוֹלָם אַל יְחַסְּרֵנוּ. (אָמֵן. —Others)

הָרַחֲמָן הוּא יִמְלוֹךְ עָלֵינוּ לְעוֹלָם וָעֶד. הָרַחֲמָן הוּא יִתְבָּרַךְ בַּשָּׁמַיִם וּבָאָרֶץ. הָרַחֲמָן הוּא יִשְׁתַּבַּח לְדוֹר דּוֹרִים, וְיִתְפָּאַר בָּנוּ לָעַד וּלְנֵצַח נְצָחִים, וְיִתְהַדַּר בָּנוּ לָעַד וּלְעוֹלְמֵי עוֹלָמִים. הָרַחֲמָן הוּא יְפַרְנְסֵנוּ בְּכָבוֹד. הָרַחֲמָן הוּא יִשְׁבּוֹר עֻלֵּנוּ מֵעַל צַוָּארֵנוּ, וְהוּא יוֹלִיכֵנוּ קוֹמְמִיּוּת לְאַרְצֵנוּ. הָרַחֲמָן הוּא יִשְׁלַח לָנוּ בְּרָכָה מְרֻבָּה בַּבַּיִת הַזֶּה, וְעַל שֻׁלְחָן זֶה שֶׁאָכַלְנוּ עָלָיו. הָרַחֲמָן הוּא יִשְׁלַח לָנוּ אֶת אֵלִיָּהוּ הַנָּבִיא זָכוּר לַטּוֹב, וִיבַשֶּׂר לָנוּ בְּשׂוֹרוֹת טוֹבוֹת יְשׁוּעוֹת וְנֶחָמוֹת.

The following text — for a guest to recite at his host's table —
appears in *Shulchan Aruch, Orach Chaim* 201.

יְהִי רָצוֹן שֶׁלֹּא יֵבוֹשׁ וְלֹא יִכָּלֵם בַּעַל הַבַּיִת הַזֶּה, לֹא בָעוֹלָם הַזֶּה וְלֹא בָעוֹלָם הַבָּא, וְיַצְלִיחַ בְּכָל נְכָסָיו, וְיִהְיוּ נְכָסָיו מוּצְלָחִים וּקְרוֹבִים לָעִיר, וְאַל יִשְׁלוֹט שָׂטָן בְּמַעֲשֵׂה יָדָיו, וְאַל יִזְדַּקֵּק לְפָנָיו שׁוּם דְּבַר חֵטְא וְהִרְהוּר עָוֹן, מֵעַתָּה וְעַד עוֹלָם.

Those eating at their own table recite the following,
adding the appropriate parenthesized phrases:

הָרַחֲמָן הוּא יְבָרֵךְ אוֹתִי
(וְאֶת אִשְׁתִּי/בַּעֲלִי וְאֶת זַרְעִי) וְאֶת כָּל אֲשֶׁר לִי.

During the reign of the Roman Emperor Hadrian, Betar was the base of Bar Kochba's ill-fated rebellion. When the Romans defeated the Jewish army, the victors avenged themselves by slaughtering hundreds of thousands of Betar's inhabitants — and then by denying the Jews the right to bury their brethren. After the passage of years, Rabban Gamliel and his court fasted and prayed for many days and Rabban Gamliel depleted his fortune to satisfy the Roman despots. Finally permission for burial was granted. Miraculously, the dead bodies were still fresh and whole. The rabbinical court instituted a blessing to thank God for His double graciousness: הַטּוֹב, *the Good* — for having preserved their remains, וְהַמֵּטִיב, *Who does good* — for allowing them to receive the final honor of burial (*Berachos* 48b). As an acknowledgement of God's goodness, the blessing was included

and with mercy, with relief, salvation, success, blessing, help, consolation, sustenance, support, mercy, life, peace, and all good. And of all good things may He never deprive us.

(Others — Amen.)

The compassionate One! May He reign over us forever. The compassionate One! May He be blessed on heaven and on earth. The compassionate One! May He be praised throughout all generations, may He be glorified through us to the ultimate ends, and be honored through us to the inscrutable everlasting. The compassionate One! May He sustain us in honor. The compassionate One! May He break the yoke of oppression from our necks and guide us erect to our land. The compassionate One! May He send us abundant blessing to this house, and upon this table at which we have eaten. The compassionate One! May He send us Elijah, the prophet — may he be remembered for good — to proclaim to us good tidings, salvations, and consolations.

The following text — for a guest to recite at his host's table — appears in Shulchan Aruch, Orach Chaim *201.*

May it be God's will that this host not be shamed nor humiliated in This World or in the World to Come. May he be successful in all his dealings. May his dealings be successful and conveniently close at hand. May no evil impediment reign over his handiwork, and may no semblance of sin or iniquitous thought attach itself to him from this time and forever.

Those eating at their own table recite the following, adding the appropriate parenthesized phrases:

The compassionate One! May He bless me,
(my wife/husband and family) and all that is mine.

---

in *Bircas HaMazon*, because meals are generally festive occasions. In a shorter form, the blessing is recited when more then one type of wine is drunk at a gathering, when very good news is heard and for such happy events as rainfall after a drought (*Avudraham*).

וְהוּא יוֹלִיכֵנוּ קוֹמְמִיּוּת לְאַרְצֵנוּ – *And guide us erect to our land.* One who has borne a heavy yoke for a

long time often remains hunchbacked even after the yoke is removed. When the Final Redemption arrives, not only will God remove the painful weight of the exile experience from us by breaking and shattering it, He will also lead us *erect* to our land. Not a telltale sign of the burden of exile will remain with us (*Shiras HaGeulah*).

Guests recite the following. Children at their parents' table add the words in parentheses.

הָרַחֲמָן הוּא יְבָרֵךְ אֶת (אָבִי מוֹרִי) בַּעַל הַבַּיִת הַזֶּה,

וְאֶת (אִמִּי מוֹרָתִי) בַּעֲלַת הַבַּיִת הַזֶּה,

All guests recite the following:

אוֹתָם וְאֶת בֵּיתָם וְאֶת זַרְעָם וְאֶת כָּל אֲשֶׁר לָהֶם.

All continue here:

אוֹתָנוּ וְאֶת כָּל אֲשֶׁר לָנוּ, כְּמוֹ שֶׁנִּתְבָּרְכוּ אֲבוֹתֵינוּ אַבְרָהָם יִצְחָק וְיַעֲקֹב בַּכֹּל מִכֹּל כֹּל,[1] כֵּן יְבָרֵךְ אוֹתָנוּ כֻּלָּנוּ יַחַד בִּבְרָכָה שְׁלֵמָה, וְנֹאמַר, אָמֵן.

בַּמָּרוֹם יְלַמְּדוּ עֲלֵיהֶם וְעָלֵינוּ זְכוּת, שֶׁתְּהֵא לְמִשְׁמֶרֶת שָׁלוֹם. וְנִשָּׂא בְרָכָה מֵאֵת יהוה, וּצְדָקָה מֵאֱלֹהֵי יִשְׁעֵנוּ, וְנִמְצָא חֵן וְשֵׂכֶל טוֹב בְּעֵינֵי אֱלֹהִים וְאָדָם.[2]

On the Sabbath add the following sentence:

הָרַחֲמָן הוּא יַנְחִילֵנוּ יוֹם שֶׁכֻּלּוֹ שַׁבָּת וּמְנוּחָה לְחַיֵּי הָעוֹלָמִים.

The words in parentheses are added on the two Seder nights in some communities.

הָרַחֲמָן הוּא יַנְחִילֵנוּ יוֹם שֶׁכֻּלּוֹ טוֹב (יוֹם שֶׁכֻּלּוֹ אָרוֹךְ, יוֹם שֶׁצַּדִּיקִים יוֹשְׁבִים וְעַטְרוֹתֵיהֶם בְּרָאשֵׁיהֶם וְנֶהֱנִים מִזִּיו הַשְּׁכִינָה, וִיהִי חֶלְקֵנוּ עִמָּהֶם).

הָרַחֲמָן הוּא יְזַכֵּנוּ לִימוֹת הַמָּשִׁיחַ וּלְחַיֵּי הָעוֹלָם הַבָּא. מִגְדּוֹל יְשׁוּעוֹת מַלְכּוֹ וְעֹשֶׂה חֶסֶד לִמְשִׁיחוֹ לְדָוִד וּלְזַרְעוֹ עַד עוֹלָם.[3] עֹשֶׂה שָׁלוֹם בִּמְרוֹמָיו, הוּא יַעֲשֶׂה שָׁלוֹם עָלֵינוּ וְעַל כָּל יִשְׂרָאֵל. וְאִמְרוּ, אָמֵן.

יְראוּ אֶת יהוה קְדֹשָׁיו, כִּי אֵין מַחְסוֹר לִירֵאָיו. כְּפִירִים רָשׁוּ וְרָעֵבוּ, וְדֹרְשֵׁי יהוה לֹא יַחְסְרוּ כָל טוֹב.[4] הוֹדוּ

יוֹם שֶׁכֻּלּוֹ אָרוֹךְ — *That everlasting day.* This prayer is a special addition recited only on

the Seder night. Having experienced a revelation of God's Presence on this night when He smote

Guests recite the following. Children at their parents' table add the words in parentheses.

The compassionate One! May He bless
(my father, my teacher) the master of this house, and
(my mother, my teacher) lady of this house

All guests recite the following:

them, their house, their family, and all that is theirs,

All continue here:

ours and all that is ours — just as our forefathers Abraham, Isaac, and Jacob were blessed in everything from everything, with everything.[1] So may He bless us all together with perfect blessing. And let us say: Amen!

On high, may merit be pleaded upon them and upon us, for a safeguard of peace. May we receive a blessing from HASHEM, and just kindness from the God of our salvation, and find favor and understanding in the eyes of God and man.[2]

On the Sabbath add the following sentence:

The Compassionate One ! May He cause us to inherit the day which will be completely a Sabbath and rest day for eternal life.

The words in parentheses are added on the two Seder nights in some communities.

The compassionate One! May He cause us to inherit that day which is altogether good, (that everlasting day, the day when the just sit with crowns on their heads, enjoying the reflection of God's majesty — and may our portion be with them)!

The compassionate One! May He make us worthy to attain the days of Messiah and the life of the World to Come. He Who is a tower of salvations to His king and shows lovingkindness to His anointed, to David and his descendants forever.[3] He Who makes harmony in His heavenly heights, may He make harmony for us and for all Israel. Say: Amen!

Fear HASHEM, His holy ones, for those who fear Him feel no depravation. Young lions may feel want and hunger, but those who seek HASHEM will not lack any good.[4] Give thanks

(1) Cf. *Genesis* 24:1; 27:33; 33:11. (2) Cf. *Proverbs* 3:4. (3) *Psalms* 18:51. (4) 34:10-11.

the firstborn of the Egyptians, we pray that we may once again be able to *enjoy the reflection of* *God's Majesty (Seder HaAruch).*

לַיהוה כִּי טוֹב, כִּי לְעוֹלָם חַסְדּוֹ.[1] פּוֹתֵחַ אֶת יָדֶךָ, וּמַשְׂבִּיעַ לְכָל חַי רָצוֹן.[2] בָּרוּךְ הַגֶּבֶר אֲשֶׁר יִבְטַח בַּיהוה, וְהָיָה יהוה מִבְטַחוֹ.[3] נַעַר הָיִיתִי גַּם זָקַנְתִּי, וְלֹא רָאִיתִי צַדִּיק נֶעֱזָב, וְזַרְעוֹ מְבַקֶּשׁ לָחֶם.[4] יהוה עֹז לְעַמּוֹ יִתֵּן, יהוה יְבָרֵךְ אֶת עַמּוֹ בַשָּׁלוֹם.[5]

Upon completion of *Bircas HaMazon* the blessing over wine is recited and the third cup is drunk while reclining on the left side. It is preferable to drink the entire cup, but at the very least, most of the cup should be drained.

בָּרוּךְ אַתָּה יהוה אֱלֹהֵינוּ מֶלֶךְ הָעוֹלָם, בּוֹרֵא פְּרִי הַגָּפֶן.

The fourth cup is poured. According to most customs, the Cup of Elijah is poured at this point, after which the door is opened in accordance with the verse, "It is a guarded night." Then the following paragraph is recited.

שְׁפֹךְ חֲמָתְךָ אֶל הַגּוֹיִם אֲשֶׁר לֹא יְדָעוּךָ וְעַל מַמְלָכוֹת אֲשֶׁר בְּשִׁמְךָ לֹא קָרָאוּ. כִּי

שְׁפֹךְ חֲמָתְךָ — *Pour Your wrath.* We now pour the fourth cup, over which we recite the continuation of *Hallel.* As explained earlier, the first part of *Hallel* praises God for the Egyptian Exodus, while the second half is both praise and a prayer for the ultimate future Redemption.[1] It portrays our servitude to the nations, the pangs of the Messianic Redemption, the war with Gog of Magog (see

Ezekiel ch. 38), and finally the Messianic Era, the Resurrection of the Dead and the World to Come (*Pesachim* 118a, *Yalkut*). We introduce this part of *Hallel* by reciting שְׁפֹךְ חֲמָתְךָ, *Pour out Your wrath,* thus expressing the resolute hope that God will indeed bring these events about, and that He has not forsaken us (*R' Yehudah ben Yakar*).[2]

Just as the redemption from Egypt was accom-

---

1. **We Are Always Indebted.** After thanking God for His kindness in the past, we implore Him to continue showering us with His kindness. Having experienced His beneficence in the past, we must display our firm confidence in His endless ability to continue helping us. We must never view our expression of gratitude as full payment for our debt to God. Thus, whenever we thank God, we add a prayer for the future, as if to say, "We want to be indebted to You always." King David alludes to this dual obligation with the words *I will raise the cup of salvations* to thank You for all You have done for me, and *I will invoke the Name of HASHEM* (*Psalms* 116:13) asking for continued displays of His love and kindness. The Matriarch Leah was punished for lacking sensitivity to this truth. Although she thanked God for granting her more than her fair share of children (*Genesis* 29:35), she stopped bearing children for a few years because she did not pray to God for more (*Tur, Degel Machaneh Ephraim*).

2. **Royal Retribution.** Why do we wait until after the meal to offer our plea that God bring retribution upon our tormentors? *Minchas Elazar* explains with a parable:

A powerful king employed a talented and loyal gourmet chef who always prepared fine feasts for him. In honor of a special occasion, the chef spent many hours preparing delectable dishes, served with an assortment of wines. At the banquet, the chef brought the food and the drinks to the head of the table, where the king sat surrounded by his guests.

to HASHEM for He is good; His lovingkindness is eternal.[1] You open Your hand and satisfy the desire of every living thing.[2] Blessed is the man who trusts in HASHEM, and HASHEM will be his trust.[3] I was a youth and also have aged, and I have not seen a righteous man forsaken, with his children begging for bread.[4] HASHEM will give might to His nation; HASHEM will bless His nation with peace.[5]

Upon completion of *Bircas HaMazon* the blessing over wine is recited and the third cup is drunk while reclining on the left side. It is preferable to drink the entire cup, but at the very least, most of the cup should be drained.

Blessed are You, HASHEM, our God, King of the universe, Who creates the fruit of the vine.

The fourth cup is poured. According to most customs, the Cup of Elijah is poured at this point, after which the door is opened in accordance with the verse, "It is a guarded night." Then the following paragraph is recited.

Pour Your wrath upon the nations that do not recognize You and upon kingdoms that do not call upon Your Name. For

(1) *Psalms* 136:1 et al. (2) 145:16. (3) *Jeremiah* 17:7. (4) *Psalms* 37:25. (5) 29:11.

panied by God's venting His wrath on the Egyptians, so we pray that God punish all our oppressors and pour forth His wrath and indignation on them.

According to one opinion in the *Talmud Yerushalmi* (*Pesachim* 10:1) the Four Cups of the Seder represent the "four cups of Hashem's wrath" that the nations of the world will be forced to drink when the Messianic Era arrives. Thus the cups symbolize the overthrow of the four great empires which have in turn subjugated the Jewish people

since the destruction of the First Temple (Babylonia, Persia, Greece and, finally, Rome, which represents the present Exile as well; see *Shemos Rabbah* 6:26). The pouring of this fourth cup, therefore, evokes our prayer that God punish our present oppressors and bring about our ultimate redemption (*Meiri*).

Since the Seder night is ליל שִׁמֻּרִים, *the night of protection* (see *Targum Yerushalmi, Exodus* 12:42), when Jews are protected against harm, we affirm our trust in God and pray that He permanently

As the chef passed through the courtyard on his way to the banquet hall, some dogs smelled the tantalizing aroma of the food and wildly attacked. The trays crashed to the ground, breaking all the plates as the canines devoured the meat and licked up the wine. Brokenhearted, the chef took the little bit of salvageable wine, put it on the tray, and entered the banquet hall. "Your Majesty," he said contritely, "I did my best. I roasted the meat to your taste, but the brazen dogs came and ate it all. Nothing of the magnificent banquet I prepared for you is left except a little bit of wine and some bread. Please, Your Majesty, banish the arrogant dogs so that they can no longer destroy your banquet!"

In Temple times we would prepare roast meat of the *pesach* offering and the four cups of wine, exactly according to the specifications of our King. Then heathen dogs came, destroyed the Temple and devoured the meat. All we have left is a little wine and matzah. Saddened by our failure to provide the proper royal banquet, we pour the fourth and final cup of wine and implore God to remove the impudent marauders, the dogs who have devoured Jacob and have destroyed his abode, so that we may again prepare the banquet for the real King.

silence all those nations who defame His Name and seek to destroy His people. *Targum Yonasan* interprets שִׁמֻּרִים as *a night of [patient] waiting*. Since establishing this night during the Exodus as a time for redemption, God, as it were, is waiting for the opportune moment to bring about our final redemption. The process that began in Egypt will come to full fruition with the destruction of all evil and the triumph of good.

Thus, on Pesach night we proclaim our faith in the coming of the Messiah, and pray that through the merit of this trust itself, we may deserve to witness his arrival even sooner (*Matteh Moshe, Or Zarua*). This is why we open the door at שְׁפֹךְ חֲמָתְךָ — to show that we have no fear of our enemies (see *Rema O.C.* 480), and that we expect our deliverance to come imminently, heralded by Elijah, the messenger of the redemption.[1] The custom has arisen to also pour a special cup in his honor. Some even have the custom of calling out בָּרוּךְ הַבָּא, *Welcome*, when opening the door.[2]

אֲשֶׁר לֹא יְדָעוּךְ — *That do not recognize You*. The Ten Plagues and the miraculous display of God's might that accompanied the Exodus served a dual purpose: (a) to counteract Pharaoh's impudent declaration, *Who is HASHEM that I should heed His voice . . . ? I do not know HASHEM!* (see *Exodus* 5:2); and (b) to punish the Egyptians for their inhumane cruelty to the Jews. We ask that God pour His wrath on the purveyors of evil for these two same reasons. *Pour Your wrath upon the nations that do not recognize You and upon the kingdoms that do not invoke Your Name.*[3]

1. **Open-door Policy.** When the Jews left Egypt they were commanded, *And as for you, you shall not leave the entrance of your home until morning* (*Exodus* 12:22). Since the Jews had little, if any, merit at the time, they were vulnerable to be destroyed during the slaying of the firstborn, as the Sages teach, "Once the destroyer is granted permission to kill, it does not differentiate between the righteous and the wicked" (*Rashi*, ibid.). Even righteous people may not expose themselves to mortal danger and expect to be saved. In such circumstances, it might often take a miracle to prevent someone from being harmed, and one may not rely on a miracle. Thus, Jews were taught that anyone who left his safe premises was in danger. Unlike the time of the Exodus, however, when the Messiah comes we will all be able to witness clearly the crumbling of evil. In the words of the prophet, *for they will see it with their own eyes when HASHEM returns to Zion* (*Isaiah* 52:8). Thus, as we pray for the downfall of evil and our own redemption, we open the door, symbolic of the open revelation that will abound in the Messianic Era (*Sfas Emes*).

2. **Soul Model.** According to tradition, the prophet Elijah, who is known as "the Angel of the Covenant" (*Malachi* 3:1), attends, in spirit, circumcisions throughout the ages. Likewise the prophet Malachi describes him as the harbinger of the Final Redemption, who will *turn back [to God] the hearts of fathers with [their] sons and the hearts of sons with their fathers* (ibid. 3:24), by ushering in the era of repentance that will precede the Final Redemption. Thus Elijah will remove both the physical and spiritual impediments to redemption. We symbolically open the door for him on this night so that he may accomplish both tasks and prepare Israel for true freedom (*Toras Emes*).

⋖§ **Believing Is More Than Seeing.** The *Chidushei HaRim* spoke glowingly of the great piety of the *Noda BiYehudah*. "Once on the Seder night after reciting שְׁפֹךְ חֲמָתְךָ, the *Noda BiYehudah* accompanied Elijah all the way down the steps in front of the house. When questioned, the *Noda BiYehudah* said about this, 'I accompanied him not because I saw him, but because I have full faith that he comes on this night to every Jewish home — even mine.' " The *Chidushei HaRim* concluded, "Such pristine faith is even more meaningful than if Elijah would actually reveal himself to the person!"

⋖§ **Cup of Doubt.** The *Vilna Gaon* suggests that the special cup that we call by Elijah's name is meant to represent a *fifth* cup that should be drunk according to some opinions (e.g., *Rif* to *Pesachim* 118a). Since others disagree with this ruling, we pour the cup but leave it on the table to await the coming of Elijah who, according to tradition, will resolve all pending halachic questions. Thus the fifth cup awaits the redemption, and is a symbol of our future deliverance.

3. **Too Committed.** God ordained that the Jews should suffer from the nations on account of their sins. If the nations had carried out their task as they were meant to, without undue cruelty and in order to bring the Jews back to God, they would not have deserved punishment (see *Ramban, Genesis* 15:14). But they

By venting Your anger upon them, You will cause the world at large to acknowledge You. Secondly, they deserve to be punished for all they have done to Your people. *For they have devoured Jacob and destroyed his habitation* (Abarbanel).

וְעַל מַמְלָכוֹת אֲשֶׁר בְּשִׁמְךָ לֹא קָרָאוּ — *And upon kingdoms that do not call upon Your Name.* The previous verse teaches that God will pour His wrath

אֶל הַגּוֹיִם, *upon the nations* who lack knowledge of Him in order to threaten and warn them, in the hope of awakening them to the Godly message. This phrase calls for Him to pour His wrath עַל מַמְלָכוֹת, *upon kingdoms* who *are* aware of God, yet fail to *call upon* [His] *Name.* Because they *do* know of God, yet refuse to call upon His Name and follow His spirit, their crimes are inexcusable (Malbim).[1]

went far beyond their assigned task; they persecuted the Jews with uncalled-for harshness, and not from a desire to do God's will. On the contrary, they do not acknowledge God, and have oppressed the Jews *because* they are God's people and the carriers of His word. Therefore, they are deserving of punishment (Rabbi Mordechai Benet).

1. **Haunting Hatred.** Why do we note that they neither recognize God nor call in His Name? Are not their heinous actions sufficiently despicable in and of themselves, regardless of whether or not they recognize God?

The master of the parable, the *Dubno Maggid*, illustrated the point:

For years a successful retailer bought goods from a wealthy wholesaler, with both parties profiting handsomely. Once the retailer made a few bad deals; he was wiped out and informed his creditor that he would be unable to pay off his debt.

The wholesaler thought to himself: "What shall I do — send hoodlums to threaten him? Take him to court? Have him thrown into debtor's prison? He admits he owes me the money; he is simply penniless." Turning to the embarrassed retailer he said, "Life is a merry-go-round; I'm sure your luck will eventually turn around. Don't be ashamed, I'm willing to hire you as a salesman and pay you a good wage. I will deduct half of your salary each week toward repayment of the debt and the rest will be yours to support your family in a respectable fashion."

The retailer thanked his benefactor profusely and immediately threw himself into the job in earnest. He traveled from town to town getting orders, delivering goods, collecting payment and servicing his customers. One day he arrived in a town to collect an outstanding debt from a merchant. The debtor, who had fallen on hard times, begged, "Please let me have just one more order on credit so that I can reverse my downturn. Then I will honor all my outstanding debts."

The salesman exploded, "Don't think I will let you get away with this!" Enraged, he slapped the merchant and had him arrested and confined in debtor's prison. From the prison the merchant wrote a letter of complaint to his uncle — who was none other than the wholesaler for whom the salesman worked.

When the salesman returned to his home base, he was met by local police who arrested him and had him imprisoned. Incredulously he asked, "What have I done?" The police replied, "The wholesaler filed a complaint against you for a huge outstanding debt." Shocked, the salesman asked to be allowed to speak to his employer. When the wholesaler entered his cell, the salesman cried out "Why the change of heart? You were so gracious to me in the past and saved me from embarrassment and eternal poverty. Why did you now have me arrested for a debt you know I can't pay?"

The wholesaler responded, "Being a naturally compassionate person, I was willing to give you a chance. But now that I see that you have no compassion for others who look to you for mercy, I see that you don't deserve mercy from me."

If the nations of the world had exhibited mercy toward the Jews, we would expect God to show compassion toward them. However, since they heartlessly devoured Jacob and laid waste to his dwelling, they have no legitimate right to expect Divine mercy. Thus, we ask God to pursue them with anger and obliterate them from under His skies.

⊷§ **Major Offense.** A gang of counterfeiters of bills was sentenced to twenty years at hard labor. Appealing the sentence they argued, "If those who were caught using the bills received only a year or two in prison, we, who don't even have one bill, certainly don't deserve such a stiff sentence!"

The judge replied, "What they did was criminal, but what you did was treasonous. They only *had*

אָכַל אֶת יַעֲקֹב וְאֶת נָוֵהוּ הֵשַׁמּוּ.¹ שְׁפֹךְ עֲלֵיהֶם זַעְמֶךָ וַחֲרוֹן אַפְּךָ יַשִּׂיגֵם.² תִּרְדֹּף בְּאַף וְתַשְׁמִידֵם מִתַּחַת שְׁמֵי יְהֹוָה.³

הלל

The door is closed and the recitation of the Haggadah is continued.

לֹא לָנוּ יְהֹוָה לֹא לָנוּ, כִּי לְשִׁמְךָ תֵּן כָּבוֹד, עַל חַסְדְּךָ עַל אֲמִתֶּךָ. לָמָּה יֹאמְרוּ הַגּוֹיִם, אַיֵּה נָא אֱלֹהֵיהֶם.

כִּי אָכַל אֶת יַעֲקֹב —*For they* [lit. *it*] *have devoured Jacob*. The verse begins by speaking of the *nations* in plural, and then changes to the singular כִּי אָכַל, *for [it] has devoured*. This is the insidious nature of anti-Semitism; it unifies even hated rivals. The many nations were able to overcome their bitter rivalries and unite as one in order to devour the people of Israel [see *Rashi* to *Numbers* 22:4] (*Ohr LaYesharim*).

וְאֶת נָוֵהוּ הֵשַׁמּוּ — *And destroyed His habitation*. The ultimate proof of the gentiles' impure intentions is their wanton, malicious devastation of Your Temple. If they had the slightest concern for spreading the recognition of Your Name, why didn't they spare at least a vestige of this unique habitation where Your spirit dwelled in clearly revealed grandeur? (*Chozeh David*).[1]

שְׁפֹךְ עֲלֵיהֶם זַעְמֶךָ — *Pour Your fury upon them.* The

Midrash comments that God mercifully diverted His anger from the Jews themselves. He poured out His wrath upon the sticks and stones of the Temple rather than upon the Jewish nation. (See ArtScroll *Eichah*, comm. to 2:56; and 4:11.) The cruel enemies of Israel, however, do not deserve this Divine compassion. Therefore, unleash the full measure of Your fury directly upon them! (*Shaarei Chaim*).

⏴§ **Introduction to Psalm 115, the Continuation of Hallel**

Psalm 114, which was recited before the meal, vividly depicts the awe that God's miraculous deliverance of His people inspired in all of mankind. This, however, dissipated over the course of time. While God's intervention in history left an indelible mark of faith upon the Jewish heart, the gentile nations were quick to forget the miraculous display of Divine might. The moment God con-

counterfeit currency; you *produced* it, thus undermining the integrity of the government!''

Likewise, the cruelty exhibited by the nations is unpardonable, but it pales in significance compared to their disregard for God and His word, which is the source of all their bloody and torturous mistreatment of Jews. Devouring Jacob and his habitat is a terrible thing, but it is the godlessness of the nations that caused it to happen. Thus we ask God to pour out His full wrath on them because they maintain societies that foster evil, born of godlessness (*R' Leib Chasman*).

1. **Lacking Inspiration.** The Temple had a ripple effect on the nations of the world, causing them to some degree to also recognize Hashem. The spiritual level of the Jewish people always affects society at large; King David expressed this spiritual linkage, saying: *May my mouth declare the praise of HASHEM and may all flesh bless His Holy Name forever and ever* (*Psalms* 145:21). As a result of our own verbalization of Hashem's praise, other nations will be inspired to bless Him. Once the heathens destroyed the Temple, however, they lacked a source of inspiration to recognize God. Thus, by destroying His Habitation, they became ''nations that did not recognize God and kingdoms that do not call upon His Name'' (*R' Eliyahu Kitov*).

they have devoured Jacob and destroyed His habitation.[1] Pour Your fury upon them and let Your fiery wrath overtake them.[2] Pursue them with wrath and annihilate them from beneath the heavens of HASHEM.[3]

HALLEL

The door is closed and the recitation of the *Haggadah* is continued.

Not for our sake, HASHEM, not for our sake, but for Your Name's sake give glory, for the sake of Your kindness and Your truth! Why should the nations say: "Where now is their God?"

---

(1) *Psalms* 79:6-7. (2) 69:25. (3) *Lamentations* 3:66.

---

cealed His presence, the gentiles taunted the Jews saying, "Where now is their God?" (verse 2).

Therefore, we beseech God to disabuse the scoffers, by intervening again, *Not for our sake, HASHEM, not for our sake . . . but for the sake of Your kindness and Your truth!* (verse 1). Give us an opportunity to silence the heretics who mock You, and then, *we will bless God, henceforth and forever* (verse 18).

Furthermore, these are lessons that we ourselves must inculcate and internalize in order to be fit for a Messianic world. The lesson of the Exodus, that *I am HASHEM in the midst of the land* (*Exodus* 8:18), must be taken to heart. At the Splitting of the Sea, the Jews exclaimed, *This is my God* (*Exodus* 15:2); the future redemption will be marked by our raising this same cry, *Behold, He is our God* (*Isaiah* 25:9). The psalms of praise that form *Hallel* are meant to awaken in us this same awareness of God. At the same time, we hope and pray that our sincere acknowledgment of God's Kingship will in turn evoke a Heavenly response, and God will acknowledge us as His people and redeem us from Exile. Thus the psalm is a plea for the revelation of God's power in the Messianic Age, when He will enjoy universal recognition (*R' A. C. Feuer*).

לֹא לָנוּ ה' לֹא לָנוּ כִּי לְשִׁמְךָ תֵּן כָּבוֹד — *Not for our sake, HASHEM, not for our sake, but for Your Name's sake give glory.* We beg You to redeem us, Hashem, not because we are personally worthy, nor because of the merit of our forefathers; rather, we seek salvation on behalf of Your glorious Name, so that the gentiles have no opportunity to deny Your mastery and dominion (*Radak*).[1]

According to *Kedushas Levi* this refers to our requests for prosperity. We ask for financial success not for our own personal pleasure, but in order to perform *mitzvos*, provide for the needy, support Torah scholars and do other activities that add glory to God's Name.

עַל חַסְדְּךָ עַל אֲמִתֶּךָ — *For the sake of Your kindness and Your truth.* Our personal merit is insufficient to warrant Your assistance, but You are the God of kindness Who helps even the unworthy. You also made a covenant with the Patriarchs and promised not to abandon their children, and You must abide by this *truth* (*Malbim; Iyun Tefillah*).

לָמָּה יֹאמְרוּ הַגּוֹיִם אַיֵּה נָא אֱלֹהֵיהֶם — *Why should the nations say: "Where now is their God?"* The translation of נָא as *now* follows *Targum* and *Metzudos*.

---

1. **Godly Salvation.** Chassidic masters interpreted a phrase in the weekday *Shemoneh Esrei* in this vein. כִּי לִישׁוּעָתְךָ קִוִּינוּ כָּל הַיּוֹם, *For we hope for Your salvation all day long*. With the advent of the Messiah, God Himself will be "saved," as it were, for at that time all men will come to recognize Him. Thus it is for *His* salvation, in addition to our own, that we pray.

וֵאלֹהֵינוּ בַשָּׁמֵיִם, כֹּל אֲשֶׁר חָפֵץ עָשָׂה. עֲצַבֵּיהֶם כֶּסֶף וְזָהָב,
מַעֲשֵׂה יְדֵי אָדָם. פֶּה לָהֶם וְלֹא יְדַבֵּרוּ, עֵינַיִם לָהֶם וְלֹא
יִרְאוּ. אָזְנַיִם לָהֶם וְלֹא יִשְׁמָעוּ, אַף לָהֶם וְלֹא יְרִיחוּן. יְדֵיהֶם
וְלֹא יְמִישׁוּן, רַגְלֵיהֶם וְלֹא יְהַלֵּכוּ, לֹא יֶהְגּוּ בִּגְרוֹנָם. כְּמוֹהֶם
יִהְיוּ עֹשֵׂיהֶם, כֹּל אֲשֶׁר בֹּטֵחַ בָּהֶם. יִשְׂרָאֵל בְּטַח בַּיהוה,

---

The nations admit that God performed miracles for Israel in the past, but they claim that *now* He has withdrawn into His heavenly abode and abandoned them (*Maharam Arma'ah*).[1]

We beg of You to display Your total control of human affairs so as to silence their mockery and thus sanctify Your Name.

Those who mock us don't realize that their idols, while physically present, are impotent to help them, while our God, in the highest heavens, rules over the most minute detail of what occurs on earth. Totally unrestrained, He is able to do as He pleases.[2]

1. **Squandered Fortune.** There once was a pauper who could not marry off his daughter because he could not provide a dowry. Brokenhearted, he turned to his wealthy brother for help. Magnanimously, the brother replied, ''I am willing to give you 10,000 rubles as a dowry for your daughter.''

Immediately matchmakers swarmed to the pauper with proposals, and eventually a fine young man from an upstanding family was selected. The brother provided the 10,000 rubles without hesitation, and the pauper thanked him emotionally and profusely. From this money, the pauper catered a festive engagement party, bought gifts for the groom, had clothes tailored for the bride, her mother and sisters, and paid off some of his more pressing creditors. In no time at all the money was almost completely gone.

Left without any money for the dowry or to pay for the wedding, the father of the bride had no choice but to go to his wealthy brother again. But how could he ask for more after he had squandered the 10,000 rubles? A close friend gave him the following advice: ''Take the groom along with you when you go to speak to your brother. Tell him what happened, how you spent the money, and then say to him, 'I'm not asking for the money for myself; give it directly to the groom.' ''

This is what we ask of God, explained *The Dubno Maggid*: ''Hashem, You have been so good to us in the past and provided us with beneficence far beyond what we deserve. However, in our poverty (both literal and spiritual) we have wasted everything You have given us on foolish pursuits, or simply to provide for ourselves and our families so that we might survive the ravaging exile. By what right are we entitled to ask You to redeem us yet again? Nonetheless, we beg of You, ''*Not for our own sake, HASHEM,* do we ask You for the dowry and the 'Great Wedding' — the Final Redemption. *Not for our own sake, HASHEM,* but only so that You, our Groom (see *Rashi* to *Deuteronomy* 33:2), will finally receive the real dowry for the Great Wedding between You and Your nation.''

⏴§ **Show Them Now.** We believe firmly that in the future all the terrible ordeals and tribulations of the exile will disappear as God raises us above all the nations. However, what will be until then? We ask God to redeem us *now* so that the scornful nations cease to mock us: ''Fine, you have a rosy future; but where is your God *now*?'' (*R' Levi Yitzchak of Berditchev*).

2. **Misappropriation.** A man apprenticed his son to a shoemaker, and committed himself to send food for his son so that the shoemaker not be burdened with another mouth to feed. The father kept his word, sending not only tasty and nutritious food for his son, but even providing enough for the shoemaker and his family. The shoemaker, however, was cruel and took all the food for himself and his family; for his young apprentice he gave nothing but hard bread and water. As if to add insult to injury, the shoemaker constantly taunted the youngster, ''See how your heartless father refuses to send you decent food?''

The young lad was devastated over his situation and even more so over the snide mockery of his cruel

Our God is in the heavens; whatever He pleases, He does! Their idols are silver and gold, the handiwork of man. They have a mouth, but cannot speak; they have eyes, but cannot see; they have ears, but cannot hear; they have a nose, but cannot smell; their hands — they cannot feel; their feet — they cannot walk; nor can they utter a sound with their throat. Those who make them shall become like them, whoever trusts in them. O Israel! Trust in HASHEM —

עֲצַבֵּיהֶם כֶּסֶף וְזָהָב מַעֲשֵׂה יְדֵי אָדָם — *Their idols are silver and gold, the handiwork of man.* The word עֲצַבֵּיהֶם, *idols*, is related to עֶצֶב, *sorrow,* because the helpless idols only disappoint their worshipers, causing them heartbreak and sorrow.[1] How can idols help a man, when they are the work of his own hands? Certainly they have no more power than their maker (*Ibn Ezra; Radak*). As an illustration of their impotence, the Psalmist contends that the idols lack even the five senses of ordinary human beings.

אַף לָהֶם וְלֹא יְרִיחוּן — *They have a nose, but cannot smell.* Homiletically, the subject of this verse may be the idol worshipers. The Creator fashioned Adam, the father of all mankind, in His own image, and blew the breath of life into his nostrils. Every breath of fresh air is a reminder to man that God is

his Creator and that his life is in God's hands. The idolater's nose is physically identical to that of the believer, yet, he fails to sense the presence and the kindness of the Creator with his every breath (*R' A.C. Feuer*).

כְּמוֹהֶם יִהְיוּ עֹשֵׂיהֶם — *Those who make them shall become like them.* Just as man is truly created in the image of God, so those who falsely believe in idols will assume their image and lose the use of their own senses.

יִשְׂרָאֵל בְּטַח בַּה׳ — *O Israel! Trust in HASHEM.* The Psalmist contrasts the Children of Israel, who trust in Hashem alone, with those described in the previous verse, who trust in the lifeless and helpless idols (*Ibn Ezra*).

Maharal comments that the final three verses of the paragraph refer to three categories of Jews,

---

master. Finally, unable to bear his predicament any longer, he ran away and went back to his parents. Overjoyed to see his son, the father welcomed him back with open arms. "But what happened to you, my son? Why are you so thin and emaciated looking?"

"What do you mean?" the boy cried out. "I had nothing to eat." The father, shocked at his son's words, enumerated all of the delicacies he had sent for his dear son.

"I received none of it," said the boy. "Not only that, but the shoemaker taunted me over the heartless father I have. Please, Father, allow me to remain with you so that I need not be subject to the torture of feeling that you have abandoned me."

God sends us into exile because there are lessons that can be learned only through hardship and deprivation. Often He showers our host nations with great prosperity, only so that they would be sure to provide us with our needs. What do they do? They take all of God's gifts and use them for themselves, denigrating us to Spartan conditions or worse. And they revile us over how our Father has abandoned us! Thus, we turn to God and cry out, *Why should the nations say, "Where, now, is their God?* Please, Father, bring us home to You so that we will be saved from their merciless mockery"* (*Yerios HaOhel*).

1. **Frazzled Over Finance.** Homiletically, the *Kotzker Rebbe* would teach concerning this verse that man suffers from sorrow (עֲצַבֵּיהֶם) because he mistakenly thinks that כֶּסֶף וְזָהָב מַעֲשֵׂה יְדֵי אָדָם, *silver and gold* (i.e. material riches) *are the handiwork of man.* Consequently, he wearies himself and wastes away his life trying to make money and becomes sorrowful at its loss, not realizing that man's income is determined by the will of God.

עֶזְרָם וּמָגִנָּם הוּא. בֵּית אַהֲרֹן בִּטְחוּ בַיהוה, עֶזְרָם וּמָגִנָּם הוּא. יִרְאֵי יהוה בִּטְחוּ בַיהוה, עֶזְרָם וּמָגִנָּם הוּא.

יהוה זְכָרָנוּ יְבָרֵךְ, יְבָרֵךְ אֶת בֵּית יִשְׂרָאֵל, יְבָרֵךְ אֶת בֵּית אַהֲרֹן. יְבָרֵךְ יִרְאֵי יהוה, הַקְּטַנִּים עִם הַגְּדֹלִים. יֹסֵף יהוה עֲלֵיכֶם, עֲלֵיכֶם וְעַל בְּנֵיכֶם. בְּרוּכִים אַתֶּם לַיהוה, עֹשֵׂה שָׁמַיִם וָאָרֶץ. הַשָּׁמַיִם שָׁמַיִם לַיהוה, וְהָאָרֶץ נָתַן לִבְנֵי אָדָם. לֹא הַמֵּתִים יְהַלְלוּ יָהּ, וְלֹא כָּל יֹרְדֵי דוּמָה. וַאֲנַחְנוּ נְבָרֵךְ יָהּ, מֵעַתָּה וְעַד עוֹלָם, הַלְלוּיָהּ.[1]

---

each with a different motive for serving God. Some Jews cling to Him simply because they feel that He is their Father, and they are His devoted children. These are called יִשְׂרָאֵל, *Israel,* God's chosen, beloved nation. The next verse, *the House of Aaron,* refers to those who serve God out of love. They do not approach Him sporadically, when seized by a fleeting impulse; rather, they constantly concentrate their hearts on His service and cling to Him in all situations. Thus they resemble the *House of Aaron,* i.e., the *Kohanim* who never betrayed God and were therefore designated to stand in His presence, in the Temple, for all time. *Those who fear HASHEM* are yet a third group: those who fear Him and serve Him out of awe and reverence.

The Psalmist assures all three groups of devotees that they can *trust* wholeheartedly, that God will be their unfailing *shield* (*Radak*).

When they undertake an action, they put their trust in God and *He is their help*. When they need protection from any negative, harmful force, *He is their shield* (*R' Vidal HaTzarfati*). As long as the exile

continues, God will be our *shield* protecting us from our enemies. Hopefully, He soon will act as our *help* and redeem us.

ה׳ זְכָרָנוּ יְבָרֵךְ — *HASHEM Who has remembered us will bless.* Hashem *has remembered* the complex makeup of the Jewish nation and recognizes the diverse levels of faith (see previous section). He will bless each individual in accordance with his special characteristics. Furthermore, having created them all He intimately knows the needs of each individual and will provide accordingly.

יְבָרֵךְ יִרְאֵי ה׳ הַקְּטַנִּים עִם הַגְּדֹלִים — *He will bless those who fear HASHEM, the small as well as the great.* When the Psalmist exhorted all elements of the Jewish nation to *trust in HASHEM* (verses 9-11), he made no special reference to young children, because minors lack the experience and maturity necessary for complete trust in Hashem. However, now that the Psalmist calls upon God to bless *those who fear HASHEM,* the children are included because they observe the piety of their elders and learn from their example (*R' A.C. Feuer*).[1]

1. **Self-made Greatness.** The Psalmist speaks of the *House of Israel* and the *House of Aaron,* yet those who fear Hashem are not referred to as "a house." *R' Yechezkel Abramsky* explained: One is a Jew if he comes from a Jewish home and parents. Likewise, being a *Kohen* is an inherited status. Not so fear of God. Just because one's parents are God fearing, this does not necessarily guarantee that he will be so. *One who fears HASHEM* is a title that one must work hard in order to attain. The Midrash (*Bamidbar Rabbah* 8) teaches that for this reason *God loves the righteous* (*Psalm* 146), for they are self-made.

He is their help and shield! House of Aaron! Trust in HASHEM! He is their help and shield. Those who fear HASHEM! Trust in HASHEM, He is their help and shield!

HASHEM Who has remembered us will bless — He will bless the House of Israel; He will bless the House of Aaron; He will bless those who fear HASHEM, the small as well as the great. May HASHEM add upon you, upon you and upon your children! You are blessed of HASHEM, Maker of heaven and earth. As for the heaven — the heaven is HASHEM's, but the earth He has given to mankind. The dead cannot praise God, nor any who descend into silence; but we will bless God henceforth and forever. Halleluyah![1]

_____

(1) *Psalms* 115.

Alternatively, God's blessing will come to us only when we are united — *the small together with the great* (*Pri Chaim*).

יֹסֵף ה' עֲלֵיכֶם וְעַל בְּנֵיכֶם — *May HASHEM add upon you, upon you and upon your children.* Abarbanel explains that the Psalmist foresaw prophetically that in exile, Israel would suffer from attrition and become afraid that they may never be redeemed because they will seem to be close to extinction. The Psalmist encourages Israel with the assurance that at the advent of the Messiah, their numbers will increase dramatically. In fact the Talmud teaches that the Messiah will come only when all the souls in the Heavenly storehouse will have been placed in bodies and come to this world (see *Yevamos* 62a).

הַשָּׁמַיִם שָׁמַיִם לַה' וְהָאָרֶץ נָתַן לִבְנֵי אָדָם — *As for the heaven — the heaven is HASHEM's* [lit., *to HASHEM*], *but the earth He has given to mankind.* Although God made both heaven and earth, He kept only heaven under His exclusive control, for He gave man control over the earth, as Psalm 8:7 states: *You gave him dominion over the works of Your hand, You placed everything under his feet*, i.e., God allowed man a degree of physical control over nature, and allowed His guidance of the universe to be conditioned by man's allegiance to the Torah.

Chidushei HaRim explained this verse homiletically. Heaven is already HASHEM's, i.e., dedicated to the holiness of God and His service; man need not perfect heaven. But the earth is man's province. We are bidden to perfect it and transform its material nature into something spiritual. Indeed, we are charged to make the earth heavenly.

לֹא הַמֵּתִים יְהַלְלוּ יָהּ — *The dead cannot praise God.* The people who fail to recognize God's omnipresence and influence over the world resemble *the dead*, who are insensitive to all external stimuli and who are oblivious to the reality of the Living God (*Binah Leltim*). We, however, who are inextricably linked to the Source of all life will praise Hashem henceforth and forever.[1]

1. **Back to Square One.** *Beis Avraham* comments that a person's prayers are often disturbed by the memories of his many sins, causing him to wonder how he can dare pray to God. The Evil Inclination seeks to depress man's spirits, because depressed people cannot raise themselves to higher spiritual levels. Someone who is beset by thoughts of his deficiencies should therefore resolve to begin anew and to forget his earlier failures. This is the Psalmist's call, *We will bless HASHEM henceforth and forever*; even though we have failed previously, we are determined to make a fresh start.

אָהַבְתִּי כִּי יִשְׁמַע יהוה, אֶת קוֹלִי תַּחֲנוּנָי. כִּי הִטָּה אָזְנוֹ לִי, וּבְיָמַי אֶקְרָא. אֲפָפְוּנִי חֶבְלֵי מָוֶת, וּמְצָרֵי שְׁאוֹל מְצָאְוּנִי, צָרָה וְיָגוֹן אֶמְצָא. וּבְשֵׁם יהוה אֶקְרָא, אָנָּה יהוה מַלְּטָה נַפְשִׁי. חַנּוּן יהוה וְצַדִּיק, וֵאלֹהֵינוּ מְרַחֵם. שֹׁמֵר פְּתָאִים יהוה, דַּלּוֹתִי וְלִי יְהוֹשִׁיעַ. שׁוּבִי נַפְשִׁי לִמְנוּחָיְכִי, כִּי יהוה גָּמַל עָלָיְכִי. כִּי חִלַּצְתָּ נַפְשִׁי מִמָּוֶת, אֶת עֵינִי מִן דִּמְעָה, אֶת רַגְלִי מִדֶּחִי. אֶתְהַלֵּךְ לִפְנֵי יהוה, בְּאַרְצוֹת הַחַיִּים. הֶאֱמַנְתִּי כִּי אֲדַבֵּר, אֲנִי עָנִיתִי מְאֹד. אֲנִי אָמַרְתִּי בְחָפְזִי, כָּל הָאָדָם כֹּזֵב.

אָהַבְתִּי כִּי יִשְׁמַע ה׳ אֶת קוֹלִי תַּחֲנוּנָי – *I love [Him] for HASHEM hears my voice, my supplications.* According to *Abarbanel*, the Psalmist addresses Israel's loneliness in the exile. The nations taunt them, "Your prayers and pleading are worthless, because God has turned a deaf ear to you." Therefore, this psalm was composed to encourage the downcast exiles with the assurance that indeed Hashem "hears my voice, my supplications."[1]

By drawing upon our experience in Egypt and the overwhelming care and love that God showed us then, we strengthen our resolve to keep pleading for the ultimate redemption: "I love my prayers and will not abandon them because I firmly believe that God *hears my voice and* will hearken to my prayers.[2] Having experienced *how He inclined His ear to me* when I cried out from the torment of the Egyptians, I am sure He will redeem us again.

1. **Listening With Love.** God hearkens to one's prayers in proportion to the love the person has in his heart for other Jews. For this reason the *Arizal* suggested that before beginning to pray, one should verbalize a resolution to fulfill the *mitzvah* of *Love your neighbor as yourself* (*Leviticus* 19:18).

This practice is alluded to in our verse: אָהַבְתִּי כִּי יִשְׁמַע ה׳ אֶת, *I [accept upon myself total] love [of all Jews]*, קוֹלִי תַּחֲנוּנָי, *and then God listens to my voice, to my supplication* (*Bircas HaShir*).

2. **Forced to Come Closer.** The Talmud (*Pesachim* 118b) expounds on this verse: "When are we considered beloved in Your eyes, Hashem? When You hearken to my voice." When God fails to provide us easily with our needs, forcing us to pray, it is a sign of His love for us. He wants to hear our voice raised in prayer, so He gives us cause to pray.

The order given in the verse seems to be reversed; first one inclines his ear and only then does he hear the voice. Why is the order reversed here? *Rabbi Yitzchok Hutner* explains: God inclines His ear to our plea not merely to hear our plea; rather He inclines His ear to indicate our closeness to Him. The fulfillment of one's request is a natural outgrowth of that closeness. Crises come upon us in order to force us to turn to him in recognition that the power to help is His alone. Once we have done so, the goal has been achieved and there is no further need for the threat of calamity.

Thus, the psalm teaches that God has heeded and responded to our prayer — because we have been able to establish a new closeness to Him; He has responded to our overtures for a closer relationship.

Imrei Emes views the order as teaching the efficacy of prayer. Not only when we are close to God and living according to His will does He hear our prayers; even if He must incline His ear, as it were, indicating that the prayer is coming from someone spiritually far away, He is also ready to do so.

I love [Him] for HASHEM hears my voice, my supplications. For He has inclined His ear to me, in my days I will call upon Him. The ropes of death encircled me; the confines of the grave have found me; trouble and sorrow I have found. Then I called upon the Name of HASHEM: "Please, HASHEM, save my soul." Gracious is HASHEM, and righteous, our God is merciful. HASHEM protects the simple; I was brought low but He saved me. Return my soul, to your rest, for HASHEM has been kind to you. You delivered my soul from death, my eyes from tears and my feet from stumbling. I shall walk before HASHEM in the lands of the living. I have kept faith although I say: "I suffer exceedingly." I said in my haste: "All mankind is deceitful."

Thus, even in bad times, *in my days I will call upon Him.* [1]

Though the *ropes of death* and the destruction of so many communities in sanctification of God's Name *have encircled me* in this exile, though *I find trouble and sorrow, I* will still *call upon the Name of HASHEM* and beseech Him — *save my soul!*

Since the ultimate redemption is contingent on the repentance of the Jewish people, we call for a collective return. Therefore we urge, *"Return, my soul, to your rest." For Hashem has been kind to you* in the past; *You,* Hashem, *have delivered my soul from* [spiritual] *death* in the terrible impurity of Egypt. Just as we were saved from that formidable tragedy, so we are sure that You will redeem us and bring us to a renewed Land of Israel, the land whose climate is so conducive to authentic spiritual life.

הֶאֱמַנְתִּי כִּי אֲדַבֵּר אֲנִי עָנִיתִי מְאֹד — *I have kept faith although I say: "I suffer exceedingly."* [2] Just as we sit at the Seder and recall the travails of our ancestors in Egypt and how God saved them, so *I have kept faith* that some day *I will say* about the current exile, with the same air of gratitude and contentment, *I suffer[ed] exceedingly.* but Hashem saved me from those afflictions as well. At that time I will reflect upon my despair in the exile, and think about how *I said in my haste, "All mankind —*

1. **In Good and in Bad.** A Jew calls to God in all seasons. In good times and in bad he always realizes that God is with him. In times of trouble he entreats God for His help; when He finally redeems us we call to Him in praise (*Rashi*).

R' Yaakov Yosef of Skvere would often complain, "Do you know why I suffer from heart disease? When people undergo troubles and difficulties they come to me to unburden their hearts and share their woes. I take it all to heart. But when God helps them and their situation improves, few people bother to call me and let me know the good news. While they rejoice in the salvation of God I am still walking around with the pain in my heart. Is it any wonder that I suffer from heart disease?"

Jews do not only call to God to pour out their troubles and woes; Jews also return to Him to "report" and praise Him for their new-found good fortune. Thus we call to God *all the days* of our lives (*Maharal Diskin*).

2. **Veracity Verbalized.** Faith becomes stronger and more profound the more one speaks about it. Verbalization of self-evident truths inculcates them deeper into the mind and heart, causing one to internalize them until they become a natural reaction. This is homiletically alluded to here: I believe because I constantly spoke about these truths (*R' Moshe of Kobrin*).

מָה אָשִׁיב לַיהוה, כָּל תַּגְמוּלְוֹהִי עָלָי. כּוֹס יְשׁוּעוֹת אֶשָּׂא, וּבְשֵׁם יהוה אֶקְרָא. נְדָרַי לַיהוה אֲשַׁלֵּם, נֶגְדָה נָּא לְכָל עַמּוֹ. יָקָר בְּעֵינֵי יהוה, הַמָּוְתָה לַחֲסִידָיו. אָנָּה יהוה כִּי אֲנִי עַבְדֶּךָ, אֲנִי עַבְדְּךָ, בֶּן אֲמָתֶךָ, פִּתַּחְתָּ לְמוֹסֵרָי. לְךָ אֶזְבַּח זֶבַח תּוֹדָה, וּבְשֵׁם יהוה אֶקְרָא. נְדָרַי לַיהוה אֲשַׁלֵּם, נֶגְדָה נָּא לְכָל עַמּוֹ. בְּחַצְרוֹת בֵּית יהוה, בְּתוֹכֵכִי יְרוּשָׁלָיִם הַלְלוּיָהּ.[1]

---

all the prophets from Moses and on, who prophesied redemption and consolation — *is deceitful*" (*Abarbanel*).[1]

מָה אָשִׁיב לַה' — *How can I repay* HASHEM. What gift can I give to the King Who owns everything? (*Ibn Ezra*). How can I possibly repay His acts of kindness, for they are too numerous to recount (*Radak*).[2]

Sforno views this as the declaration of the Jewish people when the Final Redemption finally arrives.

When God gathers in the scattered survivors of the long exile, they will remember that God delivered them from many extremely dangerous situations, and they will feel incapable of expressing their appreciation adequately.

כּוֹס יְשׁוּעוֹת אֶשָּׂא — *I will raise the cup of salvations.* Nonetheless, just as we do this evening when we celebrate God's salvation in saving us from spiritual oblivion in Egypt, so in the future we will raise the cup of salvations, celebrating the numerous

---

1. **Volunteer Firefighters.** Cynically, we often scoff at rebuke or at sound advice offered by teachers, parents, rabbis or mentors, with the rationalization that "to offer rebuke is his job." The foolishness of this attitude may be illustrated by an analogy:

In a small village all the homes were built of wood with straw roofs and floors. One night after his wife went upstairs to sleep, a man sat down to read by candlelight. Suddenly they heard a policeman scream out, "Be careful that nothing catches fire." The woman woke up and called down to her husband, "Chaim, be careful not to fall asleep while the candles are still burning. Listen to what the policeman says."

Replied the indignant husband, "Foolish wife! Do you think the policeman really means what he says? He gets paid to say it. If they would pay him to tell us all to burn down our houses he would announce that also. Do you really expect me to take the policeman seriously?"

Sure enough, he ignored all the warnings and succeeded in having the candle ignite the straw floor in his house. Quickly the fire spread and burned the town down.

Likewise, when a rabbi or a friend seeks to offer spiritual guidance, let us never brush it off with the irrelevant excuse, "He says so because it's his job." It might spell the difference between spiritual life and death (*Ohr LaYesharim*).

2. **Abusing Credit.** One who buys on credit can hope that the storekeeper will extend him further credit only if he makes at least minimal payments on his bill. If, however, he does nothing to bring his balance down, he is too embarrassed to ask for more goods on credit. Thus, we tell God: What shall I say to God? How can I ask Him to continue to provide for me when all His beneficence is still upon me; I have done nothing to even begin to repay Him (*Chafetz Chaim*).

What will I answer when God calls me to task for my failings? What will I be able to say when He points out that I have abused His kindness, using it all only for my own personal agenda, never stopping to think that He provides for me so that I may serve Him (*R' Moshe of Kobrin*).

How can I repay HASHEM for all His kindness to me? I will raise the cup of salvations, and the Name of HASHEM will I invoke . My vows to HASHEM will I pay in the presence His entire people. Precious in the eyes of HASHEM is the death for His devout ones. Please, HASHEM — for I am Your servant, I am Your servant, the son of Your handmaid — You have released my bonds. To You I sacrifice thanksgiving offerings, and the Name of HASHEM will I invoke. My vows to HASHEM will I pay in the presence now of His entire people; in the courtyards of the House of HASHEM, in your midst, O Jerusalem, Halleluyah.[1]

---

(1) *Psalms* 116.

---

times throughout the exile when God saved us. By pointing to the source of our salvation, we *will invoke the Name of HASHEM* and proclaim His omnipotence to all mankind (*Abarbanel*).

נְדָרַי לַה' אֲשַׁלֵּם נֶגְדָה נָּא לְכָל עַמּו — *My vows to HASHEM will I pay in the presence, now, of His entire people.* Sforno views this as a pledge by the Jewish people to rededicate themselves to the very first vow that they made at Sinai, נַעֲשֶׂה וְנִשְׁמַע, *We shall do and we shall listen* (*Exodus* 24:7).

This I will do in the presence of all Jews, especially the sinners who have neglected their own obligations and vows, either intentionally or unintentionally. My service will thus set an example for them.

אָנָה ה' כִּי אֲנִי עַבְדֶּךָ — *Please, HASHEM — for I am Your servant.* This translation follows *Targum*, who translates אָנָה as בְּבָעוּ, *please* (like אָנָּא with an *aleph*, as in אָנָּא ה' הוֹשִׁיעָה נָא below). *Sforno* interprets: Please, God, let me live to see the days of the Messiah. I realize that precious reward awaits the pious in the afterlife, yet since *I am Your servant,* I wish to live to see the time when all men will serve

You in this world.

Ibn Ezra renders אָנָה as *I thank You*, i.e., I give thanks to Hashem for allowing me the privilege of being His servant.[1]

אֲנִי עַבְדְּךָ בֶּן אֲמָתֶךָ — *I am Your servant, son of Your handmaid.* The slave born to a slave (i.e., *hand-maid*) is far more submissive than someone born free who became a slave (*Rashi*). The former serves his master naturally and instinctively, whereas the latter serves him only in response to external threats (*Sforno*).

פִּתַּחְתָּ לְמוֹסֵרָי — *You have released my bonds.* A free man impressed into slavery constantly seeks to escape; therefore he must be tightly bound and shackled. However, one born into slavery has an ingrained allegiance to his master and gladly remains under his domination. His bonds may be loosened, for he will not attempt to escape (*Al-shich*).

Thus, David declares: I have inherited a legacy of love for You, O God! My ancestress Ruth made immense sacrifices in order to join the Jewish people and accept the yoke of Torah. From her I

---

1. **Do It for Me.** When the *Imrei Emes* succeeded his father (the *Sfas Emes*) as Gerer Rebbe, a group of older *chassidim* asked him, "Your father promised us that if we would recite the verse 'אָנָה ה' (*Please, HASHEM*) in the *Hallel* service with great devotion and intent, all our wishes would be granted from Heaven. We tried. Why didn't it work?" The new *Rebbe* replied: "Which 'אָנָה ה' do you think my father meant: אָנָּא ה' הוֹשִׁיעָה נָא, *Please, HASHEM, save now*? No! He meant אָנָה ה' כִּי אֲנִי עַבְדֶּךָ, *Please, HASHEM, for I am Your servant* (*Psalms* 116:16). Just as a mortal master must provide all the needs of his servants, so God provides for His true servants. But first we must commit ourselves to His service."

הַלְלוּ אֶת יהוה, כָּל גּוֹיִם, שַׁבְּחוּהוּ כָּל הָאֻמִּים. כִּי גָבַר עָלֵינוּ חַסְדּוֹ, וֶאֱמֶת יהוה לְעוֹלָם, הַלְלוּיָהּ.[1]

הוֹדוּ לַיהוה כִּי טוֹב,   כִּי לְעוֹלָם חַסְדּוֹ.
יֹאמַר נָא יִשְׂרָאֵל,   כִּי לְעוֹלָם חַסְדּוֹ.
יֹאמְרוּ נָא בֵית אַהֲרֹן,   כִּי לְעוֹלָם חַסְדּוֹ.
יֹאמְרוּ נָא יִרְאֵי יהוה,   כִּי לְעוֹלָם חַסְדּוֹ.

---

inherited an instinctive devotion to do Your will, so I need no external bonds to harness me to Your service (*Bach*).[1]

הַלְלוּ אֶת ה׳ כָּל גּוֹיִם — *Praise HASHEM, all nations!* At the time of the Exodus, the Jews, unlike other nations, reinforced their faith in Hashem and praised Him. At the time of the future redemption, however, *all nations* will *praise Hashem* because they will recognize that *His love for us is strong,* and they will acknowledge that *the truth of Hashem is eternal* (*Abarbanel*).

כִּי גָבַר עָלֵינוּ חַסְדּוֹ — *For His kindness to us was*

overwhelming. A Russian prince asked *R' Yitzchak* (*Reb Itzeleh*) of Volozhin why *gentile nations* should praise Hashem for overwhelming *Israel* with Divine kindness? *R' Yitzchak* replied without hesitation, "You princes plan countless anti-Semitic schemes with which to destroy us, but our Merciful God always manages to foil your plots. Your secret councils are so well guarded that we Jews never know all the ways in which you intended to harm us, nor how God saved us. Only you gentiles see clearly how *His kindness to us was overwhelming;* therefore it is only you who can praise Him adequately!"[2]

---

1. **The Freest of Men.** The servant of God considers himself the freest of all. The fact that *I am Your servant, son of Your handmaid* is itself the way in which *You have released my bonds.* By living a Torah life, one can slip away from the grip of emotionally crippling desire. In the words of the great poet of Israel, *R' Yehudah HaLevi:* "Those indentured to the temporal are slaves of [other] slaves; only the servant of God is truly free!" (*Kozhnitzer Maggid*).

2. **It's Mere Child's Play.** In the times of the *Vilna Gaon,* Valentin Potocki, a young noble and heir to the Count Potocki fortune, converted to Judaism and assumed the name of Abraham ben Abraham. The Catholic Church was infuriated by his conversion and condemned him to be burned at the stake. As he was led to his death, his executioner realized that he was about to kill a holy man and begged Abraham ben Abraham not to seek revenge against him in the afterlife.

The convert calmed the executioner, saying, "When I was a little boy I wandered from the palace and got lost in the woods. A farmer took me into his home and treated me like his own son. Once I made some soldiers out of clay, but the farmer's son was jealous and smashed my precious soldiers. I was sad and angry. Eventually I was found and returned to my palace. A few days later the farmer and his son, trembling with fear, came to see me. The farmer begged me not to punish his son for breaking my soldiers.

"I calmed him, saying, 'When I was with you I had nothing but those mud soldiers, so their destruction grieved me. But in my palace I have more splendid toys and playthings than I can ever use. Now the loss of coarse mud figurines means nothing to me.' "

Passionately, the devout convert turned to his executioner, "While I am alive, my flesh and blood are precious to me and certainly I would be bitter towards anyone who hurt me. But now I am entering a new world, a spiritual place of eternal bliss and glory. In that world, my body will seem like crude clay and mud and its pain and destruction will be meaningless to me." (*R' A. C. Feuer;* see ArtScroll *Pirkei*

Praise HASHEM, all nations; praise Him, all you peoples! For His kindness to us was overwhelming, and the truth of HASHEM is eternal. Halleluyah![1]

Give thanks to HASHEM for He is good;

For His kindness endures forever!

Let Israel say: For His kindness endures forever!

Let the House of Aaron say: For His kindness endures forever!

Let those who fear HASHEM say now:

For His kindness endures forever!

---

(1) *Psalms* 117.

Although all of *Hallel* should be recited joyfully, it is particularly important to do so for the four verses that end with כִּי לְעוֹלָם חַסְדּוֹ, *for His kindness endures forever*. Ideally, these verses should be recited responsively, with the leader of the Seder reciting each of the verses aloud, and the other participants responding with the full verse . . . הוֹדוּ לַה' כִּי טוֹב, *Give thanks to HASHEM for He is good* . . . It is commendable to have at least three men at the Seder, so that two can respond to the leader's invitation to praise God. If there are not three men present, women and children can provide the response.

This psalm reflects the joy of the final redemption, when Israel will return to its former glory and revive its noble traditions and institutions. Every segment of Jewish society will be affected by God's concern, and all will enthusiastically proclaim: *His kindness endures forever!*

הוֹדוּ לַה' כִּי טוֹב — *Give thanks to HASHEM for He is good.* This is a general expression of thanks to God. No matter what occurs, God is always good and

everything He does is for the best, even though this may not be immediately apparent to man.

Seder HaAruch renders "for *it* is good," that is, it is good to give thanks to Hashem. There is nothing more helpful for man in his search for God than to verbalize his thanks for all that He does on man's behalf. It allows us to focus on God's "fingerprints" wherever we turn.

כִּי לְעוֹלָם חַסְדּוֹ — *For His kindness endures forever!* The phrase refers to clearly revealed acts of kindness. Though this visible *kindness* may often be followed by periods of הֶסְתֵּר פָּנִים, *concealment of the Divine Presence*, the Psalmist reassures Israel that God's *kindness endures forever* and that it will definitely manifest itself again after each period of concealment (*Abarbanel*).

יֹאמְרוּ נָא יִרְאֵי ה' כִּי לְעוֹלָם חַסְדּוֹ — *Let those who fear HASHEM say now: "For His kindness endures forever!"* With the advent of the Messianic Era, Israel will thank God for releasing them from the need to fear other men, thereby enabling them to concentrate on the fear of God (*Radak*).[1]

Avos Treasury for a slightly different version.)

Likewise, in the Messianic Age God will bestow such overwhelming kindness upon His people that all the torment they received in the past from the nations of the world will seem trivial. Thus, it is the other nations who will thank God for the kindness that He bestows on us, for in its wake Jews will lose their desire for revenge against their tormentors.

1. **An Issue of Perspective.** A savage from the deepest recesses of the Amazon jungle was once brought to watch an open-heart surgical team. Lying on the table was a person with all kinds of tubes and wires attached to him. Surrounding by whispering, masked people, the man on the table looked like an unwilling participant in a tribal rite. Suddenly a person dressed in a flowing green gown with a mask on his face and a kerchief on his head cried out, "Scalpel!" He took the knife in his hand and with one swipe made an incision in the patient's chest. "Oh!" shrieked the Amazonian visitor, "What unspeakable cruelty! This is

מִן הַמֵּצַר קָרָאתִי יָּה, עָנָנִי בַמֶּרְחָב יָה. יהוה לִי לֹא אִירָא, מַה יַּעֲשֶׂה לִי אָדָם. יהוה לִי בְּעֹזְרָי, וַאֲנִי אֶרְאֶה בְשׂנְאָי. טוֹב לַחֲסוֹת בַּיהוה, מִבְּטֹחַ בָּאָדָם. טוֹב לַחֲסוֹת בַּיהוה, מִבְּטֹחַ בִּנְדִיבִים. כָּל גּוֹיִם סְבָבוּנִי, בְּשֵׁם יהוה כִּי אֲמִילַם. סַבּוּנִי גַם סְבָבוּנִי, בְּשֵׁם יהוה כִּי אֲמִילַם. סַבּוּנִי כִדְבֹרִים דֹּעֲכוּ כְּאֵשׁ קוֹצִים, בְּשֵׁם יהוה כִּי אֲמִילַם. דָּחֹה דְחִיתַנִי לִנְפֹּל, וַיהוה עֲזָרָנִי. עָזִּי וְזִמְרָת יָה, וַיְהִי לִי לִישׁוּעָה. קוֹל רִנָּה וִישׁוּעָה, בְּאָהֳלֵי צַדִּיקִים, יְמִין יהוה עֹשָׂה חָיִל. יְמִין יהוה רוֹמֵמָה, יְמִין יהוה עֹשָׂה חָיִל.

מִן הַמֵּצַר קָרָאתִי יָּה עָנָנִי בַמֶּרְחָב יָה — *From the straits did I call to God; God answered me with expansiveness.* In place of the *straits* of our earthly existence (מֵצַר), God substitutes true *expansiveness* of freedom (מֶרְחָב). The soul of man, weighted down by mundane forces, yearns to soar and be free to achieve self-actualization. In the days of the Final Redemption, man will shout in joy at his newfound spiritual freedom.

This declaration is an eloquent expression of one of David's most cherished credos: Never be discouraged by the burdens of life, for every frustrating, enfeebling situation is actually a Divinely ordained opportunity to overcome adversity by fully utilizing one's talents and abilities. Thus, every distress which threatens to limit or diminish an individual can be a springboard for broadening one's scope and elevating his perspective.

ה׳ לִי בְּעֹזְרָי וַאֲנִי אֶרְאֶה בְשׂנְאָי — *HASHEM is for me*

through my helpers; therefore I can face my foes. Sometimes our enemies display their hatred openly; knowing their feelings, we can take precautions to protect ourselves. But how can one protect himself against someone who on the surface projects the image of being a good friend, but is in fact a sworn enemy? Thus, we ask God, "Be with me when it comes to those who pretend to be *my helpers,* so that I may have a clear picture and see who my enemies are" (*Midrash Shmuel*).[1]

טוֹב לַחֲסוֹת בַּה׳ מִבְּטֹחַ בָּאָדָם — *It is better to take refuge in HASHEM than to rely on man.* R' Bachya and the *Vilna Gaon* explain the difference between the two related words חִסָּיוֹן, *refuge,* and בִּטָּחוֹן, *reliance.* The former denotes absolute confidence, even when no guarantees have been given. Thus, one may seek *refuge* behind a boulder or under a sturdy roof, for although neither the boulder nor the roof has pledged shelter, one has confidence in their

---

even worse than what goes on in the jungle."

Had he known about bypass surgery, he would have realized that the scalpel-wielding man in green is an angel of mercy, not a heartless demon.

Here we declare that we know God is intrinsically and absolutely good; therefore we are sure that His kindness is eternal, although we don't always realize how this is so.

1. An Awesome Parable. In the Hoshana prayers we say כְּבוּשָׁה בַּגּוֹלָה לוֹמֶדֶת יִרְאָתֶךָ, *confined in exile, learning the fear of You.* The trepidation we endure from our captors while in exile is a lesson on how we should fear God (*Bnei Yisas'char*). Thus, when God will finally free us from their rule, we will be able to apply the lesson to its fullest and no longer waste our capacity to fear on anything else besides Him (*Simchas Aharon*).

From the straits did I call to God; God answered me with expansiveness. HASHEM is with me, I have no fear; how can man affect me? HASHEM is for me through my helpers; therefore I can face my foes. It is better to take refuge in HASHEM than to rely on man. It is better to take refuge in HASHEM than to rely on princes. All nations surround me; in the Name of HASHEM I cut them down. They encirlce me, they also surround me; in the Name of HASHEM I cut them down. They encircle me like bees, but they are extinguished as a fire does thorns; in the Name of HASHEM I cut them down! You pushed me hard that I might fall, but HASHEM assisted me. My strength and song is God; He became my salvation. The sound of rejoicing and salvation is in the tents of the righteous. "The right hand of HASHEM does valiantly! The right hand of HASHEM is raised triumphantly! The right hand of HASHEM does valiantly!"

indestructibility. The word *reliance*, however, implies a promise of protection, such as a הַבְטָחָה, *pledge,* of protection from a military power. The Psalmist says that it is far better to put one's trust in God's protection, even without a pledge from Him, than to rely on the most profound assurances of human beings.[1]

סַבּוּנִי כִדְבֹרִים — *They encircle me like bees. Maharam Aramah* observes that there is a species of bee that stings only once in its lifetime, and for that one sting it pays with its life, because it leaves its stinger inside its victim and remains mortally wounded. Similarly, David's enemies were so consumed with hatred that they fought him even though they knew that they would surely forfeit their lives in the conflict.[2]

דָּחֹה דְּחִיתַנִי לִנְפֹּל וַה' עֲזָרָנִי — *You pushed me hard that I might fall, but HASHEM assisted me.* The *Zohar* (*Parashas Vayishlach*) identifies the foe being addressed as man's greatest adversary, the Evil Inclination, which always tempts him. This enemy must be dealt with directly and decisively.

The Talmud teaches that man's Evil Inclination renews its efforts every day, seeking to spiritually assassinate him. Only due to Heavenly assistance can we overcome it (see *Succah* 52b).

1. **Enduring Arsenal.** At the end of the days, when we look back on our history and how we survived the exile, it will become clear that we were able to prevail against our enemies only when we stood against them in the Name of God. Efforts to save ourselves by political or military means, or by diplomatic reliance on other nations have always proven to be futile, if not disastrous (*R' S. R. Hirsch*).

◆§ **Disappointment and Dependence.** The verse does not come to present a study in contrasts between trust in God and in mortals. How can one even compare the protection of the all-powerful Master of the World with that of puny and fleeting human beings? Rather, King David teaches that man can truly appreciate God and sense the security of relying on Him only after having tasted the bitter disappointment of trust in man. Only on top of the ruins of the hollow human promise does man really realize that only in God can we trust. The verse may thus be rendered, "That it is good to take refuge in Hashem, [we learn] from trusting in man"(*R' Shmuel Walkin*).

2. **Obsessive Hatred.** This pattern repeats itself throughout history. Blinded by the fury of their hatred for the Jews, our enemies pursue courses of self-destruction in their rabid obsession with eradicating us. Hitler ימ"ש, crazed by his delusions of a historical calling to make Europe *Judenrein,* diverted trains desperately needed to bring supplies to the Russian front in order to transport Hungarian Jews to Auschwitz.

לֹא אָמוּת כִּי אֶחְיֶה, וַאֲסַפֵּר מַעֲשֵׂי יָהּ. יַסֹּר יִסְּרַנִּי יָּהּ, וְלַמָּוֶת לֹא נְתָנָנִי. פִּתְחוּ לִי שַׁעֲרֵי צֶדֶק, אָבֹא בָם אוֹדֶה יָהּ. זֶה הַשַּׁעַר לַיהוה, צַדִּיקִים יָבֹאוּ בוֹ. אוֹדְךָ כִּי עֲנִיתָנִי, וַתְּהִי לִי לִישׁוּעָה. אוֹדְךָ כִּי עֲנִיתָנִי, וַתְּהִי לִי לִישׁוּעָה. אֶבֶן מָאֲסוּ הַבּוֹנִים, הָיְתָה לְרֹאשׁ פִּנָּה. אֶבֶן מָאֲסוּ הַבּוֹנִים, הָיְתָה לְרֹאשׁ פִּנָּה. מֵאֵת יהוה הָיְתָה זֹּאת, הִיא נִפְלָאת בְּעֵינֵינוּ. מֵאֵת יהוה הָיְתָה זֹּאת, הִיא נִפְלָאת בְּעֵינֵינוּ. זֶה הַיּוֹם עָשָׂה יהוה, נָגִילָה וְנִשְׂמְחָה בוֹ. זֶה הַיּוֹם עָשָׂה יהוה, נָגִילָה וְנִשְׂמְחָה בוֹ.

אָנָּא יהוה הוֹשִׁיעָה נָּא. אָנָּא יהוה הוֹשִׁיעָה נָּא. אָנָּא יהוה הַצְלִיחָה נָּא. אָנָּא יהוה הַצְלִיחָה נָּא.

בָּרוּךְ הַבָּא בְּשֵׁם יהוה, בֵּרַכְנוּכֶם מִבֵּית יהוה. בָּרוּךְ הַבָּא בְּשֵׁם יהוה, בֵּרַכְנוּכֶם מִבֵּית יהוה. אֵל יהוה וַיָּאֶר לָנוּ,

---

According to *Ibn Yachya*, the double expression refers to the future war of Gog and Magog and the two-stage unfolding of the Messianic drama. At first the enemy will be successful, and מָשִׁיחַ בֶּן יוֹסֵף *the Messiah, the son of Joseph,* will be slain. The enemy will strike again and again, chasing the defeated Jews to the mountains and the wilderness. Ultimately, however, Hashem will help Israel, with the advent of the eternal Messiah, the son of David.

לֹא אָמוּת כִּי אֶחְיֶה וַאֲסַפֵּר מַעֲשֵׂי יָהּ — *I shall not die! But I shall live and relate the deeds of God.* My refusal to die is not merely in order to live; I seek life in order to praise God (*Maharal*).

R' Moshe of Kobrin offered a homiletical rendering: *I will not die while I am alive.* I will never allow myself, as long as I am physically alive, to become spiritually dead. How will I assure this? By relating the deeds of God.

פִּתְחוּ לִי שַׁעֲרֵי צֶדֶק אָבֹא בָם אוֹדֶה יָהּ — *Open for me the gates of righteousness, I will enter them and thank God.* The *Zohar* (*Parashas Emor*) explains that the righteous man's plea echoes the Heavenly call to those who love God: "Open your hearts to Me, even with an opening as tiny as a pinpoint, and I will make you an opening as wide as that of a hall!"[1]

זֶה הַיּוֹם עָשָׂה ה׳ נָגִילָה וְנִשְׂמְחָה בוֹ — *This is the day HASHEM has made; we will rejoice and be glad on it!* In the future it will be obvious that the events

---

1. **The Humble Combination.** The constant plea to enter the gates of righteousness is itself the key to unlocking them. *Kedushas Levi* explains that this plea reflects the yearning of a righteous person to ascend to new heights of sanctity and devotion. When he reaches a plateau of piety, he is not satisfied; he seeks to climb even closer to God. It is precisely this intense yearning that infuses him with the strength to overcome all obstacles in his path. Thus, although certain doors may be closed even to the righteous, his yearning itself is the key to opening them.

I shall not die! But I shall live and relate the deeds of God. God chastised me exceedingly but He did not let me die. Open for me the gates of righteousness, I will enter them and thank God. This is the gate of HASHEM; the righteous shall enter through it. I thank You for You answered me and become my salvation! I thank You for You answered me and become my salvation! The stone which the builders despised has become the cornerstone. The stone which the builders despised has become the cornerstone. This emanated from HASHEM; it is wondrous in our eyes. This emanated from HASHEM; it is wondrous in our eyes. This is the day HASHEM has made; let us rejoice and be glad on it. This is the day HASHEM has made; let us rejoice and be glad on it.

Please, HASHEM, save now!
Please, HASHEM, save now!
Please, HASHEM, bring success now!
Please, HASHEM, bring success now!

Blessed is he who comes in the Name of HASHEM; we bless you from the House of HASHEM. Blessed is he who comes in the Name of HASHEM; we bless you from the House of HASHEM. HASHEM is God and He illuminated for us.

---

transpiring for the benefit of Israel are supernatural. Then everyone will admit: *This is the day HASHEM has made* (*Radak*).

אָנָּא ה׳ הוֹשִׁיעָה נָּא — *Please, HASHEM, save now!* Having praised God and described the salvation He has offered, we now pray for the future. This declaration is not only a plea for the future, but also serves as a declaration of our faith in God's ability to solve all our problems (see *R' Yonah to Berachos 4b*).

בָּרוּךְ הַבָּא בְּשֵׁם ה׳ — *Blessed is he who comes, in the Name of Hashem.* In the course of the exile, many

Jews became estranged from their own tradition and no longer felt at home within their own heritage. In the future, however, righteous and congenial teachers will welcome back all those who strayed from the fold and will bless them *in the Name of HASHEM* (see *Sforno*).

אֵל ה׳ וַיָּאֶר לָנוּ — *HASHEM is God and He illuminated for us.* Exile is equated with darkness, while the advent of the Messiah, which will usher in an era of spiritual illumination, is compared to light. Thus we pray daily: אוֹר חָדָשׁ עַל צִיּוֹן תָּאִיר וְנִזְכֶּה כֻלָּנוּ מְהֵרָה לְאוֹרוֹ, *May You shine a new light upon Zion and may we all speedily merit to see its light.*

R' Baruch of Mezhibuzh views humility as the key to open all doors. Man entreats God to open the gates so that, despite his unworthiness, he may enter the Heavenly realms and so that God may enter man's life. God answers, *This is the gate to HASHEM.* Your humility and the feeling that you are unworthy are themselves the greatest entrance pass. It is only because you feel that you are still on the outside, far away from any significant spiritual plateau, that you are really fit to enter the gates.

אִסְרוּ חַג בַּעֲבֹתִים, עַד קַרְנוֹת הַמִּזְבֵּחַ. אֵל יהוה וַיָּאֶר לָנוּ, אִסְרוּ חַג בַּעֲבֹתִים, עַד קַרְנוֹת הַמִּזְבֵּחַ. אֵלִי אַתָּה וְאוֹדֶךָּ, אֱלֹהַי אֲרוֹמְמֶךָּ. אֵלִי אַתָּה וְאוֹדֶךָּ, אֱלֹהַי אֲרוֹמְמֶךָּ. הוֹדוּ לַיהוה כִּי טוֹב, כִּי לְעוֹלָם חַסְדּוֹ. הוֹדוּ לַיהוה כִּי טוֹב, כִּי לְעוֹלָם חַסְדּוֹ.[1]

יְהַלְלוּךָ יהוה אֱלֹהֵינוּ כָּל מַעֲשֶׂיךָ, וַחֲסִידֶיךָ צַדִּיקִים עוֹשֵׂי רְצוֹנֶךָ, וְכָל עַמְּךָ בֵּית יִשְׂרָאֵל בְּרִנָּה יוֹדוּ וִיבָרְכוּ וִישַׁבְּחוּ וִיפָאֲרוּ וִירוֹמְמוּ וְיַעֲרִיצוּ וְיַקְדִּישׁוּ וְיַמְלִיכוּ אֶת שִׁמְךָ מַלְכֵּנוּ, כִּי לְךָ טוֹב לְהוֹדוֹת וּלְשִׁמְךָ נָאֶה לְזַמֵּר, כִּי מֵעוֹלָם וְעַד עוֹלָם אַתָּה אֵל.

הוֹדוּ לַיהוה כִּי טוֹב   כִּי לְעוֹלָם חַסְדּוֹ.
הוֹדוּ לֵאלֹהֵי הָאֱלֹהִים   כִּי לְעוֹלָם חַסְדּוֹ.

יְהַלְלוּךָ ה׳ אֱלֹהֵינוּ כָּל מַעֲשֶׂיךָ — *All Your works, HASHEM, our God, will praise You.* This is not part of *Psalms*, but a concluding blessing that sums up the broad theme of *Hallel* — that Israel and the entire universe will join in praising God. *All Your works will praise You* means that in the perfect world of the future, the entire universe, including the vast variety of human beings, will function harmoniously according to God's will. This is the highest form of praise, for it expresses the goal of Creation.

The correct position of this paragraph at the Seder is a matter of dispute. According to the Ashkenazic custom it is recited at this point, while the Sefardic custom is to say it later, after *Yishtabach*. The *Vilna Gaon* (*Maaseh Rav* 191) held that it should be omitted altogether.

הוֹדוּ לַה׳ — *Give thanks to* HASHEM. This psalm, designated by the Talmud (*Pesachim* 118a) as הַלֵּל הַגָּדוֹל, *The Great Hallel*, delineates the prime elements of the creation of the universe and records

the major events of the Exodus and the subsequent conquest of Canaan. The psalm is appended to the *Hallel* at the Passover Seder because it describes many of the miracles that God performed as He redeemed Israel from Egypt.

The list of kindnesses for which we thank God in this psalm concludes with the declaration: *He gives food to all living creatures, for His kindness endures forever.* Thus the Psalmist equates such awesome miracles as the Splitting of the Sea with the apparently routine task of providing daily sustenance. This teaches that "the provision of daily sustenance is as significant as the Splitting of the Sea." History unfolds every day as God choreographs the countless details that provide every creature with its daily needs. God's kindness is eternal and enduring. Thus we are sure that in due course He will bring about the Final Redemption, as well.

כִּי לְעוֹלָם חַסְדּוֹ — *For His Kindness endures forever.* The refrain in each verse stresses the idea of God's

Bind the festival sacrifice with cords, leading it up to the corners of the altar. HASHEM is God and He illuminated for us. Bind the festival sacrifice with cords, leading it up to the corners of the altar. You are my God and I will thank You. My God — I will exalt You. You are my God and I will thank You. My God — I will exalt You. Give thanks to HASHEM for He is good, for His kindness endures forever. Give thanks to HASHEM for He is good, for His kindness endures forever.[1]

All Your works, HASHEM, our God, will praise You, and Your pious ones, the righteous who perform Your will. And all Your people, the House of Israel, with song, will thank, bless, laud, glorify, exalt, adulate, sanctify, and acknowledge the majesty of Your Name, our King, for to You it is good to give thanks, and to Your Name it is proper to sing, because You are God for eternity.

Give thanks to HASHEM for He is good
      — for His kindness endures forever.
Give thanks to the God of gods
      — for His kindness endures forever.

---

(1) *Psalms* 118.

Providence and lovingkindness. The number of verses in this Psalm is significant in this regard as well:. There are twenty-six verses, corresponding to the numerical *gematria* value of the Four-letter Divine Name יְ-הֹ-וָ-ה (HASHEM), which designates God as Creator and Master of world affairs and history, indicating especially His מִדַּת הָרַחֲמִים, quality of mercy.[1]

---

1. **Earning our Keep.** The Talmud (*Pesachim* 118a) notes that the refrain *for His kindness endures forever* is repeated twenty-six times in this psalm. This corresponds, it explains, to the twenty-six generations of mankind that lived in the time period between Creation and the Giving of the Torah at Sinai. The Talmud certainly does not mean to imply that the giving of the Torah signaled a diminishment of God's kindness. Rather, it means to teach that God created the world so that mortals might be provided with the opportunity to earn Divine recompense by studying the Torah and obeying its dictates. God showers His blessings of sustenance upon people so that they may have the wherewithal to accomplish this task.

Mankind was not ready to receive the Torah until twenty-six generations had passed. In the strictest sense, these generations had no way to earn their sustenance and upkeep, yet God, in His great kindness, provided even for these generations and sustained them. God's kindness continued forever and was deepened with the giving of the Torah, because the ultimate kindness bestowed upon man was the gift of the Torah which provides the soul with the opportunity to earn its Divine reward. The pre-Torah kindness resembles alms given to a pauper. The post-Torah kindness is comparable to providing the pauper with a job so that he may earn a living on his own (*R' Yitzchak Hutner*).

כִּי לְעוֹלָם חַסְדּוֹ.	הוֹדוּ לַאדֹנֵי הָאֲדֹנִים
כִּי לְעוֹלָם חַסְדּוֹ.	לְעֹשֵׂה נִפְלָאוֹת גְּדֹלוֹת לְבַדּוֹ
כִּי לְעוֹלָם חַסְדּוֹ.	לְעֹשֵׂה הַשָּׁמַיִם בִּתְבוּנָה
כִּי לְעוֹלָם חַסְדּוֹ.	לְרֹקַע הָאָרֶץ עַל הַמָּיִם
כִּי לְעוֹלָם חַסְדּוֹ.	לְעֹשֵׂה אוֹרִים גְּדֹלִים
כִּי לְעוֹלָם חַסְדּוֹ.	אֶת הַשֶּׁמֶשׁ לְמֶמְשֶׁלֶת בַּיּוֹם
כִּי לְעוֹלָם חַסְדּוֹ.	אֶת הַיָּרֵחַ וְכוֹכָבִים לְמֶמְשְׁלוֹת בַּלָּיְלָה
כִּי לְעוֹלָם חַסְדּוֹ.	לְמַכֵּה מִצְרַיִם בִּבְכוֹרֵיהֶם
כִּי לְעוֹלָם חַסְדּוֹ.	וַיּוֹצֵא יִשְׂרָאֵל מִתּוֹכָם
כִּי לְעוֹלָם חַסְדּוֹ.	בְּיָד חֲזָקָה וּבִזְרוֹעַ נְטוּיָה
כִּי לְעוֹלָם חַסְדּוֹ.	לְגֹזֵר יַם סוּף לִגְזָרִים
כִּי לְעוֹלָם חַסְדּוֹ.	וְהֶעֱבִיר יִשְׂרָאֵל בְּתוֹכוֹ
כִּי לְעוֹלָם חַסְדּוֹ.	וְנִעֵר פַּרְעֹה וְחֵילוֹ בְיַם סוּף
כִּי לְעוֹלָם חַסְדּוֹ.	לְמוֹלִיךְ עַמּוֹ בַּמִּדְבָּר
כִּי לְעוֹלָם חַסְדּוֹ.	לְמַכֵּה מְלָכִים גְּדֹלִים

לְעֹשֵׂה הַשָּׁמַיִם בִּתְבוּנָה – *To Him who made the heavens with understanding.* According to *Reb Simchah Bunim of P'shis'cha,* God *made the heavens* [in order] to bestow *understanding* upon the man who studies them, as the prophet says, *Lift up your eyes on high and behold Who created these [things]! He brings forth their legions by number, He calls to each of them by name* (Isaiah 40:26).

לְמַכֵּה מִצְרַיִם בִּבְכוֹרֵיהֶם – *To Him Who smote the Egyptians through their firstborn.* The terminology of the Psalmist is very precise. He does not say that "God struck the firstborn of Egypt"; rather, *He smote the Egyptians through their firstborn.* This is explained in the Midrash cited by *Rashi:* Upon hearing that they would be the victims of the last plague, the firstborn insisted that Israel be released immediately. When the other Egyptians refused to accede to their pleas, the desperate firstborn attacked their fellow Egyptians and precipitated a civil war. Thus, the tenth plague was a double blow to Egypt — not only did God kill the firstborn of Egypt Himself, but also many other Egyptians were killed by the angry firstborn.

Even in smiting the firstborn, God was showing kindness to the world, for He taught mankind that He punishes מִדָּה כְּנֶגֶד מִדָּה, *measure for measure.* Since the Egyptians had oppressed Israel, *God's firstborn son* (Exodus 4:22), their own firstborn were killed. Furthermore, God killed the firstborn of Egypt Himself, instead of dispatching an angel or agent. This demonstrated the extent of God's involvement in the affairs of the world for the sake of His beloved nation, Israel (*Alshich*).

וַיּוֹצֵא יִשְׂרָאֵל מִתּוֹכָם – *And brought Israel forth from their midst.* Not a single Jew was left behind because of infirmity, for, as the Psalmist (105:37) puts it: *He took them out with silver and gold, and among His tribes was none who stumbled* (*Sforno*).

Give thanks to the Master of masters

    — for His kindness endures forever.

To Him Who does great wonders alone

    — for His kindness endures forever.

To Him Who made the heavens with understanding

    — for His kindness endures forever.

To Him Who stretches the earth over the water

    — for His kindness endures forever.

To Him Who makes the great lights

    — for His kindness endures forever.

The sun for the reign of day

    — for His kindness endures forever.

The moon and the stars for the reign of night

    — for His kindness endures forever.

To Him Who smote the Egyptians through their firstborn

    — for His kindness endures forever.

And brought Israel forth from their midst

    — for His kindness endures forever.

With a strong hand and an outstretched arm

    — for His kindness endures forever.

To Him Who divided the Reed Sea into parts

    — for His kindness endures forever.

And had Israel pass through it

    — for His kindness endures forever.

And threw Pharaoh and his army into the Sea of Reeds

    — for His kindness endures forever.

To Him Who led His people through the desert

    — for His kindness endures forever.

To Him Who smote great kings

    — for His kindness endures forever.

וַיְנַעֵר פַּרְעֹה וְחֵילוֹ בְיַם סוּף – *And threw Pharaoh and his army into the Sea of Reeds.* God forcefully threw the Egyptians into the sea and made an open spectacle of their drowning, so that the Jews would witness it and have no doubts as to the fate of their pursuers. The Jews did not feel truly liberated until they actually saw the destruction of their taskmasters (*Ibn Ezra; Radak*).

If the sea waters had merely returned to their original place, the drowning of the Egyptians could have been misconstrued as a natural death. But God did not wait for the waters to engulf the Egyptians; rather, He catapulted them into the walls of water to demonstrate that He was executing them for their evil deeds. Thus He dealt kindly with the world by teaching mankind that God chastises the wicked with a punishment to fit the crime (*Alshich*).

כִּי לְעוֹלָם חַסְדּוֹ.	וַיַּהֲרֹג מְלָכִים אַדִּירִים
כִּי לְעוֹלָם חַסְדּוֹ.	לְסִיחוֹן מֶלֶךְ הָאֱמֹרִי
כִּי לְעוֹלָם חַסְדּוֹ.	וּלְעוֹג מֶלֶךְ הַבָּשָׁן
כִּי לְעוֹלָם חַסְדּוֹ.	וְנָתַן אַרְצָם לְנַחֲלָה
כִּי לְעוֹלָם חַסְדּוֹ.	נַחֲלָה לְיִשְׂרָאֵל עַבְדּוֹ
כִּי לְעוֹלָם חַסְדּוֹ.	שֶׁבְּשִׁפְלֵנוּ זָכַר לָנוּ
כִּי לְעוֹלָם חַסְדּוֹ.	וַיִּפְרְקֵנוּ מִצָּרֵינוּ
כִּי לְעוֹלָם חַסְדּוֹ.	נֹתֵן לֶחֶם לְכָל בָּשָׂר
כִּי לְעוֹלָם חַסְדּוֹ.[1]	הוֹדוּ לְאֵל הַשָּׁמָיִם

נִשְׁמַת כָּל חַי תְּבָרֵךְ אֶת שִׁמְךָ יהוה אֱלֹהֵינוּ, וְרוּחַ כָּל בָּשָׂר תְּפָאֵר וּתְרוֹמֵם זִכְרְךָ מַלְכֵּנוּ תָּמִיד. מִן הָעוֹלָם וְעַד הָעוֹלָם אַתָּה אֵל, וּמִבַּלְעָדֶיךָ אֵין לָנוּ מֶלֶךְ גּוֹאֵל וּמוֹשִׁיעַ. פּוֹדֶה וּמַצִּיל וּמְפַרְנֵס וּמְרַחֵם בְּכָל עֵת צָרָה וְצוּקָה.

וַיִּפְרְקֵנוּ מִצָּרֵינוּ – *And released us from our tormentors. Tormentors*, according to *Rashi*, refers to our Egyptian taskmasters. According to *Radak*, however, this refers to the Jews' survival in exile among the nations. Although they persistently torment us, God gives us the strength to endure, and ultimately He will redeem us from exile and release us completely from their power.

נִשְׁמַת כָּל חַי — *The soul of every living being.* At this point a lengthy blessing begins, which extends all the way to the passage יִשְׁתַּבַּח, *May Your Name be praised.* The Sages (*Pesachim* 118a) referred to this blessing as בִּרְכַּת הַשִּׁיר, *the Blessing of the Song,* because it is recited in the Sabbath and holiday morning prayers as a conclusion to the readings from *Psalms* (the *songs* of King David), or because

it continues on the theme of the *Song* of the Sea which is recited immediately before it.

This beautiful and moving prayer is an outpouring of praise and gratitude to God. Lyrically, it depicts our utter dependency on God's mercy, our total inadequacy to laud Him properly and our enthusiastic resolve to dedicate ourselves to His service.

It is the "prayer of prayers," complete with all the various aspects of prayer: praise of God; expression of faith, trust and hope; man's humility, and at the same time, his greatness. Rapturously poetic, it strums on every string of the harp of one's soul.[1]

So highly was this prayer regarded that such great commentators as *Rabbi Yehudah HaLevi* and *Ibn Ezra* composed poetic introductions to *Nish-*

---

1. **A Study in Contrasts.** The reconciliation of self-esteem and humility could not be better done than it is in *Nishmas*. "Were our mouths as full of song as the sea, and our tongues as full of joyous melody as its multitude of waves, and our lips as full of praise as the breadth of the heavens, and our eyes as brilliant as the sun . . .we still could not sufficiently thank You." Thus we express human inadequacy, out of our

And killed mighty kings — for His kindness endures forever.
Sichon, king of the Emorites
— for His kindness endures forever.

And Og, king of Bashan — for His kindness endures forever.
And gave their lands as an inheritance
— for His kindness endures forever.

An inheritance to Israel, His servant
— for His kindness endures forever.

Who remembered us in our lowliness
— for His kindness endures forever.

And released us from our tormentors
— for His kindness endures forever.

He gives food to all living creatures
— for His kindness endures forever.

Give thanks to God of the heavens
— for His kindness endures forever.[1]

The soul of every living being will bless Your Name, HASHEM, our God, and the spirit of all flesh will constantly glorify and exalt Your remembrance, our King. You are God forever, and besides You we have no king, redeemer, savior, liberator, deliverer, supporter, or source of mercy in every time of distress and anguish.

---

(1) *Psalms* 136.

mas. That of *Ibn Ezra,* צָמְאָה נַפְשִׁי לֵאלֹהִים, *My soul thirsts for God,* is sung by many as part of the Sabbath Eve *Zemiros.* Its final stanza ends with the opening words of *Nishmas:* אֶפְתַּח פִּי ״בְּנִשְׁמַת כָּל חָי״, *I will open my mouth with [the words] "The soul of every living being."*

Nishmas is included in the Pesach Seder since it places the Exodus in the context of God's ongoing role as Savior and Protector of His people. Hence it gives heartfelt expression to the lessons in faith that should be our spiritual inheritance from that seminal experience.

According to *Kol Bo, Nishmas* was composed by

R' *Shimon ben Shetach* during the Hasmonean period.

וְרוּחַ כָּל בָּשָׂר — *The spirit of all flesh.* Not only those endowed with a soul sensitive enough to perceive God in all of creation, but even those whose sense of God is very mundane (*all flesh*) also relate to Him through the "ordinary" favors that He does for us. Thus, every person, no matter what his spiritual level, has ample reason to praise God profusely.

בְּכָל עֵת צָרָה וְצוּקָה — *In every time of distress and anguish.* Commonly, people express gratitude in happy times and pray for salvation in hard times.

---

humility."Therefore, the organs which You have set within us, and the spirit and soul that You breathed into our nostrils, and the tongue which You have placed in our mouth . . . they shall all . . . praise and glorify . . . Your Name." In other words, we ourselves are nothing, but with the greatness that God has instilled within us, we can approach the Infinite (*R' A. J. Twerski*).

אֵין לָנוּ מֶלֶךְ אֶלָּא אָתָּה. אֱלֹהֵי הָרִאשׁוֹנִים וְהָאַחֲרוֹנִים אֱלוֹהַּ כָּל בְּרִיּוֹת אֲדוֹן כָּל תּוֹלָדוֹת הַמְהֻלָּל בְּרֹב הַתִּשְׁבָּחוֹת הַמְנַהֵג עוֹלָמוֹ בְּחֶסֶד וּבְרִיּוֹתָיו בְּרַחֲמִים וַיהוה לֹא יָנוּם וְלֹא יִישָׁן. הַמְעוֹרֵר יְשֵׁנִים וְהַמֵּקִיץ נִרְדָּמִים וְהַמֵּשִׂיחַ אִלְּמִים וְהַמַּתִּיר אֲסוּרִים וְהַסּוֹמֵךְ נוֹפְלִים וְהַזּוֹקֵף כְּפוּפִים. לְךָ לְבַדְּךָ אֲנַחְנוּ מוֹדִים. אִלּוּ פִינוּ מָלֵא שִׁירָה כַּיָּם וּלְשׁוֹנֵנוּ רִנָּה כַּהֲמוֹן גַּלָּיו וְשִׂפְתוֹתֵינוּ שֶׁבַח כְּמֶרְחֲבֵי רָקִיעַ וְעֵינֵינוּ מְאִירוֹת כַּשֶּׁמֶשׁ וְכַיָּרֵחַ וְיָדֵינוּ פְרוּשׂוֹת כְּנִשְׁרֵי שָׁמָיִם וְרַגְלֵינוּ קַלּוֹת כָּאַיָּלוֹת, אֵין אֲנַחְנוּ מַסְפִּיקִים לְהוֹדוֹת לְךָ יהוה אֱלֹהֵינוּ וֵאלֹהֵי אֲבוֹתֵינוּ וּלְבָרֵךְ אֶת שְׁמֶךָ עַל אַחַת מֵאָלֶף אֶלֶף אַלְפֵי אֲלָפִים וְרִבֵּי רְבָבוֹת פְּעָמִים הַטּוֹבוֹת שֶׁעָשִׂיתָ עִם אֲבוֹתֵינוּ וְעִמָּנוּ. מִמִּצְרַיִם גְּאַלְתָּנוּ יהוה אֱלֹהֵינוּ וּמִבֵּית עֲבָדִים פְּדִיתָנוּ בְּרָעָב זַנְתָּנוּ וּבְשָׂבָע כִּלְכַּלְתָּנוּ מֵחֶרֶב הִצַּלְתָּנוּ וּמִדֶּבֶר מִלַּטְתָּנוּ וּמֵחֳלָיִם רָעִים וְנֶאֱמָנִים דִּלִּיתָנוּ. עַד הֵנָּה עֲזָרוּנוּ רַחֲמֶיךָ וְלֹא עֲזָבוּנוּ חֲסָדֶיךָ

We go further, however — even when we suffer *distress and* anguish, we express our gratitude to God for allowing us to survive the attacks of our enemies and the travails of life.

אֱלֹהֵי הָרִאשׁוֹנִים וְהָאַחֲרוֹנִים — *God of the first and of the last.* When God initiates a course of action, He takes into account the results it will bring about centuries into the future. Thus, He is the Master of the *first* set of events as well as of the *last* (R' Moshe Cordevero).

הַמְנַהֵג עוֹלָמוֹ בְּחֶסֶד וּבְרִיּוֹתָיו בְּרַחֲמִים — *Who guides His world with lovingkindness and His creatures with mercy.* The physical, inanimate world, which can be neither meritorious nor guilty, is guided by God with a spirit of lovingkindness and care. He shows His mercy even to people (God's *creatures*) who often ignore His demands (R' Eliyahu Kitov).

וְהַמַּתִּיר אֲסוּרִים — *He frees the bound.* Prisoners of our bad habits, we frequently are so bound by the chains of our Evil Inclination that we find it nearly impossible to free ourselves of its shackles.

God grants us both the ability and inspiration to become free by repenting from our past and opening up a new beginning to our lives (Siach Yitzchak).

אִלּוּ פִינוּ — *Were our mouths...* Having stated that God is All-powerful and All-merciful, and thus worthy of our grateful thanks, we now begin to explain that no creature could do justice to this task — even if he were endowed with superhuman

We have no King but You, God of the first and of the last, God of all creatures, Master of all generations, extolled with many praises, Who guides His world with lovingkindness and His creatures with mercy. HASHEM does not doze or slumber. He wakes those who sleep and arouses those who slumber. He makes the mute speak. He frees the bound, supports those who fall, and straightens those who are bent over. You alone we thank. Were our mouths as full of song as the sea, and our tongues as full of joyous melody as its multitude of waves, and our lips as full of praise as the breadth of the heavens, and our eyes as brilliant as the sun and the moon, and our arms spread wide as the eagles of the skies, and our feet as fleet as antelopes, we still could not sufficiently thank You or bless Your Name, HASHEM, our God and the God of our fathers, for even one of the thousand thousand, thousands of thousands and myriad myriads of favors that you performed for our ancestors and for us. You redeemed us from Egypt, HASHEM, our God, and delivered us from the house of bondage. In famine You nourished us and in plenty you sustained us. You have saved us from the sword, rescued us from epidemic, and spared us from severe and enduring diseases. Until now Your mercy has helped us and Your kindness has not abandoned us.

---

qualities.[1]

בְּרָעָב זַנְתָּנוּ וּבְשָׂבָע כִּלְכַּלְתָּנוּ — *In famine You nourished us and in plenty You sustained us.* Only someone with an appetite for spiritual growth can actually grow; complacent people almost always stagnate. Thus, it is spiritual famine and the sense that one has not yet achieved enough that drives

one to higher and higher levels of growth. Accordingly, this phrase might be rendered as: *Through famine You nourished us.* By making us suffer spiritual hunger, God forces us to make the efforts from which spiritual greatness emerges.

עַד הֵנָּה עֲזָרוּנוּ רַחֲמֶיךָ — *Until now Your mercy has helped us.* All You have done for us in the past was

1. **Happy for Him.** First we speak of God as the Eternal Power and then as our only hope for redemption and salvation.

The *Dubno Maggid* likened this to a person whose brother came into fantastic wealth. Informed of the news, the poor brother rejoiced over his brother's good fortune. A bystander wondered why the poor brother was so happy. "Who says your brother will help you with his newfound wealth? Maybe he will ignore your plight!"

Replied the poor but loyal brother, "If he helps me, fine. But even if he does not, I am first and foremost happy over *his* success."

Likewise, Jews first and foremost rejoice over the fact that God is the ruler of the world and all it contains. Only secondary to that is the help that He provides us in times of need.

וְאַל תִּטְּשֵׁנוּ יהוה אֱלֹהֵינוּ לָנֶצַח. עַל כֵּן אֵבָרִים שֶׁפִּלַּגְתָּ בָּנוּ וְרוּחַ וּנְשָׁמָה שֶׁנָּפַחְתָּ בְּאַפֵּינוּ וְלָשׁוֹן אֲשֶׁר שַׂמְתָּ בְּפֵינוּ הֵן הֵם יוֹדוּ וִיבָרְכוּ וִישַׁבְּחוּ וִיפָאֲרוּ וִירוֹמְמוּ וְיַעֲרִיצוּ וְיַקְדִּישׁוּ וְיַמְלִיכוּ אֶת שִׁמְךָ מַלְכֵּנוּ. כִּי כָל פֶּה לְךָ יוֹדֶה וְכָל לָשׁוֹן לְךָ תִשָּׁבַע וְכָל בֶּרֶךְ לְךָ תִכְרַע וְכָל קוֹמָה לְפָנֵיךָ תִשְׁתַּחֲוֶה וְכָל לְבָבוֹת יִירָאוּךָ וְכָל קֶרֶב וּכְלָיוֹת יְזַמְּרוּ לִשְׁמֶךָ. כַּדָּבָר שֶׁכָּתוּב כָּל עַצְמֹתַי תֹּאמַרְנָה יהוה מִי כָמוֹךָ, מַצִּיל עָנִי מֵחָזָק מִמֶּנּוּ וְעָנִי וְאֶבְיוֹן מִגֹּזְלוֹ.¹ מִי יִדְמֶה לָךְ וּמִי יִשְׁוֶה לָּךְ וּמִי יַעֲרָךְ לָךְ הָאֵל הַגָּדוֹל הַגִּבּוֹר וְהַנּוֹרָא אֵל עֶלְיוֹן קֹנֵה שָׁמַיִם וָאָרֶץ. נְהַלֶּלְךָ וּנְשַׁבֵּחֲךָ וּנְפָאֶרְךָ וּנְבָרֵךְ אֶת שֵׁם קָדְשֶׁךָ כָּאָמוּר לְדָוִד בָּרְכִי נַפְשִׁי אֶת יהוה וְכָל קְרָבַי אֶת שֵׁם קָדְשׁוֹ.²

הָאֵל בְּתַעֲצֻמוֹת עֻזֶּךָ הַגָּדוֹל בִּכְבוֹד שְׁמֶךָ הַגִּבּוֹר לָנֶצַח וְהַנּוֹרָא בְּנוֹרְאוֹתֶיךָ הַמֶּלֶךְ הַיּוֹשֵׁב עַל כִּסֵּא רָם וְנִשָּׂא.

---

a result of Your mercy. Though we were undeserving, Your kindness, rather than our merit, did not forsake us. Thus, we are confident that likewise in the future You will not abandon us forever (*Vilna Gaon*).[1]

עַל כֵּן אֵבָרִים שֶׁפִּלַּגְתָּ בָּנוּ — *Therefore the organs which You have set within us.* Though unable to

encompass the full scope of praise with which we should laud God, we are committed to use every God-given faculty to at least attempt to thank God for all he does for us. *The Maggid of Mezritch* offers an analogy: A king instructed one of his subjects to prepare a feast. Unsure of how lavish the banquet should be, the frightened subject could not decide how to prepare. Finally, he decided to ask the king

---

1. **Eternally Magnanimous.** One who lends money is entitled to demand repayment, but once the full amount has been returned, he no longer has a right to make demands. On the other hand, an abjectly poor individual who depends on charity for his survival may continuously return to the wealthy individual who provides for him and ask that his benefactor continue to provide for him. Since he appeals to the magnanimity of his benefactor rather than demanding an entitlement, there is no limit to how much or how frequently he may ask.

Had we come to God and made demands based on our merits, we would quickly deplete our entitlement. However, we realize that we have thrown ourselves on His mercy in the past, and will continue to do so in the future (*Vilna Gaon*).

HASHEM, our God, do not ever desert us. Therefore the organs which You have set within us, and the spirit and soul that You breathed into our nostrils, and the tongue which You have placed in our mouth — they shall all thank, bless, praise, glorify, exalt, adulate, sanctify, and do homage to Your Name, our King. For every mouth gives thanks to You, every tongue vows allegiance to You, every knee bends to You, every erect spine shall prostrate itself before You, every heart fears You, and all internal organs sing out to Your Name. As it is written, "All my bones shall say, HASHEM: Who is like You, Who saves the poor man from one stronger than he, and the poor and impoverished from the one who seeks to rob him?"[1] Who can resemble You? Who can compare to You? Who can estimate You? The great, mighty, and awesome God, the supreme God, Creator of heavens and earth. We will praise You, laud You, glorify You, and bless Your holy Name, as it says: "Of David: Bless HASHEM O my soul, and my whole inner being [bless] His holy Name."[2]

O God, in the supremacies of Your might! You Who are great in the glory of Your name, Who are mighty forever and fearful through Your awe-inspiring deeds! The King Who sits upon a high and exalted throne!

(1) *Psalms* 35:10. (2) 103:1.

---

to send him all the items he would need for the feast. Thus he would no longer need to be concerned; whatever the king would send him he would use to prepare the royal meal.

Similarly, we are constantly afraid that our praise of God will fall short. In order to be sure, we commit every fiber of our being, all the natural ability that we have, to laud and serve Him.

וְכָל קוֹמָה לְפָנֶיךָ תִשְׁתַּחֲוֶה — *Every erect spine shall prostrate itself before You.* One must bow to God even while he is standing erect. "Bowing" is not only a physical action; it must also be done in the heart and mind (*R' Feivel of Mezhibuzh*).

כָּל עַצְמוֹתַי תֹּאמַרְנָה — *All my bones shall say.* Having just described how each limb and organ

will offer praise to God, we cite the Scriptural source for this obligation. The verse concludes with the inspiring praise that God's greatness is manifested in His rescue of the powerless from their oppressors. This is meant both literally and figuratively, for, as *Radak* explains, God rescues the seemingly overpowered Good Inclination from the seductions of the Evil Inclination.

בָּרְכִי נַפְשִׁי אֶת ה' — *Bless HASHEM, O my soul.* The soul is given to us by God, and is our closest link to Him; He breathed it into us as part of His own Divine essence.

Moreover, the Midrash likens the soul's role within a person to God's role in the universe: The soul occupies the entire body but dwells in its innermost recesses, it sees but is not seen, and it

שׁוֹכֵן עַד מָרוֹם וְקָדוֹשׁ שְׁמוֹ. וְכָתוּב רַנְּנוּ צַדִּיקִים בַּיהוה לַיְשָׁרִים נָאוָה תְהִלָּה. בְּפִי יְשָׁרִים תִּתְהַלָּל וּבְדִבְרֵי צַדִּיקִים תִּתְבָּרַךְ וּבִלְשׁוֹן חֲסִידִים תִּתְרוֹמָם וּבְקֶרֶב קְדוֹשִׁים תִּתְקַדָּשׁ:

וּבְמַקְהֲלוֹת רִבְבוֹת עַמְּךָ בֵּית יִשְׂרָאֵל בְּרִנָּה יִתְפָּאַר שִׁמְךָ מַלְכֵּנוּ בְּכָל דּוֹר וָדוֹר שֶׁכֵּן חוֹבַת כָּל הַיְצוּרִים לְפָנֶיךָ יהוה אֱלֹהֵינוּ וֵאלֹהֵי אֲבוֹתֵינוּ לְהוֹדוֹת לְהַלֵּל לְשַׁבֵּחַ לְפָאֵר לְרוֹמֵם לְהַדֵּר לְבָרֵךְ לְעַלֵּה וּלְקַלֵּס עַל כָּל דִּבְרֵי שִׁירוֹת וְתִשְׁבְּחוֹת דָּוִד בֶּן יִשַׁי עַבְדְּךָ מְשִׁיחֶךָ.

יִשְׁתַּבַּח שִׁמְךָ לָעַד מַלְכֵּנוּ הָאֵל הַמֶּלֶךְ הַגָּדוֹל וְהַקָּדוֹשׁ בַּשָּׁמַיִם וּבָאָרֶץ כִּי לְךָ נָאֶה יהוה אֱלֹהֵינוּ וֵאלֹהֵי אֲבוֹתֵינוּ שִׁיר וּשְׁבָחָה הַלֵּל וְזִמְרָה עֹז וּמֶמְשָׁלָה נֶצַח גְּדֻלָּה וּגְבוּרָה תְּהִלָּה וְתִפְאֶרֶת קְדֻשָּׁה וּמַלְכוּת בְּרָכוֹת וְהוֹדָאוֹת מֵעַתָּה וְעַד עוֹלָם: בָּרוּךְ אַתָּה יהוה אֵל מֶלֶךְ גָּדוֹל בַּתִּשְׁבָּחוֹת אֵל הַהוֹדָאוֹת אֲדוֹן הַנִּפְלָאוֹת הַבּוֹחֵר בְּשִׁירֵי זִמְרָה מֶלֶךְ אֵל חֵי הָעוֹלָמִים.

sustains the whole organism. Therefore, the soul is called upon first to give praise to God — but so is כָּל קְרָבַי, *my whole inner being,* i.e., all the physical organs that are the soul's tools to carry out God's will. Man's power to praise God by word of mouth is limited; instead he is called upon to use all the faculties of his body and soul in order to turn his life into a symphonic poem of praise for God.

בְּפִי יְשָׁרִים — *By the mouth of the upright.* Four categories of people are listed as praising God: יְשָׁרִים, צַדִּיקִים, חֲסִידִים, קְדוֹשִׁים, *upright, righteous, devout* and *holy.* The initials of these four

words spell יִצְחָק, leading some to speculate that it is the signature of the unknown author of *Nishmas.*

R' Shraga Feivel Mendlowitz noted in the name of *R' Yisrael of Rizhin* that these four categories seem to be listed in ascending order of their spiritual accomplishment, the lowest being the upright, fair-minded people and the highest being the holy ones. The higher the level of the person, the more meaningful the manner in which he praises God. While the *upright* person praises God with his *mouth,* the *righteous* one uses articulated *words.* The *devout* one uses his *tongue,* implying that the praise comes from deep

He Who dwells in eternity, high and holy is His Name. As it is written, "Let the righteous rejoice in HASHEM. It is fitting for upright to extol."[1] By the mouth of the upright You shall be praised. And by the words of the righteous You shall be blessed. And by the tongue of the devout You shall be exalted. And amid the holy You shall be sanctified.

And in the assemblies of the myriads of Your people, the House of Israel, Your Name shall be extolled in song, our King, in each and every generation. For it is the duty of all that is created: in Your presence, HASHEM, our God and the God of our fathers, to thank, praise, laud, glorify, exalt, adorn, bless, elevate, and celebrate beyond all the songs and praises of David the son of Yishai, Your servant, Your anointed.

May Your Name be praised forever, our King, the God and King, great and holy, in the heavens and the earth. For hymn and praise befit You, HASHEM, our God and the God of our fathers — accolade and song, strength and sovereignty, eternity, greatness and might, fame and glory, sanctity and majesty, blessing and thanksgiving, for all eternity. Blessed are You, HASHEM, God, King, great in praises, the God to whom we owe thanks, Master of wonders, Who chooses musical songs — King, God, Life of the worlds.

---

(1) *Psalms* 33:1.

---

within himself. The *holy* person, however, praises God with his very *essence* (קֶרֶב, literally, *inner being*).[1]

הַבּוֹחֵר בְּשִׁירֵי זִמְרָה — *Who chooses musical songs.* R' Simcha Bunam of P'shis'cha homiletically ex-

plained the word שִׁירֵי as being related to *remnants* (from שִׁירַיִם, *leftovers*). God wants to see how much of the lofty sentiments we express in our prayers remain with us after we close the *siddur*. Thus He prefers what is *left over* after the prayers have been concluded.

1. **People Power.** After describing the four levels of individuals who serve God and their particular modes of service, we then describe the praise of God that is found *in the assemblies of the myriads of Your people the House of Israel.* When the multitude of Jews unite as an assembly and turn to God in prayer and praise, they are as potent a force as the most upright, righteous, devout and holy of God's servants. The Talmud (*Berachos* 8a) teaches that God never rejects the prayers of the collective congregation.

R' Asher of Stolin was once overheard praying to God: "I may not be among the upright or the righteous, I may not even be numbered among the devout or the holy ones. I include myself among the masses of simple Jews and by that right I allow myself the privilege to praise You and pray to You."

The blessing over wine is recited and the fourth cup is drunk while reclining to the left side.
It is preferable that the entire cup be drunk.

בָּרוּךְ אַתָּה יהוה אֱלֹהֵינוּ מֶלֶךְ הָעוֹלָם, בּוֹרֵא פְּרִי הַגָּפֶן.

After drinking the fourth cup, the concluding blessing is recited.
On the Sabbath include the passage in parentheses.

בָּרוּךְ אַתָּה יהוה אֱלֹהֵינוּ מֶלֶךְ הָעוֹלָם, עַל הַגֶּפֶן וְעַל פְּרִי הַגֶּפֶן וְעַל תְּנוּבַת הַשָּׂדֶה וְעַל אֶרֶץ חֶמְדָּה טוֹבָה וּרְחָבָה שֶׁרָצִיתָ וְהִנְחַלְתָּ לַאֲבוֹתֵינוּ לֶאֱכֹל מִפִּרְיָהּ וְלִשְׂבּוֹעַ מִטּוּבָהּ. רַחֵם נָא יהוה אֱלֹהֵינוּ עַל יִשְׂרָאֵל עַמֶּךָ וְעַל יְרוּשָׁלַיִם עִירֶךָ וְעַל צִיּוֹן מִשְׁכַּן כְּבוֹדֶךָ וְעַל מִזְבְּחֶךָ וְעַל הֵיכָלֶךָ. וּבְנֵה יְרוּשָׁלַיִם עִיר הַקֹּדֶשׁ בִּמְהֵרָה בְיָמֵינוּ וְהַעֲלֵנוּ לְתוֹכָהּ וְשַׂמְּחֵנוּ בְּבִנְיָנָהּ וְנֹאכַל מִפִּרְיָהּ וְנִשְׂבַּע מִטּוּבָהּ וּנְבָרֶכְךָ עָלֶיהָ בִּקְדֻשָּׁה וּבְטָהֳרָה. [וּרְצֵה וְהַחֲלִיצֵנוּ בְּיוֹם הַשַּׁבָּת הַזֶּה]

The final cup of wine of the Seder was instituted to be drunk in connection with the completion of *Hallel*. However, *Maharam Rothenberg* used to drink it at the end of the Haggadah; since it is forbidden to drink after the fourth cup, he wanted to drink it as late as possible so that he should not become thirsty later in the night. Many people follow this practice today.

The requirement of drinking four cups at the Seder may be fulfilled by drinking most of the wine in each cup (although there is also an opinion that it is preferable to drink the whole cup). However, there is a disagreement among the early halachic authorities regarding how much wine obligates one to recite the concluding blessing *Al HaGefen*; opinions range from a *kezayis* (approx. 1 fl. oz.) to a *revi'is* (approx. 3-4 fl. oz.). It is therefore advisable at the Seder to drink enough wine so that the requirement to recite the *Al HaGefen* blessing will not be in doubt. Since the blessing is recited after the fourth cup, one should be careful to drink a full *revi'is*.

**עַל הַגֶּפֶן וְעַל פְּרִי הַגֶּפֶן — *For the vine and the fruit of the vine.* The Sages instituted a special blessing of thanks to be recited after partaking of any of the

Seven Species of food for which the Torah praises *Eretz Yisrael* (*Deuteronomy* 8:8). The blessing is known as בְּרָכָה אַחַת מֵעֵין שָׁלֹשׁ — literally, "a single blessing that is an abridgement of three" — because it summarizes the three Scripturally ordained blessings of *Bircas HaMazon* recited after eating bread. The fourth blessing of *Bircas HaMazon* (הַטּוֹב וְהַמֵּטִיב) is also condensed in the prayer, but the title ("abridgement of three") does not allude to it, because it is of later, Rabbinic origin.

**וְנֹאכַל מִפִּרְיָהּ וְנִשְׂבַּע מִטּוּבָהּ — *Let us eat of its fruits and be satisfied with its goodness.* The Talmud (*Sotah* 14a) teaches: "Why did Moses so passionately desire to enter *Eretz Yisrael*? Was it merely to eat of its fruits or to become satisfied with its bounty? Rather, his desire was to fulfill the commandments that can be performed only in the land." Seemingly, the blessing's request that we merit the rebuilding of Jerusalem in order to eat of its fruits might be deemed materialistic and inappropriate.

R' Yitzchak Zev Soloveitchik explains that this phrase refers not to ordinary food, but to *maaser sheini*, the yearly tithe taken (four years out of

The blessing over wine is recited and the fourth cup is drunk while reclining to the left side. It is preferable that the entire cup be drunk.

Blessed are You, HASHEM, our God, King of the universe, Who creates the fruit of the vine.

After drinking the fourth cup, the concluding blessing is recited.
On the Sabbath include the passage in parentheses.

Blessed are You, HASHEM, our God, King of the universe, for the vine and the fruit of the vine, and the produce of the field, and for the precious, good, and spacious land that You willed to give as an inheritance to our ancestors, to eat of its fruit and to be sated by its goodness. Have mercy, please, HASHEM, our God, on Israel, Your people, and on Jerusalem, Your city, and on Zion, the abode of Your glory, and on Your altar and on Your Temple. Rebuild Jerusalem, the city of sanctity, speedily in our lifetimes. Bring us up into it and let us rejoice in its reconstruction. Let us eat of its fruits and be satisfied with its goodness. And we will bless You for it in holiness and purity (and may it be Your will to fortify us on this Sabbath day),

seven) from all produce, which was to be eaten in a state of "holiness and purity" within the city of Jerusalem.[1]

וּנְבָרֶכְךָ עָלֶיהָ בִּקְדֻשָׁה וּבְטָהֲרָה — And we will bless You for it in holiness and purity. According to the Lev Simcha of Gur, this prayer is based on the Talmud's teaching that with the destruction of the Temple a spiritual impurity descended on the world, causing fruit to lose its succulent taste and aroma (Sotah 48a). Thus we pray for the restoration of the Temple, when we will again eat tasty fruits in a purer, more refined atmosphere. Others comment that the request is added specifically to this blessing because it thanks God not only for bread, the staple of life, but for wine and some fruits, which are luxuries that tend to arouse desires for mundane pleasures. We therefore pray that we may experience even luxuries in an atmosphere of holiness and purity.

נִרְצָה — Our Observance Is Accepted.

The intent of the word נִרְצָה, Acceptance, is in dispute. Shelah, Maggid Meisharim and others view it as marking the end of the formal part of the Haggadah and expressing our prayer that our

1. **Succulently Spiritual.** The fruits of Eretz Yisrael bear within themselves a special spiritual quality. The special sanctity of the land permeates even the fruits which lie deep inside the holy earth of Eretz Yisrael. When one partakes of those fruits he too is imbued with the sanctity of the land over which "God constantly watches" (see Bach to O.C. 208).

According to R' Tzadok HaKohen, true sanctity is the ability to derive full enjoyment from the permitted pleasures of this world, while subjugating one's pleasure to serve as a tool with which to serve God. R' Yehudah HaNasi was the epitome of this approach. On one hand he was so wealthy that even rare and out-of-season produce could always be found on his table (Avodah Zarah 11a). On the other hand, on his deathbed he lifted his ten fingers and declared that he had not derived even the slightest bit of enjoyment from this world (Kesubos 104a). Both statements were true — he lived very well, but never in a narcissistic or hedonistic way. For him, this world was truly a means to the World to Come.

וְשַׂמְּחֵנוּ בְּיוֹם חַג הַמַּצּוֹת הַזֶּה. כִּי אַתָּה יהוה טוֹב וּמֵטִיב לַכֹּל וְנוֹדֶה לְּךָ עַל הָאָרֶץ וְעַל פְּרִי הַגָּפֶן. בָּרוּךְ אַתָּה יהוה עַל הָאָרֶץ וְעַל פְּרִי הַגָּפֶן.

נרצה

חֲסַל סִדּוּר פֶּסַח כְּהִלְכָתוֹ. כְּכָל מִשְׁפָּטוֹ וְחֻקָּתוֹ. כַּאֲשֶׁר זָכִינוּ לְסַדֵּר אוֹתוֹ. כֵּן נִזְכֶּה לַעֲשׂוֹתוֹ. זָךְ שׁוֹכֵן מְעוֹנָה. קוֹמֵם קְהַל עֲדַת מִי מָנָה. בְּקָרוֹב נַהֵל נִטְעֵי כַנָּה. פְּדוּיִם לְצִיּוֹן בְּרִנָּה.

Seder observance be found *acceptable* by God, a theme which is conveyed by the passage חֲסַל סִדּוּר פֶּסַח, *The order of Pesach is now concluded.* According to *Maharal* and *Chida*, this part of the Seder is connected with the preceding portion of *Hallel*. As explained earlier, the first half of *Hallel* praises God for saving us from Egypt and for all the accompanying miracles and spiritual wealth (manna, Torah, *Eretz Yisrael*, the Temple) that He showered upon us, then and later. The second half of *Hallel* is a prayer for the ultimate, complete redemption. Thus, by reciting *Hallel*, we are begging God to find us *acceptable* in His eyes so that He may again do wonders on our behalf and grant us everlasting salvation.[1]

Midrash Shocher Tov (18) teaches that whoever responds to God's miracles by singing His praises in joyful song will be granted full pardon for all his sins and will be spiritually reborn (see *Midrash Rabbah* to *Exodus* 15:22). As we view ourselves on this night as having personally left Egypt and experienced miraculous redemption, we recite the joyous song of *Hallel* in the hope that our sins be forgiven and absolved. We therefore conclude our Seder with the cry of נִרְצָה, as the prophet Isaiah (40:2) uses the term נִרְצָה עֲוֹנָהּ, *her iniquity has been atoned for* (*Haggadas Chodesh HaAviv*).

חֲסַל — *The order of Pesach is now concluded.* This passage is taken from the conclusion of the lengthy פִּיּוּט (liturgical poem), written by *Rabbi Yosef Tov Elem (Bonfils)* for *Shabbos HaGadol*, in which he summarized in verse the laws and customs of Pesach.

The original intention of the word לְסַדֵּר in the liturgy of the Sabbath before Pesach was: "As we have verbalized the plans for Pesach's observance, so may we merit to actually perform them all (לַעֲשׂוֹתוֹ) properly when the holiday comes in a few more days." In the Haggadah we must understand it in a slightly different sense: "As we have carried out (לְסַדֵּר) the Pesach observances of this Seder, so may we merit to fulfill the Pesach requirements in their entirety (לַעֲשׂוֹתוֹ) in the future — with the offer-

---

1. **Proud of His Proud Children.** A father who was angry with his son once heard how the son was praising him to strangers. The father thought, "How can I continue to be angry with my son when he is so proud of me?"

When we praise God and express our pride that He is our Father Who cares so much for us and does so much on our behalf, how can He not find us and our service acceptable? Thus, we are sure that *Hallel*, our praise of Him, results in נִרְצָה, *Acceptance* (*Avnei Azel*).

and may You bring us joy on this day of the Festival of Matzos. For You, HASHEM, are good and do good to all, and we thank You for the land and the fruit of the vine. Blessed are You, HASHEM, for the land and the fruit of the vine.

NIRTZAH

The order of Pesach is now concluded in accordance with its Halachah, in accordance with all of its laws and statutes. As we have carried out the Pesach observance [of this Seder], so may we merit to fulfill the Pesach requirements [in their entirety] in the future. Pure One, Who dwells on high, raise up the countless congregation of Israel. In the near future, lead the shoots You have planted to Zion, redeemed, joyously.

---

ing of the *pesach* sacrifice in the rebuilt Temple."[1]

This prayer is offered in the spirit of the Talmudic statement, "If one thought to perform a *mitzvah* and, due to unforeseen circumstances, was unable to do so, the Torah considers it as if he did it." Thus we declare that we have performed all the observances we could, and spoken of the others. Therefore, we look forward to the opportunity to perform them all [see *Berachos* 6a and *Kiddushin* 40a] (*Haggadas Chodesh HaAviv*).

זָךְ שׁוֹכֵן מְעוֹנָה — *O Pure One, Who dwells on high.*

We beg of God *Who dwells on high* that He figuratively reach down to raise us up and lead us to freedom in a reestablished Jerusalem.[2]

בְּקָרוֹב נַהֵל — *In the near future,* lead. בְּקָרוֹב may also be rendered *from up close*. When a child plays in the park, his mother, fearful of the sharp rocks and open ditches, stays nearby to keep an eye on him. Sometimes she sits right next to him, almost like a shadow, preventing anything from happening to him. Other times she remains at a distance, unseen, but her eyes are constantly on her child,

1. **Filling the Well.** The Pesach Seder sets the tone for one's spiritual accomplishments throughout the year. The degree of faith and commitment that one reaches on this night when we retell the greatness of God and His care for us serves as the wellspring of faith from which we may draw for the rest of the year. Thus, we pray that just as we have *arranged* (לְסַדֵּר) our spiritual priorities on this night, so may we merit to see our spiritual planting bear fruit (לַעֲשׂוֹתוֹ), as our newly heightened faith is translated into action (*Eretz Tzvi*).

2. **Raising the Dust.** The poem refers to the nation of Israel as *the congregation which is without number* (lit., "the congregation that who can count?"). This appellation is based on *Numbers* 23:10: *Who can count the dust of Jacob?* According to *Rashi* (ad loc.) this expression alludes to the *mitzvos* we do with the dirt of the earth. Jews employ every level of nature for the service of God — be it fire for the Altar and the Shabbos candles, be it water for washing the hands or making the water libation on Succos — we harness all of creation to serve its Creator. Even the lowly dust of the earth can be used as a vehicle for a *mitzvah* (e.g. covering over the blood of a slaughtered fowl or wild animal).

When Jews sink to their lowest level, figuratively falling down to the dirt of the earth, God saves them in the merit of such commandments. Thus, we ask God to save us from the pitiful spiritual state we suffer in exile by remembering how we employ even the lowly earth as a means to honor Him (*Yisa Berachah*). Just as we elevate the lowly earth by bringing it closer to God, so He will raise us and bring us close to Him.

לְשָׁנָה הַבָּאָה בִּירוּשָׁלָיִם.

On the first night recite the following. On the second night continue on page 232.

וּבְכֵן וַיְהִי בַּחֲצִי הַלַּיְלָה.

בַּלַּיְלָה.   אָז רוֹב נִסִּים הִפְלֵאתָ

הַלַּיְלָה.   בְּרֹאשׁ אַשְׁמוֹרֶת זֶה

לַיְלָה.   גֵּר צֶדֶק נִצַּחְתּוֹ כְּנֶחֱלַק לוֹ

       וַיְהִי בַּחֲצִי הַלַּיְלָה.

הַלַּיְלָה.   דָּנְתָּ מֶלֶךְ גְּרָר בַּחֲלוֹם

---

ready to respond immediately if something should happen. If the child falls, the mother will rush over quickly and pick him up; if he is bruised, she will tend to his injuries; if other children attack, the mother will come to his defense. But if she is not nearby, the child will be hurt by the time she comes to his rescue.

Similarly, God watches over us. When we merit it, His care is immediate — from close up, so to speak. Under such circumstances, not only are we saved from all pain and enemies, we are also spiritually uplifted by our close proximity to Him. Sometimes God hides His countenance from us, as it were, and we find ourselves removed from Him. At such times we remain vulnerable to our physical and spiritual enemies. Even at such moments in our history, God is watching over us — but it is from a distance.

On this night, as we relive the Exodus we reexperience the loving caress of God's Hand as He guides history. Tonight we ask God to lead us בְּקָרוֹב, *from up close,* so that we may experience His closeness and become worthy of ultimate redemption (R' Chaim of Chernowitz).

לְשָׁנָה הַבָּאָה בִּירוּשָׁלָיִם — *Next year in Jerusalem.* Our request that we merit to bring the *pesach* offering, just as we have now performed the Seder ritual, ends with the cry "Next year in Jerusalem!"

This prayer is exclaimed twice a year — at the end of the Yom Kippur service and at the conclusion of the Pesach Seder. This reflects the Talmudic dispute as to whether the coming of the Messiah and the accompanying Final Redemption are more likely to take place in the month of Tishrei, when Yom Kippur occurs, or in Nissan, the Pesach season (see *Rosh Hashanah* 11a). In our fervent hope for redemption we pray in both seasons, whichever is the more appropriate one (*Yismach Moshe*).

R' Eliyahu Kitov comments on the twice-yearly recitation: There are no more joyous moments in the Jewish calendar than the Seder night and the final moments of Yom Kippur. On Pesach we celebrate and relive the joyous moment of national redemption, when we were freed from the physical bondage and spiritual impurity of Egypt. Yom Kippur, the day God granted us so that we may free ourselves from the spiritual albatross of sin, is referred to by the Sages as the day when "God's heart rejoices" (see *Song of Songs* 3:11). At the climax of Yom Kippur, when we rejoice over our personal redemption as God lifts the weight of sin from our shoulders, we echo the call of King David always to elevate Jerusalem above our foremost joy (see *Psalms* 37:6).[1]

---

1. **Tempered Joy.** This verse is the source for the custom for a bridegroom to place ashes on his head before the marriage ceremony (*Tosefta, Sotah* 15:4,5) and the custom to break a glass after the wedding ceremony in memory of Jerusalem (*Rama, Orach Chaim* 360).

Next year in Jerusalem!

On the first night recite the following. On the second night continue on page 232.

It happened at midnight.

Then You performed wondrous miracles at night.
At the first watch of this night.
You brought victory to the righteous convert
[Abraham] by dividing for him the night.
It happened at midnight.
You judged the king of Gerar [Abimelech]
in a dream of the night.

At the height of these two most joyous occasions we place Jerusalem at the head of our priorities. At the Seder we plead that we may merit *in the year to come,* to conduct our Seder along with the *pesach* offering in the newly rebuilt Jerusalem. Similarly, in the waning moments of Yom Kippur we pray that our next Yom Kippur be spent in the Holy Temple, involved with the details of the day's special sacrificial service. Next year in Jerusalem.

The joy of this night is even greater than that of Yom Kippur. On Yom Kippur we achieve sanctity through abstinence; tonight it is our eating and singing that allow us to ascend the ladder of holiness and truly free ourselves. When a Jew senses himself free, he is inspired to focus his mind and heart on the crux of his hopes and dreams, the Holy City.

וּבְכֵן וַיְהִי בַּחֲצִי הַלַּיְלָה — *It happened at midnight.* Borrowed from the liturgy of the morning of the first day of Pesach, this poem is attributed to Yannai, one of the earliest liturgical poets known to us. He lived in *Eretz Yisrael,* just after the Talmudic period.

The night of Pesach is referred to by the Torah as לֵיל שִׁמֻּרִים . . . לְדֹרֹתָם, *a night of watching . . . for their generations (Exodus 12:42).* On that night God protected the Jews from the ravaging plague of the firstborn, and from then on, the first night of Pesach became a time when God extended protection to the Jewish people.[1]

גֵּר צֶדֶק וכו׳ — *The righteous convert . . .* This line refers to Abraham's victorious military campaign against the four kings described in *Genesis 14,* which, according to the Midrash (alluded to by *Rashi* in *Genesis 14:15*), took place during the first half of the night, leaving the second half "free" for the miracle of the Exodus.

דַּנְתָּ מֶלֶךְ גְּרָר וכו׳ — *You judged the king of Gerar . . .* In this stanza, the poet refers first to God's stern warning to Abimelech to return Sarah to Abraham (ibid. 31:29). Then he mentions God's warning to Laban not to harm Jacob (ibid. 20:3) and Israel's victorious struggle with the angel in *Genesis 32:28.*

---

1. **Seeing the Light.** In Torah literature "light" is often used to indicate truth, clarity of vision and reality, whereas "darkness" refers to the sinister, to folly and to the distortion of reality. *Ecclesiastes* states, *The superiority of wisdom over folly is like that of light over darkness . . . The fool walks in darkness (2:13-14).* As important as physical vision is to a person, wisdom is even more important. In this sense it is possible for a person with healthy vision to distort reality and walk through life, as it were, in total darkness, stumbling into obstacles that he does not perceive.

On this festival of liberation, we pray for the ultimate Redemption, for a day when there will be a Divine revelation, when all evil will be eradicated, and humanity will be privileged to see the truth. With this Divine light, there will be no difference between day and night (*R' A. J. Twerski*).

הִפְחַדְתָּ אֲרַמִּי בְּאֶמֶשׁ   לַיְלָה.

וַיָּשַׂר יִשְׂרָאֵל לְמַלְאָךְ וַיּוּכַל לוֹ   לַיְלָה.

וַיְהִי בַּחֲצִי הַלַּיְלָה.

זֶרַע בְּכוֹרֵי פַתְרוֹס מָחַצְתָּ בַּחֲצִי   הַלַּיְלָה.

חֵילָם לֹא מָצְאוּ בְּקוּמָם   בַּלַּיְלָה.

טִיסַת נְגִיד חֲרוֹשֶׁת סִלִּיתָ בְּכוֹכְבֵי   לַיְלָה.

וַיְהִי בַּחֲצִי הַלַּיְלָה.

יָעַץ מְחָרֵף לְנוֹפֵף אִוּוּי הוֹבַשְׁתָּ פְגָרָיו   בַּלַּיְלָה.

כָּרַע בֵּל וּמַצָּבוֹ בְּאִישׁוֹן   לַיְלָה.

לְאִישׁ חֲמוּדוֹת נִגְלָה רָז חֲזוֹת   לַיְלָה.

וַיְהִי בַּחֲצִי הַלַּיְלָה.

מִשְׁתַּכֵּר בִּכְלֵי קֹדֶשׁ נֶהֱרַג בּוֹ   בַּלַּיְלָה.

נוֹשַׁע מִבּוֹר אֲרָיוֹת פּוֹתֵר בִּעֲתוּתֵי   לַיְלָה.

שִׂנְאָה נָטַר אֲגָגִי וְכָתַב סְפָרִים   בַּלַּיְלָה.

וַיְהִי בַּחֲצִי הַלַּיְלָה.

עוֹרַרְתָּ נִצְחֲךָ עָלָיו בְּנֶדֶד שְׁנַת   לַיְלָה.

זֶרַע בְּכוֹרֵי פַתְרוֹס **זֶרַע בְּכוֹרֵי פַּתְרוֹס** — *The firstborn offspring of Pathros . . .* Pathros was one of the Egyptian tribes mentioned in *Genesis* 10:14, and is used here as a poetic synonym for Egypt itself. The first two lines of this stanza speak of the plague of the firstborn, when the Egyptians could not find the *strength* to hold onto the Jews any longer. The third line refers to the defeat of *the prince* Sisera at *Harosheth* (*Judges* 4:13), when God turned the very stars of the heavens against the Canaanite persecu- tors of Israel (ibid. 5:20).

יָעַץ מְחָרֵף וכו׳ — *The blasphemer schemed . . .* This stanza deals first with the blasphemous Sennach- erib's miraculous downfall at the gates of Jerusalem, described in *II Kings* 19:35, and then it speaks of the collapse of *Bel*, the chief Babylonian idol, in Nebuchadnezzar's dream (*Daniel* 2). The dream was interpreted by Daniel, called the *beloved man* (ibid.).[1]

1. **Unconquerable Spirit.** During Sennacherib's siege of Jerusalem, Rabshakeh rebelled against his Jewish heritage, became a heretic and deserted to Sennacherib's camp. On Erev Pesach, he stood on the wall of the city and blasphemed God. That night he looked over the wall and heard the Jews reciting the *Hallel* and singing God's praises. He went to Sennacherib and suggested he cancel the planned invasion. "Tonight miracles will occur for them," he warned Sennacherib. The king arrogantly dismissed the advice. What was

You terrified the Aramean [Laban] in the dark of　　　　　　　night.
And Israel [Jacob] fought with an angel
　　and overcame him at　　　　　　　　　　　　　　　night.
　　　　It happened at midnight.
You bruised the firstborn offspring of Pasros [Egypt] at midnight.
They did not find their strength when they arose at　　　night.
The swift armies of the prince of Harosheth [Sisera]
　　You crushed with the stars of　　　　　　　　　　night.
　　　　It happened at midnight.
The blasphemer [Sennacherib] schemed to raise
　　his hand menacingly [over the precious city].
　　You made his corpses rot at　　　　　　　　　　night.
Bel [the Babylonian pagan deity] and his
　　pedestal fell in the black of　　　　　　　　　　night.
To the beloved man [Daniel] was revealed
　　the secret of the visions of　　　　　　　　　　night.
　　　　It happened at midnight.
He who guzzled out of the sacred vessels
　　[Belshazzar, king of Babylonia] was killed on that　　night.
The one who was saved from the lions' den
　　interpreted the terrors of the　　　　　　　　　night.
The Agagite [Haman] nurtured hatred
　　and wrote decrees at　　　　　　　　　　　　　night.
　　　　It happened at midnight.
You aroused Your triumph over him
　　by disturbing the sleep [of Ahasuerus] at　　　　night.

מִשְׁתַּכֵּר בִּכְלֵי קֹדֶשׁ וכו׳ — *He who guzzled out of the holy vessels* . . . The poet continues to refer to the drunken feast in which Belshazzar desecrated the Temple vessels; Belshazzar *was killed on that very night* (*Daniel* 5:30). The next line is a reference to Daniel's miraculous salvation from the *lion's den* (*Daniel* 6), which, according to the Midrash, oc-

curred on the night of Pesach. The final line of the stanza speaks of Haman (the *Agagite*) penning his evil decrees against the Jews at night (*Esther* 3:12).

עוֹרַרְתָּ נִצְחֲךָ עָלָיו וכו׳ — *You aroused Your triumph over him* . . . The poet mentions the beginning of Haman's downfall, when King Ahasuerus' sleep

---

it that convinced the apostate Rabshakeh that the invasion was futile?
　　R' Betzalel Zolty explained that the source of the Jews' indomitable spirit is their ability to praise God in the worst of times. Sure of His power and will to save us, we praise Him even for salvations that are yet to come. This unprecedented display of faith and hope struck a deep chord in Rabshakeh's Jewish soul, convincing him that the Jews were unconquerable.

מִלַּיְלָה.   **פּוּרָה** תִדְרוֹךְ לְשֹׁמֵר מַה

לַיְלָה.   צָרַח כַּשּׁוֹמֵר וְשָׂח אָתָא בֹקֶר וְגַם

וַיְהִי בַּחֲצִי הַלַּיְלָה.

לַיְלָה.   קָרֵב יוֹם אֲשֶׁר הוּא לֹא יוֹם וְלֹא

הַלַּיְלָה.   רָם הוֹדַע כִּי לְךָ הַיּוֹם אַף לְךָ

הַלַּיְלָה.   שׁוֹמְרִים הַפְקֵד לְעִירְךָ כָּל הַיּוֹם וְכָל

לַיְלָה.   תָּאִיר כְּאוֹר יוֹם חֶשְׁכַּת

וַיְהִי בַּחֲצִי הַלַּיְלָה.

On the first night continue on page 236. On the second night recite the following.

וּבְכֵן וַאֲמַרְתֶּם זֶבַח פֶּסַח:

בַּפֶּסַח.   **אֹמֶץ** גְּבוּרוֹתֶיךָ הִפְלֵאתָ

פֶּסַח.   **בְּרֹאשׁ** כָּל מוֹעֲדוֹת נִשֵּׂאתָ

פֶּסַח.   **גִּלִּיתָ** לְאֶזְרָחִי חֲצוֹת לֵיל

וַאֲמַרְתֶּם זֶבַח פֶּסַח.

בַּפֶּסַח.   **דְּלָתָיו** דָּפַקְתָּ כְּחֹם הַיּוֹם

בַּפֶּסַח.   **הִסְעִיד** נוֹצְצִים עֻגוֹת מַצּוֹת

פֶּסַח.   **וְאֶל** הַבָּקָר רָץ זֵכֶר לְשׁוֹר עֵרֶךְ

וַאֲמַרְתֶּם זֶבַח פֶּסַח.

---

was disturbed (ibid. 6:1). The rest of the poem contains references to, and prayers for, our future redemption in Messianic times, which, according to tradition, will occur on Pesach night. The poet's descriptions of the final salvation borrow expressions from *Isaiah* 63:3, ibid. 21:11-12, *Zechariah* 14:7, *Psalms* 74:16 and *Isaiah* 62:6. The poem concludes with a plea to God to change the "darkness" of our oppression into the "bright light" of redemption.

וּבְכֵן וַאֲמַרְתֶּם זֶבַח פֶּסַח — *And you shall say: This is the Feast of Pesach.* The author of this poem is Rabbi Elazar HaKalir, who also lived just after the Talmudic era in *Eretz Yisrael*. It is borrowed here from our morning liturgy of the second day of Pesach.

The poem begins by declaring that Pesach has always been a time when God displays His miraculous power. The poet then notes that Pesach is the most exalted of all holidays, always mentioned first

You will tread a winepress [in peace after victory]
  for him who cries out [Israel]: Our Guardian!
    What will be of this   night?
Like a guardian You will call out in response:
  The morning has come, as well as the   night.
    It happened at midnight.
The day is approaching which is neither day nor   night.
Most High! Make it known that Yours are
  both the day and the   night.
Appoint watchmen over Your city all day and all   night.
Illuminate like the light of day the darkness of   night.
    It will happen at midnight.

On the first night continue on page 236. On the second night recite the following.

And you will say: this is the feast of Pesach.

The power of Your mighty deeds
  You showed wondrously on   Pesach.
Foremost of all festivals You exalted   Pesach.
You revealed to the Easterns One [Abraham]
  the events of the night of   Pesach.
    And you will say: This is the feast of Pesach.
You knocked on his doors
  during the heat of the day on   Pesach.
He gave bright angels a meal of cakes of
  matzah on   Pesach.
He ran to fetch an ox in commemoration of
  the ox sacrificed [as the *korban chagigah* —
  the festival offering] on   Pesach.
    And you will say: This is the feast of Pesach.

---

in the Torah's list of holidays. Then, like the previous poem, it enumerates various Biblical incidents that took place on Pesach.

גְּלִיתָ לְאֶזְרָחִי וכו׳ — *You revealed to the Eastern One*. Abraham was known as the *Eastern One* (*Bava Basra* 15a). According to the Midrash, at the

Covenant Between the Parts (*Genesis* 15), God told Abraham the exact date of the Exodus.

דְּלָתָיו דָּפַקְתָ וכו׳ — *You knocked on his door* . . . This stanza refers to God's appearance to Abraham and the latter's hospitality to the three angels that God sent to him on that occasion (*Genesis* 18).

זוֹעֲמוּ סְדוֹמִים וְלוֹהֲטוּ בָּאֵשׁ   בַּפֶּֽסַח.

חֻלַּץ לוֹט מֵהֶם וּמַצּוֹת אָפָה בְּקֵץ   פֶּֽסַח.

טֵאטֵאתָ אַדְמַת מוֹף וְנוֹף בְּעָבְרְךָ   בַּפֶּֽסַח.

וַאֲמַרְתֶּם זֶֽבַח פֶּֽסַח.

יָהּ רֹאשׁ כָּל אוֹן מָחַֽצְתָּ בְּלֵיל שִׁמּוּר   פֶּֽסַח.

כַּבִּיר עַל בֵּן בְּכוֹר פָּסַֽחְתָּ בְּדַם   פֶּֽסַח.

לְבִלְתִּי תֵּת מַשְׁחִית לָבֹא בִּפְתָחַי   בַּפֶּֽסַח.

וַאֲמַרְתֶּם זֶֽבַח פֶּֽסַח.

מְסֻגֶּֽרֶת סֻגָּֽרָה בְּעִתּֽוֹתֵי   פֶּֽסַח.

נִשְׁמְדָה מִדְיָן בִּצְלִיל שְׂעוֹרֵי עֹֽמֶר   פֶּֽסַח.

שׂוֹרְפוּ מִשְׁמַנֵּי פּוּל וְלוּד בִּיקַד יְקוֹד   פֶּֽסַח.

וַאֲמַרְתֶּם זֶֽבַח פֶּֽסַח.

עוֹד הַיּוֹם בְּנֹב לַעֲמוֹד עַד גָּֽעָה עֽוֹנַת   פֶּֽסַח.

פַּס יַד כָּתְבָה לְקַעֲקֵֽעַ צוּל   בַּפֶּֽסַח.

צָפֹה הַצָּפִית עָרוֹךְ הַשֻּׁלְחָן   בַּפֶּֽסַח.

וַאֲמַרְתֶּם זֶֽבַח פֶּֽסַח.

זוֹעֲמוּ סְדוֹמִים וכו׳ — *The Sodomites provoked (God) and were devoured by fire on Pesach.*[1] Sodom was destroyed the day after the angels visited Abraham (which was still during Pesach), after Lot invited them in and served them matzos (*Genesis* 19:3).

טֵאטֵאתָ וכו׳ — *You swept.* This line, as well as the entire next stanza, refers to God's smiting of the firstborn of Egypt on the night of the first Pesach, while protecting the Jewish homes from the plague.

מְסֻגֶּֽרֶת סֻגָּֽרָה — *The closed city (Jericho) was besieged.* The siege of Jericho took place just after the beginning of Pesach (*Joshua* 6).

נִשְׁמְדָה מִדְיָן — *Midian was destroyed.* According to the Midrash (alluded to by *Rashi* in *Judges* 7:13), Israel's miraculous defeat of Midian in the days of Gideon was in the merit of the *Omer* offering, a barley meal offering brought on the second day of Pesach.

---

1. **Holy Fire.** R' Pinchas of Koritz suggests an alternative text: "They were devoured by the fire *of the pesach.*" The Sages teach that our forefathers fulfilled the Torah long before it was given. When Abraham himself brought a *pesach* offering, he brought a great and holy fire into this world. His message that One God made and controls everything was symbolized by the future *pesach* offering, which carries that very same message. That was the "fire" that consumed Sodom.

The Sodomites provoked God
and were devoured by fire on   Pesach.
Lot escaped from them and baked matzos
at the end of   Pesach.
You swept clean the land of *Mof* and *Nof*
[Egyptian cities] on   Pesach.
       And you will say: This is the feast of Pesach.
God, the first issue of strength You bruised
on the watchful night of   Pesach.
Mighty One, You skipped over the firstborn son
because of the blood of   Pesach,
Not to allow the destroyer to enter my doors on Pesach.
       And you will say: This is the feast of Pesach.
The closed city [Jericho] was besieged
at the time of   Pesach.
Midian was destroyed [by the Jews
under the leadership of Gidon]
through the merit of a cake of the *omer* on   Pesach.
The mighty nobles of Pul and Lud [the Assyrians
in the days of King Hezekiah]
were burnt in a conflagration on   Pesach.
       And you will say: This is the feast of Pesach.
He [Sennacherib] would have stood at Nob,
but the time of Pesach arrived.
A hand inscribed the decree of annihilation against Zul
[Babylonia] on   Pesach.
Their scout went to look for the enemy while their table
was festively set on   Pesach.
       And you will say: This is the feast of Pesach.

שׂוֹרְפוּ וכו׳ — *Were burnt.* The choice warriors of the army of Assyria (*Lud and Pul*) were annihilated in one night (*II Kings* 19:35) — Pesach eve. *Lud* was a kinsman of Asshur, the founder of Assyria (*Genesis* 10:22). *Pul* is mentioned together with *Lud* in *Isaiah* 66:19.

עוֹד הַיּוֹם בְּנֹב לַעֲמֹד — *He (Sennacherib) would have stood that day at Nob.* According to the Talmud's interpretation of *Isaiah* 10:32 (*Sanhedrin*

94b), Sennacherib, king of Assyria, rushed his army to Nob, in the environs of Jerusalem, in one day.

פַּס יַד כָּתְבָה — *A hand inscribed.* This line and the next refer to the episode of the "handwriting on the wall" at Belshazzar's feast, described in *Daniel* 5 and alluded to prophetically in *Isaiah* 21:5. Babylonia is called *Zulah* in *Isaiah* 44:27, according to the Talmud (*Sanhedrin* 93a).

קָהָל כִּנְּסָה הֲדַסָּה צוֹם לְשַׁלֵּשׁ   בַּפֶּסַח.

רֹאשׁ מִבֵּית רָשָׁע מָחַצְתָּ בְּעֵץ חֲמִשִּׁים   בַּפֶּסַח.

שְׁתֵּי אֵלֶּה רֶגַע תָּבִיא לְעוּצִית   בַּפֶּסַח.

תָּעֹז יָדְךָ וְתָרוּם יְמִינְךָ כְּלֵיל הִתְקַדֶּשׁ חַג   פֶּסַח.

וַאֲמַרְתֶּם זֶבַח פֶּסַח.

On both nights continue here:

כִּי לוֹ נָאֶה, כִּי לוֹ יָאֶה:

אַדִּיר בִּמְלוּכָה, בָּחוּר כַּהֲלָכָה, גְּדוּדָיו יֹאמְרוּ לוֹ, לְךָ וּלְךָ, לְךָ כִּי לְךָ, לְךָ אַף לְךָ, לְךָ יהוה הַמַּמְלָכָה, כִּי לוֹ נָאֶה, כִּי לוֹ יָאֶה.

קָהָל כִּנְּסָה הֲדַסָּה — *Hadassah gathered a congregation.* Esther (Hadassah) called a three-day fast, beginning with the day before Pesach, to pray for her success in begging King Ahasuerus to annul Haman's genocidal decree (*Esther* 3:12-4:16).[1] The day after the fast Haman was hanged on a fifty-cubit gallows (*Esther*, Chaps. 5,7).

שְׁתֵּי אֵלֶּה רֶגַע תָּבִיא — *Bring double misfortune . . . in an instant.* This is a quote from *Isaiah* 47:9, and refers to the double misfortune of widowhood and being bereft of children. *Utzis* refers to Edom (as in *Lamentations* 4:21). In this line and the following one, the poet offers his plea to God to end our present state of exile and demonstrate His glory to all mankind with the dawn of the Messianic Age, which, the Sages tell us, will take place in Nissan, the month of Pesach.

כִּי לוֹ נָאֶה — *To Him [praise] is fitting.* The author of

this poem is not known, although *Iyun Tefillah* conjectures that it may have been R' Elazar HaKalir. In any case, it was added to the Haggadah as long as 700 years ago, in the time of *Maharam of Rothenburg*.

The song's refrain is based on three verses: לְךָ וּלְךָ, meaning *To You, and to You*, comes from the verse, "*To You* belongs praise, O God, in Zion, *and to You* a vow should be paid" (*Psalms* 65:2). לְךָ כִּי לְךָ, meaning *To You, for to You*, alludes to the verse, "*To You*, HASHEM, belong greatness, might, glory, victory and majesty, *for* all that is in the heaven and in the earth belong *to You*" (I Chronicles 29:11). Finally, לְךָ אַף לְךָ, meaning *To you, also to You*, refers to the verse, "*To You* belongs the day, and, *also, to you* belongs the night" (*Psalms* 74:16). The last phrase of the refrain, לְךָ ה' הַמַּמְלָכָה, *To you, HASHEM, is the sovereignty*, is the conclusion of the verse in *Chronicles*.[2]

---

1. **Purim on Pesach.** According to *Magen Avraham*, it is customary for this reason to make some type of commemoration of the Purim miracle on the second day of Pesach (see *Magen Avraham* to O.C. 490).

2. **Crystal Connection.** One of God's greatest gifts to man is the ability to crown Him King of the universe. We do not speak here of God having מְלוּכָה, *sovereignty*, but rather of מַמְלָכָה, the power to *make kings*. We praise God and express our realization that everything we have, even our ability to declare Him King, is His. In His kindness He grants us this power (*Kozhnitzer Maggid*).

Sfas Emes elaborates. לְךָ, even that which we do *for You*, dear God, אַף לְךָ is *also Yours*. Our ability to praise You and perform Your commandments is Yours, a gift You granted us.

Hadassah [Esther] gathered a congregation for
  a three-day fast on   Pesach.
The head of the evil house [Haman] You killed
  on a fifty-cubit pole on   Pesach.
Bring double misfortune [bereavement and widowhood]
  to Utzis [Edom] in an instant on   Pesach.
Strengthen Your hand,
  raise Your right hand as on the night
        that the festival of Pesach was sanctified.
And you will say: This is the feast of Pesach.

On both nights continue here:

To Him it is fitting. To Him it is due.

Powerful in Kingship, chosen by right, His legions say to Him:
  To You, and to You; to You, for to You; to You, also to You; to
  You, HASHEM, is the sovereignty. To Him it is fitting. To Him it is
  due.

Because the miraculous events of the Exodus were a clear indication of God's limitless sovereignty and His ability to crush all opponents, we sing tonight of how powerful His Kingship is and how fitting it is to praise Him (*Abarbanel, Yaavetz*).

According to *Iyun Tefillah*, the stanzas alternate between describing the praises the angels offer to God and those sung by Israel. *Maaseh Nissim* comments that the alternating themes are God's appearance at the Exodus and the Sea of Reeds on the one hand, and His revelation at Mount Sinai on the other.

אַדִּיר בִּמְלוּכָה בָּחוּר כַּהֲלָכָה — *Powerful in Kingship, chosen by right.* According to *Maaseh Nissim*, this refers to God's posture at the Sea of Reeds, where the Sages say He appeared as a young

warrior, a בָּחוּר. Thus, God acted as a young warrior when He battled and defeated the Egyptians at the Sea.[1]

R' Yaakov Kantorowitz renders בָּחוּר as *chosen*. The Talmud teaches that God suspended Mount Sinai above the heads of the Jewish people and forced them to accept the Torah, God's royal edict. Thus He exhibited His power when He established Himself as the King (אַדִּיר בִּמְלוּכָה). Yet, in spite of this coercion, the Jewish people accepted God authentically and wholeheartedly. This is because, as *Rambam* (*Hilchos Gerushin* 2:21-22) explains, the intrinsic orientation of a Jew is to be a loyal servant of God. Man's Evil Inclination seeks to impede that inner, true will from emerging, so we must sometimes coerce the Evil Inclination to desist from dissuading the individual from being his true self. Thus, He is truly the *chosen God* of His people, just as they are His chosen people.

> 1. **Varied Approach.** This idea is mirrored in the Song of Glory: *Aged on judgment day and virile on the day of battle, like a man of war whose powers are many.* In judgment, God displays the balanced approach that comes with age, and in battle against His enemies and the enemies of His people, He assumes the virility of youth.

דָּגוּל בִּמְלוּכָה, הָדוּר כַּהֲלָכָה, וָתִיקָיו יֹאמְרוּ לוֹ,
לְךָ וּלְךָ, לְךָ כִּי לְךָ, לְךָ אַף לְךָ, לְךָ יהוה הַמַּמְלָכָה, כִּי לוֹ
נָאֶה, כִּי לוֹ יָאֶה.

זַכַּאי בִּמְלוּכָה, חָסִין כַּהֲלָכָה, טַפְסְרָיו יֹאמְרוּ לוֹ,
לְךָ וּלְךָ, לְךָ כִּי לְךָ, לְךָ אַף לְךָ, לְךָ יהוה הַמַּמְלָכָה, כִּי לוֹ
נָאֶה, כִּי לוֹ יָאֶה.

יָחִיד בִּמְלוּכָה, כַּבִּיר כַּהֲלָכָה, לִמּוּדָיו יֹאמְרוּ לוֹ,
לְךָ וּלְךָ, לְךָ כִּי לְךָ, לְךָ אַף לְךָ, לְךָ יהוה הַמַּמְלָכָה, כִּי לוֹ
נָאֶה, כִּי לוֹ יָאֶה.

מוֹשֵׁל בִּמְלוּכָה, נוֹרָא כַּהֲלָכָה, סְבִיבָיו יֹאמְרוּ לוֹ,
לְךָ וּלְךָ, לְךָ כִּי לְךָ, לְךָ אַף לְךָ, לְךָ יהוה הַמַּמְלָכָה, כִּי לוֹ
נָאֶה, כִּי לוֹ יָאֶה.

עָנָו בִּמְלוּכָה, פּוֹדֶה כַּהֲלָכָה, צַדִּיקָיו יֹאמְרוּ לוֹ,

---

עָנָו בִּמְלוּכָה – *Humble in Kingship.* A mortal king may not exhibit excessive humility, because he must command respect from the nation. As the Talmud teaches, he may not forgo the honor due his office (*Kiddushin* 32a). God, however, the King over all others, has such complete, absolute kingship that He may act with humility. Even in Kingship He is Humble (see *Maharsha* to *Kiddushin* 32a).

פּוֹדֶה כַּהֲלָכָה – *Redeeming by right. Imrei Emes* renders homiletically, *He redeems legitimately.* God granted the Jews in Egypt the commandments of circumcision and the *pesach* offering, so that He could have legitimate cause to redeem them. The final redemption will also be justified by our actions and the great spiritual awakening that will accompany it. In the words of *Isaiah* (7:27), *Zion shall be redeemed with justice.* Hence, God *redeems legitimately.* Alternatively, His redemption of us after only 210 years instead of the promised 400 years of servitude was justified ("legitimate"), for the intensity of the slavery compensated for the decreased sentence time (*Seder HeAruch*).

רַחוּם כַּהֲלָכָה – *Merciful of right.* The Torah (*Deuteronomy* 22:1-4) commands that if someone comes across a lost item, he may not ignore it; he must pick it up and make the effort to return it to its owner. However, if the finder is a distinguished person who would not even retrieve his own item in similar circumstances (because it would be degrading for him), he is permitted to ignore his friend's lost object as well. Thus, in the liturgical poem *Yedid Nefesh,* when we ask God to have pity on us and redeem us, we say וְחוּסָה נָא וְאַל תִּתְעַלָּם, *Have pity and do not ignore us.* Even if we have gone so far astray that it is, as it were, beneath God's dignity to be involved in our plight, we still ask Him to have pity and return us to Himself, even if we are undeserving. Therefore we address God as the One Who is legitimately merciful, Who follows the dictates of His own Torah not to ignore a lost object (*R' Yechezkel of Kuzmir*).[1]

Distinguished in Kingship, glorious of right. His faithful say to Him: To You, and to You; to You, for to You; to You, also to You; to You, HASHEM, is the sovereignty. To Him it is fitting. To Him it is due.

Pure in Kingship, firm of right. His courtiers say to Him: To You, and to You; to You, for to You; to You, also to You; to You, HASHEM, is the sovereignty. To Him it is fitting. To Him it is due.

Unique in Kingship, mighty of right. His disciples say to Him: To You, and to You; to You, for to You; to You, also to You; to You, HASHEM, is the sovereignty. To Him it is fitting. To Him it is due.

Ruling in Kingship, feared of right. Those who surround Him say to Him: To You, and to You; to You, for to You; to You, also to You; to You, HASHEM, is the sovereignty. To Him it is fitting. To Him it is due.

Humble in Kingship, redeeming by right. His righteous ones say

1. **Relatively Humble.** *Yad Yechezkel* elaborates on this theme, based on a famous incident involving R' Akiva Eiger, the great *gaon* of Posen, who traveled to Warsaw to attend a rabbinic function. While there, he said that he wished to visit a cousin of his, a poor shoemaker who lived in a suburban village. A crowd followed close behind. When he arrived, his cousin greeted him warmly and offered him the only chair in his shop — his own.

The great *gaon* spent some time with his cousin and then began his trip back to Warsaw. En route, one of the people accompanying Rabbi Eiger asked, "Why did you go to the trouble of traveling to see your cousin? Surely he could have come to greet you as so many others did. Besides, it does not befit a man of your stature to make such a trip."

The rabbi replied, "In commanding Jews to return a lost item, the Torah says: *You may not ignore it* (Deuteronomy 22:3; see also ibid. 22:1). The Talmud (*Bava Metzia* 30a) teaches that there is a time, however, when a Talmudic scholar may ignore a lost item — if it would be humiliating for him to be seen carrying such an item. A *talmid chacham* need not suffer embarrassment to fulfill the *mitzvah* of returning a lost item.

"Interestingly, similar wording is used by the prophet Isaiah (58:7) when he exhorts, וּמִבְּשָׂרְךָ לֹא תִתְעַלָּם, *And do not ignore your flesh (relatives)* (see *Rashi*). But here the Talmud does not make the exception for a case where it might be embarrassing; only in regard to a lost item does the Torah allow a Talmudic scholar to look away. No one may ignore a relative — even if it is humiliating. That's why I had no hesitation in going to visit my cousin."

As children of God, we implore God to have pity on us and not ignore our plight. Even though it might be below His dignity to return us to our place, we implore Him to do so since we are His children. Thus He is "legitimately merciful."

Sifsei Tzaddik explains the phrase based on the Talmudic dictum (*Berachos* 33a) that one may not have mercy on a fool. However, taught *Chidushei HaRim*, one should *pray* on his behalf that God grant him intelligence. Likewise, even when we act foolishly and sin, God does not simply have mercy. Instead, He grants us the intelligence and enlightenment to repent from our foolishness. Thus, He is רַחוּם כַּהֲלָכָה, *legitimately merciful.*

לְךָ וּלְךָ, לְךָ כִּי לְךָ, לְךָ אַף לְךָ, לְךָ יהוה הַמַּמְלָכָה, כִּי לוֹ נָאֶה, כִּי לוֹ יָאֶה.

קָדוֹשׁ בִּמְלוּכָה, **רַ**חוּם כַּהֲלָכָה, **שִׁ**נְאַנָּיו יֹאמְרוּ לוֹ, לְךָ וּלְךָ, לְךָ כִּי לְךָ, לְךָ אַף לְךָ, לְךָ יהוה הַמַּמְלָכָה, כִּי לוֹ נָאֶה, כִּי לוֹ יָאֶה.

תַּקִּיף בִּמְלוּכָה, **תּוֹ**מֵךְ כַּהֲלָכָה, **תְּ**מִימָיו יֹאמְרוּ לוֹ, לְךָ וּלְךָ, לְךָ כִּי לְךָ, לְךָ אַף לְךָ, לְךָ יהוה הַמַּמְלָכָה, כִּי לוֹ נָאֶה, כִּי לוֹ יָאֶה.

אַדִּיר הוּא יִבְנֶה בֵיתוֹ בְּקָרוֹב, בִּמְהֵרָה, בִּמְהֵרָה, בְּיָמֵינוּ בְּקָרוֹב. אֵל בְּנֵה, אֵל בְּנֵה, בְּנֵה בֵיתְךָ בְּקָרוֹב.

בָּחוּר הוּא. **גָּ**דוֹל הוּא. **דָּ**גוּל הוּא. יִבְנֶה בֵיתוֹ בְּקָרוֹב, בִּמְהֵרָה, בִּמְהֵרָה, בְּיָמֵינוּ בְּקָרוֹב. אֵל בְּנֵה, אֵל בְּנֵה, בְּנֵה בֵיתְךָ בְּקָרוֹב.

הָדוּר הוּא. **וָ**תִיק הוּא. **זַ**כַּאי הוּא. **חָ**סִיד הוּא. יִבְנֶה בֵיתוֹ בְּקָרוֹב, בִּמְהֵרָה, בִּמְהֵרָה, בְּיָמֵינוּ בְּקָרוֹב. אֵל בְּנֵה, אֵל בְּנֵה, בְּנֵה בֵיתְךָ בְּקָרוֹב.

טָהוֹר הוּא. **יָ**חִיד הוּא. **כַּ**בִּיר הוּא. **לָ**מוּד הוּא. **מֶ**לֶךְ הוּא. **נוֹ**רָא הוּא. **סַ**גִּיב הוּא. **עִ**זּוּז הוּא. **פּוֹ**דֶה הוּא. **צַ**דִּיק הוּא.

אַדִּיר הוּא — *Mighty is He.* This poem and the following two were composed in Germany approximately five centuries ago.

אַדִּיר הוּא expresses our passionate yearning for the rebuilding of the Holy Temple, and it presents the encouraging message that even if we are unde-serving, God will redeem us in His great mercy and kindness. We pour out our heartfelt wishes and sincere longing for the Messiah with the hope that our yearnings will speed his coming and the rebuilding of the Temple. At the Seder, we relive the Exodus, and we also prepare for the future deliverance.[1]

---

1. **Heavenly Speed.** Even though human beings may not build the Temple on the Sabbath, on *Yom Tov*, or at night, the future Temple may be built at such times, since God Himself will bring it down from Heaven (see *Rashi* to *Rosh Hashanah* 30a, s.v. לא צריכא). Thus, on this night of Pesach we ask God to rebuild the Temple *speedily and soon* (*Tosafos Binyamin*, R' *Yissachar Dov of Belz*).

to Him: To You, and to You; to You, for to You; to You, also to You; to You, HASHEM, is the sovereignty. To Him it is fitting. To Him it is due.

Holy in Kingship, merciful of right. His angels say to Him: To You, and to You; to You, for to You; to You, also to You; to You, HASHEM, is the sovereignty. To Him it is fitting. To Him it is due.

Powerful in Kingship, sustaining of right. His perfect ones say to Him: To You, and to You; to You, for to You; to You, also to You; to You, HASHEM, is the sovereignty. To Him it is fitting. To Him it is due.

Mighty is He. May He build His house soon; quickly, quickly, in our lifetimes, soon. God, build; God, build; build Your house soon.

Exalted is He, great is He, distinguished is He. May He build His house soon; quickly, quickly, in our lifetimes, soon. God, build; God, build; build Your house soon.

Glorious is He, faithful is He, guiltless is He, righteous is He. May He build His house soon; quickly, quickly, in our lifetimes, soon. God, build; God, build; build Your house soon.

Pure is He, unique is He, powerful is He, all-wise is He, the King is He, awesome is He, sublime is He, all-powerful is He, the Redeemer is He, all-righteous is He. May He

---

חָסִיד הוּא — *Righteous is He.* [1]

לָמוּד הוּא — *All-wise is He. Sfas Emes* renders homiletically *He can be learned,* i.e., He can become known and understood, to a degree. God, Whose essence is unfathomable, took a diminished form of His light and gave it tangible form in the Torah, so that we might in some

limited fashion be able to learn something of His essence.

פּוֹדֶה הוּא — *The Redeemer is He.* God provides us with many ways to redeem ourselves. We sometimes suffer difficulties without realizing that God is giving us a way to atone for our sins and be spiritually redeemed (*R' Tzadok HaKohen*).

1. **True Chasid.** The *Kaddish* in the *Nusach Sefard* rite, which is followed by chassidic Jews, includes a plea that God send the Messiah: וְיַצְמַח פֻּרְקָנֵהּ וִיקָרֵב מְשִׁיחֵהּ, *May He cause His salvation to sprout and bring near His Messiah. R' Naftali Ropschitzer,* while yet a child, asked his father, "If God is a *Chassid* (חָסִיד הוּא), why doesn't He fulfill this part of the *Kaddish?*"

יִבְנֶה בֵיתוֹ בְּקָרוֹב, בִּמְהֵרָה, בִּמְהֵרָה, בְּיָמֵינוּ בְּקָרוֹב. אֵל בְּנֵה, אֵל בְּנֵה, בְּנֵה בֵיתְךָ בְּקָרוֹב.

קָדוֹשׁ הוּא. רַחוּם הוּא. שַׁדַּי הוּא. תַּקִּיף הוּא. יִבְנֶה בֵיתוֹ בְּקָרוֹב, בִּמְהֵרָה, בִּמְהֵרָה, בְּיָמֵינוּ בְּקָרוֹב. אֵל בְּנֵה, אֵל בְּנֵה, בְּנֵה בֵיתְךָ בְּקָרוֹב.

Those who do not count the *Omer* at this point, turn to p. 246.

ספירת העומר

The *Omer* is counted from the second night of Pesach until the night before Shavuos. While most communities begin to count the *Omer* at *Maariv*, some have the custom to begin counting at the Seder. Many recite the following Kabbalistic prayer before the counting of the *Omer*.

לְשֵׁם יִחוּד קוּדְשָׁא בְּרִיךְ הוּא וּשְׁכִינְתֵּיהּ, בִּדְחִילוּ וּרְחִימוּ לְיַחֵד שֵׁם יוּ"ד הֵ"א בְּוָא"ו הֵ"א בְּיִחוּדָא שְׁלִים, בְּשֵׁם כָּל יִשְׂרָאֵל. הִנְנִי מוּכָן וּמְזוּמָּן לְקַיֵּם מִצְוַת עֲשֵׂה שֶׁל סְפִירַת הָעוֹמֶר, כְּמוֹ שֶׁכָּתוּב בַּתּוֹרָה: וּסְפַרְתֶּם לָכֶם מִמָּחֳרַת הַשַּׁבָּת, מִיּוֹם הֲבִיאֲכֶם אֶת עֹמֶר הַתְּנוּפָה, שֶׁבַע שַׁבָּתוֹת תְּמִימֹת תִּהְיֶינָה. עַד מִמָּחֳרַת הַשַּׁבָּת הַשְּׁבִיעִת תִּסְפְּרוּ חֲמִשִּׁים יוֹם, וְהִקְרַבְתֶּם מִנְחָה חֲדָשָׁה לַיהוה.¹ וִיהִי נֹעַם אֲדֹנָי אֱלֹהֵינוּ עָלֵינוּ, וּמַעֲשֵׂה יָדֵינוּ כּוֹנְנָה עָלֵינוּ, וּמַעֲשֵׂה יָדֵינוּ כּוֹנְנֵהוּ.²

שַׁדַּי הוּא – *Almighty is He.* The name שַׁדַּי is explained in the Talmud (*Chagigah* 12a) as an acronym for שֶׁאָמַר לְעוֹלָמוֹ דַּי, *Who said to His world, "It is enough!"* At Creation, as the universe took shape and grew, the Infinite Creator said to His world, "Enough," thus giving it finite form. We thus implore God that just as He told His world, "Enough," so may He put an end to the troubles and travails of exile (see *Zohar* 3:251b; *Rashi, Genesis* 43:14).

סְפִירַת הָעֹמֶר — *Counting the Omer.* In the days of the Temple, an offering called the *Omer* (a meal offering made of barley flour)[1] was brought

1. **Torah Humanizes.** The *Omer*, offered on Pesach, was of barley flour, while the offering of the Two Loaves brought on Shavuos was of wheat flour. By the time the Jews left Egypt, they were so spiritually contaminated by the forty-nine degrees of Egyptian impurity that the animalistic tendencies in them were substantial, and even dominant. On Pesach, therefore, we symbolically offer barley, an animal food. Day by day throughout the forty-nine-day *Sefirah* period, the Jews gradually shed this impurity and replaced it with new levels of sanctity, so that by Shavuos their souls had become fully human again. Thus, on that day they offered an offering made of wheat, the basic human staple. It is only with Torah that man can truly reach the optimum level of a human being.

build His house soon; quickly, quickly, in our lifetimes, soon. God, build; God, build; build Your house soon.

Holy is He, compassionate is He, Almighty is He, Omnipotent is He. May He build His house soon; quickly, quickly, in our lifetimes, soon. God, build; God, build; build Your house soon.

Those who do not count the *Omer* at this point, turn to p. 246

COUNTING THE OMER

The *Omer* is counted from the second night of Pesach until the night before Shavuos. While most communities begin to count the *Omer* at *Maariv*, some have the custom to begin counting at the Seder.

Many recite the following Kabbalistic prayer before the counting of the *Omer*.

For the sake of the unification of the Holy One, Blessed is He, and His Presence, in fear and love to unify the Name Yud-Kei with Vav-Kei in perfect unity, in the name of all Israel. Behold I am prepared and ready to perform the commandment of counting the Omer, as it is written in the Torah: "You are to count for yourselves from the morrow of the rest day, from the day you brought the Omer-offering that is waved — they are to be seven complete weeks — until the morrow of the seventh week you are to count fifty days, and then offer a new meal-offering to HASHEM."[1] May the pleasantness of my Lord, our God, be upon us — may He establish our handiwork for us; our handiwork, may He establish.[2]

(1) *Leviticus* 23:15-16. (2) *Psalms* 90:17.

on the second day of Pesach. After this offering, forty-nine days were counted (called "counting the *Omer*"),[1] leading up to the festival of Shavuos.

Nowadays, when there is no Temple and the *Omer* offering cannot be brought, most authorities take the view that the counting of the *Omer* is a

1. **We Can't Wait.** *Sefer HaChinuch* (30b) writes: The intrinsic character of the Jewish people is inextricably linked to the Torah. God redeemed us from the slavery and spiritual impurity of Egypt only so that we could be prepared to receive the Torah on Mount Sinai. For this reason we were commanded to count the days from our Exodus until we received the Torah, in order to exhibit our great eagerness for that special day to arrive. Like a slave who anxiously awaits the day when he will finally be granted his freedom, we count every day, passionately awaiting the spiritual freedom that results from accepting the Torah.

The *Baal HaTanya* offers a different perspective. One who finds a large treasure trove first grabs all that he can. Only later, when he has time to count his take, does he realized what he has gained. Likewise, the spiritual treasure granted us along with our freedom must be counted before it can be fully appreciated. Throughout the days of the *Sefirah*, we take stock of the spiritual potential God granted us at the Exodus.

בָּרוּךְ אַתָּה יהוה אֱלֹהֵינוּ מֶלֶךְ הָעוֹלָם, אֲשֶׁר קִדְּשָׁנוּ בְּמִצְוֹתָיו וְצִוָּנוּ עַל סְפִירַת הָעֹמֶר.

הַיּוֹם יוֹם אֶחָד לָעֹמֶר.

הָרַחֲמָן הוּא יַחֲזִיר לָנוּ עֲבוֹדַת בֵּית הַמִּקְדָּשׁ לִמְקוֹמָהּ, בִּמְהֵרָה בְיָמֵינוּ. אָמֵן סֶלָה.

לַמְנַצֵּחַ בִּנְגִינֹת מִזְמוֹר שִׁיר. אֱלֹהִים יְחָנֵּנוּ וִיבָרְכֵנוּ, יָאֵר פָּנָיו אִתָּנוּ סֶלָה. לָדַעַת בָּאָרֶץ דַּרְכֶּךָ, בְּכָל גּוֹיִם יְשׁוּעָתֶךָ. יוֹדוּךָ עַמִּים אֱלֹהִים, יוֹדוּךָ עַמִּים כֻּלָּם. יִשְׂמְחוּ וִירַנְּנוּ לְאֻמִּים, כִּי תִשְׁפֹּט עַמִּים מִישֹׁר, וּלְאֻמִּים בָּאָרֶץ תַּנְחֵם סֶלָה. יוֹדוּךָ עַמִּים אֱלֹהִים, יוֹדוּךָ עַמִּים כֻּלָּם. אֶרֶץ נָתְנָה יְבוּלָהּ, יְבָרְכֵנוּ אֱלֹהִים אֱלֹהֵינוּ. יְבָרְכֵנוּ אֱלֹהִים, וְיִירְאוּ אוֹתוֹ כָּל אַפְסֵי אָרֶץ.[1]

אב״ג ית״ץ	אָנָּא בְּכֹחַ גְּדֻלַּת יְמִינְךָ תַּתִּיר צְרוּרָה.
קר״ע שט״ן	קַבֵּל רִנַּת עַמְּךָ שַׂגְּבֵנוּ טַהֲרֵנוּ נוֹרָא.
נג״ד יכ״ש	נָא גִבּוֹר דּוֹרְשֵׁי יִחוּדְךָ כְּבָבַת שָׁמְרֵם.
בט״ר צת״ג	בָּרְכֵם טַהֲרֵם רַחֲמֵם צִדְקָתְךָ תָּמִיד גָּמְלֵם.
חק״ב טנ״ע	חֲסִין קָדוֹשׁ בְּרוֹב טוּבְךָ נַהֵל עֲדָתֶךָ.

Rabbinic duty only.[1]

Generally, the *Omer* is counted at the conclusion of *Maariv*, the evening prayer, as soon as possible after nightfall. It is particularly important to fulfill this *mitzvah* before sitting down to a meal, to avoid the possibility of forgetting to do so afterwards. *Yaavetz* held that this should be the practice on the Seder evening as well. Others, however, point out

1. **Recuperative Rest.** On Pesach the nation of Israel underwent radical ''surgery'' to remove the spiritually ''cancerous growth'' of Egyptian culture and values that had invaded its system. Over the course of the *Sefirah* period, God slowly healed them of the remaining vestiges of the cancer, so that by the time Shavuos arrived they enjoyed the spiritual health necessary to receive the Torah. Every year this process repeats itself. On Pesach, as we eat the matzah, the food of spiritual health, God begins the process of curing us of the spiritually wasted ''tissue'' within our personalities. The seven weeks that follow serve as a recuperative period when we are slowly nursed back to spiritual health (*Zichron Kodesh*).

Blessed are You, HASHEM, our God, King of the universe, Who has sanctified us with His commandments and has commanded us regarding the counting of the Omer.

Today is one day of the Omer.

The Compassionate One! May He return for us the service of the Temple to its place, speedily, in our days. Amen, selah!

For the Conductor, upon Neginos, a psalm, a song. May God favor us and bless us, may He illuminate His countenance with us, Selah. To make known Your way on earth, among all the nations Your salvation. The peoples will acknowledge You, O God, the peoples will acknowledge You, all of them. Nations will be glad and sing for joy, because You will judge the people fairly and guide the nations on earth, Selah. The peoples will acknowledge You, O God, the peoples will acknowledge You, all of them. The earth has yielded its produce, may God, our own God, bless us. May God bless us and may all the ends of the earth fear him.[1]

We beg You! With the strength of Your right hand's greatness, untie the bundled sins. Accept the prayer of Your nation; strengthen us, purify us, O Awesome One. Please, O Strong One — those who foster Your Oneness, guard them like the apple of an eye. Bless them, purify them, show them pity, may Your righteousness always recompense them. Powerful Holy One, with Your abundant goodness guide Your congregation.

(1) *Psalms* 67.

the incongruity of counting the *Omer* — which is a clear recognition of the fact that tonight is the second day of Pesach (and thus the beginning of *Chol HaMoed*) — and then celebrating a Seder, which marks the first night of Pesach (*Birkei Yosef*). They hold that on this night the *Omer* should be counted after the Seder.[1]

1. **Shining Our Souls.** The Torah describes the commandment as, *You shall count for yourselves from the morrow of the rest day* (*Leviticus* 23:15), i.e. from the second day of Pesach. *Beis Avraham* homiletically links וּסְפַרְתֶּם, *you shall count,* to סַפִּיר, *a sapphire,* i.e., *you shall make a sapphire.* After God freed us from the spiritually dark dungeon of Egypt, it is incumbent upon us to add brilliance to our newly freed souls. From the morrow of the first day of freedom, we must exert ourselves to enlighten our souls through our own efforts, to reinforce and retain the spiritual illumination God gave us through the Exodus.

יָחִיד גֵּאֶה לְעַמְּךָ פְּנֵה זוֹכְרֵי קְדֻשָּׁתֶךָ. יג״ל פז״ק

שַׁוְעָתֵנוּ קַבֵּל וּשְׁמַע צַעֲקָתֵנוּ יוֹדֵעַ תַּעֲלֻמוֹת. שק״ו צי״ת

בָּרוּךְ שֵׁם כְּבוֹד מַלְכוּתוֹ לְעוֹלָם וָעֶד.

רִבּוֹנוֹ שֶׁל עוֹלָם, אַתָּה צִוִּיתָנוּ עַל יְדֵי מֹשֶׁה עַבְדֶּךָ לִסְפּוֹר סְפִירַת הָעֹמֶר, כְּדֵי לְטַהֲרֵנוּ מִקְּלִפּוֹתֵינוּ וּמִטֻּמְאוֹתֵינוּ, כְּמוֹ שֶׁכָּתַבְתָּ בְּתוֹרָתֶךָ: וּסְפַרְתֶּם לָכֶם מִמָּחֳרַת הַשַּׁבָּת מִיּוֹם הֲבִיאֲכֶם אֶת עֹמֶר הַתְּנוּפָה, שֶׁבַע שַׁבָּתוֹת תְּמִימֹת תִּהְיֶינָה. עַד מִמָּחֳרַת הַשַּׁבָּת הַשְּׁבִיעִית תִּסְפְּרוּ חֲמִשִּׁים יוֹם.[1] כְּדֵי שֶׁיִּטַּהֲרוּ נַפְשׁוֹת עַמְּךָ יִשְׂרָאֵל מִזֻּהֲמָתָם. וּבְכֵן יְהִי רָצוֹן מִלְּפָנֶיךָ יהוה אֱלֹהֵינוּ וֵאלֹהֵי אֲבוֹתֵינוּ, שֶׁבִּזְכוּת סְפִירַת הָעֹמֶר שֶׁסָּפַרְתִּי הַיּוֹם, יְתֻקַּן מַה שֶּׁפָּגַמְתִּי בִּסְפִירָה חֶסֶד שֶׁבְּחֶסֶד. וְאֶטָּהֵר וְאֶתְקַדֵּשׁ בִּקְדֻשָּׁה שֶׁל מַעְלָה, וְעַל יְדֵי זֶה יֻשְׁפַּע שֶׁפַע רַב בְּכָל הָעוֹלָמוֹת. וּלְתַקֵּן אֶת נַפְשׁוֹתֵינוּ, וְרוּחוֹתֵינוּ, וְנִשְׁמוֹתֵינוּ, מִכָּל סִיג וּפְגַם, וּלְטַהֲרֵנוּ וּלְקַדְּשֵׁנוּ בִּקְדֻשָּׁתְךָ הָעֶלְיוֹנָה. אָמֵן סֶלָה.

אֶחָד מִי יוֹדֵעַ? אֶחָד אֲנִי יוֹדֵעַ. אֶחָד אֱלֹהֵינוּ שֶׁבַּשָּׁמַיִם וּבָאָרֶץ.

שְׁנַיִם מִי יוֹדֵעַ? שְׁנַיִם אֲנִי יוֹדֵעַ. שְׁנֵי לֻחוֹת הַבְּרִית, אֶחָד אֱלֹהֵינוּ שֶׁבַּשָּׁמַיִם וּבָאָרֶץ.

אֶחָד מִי יוֹדֵעַ — *Who knows one?*[1] Ostensibly, the song has no direct connection to either the

Egyptian Exodus or to the future Redemption. *Ateres Yehoshua*, however, views its contents as

---

1. **Humble Knowledge.** Humility is the key to real knowledge; one who earnestly believes that he knows little has the most potential to know much. According to *Toldos Adam* this is homiletically reflected in the question-and-answer format of this song. Because one humbly says, "מִי יוֹדֵעַ, *Who knows?*" he may legitimately say, "אֲנִי יוֹדֵעַ, *I know.*"

One and only Exalted One, turn to Your nation, which proclaims Your holiness. Accept our entreaty and hear our cry, O Knower of mysteries. Blessed is the Name of His glorious Kingdom for all eternity.

Master of the universe, You commanded us through Moses, Your servant, to count the Omer Count in order to cleanse us from our encrustations of evil and from our contaminations, as You have written in Your Torah: You are to count for yourselves from the morrow of the rest day, from the day you brought the Omer-offering that is waved — they are to be seven complete weeks — until the morrow of the seventh week you are to count fifty days,[1] so that the souls of Your people Israel be cleansed from their contamination. Therefore, may it be Your will, HASHEM, our God and the God of our forefathers, that in the merit of the Omer Count that I have counted today, may there be corrected whatever blemish I have caused in the *sefirah chesed shebechesed*. May I be cleansed and sanctified with the holiness of Above, and through this may abundant bounty flow in all the worlds. And may it correct our lives, spirits, and souls from all sediment and blemish; may it cleanse us and sanctify us with Your exalted holiness. Amen, Selah!

Who knows one? I know one.
One is our God in the heavens and the earth.
Who knows two? I know two. Two are the Tablets of the Covenant. One is our God in the heavens and the earth.

---

(1) *Leviticus* 23:15-16.

---

sources of merit that helped the redemption become a reality. The belief in One God that Jews increasingly demonstrated throughout the different stages of the Exodus was the primary force that brought about their freedom. Furthermore, their acceptance at Sinai of the *two Tablets* containing the fundamental principles of the Torah gave meaning to their liberty. As Moses was told at the burning bush at Mount Sinai, *When you take the people out of Egypt, you will serve God on this mountain* (*Exodus* 3:12). Although at the time of the Exodus they had little personal merit, God honored His covenant with the three *Patriarchs* and remembered the merit of the four *Matriarchs*. Having found them to be the appropriate bearers of His message in the world, God granted them the Written Torah, the *Five Books of the Torah*, and the Oral law as encapsulated in the *Six Orders of the*

שְׁלֹשָׁה מִי יוֹדֵעַ? שְׁלֹשָׁה אֲנִי יוֹדֵעַ. שְׁלֹשָׁה אָבוֹת, שְׁנֵי לֻחוֹת הַבְּרִית, אֶחָד אֱלֹהֵינוּ שֶׁבַּשָּׁמַיִם וּבָאָרֶץ.

אַרְבַּע מִי יוֹדֵעַ? אַרְבַּע אֲנִי יוֹדֵעַ. אַרְבַּע אִמָּהוֹת, שְׁלֹשָׁה אָבוֹת, שְׁנֵי לֻחוֹת הַבְּרִית, אֶחָד אֱלֹהֵינוּ שֶׁבַּשָּׁמַיִם וּבָאָרֶץ.

חֲמִשָּׁה מִי יוֹדֵעַ? חֲמִשָּׁה אֲנִי יוֹדֵעַ. חֲמִשָּׁה חֻמְשֵׁי תוֹרָה, אַרְבַּע אִמָּהוֹת, שְׁלֹשָׁה אָבוֹת, שְׁנֵי לֻחוֹת הַבְּרִית, אֶחָד אֱלֹהֵינוּ שֶׁבַּשָּׁמַיִם וּבָאָרֶץ.

שִׁשָּׁה מִי יוֹדֵעַ? שִׁשָּׁה אֲנִי יוֹדֵעַ. שִׁשָּׁה סִדְרֵי מִשְׁנָה, חֲמִשָּׁה חֻמְשֵׁי תוֹרָה, אַרְבַּע אִמָּהוֹת, שְׁלֹשָׁה אָבוֹת, שְׁנֵי לֻחוֹת הַבְּרִית, אֶחָד אֱלֹהֵינוּ שֶׁבַּשָּׁמַיִם וּבָאָרֶץ.

שִׁבְעָה מִי יוֹדֵעַ? שִׁבְעָה אֲנִי יוֹדֵעַ. שִׁבְעָה יְמֵי שַׁבַּתָּא, שִׁשָּׁה סִדְרֵי מִשְׁנָה, חֲמִשָּׁה חֻמְשֵׁי תוֹרָה, אַרְבַּע אִמָּהוֹת, שְׁלֹשָׁה אָבוֹת, שְׁנֵי לֻחוֹת הַבְּרִית, אֶחָד אֱלֹהֵינוּ שֶׁבַּשָּׁמַיִם וּבָאָרֶץ.

שְׁמוֹנָה מִי יוֹדֵעַ? שְׁמוֹנָה אֲנִי יוֹדֵעַ. שְׁמוֹנָה יְמֵי

Mishnah. Their tenacious loyalty to the *Holy Sabbath*, when they did not work for their Egyptian taskmasters, helped them retain a vestige of sanctity that allowed God to fully free them. Furthermore, the observance of Sabbath, when one ceases to perform creative work, is indicative of the internalization of the Exodus message — that we are servants of God and of no mortal man; be it Pharoah, our employers or even ourselves (see *Rashi* to *Deuteronomy* 5:15). *Circumcision*, the sign imprinted on man's body which reminds him who his Master is, was one of the two *mitzvos* God commanded us before the Exodus.

The *nine months of pregnancy* allude to the tenacity and faith of Jewish women in Egypt.

Faced with such horrible conditions and the threat of infanticide hanging over them, it would seem almost cruel to bring children into such a satanic world. And yet their firm faith in God's promises of redemption gave them the strength to bear the difficulties of pregnancy and bring a new generation of Jews into the world. It is not for naught that the Sages taught (*Sotah* 11b) that the Jews were redeemed in the merit of the righteous women of that generation. The *Ten Commandments*, the basic framework of all of Torah, form the essence of the Torah received at Sinai.

The *eleven stars* of Joseph's dream allude to the fact that eleven of the twelve tribes (excluding Levi) were subject to the temptations of the

Who knows three? I know three. Three are the Patriarchs. Two are the Tablets of the Covenant. One is our God in the heavens and the earth.

Who knows four? I know four. Four are the Matriarchs. Three are the Patriarchs. Two are the Tablets of the Covenant. One is our God in the heavens and the earth.

Who knows five? I know five. Five are the Books of the Torah. Four are the Matriarchs. Three are the Patriarchs. Two are the Tablets of the Covenant. One is our God in the heavens and the earth.

Who knows six? I know six. Six are the Orders of the *Mishnah.* Five are the Books of the Torah. Four are the Matriarchs. Three are the Patriarchs. Two are the Tablets of the Covenant. One is our God in the heavens and the earth.

Who knows seven? I know seven. Seven are the days of the week. Six are the Orders of the *Mishnah.* Five are the Books of the Torah. Four are the Matriarchs. Three are the Patriarchs. Two are the Tablets of the Covenant. One is our God in the heavens and the earth.

Who knows eight? I know eight. Eight are the days of

Egyptian melting pot; yet, like stars, they retained their distinctive names and modes of speech and dress. The *twelve tribes* fought off the cancer of assimilation on all fronts.[1]

In spite of all these merits, ultimately we will be redeemed due to God's overwhelming mercy, which finds expression in the *Thirteen Attributes of Mercy* enunciated in *Exodus* (34:6). The Talmud (*Rosh Hashanah* 17b) refers to them as the *Covenant of Thirteen*, for God promises that whenever we invoke them He will forgive our sins.

According to *R' Eliyahu Kitov*, this song serves

to focus us on the true goal of the Exodus. Having delineated the ten plagues in the three sets of דְּצַ"ךְ עֲדַ"ש בְּאַחַ"ב, we now make it clear that the main agenda of the Exodus was not vengeance against Egypt. Our main joy is that we became the beloved nation of the One God, Who granted us the Tablets of Law. Our happiness over being the loyal descendants of our Patriarchs and Matriarchs, who received the Torah and its commandments, far outweighs the thrill of seeing our enemies vanquished. Through this song we realize that the nation of Israel exists and thrives not as a result of

---

1. **Step by Step.** At each stage of the progression, we repeat all the steps from thirteen back until one. Wouldn't it be logical to start from thirteen and trace all the steps back?

The *Chidushei HaRim* concluded from this that spiritual growth must be achieved by slowly but steadily climbing the ladder. One runs great risk if he proceeds immediately to the highest rungs before conquering the lower levels, because it is dangerous to assume levels of observance that one is not capable of maintaining. Backsliding is much worse that gradual ascent.

מִילָה, שִׁבְעָה יְמֵי שַׁבַּתָּא, שִׁשָּׁה סִדְרֵי מִשְׁנָה, חֲמִשָּׁה חֻמְשֵׁי תוֹרָה, אַרְבַּע אִמָּהוֹת, שְׁלֹשָׁה אָבוֹת, שְׁנֵי לֻחוֹת הַבְּרִית, אֶחָד אֱלֹהֵינוּ שֶׁבַּשָּׁמַיִם וּבָאָרֶץ.

תִּשְׁעָה מִי יוֹדֵעַ? תִּשְׁעָה אֲנִי יוֹדֵעַ. תִּשְׁעָה יַרְחֵי לֵדָה, שְׁמוֹנָה יְמֵי מִילָה, שִׁבְעָה יְמֵי שַׁבַּתָּא, שִׁשָּׁה סִדְרֵי מִשְׁנָה, חֲמִשָּׁה חֻמְשֵׁי תוֹרָה, אַרְבַּע אִמָּהוֹת, שְׁלֹשָׁה אָבוֹת, שְׁנֵי לֻחוֹת הַבְּרִית, אֶחָד אֱלֹהֵינוּ שֶׁבַּשָּׁמַיִם וּבָאָרֶץ.

עֲשָׂרָה מִי יוֹדֵעַ? עֲשָׂרָה אֲנִי יוֹדֵעַ. עֲשָׂרָה דִבְּרַיָּא, תִּשְׁעָה יַרְחֵי לֵדָה, שְׁמוֹנָה יְמֵי מִילָה, שִׁבְעָה יְמֵי שַׁבַּתָּא, שִׁשָּׁה סִדְרֵי מִשְׁנָה, חֲמִשָּׁה חֻמְשֵׁי תוֹרָה, אַרְבַּע אִמָּהוֹת, שְׁלֹשָׁה אָבוֹת, שְׁנֵי לֻחוֹת הַבְּרִית, אֶחָד אֱלֹהֵינוּ שֶׁבַּשָּׁמַיִם וּבָאָרֶץ.

אַחַד עָשָׂר מִי יוֹדֵעַ? אַחַד עָשָׂר אֲנִי יוֹדֵעַ. אַחַד עָשָׂר כּוֹכְבַיָּא, עֲשָׂרָה דִבְּרַיָּא, תִּשְׁעָה יַרְחֵי לֵדָה, שְׁמוֹנָה יְמֵי מִילָה, שִׁבְעָה יְמֵי שַׁבַּתָּא, שִׁשָּׁה סִדְרֵי מִשְׁנָה, חֲמִשָּׁה חֻמְשֵׁי תוֹרָה, אַרְבַּע אִמָּהוֹת, שְׁלֹשָׁה אָבוֹת, שְׁנֵי לֻחוֹת הַבְּרִית, אֶחָד אֱלֹהֵינוּ שֶׁבַּשָּׁמַיִם וּבָאָרֶץ.

שְׁנֵים עָשָׂר מִי יוֹדֵעַ? שְׁנֵים עָשָׂר אֲנִי יוֹדֵעַ. שְׁנֵים עָשָׂר שִׁבְטַיָּא, אַחַד עָשָׂר כּוֹכְבַיָּא, עֲשָׂרָה דִבְּרַיָּא, תִּשְׁעָה יַרְחֵי לֵדָה, שְׁמוֹנָה יְמֵי מִילָה, שִׁבְעָה יְמֵי שַׁבַּתָּא, שִׁשָּׁה סִדְרֵי מִשְׁנָה, חֲמִשָּׁה חֻמְשֵׁי תוֹרָה, אַרְבַּע אִמָּהוֹת, שְׁלֹשָׁה אָבוֹת, שְׁנֵי לֻחוֹת הַבְּרִית, אֶחָד אֱלֹהֵינוּ שֶׁבַּשָּׁמַיִם וּבָאָרֶץ.

This song, with its refrain of faith in God and His Torah, celebrates the greatest dividend of the Exodus. In spite of our suffering in exile, we have

the plagues and punishments meted out to the Egyptians, but through the Torah and *mitzvos* of their loving Father.

circumcision. Seven are the days of the week. Six are the Orders of the *Mishnah.* Five are the Books of the Torah. Four are the Matriarchs. Three are the Patriarchs. Two are the Tablets of the Covenant. One is our God in the heavens and the earth.

Who knows nine? I know nine. Nine are the months of pregnancy. Eight are the days of circumcision. Seven are the days of the week. Six are the Orders of the *Mishnah.* Five are the Books of the Torah. Four are the Matriarchs. Three are the Patriarchs. Two are the Tablets of the Covenant. One is our God in the heavens and the earth.

Who knows ten? I know ten. Ten are the Commandments. Nine are the months of pregnancy. Eight are the days of circumcision. Seven are the days of the week. Six are the Orders of the *Mishnah.* Five are the Books of the Torah. Four are the Matriarchs. Three are the Patriarchs. Two are the Tablets of the Covenant. One is our God in the heavens and the earth.

Who knows eleven? I know eleven. Eleven are the stars [of Yosef's dream]. Ten are the Commandments. Nine are the months of pregnancy. Eight are the days of circumcision. Seven are the days of the week. Six are the Orders of the *Mishnah.* Five are the Books of the Torah. Four are the Matriarchs. Three are the Patriarchs. Two are the Tablets of the Covenant. One is our God in the heavens and the earth.

Who knows twelve? I know twelve. Twelve are the tribes. Eleven are the stars. Ten are the Commandments. Nine are the months of pregnancy. Eight are the days of circumcision. Seven are the days of the week. Six are the Orders of the *Mishnah.* Five are the Books of the Torah. Four are the Matriarchs. Three are the Patriarchs. Two are the Tablets of the Covenant. One is our God in the heavens and the earth.

---

much to be thankful for. While we no longer enjoy the physical freedom we gained upon leaving the Egyptian house of bondage, we still possess the spiritual wealth we acquired at the time. Even while under the sovereignty of other foreign rulers we remain the servants of the One God, privy to all His spiritual treasures. Thus, let no one ask, "What good was the deliverance from Egypt if we are in exile again anyway?" True, we are exiled, but we are immeasurably wealthier since we have acquired national treasures that will always sustain us as His servants (*Seder HaAruch*).

שְׁלֹשָׁה עָשָׂר מִי יוֹדֵעַ? שְׁלֹשָׁה עָשָׂר אֲנִי יוֹדֵעַ. שְׁלֹשָׁה עָשָׂר מִדַּיָּא, שְׁנֵים עָשָׂר שִׁבְטַיָּא, אַחַד עָשָׂר כּוֹכְבַיָּא, עֲשָׂרָה דִבְּרַיָּא, תִּשְׁעָה יַרְחֵי לֵדָה, שְׁמוֹנָה יְמֵי מִילָה, שִׁבְעָה יְמֵי שַׁבַּתָּא, שִׁשָּׁה סִדְרֵי מִשְׁנָה, חֲמִשָּׁה חֻמְשֵׁי תוֹרָה, אַרְבַּע אִמָּהוֹת, שְׁלֹשָׁה אָבוֹת, שְׁנֵי לֻחוֹת הַבְּרִית, אֶחָד אֱלֹהֵינוּ שֶׁבַּשָּׁמַיִם וּבָאָרֶץ.

חַד גַּדְיָא, חַד גַּדְיָא, דְּזַבִּין אַבָּא בִּתְרֵי זוּזֵי, חַד גַּדְיָא חַד גַּדְיָא.

וְאָתָא שׁוּנְרָא וְאָכְלָה לְגַדְיָא, דְּזַבִּין אַבָּא בִּתְרֵי זוּזֵי, חַד גַּדְיָא חַד גַּדְיָא.

חַד גַּדְיָא חַד גַּדְיָא — *A kid, a kid.* This last song of the Haggadah ostensibly tells the simple tale of a kid, a dog, a cat and other such creatures. However, one who listens closely will really hear a metaphor for the history of the Jewish people. According to the *Vilna Gaon*, the poem describes the sequence of events that led to Jacob and his family's descent to Egypt and the fluctuating pattern of exile and redemption, both in the past and in the future.

The initial event which began the chain of Jewish history was the sale of the birthright by Esau. For a paltry, two-course meal of beans and bread, he sold away his firstborn's right to be blessed by his father. When Jacob came surreptitiously disguised as Esau in order to be blessed, he brought his father food from *two young goats*. Jacob in turn granted the firstborn status and the accompanying blessings to Joseph. *The cat* — which alludes to the jealousy of Joseph's brothers — *came and devoured the kid*, by selling Joseph into slavery in Egypt. Irked by the favoritism

shown Joseph by Jacob, the brothers took the multicolored coat given him by Jacob and dipped it in the blood of a goat (see *Genesis* 37:23).

As a result of this episode, born of jealousy, the family of Jacob descended to Egypt where *the dog came and bit the cat*, i.e., the Egyptians (see *Psalms* 59:7) enslaved the Jews.

When God decided to free the Jews He brought this about by sending *the stick to beat the dog*. The staff of Moses was the agent of God to bring plagues on the Egyptians and thus release the Jews from bondage. This staff was passed from leader to leader. Joshua, the Judges, the Prophets, up to the time of King David, all performed supernatural feats on behalf of the Jewish people by means of this staff. The situation changed when the burning passion for idolatry became so overwhelming that it brought about the destruction of the Temple and rendered the staff powerless. *The fire came and burned the stick.*

The sway of idolatry was so potent that it became almost impossible to combat.[1] In an

---

1. **Burning Temptation.** The Talmud (*Sanhedrin* 102b) relates that King Menasheh, under whose reign idolatry flourished, once appeared to R' Ashi in a dream. R' Ashi asked him, "Since you are so learned, why did you worship idols?" King Menasheh replied, "Had you been living in my time, you yourself would have lifted up

Who knows thirteen? I know thirteen. Thirteen are the Attributes of God. Twelve are the tribes. Eleven are the stars. Ten are the Commandments. Nine are the months of pregnancy. Eight are the days of circumcision. Seven are the days of the week. Six are the Orders of the *Mishnah.* Five are the Books of the Torah. Four are the Matriarchs. Three are the Patriarchs. Two are the Tablets of the Covenant. One is our God in the heavens and the earth.

One kid, one kid that father bought for two *zuzim.* One kid, one kid.

And the cat came and ate the kid that father bought for two *zuzim.* One kid, one kid.

---

unprecedented step the Men of the Great Assembly successfully eradicated the lust for idolatry through prayer and fasting (*Yoma* 69b). Thus the *water,* symbolic of the Torah (as embodied by the Great Assembly), *came and doused the fire.* These very same men, led by Ezra and Nehemiah, were the vanguard of building the Second Temple. Only when the *ox,* symbol of the Roman Empire which descended from Esau, drank the water was the Second Temple destroyed. By brutally suppressing the study of Torah, the Romans sought to choke off the life supply of the Jewish people. The unrestrained reign of Esau and his cohorts will, however, not continue forever. Eventually, the Messiah the son of Joseph will vanquish Esau: *The slaughterer will come and slaughter the ox.*

According to the Talmud (*Succah* 52a), this first Messiah will die soon after accomplishing his historic task. Thus, *the angel of death will come and slaughter the slaughterer.* Finally, *God* Himself *will come* and, with the advent of the Messiah the son of David, He will forever vanquish death and raise

us eternally above all the nations.

Maaseh Nissim views the poem as an allegorical account of the saga of the Temple and the wandering exile of Israel which will end with the coming of the Messiah.

The kid (גְּדִי — *gedi*) alludes to the Temple, which is symbolized in *Song of Songs* (1:14) as *the vineyards of En-gedi.* King David bought it from Arauna the Jebusite with the two gold *dinarim* which he levied from each of the tribes (see *Zevachim* 11b). Then the cat (שׁוּנְרָא) came. This refers to Nebuchadnezzar, king of Babylonia, the שׂוֹנֵא רַע, *evil enemy,* who destroyed the First Temple. Babylonia was soon destroyed by Cyrus, when he killed Belshazzar. The machinations of the nations will eventually end with the vanquishing of death and the full blossom of Godliness in the third, eternal Temple.

The heightened sense of faith that we gain from this recitation of God's salvation brings the realization that, appearances notwithstanding, God rewards those who follow His will and punishes those

---

your garment so that it should not impede your headlong rush to the place of idolatry!'' Menasheh meant to say that R' Ashi could not comprehend how potent the temptation to worship idols was in those days.

Menasheh's words show that idolatry, which to us appears so absurd, was as tempting in his age as other sins are today. If we do not feel the same way today, it is because the Men of the Great Assembly beseeched God to banish the passion for idolatry (see *Yoma* 69b). If we could be freed from our lust for the sins that are common today, those sins would appear as ludicrous to us as idolatry (*R' Chaim Shmulevitz,* see *Michtav MeEliyahu* vol. 4, p.134).

וְאָתָא **כַלְבָּא** וְנָשַׁךְ לְשׁוּנְרָא, דְּאָכְלָה לְגַדְיָא, דְּזַבִּין אַבָּא בִּתְרֵי זוּזֵי, חַד גַּדְיָא חַד גַּדְיָא.

וְאָתָא **חוּטְרָא** וְהִכָּה לְכַלְבָּא, דְּנָשַׁךְ לְשׁוּנְרָא, דְּאָכְלָה לְגַדְיָא, דְּזַבִּין אַבָּא בִּתְרֵי זוּזֵי, חַד גַּדְיָא חַד גַּדְיָא.

וְאָתָא **נוּרָא** וְשָׂרַף לְחוּטְרָא, דְּהִכָּה לְכַלְבָּא, דְּנָשַׁךְ לְשׁוּנְרָא, דְּאָכְלָה לְגַדְיָא, דְּזַבִּין אַבָּא בִּתְרֵי זוּזֵי, חַד גַּדְיָא חַד גַּדְיָא.

וְאָתָא **מַיָּא** וְכָבָה לְנוּרָא, דְּשָׂרַף לְחוּטְרָא, דְּהִכָּה לְכַלְבָּא, דְּנָשַׁךְ לְשׁוּנְרָא, דְּאָכְלָה לְגַדְיָא, דְּזַבִּין אַבָּא בִּתְרֵי זוּזֵי, חַד גַּדְיָא חַד גַּדְיָא.

וְאָתָא **תוֹרָא** וְשָׁתָה לְמַיָּא, דְּכָבָה לְנוּרָא, דְּשָׂרַף לְחוּטְרָא, דְּהִכָּה לְכַלְבָּא, דְּנָשַׁךְ לְשׁוּנְרָא, דְּאָכְלָה לְגַדְיָא, דְּזַבִּין אַבָּא בִּתְרֵי זוּזֵי, חַד גַּדְיָא חַד גַּדְיָא.

וְאָתָא **הַשּׁוֹחֵט** וְשָׁחַט לְתוֹרָא, דְּשָׁתָה לְמַיָּא, דְּכָבָה לְנוּרָא, דְּשָׂרַף לְחוּטְרָא, דְּהִכָּה לְכַלְבָּא, דְּנָשַׁךְ לְשׁוּנְרָא, דְּאָכְלָה לְגַדְיָא, דְּזַבִּין אַבָּא בִּתְרֵי זוּזֵי, חַד גַּדְיָא חַד גַּדְיָא.

וְאָתָא **מַלְאַךְ הַמָּוֶת** וְשָׁחַט לְשׁוֹחֵט, דְּשָׁחַט לְתוֹרָא, דְּשָׁתָה לְמַיָּא, דְּכָבָה לְנוּרָא, דְּשָׂרַף לְחוּטְרָא, דְּהִכָּה לְכַלְבָּא, דְּנָשַׁךְ לְשׁוּנְרָא, דְּאָכְלָה לְגַדְיָא, דְּזַבִּין אַבָּא בִּתְרֵי זוּזֵי, חַד גַּדְיָא חַד גַּדְיָא.

וְאָתָא **הַקָּדוֹשׁ בָּרוּךְ הוּא** וְשָׁחַט לְמַלְאַךְ הַמָּוֶת, דְּשָׁחַט לְשׁוֹחֵט, דְּשָׁחַט לְתוֹרָא, דְּשָׁתָה לְמַיָּא, דְּכָבָה לְנוּרָא, דְּשָׂרַף לְחוּטְרָא, דְּהִכָּה לְכַלְבָּא, דְּנָשַׁךְ לְשׁוּנְרָא, דְּאָכְלָה לְגַדְיָא, דְּזַבִּין אַבָּא בִּתְרֵי זוּזֵי, חַד גַּדְיָא חַד גַּדְיָא.

Although the Haggadah formally ends at this point, one should continue to occupy himself with the story of the Exodus, and the laws of Pesach, until sleep overtakes him. Many recite *Shir HaShirim/Song of Songs* after the Haggadah.

And the dog came and bit the cat that ate the kid that father bought for two *zuzim*. One kid, one kid.

And the stick came and beat the dog that bit the cat that ate the kid that father bought for two *zuzim*. One kid, one kid.

And the fire came and burned the stick that beat the dog that bit the cat that ate the kid that father bought for two *zuzim*. One kid, one kid.

And the water came and doused the fire that burned the stick that beat the dog that bit the cat that ate the kid that father bought for two *zuzim*. One kid, one kid.

And the ox came and drank the water that doused the fire that burned the stick that beat the dog that bit the cat that ate the kid that father bought for two *zuzim*. One kid, one kid.

And the slaughterer came and slaughtered the ox that drank the water that doused the fire that burned the stick that beat the dog that bit the cat that ate the kid that father bought for two *zuzim*. One kid, one kid.

And the angel of death came and slaughtered the slaughterer who slaughtered the ox that drank the water that doused the fire that burned the stick that beat the dog that bit the cat that ate the kid that father bought for two *zuzim*. One kid, one kid.

The Holy One, Blessed is He, then came and slaughtered the angel of death who slaughtered the slaughterer who slaughtered the ox that drank the water that doused the fire that burned the stick that beat the dog that bit the cat that ate the kid that father bought for two *zuzim*. One kid, one kid.

Although the Haggadah formally ends at this point, one should continue to occupy himself with the story of the Exodus, and the laws of Pesach, until sleep overtakes him. Many recite *Shir HaShirim/Song of Songs* after the Haggadah.

---

who flout it. Thus the poem reflects the eternal truth expressed in *Avos* (2:6), where it is related that Hillel remarked upon seeing a skull floating on the water, "Because you drowned others you were drowned, and those who drowned you will themselves be drowned eventually." While throughout our history many have cruelly inflicted suffering upon the Jewish people, they all eventually were brought to the bar of Divine justice.[1]

1. **Coming Together or Moving Closer.** According to *R' Leibel Eiger* the *kid* is the nation of Israel, which God, the Father, irreversibly acquired as His own by dint of two types of movement. (The word גַּדְיָא is related to זז, *move*.) Sometimes we become closer to God through our own initiative to perform good deeds. At other times, when we are unmotivated, God draws us into His orbit by moving toward us, either with an outpouring of His love for us or by imbuing us with the inspiration to approach Him.

שיר השירים
SHIR HASHIRIM/SONG OF SONGS

שִׁיר הַשִּׁירִים אֲשֶׁר לִשְׁלֹמֹה: יִשָּׁקֵנִי מִנְּשִׁיקוֹת פִּיהוּ כִּי־טוֹבִים דֹּדֶיךָ מִיָּיִן: א-ב

לְרֵיחַ שְׁמָנֶיךָ טוֹבִים שֶׁמֶן תּוּרַק שְׁמֶךָ עַל־כֵּן עֲלָמוֹת אֲהֵבוּךָ: מָשְׁכֵנִי אַחֲרֶיךָ ג-ד

נָּרוּצָה הֱבִיאַנִי הַמֶּלֶךְ חֲדָרָיו נָגִילָה וְנִשְׂמְחָה בָּךְ נַזְכִּירָה דֹדֶיךָ מִיַּיִן מֵישָׁרִים

אֲהֵבוּךָ: שְׁחוֹרָה אֲנִי וְנָאוָה בְּנוֹת יְרוּשָׁלָ͏ִם כְּאָהֳלֵי קֵדָר כִּירִיעוֹת ה

שְׁלֹמֹה: אַל־תִּרְאֻנִי שֶׁאֲנִי שְׁחַרְחֹרֶת שֶׁשֱּׁזָפַתְנִי הַשָּׁמֶשׁ בְּנֵי אִמִּי נִחֲרוּ־בִי ו

שָׂמֻנִי נֹטֵרָה אֶת־הַכְּרָמִים כַּרְמִי שֶׁלִּי לֹא נָטָרְתִּי: הַגִּידָה לִּי שֶׁאָהֲבָה נַפְשִׁי ז

אֵיכָה תִרְעֶה אֵיכָה תַּרְבִּיץ בַּצָּהֳרָיִם שַׁלָּמָה אֶהְיֶה כְּעֹטְיָה עַל עֶדְרֵי חֲבֵרֶיךָ:

אִם־לֹא תֵדְעִי לָךְ הַיָּפָה בַּנָּשִׁים צְאִי־לָךְ בְּעִקְבֵי הַצֹּאן וּרְעִי אֶת־גְּדִיֹּתַיִךְ עַל ח

מִשְׁכְּנוֹת הָרֹעִים: לְסֻסָתִי בְּרִכְבֵי פַרְעֹה דִּמִּיתִיךְ רַעְיָתִי: נָאווּ ט-י

לְחָיַיִךְ בַּתֹּרִים צַוָּארֵךְ בַּחֲרוּזִים: תּוֹרֵי זָהָב נַעֲשֶׂה־לָּךְ עִם נְקֻדּוֹת הַכָּסֶף: יא

NOTES INCLUDING PHRASE-BY-PHRASE LITERAL TRANSLATION

1:1. שִׁיר הַשִּׁירִים — *The song that excels all songs* [lit., *The song of songs*]. The greatest song uttered to God by Israel.

אֲשֶׁר לִשְׁלֹמֹה — *dedicated to God, Him to Whom peace belongs* [lit., *which is Solomon's*]. In *Proverbs* and *Ecclesiastes*, Solomon is identified as the "son of David." The omission of David's name here implies that there is a second מֶלֶךְ שֶׁהַשָּׁלוֹם, namely שְׁלֹמֹה, שֶׁלּוֹ, "the King to Whom peace belongs," i.e., God, the Source of peace.

1:2. יִשָּׁקֵנִי מִנְּשִׁיקוֹת פִּיהוּ — *Communicate Your innermost wisdom to me again in loving closeness* [lit., *May He kiss me with the kisses of His mouth*]. Exiled Israel longs for God to teach the Torah, "mouth to mouth," as at Sinai.

כִּי טוֹבִים דֹּדֶיךָ מִיַּיִן — *for Your love is dearer to me than all earthly delights* [lit., *for Your love is better than wine*]. The love You showed when You redeemed us from Egypt and gave us the Torah is dearer to us than wine or any other earthly pleasure.

1:3. לְרֵיחַ שְׁמָנֶיךָ טוֹבִים — *Like the scent of goodly oils is the spreading fame of Your great deeds* [lit., *For fragrance Your oils are good*]. The "fragrance" of God's miracles in Egypt was felt everywhere.

שֶׁמֶן תּוּרַק שְׁמֶךָ — *Your very name is "Flowing Oil"* [lit., *Your name is oil poured forth*]. Your reputation is like fine oil; the more it is poured, the more its fragrance spreads.

עַל כֵּן עֲלָמוֹת אֲהֵבוּךָ — *therefore have nations loved You* [lit., *therefore do young maidens love You*]. "Maidens" refers to the nations of the world.

1:4. מָשְׁכֵנִי אַחֲרֶיךָ נָּרוּצָה — *Upon perceiving a mere hint that You wished to draw me [near], we rushed with perfect faith after You into the wilderness* [lit., *Draw me, we will run after You!*]. We followed God faithfully, without food or drink (see *Jeremiah* 2:2,6).

הֱבִיאַנִי הַמֶּלֶךְ חֲדָרָיו — *The King brought me into His cloud-pillared chamber* [lit., *the King has brought me into His chambers*]. God protected us with His clouds of glory (see *Exodus* 13:21-22).

נָגִילָה וְנִשְׂמְחָה בָּךְ — *whatever our travail, we shall always be glad and rejoice in Your Torah* [lit., *we will rejoice and be glad in You*].

We take delight in Your Torah.

נַזְכִּירָה דֹדֶיךָ מִיַּיִן — *We recall Your love more than earthly delights* [lit., *we will commemorate Your love (better) than wine*]. We recall Your former love as the finest of all pleasures.

מֵישָׁרִים אֲהֵבוּךָ — *unrestrainedly do they love You* [lit., *sincerely do they love You*].

1:5. שְׁחוֹרָה אֲנִי וְנָאוָה — *Though I am black with sin, I am comely with virtue* [lit., *I am black, yet comely*]. Though my Husband left me because my sins blackened me, I am comely by virtue of my forefathers' deeds.

בְּנוֹת יְרוּשָׁלָ͏ִם — *O nations destined to ascend to Jerusalem* [lit., *O daughters of Jerusalem*]. Ultimately, all peoples will stream to honor Jerusalem, and you nations, earlier called "maidens" (v. 3), will become "her daughters."

כְּאָהֳלֵי קֵדָר כִּירִיעוֹת שְׁלֹמֹה — *though sullied as the tents of Kedar, I will be immaculate as the draperies of Him to whom peace belongs* [lit., *as the tents of Kedar, as the curtains of Solomon*].

1:6. אַל תִּרְאֻנִי שֶׁאֲנִי שְׁחַרְחֹרֶת — *Do not view me with contempt despite my swarthiness* [lit., *Do not look upon me that I am swarthy*].

שֶׁשֱּׁזָפַתְנִי הַשָּׁמֶשׁ — *for it is but the sun which has glared upon me* [lit., *because the sun has gazed upon me*]. My darkness, i.e., sinfulness, is not genetic; it will go away when I avoid the sun.

בְּנֵי אִמִּי נִחֲרוּ בִי — *The alien children of my mother incited me* [lit., *my mother's sons kindled in me*]. The mixed multitude of Egyptians and other aliens who accompanied us at the Exodus incited us to worship idols.

שָׂמֻנִי נֹטֵרָה אֶת הַכְּרָמִים — *and made me a keeper of the vineyards of idols* [lit., *they made me keeper of the vineyards*]. . .

כַּרְמִי שֶׁלִּי לֹא נָטָרְתִּי — *but the vineyard of my own true God I did not keep* [lit., *my own vineyard I did not guard*]. I served strange gods, but not the God of my fathers.

1:7. Israel addresses God as a woman addressing her beloved Husband, and compares herself to sheep, as she contends that the exile is too difficult for her and unbecoming to Him.

הַגִּידָה לִּי שֶׁאָהֲבָה נַפְשִׁי — *Tell me, O You Whom my soul loves* . . .

1

Prologue
Israel in exile
to God

¹ The song that excels all songs dedicated to God, Him to Whom peace belongs: ² Communicate Your innermost wisdom to me again in loving closeness, for Your love is dearer to me than all earthly delights. ³ Like the scent of goodly oils is the spreading fame of Your great deeds; Your very name is "Flowing Oil," therefore have nations loved You. ⁴ Upon perceiving a mere hint that You wished to draw me [near], we rushed with perfect faith after You into the wilderness. The King brought me into His cloud-pillared chamber; whatever our travail, we shall always be glad and rejoice in Your Torah. We recall Your love more than earthly delights, unrestrainedly do they love You.

Israel to
the nations

⁵ Though I am black with sin, I am comely with virtue, O nations destined to ascend to Jerusalem; though sullied as the tents of Kedar, I will be immaculate as the draperies of Him to Whom peace belongs. ⁶ Do not view me with contempt despite my swarthiness, for it is but the sun which has glared upon me. The alien children of my mother incited me and made me a keeper of the vineyards of idols, but the vineyard of my own true God I did not keep.

Israel
to God

⁷ Tell me, O You Whom my soul loves: Where will You graze Your flock? Where will You rest them under the fiercest sun of harshest exile? Why shall I be like one veiled in mourning among the flocks of Your fellow shepherds?

God responds
to Israel

⁸ If you know not where to graze, O fairest of nations, follow the footsteps of the sheep, your forefathers, who traced a straight, unswerving path after My Torah. Then you can graze your tender kids even among the dwellings of foreign shepherds. ⁹ With My mighty steeds who battled Pharaoh's riders I revealed that you are My beloved. ¹⁰ Your cheeks are lovely with rows of gems, your neck with necklaces, My gifts to you from the splitting sea, ¹¹ by inducing Pharaoh to engage in pursuit, to add circlets of gold to your spangles of silver.

NOTES INCLUDING PHRASE-BY-PHRASE LITERAL TRANSLATION

אֵיכָה תִרְעֶה אֵיכָה תַּרְבִּיץ בַּצָּהֳרָיִם — *Where will You graze your flock? Where will You rest them under the fiercest sun of harshest exile?* [lit., *Where will You graze (Your flock), where will You rest (them) at noon?*]. Where will You graze us, Your flock, among the seventy wolflike nations? Where will You give us rest in the fierce lands of our exile?

שַׁלָּמָה אֶהְיֶה כְּעֹטְיָה — *Why shall I be like one veiled in mourning* [lit., *for what reason should I be as one veiled*]. It is unbecoming to You that I display grief.

עַל עֶדְרֵי חֲבֵרֶיךָ — *among the flocks of Your fellow shepherds* [lit., *by the flocks of Your colleagues*]? The other nations, who are "shepherded" by their rulers.

1:8. אִם לֹא תֵדְעִי לָךְ הַיָּפָה בַּנָּשִׁים — *If you know not where to graze, O fairest of nations* [lit., *If you do not know, O fairest of women*]...

צְאִי לָךְ בְּעִקְבֵי הַצֹּאן — *follow the footsteps of the sheep, your forefathers, who traced a straight, unswerving path after My Torah* [lit., *go out in the tracks of the sheep*]. If you do not know how to safeguard your children from alien cultures, follow the example of your ancestors who observed My commandments.

וּרְעִי אֶת גְּדִיֹּתַיִךְ עַל מִשְׁכְּנוֹת הָרֹעִים — *Then you can graze your tender kids even among the dwellings of foreign shepherds* [lit., *and graze your kids by the shepherds' tents*]. Then you will be able to raise your children among the nations.

1:9. לְסֻסָתִי בְּרִכְבֵי פַרְעֹה — *With My mighty steeds who battled Pharaoh's riders* [lit., *To a steed in Pharaoh's chariot*]. God saved the Jews from Pharaoh's army at the Sea of Reeds (*Exodus* Chs. 14-15).

דִּמִּיתִיךְ רַעְיָתִי — *I revealed that you are My beloved* [lit., *I have compared you, My beloved*].

1:10. נָאווּ לְחָיַיִךְ בַּתֹּרִים צַוָּארֵךְ בַּחֲרוּזִים — *Your cheeks are lovely with rows of gems, your neck with necklaces, My gifts to you from the splitting sea* [lit., *your cheeks are comely with circlets, your neck with strings of jewels*]...

1:11. תּוֹרֵי זָהָב נַעֲשֶׂה לָּךְ עִם נְקֻדּוֹת הַכָּסֶף — *by inducing Pharaoh to engage in pursuit, to add circlets of gold to your spangles of silver* [lit., *circlets of gold will We make for you and points of silver*]. God influenced the pursuing Egyptians to wear their treasures, so that, upon their defeat, Israel could claim the booty.

עַד־שֶׁהַמֶּ֙לֶךְ֙ בִּמְסִבּ֔וֹ נִרְדִּ֖י נָתַ֥ן רֵיחֽוֹ: צְר֨וֹר הַמֹּ֤ר ׀ דּוֹדִי֙ לִ֔י בֵּ֥ין שָׁדַ֖י יָלִֽין: אֶשְׁכֹּ֨ל   יב־יד

הַכֹּ֤פֶר ׀ דּוֹדִי֙ לִ֔י בְּכַרְמֵ֖י עֵ֥ין גֶּֽדִי: הִנָּ֤ךְ יָפָה֙ רַעְיָתִ֔י הִנָּ֥ךְ יָפָ֖ה עֵינַ֥יִךְ   טו

יוֹנִֽים: הִנְּךָ֨ יָפֶ֤ה דוֹדִי֙ אַ֣ף נָעִ֔ים אַף־עַרְשֵׂ֖נוּ רַֽעֲנָנָֽה: קֹר֤וֹת בָּתֵּ֙ינוּ֙ אֲרָזִ֔ים °רַחִיטֵ֖נוּ   טז־יז

[רהיטנו ק] בְּרוֹתִֽים: אֲנִי֙ חֲבַצֶּ֣לֶת הַשָּׁר֔וֹן שֽׁוֹשַׁנַּ֖ת הָעֲמָקִֽים: כְּשֽׁוֹשַׁנָּה֙ בֵּ֣ין   א־ב   **ב**

הַ֣חוֹחִ֔ים כֵּ֥ן רַעְיָתִ֖י בֵּ֥ין הַבָּנֽוֹת: כְּתַפּ֙וּחַ֙ בַּעֲצֵ֣י הַיַּ֔עַר כֵּ֥ן דּוֹדִ֖י בֵּ֣ין הַבָּנִ֑ים בְּצִלּוֹ֙   ג

חִמַּ֣דְתִּי וְיָשַׁ֔בְתִּי וּפִרְי֖וֹ מָת֥וֹק לְחִכִּֽי: הֱבִיאַ֙נִי֙ אֶל־בֵּ֣ית הַיָּ֔יִן וְדִגְל֥וֹ עָלַ֖י אַהֲבָֽה: ד

סַמְּכ֙וּנִי֙ בָּֽאֲשִׁישׁ֔וֹת רַפְּד֖וּנִי בַּתַּפּוּחִ֑ים כִּי־חוֹלַ֥ת אַהֲבָ֖ה אָֽנִי: שְׂמֹאלוֹ֙ תַּ֣חַת   ה־ו

לְרֹאשִׁ֔י וִֽימִינ֖וֹ תְּחַבְּקֵֽנִי: הִשְׁבַּ֨עְתִּי אֶתְכֶ֜ם בְּנ֤וֹת יְרֽוּשָׁלַ֙͏ִם֙ בִּצְבָא֔וֹת א֖וֹ בְּאַיְל֣וֹת   ז

הַשָּׂדֶ֑ה אִם־תָּעִ֧ירוּ ׀ וְֽאִם־תְּעֽוֹרְר֛וּ אֶת־הָאַהֲבָ֖ה עַ֥ד שֶׁתֶּחְפָּֽץ: ק֣וֹל דּוֹדִ֔י   ח

הִנֵּה־זֶ֖ה בָּ֑א מְדַלֵּג֙ עַל־הֶ֣הָרִ֔ים מְקַפֵּ֖ץ עַל־הַגְּבָעֽוֹת: דּוֹמֶ֤ה דוֹדִי֙ לִצְבִ֔י א֖וֹ לְעֹ֣פֶר   ט

הָֽאַיָּלִ֑ים הִנֵּה־זֶ֤ה עוֹמֵד֙ אַחַ֣ר כׇּתְלֵ֔נוּ מַשְׁגִּ֙יחַ֙ מִן־הַֽחַלֹּנ֔וֹת מֵצִ֖יץ מִן־הַחֲרַכִּֽים:

NOTES INCLUDING PHRASE-BY-PHRASE LITERAL TRANSLATION

1:12. עַד שֶׁהַמֶּלֶךְ בִּמְסִבּוֹ נִרְדִּי נָתַן רֵיחוֹ — *While the King was yet at Sinai my malodorous deed gave forth its scent as my Golden Calf defiled the covenant* [lit., *While the King was (still) at His table, my nard gave forth its fragrance*]. Nard is a fragrant herb, but is used here as a euphemism for the bad odor of idolatry.

1:13. צְרוֹר הַמֹּר דּוֹדִי לִי — *But my Beloved responded with a bundle of myrrh, the fragrant atonement of erecting a Tabernacle* [lit., *A bag of myrrh is my Beloved to me*]. After the disaster of the Golden Calf, God offered me a new fragrance. "Contribute toward the construction of the Tabernacle to atone for the gold you gave to make the Calf."

בֵּין שָׁדַי יָלִין — *where His Presence would dwell between the Holy Ark's staves* [lit., *lodged between my breasts*], i.e., the Shechinah (God's immanent Presence) dwelled between the two staves of the Ark. The long staves of the Ark pressed against the curtain that separated between it and the other appurtenances of the Tabernacle, causing breastlike protrusions on the other side of the curtain (*Yoma* 54a; *Menachos* 98a).

1:14. אֶשְׁכֹּל הַכֹּפֶר דּוֹדִי לִי בְּכַרְמֵי עֵין גֶּדִי — *Like a cluster of henna in En-gedi vineyards has my Beloved multiplied His forgiveness to me* [lit., *A cluster of henna is my Beloved to me, in the vineyards of En-gedi*]. The word כֹּפֶר, "henna," is linguistically related to כַּפָּרָה, "atonement."

1:15. הִנָּךְ יָפָה רַעְיָתִי הִנָּךְ יָפָה עֵינַיִךְ יוֹנִים — *He said, "I forgive you, My friend, for you are lovely in deed and lovely in resolve. The righteous among you are loyal as a dove"* [lit., *Behold, you are beautiful, My beloved; behold, you are beautiful, your eyes are doves*]. Your righteous leaders — the "eyes" of the generation — have cleaved to Me like doves, who are faithful to their mates.

1:16. הִנְּךָ יָפֶה דוֹדִי אַף נָעִים — *It is You Who are lovely, my Beloved, so pleasant that You pardoned my sin* [lit., *You are handsome, my Beloved, indeed pleasant*]. The beauty is Yours, for having forgiven us.

אַף עַרְשֵׂנוּ רַעֲנָנָה — *enabling our Temple to make me ever fresh* [lit., *even our couch is full of vigor*]. "Couch" refers to the Tabernacle, whose existence led to flourishing growth of the Jewish population.

1:17. קֹרוֹת בָּתֵּינוּ אֲרָזִים רַחִיטֵנוּ בְּרוֹתִים — *The beams of our houses are cedar, our panels are cypress.*

2:1. אֲנִי חֲבַצֶּלֶת הַשָּׁרוֹן שׁוֹשַׁנַּת הָעֲמָקִים — *I am but a rose of Sharon, even an ever-fresh rose of the valleys* [lit., *I am a rose of the Sharon, a rose of the valleys*].

2:2. כְּשׁוֹשַׁנָּה בֵּין הַחוֹחִים כֵּן רַעְיָתִי בֵּין הַבָּנוֹת — *Like the rose maintaining its beauty among the thorns, so is My faithful beloved among the nations* [lit., *As a rose among thorns, so is My beloved among the daughters*]. Just as the rose retains its beauty though surrounded by thorns, so My beloved people maintains her faith despite the torments of her neighbors.

2:3. כְּתַפּוּחַ בַּעֲצֵי הַיַּעַר כֵּן דּוֹדִי בֵּין הַבָּנִים — *Like the fruitful, fragrant apple among the barren trees of the forest, so is my Beloved among the gods* [lit., *Like an apple tree among the trees of the forest, so is my Beloved among the sons*]. God is superior to all the fruitless idols of the nations.

בְּצִלּוֹ חִמַּדְתִּי וְיָשַׁבְתִּי — *In His shade I delighted and [there] I sat . . .*

וּפִרְיוֹ מָתוֹק לְחִכִּי — *and the fruit of His Torah was sweet to my palate* [lit., *and His fruit is sweet to my palate*]. We spent twelve months at Mount Sinai enjoying the sweetness of His Torah.

2:4. הֱבִיאַנִי אֶל בֵּית הַיָּיִן — *He brought me to the chamber of Torah delights* [lit., *He has brought me to the house of wine*]; an allusion to the Tent of the Meeting, where Moses expounded the Torah's commandments.

וְדִגְלוֹ עָלַי אַהֲבָה — *and clustered my encampments about Him in love* [lit., *and His banner upon me is love*]. He gathered the tribes about His Tabernacle.

2:5. סַמְּכוּנִי בָּאֲשִׁישׁוֹת רַפְּדוּנִי בַּתַּפּוּחִים — *I say to Him, "Sustain me in exile with dainty cakes, spread fragrant apples about me to comfort my dispersion* [lit., *Sustain me with dainties, spread out apples around me*]. . .

כִּי חוֹלַת אַהֲבָה אָנִי — *for, bereft of Your Presence, I am sick with*

Israel about God

¹² *While the King was yet at Sinai my malodorous deed gave forth its scent as my Golden Calf defiled the covenant.* ¹³ *But my Beloved responded with a bundle of myrrh, the fragrant atonement of erecting a Tabernacle where His Presence would dwell between the Holy Ark's staves.* ¹⁴ *Like a cluster of henna in En-gedi vineyards has my Beloved multiplied His forgiveness to me.* ¹⁵ *He said, "I forgive you, My friend, for you are lovely in deed and lovely in resolve. The righteous among you are loyal as a dove."*

Israel to God

2

¹⁶ *It is You Who are lovely, my Beloved, so pleasant that You pardoned my sin enabling our Temple to make me ever fresh.* ¹⁷ *The beams of our houses are cedar, our panels are cypress.* ¹ *I am but a rose of Sharon, even an ever-fresh rose of the valleys.*

God to Israel

² *Like the rose maintaining its beauty among the thorns, so is My faithful beloved among the nations.*

Israel reminisces . . .

³ *Like the fruitful, fragrant apple among the barren trees of the forest, so is my Beloved among the gods. In His shade I delighted and [there] I sat, and the fruit of His Torah was sweet to my palate.* ⁴ *He brought me to the chamber of Torah delights and clustered my encampments about Him in love.* ⁵ *I say to Him, "Sustain me in exile with dainty cakes, spread fragrant apples about me to comfort my dispersion, for, bereft of Your Presence, I am sick with love."* ⁶ *With memories of His loving support in the desert, of His left hand under my head, of His right hand enveloping me.*

. . . turns to the nations . . .

⁷ *I adjure you, O nations destined to ascend to Jerusalem, for if you violate your oath, you will become as defenseless as gazelles or hinds of the field, if you dare provoke God to hate me or disturb His love for me while He still desires it.*

. . . then reminisces further

⁸ *The voice of my Beloved! Behold, it came suddenly to redeem me, as if leaping over mountains, skipping over hills.* ⁹ *In His swiftness to redeem me, my Beloved is like a gazelle or a young hart. I thought I would be forever alone, but behold! He was standing behind our wall, observing through the windows, peering through the lattices.*

NOTES INCLUDING PHRASE-BY-PHRASE LITERAL TRANSLATION

love" [lit., *for I am sick with love*]. In exile, I am sick for want of His love; I thirst for Him here in exile.

2:6. שְׂמֹאלוֹ תַּחַת לְרֹאשִׁי וִימִינוֹ תְּחַבְּקֵנִי — *With memories of His loving support in the desert, of His left hand under my head, of His right hand enveloping me* [lit., *His left hand is under my head and His right arm embraces me*]. Ecstatically, I recall how I was accompanied by God's Ark, enveloped in His cloud, eating His manna.

2:7. הִשְׁבַּעְתִּי אֶתְכֶם בְּנוֹת יְרוּשָׁלִַם — *I adjure you, O nations destined to ascend to Jerusalem* [lit., *I have adjured you, O daughters of Jerusalem*]. See 1:5.

בִּצְבָאוֹת אוֹ בְּאַיְלוֹת הַשָּׂדֶה — *for if you violate your oath, you will become as defenseless as gazelles or hinds of the field* [lit., *by gazelles or by hinds of the field*] . . .

אִם תָּעִירוּ וְאִם תְּעוֹרְרוּ אֶת הָאַהֲבָה עַד שֶׁתֶּחְפָּץ — *if you dare provoke God to hate me or disturb His love for me while He still desires it* [lit., *should you wake or rouse the love until it pleases*].

2:8. With this verse, Israel begins a recapitulation of God's remembrance of His people in Egypt.

קוֹל דּוֹדִי הִנֵּה זֶה בָּא — *The voice of my Beloved! Behold it came*

suddenly to redeem me [lit., *The voice of my Beloved! Behold He comes*] . . .

מְדַלֵּג עַל הֶהָרִים מְקַפֵּץ עַל הַגְּבָעוֹת — *as if leaping over mountains, skipping over hills* [lit., *leaping upon the mountains skipping upon the hills*]. God leaped and skipped, so to speak, redeeming the Jews one hundred and ninety years before the completion of the prophecy of four hundred years of bondage.

2:9. דּוֹמֶה דוֹדִי לִצְבִי אוֹ לְעֹפֶר הָאַיָּלִים — *In His swiftness to redeem me, my Beloved is like a gazelle or a young hart* [lit., *My Beloved is like a gazelle or a young hart*].

הִנֵּה זֶה עוֹמֵד אַחַר כָּתְלֵנוּ מַשְׁגִּיחַ מִן הַחַלֹּנוֹת מֵצִיץ מִן הַחֲרַכִּים — *I thought I would be forever alone, but behold! He was standing behind our wall, observing through the windows, peering through the lattices* [lit., *behold He stands behind our wall looking through the windows, peering through the lattices*]. I was like a woman resigned to being an *agunah* (bereft of husband, yet legally bound to him), for a still undetermined period of time. Then, suddenly, He came to tell me that He is peering through the windows of the heavens taking notice of my plight (see *Exodus 3:7*), reassuring me that whatever my travail, He will never fail to keep the closest watch over me.

עָנָה דוֹדִי וְאָמַר לִי קוּמִי לָךְ רַעְיָתִי יָפָתִי וּלְכִי־לָךְ: כִּי־הִנֵּה הַסְּתָו עָבָר יא-יא

הַגֶּשֶׁם חָלַף הָלַךְ לוֹ: הַנִּצָּנִים נִרְאוּ בָאָרֶץ עֵת הַזָּמִיר הִגִּיעַ וְקוֹל הַתּוֹר יב

נִשְׁמַע בְּאַרְצֵנוּ: הַתְּאֵנָה חָנְטָה פַגֶּיהָ וְהַגְּפָנִים ׀ סְמָדַר נָתְנוּ רֵיחַ קוּמִי °לְכִי יג

°לָךְ] ק רַעְיָתִי יָפָתִי וּלְכִי־לָךְ: יוֹנָתִי בְּחַגְוֵי הַסֶּלַע בְּסֵתֶר יד

הַמַּדְרֵגָה הַרְאִינִי אֶת־מַרְאַיִךְ הַשְׁמִיעִנִי אֶת־קוֹלֵךְ כִּי־קוֹלֵךְ עָרֵב וּמַרְאֵיךְ

נָאוֶה: אֶחֱזוּ־לָנוּ שֻׁעָלִים שֻׁעָלִים קְטַנִּים מְחַבְּלִים כְּרָמִים וּכְרָמֵינוּ טו

סְמָדַר: דּוֹדִי לִי וַאֲנִי לוֹ הָרֹעֶה בַּשּׁוֹשַׁנִּים: עַד שֶׁיָּפוּחַ הַיּוֹם וְנָסוּ הַצְּלָלִים טז-יז

סֹב דְּמֵה־לְךָ דוֹדִי לִצְבִי אוֹ לְעֹפֶר הָאַיָּלִים עַל־הָרֵי בָתֶר: עַל־ ג א

מִשְׁכָּבִי בַּלֵּילוֹת בִּקַּשְׁתִּי אֵת שֶׁאָהֲבָה נַפְשִׁי בִּקַּשְׁתִּיו וְלֹא מְצָאתִיו:

אָקוּמָה נָּא וַאֲסוֹבְבָה בָעִיר בַּשְּׁוָקִים וּבָרְחֹבוֹת אֲבַקְשָׁה אֵת שֶׁאָהֲבָה ב

נַפְשִׁי בִּקַּשְׁתִּיו וְלֹא מְצָאתִיו: מְצָאוּנִי הַשֹּׁמְרִים הַסֹּבְבִים בָּעִיר אֵת שֶׁאָהֲבָה ג

נַפְשִׁי רְאִיתֶם: כִּמְעַט שֶׁעָבַרְתִּי מֵהֶם עַד שֶׁמָּצָאתִי אֵת שֶׁאָהֲבָה נַפְשִׁי ד

NOTES INCLUDING PHRASE-BY-PHRASE LITERAL TRANSLATION

2:10. עָנָה דוֹדִי וְאָמַר לִי — *When He redeemed me from Egypt, my Beloved called out and said to me,* [lit., *My Beloved lifted His voice and said to me,*]...

קוּמִי לָךְ רַעְיָתִי יָפָתִי וּלְכִי־לָךְ — *"Arise My love, My fair one, and go forth* [lit., *Arise My love, My fair one, and go forth for yourself*]. "Carry out My precepts, and I will bring you up out of the affliction of Egypt" (*Exodus* 3:17).

2:11-13. A poetic picture describing the season of Redemption. Metaphorically, the verses conjure up an image of the worst being over, of redemption being at hand.

2:11. כִּי־הִנֵּה הַסְּתָו עָבָר — *For the winter of bondage has passed* [lit., *For, behold, the winter is past*]. The years of bondage are over. It is time to travel forth.

הַגֶּשֶׁם חָלַף הָלַךְ לוֹ — *the deluge of suffering is over and gone* [lit., *the rain is over and gone*].

2:12. הַנִּצָּנִים נִרְאוּ בָאָרֶץ — *The righteous blossoms are seen in the land* [lit., *The blossoms have appeared in the land*]. The "blossoms" are Moses and Aaron who blossomed in response to Israel's needs.

עֵת הַזָּמִיר הִגִּיעַ — *The time of your song has arrived* [lit., *the time of singing has come*], to praise God, by singing the Song of the Sea (*Exodus* Ch. 15).

וְקוֹל הַתּוֹר נִשְׁמַע בְּאַרְצֵנוּ — *and the voice of your guide is heard in the land* [lit., *and the voice of the turtledove is heard in the land*]. The word תּוֹר, "turtledove," is linguistically related to תַּיָּר, "guide," an allusion to Moses.

2:13. הַתְּאֵנָה חָנְטָה פַגֶּיהָ וְהַגְּפָנִים סְמָדַר נָתְנוּ רֵיחַ — *The fig tree has formed its first small figs, ready for ascent to the Temple; the vines are in blossom, their fragrance declaring they are ready for libation* [lit., *The fig tree has formed its first figs, and the vines in blossom give forth fragrance*]. The time is drawing near for you to bring the first fruits and the wine libations in the Temple.

קוּמִי לָךְ רַעְיָתִי יָפָתִי וּלְכִי־לָךְ — *Arise, My beloved, My fair one, and go forth"* [lit., *Arise, My beloved, My fair one, and go forth for yourself*].

2:14. יוֹנָתִי בְּחַגְוֵי הַסֶּלַע בְּסֵתֶר הַמַּדְרֵגָה — *At the sea, He said to me, "O My dove, trapped at the sea as if in the clefts of the rock, the concealment of the terrace* [lit., *O My dove, in the crannies of the rock, in the covert of the step*]. When the Jews were trapped between the sea and the Egyptian army, they were like a dove fleeing a hawk. It flew into the cleft of a rock, and found a serpent lurking there. It could neither enter, because of the snake, nor turn back, because of the hawk.

הַרְאִינִי אֶת־מַרְאַיִךְ — *"Show Me your prayerful gaze* [lit., *show Me your countenance*]. Show Me to whom you turn when you are in trouble.

הַשְׁמִיעִנִי אֶת־קוֹלֵךְ — *let Me hear your supplicating voice* [lit., *let Me hear your voice*]...

כִּי קוֹלֵךְ עָרֵב וּמַרְאֵיךְ נָאוֶה — *for your voice is sweet and your countenance comely."*

2:15. אֶחֱזוּ לָנוּ שֻׁעָלִים שֻׁעָלִים קְטַנִּים מְחַבְּלִים כְּרָמִים וּכְרָמֵינוּ סְמָדַר — *Then He told the sea, "Seize for us the Egyptian foxes, even the small foxes who spoiled Israel's vineyards while our vineyards had just begun to blossom"* [lit., *The foxes have seized us, the little foxes that ruin the vineyard, and our vineyards were in blossom*].

2:16. דּוֹדִי לִי וַאֲנִי לוֹ — *My Beloved is mine, He fills all my needs and I seek from Him and none other* [lit., *My Beloved is mine, and I am His*]. He makes demands upon us and we rely on none other but Him.

הָרֹעֶה בַּשּׁוֹשַׁנִּים — *He grazes me in roselike bounty* [lit., *Who grazes (others) among the roses*]. God grazes us, His flock, in pastures of tranquil beauty.

2:17. עַד שֶׁיָּפוּחַ הַיּוֹם וְנָסוּ הַצְּלָלִים — *Until my sin blows His friendship away and sears me like the midday sun and His protection departs* [lit., *until the day blows and the shadows flee*]. The condition of "My Beloved is mine, and I am His" was dispelled when the sins of the Golden Calf (*Exodus* Ch. 32) and the Spies (*Numbers* Chs. 13-14) blackened us with the ferocity of the noontime sun.

¹⁰ *When He redeemed me from Egypt, my Beloved called out and said to me, "Arise My love, My fair one, and go forth.* ¹¹ *For the winter of bondage has passed, the deluge of suffering is over and gone.* ¹² *The righteous blossoms are seen in the land, the time of your song has arrived, and the voice of your guide is heard in the land.* ¹³ *The fig tree has formed its first small figs, ready for ascent to the Temple; the vines are in blossom, their fragrance declaring they are ready for libation. Arise, My beloved, My fair one, and go forth!"*

¹⁴ *At the sea, He said to me, "O My dove, trapped at the sea as if in the clefts of the rock, the concealment of the terrace. Show Me your prayerful gaze, let Me hear your supplicating voice, for your voice is sweet and your countenance comely."* ¹⁵ *Then He told the sea, "Seize for us the Egyptian foxes, even the small foxes who spoiled Israel's vineyards while our vineyards had just begun to blossom."*

¹⁶ *My Beloved is mine, He fills all my needs and I seek from Him and none other. He grazes me in roselike bounty.* ¹⁷ *Until my sin blows His friendship away and sears me like the midday sun and His protection departs. My sin caused Him to turn away.*

I say to him, "My Beloved, You became like a gazelle or like a young hart on the distant mountains."

3
Israel to the nations

¹ *As I lay on my bed in the night of my desert travail, I sought Him Whom my soul loves. I sought Him but I found Him not, for He maintained His aloofness.* ² *I resolved to arise then, and roam through the city, in the streets and squares; that through Moses I would seek Him Whom my soul loved. I sought Him, but I found Him not.* ³ *They, Moses and Aaron, the watchmen patrolling the city, found me. "You have seen Him Whom my soul loves; what has He said?"* ⁴ *Scarcely had I departed from them, when, in the days of Joshua, I found Him Whom my soul loves.*

סב — *My sin caused Him to turn away* [lit., *turn*].

דְּמֵה לְךָ דוֹדִי לִצְבִי אוֹ לְעֹפֶר הָאַיָּלִים — *I say to him, "My Beloved, You became like a gazelle or like a young hart* [lit., *My Beloved, and be like a gazelle or a young hart*]. Through my sins I caused Him to depart from me, as swiftly as a gazelle. . .

עַל הָרֵי בָתֶר — *on the distant mountains"* [lit., *upon the mountains of separation*], out of reach.

3:1. עַל מִשְׁכָּבִי בַּלֵּילוֹת בִּקַּשְׁתִּי אֵת שֶׁאָהֲבָה נַפְשִׁי — *As I lay on my bed in the night of my desert travail, I sought Him Whom my soul loves* [lit., *Upon my bed during the nights I sought the One my soul loves*]. After the sin of the Spies, God did not speak directly to Moses for thirty-eight years (see *Deuteronomy* 2:14-17), a period depicted as "during the nights." This chapter depicts the anguish of Israel, bereft of its former uninhibited relationship with God, longing for a resumption of His love.

בִּקַּשְׁתִּיו וְלֹא מְצָאתִיו — *I sought Him, but I found Him not, for He maintained His aloofness* [lit., *I sought Him, but I found Him not*]. As He warned, "For I will not go up in your midst" (*Exodus* 33:3); "For I am not among you" (*Deuteronomy* 1:42).

3:2. אָקוּמָה נָּא וַאֲסוֹבְבָה בָעִיר בַּשְּׁוָקִים וּבָרְחֹבוֹת — *I resolved to arise then, and roam through the city, in the streets and squares* [lit., *I*

will rise now and roam about the city, through the streets and through the squares]. We were determined to seek God by every possible avenue.

אֲבַקְשָׁה אֵת שֶׁאָהֲבָה נַפְשִׁי — *that through Moses I would seek Him Whom my soul loved* [lit., *I will seek the One I love*]. As Moses said, "I will go up to HASHEM; perhaps I can win atonement for your sins" (*Exodus* 32:30).

בִּקַּשְׁתִּיו וְלֹא מְצָאתִיו — *I sought Him, but I found Him not.*

3:3. מְצָאוּנִי הַשֹּׁמְרִים הַסֹּבְבִים בָּעִיר — *They, Moses and Aaron, the watchmen patrolling the city, found me* [lit., *The watchmen who circle the city found me*]. Moses and Aaron went among us to instill us with the love of God. They guided us, and inspired us to be patient, for Redemption was at hand.

אֵת שֶׁאָהֲבָה נַפְשִׁי רְאִיתֶם — *"You have seen Him Whom my soul loves; what has He said?"* [lit., *Have you seen Him Whom my soul loves?*].

3:4. כִּמְעַט שֶׁעָבַרְתִּי מֵהֶם עַד שֶׁמָּצָאתִי אֵת שֶׁאָהֲבָה נַפְשִׁי — *Scarcely had I departed from them, when, in the days of Joshua, I found Him Whom my soul loves* [lit., *Scarcely had I passed them, when I found Him Whom my soul loves*]. When Moses and Aaron died, God remained with Joshua, helping him to conquer the thirty-one kings of Canaan.

ה אֲחַזְתִּיו וְלֹא אַרְפֶּנּוּ עַד־שֶׁהֲבֵיאתִיו אֶל־בֵּית אִמִּי וְאֶל־חֶדֶר הוֹרָתִי: הִשְׁבַּעְתִּי
אֶתְכֶם בְּנוֹת יְרוּשָׁלַם בִּצְבָאוֹת אוֹ בְּאַיְלוֹת הַשָּׂדֶה אִם־תָּעִירוּ| וְאִם־תְּעוֹרְרוּ
אֶת־הָאַהֲבָה עַד שֶׁתֶּחְפָּץ: ו מִי זֹאת עֹלָה מִן־הַמִּדְבָּר כְּתִימֲרוֹת
עָשָׁן מְקֻטֶּרֶת מֹר וּלְבוֹנָה מִכֹּל אַבְקַת רוֹכֵל: ז הִנֵּה מִטָּתוֹ שֶׁלִּשְׁלֹמֹה שִׁשִּׁים
גִּבֹּרִים סָבִיב לָהּ מִגִּבֹּרֵי יִשְׂרָאֵל: ח כֻּלָּם אֲחֻזֵי חֶרֶב מְלֻמְּדֵי מִלְחָמָה אִישׁ חַרְבּוֹ
עַל־יְרֵכוֹ מִפַּחַד בַּלֵּילוֹת: ט אַפִּרְיוֹן עָשָׂה לוֹ הַמֶּלֶךְ שְׁלֹמֹה מֵעֲצֵי
הַלְּבָנוֹן: י עַמּוּדָיו עָשָׂה כֶסֶף רְפִידָתוֹ זָהָב מֶרְכָּבוֹ אַרְגָּמָן תּוֹכוֹ רָצוּף אַהֲבָה
מִבְּנוֹת יְרוּשָׁלָם: יא צְאֶינָה| וּרְאֶינָה בְּנוֹת צִיּוֹן בַּמֶּלֶךְ שְׁלֹמֹה בָּעֲטָרָה
שֶׁעִטְּרָה־לּוֹ אִמּוֹ בְּיוֹם חֲתֻנָּתוֹ וּבְיוֹם שִׂמְחַת לִבּוֹ: ד א הִנָּךְ יָפָה רַעְיָתִי
הִנָּךְ יָפָה עֵינַיִךְ יוֹנִים מִבַּעַד לְצַמָּתֵךְ שַׂעְרֵךְ כְּעֵדֶר הָעִזִּים שֶׁגָּלְשׁוּ מֵהַר גִּלְעָד:
ב שִׁנַּיִךְ כְּעֵדֶר הַקְּצוּבוֹת שֶׁעָלוּ מִן־הָרַחְצָה שֶׁכֻּלָּם מַתְאִימוֹת וְשַׁכֻּלָה אֵין בָּהֶם:

NOTES INCLUDING PHRASE-BY-PHRASE LITERAL TRANSLATION

אֲחַזְתִּיו וְלֹא אַרְפֶּנּוּ — *I grasped Him, determined that my deeds would never again cause me to lose hold of Him* [lit., *I have grasped Him and I would not let Him go*]...

עַד שֶׁהֲבֵיאתִיו אֶל בֵּית אִמִּי וְאֶל חֶדֶר הוֹרָתִי — *until I brought His Presence to the Tabernacle of my mother and to the chamber of the one who conceived me* [lit., *until I brought Him to my mother's house, and to the chamber of the one who conceived me*]. I built the Tabernacle at Shiloh, in return for all that He wrought for me.

3:5. הִשְׁבַּעְתִּי אֶתְכֶם בְּנוֹת יְרוּשָׁלַם — *I adjure you, O nations destined to ascend to Jerusalem* [lit., *I have adjured you, O daughters of Jerusalem*]. See 1:5.

בִּצְבָאוֹת אוֹ בְּאַיְלוֹת הַשָּׂדֶה — *for if you violate your oath, you will become as defenseless as gazelles or hinds of the field* [lit., *by gazelles or by hinds of the field*]...

אִם תָּעִירוּ וְאִם תְּעוֹרְרוּ אֶת הָאַהֲבָה עַד שֶׁתֶּחְפָּץ — *if you dare provoke God to hate me or disturb His love for me while He still desires it* [lit., *if you will wake or rouse the love until it pleases*].

3:6. מִי זֹאת עֹלָה מִן הַמִּדְבָּר — *You nations have asked, "Who is this ascending from the wilderness* [lit., *Who is it that rises up from the wilderness*]. In the wilderness, Israel was led by the pillar of fire and the pillar of cloud (*Exodus* 13:21 ff), which killed snakes and scorpions, and burned thorns and thistles to clear the way. The nations exclaimed: "Who is this [i.e., How great is this spectacle] that comes up from the wilderness?"

כְּתִימֲרוֹת עָשָׁן — *its way secured and smoothed by palmlike pillars of smoke* [lit., *like columns of smoke*]. The word תִּימֲרָה, "column," is linguistically related to תָּמָר, "date-palm." The pillar of clouds that accompanied Israel through the wilderness was tall and erect as a palm tree...

מְקֻטֶּרֶת מֹר וּלְבוֹנָה מִכֹּל אַבְקַת רוֹכֵל — *burning fragrant myrrh and frankincense, of all the perfumer's powders?"* [lit., *perfumed with myrrh and frankincense, with every powder of the merchant*]... like the "cloud of the incense" (*Leviticus* 16:13) that ascended from the Altar in the Tabernacle.

3:7. הִנֵּה מִטָּתוֹ שֶׁלִּשְׁלֹמֹה — *Behold the resting place of Him to Whom peace belongs* [lit., *Behold, it is the couch of Solomon*], i.e., the Tent of Meeting and the Ark...

שִׁשִּׁים גִּבֹּרִים סָבִיב לָהּ מִגִּבֹּרֵי יִשְׂרָאֵל — *with sixty myriads of Israel's mighty encircling it* [lit., *sixty mighty men round about it, of the mighty men of Israel*]. Sixty times ten thousand men were eligible to fight in the Israelite army (see *Numbers* 1:45-46).

3:8. כֻּלָּם אֲחֻזֵי חֶרֶב מְלֻמְּדֵי מִלְחָמָה — *All of them gripping the sword of tradition, skilled in the battle of Torah* [lit., *They all handle the sword, learned in warfare*].

אִישׁ חַרְבּוֹ עַל יְרֵכוֹ מִפַּחַד בַּלֵּילוֹת — *each with his sword ready at his side, lest he succumb in the nights of exile* [lit., *each with his sword on his thigh, because of terror in the nights*]. "Sword" refers to the means by which to transmit the Torah intact from one generation to the next.

3:9. אַפִּרְיוֹן עָשָׂה לוֹ הַמֶּלֶךְ שְׁלֹמֹה מֵעֲצֵי הַלְּבָנוֹן — *A Tabernacle for His Presence has the King to Whom peace belongs made of the wood of Lebanon* [lit., *A sedan chair has King Solomon made unto Him, of the wood of Lebanon*], a metaphor for a private chamber for His glory.

3:10. עַמּוּדָיו עָשָׂה כֶסֶף — *Its pillars He made of silver.* A reference to the silver hooks of the Tabernacle's courtyard pillars (see *Exodus* 27:10).

רְפִידָתוֹ זָהָב — *His resting place was gold* [lit., *its covering was gold*]. God's Presence rested upon the golden Cover of the Ark, from which He spoke to Moses (see *Exodus* 27:17,22).

מֶרְכָּבוֹ אַרְגָּמָן — *Its suspended curtain was purple wool* [lit., *its seat was purple wool*]. The dominant color of the *Paroches* (Curtain) between the Holy and the Holy of Holies was purple (see *Exodus* 26:31-33).

תּוֹכוֹ רָצוּף אַהֲבָה — *Its midst was decked with implements bespeaking love* [lit., *its inner side was decked with love*]. The Ark, its Cover, its Cherubim and Tablets were all symbolic of the love between God and Israel.

מִבְּנוֹת יְרוּשָׁלָם — *by the daughters of Jerusalem.* Throughout the rest of the Book (see, e.g., 1:5) "daughters of Jerusalem" refers

I grasped Him, determined that my deeds would never again cause me to lose hold of Him, until I brought His Presence to the Tabernacle of my mother and to the chamber of the one who conceived me. ⁵ I adjure you, O nations destined to ascend to Jerusalem, for if you violate your oath, you will become as defenseless as gazelles or hinds of the field, if you dare provoke God to hate me or disturb His love for me while He still desires it.

Quoting the nations *⁶ You nations have asked, "Who is this ascending from the wilderness, its way secured and smoothed by palmlike pillars of smoke, burning fragrant myrrh and frankincense, of all the perfumer's powders?" ⁷ Behold the resting place of Him to Whom peace belongs, with sixty myriads of Israel's mighty encircling it. ⁸ All of them gripping the sword of tradition, skilled in the battle of Torah, each with his sword ready at his side, lest he succumb in the nights of exile.*

⁹ A Tabernacle for His presence has the King to Whom peace belongs made of the wood of Lebanon: ¹⁰ Its pillars He made of silver; His resting place was gold; its suspended curtain was purple wool, its midst was decked with implements bespeaking love by the daughters of Jerusalem. ¹¹ Go forth and gaze, O daughters distinguished by loyalty to God, upon the King to Whom peace belongs adorned with the crown His nation made for Him, on the day His Law was given and He became one with Israel, and on the day His heart was gladdened by His Tabernacle's consecration.

4 God to Israel *¹ **B**ehold, you are lovely, My beloved, behold you are lovely, your very appearance radiates dovelike constancy. The most common sons within your encampments are as dearly beloved as the children of Jacob in the goatlike procession descending the slopes of Mount Gilead. ² Accountable in deed are your mighty leaders like a well-numbered flock come up from the washing, all of them unblemished with no miscarriage of action in them.*

---

to the heathen nations who will flock to Jerusalem in the future; here it refers to the Jews.

3:11. צְאֶינָה וּרְאֶינָה בְּנוֹת צִיּוֹן בַּמֶּלֶךְ שְׁלֹמֹה — *Go forth and gaze, O daughters distinguished by loyalty to God, upon the King to Whom peace belongs* [lit., *Go forth and gaze, O daughters of Zion, upon King Solomon*]. צִיּוֹן, "Zion," is linguistically related to צִיּוּן, "distinguishing mark." The daughters of Zion, Israel, are distinguished in their loyalty to God and to His commandments.

בָּעֲטָרָה שֶׁעִטְּרָה לּוֹ אִמּוֹ — *adorned with the crown His nation made for Him* [lit., *with the crown with which his mother crowned him*]. The Tabernacle was "crowned" with coverings of colored skins; of blue, purple and scarlet wool, and fine linen; and of goat's hair (*Exodus* 26:1,7,14).

בְּיוֹם חֲתֻנָתוֹ — *on the day His Law was given and He became one with Israel* [lit., *on His wedding day*]; the day the Torah was given.

וּבְיוֹם שִׂמְחַת לִבּוֹ — *and on the day His heart was gladdened by His Tabernacle's consecration* [lit., *and on the day of His heart's bliss*]. The dedication day of the Tabernacle in the wilderness.

4:1. הִנָּךְ יָפָה רַעְיָתִי הִנָּךְ יָפָה עֵינַיִךְ יוֹנִים — *Behold, you are lovely, My beloved, behold you are lovely, your very appearance radiates*

dovelike constancy [lit., *Behold, you are beautiful, My beloved; behold you are beautiful, your eyes are doves*]. You are like the dove which is loyal to its mate.

מִבַּעַד לְצַמָּתֵךְ שַׂעְרֵךְ כְּעֵדֶר הָעִזִּים שֶׁגָּלְשׁוּ מֵהַר גִּלְעָד — *The most common sons within your encampments are as dearly beloved as the children of Jacob in the goatlike procession descending the slopes of Mount Gilead* [lit., *Within your kerchief, your hair is like a flock of goats streaming down from Mount Gilead*]. Even your common people, whose merits are hidden by veils, are as dear to Me as Jacob and his sons who streamed down Mount Gilead when Laban pursued them (see *Genesis* 31:23ff).

4:2. שִׁנַּיִךְ כְּעֵדֶר הַקְּצוּבוֹת שֶׁעָלוּ מִן הָרַחְצָה — *Accountable in deed are your mighty leaders like a well-numbered flock come up from the washing* [lit., *Your teeth are like a flock well counted, which have come up from the washing*]. Israel's warriors who "tear apart and consume" their enemies are allegorized as teeth. By refraining from plunder and lewdness, the warriors remain untainted by sin, as if they "came up from the washing."

שֶׁכֻּלָּם מַתְאִימוֹת וְשַׁכֻּלָה אֵין בָּהֶם — *all of them unblemished with no miscarriage of action in them* [lit., *all of them are perfect and there is none blemished among them*].

ג כְּחוּט הַשָּׁנִי שִׂפְתוֹתַ֫יִךְ וּמִדְבָּרֵ֖ךְ נָאוֶה כְּפֶ֫לַח הָרִמּוֹן רַקָּתֵ֔ךְ מִבַּ֖עַד לְצַמָּתֵֽךְ:

ד כְּמִגְדַּל דָּוִיד צַוָּארֵ֔ךְ בָּנ֖וּי לְתַלְפִּיּ֑וֹת אֶ֤לֶף הַמָּגֵן֙ תָּל֣וּי עָלָ֔יו כֹּ֖ל שִׁלְטֵ֥י הַגִּבֹּרִֽים:

ה־ו שְׁנֵ֥י שָׁדַ֖יִךְ כִּשְׁנֵ֣י עֳפָרִ֑ים תְּאוֹמֵ֣י צְבִיָּ֔ה הָרֹעִ֖ים בַּשּֽׁוֹשַׁנִּֽים: עַ֤ד שֶׁיָּפ֙וּחַ֙ הַיּ֔וֹם

ז וְנָ֖סוּ הַצְּלָלִ֑ים אֵ֤לֶךְ לִי֙ אֶל־הַ֣ר הַמּ֔וֹר וְאֶל־גִּבְעַ֖ת הַלְּבוֹנָֽה: כֻּלָּ֤ךְ יָפָה֙ רַעְיָתִ֔י

ח וּמ֖וּם אֵ֥ין בָּֽךְ: אִתִּ֤י מִלְּבָנוֹן֙ כַּלָּ֔ה אִתִּ֖י מִלְּבָנ֣וֹן תָּב֑וֹאִי

ט תָּשׁ֣וּרִי ׀ מֵרֹ֣אשׁ אֲמָנָ֗ה מֵרֹ֤אשׁ שְׂנִיר֙ וְחֶרְמ֔וֹן מִמְּעֹנ֣וֹת אֲרָי֔וֹת מֵהַֽרְרֵ֖י נְמֵרִֽים: לִבַּבְתִּ֖נִי

אֲחֹתִ֣י כַלָּ֑ה לִבַּבְתִּ֙נִי֙ °באחד [בְּאַחַ֣ת ק] מֵֽעֵינַ֔יִךְ בְּאַחַ֥ד עֲנָ֖ק מִצַּוְּרֹנָֽיִךְ:

י מַה־יָּפ֥וּ דֹדַ֖יִךְ אֲחֹתִ֣י כַלָּ֑ה מַה־טֹּ֤בוּ דֹדַ֙יִךְ֙ מִיַּ֔יִן וְרֵ֥יחַ שְׁמָנַ֖יִךְ מִכָּל־בְּשָׂמִֽים:

יא נֹ֛פֶת תִּטֹּ֥פְנָה שִׂפְתוֹתַ֖יִךְ כַּלָּ֑ה דְּבַ֤שׁ וְחָלָב֙ תַּ֣חַת לְשׁוֹנֵ֔ךְ וְרֵ֥יחַ שַׂלְמֹתַ֖יִךְ

יב כְּרֵ֥יחַ לְבָנֽוֹן: גַּ֥ן ׀ נָע֖וּל אֲחֹתִ֣י כַלָּ֑ה גַּ֥ל נָע֖וּל מַעְיָ֥ן חָתֽוּם:

יג־יד שְׁלָחַ֙יִךְ֙ פַּרְדֵּ֣ס רִמּוֹנִ֔ים עִ֖ם פְּרִ֣י מְגָדִ֑ים כְּפָרִ֖ים עִם־נְרָדִֽים: נֵ֣רְדְּ ׀ וְכַרְכֹּ֗ם

קָנֶה֙ וְקִנָּמ֔וֹן עִ֖ם כָּל־עֲצֵ֣י לְבוֹנָ֑ה מֹ֚ר וַֽאֲהָל֔וֹת עִ֖ם כָּל־רָאשֵׁ֥י בְשָׂמִֽים:

NOTES INCLUDING PHRASE-BY-PHRASE LITERAL TRANSLATION

4:3. כְּחוּט הַשָּׁנִי שִׂפְתוֹתַיִךְ — *Like the scarlet thread, guarantor of Rahab's safety, is the sincerity of your lips* [lit., *Your lips are like a thread of scarlet*]. This refers to the sincere pledge that Joshua's spies made to Rahab in Jericho. They guaranteed her safety if she would display a scarlet thread as a signal to the conquering Jews (see *Joshua* Ch. 2).

וּמִדְבָּרֵךְ נָאוֶה — *and your word is unfeigned* [lit., *and your speech is comely*].

כְּפֶלַח הָרִמּוֹן רַקָּתֵךְ מִבַּעַד לְצַמָּתֵךְ — *As many as a pomegranate's seeds are the merits of your unworthiest within your modest veil* [lit., *Your cheeks are like a slice of pomegranate, from behind your veil*]. The word רַקָּה, "cheeks," is linguistically related to רַק, "empty," and is a metaphor for those who are relatively empty of mitzvos; rosy cheeks also resemble a pomegranate. Even the comparatively few merits of the lowest among you are as numerous as a pomegranate's seeds.

4:4. כְּמִגְדַּל דָּוִיד צַוָּארֵךְ בָּנוּי לְתַלְפִּיּוֹת — *As stately as the Tower of David is the site of your Sanhedrin built as a model to emulate* [lit., *Your neck is the Tower of David, built as an ornament*]. The verse alludes to the Stronghold of Zion, a beautiful, stately fortification, and to the chamber of the Sanhedrin, the spiritual stronghold of Israel.

אֶלֶף הַמָּגֵן תָּלוּי עָלָיו כֹּל שִׁלְטֵי הַגִּבֹּרִים — *with a thousand shields of Torah armor hung upon it, all the disciple-filled quivers of the mighty* [lit., *a thousand shields are hung upon it; all the quivers of the mighty men*]. Students are likened to arrows (see *Psalms* 127:4-5).

4:5. שְׁנֵי שָׁדַיִךְ כִּשְׁנֵי עֳפָרִים תְּאוֹמֵי צְבִיָּה — *Moses and Aaron, your two sustainers, are like two fawns, twins of the gazelle* [lit., *Your breasts are like two fawns, twins of a gazelle*]. Moses and Aaron are like the breasts that nurtured Israel. They are called "twins" because they were of equal stature.

הָרֹעִים בַּשּׁוֹשַׁנִּים — *who graze their sheep in roselike bounty* [lit., *who feed among the roses*]. Like shepherds, Moses and Aaron guided their nation along tranquil paths.

4:6. עַד שֶׁיָּפוּחַ הַיּוֹם וְנָסוּ הַצְּלָלִים — *Until My sunny benevolence was withdrawn from Shiloh and the protective shadows were dispersed by your sin* [lit., *Until the day breathes and the shadows flee*]. God had been Israel's protective shade, until they sinned.

אֵלֶךְ לִי אֶל הַר הַמּוֹר וְאֶל גִּבְעַת הַלְּבוֹנָה — *I will go to Mount Moriah and the hill of frankincense* [lit., *I will get me to the mountain of myrrh, and to the hill of frankincense*]. After His anger abated, He chose Mount Moriah as the site of the Temple, where incense would be offered.

4:7. כֻּלָּךְ יָפָה רַעְיָתִי וּמוּם אֵין בָּךְ — *where [on Mount Moriah] you will be completely fair, My beloved, and no blemish will be in you* [lit., *You are entirely fair, My beloved, and there is no blemish in you*].

4:8. אִתִּי מִלְּבָנוֹן כַּלָּה אִתִּי מִלְּבָנוֹן תָּבוֹאִי — *With Me will you be exiled from the Temple, O bride, with Me from the Temple until you return* [lit., *With Me from Lebanon, O bride! With Me from Lebanon shall you come*]. The Temple is called Lebanon (לְבָנוֹן, lit., "whitener") because it whitens the sins of Israel (Talmud, *Yoma* 39b). You will be exiled "with Me," says God, "for in all your afflictions, I, too, am afflicted" (see *Isaiah* 63:9).

תָּשׁוּרִי מֵרֹאשׁ אֲמָנָה — *then to contemplate the fruits of your faith from its earliest beginnings* [lit., *Look from the peak of Amanah*]. The word ראש means both "head (or, peak)" and "beginning"; אֲמָנָה means "covenant of faith" and is the name of a mountain on the northern border of the Land of Israel.

מֵרֹאשׁ שְׂנִיר וְחֶרְמוֹן מִמְּעֹנוֹת אֲרָיוֹת מֵהַרְרֵי נְמֵרִים — *from your first arrival at the summits of Senir and Hermon, the lands of mighty Sihon and Og, as impregnable as dens of lions, and as mountains of leopards* [lit., *from the peak of Senir and Hermon, from the dens of lions, from the mountains of leopards*].

4:9. לִבַּבְתִּנִי אֲחֹתִי כַלָּה — *You have captured My heart, My sister, O bride*.

לִבַּבְתִּנִי בְּאַחַת מֵעֵינַיִךְ בְּאַחַד עֲנָק מִצַּוְּרֹנָיִךְ — *you have captured My heart with but one of your virtues, with but one of the precepts that adorn you like beads of a necklace resplendent* [lit., *You have*

³ *Like the scarlet thread, guarantor of Rahab's safety, is the sincerity of your lips, and your word is unfeigned. As many as a pomegranate's seeds are the merits of your unworthiest within your modest veil.* ⁴ *As stately as the Tower of David is the site of your Sanhedrin built as a model to emulate, with a thousand shields of Torah armor hung upon it, all the disciple-filled quivers of the mighty.* ⁵ *Moses and Aaron, your two sustainers, are like two fawns, twins of the gazelle, who graze their sheep in roselike bounty.*

⁶ *Until My sunny benevolence was withdrawn from Shiloh and the protective shadows were dispersed by your sin. I will go to Mount Moriah and the hill of frankincense —* ⁷ *where you will be completely fair, My beloved, and no blemish will be in you.*

⁸ *With Me will you be exiled from the Temple, O bride, with Me from the Temple until you return; then to contemplate the fruits of your faith from its earliest beginnings, from your first arrival at the summits of Senir and Hermon, the lands of mighty Sihon and Og, as impregnable as dens of lions, and as mountains of leopards.*

⁹ *You have captured My heart, My sister, O bride; you have captured My heart with but one of your virtues, with but one of the precepts that adorn you like beads of a necklace resplendent.* ¹⁰ *How fair was your love in so many settings, My sister, O bride; so superior is your love to wine and your spreading fame to all perfumes.*

¹¹ *The sweetness of Torah drips from your lips, like honey and milk it lies under your tongue; your very garments are scented with precepts like the scent of Lebanon.* ¹² *As chaste as a garden locked, My sister, O bride; a spring locked up, a fountain sealed.* ¹³ *Your least gifted ones are a pomegranate orchard with luscious fruit; henna with nard;* ¹⁴ *nard and saffron, calamus and cinnamon, with all trees of frankincense, myrrh and aloes with all the chief spices;*

---

captured my heart with one of your eyes, with one bead of your necklace]. I would have loved you even had you possessed only one of your endearing qualities; how much more so since you possess so many!

4:10. מַה יָּפוּ דֹדַיִךְ אֲחֹתִי כַלָּה — *How fair was your love in so many settings, My sister, O bride* [lit., *How fair was your love, My sister O bride!*]. Your love is pleasing everywhere, whether in the Tabernacle or in the Temple.

מַה טֹּבוּ דֹדַיִךְ מִיַּיִן וְרֵיחַ שְׁמָנַיִךְ מִכָּל בְּשָׂמִים — *so superior is your love to wine and your spreading fame to all perfumes* [lit., *how much better your love than wine, and the fragrance of your oils than all spices!*].

4:11. נֹפֶת תִּטֹּפְנָה שִׂפְתוֹתַיִךְ כַּלָּה דְּבַשׁ וְחָלָב תַּחַת לְשׁוֹנֵךְ — *The sweetness of Torah drips from your lips, like honey and milk it lies under your tongue* [lit., *Honey drops from your lips, O bride, honey and milk are under your tongue*].

וְרֵיחַ שַׂלְמֹתַיִךְ כְּרֵיחַ לְבָנוֹן — *your very garments are scented with precepts like the scent of Lebanon* [lit., *and the scent of your garments is like the scent of Lebanon*]. This refers to the precepts

associated with clothing, such as the commandment of wearing *tzitzis* and the prohibition against wearing *shaatnez* (see Deuteronomy 22:11).

4:12. גַּן נָעוּל אֲחֹתִי כַלָּה גַּל נָעוּל מַעְיָן חָתוּם — *As chaste as a garden locked, My sister, O bride; a spring locked up, a fountain sealed* [lit., *A garden locked up is my sister, the bride, a spring locked up, a fountain sealed*]. The beauty and charm of the daughters of Israel are guided by modesty and purity.

4:13. שְׁלָחַיִךְ פַּרְדֵּס רִמּוֹנִים עִם פְּרִי מְגָדִים — *Your least gifted ones are a pomegranate orchard with luscious fruit* [lit., *Your arid areas are an orchard of pomegranates with precious fruits*]. Like a field in need of irrigation, your youngsters strive to be "moistened" with Torah and good deeds.

כְּפָרִים עִם נְרָדִים — *henna with nard.* Types of spices (see 1:14).

4:14. נֵרְדְּ וְכַרְכֹּם קָנֶה וְקִנָּמוֹן עִם כָּל עֲצֵי לְבוֹנָה מֹר וַאֲהָלוֹת עִם כָּל רָאשֵׁי בְשָׂמִים — *Nard and saffron, calamus and cinnamon, with all trees of frankincense, myrrh, and aloes, with all the chief spices.*

מַעְיַ֣ן גַּנִּ֔ים בְּאֵ֖ר מַ֣יִם חַיִּ֑ים וְנֹזְלִ֖ים מִן־לְבָנֽוֹן: ע֤וּרִי צָפוֹן֙ וּב֣וֹאִי תֵימָ֔ן הָפִ֥יחִי גַנִּ֖י   טו-טז

יִזְּל֣וּ בְשָׂמָ֑יו יָבֹ֤א דוֹדִי֙ לְגַנּ֔וֹ וְיֹאכַ֖ל פְּרִ֥י מְגָדָֽיו: בָּ֣אתִי לְגַנִּי֮ אֲחֹתִ֣י כַלָּה֒ אָרִ֤יתִי   א

מוֹרִי֙ עִם־בְּשָׂמִ֔י אָכַ֤לְתִּי יַעְרִי֙ עִם־דִּבְשִׁ֔י שָׁתִ֥יתִי יֵינִ֖י עִם־חֲלָבִ֑י אִכְל֣וּ רֵעִ֔ים

שְׁת֥וּ וְשִׁכְר֖וּ דּוֹדִֽים: אֲנִ֥י יְשֵׁנָ֖ה וְלִבִּ֣י עֵ֑ר ק֣וֹל ׀ דּוֹדִ֣י דוֹפֵ֗ק פִּתְחִי־לִ֞י   ב

אֲחֹתִ֤י רַעְיָתִי֙ יוֹנָתִ֣י תַמָּתִ֔י שֶׁרֹּאשִׁי֙ נִמְלָא־טָ֔ל קְוֻּצּוֹתַ֖י רְסִ֥יסֵי לָֽיְלָה: פָּשַׁ֙טְתִּי֙   ג

אֶת־כֻּתָּנְתִּ֔י אֵיכָ֖כָה אֶלְבָּשֶׁ֑נָּה רָחַ֥צְתִּי אֶת־רַגְלַ֖י אֵיכָ֥כָה אֲטַנְּפֵֽם: דּוֹדִ֗י שָׁלַ֤ח   ד

יָדוֹ֙ מִן־הַ֣חֹ֔ר וּמֵעַ֖י הָמ֥וּ עָלָֽיו: קַ֥מְתִּֽי אֲנִ֖י לִפְתֹּ֣חַ לְדוֹדִ֑י וְיָדַ֣י נָֽטְפוּ־מ֗וֹר   ה

וְאֶצְבְּעֹתַי֙ מ֣וֹר עֹבֵ֔ר עַ֖ל כַּפּ֥וֹת הַמַּנְעֽוּל: פָּתַ֤חְתִּי אֲנִי֙ לְדוֹדִ֔י וְדוֹדִ֖י חָמַ֣ק עָבָ֑ר   ו

נַפְשִׁי֙ יָֽצְאָ֣ה בְדַבְּר֔וֹ בִּקַּשְׁתִּ֙יהוּ֙ וְלֹ֣א מְצָאתִ֔יהוּ קְרָאתִ֖יו וְלֹ֥א עָנָֽנִי: מְצָאֻ֧נִי   ז

הַשֹּֽׁמְרִ֛ים הַסֹּבְבִ֥ים בָּעִ֖יר הִכּ֣וּנִי פְצָע֑וּנִי נָֽשְׂא֤וּ אֶת־רְדִידִי֙ מֵֽעָלַ֔י שֹׁמְרֵ֖י הַֽחֹמֽוֹת:

NOTES INCLUDING PHRASE-BY-PHRASE LITERAL TRANSLATION

4:15. מַעְיַן גַּנִּים בְּאֵר מַיִם חַיִּים וְנֹזְלִים מִן לְבָנוֹן — *purified in a garden spring, a well of waters alive and flowing clean from Lebanon* [lit., *(You are) a garden spring; a well of living waters streams from Lebanon*]. God praises the women of Israel whose ritual immersion is like a spring enabling the fields to be fruitful.

4:16. עוּרִי צָפוֹן וּבוֹאִי תֵימָן הָפִיחִי גַנִּי יִזְּלוּ בְשָׂמָיו — *Awake from the north and come from the south! Like the winds let My exiles return to My garden, let their fragrant goodness flow in Jerusalem* [lit., *Awake, O north (wind), and come, O south! Blow (upon) my garden, let its spices flow out*]. Having found delight in you, command the winds to waft your fragrance afar. Allegorically, Israel's host nations will be so overwhelmed by the miracles preceding the Redemption that they will bring the Jews to Eretz Yisrael (see *Isaiah* 66:20). In the Temple, the Jews will say to God . . .

יָבֹא דוֹדִי לְגַנּוֹ וְיֹאכַל פְּרִי מְגָדָיו — *Let but my Beloved come to His garden and enjoy His precious people* [lit., *Let my Beloved come to His garden and eat its precious fruit*]. If You are there, all is there.

5:1. בָּאתִי לְגַנִּי אֲחֹתִי כַלָּה — *To your Tabernacle Dedication, My sister, O bride, I came as if to My garden* [lit., *I have come into My garden, My sister, O bride*]. When the Tabernacle was set up, God's glory filled it (*Exodus* 40:33,34).

אָרִיתִי מוֹרִי עִם בְּשָׂמִי — *I gathered My myrrh with My spice from your princely incense* [lit., *I have gathered My myrrh with My spice*]. The princes of the tribes offered incense at the Dedication of the Tabernacle (*Numbers* Ch. 7).

אָכַלְתִּי יַעְרִי עִם דִּבְשִׁי — *I accepted your unbidden as well as your bidden offerings to Me* [lit., *I have eaten My honeycomb with My honey*]. After its sweetness has been sucked, the comb is discarded. However, God's love of Israel was such that, during the inauguration of the Tabernacle, He accepted even offerings that would have otherwise been inappropriate. The tribal princes brought not only incense, but also sin-offerings, even though sin-offerings are not appropriate to be brought voluntarily.

שָׁתִיתִי יֵינִי עִם חֲלָבִי — *I drank your libations pure as milk* [lit., *I have*

drunk My wine with My milk].

אִכְלוּ רֵעִים שְׁתוּ וְשִׁכְרוּ דּוֹדִים — *Eat, My beloved priests! Drink and become God-intoxicated, O friends* [lit., *Eat, friends; drink and become intoxicated, O beloved ones*], you who partook of the flesh of the peace-offerings.

5:2. [The following verses allegorize the period of the First Temple and its destruction, Israel's sins, God's pleas for repentance, and Israel's recalcitrance — until it was too late.]

אֲנִי יְשֵׁנָה וְלִבִּי עֵר — *I let my devotion slumber, but the God of my heart was awake* [lit., *I (was) asleep but my heart (was) awake*]. Secure in the peaceful period of feeling secure, Israel neglected the service of God, as if asleep, but, "my heart," i.e., God, was wakeful to guard me and grant me goodness.

קוֹל דּוֹדִי דוֹפֵק — *A sound! My Beloved knocks* [lit., *The sound of my Beloved knocking!*]. Throughout my slumber, He issued daily warnings through the prophets (see *Jeremiah* 7:25).

פִּתְחִי לִי אֲחֹתִי רַעְיָתִי יוֹנָתִי תַמָּתִי — *He said, "Open your heart to Me, My sister, My love, My dove, My perfection* [lit., *Open to Me* (i.e., Let Me in), *My sister, My love, My dove, My perfect one*]. Do not cause Me to depart from you.

שֶׁרֹּאשִׁי נִמְלָא טָל — *admit Me and My head is filled with dewlike memories of Abraham* [lit., *for My head is filled with dew*]. Through His prophets, He said to me, "Abraham's deeds were pleasing to Me as dew, and I will shower you with blessings if you will but return to Me."

קְוֻּצּוֹתַי רְסִיסֵי לָיְלָה — *spurn Me and I bear collections of punishing rains in exile-nights* [lit., *My locks (with) the rains of the night*].

5:3. פָּשַׁטְתִּי אֶת כֻּתָּנְתִּי אֵיכָכָה אֶלְבָּשֶׁנָּה רָחַצְתִּי אֶת רַגְלַי אֵיכָכָה אֲטַנְּפֵם — *And I responded, "I have doffed my robe of devotion; how can I don it? I have washed my feet that trod Your path; how can I soil them?"* [lit., *I have taken off my robe, how shall I don it? I have washed my feet, how shall I soil them?*]. In reaction to God's knock on the door, we thought, "We have accustomed ourselves to serve other gods — how can we return to our God?"

5:4. דּוֹדִי שָׁלַח יָדוֹ מִן הַחֹר — *In anger at my recalcitrance, my Beloved sent forth His hand from the portal in wrath* [lit., *My*

15 purified in a garden spring, a well of waters alive and flowing clean from Lebanon.

16 Awake from the north and come from the south! Like the winds let My exiles return to My garden, let their fragrant goodness flow in Jerusalem.

Israel responds

Let but my Beloved come to His garden and enjoy His precious people.

5

God replies

1 To your Tabernacle Dedication, My sister, O bride, I came as if to My garden. I gathered My myrrh with My spice from your princely incense; I accepted your unbidden as well as your bidden offerings to Me; I drank your libations pure as milk. Eat, My beloved priests! Drink and become God-intoxicated, O friends!

Israel reminisces regretfully

2 I let my devotion slumber, but the God of my heart was awake! A sound! My Beloved knocks!

He said, "Open your heart to Me, My sister, My love, My dove, My perfection; admit Me and My head is filled with dewlike memories of Abraham; spurn Me and I bear collections of punishing rains in exile-nights."

3 And I responded, "I have doffed my robe of devotion; how can I don it? I have washed my feet that trod Your path; how can I soil them?"

4 In anger at my recalcitrance, my Beloved sent forth His hand from the portal in wrath, and my intestines churned with longing for Him. 5 I arose to open for my Beloved and my hands dripped myrrh of repentant devotion to Torah and God, and my fingers flowing with myrrh to remove the traces of my foolish rebuke from the handles of the lock. 6 I opened for my Beloved; but, alas, my Beloved had turned His back on my plea and was gone. My soul departed at His decree! I sought His closeness, but could not find it; I beseeched Him, but He would not answer.

7 They found me, the enemy watchmen patrolling the city; they struck me, they bloodied me wreaking God's revenge on me. They stripped my mantle of holiness from me, the angelic watchmen of the wall.

NOTES INCLUDING PHRASE-BY-PHRASE LITERAL TRANSLATION

Beloved sent forth His hand from the portal]. When we spurned Him, God brought Aram upon us and our king, Ahaz (see *II Chronicles* 28:5,6).

וּמֵעַי הָמוּ עָלָיו — *and my intestines churned with longing for Him* [lit., *and my intestines stirred for Him*]. We changed our ways, and became righteous in the service of God.

5:5. קַמְתִּי אֲנִי לִפְתֹּחַ לְדוֹדִי וְיָדַי נָטְפוּ מוֹר — *I arose to open for my Beloved and my hands dripped myrrh of repentant devotion to Torah and God* [lit., *I rose to open for my Beloved and my hands dripped with myrrh*]. Hezekiah, Ahaz's son, became a model of piety. His entire generation was perfect; and there never arose another generation like it (*Talmud, Sanhedrin* 94b).

וְאֶצְבְּעֹתַי מוֹר עֹבֵר עַל כַּפּוֹת הַמַּנְעוּל — *and my fingers flowing with myrrh to remove the traces of my foolish rebuke from the handles of the lock* [lit., *and my fingers flowing with myrrh upon the handles of the lock*].

5:6. But, His Decree was to be enforced.

פָּתַחְתִּי אֲנִי לְדוֹדִי וְדוֹדִי חָמַק עָבָר — *I opened for my Beloved; but, alas, my Beloved had turned His back on my plea and was gone* [lit., *I opened for my Beloved, but my Beloved had turned and gone*]. Belatedly, I responded to my Beloved, but, alas, He did not

annul His decree.

נַפְשִׁי יָצְאָה בְדַבְּרוֹ — *My soul departed at His decree* [lit., *my soul departed* (i.e., I became faint) *as He spoke*]. In effect, He said, "I will not enter, since at first you had refused to let Me in."

בִּקַּשְׁתִּיהוּ וְלֹא מְצָאתִיהוּ — *I sought His closeness, but could not find it* [lit., *I sought Him, but did not find Him*].

קְרָאתִיו וְלֹא עָנָנִי — *I beseeched Him, but He would not answer* [lit., *I called Him, but He did not answer me*].

5:7. מְצָאֻנִי הַשֹּׁמְרִים הַסֹּבְבִים בָּעִיר — *They found me, the enemy watchmen patrolling the city* [lit., *The watchmen who circle the city found me*]. Nebuchadnezzar's forces lay siege to Jerusalem . . .

הִכּוּנִי פְצָעוּנִי — *they struck me, they bloodied me, wreaking God's revenge on me* [lit., *they struck me, they wounded me*]. The Destruction of the First Temple was beginning.

נָשְׂאוּ אֶת רְדִידִי מֵעָלַי שֹׁמְרֵי הַחֹמוֹת — *They stripped my mantle of holiness from me, the angelic watchmen of the wall* [lit., *the guards of the walls stripped my mantle from me*]. Even the angels that had formerly been assigned to protect the city now took part in the destruction (see *Lamentations* 1:13).

ח הִשְׁבַּעְתִּי אֶתְכֶם בְּנוֹת יְרוּשָׁלִַם אִם־תִּמְצְאוּ אֶת־דּוֹדִי מַה־תַּגִּידוּ לוֹ שֶׁחוֹלַת

ט אַהֲבָה אָנִי: מַה־דּוֹדֵךְ מִדּוֹד הַיָּפָה בַּנָּשִׁים מַה־דּוֹדֵךְ מִדּוֹד שֶׁכָּכָה הִשְׁבַּעְתָּנוּ:

י־יא דּוֹדִי צַח וְאָדוֹם דָּגוּל מֵרְבָבָה: רֹאשׁוֹ כֶּתֶם פָּז קְוֻצּוֹתָיו תַּלְתַּלִּים שְׁחֹרוֹת

יב־יג כָּעוֹרֵב: עֵינָיו כְּיוֹנִים עַל־אֲפִיקֵי מָיִם רֹחֲצוֹת בֶּחָלָב יֹשְׁבוֹת עַל־מִלֵּאת: לְחָיָו

יד כַּעֲרוּגַת הַבֹּשֶׂם מִגְדְּלוֹת מֶרְקָחִים שִׂפְתוֹתָיו שׁוֹשַׁנִּים נֹטְפוֹת מוֹר עֹבֵר: יָדָיו

טו גְּלִילֵי זָהָב מְמֻלָּאִים בַּתַּרְשִׁישׁ מֵעָיו עֶשֶׁת שֵׁן מְעֻלֶּפֶת סַפִּירִים: שׁוֹקָיו עַמּוּדֵי

טז שֵׁשׁ מְיֻסָּדִים עַל־אַדְנֵי־פָז מַרְאֵהוּ כַּלְּבָנוֹן בָּחוּר כָּאֲרָזִים: חִכּוֹ מַמְתַקִּים וְכֻלּוֹ

א מַחֲמַדִּים זֶה דוֹדִי וְזֶה רֵעִי בְּנוֹת יְרוּשָׁלִָם: אָנָה הָלַךְ דּוֹדֵךְ הַיָּפָה בַּנָּשִׁים אָנָה

ב פָּנָה דוֹדֵךְ וּנְבַקְשֶׁנּוּ עִמָּךְ: דּוֹדִי יָרַד לְגַנּוֹ לַעֲרוּגוֹת הַבֹּשֶׂם לִרְעוֹת בַּגַּנִּים

ג וְלִלְקֹט שׁוֹשַׁנִּים: אֲנִי לְדוֹדִי וְדוֹדִי לִי הָרֹעֶה בַּשּׁוֹשַׁנִּים:

NOTES INCLUDING PHRASE-BY-PHRASE LITERAL TRANSLATION

5:8. הִשְׁבַּעְתִּי אֶתְכֶם בְּנוֹת יְרוּשָׁלִַם — *I adjure you, O nations destined to ascend to Jerusalem* [lit., *I adjure you, O daughters of Jerusalem*]. You, our oppressors, should testify that we remained loyal to our God.

אִם־תִּמְצְאוּ אֶת־דּוֹדִי — *when you see my Beloved on the future Day of Judgment* [lit., *If you find my Beloved*], when the nations will be called upon to bear witness for Israel . . .

מַה־תַּגִּידוּ לוֹ שֶׁחוֹלַת אַהֲבָה אָנִי — *will you not tell Him that I bore all travails for love of Him?* [lit., *What shall you tell him? That I am sick with love*]. Tell Him that only for love of Him were we afflicted with harsh suffering.

5:9. מַה־דּוֹדֵךְ מִדּוֹד הַיָּפָה בַּנָּשִׁים — *With what does your beloved God excel all others that you suffer for His Name, O fairest of nations?* [lit., *What (makes) your Beloved (better) than (another) beloved, O fairest among women?*]. How is your God so superior to other gods that you are ready to be burned and tortured for Him? You are handsome, you are mighty; come intermingle with us!

מַה־דּוֹדֵךְ מִדּוֹד שֶׁכָּכָה הִשְׁבַּעְתָּנוּ — *With what does your beloved God excel all others that you dare to adjure us?* [lit., *What (makes) your Beloved (better) than (another) beloved, that you so adjure us?*].

5:10. דּוֹדִי צַח וְאָדוֹם — *My Beloved is pure and purifies sin, and is ruddy with vengeance to punish betrayers* [lit., *My Beloved is white, yet ruddy*]. Even when He sits in judgment, He is anxious to purify my deeds. But when exacting retribution from His enemies, He is depicted as clad in blood-red vestments (see *Isaiah 63:2*).

דָּגוּל מֵרְבָבָה — *surrounded with myriad angels* [lit., *preeminent above ten thousand*].

5:11. רֹאשׁוֹ כֶּתֶם פָּז — *His opening words were finest gold* [lit., *His head is finest gold*]. When He gave us the Ten Commandments, His words were like fine gold.

קְוֻצּוֹתָיו תַּלְתַּלִּים — *His crowns hold mounds of statutes* [lit., *His locks are wavy*]. From every one of the scribal crowns that adorn the tops of many letters in the Torah script, mounds and mounds of laws can be derived (*Eruvin 21b*).

שְׁחֹרוֹת כָּעוֹרֵב — *written in raven-black flame* [lit., *black as the raven*]. In Heaven, the Torah is written in black fire upon white fire.

5:12. עֵינָיו כְּיוֹנִים עַל־אֲפִיקֵי מָיִם — *Like the gaze of doves toward their cotes, His eyes are fixed on the waters of Torah* [lit., *His eyes are like doves besides brooks of water*].

רֹחֲצוֹת בֶּחָלָב — *bathing all things in clarity* [lit., *bathing in milk*]. God's "eyes" see clearly, rewarding the righteous, and condemning the wicked.

יֹשְׁבוֹת עַל־מִלֵּאת — *established upon Creation's fullness* [lit., *sitting upon the fullness*]. His judgment is upon the fullness of the earth.

5:13. לְחָיָו כַּעֲרוּגַת הַבֹּשֶׂם מִגְדְּלוֹת מֶרְקָחִים — *Like a bed of spices are His words at Sinai, like towers of perfume* [lit., *His cheeks are like a bed of spices, towers of perfume*]. God's utterances at Mount Sinai during which He displayed a friendly, smiling demeanor were like beds of spices and mounds of sweet herbs to be processed into perfumes.

שִׂפְתוֹתָיו שׁוֹשַׁנִּים נֹטְפוֹת מוֹר עֹבֵר — *His comforting words from the Tabernacle are roses dripping flowing myrrh* [lit., *His lips are like roses; they drip flowing myrrh*]. In the Tabernacle, God taught us about the offerings that atone for sin.

5:14. יָדָיו גְּלִילֵי זָהָב — *The Tablets, His handiwork, are desirable above even rolls of gold* [lit., *His arms are rods of gold*]. The Tablets of the Ten Commandments, written by the "finger" of God (*Exodus 31:18*), "are more desirable than gold, than even much fine gold" (*Psalms 19:11*).

מְמֻלָּאִים בַּתַּרְשִׁישׁ — *they are studded with commandments precious as gems* [lit., *studded with crystal*].

מֵעָיו עֶשֶׁת שֵׁן מְעֻלֶּפֶת סַפִּירִים — *the Torah's innards are sparkling as ivory intricately inlaid with precious stone* [lit., *his innards are as shiny as ivory inlaid with sapphires*].

5:15. שׁוֹקָיו עַמּוּדֵי שֵׁשׁ מְיֻסָּדִים עַל־אַדְנֵי־פָז — *The Torah's columns are marble set in contexts of finest gold* [lit., *His legs are pillars of marble set upon sockets of fine gold*] . . .

מַרְאֵהוּ כַּלְּבָנוֹן בָּחוּר כָּאֲרָזִים — *its contemplation flowers like Lebanon, it is sturdy as cedars* [lit., *his appearance is like (the forest of) Lebanon, choicest among cedars*]. Just as one sees beautiful

Israel to the nations

⁸ *I adjure you, O nations destined to ascend to Jerusalem, when you see my Beloved on the future Day of Judgment, will you not tell Him that I bore all travails for love of Him?*

The nations ask Israel

⁹ *With what does your beloved God excel all others that you suffer for His Name, O fairest of nations? With what does your beloved God excel all others that you dare to adjure us?*

Israel responds

¹⁰ *My Beloved is pure and purifies sin, and is ruddy with vengeance to punish betrayers, surrounded with myriad angels.* ¹¹ *His opening words were finest gold, His crowns hold mounds of statutes written in raven-black flame.*

¹² *Like the gaze of doves toward their cotes, His eyes are fixed on the waters of Torah, bathing all things in clarity, established upon Creation's fullness.* ¹³ *Like a bed of spices are His words at Sinai, like towers of perfume. His comforting words from the Tabernacle are roses dripping flowing myrrh.* ¹⁴ *The Tablets, His handiwork, are desirable above even rolls of gold; they are studded with commandments precious as gems, the Torah's innards are sparkling as ivory intricately inlaid with precious stone.* ¹⁵ *The Torah's columns are marble set in contexts of finest gold, its contemplation flowers like Lebanon, it is sturdy as cedars.* ¹⁶ *The words of His palate are sweet and He is all delight.*

This is my Beloved and this is my Friend, O nations destined to ascend to Jerusalem.

6 *The nations, derisively, to Israel*

¹ **W**here has your Beloved gone, O fairest among women? Where has your Beloved turned to rejoin you? Let us seek Him with you and build His Temple with you.

Israel responds

² *My Beloved has descended to His Temple garden, to His Incense Altar, yet still He grazes my brethren remaining in gardens of exile to gather the roseate fragrance of their words of Torah.* ³ *I alone am my Beloved's and my Beloved is mine, He Who grazes His sheep in roselike pastures.*

---

flowers and lofty trees in a forest, so one discovers limitless wisdom in the Torah.

5:16. חִכּוֹ מַמְתַקִּים וְכֻלּוֹ מַחֲמַדִּים — *The words of His palate are sweet and He is all delight* [lit., *His palate is most sweet; and all of him is a delight*].

זֶה דוֹדִי וְזֶה רֵעִי בְּנוֹת יְרוּשָׁלָם — *This is my Beloved and this is my Friend, O nations destined to ascend to Jerusalem* [lit., *this is my Beloved, and this is my Friend, O daughters of Jerusalem*].

6:1. The nations continue to taunt Israel:

אָנָה הָלַךְ דּוֹדֵךְ הַיָּפָה בַּנָּשִׁים — *Where has your Beloved gone, O fairest among women?* Why has He left you alone, widowed?

אָנָה פָּנָה דוֹדֵךְ וּנְבַקְשֶׁנּוּ עִמָּךְ — *Where has your Beloved turned to rejoin you? Let us seek Him with you and build His Temple with you* [lit., *Where has your Beloved turned, that we may seek Him with you?*]. When King Cyrus permitted the rebuilding of the Temple, the heathens tried to undermine the work by joining the builders and sabotaging the construction (see *Ezra 4:1-2*).

6:2. דּוֹדִי יָרַד לְגַנּוֹ לַעֲרֻגוֹת הַבֹּשֶׂם — *My Beloved has descended to His Temple garden, to His Incense Altar* [lit., *My Beloved has gone down to His garden, to the beds of spices*]. He commanded us to build His Temple, and He will surely be there with us.

לִרְעוֹת בַּגַּנִּים וְלִלְקֹט שׁוֹשַׁנִּים — *yet still He grazes my brethren remaining in gardens of exile to gather the roseate fragrance of their words of Torah* [lit., *to graze in the gardens and to pick roses*]. God did not neglect those of His children who chose not to return to the land. He manifested His Presence in their synagogues and study halls.

6:3. In reply to the nations' insincere offer to help Israel:

אֲנִי לְדוֹדִי — *I alone am my Beloved's* [lit., *I am My Beloved's*]. I, alone, am my Beloved's. You are not His, and you will not assist us in the construction (see *Ezra 4:3*).

וְדוֹדִי לִי — *and my Beloved is mine*.

הָרוֹעֶה בַּשׁוֹשַׁנִּים — *He Who grazes His sheep in roselike pastures* [lit., *Who feeds (others) among the roses*].

יָפָ֨ה אַ֤תְּ רַעְיָתִי֙ כְּתִרְצָ֔ה נָאוָ֖ה כִּירוּשָׁלָ֑͏ִם אֲיֻמָּ֖ה כַּנִּדְגָּלֽוֹת: הָסֵ֤בִּי עֵינַ֙יִךְ֙ מִנֶּגְדִּ֔י

שֶׁהֵ֖ם הִרְהִיבֻ֑נִי שַׂעְרֵךְ֙ כְּעֵ֣דֶר הָֽעִזִּ֔ים שֶׁגָּלְשׁ֖וּ מִן־הַגִּלְעָֽד: שִׁנַּ֙יִךְ֙ כְּעֵ֣דֶר הָֽרְחֵלִ֔ים

שֶׁעָל֖וּ מִן־הָרַחְצָ֑ה שֶׁכֻּלָּם֙ מַתְאִימ֔וֹת וְשַׁכֻּלָ֖ה אֵ֥ין בָּהֶֽם: כְּפֶ֤לַח הָֽרִמּוֹן֙ רַקָּתֵ֔ךְ

מִבַּ֖עַד לְצַמָּתֵֽךְ: שִׁשִּׁ֥ים הֵ֙מָּה֙ מְלָכ֔וֹת וּשְׁמֹנִ֖ים פִּֽילַגְשִׁ֑ים וַֽעֲלָמ֖וֹת אֵ֥ין מִסְפָּֽר:

אַחַ֥ת הִיא֙ יֽוֹנָתִ֣י תַמָּתִ֔י אַחַ֥ת הִיא֙ לְאִמָּ֔הּ בָּרָ֥ה הִ֖יא לְיֽוֹלַדְתָּ֑הּ רָא֤וּהָ

בָנוֹת֙ וַֽיְאַשְּׁר֔וּהָ מְלָכ֥וֹת וּפִֽילַגְשִׁ֖ים וַֽיְהַלְלֽוּהָ: מִי־זֹ֥את הַנִּשְׁקָפָ֖ה

כְּמוֹ־שָׁ֑חַר יָפָ֣ה כַלְּבָנָ֗ה בָּרָה֙ כַּֽחַמָּ֔ה אֲיֻמָּ֖ה כַּנִּדְגָּלֽוֹת: אֶל־גִּנַּ֤ת אֱגוֹז֙

יָרַ֔דְתִּי לִרְא֖וֹת בְּאִבֵּ֣י הַנָּ֑חַל לִרְאוֹת֙ הֲפָֽרְחָ֣ה הַגֶּ֔פֶן הֵנֵ֖צוּ הָֽרִמֹּנִֽים: לֹ֣א יָדַ֔עְתִּי

נַפְשִׁ֣י שָׂמַ֔תְנִי מַרְכְּב֖וֹת עַמִּ֥י נָדִֽיב: שׁ֤וּבִי שׁ֙וּבִי֙ הַשּׁ֣וּלַמִּ֔ית שׁ֥וּבִי שׁ֖וּבִי וְנֶֽחֱזֶה־

בָּ֑ךְ מַֽה־תֶּחֱזוּ֙ בַּשּׁ֣וּלַמִּ֔ית כִּמְחֹלַ֖ת הַֽמַּֽחֲנָֽיִם: מַה־יָּפ֧וּ פְעָמַ֛יִךְ בַּנְּעָלִ֖ים בַּת־

6:4. יָפָה אַתְּ רַעְיָתִי כְּתִרְצָה — *You are beautiful, My love, when your deeds are pleasing* [lit., *You are beautiful, My love, as Tirzah*]. Tirzah was a beautiful city that was the capital for a succession of kings of the Northern Kingdom of Israel (see *I Kings* 15:33; 16:8-9,15,23).

נָאוָה כִּירוּשָׁלָם — *as comely now as you once were in Jerusalem of old* [lit., *comely as Jerusalem*].

אֲיֻמָּה כַּנִּדְגָּלוֹת — *hosts of angels stand in awe of you* [lit., *awe inspiring as an army with banners*]. See *Ezra* Ch. 5.

6:5. הָסֵבִּי עֵינַיִךְ מִנֶּגְדִּי שֶׁהֵם הִרְהִיבֻנִי — *Turn your pleading eyes from Me lest I be tempted to bestow upon you holiness more than you can bear* [lit., *Turn your eyes away from Me, for they overwhelm Me*]. As the Second Temple was being built, God said figuratively, "You are as beautiful to Me now as you were before, but in this Temple I will not return the Ark, the Cherubim and the *Paroches*-Curtain that you had in the First Temple. They invoke special love in Me that you cannot have now that you have sinned. But in every other way you have maintained the former virtues that endeared you to Me."

שַׂעְרֵךְ כְּעֵדֶר הָעִזִּים שֶׁגָּלְשׁוּ מִן הַגִּלְעָד — *But with all your flaws, your most common sons are as dearly beloved as the children of Jacob in the goatlike procession descending the slopes of Mount Gilead* [lit., *your hair is like a flock of goats streaming down from Gilead*]. Even the young, tender and insignificant among you are praiseworthy.

6:6. שִׁנַּיִךְ כְּעֵדֶר הָרְחֵלִים שֶׁעָלוּ מִן הָרַחְצָה שֶׁכֻּלָּם מַתְאִימוֹת וְשַׁכֻּלָה אֵין בָּהֶם — *Your mighty leaders are perfect, as a flock of ewes come up from the washing, all of them unblemished with no miscarriage of action in them* [lit., *Your teeth are like a flock of ewes which have come up from the washing, all of them are perfect and there is none blemished among them*] (see 4:2).

6:7. כְּפֶלַח הָרִמּוֹן רַקָּתֵךְ מִבַּעַד לְצַמָּתֵךְ — *As many as a pomegranate's seeds are the merits of your unworthiest within your modest veil* [lit., *Your cheeks are like a slice of pomegranate, from behind your veil*] (see 4:3).

6:8. שִׁשִּׁים הֵמָּה מְלָכוֹת — *The queenly offspring of Abraham are sixty* [lit., *There are sixty queens*]. Abraham's male descendants

---

through the children of Jacob (*Genesis* 25:1-4, 12-15; 35:23-36:19) numbered sixty (see Appendix B, charts 2 and 4).

וּשְׁמֹנִים פִּילַגְשִׁים וַעֲלָמוֹת אֵין מִסְפָּר — *compared to whom the eighty Noachides and all their countless nations are like mere concubines* [lit., *and eighty concubines and maidens without number*]. Noah's descendants, until Abraham (*Genesis* Chs. 10-11), numbered eighty (See Appendix B, chart 1). Each of them branched out into many families.

6:9. אַחַת הִיא יוֹנָתִי תַמָּתִי — *Unique is she, My constant dove, My perfect one* [lit., *One is My dove, My perfect one*]. Israel is My chosen nation, like a perfect dove, loyal to her mate.

אַחַת הִיא לְאִמָּהּ — *Unique is she, this nation striving for the truth* [lit., *one is she to her mother*]. To comprehend Torah in its fundamentals and its truth.

בָּרָה הִיא לְיוֹלַדְתָּהּ — *pure is she to Jacob who begot her* [lit., *she is pure to the one that begot her*]. All of Jacob's sons were righteous.

רָאוּהָ בָנוֹת וַיְאַשְּׁרוּהָ מְלָכוֹת וּפִילַגְשִׁים וַיְהַלְלוּהָ — Nations [lit., *maidens*] *saw her and they extolled her; queens and concubines, and they praised her* (see *Malachi* 3:12).

6:10. God now quotes to Israel how the nations will extol and praise her:

מִי זֹאת הַנִּשְׁקָפָה כְּמוֹ שָׁחַר — *"Who is this that gazes down from atop the Temple Mount, brightening like the dawn* [lit., *Who is that gazing down like dawn*?]. Like a steadily brightening dawn, Israel began the Second Temple era in subjugation, but later became independent under the Hasmonean dynasty.

יָפָה כַלְּבָנָה בָּרָה כַּחַמָּה — *beautiful as the moon, brilliant as the sun* [lit., *beautiful as the moon, pure as the sun*]. At first, Israel was like the moon, because it could only reflect the power permitted it by King Cyrus.

אֲיֻמָּה כַּנִּדְגָּלוֹת — *awesome as the bannered hosts of kings?"* [lit., *awe inspiring as an army with banners*].

6:11. אֶל גִּנַּת אֱגוֹז יָרַדְתִּי — *I descended upon the deceptively simple holiness of the Second Temple* [lit., *I went down to the garden of nuts*]. Israel is modest and unpretentious; her scholars are not

God to Israel ⁴ *You are beautiful, My love, when your deeds are pleasing, as comely now as you once were in Jerusalem of old, hosts of angels stand in awe of you.* ⁵ *Turn your pleading eyes from Me lest I be tempted to bestow upon you holiness more than you can bear. But with all your flaws, your most common sons are as dearly beloved as the children of Jacob in the goatlike procession descending the slopes of Mount Gilead.* ⁶ *Your mighty leaders are perfect, as a flock of ewes come up from the washing, all of them unblemished with no miscarriage of action in them.* ⁷ *As many as a pomegranate's seeds are the merits of your unworthiest within your modest veil.* ⁸ *The queenly offspring of Abraham are sixty, compared to whom the eighty Noachides and all their countless nations are like mere concubines.*

⁹ *Unique is she, My constant dove, My perfect one. Unique is she, this nation striving for the truth; pure is she to Jacob who begot her. Nations saw her and they extolled her; queens and concubines, and they praised her:* ¹⁰ *"Who is this that gazes down from atop the Temple Mount, brightening like the dawn, beautiful as the moon, brilliant as the sun, awesome as the bannered hosts of kings?"*

¹¹ *I descended upon the deceptively simple holiness of the Second Temple to see your moisture-laden deeds in the river beds; to see whether your Torah scholars had budded on the vine, whether your merit-laden righteous had flowered like the pomegranates filled with seeds.*

Israel responds sadly ¹² *Alas, I knew not how to guard myself from sin! My own devices harnessed me, like chariots subject to a foreign nation's mercies.*

7 ¹*The nations have said to me, "Turn away, turn away from God, O nation whose faith in Him is perfect, turn away, turn away, and we shall choose nobility from you."*

But I replied to them, "What can you bestow upon a nation of perfect faith commensurate even with the desert camps encircling?"

The nations to Israel ² *But your footsteps were so lovely when shod in pilgrim's sandals, O daughter*

conspicuous, but they are full of wisdom.

לִרְאוֹת בְּאִבֵּי הַנַּחַל — *to see your moisture-laden deeds in the river beds* [lit., *to look at the green plants of the streams*], to examine the good deeds that I could find in you . . .

לִרְאוֹת הֲפָרְחָה הַגֶּפֶן — *to see whether your Torah scholars had budded on the vine* [lit., *to see whether the vine has budded*] . . .

הֵנֵצוּ הָרִמֹּנִים — *whether your merit-laden righteous had flowered like the pomegranates filled with seeds* [lit., *if the pomegranates were in flower*].

6:12. Hearing God's praise of her glorious past, Israel reflects on her current plight and responds sadly:

לֹא יָדַעְתִּי נַפְשִׁי שָׂמַתְנִי מַרְכְּבוֹת עַמִּי נָדִיב — *Alas, I knew not how to guard myself from sin! My own devices harnessed me, like chariots subject to a foreign nation's mercies* [lit., *I did not know; my soul set me (as) chariots of a noble nation*]. Instead of avoiding sin, I stumbled into the sin of hatred and controversy, which caused Jews to invite Rome into the land and take control. From that point, I became a chariot driven by foreign nations.

7:1. שׁוּבִי שׁוּבִי הַשּׁוּלַמִּית — *The nations have said to me, "Turn*

away, turn away from God, O nation whose faith in Him is perfect [lit., *Turn, turn, O Shulammite*]. The word שׁוּלַמִּית, "Shulammite," is linguistically related to שָׁלֵם, "whole, perfect."

שׁוּבִי שׁוּבִי וְנֶחֱזֶה בָּךְ — *turn away, turn away, and we shall choose nobility from you"* [lit., *turn, turn, that we may see you*]. Join us and we will discern what greatness to bestow upon you.

מַה תֶּחֱזוּ בַּשּׁוּלַמִּית כִּמְחֹלַת הַמַּחֲנָיִם — *But I replied to them, "What can you bestow upon a nation of perfect faith commensurate even with the desert camps encircling?"* [lit., *What will you see in the Shulammite like a dance of the camps?*]. Your highest honors are not equal even to the greatness of the encircling encampments in the desert. See *Numbers* Ch. 2.

7:2. מַה יָּפוּ פְעָמַיִךְ בַּנְּעָלִים בַּת נָדִיב — *But your footsteps were so lovely when shod in pilgrim's sandals, O daughter of nobles* [lit., *How lovely are your steps in sandals, O daughter of nobility!*]. The word פְּעָמִים means both "footsteps," (hence, "pilgrimage") and "times, repeated occasions." The nations were impressed by Israel's pilgrimages to the Temple three times each year to celebrate the festivals.

גֹ נָדִיב חֲמוּקֵי יְרֵכַיִךְ כְּמוֹ חֲלָאִים מַעֲשֵׂה יְדֵי אָמָּן: שָׁרְרֵךְ אַגַּן הַסַּהַר

דֹ אַל־יֶחְסַר הַמָּזֶג בִּטְנֵךְ עֲרֵמַת חִטִּים סוּגָה בַּשּׁוֹשַׁנִּים: שְׁנֵי שָׁדַיִךְ כִּשְׁנֵי

הֹ עֳפָרִים תָּאֳמֵי צְבִיָּה: צַוָּארֵךְ כְּמִגְדַּל הַשֵּׁן עֵינַיִךְ בְּרֵכוֹת בְּחֶשְׁבּוֹן עַל־שַׁעַר

וֹ בַּת־רַבִּים אַפֵּךְ כְּמִגְדַּל הַלְּבָנוֹן צוֹפֶה פְּנֵי דַמָּשֶׂק: רֹאשֵׁךְ עָלַיִךְ כַּכַּרְמֶל וְדַלַּת

זֹ רֹאשֵׁךְ כָּאַרְגָּמָן מֶלֶךְ אָסוּר בָּרְהָטִים: מַה־יָּפִית וּמַה־נָּעַמְתְּ אַהֲבָה

ח־ט בַּתַּעֲנוּגִים: זֹאת קוֹמָתֵךְ דָּמְתָה לְתָמָר וְשָׁדַיִךְ לְאַשְׁכֹּלוֹת: אָמַרְתִּי אֶעֱלֶה

בְתָמָר אֹחֲזָה בְּסַנְסִנָּיו וְיִהְיוּ־נָא שָׁדַיִךְ כְּאֶשְׁכְּלוֹת הַגֶּפֶן וְרֵיחַ אַפֵּךְ כַּתַּפּוּחִים:

י־יא וְחִכֵּךְ כְּיֵין הַטּוֹב הוֹלֵךְ לְדוֹדִי לְמֵישָׁרִים דּוֹבֵב שִׂפְתֵי יְשֵׁנִים: אֲנִי לְדוֹדִי וְעָלַי

יב־יג תְּשׁוּקָתוֹ: לְכָה דוֹדִי נֵצֵא הַשָּׂדֶה נָלִינָה בַּכְּפָרִים: נַשְׁכִּימָה לַכְּרָמִים נִרְאֶה

אִם־פָּרְחָה הַגֶּפֶן פִּתַּח הַסְּמָדַר הֵנֵצוּ הָרִמּוֹנִים שָׁם אֶתֵּן אֶת־דֹּדַי לָךְ:

NOTES INCLUDING PHRASE-BY-PHRASE LITERAL TRANSLATION

חֲמוּקֵי יְרֵכַיִךְ כְּמוֹ חֲלָאִים מַעֲשֵׂה יְדֵי אָמָּן — *The rounded shafts for your libations' abysslike trenches, handiwork of the Master Craftsman* [lit., *The roundness of your flanks are like jewels, the work of a master's hand*]. The wine libations, poured onto the top of the Temple's Courtyard Altar, flowed through pipes into deep pits under the Altar. Those pits had been placed there by God Himself during the Six Days of Creation. They were rounded like a thigh and descended into the abyss.

7:3. שָׁרְרֵךְ אַגַּן הַסַּהַר — *At earth's very center your Sanhedrin site is a crescent basin* [lit., *Your umbilicus is like a moonshaped basin*]. The seat of the Sanhedrin (high court) was in the Temple complex, at the center of the world. Its members were seated in a semicircle, like the crescent moon, so they could see each other and speak face to face.

אַל־יֶחְסַר הַמָּזֶג — *of ceaseless, flowing teaching* [lit., *wherein no mixed wine is lacking*]. The Sanhedrin was an endless source of wisdom.

בִּטְנֵךְ עֲרֵמַת חִטִּים — *your national center an indispensable heap of nourishing knowledge* [lit., *your stomach is like a heap of wheat*]. Wheat is an indispensable staple.

סוּגָה בַּשּׁוֹשַׁנִּים — *Hedged about with roses.* Just as a hedge of roses is hardly an imposing barrier, similarly, the sanctions of the Torah are gentle reminders to refrain from trespass against the handiwork of God.

7:4. שְׁנֵי שָׁדַיִךְ כִּשְׁנֵי עֳפָרִים תָּאֳמֵי צְבִיָּה — *Your twin sustainers, the Tablets of the Law, are like two fawns, twins of the gazelle* [lit., *Your two breasts are like two fawns, twins of a gazelle*]. This refers to the twin Tablets of the Covenant (see also 4:5).

7:5. צַוָּארֵךְ כְּמִגְדַּל הַשֵּׁן — *Your Altar and Temple, erect and stately as an ivory tower* [lit., *Your neck is like a tower of ivory*]. The Sanctuary and Altar, which stood erect and tall, provided spiritual strength and protection like an ivory tower.

עֵינַיִךְ בְּרֵכוֹת בְּחֶשְׁבּוֹן עַל שַׁעַר בַּת רַבִּים — *your wise men aflow with springs of complex wisdom at the gate of the many-peopled city* [lit., *your eyes are (like the) pools in Heshbon by the gate of Bath-rabbim*]. Your wise men (the "eyes" of the nation) sit at the gates of Jerusalem (Bath-rabbim, lit., "of great population")

where they are involved in the complex calculations of the Hebrew calendar.

אַפֵּךְ כְּמִגְדַּל הַלְּבָנוֹן צוֹפֶה פְּנֵי דַמָּשֶׂק — *your face, like the tower of Lebanon, looks to your future boundary as far as Damascus* [lit., *your face is like the tower of Lebanon facing toward Damascus*]. An allusion to the prophetic vision (see *Zechariah 9:1*) that in the future the gates of Jerusalem will stretch forth until Damascus.

7:6. רֹאשֵׁךְ עָלַיִךְ כַּכַּרְמֶל — *The Godly name on your head is as mighty as Carmel* [lit., *Your head upon you is like (Mount) Carmel*]. This refers to the *tefillin* of the head, of which the verse says, "Then all the peoples of the earth will see that the Name of HASHEM is proclaimed over you, and they will revere you" (*Deuteronomy 28:10*). The *tefillin* are Israel's strength; they are as awe inspiring as the lofty cliffs of Mount Carmel.

וְדַלַּת רֹאשֵׁךְ כָּאַרְגָּמָן — *your crowning braid is royal purple* [lit., *and the locks of your head are like purple*]. The locks of your Nazirites are as comely as garments of royal purple.

מֶלֶךְ אָסוּר בָּרְהָטִים — *your King is bound in Naziritic tresses* [lit., *a king bound in tresses*]. The crown of the King (God) is associated with the Nazirite's hair (see *Numbers 6:7*).

7:7. מַה יָּפִית וּמַה נָּעַמְתְּ אַהֲבָה בַּתַּעֲנוּגִים — *How beautiful and pleasant are you, befitting the pleasures of spiritual love* [lit., *How beautiful you are, and how pleasant, love in delights*]. The nations now praise Israel's lofty spiritual ideals.

7:8. זֹאת קוֹמָתֵךְ דָּמְתָה לְתָמָר — *Such is your stature, likened to a towering palm tree* [lit., *This is your stature, like unto a palm tree*]. We witnessed your lovely stature in the days of Nebuchadnezzar, when all the nations bowed down to the statue (see *Daniel* Ch. 3).

וְשָׁדַיִךְ לְאַשְׁכֹּלוֹת — *from your teachers flow sustenance like wine-filled clusters* [lit., *and your breasts are like clusters*]. "Your breasts," your sources of spiritual nourishment, i.e., Daniel and his companions Hananiah, Mishael, and Azariah, nurtured everyone with the knowledge that there is no fear of God like yours.

7:9. אָמַרְתִּי אֶעֱלֶה בְתָמָר — *I boast on High that your deeds cause Me to ascend on your palm tree* [lit., *I said: I will ascend in the palm tree*]. I boast about you among the Celestial Hosts, that I am

of nobles. The rounded shafts for your libations' abysslike trenches, handiwork of the Master Craftsman. ³ At earth's very center your Sanhedrin site is a crescent basin of ceaseless, flowing teaching; your national center an indispensable heap of nourishing knowledge hedged about with roses. ⁴ Your twin sustainers, the Tablets of the Law, are like two fawns, twins of the gazelle. ⁵ Your Altar and Temple, erect and stately as an ivory tower; your wise men aflow with springs of complex wisdom at the gate of the many-peopled city; your face, like the tower of Lebanon, looks to your future boundary as far as Damascus.

⁶ The Godly name on your head is as mighty as Carmel; your crowning braid is royal purple, your King is bound in Naziritic tresses. ⁷ How beautiful and pleasant are you, befitting the pleasures of spiritual love. ⁸ Such is your stature, likened to a towering palm tree, from your teachers flow sustenance like wine-filled clusters.

God to Israel ⁹ I boast on High that your deeds cause Me to ascend on your palm tree, I grasp onto your branches. I beg now your teachers that they may remain like clusters of grapes from which flow strength to your weakest ones, and the fragrance of your countenance like apples, ¹⁰ and may your utterance be like finest wine.

Israel to God... I shall heed Your plea to uphold my faith before my Beloved in love so upright and honest that my slumbering fathers will move their lips in approval.

...to the nations... ¹¹ I am my Beloved's and He longs for my perfection.

...to God ¹² Come, my Beloved, let us go to the fields where Your children serve You in want, there let us lodge with Esau's children who are blessed with plenty yet still deny.

¹³ Let us wake at dawn in vineyards of prayer and study. Let us see if students of Writ have budded, if students of Oral Law have blossomed, if ripened scholars have bloomed; there I will display my finest products to You.

NOTES INCLUDING PHRASE-BY-PHRASE LITERAL TRANSLATION

elevated through your actions on earth.

אֲחֲזָה בְּסַנְסִנָּיו — *I grasp onto your branches* [lit., *I will take hold of its branches*]. I cleave to the branches, i.e., the children, of this palm tree, Israel.

וְיִהְיוּ נָא שָׁדַיִךְ כְּאֶשְׁכְּלוֹת הַגֶּפֶן וְרֵיחַ אַפֵּךְ כַּתַּפּוּחִים — *I beg now your teachers that they may remain like clusters of grapes from which flow strength to your weakest ones, and the fragrance of your countenance like apples* [lit., *and let your breasts be like clusters of the vine, and the fragrance of your countenance like apples*]. May the righteous and wise inspire the young to withstand the taunts of their heathen neighbors who wish to lead Israel astray.

7:10. וְחִכֵּךְ כְּיֵין הַטּוֹב — *and may your utterance be like finest wine* [lit., *your palate is like choice wine*]. May your response to the taunts of the heathens be as clear and potent as fine wine.

הוֹלֵךְ לְדוֹדִי לְמֵישָׁרִים — *I shall heed Your plea to uphold my faith before my Beloved in love so upright and honest* [lit., *it goes to my Beloved in righteousness*].

דּוֹבֵב שִׂפְתֵי יְשֵׁנִים — *that my slumbering fathers will move their lips in approval* [lit., *causing the lips of sleepers to speak*]. My love is so intense that even my departed ancestors will rejoice in me and be thankful for their lot.

7:11. אֲנִי לְדוֹדִי וְעָלַי תְּשׁוּקָתוֹ — *I am my Beloved's and He longs for*

my perfection [lit., *I am my Beloved's and His longing is upon me*].

7:12. לְכָה דוֹדִי נֵצֵא הַשָּׂדֶה — *Come, my Beloved, let us go to the fields where Your children serve You in want* [lit., *Come, my Beloved, let us go forth into the field*]. Do not judge me by the affluent people who indulge in robbery and immorality; come, let me show You scholars who study the Torah in poverty.

נָלִינָה בַּכְּפָרִים — *there let us lodge with Esau's children who are blessed with plenty yet still deny* [lit., *let us lodge in the villages*]. I will show You the children of Esau, upon whom You have bestowed much bounty, yet they do not believe in You.

7:13. נַשְׁכִּימָה לַכְּרָמִים — *Let us wake at dawn in vineyards of prayer and study* [lit., *Let us rise early for the vineyards*].

נִרְאֶה אִם פָּרְחָה הַגֶּפֶן פִּתַּח הַסְּמָדַר הֵנֵצוּ הָרִמּוֹנִים — *Let us see if students of Writ have budded, if students of Oral Law have blossomed, if ripened scholars have bloomed* [lit., *Let us see if the vine has budded, if the blossom has opened, if the pomegranates are in bloom*]. The stages of the ripening grape — budding, flowering, fruiting — symbolize the progress of the developing Torah scholars, from Scripture to Mishnah to Talmud.

שָׁם אֶתֵּן אֶת דֹּדַי לָךְ — *there I will display my finest products to You* [lit., *there I will give my love to You*]. I will show You my glory and my greatness, my sons and my daughters.

חַ

יד הַדּוּדָאִים נָתְנוּ־רֵיחַ וְעַל־פְּתָחֵינוּ כָּל־מְגָדִים חֲדָשִׁים גַּם־יְשָׁנִים דּוֹדִי צָפַנְתִּי

א לָךְ: מִי יִתֶּנְךָ כְּאָח לִי יוֹנֵק שְׁדֵי אִמִּי אֶמְצָאֲךָ בַחוּץ אֶשָּׁקְךָ גַּם לֹא־יָבֻזוּ לִי:

ב אֶנְהָגְךָ אֲבִיאֲךָ אֶל־בֵּית אִמִּי תְּלַמְּדֵנִי אַשְׁקְךָ מִיַּיִן הָרֶקַח מֵעֲסִיס רִמֹּנִי:

ג-ד שְׂמֹאלוֹ תַּחַת רֹאשִׁי וִימִינוֹ תְּחַבְּקֵנִי: הִשְׁבַּעְתִּי אֶתְכֶם בְּנוֹת יְרוּשָׁלַ͏ִם מַה־

ה תָּעִירוּ | וּמַה־תְּעֹרְרוּ אֶת־הָאַהֲבָה עַד שֶׁתֶּחְפָּץ: מִי זֹאת עֹלָה מִן־

הַמִּדְבָּר מִתְרַפֶּקֶת עַל־דּוֹדָהּ תַּחַת הַתַּפּוּחַ עוֹרַרְתִּיךָ שָׁמָּה חִבְּלַתְךָ אִמֶּךָ

ו שָׁמָּה חִבְּלָה יְלָדַתְךָ: שִׂימֵנִי כַחוֹתָם עַל־לִבֶּךָ כַּחוֹתָם עַל־זְרוֹעֶךָ כִּי־עַזָּה

ז כַמָּוֶת אַהֲבָה קָשָׁה כִשְׁאוֹל קִנְאָה רְשָׁפֶיהָ רִשְׁפֵּי אֵשׁ שַׁלְהֶבֶתְיָה: מַיִם רַבִּים

לֹא יוּכְלוּ לְכַבּוֹת אֶת־הָאַהֲבָה וּנְהָרוֹת לֹא יִשְׁטְפוּהָ אִם־יִתֵּן אִישׁ אֶת־כָּל־הוֹן

ח בֵּיתוֹ בָּאַהֲבָה בּוֹז יָבוּזוּ לוֹ: אָחוֹת לָנוּ קְטַנָּה וְשָׁדַיִם אֵין לָהּ מַה־

ט נַּעֲשֶׂה לַאֲחֹתֵנוּ בַּיּוֹם שֶׁיְּדֻבַּר־בָּהּ: אִם־חוֹמָה הִיא נִבְנֶה עָלֶיהָ טִירַת כָּסֶף

NOTES INCLUDING PHRASE-BY-PHRASE LITERAL TRANSLATION

7:14. הַדּוּדָאִים נָתְנוּ רֵיחַ — *All my baskets, good and bad, emit a fragrance* [lit., *The baskets yield fragrance*]. "Good figs" are an allusion to the righteous; "bad figs," to the wicked. In time, even the wicked will seek out God.

וְעַל פְּתָחֵינוּ כָּל מְגָדִים חֲדָשִׁים גַּם יְשָׁנִים — *all at our doors are the precious fruits of comely deeds, both the Scribes' new ordinances and the Torah's timeless wisdom* [lit., *and at our door are all precious fruits, both new and old*].

דּוֹדִי צָפַנְתִּי לָךְ — *for You, O Beloved, has my heart stored them* [lit., *I have hidden for You, my Beloved*]. Your commandments are in the depths of my heart.

8:1. מִי יִתֶּנְךָ כְּאָח לִי יוֹנֵק שְׁדֵי אִמִּי — *If only, despite my wrongs, You could comfort me as Joseph did, like a brother nurtured at my mother's breast* [lit., *If only You were as a brother to me, who had nursed at my mother's breast!*]. If only You would comfort me as Joseph comforted his brothers (see *Genesis* 50:21).

אֶמְצָאֲךָ בַחוּץ אֶשָּׁקְךָ גַּם לֹא יָבֻזוּ לִי — *if in the streets I found Your prophets I would kiss You and embrace You through them, nor could anyone despise me for it* [lit., *(when) I would find You in the street I would kiss You and no one would scorn me*]. I would find Your prophets speaking in Your Name and I would embrace and kiss them.

8:2. אֶנְהָגְךָ אֲבִיאֲךָ אֶל בֵּית אִמִּי תְּלַמְּדֵנִי — *I would lead You, I would bring You to my mother's Temple for You to teach me as You did in Moses' Tent* [lit., *I would lead You, I would bring You to my mother's house that You should instruct me*].

אַשְׁקְךָ מִיַּיִן הָרֶקַח מֵעֲסִיס רִמֹּנִי — *to drink I would give You spiced libations, wines like pomegranate nectar* [lit., *I would give You spiced wine to drink, of the juice of my pomegranate*].

8:3. שְׂמֹאלוֹ תַּחַת רֹאשִׁי וִימִינוֹ תְּחַבְּקֵנִי — *Despite my laments in exile, His left hand supports my head and His right hand embraces me in support* [lit., *His left hand is under my head and His right arm embraces me*].

8:4. הִשְׁבַּעְתִּי אֶתְכֶם בְּנוֹת יְרוּשָׁלַיִם מַה תָּעִירוּ וּמַה תְּעֹרְרוּ אֶת הָאַהֲבָה עַד שֶׁתֶּחְפָּץ — *I adjure you, O nations who are destined to ascend to Jerusalem, if you dare provoke God to hate me or disturb His love for me while He still desires it* [lit., *I have adjured you O daughters of Jerusalem: should you wake or rouse the love until it pleases*]. Your efforts will be of no avail! (see 2:6-7).

8:5. מִי זֹאת עֹלָה מִן הַמִּדְבָּר מִתְרַפֶּקֶת עַל דּוֹדָהּ — *How worthy she is ascending from the wilderness bearing Torah and His Presence, clinging to her Beloved!* [lit., *Who is she that rises up from the wilderness leaning upon her Beloved?*]. Israel ascended from the desert bearing wonderful gifts from God; there she rose spiritually by cleaving to the Divine Presence.

תַּחַת הַתַּפּוּחַ עוֹרַרְתִּיךָ — *Under Sinai suspended above me, there I roused Your love* [lit., *Under the apple tree I roused You*]. Remember, how, beneath Mount Sinai, which was suspended over my head like an apple ["and they stood beneath the mountain" (*Deuteronomy* 4:11)], I manifested my love for You.

שָׁמָּה חִבְּלַתְךָ אִמֶּךָ שָׁמָּה חִבְּלָה יְלָדַתְךָ — *there was Your people born; a mother to other nations, there she endured the travail of her birth* [lit., *there Your mother was in travail for You; she who bore You was in travail*].

8:6. שִׂימֵנִי כַחוֹתָם עַל לִבֶּךָ כַּחוֹתָם עַל זְרוֹעֶךָ — *For the sake of my love, place me like a seal on Your heart, like a seal to dedicate Your strength for me* [lit., *Set me as a seal upon Your heart, as a seal upon Your arm*]. And because of that love, seal me upon Your heart so that You do not forget me.

כִּי עַזָּה כַמָּוֶת אַהֲבָה — *for strong till the death is my love* [lit., *that love is strong as death*].

קָשָׁה כִשְׁאוֹל קִנְאָה — *though their zeal for vengeance is hard as the grave* [lit., *jealousy is hard as the grave*], i.e., the unjust complaints, rivalries and jealousies that the nations provoked against me because of You.

רְשָׁפֶיהָ רִשְׁפֵּי אֵשׁ שַׁלְהֶבֶתְיָה — *its flashes are flashes of fire, the flame of God*. Its flashes are of a fierce fire emanating from the flames of Gehinnom.

8:7. מַיִם רַבִּים לֹא יוּכְלוּ לְכַבּוֹת אֶת הָאַהֲבָה — *Many waters of heathen tribulation cannot extinguish the fire of this love* [lit., *Many waters*

14 All my baskets, good and bad, emit a fragrance; all at our doors have the precious fruits of comely deeds, both the Scribes' new ordinances and the Torah's timeless wisdom; for You, Beloved, has my heart stored them.

8

1 If only, despite my wrongs, You could comfort me as Joseph did, like a brother nurtured at my mother's breasts, if in the streets I found Your prophets I would kiss You and embrace You through them, nor could anyone despise me for it. **2** I would lead You, I would bring You to my mother's Temple for You to teach me as You did in Moses' Tent; to drink I would give You spiced libations, wines like pomegranate nectar.

Israel to the nations

3 Despite my laments in exile, His left hand supports my head and His right hand embraces me in support. **4** I adjure you, O nations who are destined to ascend to Jerusalem, if you dare provoke God to hate me or disturb His love for me while He still desires it.

God and the Heavenly Tribunal

5 How worthy she is ascending from the wilderness bearing Torah and His Presence, clinging to her Beloved!

Israel interjects

Under Sinai suspended above me, there I roused Your love, there was Your people born; a mother to other nations, there she endured the travail of her birth. **6** For the sake of my love, place me like a seal on Your heart, like a seal to dedicate Your strength for me, for strong till the death is my love; though their zeal for vengeance is hard as the grave, its flashes are flashes of fire, the flame of God. **7** Many waters of heathen tribulation cannot extinguish the fire of this love, nor rivers of royal seduction or torture wash it away.

God replies to Israel

Were any man to offer all the treasure of his home to entice you away from your love, they would scorn him to extreme.

The Heavenly Tribunal reflects

8 Israel desires to cleave to us, the small and humble one, but her time of spiritual maturity has not come. What shall we do for our cleaving one on the day the nations plot against her?

9 If her faith and belief are strong as a wall withstanding incursions from without, we shall become her fortress and beauty, building her city and Holy Temple;

---

cannot extinguish the love]. "Many waters" refers to the heathen nations (see *Isaiah 17:12,13*).

וּנְהָרוֹת לֹא יִשְׁטְפוּהָ — *nor rivers of royal seduction or torture wash it away* [lit., *and rivers cannot drown it*]. Their leaders and kings cannot drown it, neither by force, nor by terror, nor by seductive enticement.

אִם יִתֵּן אִישׁ אֶת כָּל הוֹן בֵּיתוֹ בָּאַהֲבָה בּוֹז יָבוּזוּ לוֹ — *Were any man to offer all the treasure of his home to entice you away from your love, they would scorn him to extreme* [lit., *If a man would give all the substance of his house in exchange for love, he would be laughed to scorn*]. God and His Tribunal bear witness to Israel's love for her Beloved.

8:8. אָחוֹת לָנוּ קְטַנָּה — *Israel desires to cleave to us, the small and humble one* [lit., *We have a little sister*]. The words אָח, "brother," and אָחוֹת, "sister," are linguistically related to the verb אחה, "to join together." The Heavenly Tribunal said, "One small, humble nation longs to join with us."

וְשָׁדַיִם אֵין לָהּ — *but her time of spiritual maturity has not come* [lit., *but she has no breasts*]. She is not yet ripe for Redemption (see *Ezekiel 16:7*).

מַה נַּעֲשֶׂה לַאֲחוֹתֵנוּ בַּיּוֹם שֶׁיְּדֻבַּר בָּהּ — *What shall we do for our cleaving one on the day the nations plot against her?* [lit., *What shall we do for our sister on the day she is spoken for?*]. How will we treat her when she seeks our protection?

8:9. אִם חוֹמָה הִיא נִבְנֶה עָלֶיהָ טִירַת כָּסֶף — *If her faith and belief are strong as a wall withstanding incursions from without, we shall become her fortress and beauty, building her city and Holy Temple* [lit., *If she be a wall, we will build upon her a turret of silver*]. Our response depends upon how she conducts herself in exile: If Israel will gird herself with faith and act toward the nations as if fortified with impenetrable "walls of copper" (*Jeremiah 1:18*), i.e., if she will neither intermarry nor intermingle with them, then we will rebuild the Holy City and Temple.

 י וְאִם־דֶּ֣לֶת הִ֔יא נָצ֥וּר עָלֶ֖יהָ ל֣וּחַ אָ֑רֶז: אֲנִ֣י חוֹמָ֔ה וְשָׁדַ֖י כַּמִּגְדָּל֑וֹת אָ֛ז הָיִ֥יתִי

יא בְעֵינָ֖יו כְּמוֹצְאֵ֥ת שָׁלֽוֹם: כֶּ֣רֶם הָיָ֤ה לִשְׁלֹמֹה֙ בְּבַ֣עַל הָמ֔וֹן נָתַ֥ן אֶת־הַכֶּ֖רֶם

יב לַנֹּטְרִ֑ים אִ֛ישׁ יָבִ֥א בְּפִרְי֖וֹ אֶ֥לֶף כָּֽסֶף: כַּרְמִ֥י שֶׁלִּ֖י לְפָנָ֑י הָאֶ֤לֶף לְךָ֙ שְׁלֹמֹ֔ה

יג וּמָאתַ֖יִם לְנֹטְרִ֥ים אֶת־פִּרְיֽוֹ: הַיּוֹשֶׁ֣בֶת בַּגַּנִּ֗ים חֲבֵרִ֛ים מַקְשִׁיבִ֥ים לְקוֹלֵ֖ךְ

יד הַשְׁמִיעִֽנִי: בְּרַ֣ח ׀ דּוֹדִ֗י וּֽדְמֵה־לְךָ֤ לִצְבִי֙ א֚וֹ לְעֹ֣פֶר הָֽאַיָּלִ֔ים עַ֖ל הָרֵ֥י בְשָׂמִֽים:

NOTES INCLUDING PHRASE-BY-PHRASE LITERAL TRANSLATION

וְאִם־דֶּלֶת הִיא נָצוּר עָלֶיהָ לוּחַ אָרֶז — *but if she wavers like a door, succumbing to every alien knock, with fragile cedar panels shall we then enclose her* [lit., *But if she be a door we will enclose her with cedar panel*]. If she is open to all blandishments, like a door that always swings open, then we will line her doors with wooden panels that will rot, thus exposing her to danger.

8:10. אֲנִי חוֹמָה וְשָׁדַי כַּמִּגְדָּלוֹת — *My faith is firm as a wall, and my nourishing synagogues and study halls are strong as towers!* [lit., *I am a wall, and my breasts are like towers!*]. I comport myself like a wall, strong in the love of my Beloved. My synagogues and study halls nurture Israel with words of Torah; they "are like towers."

אָז הָיִיתִי בְעֵינָיו כְּמוֹצְאֵת שָׁלוֹם — *Then, having said so, I become in His eyes like a bride found perfect* [lit., *Then I am in His eyes like one who found peace*].

8:11. כֶּרֶם הָיָה לִשְׁלֹמֹה בְּבַעַל הָמוֹן — *Israel was the vineyard of Him to Whom peace belongs in populous Jerusalem* [lit., *Solomon had a vineyard in Baal-hamon*]. "Solomon" refers to God (see 1:1); "vineyard" to Israel (see *Isaiah* 5:7); "Baal-hamon" [lit., "the owner of the multitude"] to Jerusalem, the greatly populated city.

נָתַן אֶת הַכֶּרֶם לַנֹּטְרִים — *He gave His vineyard to harsh, cruel guardians* [lit., *He gave over the vineyard to guardians*]. He handed over His people to harsh rulers: Babylon, Media, Greece and Rome.

אִישׁ יָבִא בְּפִרְיוֹ אֶלֶף כָּסֶף — *each one came to extort his fruit, even a thousand silver pieces* [lit., *everyone would bring for its fruit a thousand silver pieces*]. The "guardians" would impose exorbitant levies and taxes to feed their lusts.

8:12. כַּרְמִי שֶׁלִּי לְפָנָי — *The vineyard is Mine! Your iniquities are before Me!* [lit., *My vineyard, which is Mine, is before Me!*]

but if she wavers like a door, succumbing to every alien knock, with fragile cedar panels shall we then enclose her.

Israel replies proudly . . . ¹⁰ *My faith is firm as a wall, and my nourishing synagogues and study halls are strong as towers! Then, having said so, I become in His eyes like a bride found perfect.*

. . . and reminisces ¹¹ *Israel was the vineyard of Him to Whom peace belongs in populous Jerusalem. He gave His vineyard to harsh, cruel guardians; each one came to extort his fruit, even a thousand silver pieces.*

God to the nations, on judgment day ¹² *The vineyard is Mine! Your iniquities are before Me!*

The nations will reply *The thousand silver pieces are Yours, You to Whom peace belongs, and two hundred more to the Sages who guarded the fruit of Torah from our designs.*

God to Israel ¹³ *O My beloved, dwelling in far-flung gardens, your fellows, the angels, hearken to your voice of Torah and prayer. Let Me hear it, that they may then sanctify Me.*

Israel to God ¹⁴ *Flee, my Beloved, from our common exile and be like a gazelle or a young hart in Your swiftness to redeem and rest Your Presence among us on the fragrant Mount Moriah, site of Your Temple.*

Although I transferred My vineyard to you, I am still the sole owner. All your injustices against Israel are before Me; nothing eludes Me.

הָאֶלֶף לְךָ שְׁלֹמֹה — *The thousand silver pieces are Yours, You to Whom peace belongs* [lit., *You, Solomon, can have Your thousand*]. Whatever we stole from them will all be returned to You.

וּמָאתַיִם לְנֹטְרִים אֶת פִּרְיוֹ — *and two hundred more to the Sages who guarded the fruit of Torah from our designs* [lit., *and two hundred to the tenders of its fruit*]. We will recompense Israel's leaders and Sages (see *Isaiah 60:17*).

8:13. הַיּוֹשֶׁבֶת בַּגַּנִּים חֲבֵרִים מַקְשִׁיבִים לְקוֹלֵךְ — *O My beloved, dwelling in far-flung gardens, your fellows, the angels, hearken to your voice of Torah and prayer* [lit., *O you who dwell in the gardens, companions are attentive to your voice*]. The angels listen to the prayers of Israel in the Diaspora, tending the

gardens of others, and who dwell in the synagogues and study halls.

הַשְׁמִיעִנִי — *Let Me hear it, that they may then sanctify Me* [lit., *let Me hear it*]. Let Me hear your voice, for after you are finished, the ministering angels will commence to sanctify Me.

8:14. בְּרַח דּוֹדִי — *Flee, my Beloved, from our common exile* [lit., *Flee, my Beloved*]. Flee away with us, O God Who has accompanied us throughout every exile! And let us leave this exile together.

וּדְמֵה לְךָ לִצְבִי אוֹ לְעֹפֶר הָאַיָּלִים — *and be like a gazelle or a young hart in Your swiftness to redeem and rest Your Presence among us* [lit., *and be like a gazelle or a young hart*]. Hasten the Redemption.

עַל הָרֵי בְשָׂמִים — *on the fragrant Mount Moriah, site of Your Temple* [lit., *upon the mountains of spices*], may it be rebuilt speedily in our days. Amen.

משניות פסחים
MISHNAYOS PESACHIM

It is customary to study the *mishnah* of Tractate *Pesachim* during Pesach.

פרק ראשון

[א] **אוֹר** לְאַרְבָּעָה עָשָׂר בּוֹדְקִים אֶת הֶחָמֵץ לְאוֹר הַנֵּר. כָּל מָקוֹם שֶׁאֵין מַכְנִיסִין בּוֹ חָמֵץ אֵין צָרִיךְ בְּדִיקָה.

וְלָמָה אָמְרוּ: „שְׁתֵּי שׁוּרוֹת בַּמַּרְתֵּף"? מָקוֹם שֶׁמַּכְנִיסִין בּוֹ חָמֵץ. בֵּית שַׁמַּאי אוֹמְרִים: שְׁתֵּי שׁוּרוֹת עַל פְּנֵי כָל הַמַּרְתֵּף. וּבֵית הִלֵּל אוֹמְרִים: שְׁתֵּי שׁוּרוֹת הַחִיצוֹנוֹת שֶׁהֵן הָעֶלְיוֹנוֹת.

[ב] אֵין חוֹשְׁשִׁין שֶׁמָּא גֵּרְרָה חֻלְדָּה מִבַּיִת לְבַיִת, וּמִמָּקוֹם לְמָקוֹם; דְּאִם כֵּן, מֵחָצֵר לְחָצֵר וּמֵעִיר לְעִיר – אֵין לַדָּבָר סוֹף.

[ג] רַבִּי יְהוּדָה אוֹמֵר: בּוֹדְקִין אוֹר אַרְבָּעָה עָשָׂר, וּבְאַרְבָּעָה עָשָׂר שַׁחֲרִית, וּבִשְׁעַת הַבִּעוּר.

וַחֲכָמִים אוֹמְרִים: לֹא בָדַק אוֹר אַרְבָּעָה עָשָׂר, יִבְדֹּק בְּאַרְבָּעָה עָשָׂר; לֹא בָדַק בְּאַרְבָּעָה עָשָׂר, יִבְדֹּק בְּתוֹךְ הַמּוֹעֵד; לֹא בָדַק בְּתוֹךְ הַמּוֹעֵד, יִבְדֹּק לְאַחַר הַמּוֹעֵד.

וּמַה שֶּׁמְשַׁיֵּר, יַנִּיחֶנּוּ בְּצִנְעָא, כְּדֵי שֶׁלֹא יְהֵא צָרִיךְ בְּדִיקָה אַחֲרָיו.

[ד] רַבִּי מֵאִיר אוֹמֵר: אוֹכְלִין כָּל חָמֵשׁ, וְשׂוֹרְפִין בִּתְחִלַּת שֵׁשׁ. וְרַבִּי יְהוּדָה אוֹמֵר: אוֹכְלִין כָּל אַרְבַּע, וְתוֹלִין כָּל חָמֵשׁ, וְשׂוֹרְפִין בִּתְחִלַּת שֵׁשׁ.

יד אברהם

[A full treatment of these mishnayos may be found in the ArtScroll Mishnah with the *Yad Avraham* commentary, from which the following commentary has been adapted.]

Tractate Pesachim. This tractate deals with the many *mitzvos* relevant to the festival of Pesach. It is divided into two basic parts [and is for this reason named in the plural, *Pesachim*]. Chapters 1-4 and 10 deal with all the laws unrelated to the *pesach* offering, such as the prohibition to eat or even possess *chametz* during Pesach, the requirement to eat matzah on the *Seder* night, and the *mitzvah* to relate the story of the redemption from Egypt. Chapters 5-9 deal with the laws of the *pesach* offering made in Temple times on the fourteenth of Nissan.

CHAPTER ONE

1. This tractate begins with the law of בְּדִיקַת חָמֵץ, *the search for chametz*. This is predicated upon the dual *mitzvos* of: (1) eliminating *chametz* from Jewish possession; and (2) the prohibition of having *chametz* during Pesach.

אוֹר לְאַרְבָּעָה עָשָׂר — *The evening of the fourteenth* was fixed as the time for the search (rather than the day) because people are home then and a search by candlelight in the darkness is especially effective [making the illuminated area stand out]. The requirement to use a candle for the search is derived by the *Gemara* exegetically (7b; see O. Ch. 433:1).

בּוֹדְקִים אֶת הֶחָמֵץ — *One must search for the chametz* and eliminate it so as not to transgress the prohibition against keeping *chametz* on Pesach (*Rashi*). *Tosafos*, however, state that the purpose of the search is to prevent its inadvertent consumption on Pesach. [The Scriptural requirement not to possess *chametz*, however, could be met by בִּטּוּל, *nullifying* the *chametz*.]

מָקוֹם שֶׁמַּכְנִיסִין בּוֹ חָמֵץ — *A place into which chametz is [customarily] brought*. Thus a cellar used to store wine for sale does not need to be searched. Only a domestic wine cellar must be searched because servants fetching wine from there occasionally enter carrying a piece of bread.

שְׁתֵּי שׁוּרוֹת ... — *Two rows ...* It was practice to arrange the barrels so that each one rested upon the two barrels under it, very much as bricks are laid. Beis Shammai require that the entire wall of barrels facing the front of the cellar be searched from floor to ceiling, as well as the entire top layer of barrels from front to back [i.e. the layer facing the ceiling]. But Beis Hillel equate *row* with layers, of which only the two uppermost layers of the front row of barrels must be searched (*Rav*).

2. וּמִמָּקוֹם לְמָקוֹם — *Or from one place to another*, i.e. from an unsearched corner of the house to one that has been searched (*Rav*).

דְּאִם כֵּן — *For if* we have to concern ourselves that a weasel

It is customary to study the mishnah of Tractate *Pesachim* during Pesach.

CHAPTER ONE

1/1-4

[1] אוֹר *On the evening of the fourteenth [of Nissan] one must search for chametz by the light of a candle. Any place into which chametz is not [customarily] brought does not require a search. In regard to what [have the Sages] said, 'Two rows of a [wine] cellar [must be searched]'? For a place into which chametz is [customarily] brought. Beis Shammai say: Two rows over the entire front of the [wine] cellar [must be searched]. But Beis Hillel say: The two outer rows which are the uppermost.*

[2] *We need not be concerned that a weasel dragged [chametz] from one house to another, or from one place to another; for if so, [we would have to be concerned] from one courtyard to another and from one town to another — [and] there is no end to the matter.*

[3] *R' Yehudah says: One must search on the evening of the fourteenth, or on the morning of the fourteenth, or at the time of removal. But the Sages say: [If] one did not search on the evening of the fourteenth, he must search on the [day of the] fourteenth; [if] he did not search on the fourteenth, he must search during the festival; [if] he did not search during the festival, he must search after the festival.*

That which he leaves over [to eat in the morning], he should put in a safe place, so that it will not be necessary to search for it [again].

[4] *R' Meir says: One may eat [chametz] the entire fifth [hour], and he must burn [it] at the onset of the sixth [hour]. But R' Yehudah says: One may eat [it] the entire fourth [hour], but we suspend [it] the entire fifth [hour], and one must burn it at the onset of the sixth [hour].*

YAD AVRAHAM

brought *chametz* from one house to another after the search had been completed, we would also have to be concerned that *chametz* had been dragged in from another courtyard or town which had not yet been searched (*Rav*).

3. וּבְאַרְבָּעָה עָשָׂר שַׁחֲרִית — *Or on the morning of the fourteenth,* if one forgot or was unable to search at night (*Rav*).

וּבִשְׁעַת הַבִּעוּר — *Or at the time of removal,* when the left-over *chametz* must be destroyed. This is at the beginning of the sixth hour (approximately the hour before noon). R' Yehudah contends that the search may not be performed after midday, because one might inadvertently eat the *chametz* he finds and transgress a Scriptural prohibition [see m. 4] (*Rav*). The prohibition to eat *chametz* before then, however, is only Rabbinic in origin, and the search is not waived because of it.

וַחֲכָמִים אוֹמְרִים — *But the Sages* are not concerned that the searcher may eat the *chametz* he finds, because his purpose for searching is to destroy the *chametz*. Thus, he may search even on the festival.

יִבְדֹּק לְאַחַר הַמּוֹעֵד — *He must search after the festival,* since *chametz* left in a Jew's possession over Pesach is forbidden (2:5).

בְּצִנְעָא — *In a safe place,* so that it does not scatter (*Rambam*), for if one does not find the *chametz* he put aside, or if he put aside ten pieces and found only nine, it is necessary to search

again. However, if he put it in a secure spot, he may assume that it was eaten by a person and another search is unnecessary (*O. Ch. 434:1*).

4. The *Gemara* deduces from our mishnah that there is a Biblical ban on possessing *chametz* from midday of the fourteenth forward. Because many people cannot accurately estimate midday, the Sages decreed that the prohibition be observed even before noon.

רַבִּי מֵאִיר אוֹמֵר — *R' Meir says:* Hours throughout the Mishnah are שָׁעוֹת זְמַנִּיּוֹת, *seasonal hours*, in which daylight is divided into twelve equal parts; accordingly, an 'hour' may be longer or shorter than the traditional 60 minutes, depending on the season. R' Meir permits eating *chametz* on Erev Pesach until the end of the fifth hour. [For example, if the length of the day is twelve hours, from 6 a.m. to 6 p.m., one may eat *chametz* until 11 a.m.] One must then burn it at the onset of the sixth [hour], and no benefit may be derived from it. Although the *chametz* is Biblically permitted in the sixth hour, the Sages forbade its use then because one might miscalculate the end of the sixth hour (*Rav*).

וְרַבִּי יְהוּדָה אוֹמֵר — *But R' Yehudah says* that in the fifth hour we neither eat *chametz* nor destroy it, but we may derive other benefit from it, such as by feeding it to our animals (*Rav*). In his view, the Sages restricted the consumption of *chametz* two hours before the Biblical prohibition, to allow more of a margin

[ה] וְעוֹד אָמַר רַבִּי יְהוּדָה: שְׁתֵּי חַלּוֹת שֶׁל תּוֹדָה פְּסוּלוֹת מֻנָּחוֹת עַל גַּג הָאִצְטְבָא. כָּל זְמַן שֶׁמֻּנָּחוֹת, כָּל הָעָם אוֹכְלִים. נִטְּלָה אַחַת, תּוֹלִין – לֹא אוֹכְלִין וְלֹא שׂוֹרְפִין. נִטְּלוּ שְׁתֵּיהֶן, הִתְחִילוּ כָּל הָעָם שׂוֹרְפִין.

רַבָּן גַּמְלִיאֵל אוֹמֵר: חֻלִּין נֶאֱכָלִים כָּל אַרְבַּע; וּתְרוּמָה כָּל חָמֵשׁ; וְשׂוֹרְפִין בִּתְחִלַּת שֵׁשׁ.

[ו] רַבִּי חֲנִינָא, סְגַן הַכֹּהֲנִים, אוֹמֵר: מִימֵיהֶם שֶׁל כֹּהֲנִים, לֹא נִמְנְעוּ מִלִּשְׂרֹף אֶת הַבָּשָׂר שֶׁנִּטְמָא בִּוְלַד הַטֻּמְאָה עִם הַבָּשָׂר שֶׁנִּטְמָא בְּאַב הַטֻּמְאָה, אַף עַל פִּי שֶׁמּוֹסִיפִין טֻמְאָה עַל טֻמְאָתוֹ.

הוֹסִיף רַבִּי עֲקִיבָא וְאָמַר: מִימֵיהֶם שֶׁל כֹּהֲנִים, לֹא נִמְנְעוּ מִלְּהַדְלִיק אֶת הַשֶּׁמֶן שֶׁנִּפְסַל בִּטְבוּל יוֹם בְּנֵר שֶׁנִּטְמָא בִטְמֵא מֵת, אַף עַל פִּי שֶׁמּוֹסִיפִין טֻמְאָה עַל טֻמְאָתוֹ.

[ז] אָמַר רַבִּי מֵאִיר: מִדִּבְרֵיהֶם לָמַדְנוּ שֶׁשּׂוֹרְפִין תְּרוּמָה טְהוֹרָה עִם הַטְּמֵאָה בְּפֶסַח.

אָמַר לוֹ רַבִּי יוֹסֵי: אֵינָהּ הִיא הַמִּדָּה. וּמוֹדִים רַבִּי אֱלִיעֶזֶר וְרַבִּי יְהוֹשֻׁעַ

יד אברהם

of error for a cloudy day (*Gem.*). However, because this is not a common problem, the Sages did not prohibit all benefit in the fifth hour (*Pnei Yehoshua*).

The custom is to burn *chametz* before the fifth hour, in order to be able to nullify the *chametz* again after burning it, as stated by *Rama* (434:2). *Chametz* in the sixth hour is forbidden for any benefit and therefore worthless; thus it can no longer be nullified because it can no longer be considered the property of its owner.

5. [R' Yehudah now relates how the times of the prohibitions of *chametz* were made known in Jerusalem during the Temple era.]

שֶׁל תּוֹדָה — *Of a thanksgiving offering.* This is an offering brought by a person who has been delivered from misfortune, such as a dangerous sickness or sea voyage. Accompanying the animal offering are forty loaves, ten of which are *chametz* while the rest are matzah. Since a thanksgiving offering may be eaten the night after its sacrifice, it was forbidden to bring one on Erev Pesach, when the *chametz* loaves could be eaten only till midday. Therefore, numerous offerings were brought on the day before by festival pilgrims, and those that could not be finished on time became unfit at daybreak of the fourteenth. Two of these unfit loaves were used to signify the various stages of the status of *chametz* (*Gem.*).

נִטְּלָה אַחַת — *[When] one [loaf] was removed* by a messenger of the Court at the beginning of the fifth hour (approximately 10 a.m.), people stopped using *chametz*.

וּתְרוּמָה כָּל חָמֵשׁ — *Terumah [which is chametz may be eaten] the entire fifth [hour].* Because it possesses sanctity and should not be destroyed unless absolutely necessary, Rabban Gamliel

allows its consumption for an additional hour (*Rav*).

6. *Terumah* [the tithe given to the *Kohen*] must be safeguarded against *tumah*-contamination and destruction. However, on Erev Pesach, *terumah*, too, must be destroyed if it is *chametz*. The question arises whether care must be taken even during the burning to safeguard it from contamination. If so, two pyres would be required, one for uncontaminated *terumah*, and a second for all other *chametz*, so that the *terumah* not come in contact with contaminated *chametz*. It might be, however, that since destruction of the *terumah* is imminent, the mandate to safeguard it against *tumah* no longer applies. In order to resolve this question, mishnah 6 introduces a parallel situation regarding the destruction of contaminated sacrificial parts, followed by a dispute (mishnah 7) between R' Meir and R' Yose whether this situation is analogous to burning *terumah* that is *chametz*.

Tumah is a legally defined state of impurity which the Torah attaches to people or objects in certain conditions. It can be transmitted to other persons or objects, but the recipient's level of *tumah* is generally one degree lower than the transmitter's. The greatest degree of *tumah* is that of a human corpse, which is classified as אֲבִי אֲבוֹת הַטֻּמְאָה, *avi avos hatumah* [lit. *grandfather of all tumos*]. All other *sources* of *tumah* [e.g. a *zav*, *niddah*, *sheretz*; see 8:5] are classified one level lower as *av hatumah*, or primary *tumah*. A person, utensil or food that is contaminated by an *av hatumah* becomes a *rishon*, or first degree of acquired *tumah*. A *rishon* can pass *tumah* only to a food or beverage, which then becomes a *sheni*, or second degree of acquired *tumah*. In the case of unsanctified food, *tumah* can go no further. However, due to its greater sanctity, *terumah* can become *tamei* to a third degree [*shlishi*] by touching a *sheni*, while sacrifices have still one more level of possible *tumah* and

[5] *R' Yehudah also said: Two loaves of a thanksgiving offering [which had become] unfit were placed on the roof of the [Temple] portico. As long as they lay [there], the people would eat [chametz]. [When] one [loaf] was removed, they suspended [it] — neither eating nor burning [the chametz]. When both were removed, the people would begin burning [the chametz].*

Rabban Gamliel says: Non-consecrated [chametz] may be eaten the entire fourth [hour]; terumah [which is chametz may be eaten] the entire fifth [hour]; and we must burn [all chametz] at the onset of the sixth [hour].

[6] *R' Chanina, the administrator of the Kohanim, says: In all the days of the Kohanim, never did they refrain from burning [sacrificial] meat that had been contaminated by a secondary tumah together with [sacrificial] meat that had been contaminated by a primary tumah, although [by so doing] they added tumah to its tumah. R' Akiva added, saying: In all the days of the Kohanim, never did they refrain from lighting oil that had become unfit [through contact] with a tevul yom in a lamp that had been contaminated by one contaminated by a corpse, although [by so doing] they added tumah to its tumah.*

[7] *R' Meir said: From their words we may infer that we may burn uncontaminated terumah [that is chametz] with contaminated terumah on Pesach. R' Yose said to him: This is not analogous. [Furthermore, even] R' Eliezer and R' Yehoshua concur*

YAD AVRAHAM

can become a *revi'i*, fourth degree of *tumah*.

מִימֵיהֶם שֶׁל כֹּהֲנִים — *In all the days of the Kohanim* who oversaw the disposal of disqualified and contaminated offerings, i.e., as long as the Temple stood.

אֶת הַבָּשָׂר שֶׁנִּטְמָא בּוּלַד הַטֻּמְאָה — *[Sacrificial] meat that had been contaminated by a secondary tumah*, i.e. a second degree of acquired *tumah* [*sheni*]. The contaminated meat was thus a *shlishi* (*Rav*).

עִם הַבָּשָׂר שֶׁנִּטְמָא בְּאַב הַטֻּמְאָה — *Together with [sacrificial] meat that had been contaminated by a primary tumah*. By coming in contact with an *av hatumah*, this meat became a *rishon*, i.e. *tamei* in the first degree. Burning it together with meat possessing only a third-degree *tumah* imparts to the latter a greater degree of *tumah*. Nevertheless, since both are being burned in any case, we are unconcerned with the increase in *tumah* (*Rav*).

לֹא נִמְנְעוּ מִלְהַדְלִיק . . . — *Never did they refrain from lighting oil . . .* A *tevul yom* is any person who has immersed in a *mikveh* to purify himself of *tumah*. Such a person does not regain his purity in regard to *terumah* until nightfall. In the interim his status is equivalent to a *sheni* [second degree], and any *terumah* he touches becomes *tamei* in the third degree. Contaminated *terumah* must be burned, though the oil may be used to kindle a lamp in the process. If the lamp had been contaminated by someone who had touched a human corpse, it is *tamei* in the degree of *av* [primary]. This is due to the rule [exclusive to human-corpse *tumah*] that חֶרֶב הֲרֵי הוּא כֶּחָלָל, *the sword has the same status as the corpse*; i.e. that any utensil (except one made of earthenware) which touches an *avi avos hatumah* (the corpse itself) or an *av hatumah* (whatever touched the corpse) receives

the *same* degree of *tumah* as the object it touched (*Rambam*; according to some, this stringency applies only to metal utensils). Thus, the oil burned in this metal lamp will become a *rishon* (*tamei* in the first degree), whereas the unfit *terumah* oil had previously only possessed a third degree of *tumah*. Nevertheless, the Sages permitted doing this.

7. מִדְּבְרֵיהֶם לָמַדְנוּ — *From their words* [R' Chanina's and R' Akiva's in the previous mishnah] *we may infer* that the *Kohanim* burned flesh that was a third-degree *tumah* together with flesh that was a first-degree *tumah*; we may infer that we may burn uncontaminated *terumah* with contaminated *terumah* on Erev Pesach, although this contaminates the former while burning it (*Rav*). Since the uncontaminated *terumah* must be burned, it need not be safeguarded against *tumah*. The second-degree *tumah* mentioned by R' Chanina as the contaminator of the meat refers even to liquids. However, R' Meir holds that according to Biblical law, liquids cannot transmit *tumah*. Consequently, the meat touched by the liquid is *tamei* only according to Rabbinic decree, but is *tahor* on the Biblical level. Since the Sages nevertheless permitted burning it with meat that is a *rishon*, which renders it Biblically *tamei*, it is evident that even uncontaminated sacrificial parts being burned need not be protected against *tumah*.

אָמַר לוֹ רַבִּי יוֹסֵי — *R' Yose said to him* that the cases are not analogous. In his view the power of liquids to contaminate is Biblical. Accordingly, R' Chanina's precedent demonstrates only that meat which was *tamei* at least to some degree Biblically may be further contaminated while being burned. But the *terumah* of mishnah 6 is not *tamei* at all, merely *chametz*. Thus, we may not contaminate it while burning it in the sixth hour (*Rav*). [However, even R' Yose agrees that once the Biblical

---

שֶׁשּׂוֹרְפִין זוֹ לְעַצְמָהּ וְזוֹ לְעַצְמָהּ. עַל מַה נֶּחְלָקוּ? עַל הַתְּלוּיָה וְעַל הַטְּמֵאָה. שֶׁרַבִּי אֱלִיעֶזֶר אוֹמֵר תִּשָּׂרֵף זוֹ לְעַצְמָהּ וְזוֹ לְעַצְמָהּ, וְרַבִּי יְהוֹשֻׁעַ אוֹמֵר שְׁתֵּיהֶן כְּאַחַת.

פרק שני

[א] **כָּל** שָׁעָה שֶׁמֻּתָּר לֶאֱכוֹל, מַאֲכִיל לִבְהֵמָה, לְחַיָּה וּלְעוֹפוֹת, וּמוֹכְרוֹ לְנָכְרִי, וּמֻתָּר בַּהֲנָאָתוֹ. עָבַר זְמַנּוֹ, אָסוּר בַּהֲנָאָתוֹ, וְלֹא יַסִּיק בּוֹ תַּנּוּר וְכִירַיִם.

רַבִּי יְהוּדָה אוֹמֵר: אֵין בִּעוּר חָמֵץ אֶלָּא שְׂרֵפָה.

וַחֲכָמִים אוֹמְרִים: אַף מְפָרֵר וְזוֹרֶה לָרוּחַ אוֹ מַטִּיל לַיָּם.

[ב] חָמֵץ שֶׁל נָכְרִי שֶׁעָבַר עָלָיו הַפֶּסַח, מֻתָּר בַּהֲנָאָה; וְשֶׁל יִשְׂרָאֵל, אָסוּר בַּהֲנָאָה – שֶׁנֶּאֱמַר: "וְלֹא יֵרָאֶה לְךָ שְׂאֹר."

[ג] נָכְרִי שֶׁהִלְוָה אֶת יִשְׂרָאֵל עַל חֲמֵצוֹ, אַחַר הַפֶּסַח מֻתָּר בַּהֲנָאָה; וְיִשְׂרָאֵל שֶׁהִלְוָה אֶת הַנָּכְרִי עַל חֲמֵצוֹ, אַחַר הַפֶּסַח אָסוּר בַּהֲנָאָה. חָמֵץ שֶׁנָּפְלָה עָלָיו מַפֹּלֶת, הֲרֵי הוּא כִמְבֹעָר. רַבָּן שִׁמְעוֹן בֶּן גַּמְלִיאֵל אוֹמֵר: כָּל שֶׁאֵין הַכֶּלֶב יָכוֹל לְחַפֵּשׂ אַחֲרָיו.

[ד] הָאוֹכֵל תְּרוּמַת חָמֵץ בַּפֶּסַח בְּשׁוֹגֵג, מְשַׁלֵּם קֶרֶן וָחֹמֶשׁ. בְּמֵזִיד, פָּטוּר.

יד אברהם

requirement to destroy *chametz* takes effect at noon, the *terumah* may be allowed to become *tamei* in the process (*Gem.*).]

וּמוֹדִים רַבִּי אֱלִיעֶזֶר וְרַבִּי יְהוֹשֻׁעַ . . . — [*Furthermore, even*] *R' Eliezer and R' Yehoshua concur . . .* R' Eliezer and R' Yehoshua disagree whether there is a prohibition to burn *terumah* whose *tumah* is in doubt together with *terumah* that is definitely *tamei*. R' Eliezer rules that it may not be burned because there is an obligation to safeguard even doubtfully contaminated *terumah* from becoming definitely *tamei*. R' Yehoshua, however, rules that once its purity is in question and it can no longer be used, the Torah no longer requires us to safeguard it from *tumah*. [The dispute is based on different exegetical interpretations of the relevant verse.] Nevertheless, R' Yose states, they both concur that clearly uncontaminated *terumah* may not be burned with contaminated *terumah*, even in the sixth hour when it is already Rabbinically prohibited (*Rav*).

CHAPTER TWO

1. The mishnah now returns to the topic of the time limits for eating and benefiting from *chametz* on Erev Pesach.

כָּל שָׁעָה שֶׁמֻּתָּר לֶאֱכוֹל — *As long as it is permitted to eat [chametz],* one may feed it to his animals. But once the prohibition to eat *chametz* takes effect, it is forbidden for all benefit. Thus according to Rabban Gamliel (1:5) who gives *Kohanim* an extra hour for eating *terumah*, even an Israelite who must stop eating *chametz* at the beginning of the fifth hour may continue to feed *chametz* to his livestock until the onset of the sixth hour. [This

is indeed the *halachah*; see *O. Ch. 443:1*.]

וּמֻתָּר בַּהֲנָאָתוֹ — *And one is permitted to derive benefit from it.* The Gemara concludes that this [seemingly redundant] clause alludes to the rule that if *chametz* is charred before it becomes forbidden to such an extent that it is inedible even to dogs, he is permitted to derive benefit from it even after the *chametz* prohibition takes effect (*Rav*).

עָבַר זְמַנּוֹ, אָסוּר בַּהֲנָאָתוֹ — *Once its period has passed* [i.e., the fifth hour], *it is forbidden to derive benefit from it.* During the sixth hour, *chametz* is forbidden by Rabbinic injunction, and after noon, by Biblical law. Even while burning it he may not benefit from it [by using it to fire an oven] (*Rav*).

רַבִּי יְהוּדָה אוֹמֵר — *R' Yehudah* derives his rule from a comparison of *chametz* to נוֹתָר, *leftover* sacrificial meat. Since *leftover* offerings must be burned (*Ex. 12:10*), *chametz* too must be burned (*Rav*).

וַחֲכָמִים אוֹמְרִים — *The Sages* reject R' Yehudah's analogy because not all forbidden substances share the requirement of burning. Although the *halachah* follows the Sages, it is customary to burn the *chametz* (*Rama, O. Ch. 445:1*).

אוֹ מַטִּיל לַיָּם — *Or cast [it] into the sea.* Hard *chametz* or grain, which does not disintegrate rapidly, must first be crumbled; other kinds may simply be cast into the sea.

2. חָמֵץ שֶׁל נָכְרִי — The *chametz* kept by a non-Jew until the end of Pesach is permitted for a Jew's benefit, and may even be eaten.

that each is burned separately. Concerning what did they differ? Concerning questionably contaminated [terumah] and definitely contaminated [terumah]. R' Eliezer says that each must be burned separately, but R' Yehoshua says that both [may be burned] together.

CHAPTER TWO

[1] **כָּל** *As long as it is permitted to eat [chametz], one may feed [it] to livestock, beasts and birds, and sell it to a non-Jew, and one is permitted to derive benefit from it. Once its period has passed, it is forbidden to derive benefit from it, and one may not fire an oven or a stove with it.*

R' Yehudah says: Chametz may be removed only by burning. But the Sages say: He may also crumble [it] and throw [it] to the wind or cast [it] into the sea.

[2] *The chametz of a non-Jew over which Pesach has passed is permitted for benefit, but [the chametz] of a Jew is forbidden for benefit — since it is said: Nor shall leaven be seen with you (Ex. 13:7).*

[3] *[If] a non-Jew lent [money] to a Jew with his chametz [as collateral], it is permitted to benefit from it after Pesach; but if a Jew lent [money] to a non-Jew with his chametz [as collateral], it is forbidden to benefit from it after Pesach.*

If a ruin collapsed over chametz, it is regarded as removed. Rabban Shimon ben Gamliel says: Provided a dog cannot search it out.

[4] *One who eats terumah of chametz on Pesach mistakenly, must repay the principal plus a fifth. [If he eats it] deliberately, he is exempt from payment*

YAD AVRAHAM

וְשֶׁל יִשְׂרָאֵל — *But [the chametz]* kept by a Jew over Pesach is forbidden after Pesach for consumption and even benefit. According to the *Gemara's* conclusion, the post-festival prohibition is a Rabbinically imposed penalty. The mishnah quotes this verse because it is the verse upon which the Sages based their decree. *Chametz* left in a Jew's possession over Pesach is forbidden forever even if it was left over *accidentally* (O. Ch. 448:3).

3. נָכְרִי שֶׁהִלְוָה אֶת יִשְׂרָאֵל ... — *[If] a non-Jew lent [money] to a Jew* before Pesach, with the Jew pledging his *chametz* as collateral, and the Jew then defaulted on the loan, the *chametz* does not become prohibited because it belonged to the gentile over Pesach. This is true only if their agreement stipulated that in case of default the collateral would become the lender's retroactive to the time of the loan. Also, the collateral must have been held in the lender's premises during Pesach, so that he need not take any action to collect his debt (*Rav*). A Jew is permitted to purchase this *chametz* after Pesach and eat it.

וְיִשְׂרָאֵל שֶׁהִלְוָה אֶת הַנָּכְרִי — *But if a Jew lent [money] to a non-Jew,* i.e., if the situation was reversed and the non-Jew defaulted on the debt, the *chametz* is considered the lender's and consequently forbidden since it had been 'kept' by a Jew over Pesach.

חָמֵץ שֶׁנָּפְלָה עָלָיו מַפֹּלֶת — *If a ruin collapsed over chametz,* it is not necessary to remove the debris in order to find and destroy the *chametz* (*Tif. Yis.*). However, the owner must nullify it in his heart (בטול), because it is conceivable that the debris will be removed during Pesach (*Rav*).

כָּל שֶׁאֵין הַכֶּלֶב ... — *Provided a dog cannot* search it out; i.e., it is under at least three handbreadths of debris.

4. *Terumah [the portion separated from produce and given a Kohen]* may not be eaten by anyone except *Kohanim* and members of their households. If *terumah* is mistakenly [בְּשׁוֹגֵג] eaten by a non-*Kohen* (e.g. he was unaware that it was *terumah*), he must atone by repaying the principal and adding a fifth. The payment must be made in produce (not money), which is then rendered *terumah*. If he knowingly eats *terumah*, he is liable to the punishment of premature 'death at the hands of Heaven' [מִיתָה בִּידֵי שָׁמַיִם]; if he had been forewarned by two witnesses, he is liable to lashes. His only financial liability, however, is to pay damages; this can be done with money, and even if it is with produce, it does not become *terumah*.

מְשַׁלֵּם קֶרֶן וְחֹמֶשׁ — *Must repay the principal plus a fifth.* Although *chametz* on Pesach becomes forbidden forever and the *terumah* he ate was thus worthless, *terumah* is unique in that the amount repaid for eating it mistakenly does not depend on its value, but on the volume consumed. A pound of fruit must be replaced with a pound of the same kind of fruit regardless of the price at the time of repayment. Thus, the original value of the *terumah* is irrelevant.

בְּמֵזִיד ... — *[If he eats it] deliberately,* knowing that it was *terumah* and forbidden to him, he does not pay anything. In this case the obligation to pay is not determined by quantity but by the value of the damage. *Chametz* on Pesach, however, has no value (*Rav*).

[ה] אֵלּוּ דְבָרִים שֶׁאָדָם יוֹצֵא בָהֶן יְדֵי חוֹבָתוֹ בַּפֶּסַח: בְּחִטִּים, בִּשְׂעוֹרִים, בְּכֻסְּמִין, וּבְשִׁיפוֹן וּבְשִׁבֹּלֶת שׁוּעָל. וְיוֹצְאִין בִּדְמַאי, וּבְמַעֲשֵׂר רִאשׁוֹן שֶׁנִּטְּלָה תְרוּמָתוֹ, וּבְמַעֲשֵׂר שֵׁנִי וְהֶקְדֵּשׁ שֶׁנִּפְדּוּ; וְהַכֹּהֲנִים בְּחַלָּה וּבִתְרוּמָה; אֲבָל לֹא בְטֶבֶל, וְלֹא בְמַעֲשֵׂר רִאשׁוֹן שֶׁלֹּא נִטְּלָה תְרוּמָתוֹ, וְלֹא בְמַעֲשֵׂר שֵׁנִי וְהֶקְדֵּשׁ שֶׁלֹּא נִפְדּוּ.

חַלּוֹת תּוֹדָה וּרְקִיקֵי נָזִיר – עֲשָׂאָן לְעַצְמוֹ, אֵין יוֹצְאִין בָּהֶן; עֲשָׂאָן לִמְכֹּר בַּשּׁוּק, יוֹצְאִין בָּהֶן.

[ו] וְאֵלּוּ יְרָקוֹת שֶׁאָדָם יוֹצֵא בָהֶן יְדֵי חוֹבָתוֹ בַּפֶּסַח: בְּחֲזֶרֶת, וּבְעֻלְשִׁין, וּבְתַמְכָא, וּבְחַרְחֲבִינָה, וּבְמָרוֹר. יוֹצְאִין בָּהֶן בֵּין בֵּין לַחִין בֵּין יְבֵשִׁין, אֲבָל לֹא כְבוּשִׁין, וְלֹא שְׁלוּקִין, וְלֹא מְבֻשָּׁלִין. וּמִצְטָרְפִין לִכְזַיִת. וְיוֹצְאִין בְּקֶלַח שֶׁלָּהֶן; וּבִדְמַאי; וּבְמַעֲשֵׂר רִאשׁוֹן שֶׁנִּטְּלָה תְרוּמָתוֹ; וּבְמַעֲשֵׂר שֵׁנִי וְהֶקְדֵּשׁ שֶׁנִּפְדּוּ.

[ז] אֵין שׁוֹרִין אֶת הַמֻּרְסָן לַתַּרְנְגוֹלִים, אֲבָל חוֹלְטִין. הָאִשָּׁה לֹא תִשְׁרֶה אֶת הַמֻּרְסָן שֶׁתּוֹלִיךְ בְּיָדָהּ לַמֶּרְחָץ, אֲבָל שָׁפָה הִיא

יד אברהם

וּמִדְּמֵי עֵצִים — And from [liability for] its value as fuel, because chametz on Pesach may not even be burned as a fuel.

5. There is a Biblical obligation to eat matzah on the first night of Pesach. The mishnah delineates the products that may be used to fulfill this mitzvah. [Many of the other items mentioned here may be eaten on Pesach but they cannot be used to fulfill the first night's obligation.]

בְּחִטִּים . . . — With wheat . . . However, one does not discharge his obligation with millet, rice, or matzah made from any other grain but these five. It is customary to use only wheat (O. Ch. 453:1), because it is the tastiest.

בִּדְמַאי — With demai, i.e. produce purchased from a common person. The Sages decreed that such produce may not be eaten until it has been tithed, because they observed that many common people had become lax in separating tithes other than terumah. However, they did not impose this burden upon poor people, in view of the compliance of most ignorant people with the laws of tithes. Technically, anyone can avail himself of the right to eat demai by declaring his property hefker (ownerless) and becoming poor. Conasequently, fulfilling the matzah obligation with demai is not per se disqualified as a mitzvah that comes about through a transgression (Gem.).

וּבְמַעֲשֵׂר רִאשׁוֹן שֶׁנִּטְּלָה תְרוּמָתוֹ — [And] with maaser rishon whose terumah has been separated. The produce of Eretz Yisrael may not be eaten until various tithes have been separated from it.

These are: terumah (about 2% of the crop) which is given a Kohen, and maaser rishon (10% of the remainder), which goes to a Levite. Maaser, however, may not be eaten until the Levite tithes it by separating a tenth to give to a Kohen. This is called the terumah of the maaser and has all the laws of terumah. Obviously, one may use such tithed maaser for matzah. The mishnah's point is that there are circumstances in which it may be used even if only the Levite's terumah had been separated but not the general terumah which should have come first. This occurs when the maaser was separated before the terumah obligation took effect at threshing (Gem.).

וּבְמַעֲשֵׂר שֵׁנִי וְהֶקְדֵּשׁ שֶׁנִּפְדּוּ — With maaser sheni or consecrated produce that were redeemed. There is yet another tithe required. In the first, second, fourth and fifth years of the Sabbatical cycle, maaser sheni is separated (also 10%). This belongs to the owner but it must be eaten in Jerusalem. However, the owner may redeem the maaser sheni [which then loses its sanctity] and take the money to Jerusalem in place of the produce. This he uses to buy food which then assumes the maaser sheni sanctity. When redeeming his own maaser, the owner must add an extra fifth to the price. The same is true when one redeems items he has consecrated to the Temple treasury. Thus, he may fulfill his matzah obligation with redeemed maaser sheni and consecrated produce. In stating the obvious, the mishnah also teaches that even if the fifth has not yet been paid the redemption has already taken effect and the matzah obligation

and from [liability for] its value as fuel.

[5] *These are the species [of grain] with which a man fulfills his [matzah] obligation on Pesach: with wheat, barley, spelt, rye and oats. One can discharge [his obligation to eat matzah] with demai, with maaser rishon whose terumah has been separated, with maaser sheni or consecrated produce that were redeemed; and Kohanim with challah and terumah; but not with untithed produce, nor with maaser rishon whose terumah has not been separated, nor with maaser sheni or consecrated produce that were not redeemed.*

The [unleavened] loaves of the thanksgiving offering, and the nazir's wafers — [if] he made them for himself, he cannot fulfill his obligation with them; [but if] he made them to sell in the market, he can fulfill his obligation with them.

[6] *These are the [bitter] herbs with which one fulfills his [maror] obligation on Pesach: with lettuce, endives, horseradish, charchavinah, and [with] maror. One fulfills his obligation with them whether they are fresh or dry, but not soaked, nor stewed, nor boiled. These [may be] combined to [form] the olive-sized [minimum]. One can fulfill his obligation with their stalk; with demai; with maaser rishon whose terumah has been separated; and with consecrated property and maaser sheni which were redeemed.*

[7] *One may not soak bran for chickens, but one may scald it. A woman may not soak bran to take with her to the baths, but she may rub it on her skin*

YAD AVRAHAM

is fulfilled (*Gem.*).

וְהַכֹּהֲנִים בְּחַלָּה — *And Kohanim with challah.* Dough requires an additional *terumah*, called *challah*. Since *challah* and *terumah* are forbidden to non-*Kohanim*, only *Kohanim* fulfill their obligation with them.

אֲבָל לֹא בְטֶבֶל — *But not with untithed produce,* because it is prohibited and thus obviously unfit for matzah. Our mishnah means to include even Rabbinically forbidden *tevel*, i.e., grain not subject to tithing under Biblical law, but for which the Sages imposed an obligation. All the substances disqualified here are because of the principle invalidating a מִצְוָה הַבָּאָה בַּעֲבֵירָה, *mitzvah brought about by means of a transgression.*

חַלּוֹת תּוֹדָה — *Loaves of the thanksgiving offering;* see 1:5.

וּרְקִיקֵי נָזִיר — *Nazir's wafers.* When the term of a *nazir's* vow ends, he brings a set of offerings which include *a basket of unleavened bread, loaves of fine flour mixed with oil, and unleavened wafers smeared with oil* (*Num.* 6:15).

עֲשָׂאָן לְעַצְמוֹ ... — *[If] he made them for himself,* to use for his own *nazir* offering, he cannot fulfill his matzah obligation with them, because the Torah states: *you shall guard the matzos* (*Ex.* 12:17), which the Sages understand to teach that the matzah must be guarded during its preparation for the sake of the *mitzvah* of eating matzah; not for any other purpose, such as a sacrifice (*Rav*).

עֲשָׂאָן לִמְכֹּר ... — *[But if] he made them to sell* to other nazirites,

he may fulfill his first-night obligation with them. Anyone making loaves for sale stipulates beforehand: 'If it is sold, well and good; if not, I will fulfill the obligation of matzah with it' (*Gem.*).

6. חַרְחֲבִינָה — *Charchavinah.* The Gemara identifies this as a type of vine growing around palms. *Rambam* identifies it as a type of thistle, while *R' Hai Gaon* considers it a type of acacia.

וּבְמָרוֹר — *And [with] maror.* According to *Rashi*, this is wormwood (cf. *Rama O. Ch.* 473:5 and *Beur Halachah* there). *Rambam* and *Aruch* identify it as a wild lettuce.

יְבֵשִׁין — *Dry,* i.e., the stalks; the leaves, however, must be fresh (*Gem.*).

אֲבָל לֹא כְבוּשִׁין — *But not soaked* in vinegar (*Rashi*), or in water (*Mag. Av.* 473:14). Vinegar disqualifies the herbs after 18 minutes of soaking; water after 24 hours (*Tif. Yis.*).

שְׁלוּקִין — *Stewed,* i.e., cooked until they are reduced to a mush (*Rashi*). Boiling, stewing and soaking remove the herbs' bitter taste.

7. אֵין שׁוֹרִין אֶת הַמֻּרְסָן ... — *One may not soak bran* even in cold water, and even for less than eighteen minutes, because soaking causes the leavening process to begin. *But one may scald it,* because scalded grain will not leaven (just as baked matzah will not leaven). However, the *Geonim* and *Rambam* prohibited scalding grain on Pesach, for fear that people will not make the water hot enough.

אֲבָל שָׁפָה — *But she may rub* her skin with dry bran although she

בִּבְשָׂרָה יָבֵשׁ. לֹא יִלְעֹס אָדָם חִטִּין וְיַנִּיחַ עַל מַכָּתוֹ בַּפֶּסַח, מִפְּנֵי שֶׁהֵן מַחְמִיצוֹת.

[ח] אֵין נוֹתְנִין קֶמַח לְתוֹךְ הַחֲרֹסֶת אוֹ לְתוֹךְ הַחַרְדָּל. וְאִם נָתַן, יֹאכַל מִיָּד. וְרַבִּי מֵאִיר אוֹסֵר. אֵין מְבַשְּׁלִין אֶת הַפֶּסַח לֹא בְמַשְׁקִין וְלֹא בְמֵי פֵרוֹת. אֲבָל סָכִין וּמַטְבִּילִין אוֹתוֹ בָהֶן. מֵי תַשְׁמִישׁוֹ שֶׁל נַחְתּוֹם יִשָּׁפְכוּ, מִפְּנֵי שֶׁהֵן מַחְמִיצִין.

פרק שלישי

[א] **אֵלוּ עוֹבְרִין** בַּפֶּסַח: כֻּתָּח הַבַּבְלִי, וְשֵׁכָר הַמָּדִי, וְחֹמֶץ הָאֲדוֹמִי, וְזִיתוֹם הַמִּצְרִי, וְזוֹמָן שֶׁל צַבָּעִים, וַעֲמִילָן שֶׁל טַבָּחִים, וְקוֹלָן שֶׁל סוֹפְרִים. רַבִּי אֱלִיעֶזֶר אוֹמֵר: אַף תַּכְשִׁיטֵי נָשִׁים. זֶה הַכְּלָל: כֹּל שֶׁהוּא מִמִּין דָּגָן, הֲרֵי זֶה עוֹבֵר בַּפֶּסַח. הֲרֵי אֵלוּ בְאַזְהָרָה, וְאֵין בָּהֶן מִשּׁוּם כָּרֵת.

[ב] בָּצֵק שֶׁבְּסִדְקֵי עֲרֵבָה, אִם יֵשׁ כְּזַיִת בְּמָקוֹם אֶחָד, חַיָּב לְבַעֵר; וְאִם לֹא, בָּטֵל בְּמִעוּטוֹ. וְכֵן לְעִנְיַן הַטֻּמְאָה. אִם מַקְפִּיד עָלָיו, חוֹצֵץ; וְאִם רוֹצֶה

יד אברהם

is sweating because sweat is not a leavening agent. Nevertheless, it is advisable not to rub grain on the skin in any case, because one may forget to remove it before washing (O.Ch. 465:2). Saliva, however, causes leavening.

8. הַחֲרֹסֶת ... לְתוֹךְ — *Into charoses . . . mustard,* which in Mishnaic times, contained water in addition to vinegar.

יֹאכַל מִיָּד — *It must be eaten immediately.* This applies *only* to mustard, because its pungency delays the flour's leavening. *Charoses,* however, begins leavening immediately, and it should therefore be burned without delay (*Gem.*). R' Meir, however, maintains that even the sharpness of mustard will not retard the leavening process. *Rama* (*O. Ch.* 464) remarks that it is customary (among Ashkenazim) to refrain from eating mustard on Pesach altogether.

אֵין מְבַשְּׁלִין אֶת הַפֶּסַח ... — *We may not cook the Pesach offering . . .* The term *liquids* refers specifically to seven liquids: wine, honey, oil, milk, dew, blood, and water (*Machshirin* 6:4). *Fruit juices* includes any other fruit juice. In prohibiting the consumption of a cooked Pesach offering, the Torah mentions only cooking in water (*Ex.* 12:9); nevertheless the Sages found an allusion in this verse to prohibit cooking in any liquid.

מֵי תַשְׁמִישׁוֹ ... — *The water used* by a baker to cool his hands retains some of the dough which becomes *chametz.*

CHAPTER THREE

1. There are three categories of *chametz,* each with a different degree of stringency: (1) Pure, unadulterated *chametz;* (2) *chametz* mixed with other substances; (3) *chametz nuksheh.* Consumption of unadulterated *chametz* on Pesach is punishable by *kares.* Consumption of a mixture containing *chametz* is Biblically prohibited, but the severity of the prohibition is subject to dispute. If the percentage of *chametz* in the mixture is such that a person eating an amount equal to three (*Rambam*) or four (*Rashi*) eggs consumes an olive's volume of *chametz* [כְּזַיִת בִּכְדֵי אֲכִילַת פְּרָס], it is subject to a negative commandment [לֹא תַעֲשֶׂה] but not *kares* (*Rambam*). [According to *Ramban* it is even subject to *kares*.] If the proportion of *chametz* is less than this, it is certainly not subject to *kares,* but there is a Tannaitic dispute whether it is included in the negative commandment against consumption of *chametz.* R' Eliezer maintains that it is, whereas the Sages hold that it is Biblically prohibited, but by less than a negative commandment. *Chametz nuksheh* (lit. *hardened chametz*) is incomplete *chametz,* either dough whose leavening was never completed (see 3:5), or *chametz* that was never fit for consumption. Some *Tannaim* hold *chametz nuksheh* to be Biblically prohibited by a negative commandment, while others contend that it is only Rabbinically prohibited (*Gem.*).

אֵלוּ עוֹבְרִין בַּפֶּסַח — *The following must be removed* from the world, i.e., destroyed, because one is not permitted to possess them on Pesach (*Tos.*). This requirement is Rabbinic, to prevent anyone from eating them by mistake (*Ran*). The Torah prohibition to own *chametz* applies only to completed *chametz* that is unmixed.

dry. A person may not chew wheat and place it on his wound on Pesach, because it becomes chametz.

[8] *One may not put flour into charoses nor into mustard. If one did so, it must be eaten immediately. But R' Meir forbids [it]. We may not cook the Pesach offering either in liquids or in fruit juices. But we may baste it and dip it in them. The water used by a baker must be poured out, because they have become chametz.*

CHAPTER THREE

[1] אֵלּוּ *The following must be removed on Pesach: Babylonian dairy condiment, Median beer, Idumean vinegar, Egyptian zisom, dyers' broth, cooks' dough and scribes' paste. R' Eliezer says: Also women's cosmetics. This is the rule: Whatever is of a species of grain must be removed on Pesach. These are prohibited by a negative commandment but they are not subject to kares.*

[2] *When dough remains in the grooves of a kneading trough, if there is as much as an olive's [volume] in one place, he must remove [it]; but if not, it is null because of its insignificant amount. And likewise regarding the [laws of] tumah-contamination. If he objects to it, it interposes; but if he desires it to remain, it is*

YAD AVRAHAM

... כֻּתָּח הַבַּבְלִי — *Babylonian dairy condiment* consisted of sour milk, moldy bread crusts and salt (*Gem.*). *Median beer* was brewed from dates and barley, making it mixed *chametz*. By contrast, most beers in Talmudic times were brewed from dates alone. [However, contemporary beer, prepared exclusively from barley, is subject to *kares*.] *Idumean vinegar* was made from wine fermented with barley soaked in water (*Tos.*). *Egyptian zisom* was made from equal quantities of barley, saffron (or safflower) and salt, kneaded with water and used for medicinal purposes (*Rambam*). Though these four substances contain amounts of complete *chametz*, there is no *kares* for their consumption because they also contain large amounts of other ingredients. The next three listed are pure *chametz* with no admixture of foreign ingredients. However, because they are not meant for consumption (though theoretically they can be eaten), they are considered *chametz nuksheh* and therefore exempted from *kares*.

... וְזוֹמָן שֶׁל צַבָּעִים — *Dyers' broth* was made of bran mixed with water and used in the preparation of certain red dyes. *Cooks' dough* was made of flour from grain less than one-third ripe. The dough was fashioned into a pot cover which, when placed over a pot of cooking meat, drew out the muck and bad smell (*Gem.*). *Scribes' paste* was made of rye flour; it was used by tanners to paste layers of leather together and by scribes to prepare paper (*Gem.*).

רַבִּי אֱלִיעֶזֶר אוֹמֵר — *R' Eliezer says:* The *Tanna Kamma* forbade only a mixture containing complete *chametz* or pure *chametz nuksheh*, but he permitted the possession of *chametz nuksheh* as part of a mixture. R' Eliezer disagrees and rules that even a mixture containing *chametz nuksheh* is

forbidden. The cosmetics specified by him are such a mixture.

מִמִּין דָּגָן — *[Made] of* one of the five species of grain (i.e., wheat, barley, spelt, rye and oats) and mixed with water (*Rashi*).

הֲרֵי אֵלּוּ בְּאַזְהָרָה ... — *These* [substances listed above] *are prohibited by a negative commandment*, but he is not subject to *kares* for eating them. Our mishnah represents a minority opinion. The (*Gem.*) consensus of *Tannaim* is that mixtures containing pure *chametz*, as well as *chametz nuksheh*, are not included in the negative commandment prohibiting consumption of *chametz*, though they are Biblically forbidden and may not be kept on Pesach; see preface.

2. כְּזַיִת בְּמָקוֹם אֶחָד — *An olive's [volume] in one place* is too significant an amount to be nullified and considered part of the trough. However, less than an olive's volume in any *one* part of the trough is no longer considered a foodstuff but an integral part of the utensil, because it serves to seal the cracks and holes. However, if the dough does not serve as a seal, even the smaller amount must be removed before Pesach, because the owner may decide to detach it and it is thus not subsidiary to the trough.

וְכֵן לְעִנְיַן הַטֻּמְאָה — *And likewise regarding [the laws of] tumah-contamination.* Should a source of *tumah* touch an olive-sized piece of dough in the crack of a trough, its size gives it an identity independent of the trough. The dough thus intervenes between the contaminating agent and the trough, and only the dough becomes *tamei*, not the trough. [The dough cannot in turn pass its *tumah* to the utensil, for it is a cardinal rule that foodstuffs cannot pass *tumah* to people and utensils, only to other food or liquids.] If the amount of dough was less than an olive's size, it

בְּקִיּוּמוֹ, הֲרֵי הוּא כָעֲרֵבָה. בָּצֵק הַחֵרֵשׁ, אִם יֵשׁ כַּיּוֹצֵא בוֹ שֶׁהֶחְמִיץ, הֲרֵי זֶה אָסוּר.

[ג] כֵּיצַד מַפְרִישִׁין חַלָּה בְּטֻמְאָה בְּיוֹם טוֹב? רַבִּי אֱלִיעֶזֶר אוֹמֵר: לֹא תִקְרָא לָהּ שֵׁם עַד שֶׁתֵּאָפֶה.

רַבִּי יְהוּדָה בֶּן בְּתֵירָא אוֹמֵר: תַּטִּיל בְּצוֹנֵן. אָמַר רַבִּי יְהוֹשֻׁעַ: לֹא זֶה הוּא חָמֵץ שֶׁמֻּזְהָרִים עָלָיו ,,בְּבַל יֵרָאֶה" וְ,,בְּבַל יִמָּצֵא." אֶלָּא מַפְרִשְׁתָּהּ וּמַנִּחַתָּהּ עַד הָעֶרֶב; וְאִם הֶחְמִיצָה, הֶחְמִיצָה.

[ד] רַבָּן גַּמְלִיאֵל אוֹמֵר: שָׁלֹשׁ נָשִׁים לָשׁוֹת כְּאַחַת וְאוֹפוֹת בְּתַנּוּר אֶחָד, זוֹ אַחַר זוֹ. וַחֲכָמִים אוֹמְרִים: שָׁלֹשׁ נָשִׁים עוֹסְקוֹת בְּבָצֵק – אַחַת לָשָׁה, וְאַחַת עוֹרֶכֶת, וְאַחַת אוֹפָה. רַבִּי עֲקִיבָא אוֹמֵר: לֹא כָל הַנָּשִׁים וְלֹא כָל הָעֵצִים וְלֹא כָל הַתַּנּוּרִים שָׁוִין. זֶה הַכְּלָל: תָּפַח, תִּלְטוֹשׁ בְּצוֹנֵן.

[ה] שְׂאוֹר יִשָּׂרֵף, וְהָאוֹכְלוֹ פָּטוּר. סִדּוּק יִשָּׂרֵף, וְהָאוֹכְלוֹ חַיָּב כָּרֵת. אֵיזֶהוּ שְׂאוֹר? כְּקַרְנֵי חֲגָבִים. סִדּוּק? שֶׁנִּתְעָרְבוּ סִדְקָיו זֶה בָזֶה; דִּבְרֵי רַבִּי יְהוּדָה. וַחֲכָמִים אוֹמְרִים: זֶה וָזֶה הָאוֹכְלוֹ חַיָּב כָּרֵת. וְאֵיזֶהוּ שְׂאוֹר? כָּל שֶׁהִכְסִיפוּ פָנָיו, כְּאָדָם שֶׁעָמְדוּ שַׂעֲרוֹתָיו.

[ו] אַרְבָּעָה עָשָׂר שֶׁחָל לִהְיוֹת בַּשַּׁבָּת, מְבַעֲרִין אֶת הַכֹּל מִלִּפְנֵי הַשַּׁבָּת; דִּבְרֵי רַבִּי מֵאִיר. וַחֲכָמִים אוֹמְרִים: בִּזְמַנָּן. רַבִּי אֶלְעָזָר בַּר צָדוֹק אוֹמֵר: תְּרוּמָה מִלִּפְנֵי הַשַּׁבָּת וְחֻלִּין בִּזְמַנָּן.

יד אברהם

is considered part of the utensil (if the owner intends to leave it in the cracks), and any *tumah* touching it contaminates the entire utensil (*Rav*).

אִם מַקְפִּיד עָלָיו חוֹצֵץ — *If he objects to it*, and plans to remove it eventually, *it interposes*. The previous ruling that an olive-sized piece is never considered part of the trough is true only on Pesach, when the laws of *chametz* make the size of an olive a key factor in whether *chametz* may be retained. The mishnah now teaches that during the rest of the year the size of the dough is of no concern and the only consideration is whether the owner plans to leave it attached to the vessel.

בָּצֵק הַחֵרֵשׁ — *'Deaf' dough*, i.e., a dough which there is reason to suspect has leavened, but exhibits none of the symptoms of leavening outlined in mishnah 5. The dough as yet emits no sound when struck, like a deaf person who, when addressed, shows no reaction. [Emitting such a sound is considered a sign of leavening.] If there is another dough that was kneaded at the same time that has become leavened, the 'deaf' dough is also forbidden. In the absence of another dough, the dough is considered *chametz* if it has been left without being kneaded for 18 minutes. As long as it is constantly being worked upon, however, the process of leavening does not take place (*O. Ch.* 459:2).

3. כֵּיצַד מַפְרִישִׁין חַלָּה בְּטֻמְאָה בְּיוֹם טוֹב? — *How does one separate*

challah *from contaminated dough on the festival?* Challah is the portion separated from dough and given to a *Kohen*. When dough is *tamei* the *challah* is separated (to permit the remainder of the dough) and then burned, because *challah*, like *terumah*, may be eaten only *tahor*. This presents a problem on Pesach since one cannot lay the *challah* aside until evening when it can be burned because the dough will leaven, causing the owner to be in possession of *chametz*. Nor can one follow the normal Pesach procedure for *challah* of separating and baking it immediately, because cooking and baking on *Yom Tov* are permitted only for the purpose of אוֹכֶל נֶפֶשׁ, *human consumption*, which is impossible here. R' Eliezer therefore suggests that the housewife bake her dough into matzah before separating *challah*, separate some of the matzah as *challah*, and burn it after *Yom Tov*. R' Yehudah ben Beseirah advises her to separate *challah* from the dough and put it into frigid water (which prevents leavening) and leave it until nightfall for burning. [R' Eliezer rejects this option, because the water may not be cold enough to retard leavening in every case.]

אָמַר רַבִּי יְהוֹשֻׁעַ — *R' Yehoshua* rejects the need for any precaution because once dough is designated *challah* it becomes the collective property of all *Kohanim* and does not belong to the original owner any longer. Thus the *challah* dough need not be destroyed as the trough. 'Deaf' dough — if there is [dough] similar to it that has already leavened, it is forbidden.

[3] *How does one separate challah from contaminated dough on the festival? R' Eliezer says: She should not designate it with the name [challah] until it is baked. R' Yehudah ben Beseira says: She should cast into cold water. Said R' Yehoshua: This is not the leaven concerning which we are warned, it shall not be seen (Exodus 13:7) and it shall not be found (Exodus 12:19). Rather, he separates it and leaves it until the evening; and if it leavens, it leavens.*

[4] *Rabban Gamliel says: Three women may knead at the same time and bake in the same oven, one after the other. But the Sages say: Three women may be occupied with dough [simultaneously] — one kneading, another shaping, and a third baking. R' Akiva says: Not all women and not all kinds of wood and not all ovens are alike. This is the rule: [If the dough] rises, let her wet it with cold water.*

[5] *Partly leavened dough must be burned, but one who eats it is exempt [from punishment]. Furrowed dough must be burned and one who eats it is liable to kares. Which [dough] is partly leavened? [When the furrows are] like locusts' horns. [Which is] furrowed? When the furrows run into each other; [these are] the words of R' Yehudah. But the Sages say: If one eats either of these he is liable to kares. Which [then] is partly leavened dough [which is exempted]? Any [dough] whose surface has blanched, like a man whose hairs stand on end [out of fright].*

[6] *[If] the fourteenth [of Nissan] falls on the Sabbath, one must remove all chametz before the Sabbath; [these are] the words of R' Meir. But the Sages say: At its [usual] time. R' Elazar bar Tzadok says: Terumah [must be removed] before the Sabbath and chullin at its [usual] time.*

YAD AVRAHAM

because it is the property of neither the original owner nor of any specific *Kohen* (*Rav*). [However, R' Eliezer and Ben Beseira maintain that since the original owner still retains the power to give the *challah* to the *Kohen* of his choice, this constitutes a certain degree of ownership (טוֹבַת הַנָּאָה מָמוֹן). R' Yehoshua considers this right inconsequential (*Gem*.).]

4. שָׁלֹשׁ נָשִׁים לָשׁוּת בְּאַחַת — *Three women may knead at the same time* although they are using an oven large enough for only one dough. Although the third dough will be left standing until the other two bake, R' Gamliel maintains that dough does not leaven in so short a time. However, the Sages fear that the time lapse may be too long. Thus, they rule that they must stagger their work so that one kneads while the second shapes or rolls the dough and bastes it with cold water, and a third bakes, with the cycle repeating itself, so that no dough is left unattended. R' Akiva disputes R' Gamliel and concurs with the Sages because one cannot generalize about the pace at which different women work, ovens heat, or wood burns (*Rav*).

זֶה הַכְּלָל: — *This is the rule:* [This phrase is not part of R' Akiva's statement but a unanimous statement of the mishnah.] When a woman notices that dough is about to rise, she should baste it with cold water. This retards the leavening process (*Rav*).

5. שְׂאוֹר יִשָׂרֵף — *Partly leavened dough* is classified as *chametz*

nukskeh (mishnah 1) and must be burned. Nevertheless, one who eats it on Pesach is exempt from both *malkos* [lashes] and *kares*.

סְדוּק יִשָׂרֵף — *Furrowed dough must be burned.* The appearance of furrows on dough is a symptom of fermentation, indicating that the leavening process has been completed.

כְּקַרְנֵי חֲגָבִים — *Like locusts' horns.* When there are so few furrows on the dough's surface that they do not meet (*Rashi*), and they are very thin (*Rambam*). The Sages, however, maintain that furrows in any form, even if they do not run into each other, are an indication of complete leavening. Consequently, the dough classified as 'partly leavened' by R' Yehudah is categorized by the Sages as finished *chametz*, subject to *kares*. [Conversely, what the Sages classify as partly leavened is, according to R' Yehudah, matzah (albeit Rabbinically prohibited).]

6. וַחֲכָמִים אוֹמְרִים — *But the Sages say* that one may leave as much *chametz* as he likes for the Sabbath on the assumption that there will be enough people to eat it. Should any *chametz* remain, it can be eliminated when the proper time comes in those manners permissible on the Sabbath; see *O. Ch.* 444:4-5 with *Mishnah Berurah*.

רַבִּי אֶלְעָזָר בַּר צָדוֹק אוֹמֵר — *R' Elazar bar Tzadok* differentiates between *terumah*, which is forbidden to non-*Kohanim* and their

[ז] הַהוֹלֵךְ לִשְׁחֹט אֶת פִּסְחוֹ, וְלָמוּל אֶת בְּנוֹ, וְלֶאֱכֹל סְעוּדַת אֵרוּסִין בְּבֵית חָמִיו, וְנִזְכַּר שֶׁיֶּשׁ לוֹ חָמֵץ בְּתוֹךְ בֵּיתוֹ — אִם יָכוֹל לַחֲזוֹר, וּלְבַעֵר, וְלַחֲזוֹר לְמִצְוָתוֹ, יַחֲזוֹר וִיבַעֵר; וְאִם לָאו, מְבַטְּלוֹ בְּלִבּוֹ. לְהַצִּיל מִן הַגַּיִס, וּמִן הַנָּהָר, וּמִן הַלִּסְטִים, וּמִן הַדְּלֵקָה, וּמִן הַמַּפֹּלֶת, יְבַטֵּל בְּלִבּוֹ. וְלִשְׁבֹּת שְׁבִיתַת הָרְשׁוּת, יַחֲזוֹר מִיָּד.

[ח] וְכֵן מִי שֶׁיָּצָא מִירוּשָׁלַיִם וְנִזְכַּר שֶׁיֶּשׁ בְּיָדוֹ בְּשַׂר קֹדֶשׁ — אִם עָבַר צוֹפִים, שׂוֹרְפוֹ בִמְקוֹמוֹ; וְאִם לָאו, חוֹזֵר וְשׂוֹרְפוֹ לִפְנֵי הַבִּירָה מֵעֲצֵי הַמַּעֲרָכָה. וְעַד כַּמָּה הֵן חוֹזְרִין? רַבִּי מֵאִיר אוֹמֵר: זֶה וָזֶה בִּכְבֵיצָה. רַבִּי יְהוּדָה אוֹמֵר: זֶה וָזֶה בִּכְזַיִת. וַחֲכָמִים אוֹמְרִים: בְּשַׂר קֹדֶשׁ בִּכְזַיִת, וְחָמֵץ בִּכְבֵיצָה.

פרק רביעי

[א] מָקוֹם שֶׁנָּהֲגוּ לַעֲשׂוֹת מְלָאכָה בְּעַרְבֵי פְסָחִים עַד חֲצוֹת, עוֹשִׂין; מָקוֹם שֶׁנָּהֲגוּ שֶׁלֹּא לַעֲשׂוֹת, אֵין עוֹשִׂין. הַהוֹלֵךְ מִמָּקוֹם שֶׁעוֹשִׂין לְמָקוֹם שֶׁאֵין עוֹשִׂין, אוֹ מִמָּקוֹם שֶׁאֵין עוֹשִׂין לְמָקוֹם שֶׁעוֹשִׂין, נוֹתְנִין עָלָיו חֻמְרֵי מָקוֹם שֶׁיָּצָא מִשָּׁם וְחֻמְרֵי מָקוֹם שֶׁהָלַךְ לְשָׁם. וְאַל יְשַׁנֶּה אָדָם, מִפְּנֵי הַמַּחֲלֹקֶת.

[ב] כַּיּוֹצֵא בוֹ, הַמּוֹלִיךְ פֵּרוֹת שְׁבִיעִית מִמָּקוֹם שֶׁכָּלוּ לְמָקוֹם שֶׁלֹּא כָלוּ, אוֹ מִמָּקוֹם שֶׁלֹּא כָלוּ לְמָקוֹם שֶׁכָּלוּ, חַיָּב לְבַעֵר. רַבִּי יְהוּדָה אוֹמֵר: אוֹמְרִים לוֹ: ,,צֵא וְהָבֵא לְךָ אַף אַתָּה.''

יד אברהם

animals and is therefore more likely to remain uneaten, and non-*terumah*, which can easily be disposed of by human and animal consumption before the time of removal (*Rashi*).

7. ... הַהוֹלֵךְ — *[If] someone is going ...* All the actions enumerated here are *mitzvos*. Therefore, if one realizes on Erev Pesach that if he goes ahead to perform the *mitzvah* upon which he embarked, he will not have time to return home and eliminate his *chametz* before it is too late, he should nullify the *chametz* in his mind and proceed to his *mitzvah*. The Scriptural requirement of removal is fulfilled by בְּטּוּל בְּלֵב, *conscious nullification*. [According to many, this is because nullification removes the person's ownership of the *chametz*.] With that accomplished, the remaining requirement to physically remove the *chametz* is only Rabbinic, which the Rabbis waived for the sake of these *mitzvos* (*Rav*).

... לְהַצִּיל מִן הַגַּיִס — *To save [people] from a [marauding] troop ...* Because human life is endangered in this group of cases, he should fulfill his Scriptural obligation through nullification and not delay his mission by going back even if there is time to do so and still save them.

... וְלִשְׁבֹּת שְׁבִיתַת הָרְשׁוּת — *If it was but to establish a voluntary resting place.* On the Sabbath and festivals, one may not go beyond 2000 cubits (3000-4000 ft.) from the area of his domicile. [This is the law of *techum Shabbos*; see *Eruvin* ch. 5-6.] The Rabbis created a device for extending this range another 2000 cubits (in one direction). This is by designating a spot within 2000 cubits of his abode as his 'home' for the Sabbath [קּוֹנֶה שְׁבִיתָה], so that his 2000 cubits will be measured from there. To do so one must

place food sufficient for two meals at that spot before the Sabbath [*eruvei techumin*]. If his need for establishing this place is for personal rather than *mitzvah* reasons, he may not rely upon nullification, but must return home to dispose of his *chametz*.

8. בְּשַׂר קֹדֶשׁ — *Sacrificial meat* is rendered unfit by being removed from Jerusalem and must then be burned (*Rav*).

אִם עָבַר צוֹפִים — *If he has passed Tzofim* [Scopus, in Latin], from which the Temple first becomes visible (*Rashi*).

... וְאִם לָאו — *But if not,* he is still close enough to return without major inconvenience and the Sages therefore required him to do so *and burn it before the Temple*; i.e., on the Temple Mount, in the place designated for burning disqualified offerings, as derived from *Lev.* 6:23 (*Rav*; see further 7:8). Since he burns it at the Temple, he uses wood consecrated for use upon the Altar (see 8:2).

וַחֲכָמִים אוֹמְרִים — *But the Sages say* that because of the stringency attached by the Torah to leftover meat, we also take a stringent attitude and demand a return for an amount as small as an olive. In the case of *chametz*, however, where nullification satisfies the Scriptural requirement, we are more lenient and do not require the owner's return for any amount smaller than an egg (*Rav*).

CHAPTER FOUR

Chapter Four discusses the rule obligating people to follow the customs of their native towns, for a generally adopted custom has the force of halachah.

1. מְלָאכָה בְּעַרְבֵי פְסָחִים — *Abstention from work on Erev Pesach* before noon is only a custom, and is permitted

[7] *[If] someone is going to slaughter his Pesach-offering, to circumcise his son, or to dine at a betrothal feast at the house of his [future] father-in-law, and he remembers that he has chametz in his home — if he is able to return, remove [it], and [then] return to his mitzvah, he must go back and remove [it]; but if not, he nullifies it in his heart. [If he is on his way] to save [people] from a [marauding] troop, from a river, from bandits, from a fire, or from a collapsed building, he nullifies it in his heart. If it was but to establish a voluntary resting place, he must return at once.*

[8] *Similarly, [if] someone left Jerusalem and remembered that he had sacrificial meat in his hand — if he has passed Tzofim, he burns it where he is; but if not, he [must] return and burn it before the Temple with the wood of the [Altar] pyre. For how much [chametz or meat] must one return? R' Meir says: In both cases for [the equivalent of] an egg. R' Yehudah says: In both cases for [the equivalent of] an olive. But the Sages say: [For] sacrificial meat, [the equivalent of] an olive, but [for] chametz, [the equivalent of] an egg.*

CHAPTER FOUR

[1] **מָקוֹם** *Where it is customary to work on Erev Pesach until midday, one may do so; [but] where it is customary not to work, one may not do so. [If] one goes from where they work to where they do not, or from where they do not to where they do, we lay upon him the stringencies of the place which he has left and the stringencies of the place to which he has gone. And let no man deviate [from local custom], because it arouses conflict.*

[2] *Similarly, one who transports Sabbatical-year crops from a place where they have been exhausted to a place where they have not been exhausted, or from a place where they have not been exhausted to a place where they have been exhausted, is required to remove [them]. R' Yehudah says: We say to him, 'Go out and bring for yourself.'*

YAD AVRAHAM

where this custom was not adopted; after midday, however, labor is prohibited everywhere because it is not proper that a person go about his work while his Pesach offering is being sacrificed (*Yerushalmi*). [This prohibition remains in effect even today (*O. Ch.* 468:1) because there is still much to do to prepare for Pesach.] This prohibition, however, is no more stringent than that in effect on *Chol HaMoed*, and is milder in some respects (*M.B.* 468:7).

מְקוֹם שֶׁנָּהֲגוּ שֶׁלֹּא לַעֲשׂוֹת — *Where it is customary not to work*, even before midday, it was as a precaution against forgetting to remove the *chametz*, sacrifice the Pesach offering, and bake the matzah (*Rashi*). [In ancient days, it was a universal custom to bake the Seder matzos on Erev Pesach. This time-honored custom persists today in many (especially Chassidic) communities.]

נוֹתְנִין עָלָיו חֻמְרֵי... — *We lay upon him the stringencies...* If a person grew up with one custom and finds himself in a place that observes a different custom, he must keep whichever custom is stricter in the particular instance. [However, if he has no intention of returning to his home town, its customs are no longer binding upon him (*O. Ch.* 574:1; *M.B.* 468:19).]

וְאַל יְשַׁנֶּה אָדָם, מִפְּנֵי הַמַּחֲלֹקֶת — *And let no man deviate [from*

local custom], because it arouses conflict. One must follow the stricter local custom because persisting in one's more lenient native custom would arouse conflict in this place. But for a non-working visitor to remain idle while his neighbors are working would antagonize no one — observers would assume that he simply has nothing to do.

2. The Torah decrees that a Sabbatical year [known as *Sheviis*] be observed every seventh year by abstaining from cultivating and harvesting the fields, vineyards and orchards of *Eretz Yisrael* (*Lev.* 25:1-7). With certain exceptions, produce growing during *Sheviis* without cultivation is permitted for consumption, provided it is left accessible to all who wish to take it. [See Gen. Intro. to ArtScroll *Sheviis*.] The Torah states about such produce: *And the Sabbath [produce] of the land shall be food for you . . . and for your animals and for the beasts that are in your land* (*Lev.* 25:6,7). This teaches that the food gathered from the field is permitted for consumption only as long as there remains something for the beasts to eat in the field; once the fields are bare of a particular species, we are obligated to remove what remains in our houses. This is called בִּעוּר, *removal,* and its time differs from place to place.

הַמּוֹלִיךְ פֵּרוֹת שְׁבִיעִית... — *One who transports Sabbatical-year*

[ג] מָקוֹם שֶׁנָּהֲגוּ לִמְכֹּר בְּהֵמָה דַקָּה לְעוֹבֵד כּוֹכָבִים, מוֹכְרִין; מָקוֹם שֶׁלֹּא נָהֲגוּ לִמְכֹּר, אֵין מוֹכְרִין; וּבְכָל מָקוֹם אֵין מוֹכְרִין לָהֶם בְּהֵמָה גַסָּה, עֲגָלִים וּסְיָחִים, שְׁלֵמִין וּשְׁבוּרִין. רַבִּי יְהוּדָה מַתִּיר בִּשְׁבוּרָה. בֶּן בְּתֵירָא מַתִּיר בְּסוּס.

[ד] מָקוֹם שֶׁנָּהֲגוּ לֶאֱכֹל צָלִי בְּלֵילֵי פְסָחִים, אוֹכְלִין; מָקוֹם שֶׁנָּהֲגוּ שֶׁלֹּא לֶאֱכֹל, אֵין אוֹכְלִין.

מָקוֹם שֶׁנָּהֲגוּ לְהַדְלִיק אֶת הַנֵּר בְּלֵילֵי יוֹם הַכִּפּוּרִים, מַדְלִיקִין; מָקוֹם שֶׁנָּהֲגוּ שֶׁלֹּא לְהַדְלִיק, אֵין מַדְלִיקִין. וּמַדְלִיקִין בְּבָתֵּי כְנֵסִיּוֹת, וּבְבָתֵּי מִדְרָשׁוֹת, וּבִמְבוֹאוֹת הָאֲפֵלִים, וְעַל גַּבֵּי הַחוֹלִים.

[ה] מָקוֹם שֶׁנָּהֲגוּ לַעֲשׂוֹת מְלָאכָה בְּתִשְׁעָה בְאָב, עוֹשִׂין; מָקוֹם שֶׁנָּהֲגוּ שֶׁלֹּא לַעֲשׂוֹת מְלָאכָה, אֵין עוֹשִׂין; וּבְכָל מָקוֹם תַּלְמִידֵי חֲכָמִים בְּטֵלִים. רַבָּן שִׁמְעוֹן בֶּן גַּמְלִיאֵל אוֹמֵר: לְעוֹלָם יַעֲשֶׂה אָדָם עַצְמוֹ תַּלְמִיד חָכָם.

וַחֲכָמִים אוֹמְרִים: בִּיהוּדָה הָיוּ עוֹשִׂין מְלָאכָה בְּעַרְבֵי פְסָחִים עַד חֲצוֹת, וּבַגָּלִיל לֹא הָיוּ עוֹשִׂין כָּל עִקָּר. וְהַלַּיְלָה — בֵּית שַׁמַּאי אוֹסְרִין, וּבֵית הִלֵּל מַתִּירִין עַד הָנֵץ הַחַמָּה.

[ו] רַבִּי מֵאִיר אוֹמֵר: כָּל מְלָאכָה שֶׁהִתְחִיל בָּהּ קֹדֶם לְאַרְבָּעָה עָשָׂר, גּוֹמְרָהּ בְּאַרְבָּעָה עָשָׂר; אֲבָל לֹא יַתְחִיל בָּהּ בַּתְּחִלָּה בְּאַרְבָּעָה עָשָׂר, אַף עַל פִּי שֶׁיָּכוֹל לְגוֹמְרָהּ. וַחֲכָמִים אוֹמְרִים: שָׁלֹשׁ אֻמָּנִיּוֹת עוֹשִׂין מְלָאכָה בְּעַרְבֵי פְסָחִים עַד חֲצוֹת, וְאֵלּוּ הֵן: הַחַיָּטִים, הַסַּפָּרִים, וְהַכּוֹבְסִין. רַבִּי יוֹסֵי בַּר יְהוּדָה אוֹמֵר: אַף הָרַצְעָנִים.

יד אברהם

crops . . . If a traveler brings produce from a place where they have been exhausted from the fields [and are thus forbidden] to a place where some still remains of this species in the fields, and the inhabitants of the new place still eat the produce in their houses — or vice versa — he is required to remove them so as to comply with the restrictions of both the place he left and the place to which he has come. By his use of the plural *'they* have been exhausted,' the first *Tanna* indicates that if there are several species marinated together [so that each has absorbed some of the other's flavor], the 'removal' need not be made unless *all* of them have reached the stage of removal. In this, he follows the view of R' Yehoshua (*Sheviis* 9:5) who derives exegetically that a food need not be removed until *no part* of it is left in the fields. R' Yehudah disputes this and says that we tell him to go out and either find supplies of the species in question or remove it. This ruling follows the view of Rabban Gamliel (ibid.) (*Gem.*).

3. לִמְכֹּר בְּהֵמָה — *To sell livestock . . .* Small livestock are sheep and goats; large livestock are oxen, donkeys, and horses. Some places instituted the practice of not selling even small livestock to non-Jews to prevent the sale of

large animals. The latter was decreed because of the possibility that a Jew might also rent or lend his ox or donkey to a non-Jew who will work the animal on the Sabbath. The Torah, however, forbids allowing an animal owned by a Jew to be worked on the Sabbath (*Ex.* 23:12), even if it has been leased or loaned. The Rabbis were also concerned that a Jew might sell an ox on Friday just before sundown and the buyer might then ask him to get the laden animal to move. In doing so, the Jew violates the prohibition of causing an animal, even one which is not his, to work on the Sabbath [מְחַמֵּר] (*Rav*).

עֲגָלִים וּסְיָחִים, שְׁלֵמִין וּשְׁבוּרִין — *Calves or foals, healthy or maimed.* Although young animals are not fit to work and should not fall under the prohibition of selling large livestock, allowing their sale could lead to the sale of large ones as well. The same is true of maimed animals. R' Yehudah, however, permits selling maimed animals because, in contrast to calves and foals, these will never be able to work.

בֶּן בְּתֵירָא . . . — *Ben Beseira* permits selling a horse used exclusively for riding. Carrying a human being on the Sabbath [who can move on his own] is only Rabbinically

[3] *Where it is customary to sell small livestock to non-Jews, we may sell; where it is customary not to sell, we may not sell; but in all places we may not sell them large livestock, calves or foals, healthy or maimed. R' Yehudah permits [selling] in the case of a maimed one. Ben Beseira permits [selling] in the case of a horse.*

[4] *Where it is customary to eat roast [meat] on the night of Pesach, we may eat [it]; where it is customary not to eat [roast], we may not eat [it].*

Where it is customary to light [lamps] on the night of Yom Kippur, we may light [them]; where it is customary not to light [them], we may not light [them]. But [in all places] we light [lamps] in the synagogues, houses of study, dark alleys, and for the sick.

[5] *Where it is customary to do work on the Ninth of Av, we may do [it]; where it is customary not to do work, we may not do [it]; but in all places Torah scholars abstain. Rabban Shimon ben Gamliel says: A man should always adopt the behavior of a Torah scholar.*

The Sages say: In Judea they used to work on Erev Pesach until midday, while in Galilee they did not [work] at all. [As for] the night, Beis Shammai forbid [work], while Beis Hillel permit it until sunrise.

[6] *R' Meir says: Any work which one began before the fourteenth, he may finish on the fourteenth; but he may not begin it initially on the fourteenth, even if he can finish it [before midday]. But the Sages say: [Practitioners of] three crafts may work on Erev Pesach until midday; they are: tailors, barbers and launderers. R' Yose bar Yehudah says: Also shoemakers.*

YAD AVRAHAM

forbidden because of the principle of חַי נוֹשֵׂא אֶת עַצְמוֹ, *a living person [partially] carries himself* (*Shabbos* 94a). Accordingly, the Rabbis did not enact any further safeguards to prevent the inadvertent violation of the Rabbinic prohibition. The custom nowadays is to sell all kinds of animals to non-Jews. Various reasons for this are given by the *Poskim*. See *Y. D.* 151:4.

4. מְקוֹם שֶׁנָּהֲגוּ שֶׁלֹּא לֶאֱכוֹל — *Where it is customary not to eat* roast meat on the night of Pesach, to avoid the impression that one is eating a Pesach offering [which must be eaten roasted] outside Jerusalem. This indeed is the custom in Ashkenazic communities (*M.B.* 476:1).

לְהַדְלִיק אֶת הַנֵּר בְּלֵילֵי יוֹם הַכִּפּוּרִים — *To light [lamps] on the night of Yom Kippur* was forbidden in some communities [despite the festival status of Yom Kippur] because it was feared that if a husband and wife could see one another they might feel a desire to cohabit, which is prohibited on Yom Kippur. Other communities adopted a different safeguard against this, *requiring* that lamps be lit in the homes and bedrooms, on the assumption that people would thereby be discouraged from cohabitation, which is forbidden in an illuminated place [see *Niddah* 17a]. This is the custom of Ashkenazic communities (*O. Ch.* 610:2).

The *Gemara* praises both customs (each intended to preserve the sanctity of the holy day) with the verse *Your people are all righteous, they shall inherit the land forever* (Isaiah 60:21).

וּמַדְלִיקִין בְּבָתֵּי כְנֵסִיּוֹת... — *But [in all places] we light [lamps] in the synagogues* and wherever illumination is needed, for it is a *mitzvah* to light lamps in honor of the festival.

5. מְלָאכָה בְּתִשְׁעָה בְּאָב — *Work on the Ninth of Av* is avoided because *Tishah B'Av* should evoke a sense of mourning for the Temple, and work distracts a person from his mourning. The communities which permitted work reasoned that an ancient sorrow does not carry with it the extreme restrictions of a recent loss (*Meiri*). However, *talmidei chachamim* should abstain in all places because they should feel the loss of the Temple more keenly than others. Also, their abstention is not so noticeable for they refrain from work on many occasions. Rabban Shimon ben Gamliel says that even a layman may refrain from work without fear of appearing to assume the rank of scholar, because people will assume that he simply has no work to do. *Rama* states that the Ashkenazic custom is to refrain from work until noon on *Tishah B'Av*.

וַחֲכָמִים אוֹמְרִים: בִּיהוּדָה... עַד חֲצוֹת — *The Sages say: In Judea... until midday.* The mishnah now refers back to the ruling of mishnah 1 that abstaining from work on Erev Pesach morning is a matter of custom, not halachah. Our mishnah now informs us that the Sages disagree and consider its status a matter of halachic dispute, not popular custom. The Sages of Judea permitted work while those in Galilee prohibited it (*Gem.*). According to Beis Shammai, the Galileans prohibited work even on the night before, treating the fourteenth like a festival, when work is restricted from evening. Beis Hillel, however, permit it until sunrise, comparing the work prohibition to eating on fast days, when only the day is included.

6. רַבִּי מֵאִיר אוֹמֵר — *R' Meir says* that even in places where it is customary not to work before midday, it is still permitted to

[ז] מוֹשִׁיבִין שׁוֹבְכִין לְתַרְנְגוֹלִים בְּאַרְבָּעָה עָשָׂר. וְתַרְנְגֹלֶת שֶׁבָּרְחָה, מַחֲזִירִין אוֹתָהּ לִמְקוֹמָהּ; וְאִם מֵתָה, מוֹשִׁיבִין אַחֶרֶת תַּחְתֶּיהָ.

גּוֹרְפִין מִתַּחַת רַגְלֵי בְהֵמָה בְּאַרְבָּעָה עָשָׂר, וּבַמּוֹעֵד מְסַלְּקִין לַצְּדָדִין. מוֹלִיכִין וּמְבִיאִין כֵּלִים מִבֵּית הָאֻמָּן, אַף עַל פִּי שֶׁאֵינָם לְצֹרֶךְ הַמּוֹעֵד.

[ח] שִׁשָּׁה דְבָרִים עָשׂוּ אַנְשֵׁי יְרִיחוֹ; עַל שְׁלֹשָׁה מִחוּ בְיָדָם, וְעַל שְׁלֹשָׁה לֹא מִחוּ בְיָדָם. וְאֵלּוּ הֵן שֶׁלֹּא מִחוּ בְיָדָם: מַרְכִּיבִין דְּקָלִים כָּל הַיּוֹם; וְכוֹרְכִין אֶת שְׁמַע; וְקוֹצְרִין וְגוֹדְשִׁין לִפְנֵי הָעֹמֶר, וְלֹא מִחוּ בְיָדָם. וְאֵלּוּ שֶׁמִּחוּ בְיָדָם: מַתִּירִין גַּמְזִיּוֹת שֶׁל הֶקְדֵּשׁ; וְאוֹכְלִין מִתַּחַת הַנְּשָׁרִים בַּשַּׁבָּת; וְנוֹתְנִין פֵּאָה לְיָרָק, וּמִחוּ בְיָדָם חֲכָמִים.

[ט] שִׁשָּׁה דְבָרִים עָשָׂה חִזְקִיָּה הַמֶּלֶךְ, עַל שְׁלֹשָׁה הוֹדוּ לוֹ, וְעַל שְׁלֹשָׁה לֹא הוֹדוּ לוֹ. גֵּרַר עַצְמוֹת אָבִיו עַל מִטָּה שֶׁל חֲבָלִים, וְהוֹדוּ לוֹ. כִּתֵּת נְחַשׁ הַנְּחֹשֶׁת, וְהוֹדוּ לוֹ. גָּנַז סֵפֶר רְפוּאוֹת, וְהוֹדוּ לוֹ. עַל שְׁלֹשָׁה לֹא הוֹדוּ לוֹ. קִצֵּץ דַּלְתוֹת שֶׁל הֵיכָל וְשִׁגְּרָן לְמֶלֶךְ אַשּׁוּר, וְלֹא הוֹדוּ לוֹ. סָתַם מֵי גִיחוֹן הָעֶלְיוֹן, וְלֹא הוֹדוּ לוֹ. עִבֵּר נִיסָן בְּנִיסָן, וְלֹא הוֹדוּ לוֹ.

פרק חמישי

[א] **תָּמִיד** נִשְׁחָט בְּשְׁמוֹנֶה וּמֶחֱצָה וְקָרֵב בְּתֵשַׁע וּמֶחֱצָה. בְּעַרְבֵי

יד אברהם

complete tasks begun earlier, provided the work is being done for the sake of the festival (*Rav*). Similarly, the exemptions assigned by the Sages and R' Yose bar Yehudah to certain crafts are only for work needed for the festival.

7. בְּאַרְבָּעָה עָשָׂר — [All day] *on the fourteenth*, because this is not considered forbidden labor.

וְתַרְנְגֹלֶת שֶׁבָּרְחָה — *If a [brooding] hen escaped*. This refers to *Chol HaMoed*. If a hen left her fertilized eggs after sitting on them for three days, the embryo has started to form and the eggs are now fit only for hatching. The hen may therefore be returned to her place because the eggs would be a total loss [דְּבָר הָאָבֵד] otherwise. This is certainly permitted on the fourteenth as well, inasmuch as one may then even *set* the fowl to brood.

וְאִם מֵתָה — *If she died*. There is a question whether this too refers to *Chol HaMoed* or only to the fourteenth. It is much harder to set a hen on a brood that is not hers, and the extra effort may be prohibited on *Chol HaMoed* (see *O. Ch.* 536).

מוֹלִיכִין . . . כֵּלִים — *One may take utensils* to a craftsman on the fourteenth even if they are not needed for the festival. On *Chol HaMoed*, however, one may bring home only utensils needed for the festival.

8. שִׁשָּׁה דְבָרִים עָשׂוּ אַנְשֵׁי יְרִיחוֹ — *The citizens of Jericho did six things* . . . Although the Sages found all six objectionable, they reproved them for only three. The following they did not reprove them for: (1) They would graft fruit-bearing branches of a (male) palm tree onto a barren (female) palm. Grafting within the same

species is permitted, but they would graft even on the afternoon of Erev Pesach. (2) They would also recite the *Shema* without the appropriate pauses, e.g. without drawing out the word אֶחָד to allow a moment for meditating upon and accepting God's sovereignty. (3) They also reaped and stacked new grain prior to the *Omer*, although the Sages had forbidden this as a safeguard against eating some while working with it (*Menachos* 10:5).

The Sages reproved them for the following: (4) They permitted branches of sacred property for personal use. Although the Biblical prohibition of *me'ilah* for making personal use of *hekdesh* applies only to objects that had *themselves* been consecrated, not to branches that grew later, their use is nevertheless Rabbinically prohibited (*Gem.*). (5) Fruit that falls from a tree on the Sabbath is Rabbinically forbidden that day. The people of Jericho ate fallen fruit as long as it was not clear that it had fallen that day because they invoked the rule that Rabbinic prohibitions do not apply in doubtful cases. The Sages held this particular prohibition to apply even in doubtful cases (*Rambam*). (6) They also left *pe'ah* [a corner of the field for the poor] for certain kinds of vegetables. Vegetables are exempt from *pe'ah*. The Sages objected to their unwarranted designation as *pe'ah* because the poor, thinking that they were *pe'ah*, ate them untithed. [*Pe'ah* is exempt from tithes.] (*Rav*)

9. עַל שְׁלֹשָׁה הוֹדוּ לוֹ. . . — *Concerning three [the Sages] agreed with him*: (1) *He dragged the bones of his father* Achaz, a wicked king, in order to expiate his sins and sanctify God's Name by demonstrating the repulsiveness of his evil. Instead of a royal bier, a

[7] *We may set up coops for chickens on the fourteenth. If a [brooding] hen escaped, we may return her to her place; if she died, we may set another in her stead. One may sweep away [dung] from under an animal's feet on the fourteenth, but on the [Intermediate Days of the] festival he may [only] clear it away to the sides [of the stall]. One may take utensils to, and bring them back from, the house of a craftsman, even though they are not needed for the festival.*

[8] *The citizens of Jericho did six things; for three the Sages reproved them, and for three they did not reprove them. These are the things for which they did not reprove them: They grafted palms all day [of the fourteenth]; they ran together the Shema; and they reaped and stacked prior to the Omer, but they did not reprove them. These are the things for which they did reprove them: They permitted the branches of sacred property [for personal use]; they ate the fallen fruit from beneath [the trees] on the Sabbath; and they gave pe'ah from vegetables, and the Sages reproved them.*

[9] *King Chizkiah did six things. Concerning three [the Sages] agreed with him, and concerning three they did not agree with him. He dragged the bones of his father on a bier of ropes, and they agreed with him. He crushed the brazen serpent, and they agreed with him. He hid the Book of Remedies, and they agreed with him. Concerning three they did not agree with him: He cut off the doors of the Temple and sent them to the king of Assyria, but they did not agree with him. He blocked the upper waters of the Gichon, but they did not agree with him. He intercalated Nissan in Nissan, but they did not agree with him.*

CHAPTER FIVE

[1] תָּמִיד *The [afternoon] daily offering is [ordinarily] slaughtered at eight and a half [hours] and offered [on the Altar] at nine and a half [hours]. On Erev*

YAD AVRAHAM

lowly bed of ropes was used, and it was dragged to its place of interment rather than carried. Chizkiah was not obliged to honor his father since he was a wicked person (*Rashi*). (2) *He crushed the brazen serpent* which Moses had fashioned as an antidote to the plague of poisonous snakes that God had sent against the Israelites (*Num.* 21:4-9). This brazen serpent was brought to *Eretz Yisrael* where it eventually became an object of worship. (3) *He hid the Book of Remedies* which contained directions for curing all illnesses. He did so because people were cured so easily that illness failed to promote the desired spirit of contrition and humility (*Rashi*). However, *Rambam* explains that it contained either prohibited remedies (such as magical formulae) or instructions for preparing toxic substances to remedy certain sicknesses. When Chizkiah saw that people began to use it as a primer for preparing poisons, he hid it.

עַל שְׁלֹשָׁה לֹא הוֹדוּ לוֹ — *Concerning three they did not agree with him:* (4) When Sennacherib, king of Assyria, levied a heavy tribute upon Chizkiah in return for removing his armies from Judea, Chizkiah's resources were strained and he removed the gold of the Temple's doors to meet the levy (*II Kings* 18:16). The Sages did not approve, contending that he should have had faith that God would save him. (5) *He blocked the upper waters of the Gichon* to deny the water to the enemy besieging Jerusalem (*II Chronicles* 32:30). But the Sages did not approve, for God had

promised (*II Kings* 20:6, *Isaiah* 37:35), *I will protect this city.* (6) *He intercalated* [made a leap year] *in Nissan*. In ancient times the calendar was not fixed and a decision was made each year whether to declare a leap year. The leap month of the Jewish calendar is always Adar, and once Nissan begins, a second Adar can no longer be added. Chizkiah declared the extra month on the thirtieth of Adar (*Gem.*), but since the thirtieth of any month is fit to be designated the first of the following month (a lunar month has either twenty-nine or thirty days), the Sages ruled that intercalation on the thirtieth is tantamount to declaring a leap year in Nissan.

CHAPTER FIVE

The next four chapters discuss the laws of the *pesach* offering made on the afternoon of the fourteenth and eaten that night at the Seder.

1. תָּמִיד — *The [afternoon] daily offering.* As part of the regular Temple service, two lambs were offered as *olah* (burnt) offerings each day [the *tamid* offering], one in the morning and one in the afternoon. On a normal afternoon, the *tamid* was slaughtered at approximately 2:30 p.m. [eight and a half hours after a typical sunrise; see comm. to 1:4] to allow more time for private offerings. With the exception of the *pesach* and some unusual instances, no offering could be made after the afternoon *tamid*. Slaughtering the *tamid*, performing its blood service, cutting it

פְּסָחִים נִשְׁחָט בְּשֶׁבַע וּמֶחֱצָה וְקָרֵב בִּשְׁמוֹנֶה וּמֶחֱצָה, בֵּין בַּחוֹל בֵּין בַּשַּׁבָּת. חָל עֶרֶב פֶּסַח לִהְיוֹת בְּעֶרֶב שַׁבָּת, נִשְׁחָט בְּשֵׁשׁ וּמֶחֱצָה, וְקָרֵב בְּשֶׁבַע וּמֶחֱצָה, וְהַפֶּסַח אַחֲרָיו.

[ב] הַפֶּסַח שֶׁשְּׁחָטוֹ שֶׁלֹּא לִשְׁמוֹ, וְקִבֵּל וְהִלֵּךְ וְזָרַק שֶׁלֹּא לִשְׁמוֹ, אוֹ לִשְׁמוֹ וְשֶׁלֹּא לִשְׁמוֹ, אוֹ שֶׁלֹּא לִשְׁמוֹ וְלִשְׁמוֹ, פָּסוּל. כֵּיצַד לִשְׁמוֹ וְשֶׁלֹּא לִשְׁמוֹ? לְשֵׁם פֶּסַח וּלְשֵׁם שְׁלָמִים. שֶׁלֹּא לִשְׁמוֹ וְלִשְׁמוֹ? לְשֵׁם שְׁלָמִים וּלְשֵׁם פֶּסַח.

[ג] שְׁחָטוֹ שֶׁלֹּא לְאוֹכְלָיו, וְשֶׁלֹּא לִמְנוּיָיו, לַעֲרֵלִים, וְלִטְמֵאִים – פָּסוּל. לְאוֹכְלָיו וְשֶׁלֹּא לְאוֹכְלָיו, לִמְנוּיָיו וְשֶׁלֹּא לִמְנוּיָיו, לְמוּלִים וְלַעֲרֵלִים, לִטְמֵאִים וְלִטְהוֹרִים – כָּשֵׁר. שְׁחָטוֹ קֹדֶם חֲצוֹת, פָּסוּל – מִשּׁוּם שֶׁנֶּאֱמַר: ,,בֵּין הָעַרְבָּיִם.'' שְׁחָטוֹ קֹדֶם לַתָּמִיד, כָּשֵׁר, וּבִלְבַד שֶׁיְּהֵא אֶחָד מְמַסֵּס בְּדָמוֹ, עַד שֶׁיִּזָּרֵק דַּם הַתָּמִיד; וְאִם נִזְרַק, כָּשֵׁר.

[ד] הַשּׁוֹחֵט אֶת הַפֶּסַח עַל הֶחָמֵץ עוֹבֵר בְּלֹא תַעֲשֶׂה. רַבִּי יְהוּדָה אוֹמֵר: אַף הַתָּמִיד. רַבִּי שִׁמְעוֹן אוֹמֵר: הַפֶּסַח בְּאַרְבָּעָה עָשָׂר לִשְׁמוֹ חַיָּב, וְשֶׁלֹּא לִשְׁמוֹ פָּטוּר. וּשְׁאָר כָּל הַזְּבָחִים בֵּין לִשְׁמָן וּבֵין שֶׁלֹּא לִשְׁמָן, פָּטוּר.

יד אברהם

up, and placing it on the Altar consumed an hour.

בְּעַרְבֵי פְּסָחִים — *On Erev Pesach* the *tamid* is slaughtered an hour earlier, because the *pesach* must be slaughtered after the *tamid* and we must allow enough time for a multitude of *pesach* offerings to be offered before sunset. When Erev Pesach falls on Friday, more time is needed to allow the participants to roast their offerings before the beginning of the Sabbath. Roasting does not supersede the Sabbath (*Rav*).

2. The essential part of any offering is its עֲבוֹדַת הַדָּם, *blood service*, which is divided into four parts: שְׁחִיטָה, *slaughtering* the offering; קַבָּלָה, *receiving* the gushing blood in a special vessel; הוֹלָכָה, *transporting* the blood to the Altar; and זְרִיקָה, *throwing* the blood against the Altar wall. If the blood service is properly done, the offering is valid and the owner has discharged his obligation, even though the fats and meat were neither burned on the Altar nor eaten. Should any of these four *avodos* be done with the intention that it serve for another type of offering, or for a person other than its owner, the offering — in the case of a *pesach* — is invalidated. [The rule for most other types of offerings is somewhat different; see comm. end of mishnah 4.] The following mishnah focuses on disqualifications caused by improper intentions.

שֶׁלֹּא לִשְׁמוֹ — *For some other designation,* e.g. with the intention that it be a *shelamim* (peace offering). If the wrong intention was explicitly stated during this or *any* of the other three essential *avodos*, the offering is disqualified, even if the remaining *avodos* were performed properly. The mishnah states that the same is true even if he began the *avodah* with the proper intention and then completed it with an improper one, or vice versa. Any improper intention, whether indicated first or second, is sufficient to invalidate the offering when stated during any one of the four blood *avodos*.

3. שֶׁלֹּא לְאוֹכְלָיו — *For those who cannot eat it,* i.e. for someone too old, young or sick to eat at least a *kezayis* (the volume of an olive) of *pesach* meat. [This disqualification is unique to the *pesach* offering.]

וְשֶׁלֹּא לִמְנוּיָיו . . . — *For those not registered on it.* Several people may share a *pesach* offering but it may be eaten only by those who have registered to eat from that particular offering prior to its slaughter. A *pesach* slaughtered for unregistered people is thus equivalent to one slaughtered for people who cannot eat it. For this reason slaughtering it for uncircumcised men or people contaminated with *tumah* invalidates it, since these too are ineligible to eat from a *pesach* offering.

לְאוֹכְלָיו וְשֶׁלֹּא לְאוֹכְלָיו . . . כָּשֵׁר — *[If he slaughtered it] both for those who can and those who cannot eat it . . . it is valid* because the verse indicates that intent for people who cannot eat the *pesach* disqualifies it only if it is entirely for the wrong people. [This is in contrast to offering it for a different designation, where even a mixed intent invalidates.]

קֹדֶם לַתָּמִיד . . . — *Before the [afternoon] daily offering.* . . If the rule

---

Pesach it is slaughtered at seven and a half [hours] and offered at eight and a half [hours], whether it is a weekday or the Sabbath. [If] Erev Pesach falls on Friday, it is slaughtered at six and a half [hours], offered at seven and a half [hours], and the pesach [is offered] after it.

[2] [If] the pesach offering was slaughtered for some other designation, or [the Kohen] received, transported, or threw [its blood] for some other designation, or for its own designation and [then] for some other designation, or for some other designation and [then] for its own designation — it is invalid.

What is an example of 'for its own designation and [then] for some other designation'? For the designation of a pesach offering and [then] for the designation of a peace offering. [What is an example of] 'for some other designation and [then] for its own designation?' For the designation of a peace offering and [then] for the designation of a pesach offering.

[3] [If] he slaughtered it for those who cannot eat it, for those not registered on it, [or] for uncircumcised or contaminated persons — it is invalid. [If he slaughtered it] both for those who can and those who cannot eat it, for both its registrants and those not registered for it, for both circumcised and uncircumcised persons, [or] for both contaminated and for uncontaminated [persons] — it is valid.

[If] he slaughtered it before noon, it is invalid — because it says: In the afternoon (Ex. 12:6). [If] he slaughtered it before the [afternoon] daily offering, it is valid, provided someone stirs its blood until the blood of the daily offering is thrown; but if it was thrown [earlier], it is [also] valid.

[4] One who slaughters the pesach offering with chametz [in his possession] is in violation of a negative command. R' Yehudah says: The daily offering as well.

R' Shimon says: [If he slaughters] the pesach offering on the fourteenth under its own designation, he is liable; but [if] under some other designation, he is exempt. [With] all other offerings whether [he slaughters them] under their own designation or under some other designation, he is exempt.

YAD AVRAHAM

requiring the *pesach's* slaughter to follow the *tamid's* (5:1) was violated, the offering is nevertheless valid. Throwing the *pesach's* blood should be delayed until the *tamid's* blood is thrown. This requires that someone keep stirring the *pesach's* blood to prevent it from congealing and thereby becoming unfit for throwing. If, however, the *pesach* offering's blood was thrown before that of the *tamid*, it is still valid.

4. The verse *You shall not slaughter with chametz the blood of My offering* (Ex. 34:25) teaches that one is forbidden to have *chametz* in his possession at the time his *pesach* is slaughtered.

אַף הַתָּמִיד — *The daily offering as well.* If the afternoon *tamid* of the fourteenth is slaughtered by someone still in possession of *chametz*, he violates this commandment.

רַבִּי שִׁמְעוֹן אוֹמֵר — *R' Shimon says* that one transgresses this prohibition only if his *pesach* offering is valid. Therefore, if one slaughtered his *pesach* for the wrong designation while in possession of *chametz*, he does not transgress this prohibition, since the *pesach* is then invalid (5:2).

Moreover, R' Shimon disagrees with limiting the prohibition of slaughtering with *chametz* to the *pesach* and *tamid* offerings.

R' Shimon deduces by Biblical exegesis that it applies to all sacrifices during the period when *chametz* is forbidden. However, the same exegesis teaches that the prohibition does not apply to other offerings when it is in effect for the *pesach*. Thus, from noon till nightfall of Erev *pesach* one transgresses the *chametz* prohibition only if he slaughters a *pesach*. However, during the seven days of the festival, one does not transgress this prohibition by making a *pesach* offering, according to R' Shimon, because a *pesach* offering is then invalid. Thus, during these seven days the prohibition to slaughter with *chametz* applies to all other offerings.

The above is true, however, only for a *pesach* slaughtered as a *pesach* offering. But there is a rule that if a *pesach* is slaughtered for another designation [during a time inappropriate for a *pesach* offering], it becomes valid as a *shelamim* offering. It is therefore included in the category of other valid offerings, which, if slaughtered with *chametz* during the festival, are in violation of the Torah commandment (*Rav*).

וּשְׁאָר כָּל הַזְּבָחִים — *However, during the festival all other offerings* are subject to this prohibition whether they are slaughtered

וּבַמּוֹעֵד לִשְׁמוֹ פָּטוּר; שֶׁלֹּא לִשְׁמוֹ חַיָּב. וּשְׁאָר כָּל הַזְּבָחִים, בֵּין לִשְׁמָן בֵּין שֶׁלֹּא לִשְׁמָן, חַיָּב; חוּץ מִן הַחַטָּאת שֶׁשָּׁחַט שֶׁלֹּא לִשְׁמָהּ.

[ה] הַפֶּסַח נִשְׁחָט בְּשָׁלֹשׁ כִּתּוֹת, שֶׁנֶּאֱמַר: ,,וְשָׁחֲטוּ אֹתוֹ כֹּל קְהַל עֲדַת יִשְׂרָאֵל,'' קָהָל, וְעֵדָה, וְיִשְׂרָאֵל. נִכְנְסָה כַּת הָרִאשׁוֹנָה, נִתְמַלֵּאת הָעֲזָרָה, נָעֲלוּ דַלְתוֹת הָעֲזָרָה. תָּקְעוּ הֵרִיעוּ וְתָקְעוּ. הַכֹּהֲנִים עוֹמְדִים שׁוּרוֹת שׁוּרוֹת, וּבִידֵיהֶם בָּזִיכֵי כֶסֶף וּבָזִיכֵי זָהָב. שׁוּרָה שֶׁכֻּלָּהּ כֶּסֶף כֶּסֶף, וְשׁוּרָה שֶׁכֻּלָּהּ זָהָב זָהָב; לֹא הָיוּ מְעֹרָבִין. וְלֹא הָיוּ לַבָּזִיכִין שׁוּלַיִם, שֶׁמָּא יַנִּיחוּם וְיִקְרַשׁ הַדָּם.

[ו] שָׁחַט יִשְׂרָאֵל וְקִבֵּל הַכֹּהֵן; נוֹתְנוֹ לַחֲבֵרוֹ וַחֲבֵרוֹ לַחֲבֵרוֹ. וּמְקַבֵּל אֶת הַמָּלֵא וּמַחֲזִיר אֶת הָרֵיקָן. כֹּהֵן הַקָּרוֹב אֵצֶל הַמִּזְבֵּחַ זוֹרְקוֹ זְרִיקָה אַחַת כְּנֶגֶד הַיְסוֹד.

[ז] יָצְתָה כַּת רִאשׁוֹנָה וְנִכְנְסָה כַּת שְׁנִיָּה. יָצְתָה שְׁנִיָּה, נִכְנְסָה שְׁלִישִׁית. כְּמַעֲשֵׂה הָרִאשׁוֹנָה כָּךְ מַעֲשֵׂה הַשְּׁנִיָּה וְהַשְּׁלִישִׁית. קָרְאוּ אֶת הַהַלֵּל. אִם גָּמְרוּ שָׁנוּ, וְאִם שָׁנוּ שִׁלֵּשׁוּ, אַף עַל פִּי שֶׁלֹּא שִׁלְּשׁוּ מִימֵיהֶם. רַבִּי יְהוּדָה אוֹמֵר: מִימֵיהֶם שֶׁל כַּת הַשְּׁלִישִׁית לֹא הִגִּיעוּ לְ,,אָהַבְתִּי כִּי יִשְׁמַע ה','' מִפְּנֵי שֶׁעַמָּהּ מֻעָטִין.

[ח] כְּמַעֲשֵׂהוּ בְחוֹל כָּךְ מַעֲשֵׂהוּ בַּשַּׁבָּת, אֶלָּא שֶׁהַכֹּהֲנִים מְדִיחִים אֶת הָעֲזָרָה שֶׁלֹּא בִרְצוֹן חֲכָמִים. רַבִּי יְהוּדָה אוֹמֵר: כּוֹס הָיָה מְמַלֵּא מִדַּם הַתַּעֲרֹבֶת, זְרָקוֹ זְרִיקָה אַחַת עַל גַּבֵּי הַמִּזְבֵּחַ. וְלֹא הוֹדוּ לוֹ חֲכָמִים.

[ט] כֵּיצַד תּוֹלִין וּמַפְשִׁיטִין? אֻנְקְלָיוֹת שֶׁל בַּרְזֶל הָיוּ קְבוּעִים בַּכְּתָלִים וּבָעַמּוּדִים, שֶׁבָּהֶן תּוֹלִין וּמַפְשִׁיטִין. וְכָל מִי שֶׁאֵין לוֹ מָקוֹם לִתְלוֹת

יד אברהם

under their own designation or another. This is because other sacrifices are valid even when slaughtered for the wrong designation (Zevachim 1:1). The only other exception to this rule is the *chatas* (sin offering) which, like the *pesach*, is invalid when offered for the wrong designation. Therefore, a person offering a *chatas* in this manner during the festival has not violated the prohibition of slaughtering with *chametz*.

5. תָּקְעוּ — *They sounded a tekiah* . . . Communal sacrifices are accompanied by the sounding of trumpets, like the shofar blasts of Rosh Hashanah. The sounding preceded the recitation of the *Hallel* which accompanied the *pesach's* offering (Rambam).

הַכֹּהֲנִים עוֹמְדִים שׁוּרוֹת שׁוּרוֹת — *The Kohanim stood row upon row* forming lines across the Courtyard from the place of slaughter to the Altar. Each row had its own type of consecrated vessel — either silver or gold. The uniform appearance of the rows enhanced their festive spectacle and was a נוֹי מִצְוָה, *beautification of the mitzvah* (Gem.).

וְלֹא הָיוּ לַבָּזִיכִין שׁוּלַיִם — *Nor did the bowls have bases*, being wide at the top and pointed at the bottom, so that the *Kohanim* would not be able to set the bowls down and in their preoccupation with the many offerings, forget to throw the blood immediately. Congealed blood is unfit for the Altar (Rav).

6. שָׁחַט יִשְׂרָאֵל — *An Israelite* [was permitted to] *slaughter it.* Slaughtering is the only blood *avodah* that need not be performed by a *Kohen*; receiving, transporting, and throwing the blood *must* be done by a *Kohen*.

וַחֲבֵרוֹ לַחֲבֵרוֹ — *And he to his fellow*, passing it up the line of *Kohanim* to the Altar. At the same time the *Kohen* would take an empty one from up the line and return it down the line for reuse.

זְרִיקָה אַחַת כְּנֶגֶד הַיְסוֹד — *Once, opposite the base.* The blood was thrown upon the lower half of the Altar wall, on any section that stood above the Altar's base. The one-cubit-high base jutted out beyond the wall, but did *not* extend along most of the eastern and southern walls of the Altar.

7. קָרְאוּ אֶת הַהַלֵּל — *They* [the Levites] *recited the Hallel* during the

---

However, during a festival, [if he slaughters a pesach offering] under its own designation, he is exempt; [but] under some other designation, he is liable. [With] all other offerings, whether [he slaughters them] under their own designations or under some other designations, he is liable; except for a sin offering which he slaughtered under some other designation.

[5] *The pesach offering is slaughtered in three groups, for it is written (Ex. 12:6): "And the whole assembly of the congregation of Israel shall slaughter it" — 'assembly,' 'congregation' and 'Israel.' The first group entered; when the [Temple] Courtyard was filled, they closed the gates of the Courtyard. They sounded a tekiah, a teruah, and again a tekiah. The Kohanim stood row upon row, and in their hands were silver bowls and golden bowls. One row was altogether of silver, the other row was altogether of gold; and they were not mixed. Nor did the bowls have bases, lest they set them down and the blood congeal.*

[6] *An Israelite slaughtered it, and a Kohen received its [blood]; he would hand it to his fellow and he to his fellow. He would accept the full one and return the empty one. The Kohen nearest the Altar would throw it once, opposite the base.*

[7] *When the first group [concluded and] left, the second group entered. When the second left, the third entered. The procedure followed for the first [group] was repeated for the second and third [groups].*

They recited the Hallel. If they finish it, they repeat it, and if they complete the repetition they recite it a third time, although it never happened that they should recite it a third time. R' Yehudah says: The third group never reached as far as 'I love, for Hashem *hears' (Psalms 116:1), because its people were few.*

[8] *The procedure on weekdays was followed on the Sabbath as well, except that the Kohanim rinsed the Temple Courtyard without the consent of the Sages.*

R' Yehudah says: He would fill a cup with the mixed blood [and] throw it once upon the Altar [wall]. But the Sages did not agree with him.

[9] *How did they suspend and flay [them]? Iron hooks were affixed to [the Courtyard's] walls and pillars, from which they suspended [the Pesach offering] and flayed [it]. Anyone who had not place to suspend and flay [his offering,*

YAD AVRAHAM

slaughter and blood service of the multitude of *pesach* offerings. If they finished the *Hallel* before all the offerings in that group had been completed, they started the *Hallel* over again.

שֶׁעֲמָהּ מְעַטִּין — *Its people were few* because most Jews were eager to perform the *mitzvah* as early as possible.

8. כָּךְ מַעֲשֵׂהוּ בְּשַׁבָּת — *Was followed* [when Erev Pesach fell] *on the Sabbath,* because the slaughter and offering of the *pesach* supersedes the Sabbath prohibitions. The *Kohanim* even rinsed the floor of the Temple Courtyard, but this latter activity did not meet with the Rabbis' approval because of the Rabbinic prohibition of washing floors on the Sabbath. Since rinsing the Courtyard is not essential to the Temple service, they did not relax the prohibition (*Gem.*).

מִדַּם הַתַּעֲרֹבֶת — *With the mixed blood,* i.e., the accumulated blood on the floor, which was a mixture of the blood of all the sacrifices offered that day. By applying it once to the Altar, he

insured that even if the blood of a sacrifice had spilled before reaching the Altar, a drop of it would now reach via the cup of mixed blood and render the offering valid. The Sages, however, disagree because most of the blood on the Courtyard floor would be of the kind which is not valid for throwing, having drained from the animal after the initial gush, and the acceptable blood would thus have lost its legal identity in the majority. R' Yehudah's view is that a minority component does not become nullified in a majority of the same type of substance.

9. וּמַפְשִׁיטִין — *Flay.* The *pesach,* like other offerings, had to have its hide removed prior to placing its sacrificial parts on the Altar. To facilitate this, the carcass was suspended by its hind legs and skinned. R' Eliezer forbids using staves for this on the Sabbath because they are *muktzeh.* The Sages permit the use of staves because of the principle that 'Rabbinic [Sabbath] restrictions do not [usually] apply in the Temple' (*Rav*).

וּלְהַפְשִׁיט, מַקְלוֹת דַּקִּים חֲלָקִים הָיוּ שָׁם, וּמַנִּיחַ עַל כְּתֵפוֹ וְעַל כֶּתֶף חֲבֵרוֹ, וְתוֹלֶה וּמַפְשִׁיט. רַבִּי אֱלִיעֶזֶר אוֹמֵר: אַרְבָּעָה עָשָׂר שֶׁחָל לִהְיוֹת בַּשַּׁבָּת, מַנִּיחַ יָדוֹ עַל כֶּתֶף חֲבֵרוֹ, וְיַד חֲבֵרוֹ עַל כְּתֵפוֹ, וְתוֹלֶה וּמַפְשִׁיט.

[י] קְרָעוֹ וְהוֹצִיא אֵמוּרָיו, נְתָנוֹ בְּמָגִיס וְהִקְטִירָן עַל גַּבֵּי הַמִּזְבֵּחַ. יָצְתָה כַת רִאשׁוֹנָה וְיָשְׁבָה לָהּ בְּהַר הַבַּיִת, שְׁנִיָּה בַּחֵיל, וְהַשְּׁלִישִׁית בִּמְקוֹמָהּ עוֹמֶדֶת. חָשְׁכָה, יָצְאוּ וְצָלוּ אֶת פִּסְחֵיהֶן.

פרק ששי

[א] **אֵלּוּ** דְּבָרִים בַּפֶּסַח דּוֹחִין אֶת הַשַּׁבָּת: שְׁחִיטָתוֹ; וּזְרִיקַת דָּמוֹ; וּמִחוּי קְרָבָיו; וְהֶקְטֵר חֲלָבָיו. אֲבָל צְלִיָּתוֹ וַהֲדָחַת קְרָבָיו אֵינָן דּוֹחִין אֶת הַשַּׁבָּת. הַרְכָּבָתוֹ, וַהֲבָאָתוֹ מִחוּץ לַתְּחוּם, וַחֲתִיכַת יַבַּלְתּוֹ אֵין דּוֹחִין אֶת הַשַּׁבָּת. רַבִּי אֱלִיעֶזֶר אוֹמֵר: דּוֹחִין.

[ב] אָמַר רַבִּי אֱלִיעֶזֶר: "וַהֲלֹא דִין הוּא! מָה אִם שְׁחִיטָה, שֶׁהִיא מִשּׁוּם מְלָאכָה, דּוֹחָה אֶת הַשַּׁבָּת, אֵלּוּ שֶׁהֵן מִשּׁוּם שְׁבוּת, לֹא יִדְחוּ אֶת הַשַּׁבָּת?"

אָמַר לוֹ רַבִּי יְהוֹשֻׁעַ: "יוֹם טוֹב יוֹכִיחַ, שֶׁהִתִּירוּ בוֹ מִשּׁוּם מְלָאכָה, וְאָסוּר בּוֹ מִשּׁוּם שְׁבוּת."

אָמַר לוֹ רַבִּי אֱלִיעֶזֶר: "מַה זֶּה, יְהוֹשֻׁעַ? מָה רְאָיָה רְשׁוּת לְמִצְוָה?"

הֵשִׁיב רַבִּי עֲקִיבָא וְאָמַר: "הַזָּאָה תּוֹכִיחַ, שֶׁהִיא מִצְוָה, וְהִיא מִשּׁוּם שְׁבוּת, וְאֵינָהּ דּוֹחָה אֶת הַשַּׁבָּת. אַף אַתָּה אַל תִּתְמַהּ עַל אֵלּוּ, שֶׁאַף עַל פִּי שֶׁהֵן מִצְוָה, וְהֵן מִשּׁוּם שְׁבוּת, לֹא יִדְחוּ אֶת הַשַּׁבָּת."

יד אברהם

10. אֵמוּרָיו — *Its sacrificial parts,* certain of its fats and internal organs (*Lev.* 3:9-10, 14-15).

וְיָשְׁבָה לָהּ . . . — *And remained. . .* When Erev Pesach fell on the Sabbath, the first group carried out its sacrifices no further than the Temple Mount, because carrying was forbidden in the streets of Jerusalem. The second group stayed in the *Chel,* a ten-cubit-wide section of the Temple Mount between the outer Courtyard wall to the low wooden partition called the סוֹרֵג, *soreg* (see *Middos* 2:3). The third group remained in the Courtyard. After dark, they went to their residences and roasted their *pesachim;* roasting the *pesach* does not override the Sabbath (*Rav*).

CHAPTER SIX

1. דּוֹחִין אֶת הַשַּׁבָּת — *Override the Sabbath.* The *pesach* is offered on the Sabbath even though this involves acts which violate the Sabbath laws, as derived from the Torah's statement that the *pesach* be brought בְּמוֹעֲדוֹ, *in its appointed time* (*Num.* 9:2). *Slaughter* is one of the thirty-nine primary labors prohibited on the Sabbath; it must be done on the fourteenth of Nissan and cannot be postponed until nightfall. The same is true of

throwing the blood [which is in any case not a forbidden labor]. Cleaning the entrails is permitted to prevent putrefaction. Burning the sacrificial parts is an integral part of the offering which should properly be performed by day.

אֵינָן דּוֹחִין אֶת הַשַּׁבָּת — *Do not override the Sabbath,* the first two because they can wait until nightfall, and the last three because they could have been done before the Sabbath. Roasting is classified as *cooking,* and is Biblically forbidden. Rinsing the entrails would be Rabbinically prohibited as excessive bother (טִרְחָה), and once the offal has been removed, rinsing can be deferred until nightfall without risk of putrefaction. Carrying the lamb through the public domain to the Temple, or bringing it from outside the *techum* (see 3:7), could have been done before the Sabbath (*Rav*). A wart is a disqualifying blemish for a sacrifice until it is removed. However, removal is included in the labor of גּוֹזֵז, *shearing,* and could have been done before the Sabbath. These may not be done on the Sabbath even if it means that the sacrifice will not be brought (*Rav*). However, R' Eliezer's opinion is that if they are necessary, even the preliminaries (מַכְשִׁירִין) override the Sabbath.

would use a] thin smooth stave kept there, which he placed upon his shoulder and upon the shoulder of his fellow and so suspended and flayed [it]. R' Eliezer says: [If] the fourteenth fell on the Sabbath, he placed his hand on his fellow's shoulder, and the hand of his fellow upon his shoulder, and [thus] suspended and flayed [it].

[10] *He cut it open and removed its sacrificial parts, put them on a plate and burned them on the Altar.*

The first group went out and remained on the Temple Mount, the second [group] in the Chel, and the third [group] remained where they were [inside the Courtyard]. After dark, they went out and roasted their pesach offerings.

CHAPTER SIX

[1] **אֵלוּ** *The following aspects of the pesach offering override the Sabbath: Its slaughter; throwing its blood; cleaning its entrails; and burning its fats. But roasting it and rinsing its entrails do not override the Sabbath. Nor do carrying it, bringing it from outside the Sabbath limit, and cutting off its wart override the Sabbath. R' Eliezer says: These do override [it].*

[2] *Said R' Eliezer: But does not logic dictate this? If slaughtering [the pesach], which is a [Biblically prohibited] labor, overrides the Sabbath, [then] these, which are forbidden [merely] because of a Rabbinic prohibition, should certainly override the Sabbath!*

R' Yehoshua said to him: Let [the] festival [laws] demonstrate [this], for they permitted [Biblical] labor on it, but forbade on it [what is] Rabbinically proscribed.

R' Eliezer replied: What is this, Yehoshua? What proof [can be adduced from] an act [which is merely] permissible to one that is a mitzvah?

R' Akiva responded and said: Let 'sprinkling' demonstrate [this], for it is a mitzvah, and it is [forbidden] by a Rabbinic prohibition, and it does not override the Sabbath. So you should not wonder about these, that even though they are a mitzvah, and are [forbidden only] by a Rabbinic prohibition, they do not override the Sabbath.

YAD AVRAHAM

2. אָמַר רַבִּי אֱלִיעֶזֶר — *R' Eliezer* presented the following argument to support his position that one may violate the Sabbath even for the preliminaries of the *pesach*. Although R' Eliezer permitted overriding even Biblical prohibitions, his argument here is to force the first *Tanna* to concede that at least Rabbinic prohibitions should be waived.

אֵלוּ — *[Then] these.* As noted above, some of the forbidden preliminaries involve only Rabbinic prohibitions.

אָמַר לוֹ רַבִּי יְהוֹשֻׁעַ — *R' Yehoshua said to him:* The festival laws prove otherwise, since it is permissible to cook and bake on a festival, though these are labors Biblically prohibited on the Sabbath and even on festivals when not needed for the festival. Yet it is prohibited to bring food for the festival from outside the 2000-cubit *techum* — something proscribed only by Rabbinic decree (*Rav*). Thus we see that a valid basis for overriding a Biblical prohibition does not necessarily justify waiving a Rabbinic one. R' Eliezer rejected this argument because bringing food on the festival is not required for the fulfillment of a *mitzvah*; while one honors the festival by dining well, he is not *required* to do so. However, since the Torah does require

one to make a *pesach* offering on the Sabbath, Rabbinic prohibitions should be waived no less than Biblical ones.

הַזָּאָה תוֹכִיחַ — *Let sprinkling demonstrate [this].* A person *tamei* by contact with a corpse must be sprinkled with water containing the ashes of the *parah adumah* to become *tahor*.

Sprinkling is Rabbinically prohibited on the Sabbath because it is akin to מְתַקֵּן, *repairing* [the person], by permitting him to partake from offerings. Even so, if the final day of purification falls on Erev Pesach which is also the Sabbath, we do not permit sprinkling even to enable him to perform the *mitzvah* of eating the *pesach* offering. To this, R' Eliezer replied that he extends the same reasoning to permit sprinkling as well. R' Eliezer had forgotten his own teaching that sprinkling was indeed forbidden and R' Akiva tried to remind him respectfully of it by reversing the argument. For if sprinkling would indeed override the Sabbath, logic would require the untenable conclusion that even slaughter is forbidden (*Gem.*). Prior to this exchange, R' Akiva had studied under R' Eliezer for thirteen years without ever speaking up to contradict his mentor (*Yerushalmi*).

אָמַר לוֹ רַבִּי אֱלִיעֶזֶר: "וְעָלֶיהָ אֲנִי דָן. וּמָה אִם שְׁחִיטָה שֶׁהִיא מִשּׁוּם מְלָאכָה דּוֹחָה אֶת הַשַּׁבָּת, הַזָּאָה שֶׁהִיא מִשּׁוּם שְׁבוּת אֵינוֹ דִין שֶׁדּוֹחָה אֶת הַשַּׁבָּת?"

אָמַר לוֹ רַבִּי עֲקִיבָא: "אוֹ חִלּוּף! מָה אִם הַזָּאָה שֶׁהִיא מִשּׁוּם שְׁבוּת אֵינָה דּוֹחָה אֶת הַשַּׁבָּת, שְׁחִיטָה שֶׁהִיא מִשּׁוּם מְלָאכָה אֵינוֹ דִין שֶׁלֹּא תִדְחֶה אֶת הַשַּׁבָּת?"

אָמַר לוֹ רַבִּי אֱלִיעֶזֶר: "עֲקִיבָא! עָקַרְתָּ מַה שֶּׁכָּתוּב בַּתּוֹרָה, ,בֵּין הָעַרְבַּיִם . . . בְּמֹעֲדוֹ,' בֵּין בְּחוֹל בֵּין בַּשַּׁבָּת."

אָמַר לוֹ: "רַבִּי, הָבֵא לִי מוֹעֵד לְאֵלּוּ כְּמוֹעֵד לִשְׁחִיטָה."

כְּלָל אָמַר רַבִּי עֲקִיבָא: כָּל מְלָאכָה שֶׁאֶפְשָׁר לַעֲשׂוֹתָהּ מֵעֶרֶב שַׁבָּת אֵינָהּ דּוֹחָה אֶת הַשַּׁבָּת. שְׁחִיטָה שֶׁאִי אֶפְשָׁר לַעֲשׂוֹתָהּ מֵעֶרֶב שַׁבָּת דּוֹחָה אֶת הַשַּׁבָּת.

[ג] אֵימָתַי מֵבִיא חֲגִיגָה עִמּוֹ? בִּזְמַן שֶׁהוּא בָא בְּחוֹל בְּטָהֳרָה וּבְמֻעָט. וּבִזְמַן שֶׁהוּא בָא בַּשַּׁבָּת בִּמְרֻבֶּה וּבְטֻמְאָה, אֵין מְבִיאִין עִמּוֹ חֲגִיגָה.

[ד] חֲגִיגָה הָיְתָה בָּאָה מִן הַצֹּאן, מִן הַבָּקָר, מִן הַכְּבָשִׂים, וּמִן הָעִזִּים; מִן הַזְּכָרִים וּמִן הַנְּקֵבוֹת. וְנֶאֱכֶלֶת לִשְׁנֵי יָמִים וְלַיְלָה אֶחָד.

[ה] הַפֶּסַח שֶׁשְּׁחָטוֹ שֶׁלֹּא לִשְׁמוֹ בַּשַּׁבָּת, חַיָּב עָלָיו חַטָּאת. וּשְׁאָר כָּל הַזְּבָחִים שֶׁשְּׁחָטָן לְשׁוּם פֶּסַח: אִם אֵינָן רְאוּיִין, חַיָּב; וְאִם רְאוּיִין הֵן — רַבִּי אֱלִיעֶזֶר מְחַיֵּב חַטָּאת, וְרַבִּי יְהוֹשֻׁעַ פּוֹטֵר.

אָמַר רַבִּי אֱלִיעֶזֶר: מָה אִם הַפֶּסַח, שֶׁהוּא מֻתָּר לִשְׁמוֹ, כְּשֶׁשִּׁנָּה אֶת שְׁמוֹ חַיָּב,

---

יד אברהם

אָמַר לוֹ — *He [R' Akiva]* suggested to his teacher R' Eliezer that it is incorrect to compare the Biblical prohibition against slaughter with the Rabbinic prohibitions under discussion in this and the previous mishnah. Since the source for the permission to override the Sabbath is the Biblical phrase *appointed time*, this precludes any analogy to the Rabbinically prohibited acts, since their performance is not mandated for a specific time. Even the act of sprinkling, which must be performed at a specific time, is also prohibited because, unlike the other Rabbinic prohibitions under discussion, it is not intrinsically related to the *pesach* offering itself, and is therefore not included in the Biblical dispensation that requires overriding the Sabbath (Rav).

3. Along with the *pesach* sacrifice, an additional offering is brought on the fourteenth of Nissan, known as the *chagigah*. This is apart from the *chagigah* offering required for each of the three festivals [Pesach, Shavuos, and Succos]. The purpose of this *chagigah* is to enable one to satisfy his hunger and eat the *pesach* עַל הַשּׂוֹבַע, *sated*. However, since the Torah does not *require* that *chagigah* meat be eaten at the Seder, its slaughter

does not override the Sabbath nor the prohibition of making an offering in a state of *tumah*, and is therefore not brought when the fourteenth occurs on the Sabbath. [This stands in contrast to the *pesach* offering which may sometimes be sacrificed and eaten by people who are *tamei*; see 7:4,5.] It is also only necessary when there are many people registered on the *pesach*. However, when the registrants are few, they may satisfy themselves from the *pesach* offering itself before eating a final *kezayis*.

4. מִן הַצֹּאן — *From the flock.* The term צֹאן denotes both sheep and goats, as elaborated by the mishnah in the next phrase.

וְנֶאֱכֶלֶת . . . — *It may be eaten* on the fourteenth and fifteenth of Nissan, as well as the intervening night. Nevertheless, once the *chagigah* is put on the table with the *pesach*, it must be consumed before midnight, exactly like the *pesach*, lest its meat become mixed with the *pesach*'s (Rambam).

5. The prohibition to slaughter on the Sabbath is superseded by the obligation to offer a *pesach*. If the sacrifice is invalidated, however, the slaughter is considered a desecration of the Sabbath. Ordinarily one is obliged to atone for a non-

R' Eliezer replied: I apply my logic to this too. If slaughter, which is [Biblically forbidden] labor, overrides the Sabbath, [then] sprinkling, which is [forbidden only] by Rabbinic prohibition, should surely override the Sabbath!

R' Akiva said to him: Perhaps [the argument should be] reversed? If sprinkling, which is [forbidden] by Rabbinic prohibition, does not override the Sabbath, [then] slaughtering which is a [Biblically forbidden] labor, should [surely] not override the Sabbath!

R' Eliezer replied: Akiva! You have uprooted [with your argument] what is written in the Torah: 'In the afternoon . . . in its appointed time' (Numbers 9:3), [which implies] both on weekdays and on the Sabbath.

He [R' Akiva] said to him: My master! Give me an appointed time for these which is like the appointed time for slaughter.

A general rule was stated by R' Akiva: Any labor that can be performed on the eve of the Sabbath does not override the Sabbath. Slaughtering which cannot be performed on the eve of the Sabbath does override the Sabbath.

[3] When does one bring a chagigah with [the pesach]? When it is offered on a weekday, in purity, and [the pesach] is insufficient. But when [the pesach] is offered on the Sabbath, or is abundant, or in tumah-contamination, one does not bring a chagigah with [the pesach].

[4] A chagigah may be brought from the flock, from cattle, from sheep, or from goats; either male or female. It may be eaten for two days and one night.

[5] [If] one slaughtered the pesach offering for some other designation on the Sabbath, he is liable thereby for a sin offering. As for any other sacrifices that he slaughtered with the designation of a pesach offering: if they are not suitable, he is liable [for a sin offering]; but if they are suitable — R' Eliezer obligates him to bring a sin offering, while R' Yehoshua absolves [him].

Said R' Eliezer: If the pesach offering, which is permitted [on the Sabbath] for its own designation, makes him liable [for a sin offering] if he changed its designation,

---

YAD AVRAHAM

intentional [שׁוֹגֵג] desecration of the Sabbath by bringing a chatas (sin) offering. In the view of some, however, desecration of the Sabbath caused by slaughtering an invalid offering is exempt from this obligation, because it was committed in the course of an intended mitzvah.

שֶׁלֹּא לִשְׁמוֹ — For some other designation, e.g., as an olah; this invalidates the pesach (5:2).

וּשְׁאָר כָּל הַזְּבָחִים שֶׁשְּׁחָטָן . . . — Any other sacrifices that he slaughtered on the fourteenth which falls on the Sabbath with the mistaken intention of using it as a pesach offering is not valid as a pesach and he has desecrated the Sabbath. Nonetheless, this was an attempt to perform the mitzvah. His liability for a chatas depends on the following: If the animal he used was unsuitable for a pesach offering (i.e., anything other than a male sheep or goat, less than a year old), his error is too obvious to rank as an instance of טוֹעֶה בִּדְבַר מִצְוָה, erring in the commission of a mitzvah. But if it was of the proper age, gender, and species

for a pesach but had been sanctified for a different offering, R' Eliezer obligates him to bring a chatas because he does not consider the intention to perform a mitzvah a mitigating factor. R' Yehoshua, however, rules that his action does not require the atonement of a chatas offering since it resulted from an intention to perform a mitzvah.

אָמַר רַבִּי אֱלִיעֶזֶר . . . — R' Eliezer argued that if slaughtering a pesach offering invalidly on the Sabbath requires the atonement of a chatas, then slaughtering a totally unauthorized offering [even as a pesach] should certainly require one. R' Yehoshua replied that this argument is not convincing. In slaughtering a pesach for another designation the intention is to do something forbidden on the Sabbath; therefore he is liable for a chatas. By contrast, slaughtering another sacrifice as pesach expresses an intention to do something permissible on the Sabbath; therefore, it does not incur a chatas.

זְבָחִים שֶׁהֵן אֲסוּרִין לִשְׁמָן, כְּשֶׁשִּׁנָּה אֶת שְׁמָן, אֵינוֹ דִין שֶׁיְּהֵא חַיָּב? אָמַר לוֹ רַבִּי יְהוֹשֻׁעַ: לֹא! אִם אָמַרְתָּ בְּפֶסַח, שֶׁשִּׁנָּהוּ לְדָבָר אָסוּר, תֹּאמַר בִּזְבָחִים שֶׁשִּׁנָּן לְדָבָר מֻתָּר?

אָמַר לוֹ רַבִּי אֱלִיעֶזֶר: אֵמוּרֵי צִבּוּר יוֹכִיחוּ, שֶׁהֵן מֻתָּרִין לִשְׁמָן, וְהַשּׁוֹחֵט לִשְׁמָן חַיָּב.

אָמַר לוֹ רַבִּי יְהוֹשֻׁעַ: „לֹא! אִם אָמַרְתָּ בְּאֵמוּרֵי צִבּוּר שֶׁיֵּשׁ לָהֶן קִצְבָה, תֹּאמַר בַּפֶּסַח שֶׁאֵין לוֹ קִצְבָה?"

רַבִּי מֵאִיר אוֹמֵר: אַף הַשּׁוֹחֵט לְשֵׁם אֵמוּרֵי צִבּוּר, פָּטוּר.

[ו] שְׁחָטוֹ שֶׁלֹּא לְאוֹכְלָיו וְשֶׁלֹּא לִמְנוּיָיו, לַעֲרֵלִין וְלִטְמֵאִין, חַיָּב. לְאוֹכְלָיו וְשֶׁלֹּא לְאוֹכְלָיו, לִמְנוּיָיו וְשֶׁלֹּא לִמְנוּיָיו, לְמוּלִין וְלַעֲרֵלִין, לִטְהוֹרִים וְלִטְמֵאִים, פָּטוּר.

שְׁחָטוֹ וְנִמְצָא בַעַל מוּם, חַיָּב. שְׁחָטוֹ וְנִמְצָא טְרֵפָה בַסֵּתֶר, פָּטוּר. שְׁחָטוֹ וְנוֹדַע שֶׁמָּשְׁכוּ הַבְּעָלִים אֶת יָדָם, אוֹ שֶׁמֵּתוּ, אוֹ שֶׁנִּטְמְאוּ, פָּטוּר, מִפְּנֵי שֶׁשָּׁחַט בִּרְשׁוּת.

פרק שביעי

[א] **כֵּיצַד** צוֹלִין אֶת הַפֶּסַח? מְבִיאִין שַׁפּוּד שֶׁל רִמּוֹן תּוֹחֲבוֹ מִתּוֹךְ פִּיו עַד בֵּית נְקוּבָתוֹ, וְנוֹתֵן אֶת כְּרָעָיו וְאֶת בְּנֵי מֵעָיו לְתוֹכוֹ; דִּבְרֵי רַבִּי יוֹסֵי הַגְּלִילִי. רַבִּי עֲקִיבָא אוֹמֵר: כְּמִין בִּשּׁוּל הוּא זֶה; אֶלָּא תּוֹלִין חוּצָה לוֹ.

[ב] אֵין צוֹלִין אֶת הַפֶּסַח לֹא עַל הַשַּׁפּוּד וְלֹא עַל הָאַסְכְּלָא. אָמַר רַבִּי צָדוֹק: מַעֲשֶׂה בְרַבָּן גַּמְלִיאֵל שֶׁאָמַר לְטָבִי עַבְדוֹ: „צֵא וּצְלֵה לָנוּ

יד אברהם

אָמַר לוֹ רַבִּי אֱלִיעֶזֶר — *R' Eliezer responded* that the case of communal offerings [such as the daily *tamid* and festival *mussaf* offerings] proves that one who intends to perform a *mitzvah* which is permissible on the Sabbath but fails to execute it properly incurs a *chatas*. These communal sacrifices are required on the Sabbath, yet one who slaughters a personal offering for the communal one is liable for a *chatas*. To this R' Yehoshua replied that the analogy is inaccurate. Communal offerings on the Sabbath consist of only two *tamid* offerings and two *mussaf* offerings, and it is therefore easy to avoid a mistake. Thus, a mistake is not regarded as having *erred* in the commission of a *mitzvah*, but as having desecrated the Sabbath through negligence. In the case of the *pesach*, however, since an enormous number of animals were slaughtered that day, it is quite possible for someone to err, and he is regarded as having erred in the commission of a *mitzvah* (*Rav*).

רַבִּי מֵאִיר אוֹמֵר — *R' Meir* disagrees with both R' Eliezer and R' Yehoshua and absolves him from a *chatas* even in the case of a personal sacrifice slaughtered for the sake of a communal offering.

6. שְׁחָטוֹ שֶׁלֹּא לְאוֹכְלָיו — *[If] he slaughtered it* [exclusively] *for those who cannot eat it,* the *pesach* is invalid (5:3), and if it is a Sabbath, he has thus desecrated the Sabbath. [Since he intended it for something unacceptable as a *pesach*, he is liable for a *chatas* according to all opinions.] The same is true for the other cases mentioned here.

לְאוֹכְלָיו וְשֶׁלֹּא לְאוֹכְלָיו — *[However, if he slaughtered it both] for those who can eat it and those who cannot,* the offering is valid (5:3) and the Sabbath has not been desecrated.

בַּעַל מוּם . . . טְרֵפָה בַסֵּתֶר — *A blemish* invalidates an offering. Since an external blemish could have been discovered prior to the slaughter, the desecration of the Sabbath is not classified as unavoidable [אוֹנֶס] but as negligence [שׁוֹגֵג], and therefore requires a *chatas* to atone for the desecration of the Sabbath (*Rav*). However, if after slaughtering the *pesach*, one of its internal organs was found to be defective in a way that renders it *tereifah* [unkosher], the offering is invalid, but there is no *chatas* obligation. The internal status of the animal is not something that could have been detected in advance, and the

[then] other sacrifices, which are forbidden [on the Sabbath even] for their own designations, should surely make him liable [for a sin offering] when he changed their designations. R' Yehoshua replied: Not so! If you say [this] of the pesach, [it is because] he altered it to a forbidden matter; will you [therefore] say the same of [other] sacrifices, when he altered them to a permitted matter?

R' Eliezer responded: Let communal offerings prove it, for they are permitted [to be offered] for their own designation, yet one who slaughters [other sacrifices] for their designations is liable.

R' Yehoshua replied: Not so! If you say this of public offerings which are [brought in] limited numbers [on the Sabbath], will you say the same of the pesach offering which is [brought in] unlimited numbers?

R' Meir says: Even one who slaughters [other sacrifices] for the designation of public offerings is not liable.

[6] [If] he slaughtered it for those who cannot eat it or for those not registered on it, [or] for uncircumcised or tumah-contaminated [people], he is liable. [However, if he slaughtered it both] for those who can eat it and those who cannot, for those registered and those unregistered, for the circumcised and uncircumcised, [or] for those who are not contaminated and those who are contaminated, he is not liable.

[If] he slaughtered it and it was found to have a blemish, he is liable. [If] he slaughtered it and it was found to be a tereifah internally, he is not liable. [If] he slaughtered it and then it became known that the owners had withdrawn from it, or had died, or had become contaminated, he is not liable, because he slaughtered with permission.

CHAPTER SEVEN

[1] **כֵּיצַד** How does one roast the pesach? He brings a spit of pomegranate wood and thrusts it through its mouth to its anus, and places its knees and its entrails inside it; [these are] the words of R' Yose HaGlili. R' Akiva says: This is [considered] a form of cooking; rather they are hung outside it.

[2] One may not roast the pesach offering on a [metal] spit or roasting tray. R' Tzadok said: It once happened that Rabban Gamliel said to Tavi, his slave, 'Go out and

---

resulting Sabbath desecration is therefore considered to have occurred in the commission of a *mitzvah* [see mishnah 5] (*Tos.*).

שֶׁמָּשְׁכוּ הַבְּעָלִים אֶת יָדָם . . . — *That the owners had withdrawn from it* [before its slaughter] and registered on another *pesach*, leaving this offering without owners and thus invalid. The same applies if all the registrants died or became *tamei* and thus unfit to eat.

מִפְּנֵי שֶׁשָּׁחַט בִּרְשׁוּת — *Because he slaughtered with permission*, i.e., he had no way of knowing about the changed circumstances nor any reason to inquire about them.

CHAPTER SEVEN

1. כֵּיצַד צוֹלִין אֶת הַפֶּסַח — *How does one roast the pesach?* The Torah requires the *pesach* to be eaten roasted over a fire and not cooked (*Ex.* 12:9). A metal spit is unacceptable because the metal becomes hot and part of the *pesach* becomes roasted

from the heat of the spit rather than the fire. Likewise, woods other than pomegranate are forbidden because they exude moisture, thereby causing the *pesach* to be partially cooked rather than completely roasted (*Rav*).

תּוֹחֲבוֹ מִתּוֹךְ פִּיו — *And thrusts it through its mouth . . .* so that the carcass may be suspended head down, allowing the blood to drain freely from the cut in the neck.

כְּמִין בִּשּׁוּל הוּא זֶה — *This is [considered] a form of cooking*, because the entrails become cooked in the body cavity, as if in a pot (*Rav*).

2. מַעֲשֶׂה בְּרַבָּן גַּמְלִיאֵל . . . — *It once happened that Rabban Gamliel . . .* The Gemara explains that R' Gamliel referred to a grill-like tray, in which the spaces between the bars are big enough for the entire carcass to fit between them. The bars of the grill are used only to support the spit holding the offering (*Rashi*), and the spit is not of metal.

אֶת הַפֶּסַח עַל הָאִסְכְּלָא." נָגַע בְּחַרְסוֹ שֶׁל תַּנּוּר, יִקְלוֹף אֶת מְקוֹמוֹ. נָטַף מֵרָטְבּוֹ עַל הַחֶרֶס וְחָזַר עָלָיו, יִטּוֹל אֶת מְקוֹמוֹ. נָטַף מֵרָטְבּוֹ עַל הַסֹּלֶת, יִקְמוֹץ אֶת מְקוֹמוֹ.

[ג] סָכוֹ בְשֶׁמֶן תְּרוּמָה, אִם חֲבוּרַת כֹּהֲנִים, יֹאכֵלוּ. אִם יִשְׂרָאֵל, אִם חַי הוּא, יְדִיחֶנּוּ; וְאִם צָלִי הוּא, יִקְלוֹף אֶת הַחִיצוֹן.

סָכוֹ בְשֶׁמֶן שֶׁל מַעֲשֵׂר שֵׁנִי, לֹא יַעֲשֶׂנּוּ דָמִים עַל בְּנֵי חֲבוּרָה, שֶׁאֵין פּוֹדִין מַעֲשֵׂר שֵׁנִי בִּירוּשָׁלָיִם.

[ד] חֲמִשָּׁה דְבָרִים בָּאִין בְּטֻמְאָה, וְאֵינָן נֶאֱכָלִין בְּטֻמְאָה: הָעֹמֶר, וּשְׁתֵּי הַלֶּחֶם, וְלֶחֶם הַפָּנִים, וְזִבְחֵי שַׁלְמֵי צִבּוּר, וּשְׂעִירֵי רָאשֵׁי חֳדָשִׁים. הַפֶּסַח שֶׁבָּא בְטֻמְאָה נֶאֱכָל בְּטֻמְאָה, שֶׁלֹּא בָא מִתְּחִלָּתוֹ אֶלָּא לַאֲכִילָה.

[ה] נִטְמָא הַבָּשָׂר וְהַחֵלֶב קַיָּם, אֵינוּ זוֹרֵק אֶת הַדָּם. נִטְמָא הַחֵלֶב וְהַבָּשָׂר קַיָּם, זוֹרֵק אֶת הַדָּם. וּבַמֻּקְדָּשִׁין אֵינוֹ כֵן. אֶלָּא אַף עַל פִּי שֶׁנִּטְמָא הַבָּשָׂר וְהַחֵלֶב קַיָּם, זוֹרֵק אֶת הַדָּם.

[ו] נִטְמָא הַקָּהָל אוֹ רֻבּוֹ, אוֹ שֶׁהָיוּ הַכֹּהֲנִים טְמֵאִים וְהַקָּהָל טְהוֹרִים, יֵעָשֶׂה בְטֻמְאָה. נִטְמָא מִעוּט הַקָּהָל, הַטְּהוֹרִין עוֹשִׂין אֶת הָרִאשׁוֹן, וְהַטְּמֵאִין עוֹשִׂין אֶת הַשֵּׁנִי.

[ז] הַפֶּסַח שֶׁנִּזְרַק דָּמוֹ וְאַחַר כָּךְ נוֹדַע שֶׁהוּא טָמֵא, הַצִּיץ מְרַצֶּה. נִטְמָא

נָגַע בְּחַרְסוֹ שֶׁל תַּנּוּר — [If the offering] made contact with the earthen sides of the oven, the part of the meat that touched is not fire roasted, but roasted through an intermediary substance (Rav). This, however, disqualifies only the meat at the point of contact with the hot oven, which must therefore be sliced off.

נָטַף מֵרָטְבּוֹ . . . — [If] some of its juices dripped onto the walls of the oven, they become heated by the hot earthenware and thereby disqualified. When these are reabsorbed by the meat of the pesach, they disqualify it to the extent of their spread. [A forbidden (hot) liquid is assumed to penetrate a (permitted hot) solid to some depth.] Therefore, he must remove an appropriate thickness of meat, and not just slice off a thin sliver [as in the previous case] (Rashi).

נָטַף מֵרָטְבּוֹ עַל הַסֹּלֶת — [If] some of its juices dripped onto flour already seething from the fire, the drippings become cooked by the heat of the flour, thus disqualifying them. Since they become absorbed by the flour, he must remove a complete handful of flour and burn it (Rav).

3. סָכוֹ בְשֶׁמֶן תְּרוּמָה — Basting the pesach with a small amount of oil during the roasting does not constitute cooking and is permitted (Rav; see 2:8). However, his use of terumah oil bars consumption of the offering by non-Kohanim, to whom terumah is forbidden. Once the meat has been roasted, it absorbs the liquids smeared on it and he must therefore remove a thin section of the outer layer. However, since basting involves only

a minute amount of liquid, it does not result in a deep penetration of the meat and it therefore suffices to slice off a thin outer layer of the offering rather than the finger-thick layer required in the previous case of the drippings (Gem.).

מַעֲשֵׂר שֵׁנִי — Maaser sheni (see 2:5) must be eaten in Jerusalem. If the pesach was basted with such oil, the members of the group may not be charged for it, because maaser sheni may not be redeemed or sold in Jerusalem (Rav).

4. Although a person contaminated with tumah may not offer a sacrifice and invalidates it if he does, an exception is made for the regular communal sacrifices and the pesach offering. If the majority of the Kohanim in Jerusalem, or in the case of the pesach, the majority of the assembled people, are tamei, the sacrifices may be offered despite the tumah of the participants. [This exception is only for tumah arising from human corpses, not for any other kind of tumah.] This dispensation, however, extends only to offering the sacrifice, not to eating its meat portions. These must be burned like any sacrificial meat that has become tamei. The only exception to this rule is the pesach offering, which is eaten even if offered in tumah, and even by those who are tamei, because its purpose is not to atone but to provide the meat to be eaten at the Seder.

הָעֹמֶר — The Omer is an offering of barley flour made on the sixteenth of Nissan. After a kometz (handful) is removed from it and burnt on the Altar, the rest is eaten by the Kohanim.

roast for us the pesach offering on the roasting tray.' [If the offering] made contact with the earthen sides of the oven, he must slice off that part. [If] some of its juices dripped onto the earthen sides and spattered back onto it, he must remove that part. [If] some of its juices dripped onto flour, he must remove a handful from that place.

[3] *[If] he basted [the pesach] with oil of terumah, if the group is composed of Kohanim, they may eat it. If they are Israelites: if it is raw, he must rinse it; but if it is roasted, he must slice off the outer layer. [If] he basted it with oil of maaser sheni, its value may not be charged to the members of the company, since maaser sheni may not be redeemed in Jerusalem.*

[4] *Five things may be offered in a state of tumah-contamination, but may not be eaten in a state of tumah-contamination: the Omer, the Two Loaves, the Panim Breads, the communal peace offerings, and the he-goats of Rosh Chodesh. [But] the pesach offering that is offered in tumah may be eaten in tumah, because its very purpose is for eating.*

[5] *[If] the meat [of the pesach offering] became contaminated with tumah but the fat remained [uncontaminated], one may not throw the blood. [If] the fat became contaminated with tumah but the meat remained [uncontaminated], he throws the blood. But in the case of [other] consecrated animals it is not so. Rather, even when the meat became contaminated and the fat remained [uncontaminated], one throws the blood.*

[6] *[If] the entire community, or a majority of it, became contaminated with tumah, or if the Kohanim were contaminated while the community was uncontaminated, [the pesach] is offered in tumah-contamination. [If only] a minority of the community became contaminated, those uncontaminated observe the first [pesach offering], while the contaminated observe the second [pesach offering].*

[7] *[For] any pesach offering whose blood had been thrown and it was learned afterwards that it had been contaminated, the tzitz effects acceptance. [But if it was later*

YAD AVRAHAM

וּשְׁתֵּי הַלֶּחֶם — *Two Loaves* of leavened breads are brought on Shavuos together with a complement of animal sacrifices. The loaves are 'waved' [תְּנוּפָה] together with the two *shelamim* lambs, the lambs are offered, and the Loaves are eaten by the *Kohanim*. These lambs are known as שַׁלְמֵי צִבּוּר, *the communal peace offerings,* and their meat is eaten by the *Kohanim*.

וְלֶחֶם הַפָּנִים — Twelve *Panim Breads* were arranged each week on the *Shulchan* (golden table) inside the Temple, together with two spoonfuls of *levonah* (frankincense). These were replaced each Sabbath, and the old *levonah* was burned on the Altar, while the breads were eaten by the *Kohanim*.

5. אֵינוֹ זוֹרֵק אֶת הַדָּם — *One may not throw the blood.* The essential sacrificial procedure is to slaughter the animal, catch the blood spurting from its neck in a bowl, and throw the blood against the Altar wall. Throwing the blood is what renders the offering valid, not burning the fats or eating the meat. Nevertheless, the mishnah indicates that at least one of the other components must remain fit in order for the blood to be thrown. In the case of the *pesach*, it must be the meat that remains fit, because the main purpose of the *pesach* is for its meat to be eaten at the Seder. [Our mishnah discusses a situation where the community was not in a state of *tumah* but a particular *pesach* became *tamei*.]

6. נִטְמָא — *Became contaminated with the tumah* of human

corpses — the only *tumah* for which an exception is made in regard to sacrifices.

הָרִאשׁוֹן . . . הַשֵּׁנִי — *The first pesach offering* is Nissan 14, while *the second pesach offering* [known as the *pesach sheni*] is Iyar 14. This date is reserved for those unable to perform the regular offering because of *tumah* or other reasons (see 9:1-2). The dispensation for offering the *pesach* in *tumah* on Nissan 14 is only if the majority of the populace is *tamei*.

7. The following three mishnayos discuss cases in which the meat of the offering became *tamei* (but not the people). The Sages expound that where such contamination would result in the entire offering being disqualified, the צִיץ, *tzitz* [gold plate worn by the *Kohen Gadol* on his forehead], propitiates the sin of *tumah* and lifts the disqualification (*Gem.*). This atonement not only renders valid sacrifices already offered, releasing the participants from the obligation of a second offering, but even permits the completion of those still in progress. The Sages decreed, however, that if the *tumah* becomes known prior to the blood service, the blood should not be thrown.

וְאַחַר כָּךְ נוֹדַע שֶׁהוּא טָמֵא — *It was learned afterwards that it* [the blood or the meat] *had been contaminated,* the offering is valid. If the blood alone became *tamei*, the meat is eaten. If the meat has become *tamei*, however, it cannot be eaten because the

הַגּוּף, אֵין הַצִּיץ מְרַצֶּה. מִפְּנֵי שֶׁאָמְרוּ: הַנָּזִיר וְעוֹשֵׂה פֶסַח, הַצִּיץ מְרַצֶּה עַל טֻמְאַת הַדָּם, וְאֵין הַצִּיץ מְרַצֶּה עַל טֻמְאַת הַגּוּף. נִטְמָא טֻמְאַת הַתְּהוֹם, הַצִּיץ מְרַצֶּה.

[ח] נִטְמָא שָׁלֵם אוֹ רֻבּוֹ, שׂוֹרְפִין אוֹתוֹ לִפְנֵי הַבִּירָה מֵעֲצֵי הַמַּעֲרָכָה. נִטְמָא מִעוּטוֹ, וְהַנּוֹתָר, שׂוֹרְפִין אוֹתוֹ בְחַצְרוֹתֵיהֶן אוֹ עַל גַּגּוֹתֵיהֶן מֵעֲצֵי עַצְמָן. הַצַּיְקָנִין שׂוֹרְפִין אוֹתוֹ לִפְנֵי הַבִּירָה, בִּשְׁבִיל לֵהָנוֹת מֵעֲצֵי הַמַּעֲרָכָה.

[ט] הַפֶּסַח שֶׁיָּצָא אוֹ שֶׁנִּטְמָא יִשָּׂרֵף מִיָּד. נִטְמְאוּ הַבְּעָלִים אוֹ שֶׁמֵּתוּ תְּעֻבַּר צוּרָתוֹ, וְיִשָּׂרֵף בְּשִׁשָּׁה עָשָׂר. רַבִּי יוֹחָנָן בֶּן בְּרוֹקָה אוֹמֵר: אַף זֶה יִשָּׂרֵף מִיָּד, לְפִי שֶׁאֵין לוֹ אוֹכְלִין.

[י] הָעֲצָמוֹת וְהַגִּידִין וְהַנּוֹתָר יִשָּׂרְפוּ בְּשִׁשָּׁה עָשָׂר. חָל שִׁשָּׁה עָשָׂר לִהְיוֹת בַּשַּׁבָּת, יִשָּׂרְפוּ בְּשִׁבְעָה עָשָׂר, לְפִי שֶׁאֵינָן דּוֹחִין לֹא אֶת הַשַּׁבָּת וְלֹא אֶת יוֹם טוֹב.

[יא] כָּל הַנֶּאֱכָל בְּשׁוֹר הַגָּדוֹל יֵאָכֵל בִּגְדִי הָרַךְ, וְרָאשֵׁי כְנָפַיִם וְהַסְּחוּסִים. הַשּׁוֹבֵר אֶת הָעֶצֶם בַּפֶּסַח הַטָּהוֹר, הֲרֵי זֶה לוֹקֶה אַרְבָּעִים. אֲבָל הַמּוֹתִיר בַּטָּהוֹר וְהַשּׁוֹבֵר בַּטָּמֵא, אֵינוֹ לוֹקֶה אֶת הָאַרְבָּעִים.

יד אברהם

acceptance effected by the *tzitz* does not extend to lifting the prohibition against eating *tumah*-contaminated meat (*Rav*).

נִטְמָא הַגּוּף — *[But if it was later learned that] the person had been contaminated* — either the participants or the *Kohen* making the offering — the *tzitz* does not effect acceptance and the participants must bring another offering, the *pesach sheni*.

הַנָּזִיר וְעוֹשֵׂה פֶסַח — *The nazir and one making the Pesach offering.* A *nazir* is one who has taken upon himself a vow that bars him from drinking wine, cutting his hair, and contaminating himself with the *tumah* of a human corpse for a certain period of time. The term of *nezirus* cannot conclude, however, until the *nazir* brings certain offerings. By the *tzitz* effecting atonement for the contaminated offering, it permits the *nazir* to perform those acts that had been previously forbidden him (*Rav*).

טֻמְאַת הַתְּהוֹם — *Tumah-contamination of the deep* is a technical term denoting a human-corpse *tumah* that was previously unrecognized, e.g. a corpse discovered buried beneath a house. If this *tumah* was discovered after the *nazir* offered his sacrifices, or after the *pesach* service had been completed, the *tzitz* atones for the *tumah* of the person who became *tamei* by it even though it concerns a contamination of the person.

8. נִטְמָא שָׁלֵם אוֹ רֻבּוֹ — *[If] the whole or the greater part of* [the *pesach* offering] *became contaminated*, the meat must be burned like that of any contaminated offering. Although the *pesach* sacrifice may be burned throughout Jerusalem (3:8), the Sages made an exception here [where most or all of the sacrifice is affected and it can be presumed that it happened due to gross negligence] in order to embarrass them so that

they and the onlookers be more careful in the future (*Gem.*).

וְהַנּוֹתָר — Sacrificial *meat that was left past the time* prescribed for eating it must be burned even if not contaminated.

9. הַפֶּסַח שֶׁיָּצָא — *Any pesach offering taken out* of Jerusalem becomes disqualified, because it has left the area within which it may be eaten. The mishnah speaks of a case in which it was removed on the fourteenth after its service, but before sundown (*Rav*).

יִשָּׂרֵף — *Must be burned.* The Torah requires that disqualified sacrificial parts be burned. Those that have been disqualified directly, e.g., by becoming *tamei* or by leaving the area permitted for them, are burned immediately. Thus, in the case of the *pesach*, they should be burned before sunset of the fourteenth. Once night falls, however, they cannot be burned because disqualified sacrifices may not be burned at night, nor on a festival (*Gem.*).

נִטְמְאוּ הַבְּעָלִים אוֹ שֶׁמֵּתוּ — *[If] the owners became contaminated or died*, the offering has only been indirectly disqualified because there is no one to eat it. Consequently, it may not be burned until it becomes 'disfigured,' [meaning its state was changed] i.e., נוֹתָר, *leftover* past the time allowed for its consumption. This occurs for a *pesach* on the morning of the fifteenth, but the disqualified parts may not be burned then because it is the festival. Thus, it must wait for the sixteenth.

רַבִּי יוֹחָנָן בֶּן בְּרוֹקָה — *R' Yochanan ben Berokah* maintains that the disqualification resulting from the *tumah* of the owners is treated the same as the disqualification of the sacrifice itself.

learned that] if the person had been contaminated, the tzitz does not effect acceptance. For they have said [concerning] the nazir and one making the pesach offering, that the tzitz effects acceptance for contamination of the blood, but the tzitz does not effect acceptance for the contamination of the person. [If] one became contaminated from a tumah-contamination of the deep, the tzitz effects acceptance.

[8] *[If] the whole or the greater part of [the pesach offering] became contaminated, it must be burned before the Temple complex with wood [set aside] for the [Altar] pyre. [However, if] the lesser part became contaminated, or [if the meat] was left past its time, they burn it in their courtyards or on their rooftops with their own wood. The misers would burn it before the Temple complex, in order to make use of the wood of the pyre.*

[9] *Any pesach offering taken out [of Jerusalem] or which became contaminated with tumah must be burned immediately. [If] the owners became contaminated or died, it must become disfigured and be burned on the sixteenth. R' Yochanan ben Berokah says: This too must be burned immediately, because there are none to eat it.*

[10] *The bones, the sinews, and the leftover [meat] must be burned on the sixteenth. [If] the sixteenth falls on the Sabbath, they must be burned on the seventeenth, because [the mitzvah to burn] them does not override the Sabbath or the festival.*

[11] *Any parts edible in a full-grown ox must be eaten in a tender kid, including the ends of the shoulder blades and the cartilage. [If] one breaks the bone of an uncontaminated pesach offering, he incurs the [penalty of] forty lashes. But one who leaves over [meat] of an uncontaminated one, or who breaks [the bone] of a contaminated one, does not incur the [penalty of] forty lashes.*

YAD AVRAHAM

10. הָעֲצָמוֹת — *The bones* of the *pesach* may not be broken (*Ex.* 12:46). As a result, their edible marrow, which cannot be removed, becomes *leftover* and must be burned [together with the bones].

וְהַגִּידִין — The term *sinews* in this context includes such soft tissue as tendons, sinews, and nerves. Since the mishnah considers sinews distinct from meat, it is evident that it does not refer to ordinarily edible sinews. On the other hand, sinews too tough to be eaten do not become disqualified and need not be burned. The *Gemara* concludes that it refers to the fat of the thigh sinew, or the outer sinew of the thigh. The thigh sinew itself [גִּיד הַנָּשֶׁה] is Scripturally forbidden, but its fat is technically permitted, although it is not customarily eaten. The outer sinew is forbidden only by Rabbinic law, and therefore Biblically requires burning like edible meat.

11. כָּל הַנֶּאֱכָל . . . — *Any parts edible . . .* When a group registers on a *pesach* offering, there must be sufficient meat for each one to receive an *edible* portion the size of an olive (כְּזַיִת). Inedible parts do not count towards this amount, nor does the prohibition against leaving over offering meat. The mishnah now defines what is considered edible.

יֵאָכֵל בִּגְדִי הָרַךְ — *Must be eaten in a tender kid,* i.e., the *pesach* offering. However, parts of the *pesach* that will harden and be inedible in an adult goat or sheep (as in a grown ox) are not

included even though they are still soft in the young kid. The ends of the shoulder blades and the cartilage are considered edible, though they become so (in an adult ox) only after being boiled for a long period of time (*Rav*).

הַשּׁוֹבֵר אֶת הָעֶצֶם — *Breaking the bone* of a *pesach* offering is forbidden by the Torah (*Ex.* 12:10). *Chinuch* (*Mitzvah* 16) offers a reason for this. Breaking and gnawing at bones is the practice of the poor, who lack sufficient food. We, who proclaim that on this day we became *a kingdom of priests and a sanctified people* (*Ex.* 19:6), should deport ourselves in a manner befitting princes.

In general, the prohibition does not apply to a *pesach* that has become *tamei*. However, even breaking the bones of a contaminated *pesach* incurs punishment if the contamination occurred after the offering had already been permitted for consumption, i.e., after the 'throwing' of the blood.

אֲבָל הַמּוֹתִיר בְּטָהוֹר — *But one who leaves over [meat] of an uncontaminated pesach* is not liable to lashes, although he is forbidden to do so. This is because the Torah follows the prohibition with a compensatory commandment to burn the leftover, and whenever an affirmative command follows a negative command (לָאו הַנִּתָּק לַעֲשֵׂה), it is regarded as the remedy for the transgression, replacing punishment. Also, leaving over violates the prohibition passively rather than actively [לָאו שֶׁאֵין בּוֹ מַעֲשֶׂה], for which there is no penalty of lashes (*Gem.*).

[יב] אֵבֶר שֶׁיָּצָא מִקְצָתוֹ, חוֹתֵךְ עַד שֶׁמַּגִּיעַ לָעֶצֶם, וְקוֹלֵף עַד שֶׁמַּגִּיעַ לַפֶּרֶק, וְחוֹתֵךְ. וּבַמֻּקְדָּשִׁין קוֹצֵץ בְּקוֹפִיץ, שֶׁאֵין בּוֹ מִשּׁוּם שְׁבִירַת הָעֶצֶם. מִן הָאַגַּף וְלִפְנִים, כְּלִפְנִים; מִן הָאַגַּף וְלַחוּץ, כְּלַחוּץ. הַחַלּוֹנוֹת וְעֳבִי הַחוֹמָה, כְּלִפְנִים.

[יג] שְׁתֵּי חֲבוּרוֹת שֶׁהָיוּ אוֹכְלוֹת בְּבַיִת אֶחָד, אֵלּוּ הוֹפְכִין אֶת פְּנֵיהֶם הֵילָךְ וְאוֹכְלִין, וְאֵלּוּ הוֹפְכִין אֶת פְּנֵיהֶם הֵילָךְ וְאוֹכְלִין, וְהַמֵּחַם בָּאֶמְצַע. וּכְשֶׁהַשַּׁמָּשׁ עוֹמֵד לִמְזוֹג, קוֹפֵץ אֶת פִּיו וּמַחֲזִיר אֶת פָּנָיו עַד שֶׁמַּגִּיעַ אֵצֶל חֲבוּרָתוֹ, וְאוֹכֵל. וְהַכַּלָּה הוֹפֶכֶת אֶת פָּנֶיהָ וְאוֹכֶלֶת.

<h3>פרק שמיני</h3>

[א] הָאִשָּׁה בִּזְמַן שֶׁהִיא בְּבֵית בַּעְלָהּ, שָׁחַט עָלֶיהָ בַּעְלָהּ וְשָׁחַט עָלֶיהָ אָבִיהָ, תֹּאכַל מִשֶּׁל בַּעְלָהּ. הָלְכָה רֶגֶל רִאשׁוֹן לַעֲשׂוֹת בְּבֵית אָבִיהָ, שָׁחַט עָלֶיהָ אָבִיהָ וְשָׁחַט עָלֶיהָ בַּעְלָהּ, תֹּאכַל בְּמָקוֹם שֶׁהִיא רוֹצָה. יָתוֹם שֶׁשָּׁחֲטוּ עָלָיו אַפּוֹטְרוֹפְּסִין יֹאכַל בְּמָקוֹם שֶׁהוּא רוֹצֶה. עֶבֶד שֶׁל שְׁנֵי שֻׁתָּפִין לֹא יֹאכַל מִשֶּׁל שְׁנֵיהֶן. מִי שֶׁחֶצְיוֹ עֶבֶד וְחֶצְיוֹ בֶּן חוֹרִין לֹא יֹאכַל מִשֶּׁל רַבּוֹ.

[ב] הָאוֹמֵר לְעַבְדּוֹ: "צֵא וּשְׁחַט עָלַי אֶת הַפֶּסַח," שָׁחַט גְּדִי יֹאכַל, שָׁחַט טָלֶה יֹאכַל. שָׁחַט גְּדִי וְטָלֶה, יֹאכַל מִן הָרִאשׁוֹן. שָׁכַח מָה אָמַר לוֹ רַבּוֹ, כֵּיצַד יַעֲשֶׂה? יִשְׁחַט טָלֶה וּגְדִי וְיֹאמַר: "אִם גְּדִי אָמַר לִי רַבִּי, גְּדִי שֶׁלּוֹ וְטָלֶה שֶׁלִּי; וְאִם

<hr>

יד אברהם

12. אֵבֶר שֶׁיָּצָא מִקְצָתוֹ — [If] part of a limb . . . The Torah restricts an offering to certain areas and any offering that exits its permitted area is disqualified. If part of a limb of an offering extrudes beyond the permitted boundary, only that part becomes disqualified. Removing that part from a pesach offering must be done without breaking any bone. Thus, he must first cut around the bone to separate the meat that has become forbidden from the remainder that must be eaten. He then removes all the permissible meat from that bone as far back as the joint and cuts through the tendons, which are not considered bone, to separate the bone from the rest of the carcass. He then burns the disqualified meat and disposes of the bone. The boundaries for pesach offerings are the walls of Jerusalem and the group in which it is designated to be eaten (see m. 13).

13. שְׁתֵּי חֲבוּרוֹת — Two groups may eat from the same offering in the same house without any necessity of appearing like one group by facing each other. However, each individual is limited to eating with one company (Rav).

וְהַמֵּחַם בָּאֶמְצַע — With the kettle between them. In Talmudic times it was customary to dilute wine with warm water. The heater upon which the water kettle stands may be placed between the two groups for the waiter's convenience, even though it appears to divide the two groups, because a pesach may be eaten in two separate companies. However, since the waiter is a registered participant in this pesach and a member of one of these groups,

he must close his mouth and turn his face when he stands up to mix the wine for the other group, to remove any suspicion that he is eating with the other group.

וְהַכַּלָּה הוֹפֶכֶת אֶת פָּנֶיהָ — A bride may turn her face away [out of modesty and shyness] when eating, because a pesach may be eaten in two companies.

CHAPTER EIGHT

1. To partake of a pesach offering, a person must register on it before its slaughter. However, he need not purchase a portion but may have it assigned to him by a second party. Thus it may happen that an individual is registered for more than one pesach without his knowledge. But since one person may not bring more than one pesach offering, a determination must be made as to which of the two registrations is valid.

בִּזְמַן שֶׁהִיא בְּבֵית בַּעְלָהּ — While a woman resides in her husband's house, i.e., she is fully married, not merely betrothed. Also, she plans to spend the festival in her husband's house rather than with her parents. Accordingly, she eats from her husband's pesach because it is assumed that she prefers to join her husband's offering. [A woman is obligated in the mitzvah of eating the pesach offering.]

רֶגֶל רִאשׁוֹן — The first festival after marriage was customary for a woman to spend at her father's house. Thus, it is not self-evident that she intends to eat from her husband's pesach rather than

[12] *[If] part of a limb left the area [permitted for it], he cuts [it] until he reaches the bone, and pares [the meat] away until he reaches the joint and severs [the limb]. But with other offerings he may chop with a cleaver, for they are not subject to the [prohibition of] breaking a bone.*

From the jamb [of the city's gates] is considered within [the city]; from the jamb outward is considered outside [the city]. The windows and the thickness [atop] the walls are treated as within [the city].

[13] *[If] two groups were eating in the same house, one group may turn in one direction and eat, and the other group may turn in another direction and eat, with the kettle between them. When the waiter stands up to mix the wine, he must close his mouth and turn his face until he gets back to his own group, [when] he may [resume] eating. A bride may turn her face away and eat.*

CHAPTER EIGHT

[1] **הָאִשָּׁה** *While a woman resides in her husband's house, [if] her husband slaughtered [a pesach] on her behalf and her father slaughtered on her behalf, she eats from [the pesach] of her husband. [If] she went to spend the first festival in her father's house, [and] both her father and husband slaughtered on her behalf, she may eat in whichever place she desires. An orphan whose guardians slaughtered for him may eat in whichever place he desires. A slave belonging to two partners may not eat from either one's [pesach]. One who is half slave and half free may not eat from his master's.*

[2] *One who instructed his slave, 'Go out and have a pesach offering slaughtered for me,' [whether] he [arranged for] a kid to be slaughtered or a lamb [to be] slaughtered, he may eat [of it]. [If] he arranged for [both] a kid and a lamb to be slaughtered, he must eat of the first. [If] he forgot which his master had specified, what should he do? Let him slaughter a lamb and a kid and stipulate: 'If my master specified a kid, let the kid be his and the lamb mine; and if my master specified*

YAD AVRAHAM

her father's. Accordingly, though she may eat whichever she desires, she must state her preference by the time of slaughter in order to be able to eat from either one (*Gem.*). [Stating her preference at the *Seder*, however, cannot retroactively register her on one *pesach* or the other.]

יָתוֹם שֶׁשָּׁחֲטוּ עָלָיו — *An orphan* who had more than one guardian and each slaughtered a *pesach* on his behalf, may choose the *pesach* in which he will participate even after the slaughter. The problem of retroactive choice does not apply here because the Torah says (*Ex.* 12:3): *And they shall take . . . a kid for a household*, implying that the head of the household [the guardian in this case] has the power to purchase a *pesach* for his minor children without their acquiescence (*Gem.*). Thus, the subsequent choice made by the orphan does not have to be effective retroactively.

עֶבֶד שֶׁל שְׁנֵי שֻׁתָּפִין — *A* [gentile] *slave belonging to two* [Jewish] *partners* is obligated to eat the *pesach*, but may not do so unless both owners agree on which *pesach* to register him. Otherwise, since half of him belongs to each partner, neither one's registration is valid without permission from the other owner.

מִי שֶׁחֶצְיוֹ עֶבֶד — *One who is half slave* and half free, having been freed by one of his two owners, may not eat from his master's offering because it is assumed that the master of half of him did not intend to register the free half upon his offering (*Rashi*).

2. . . . הָאוֹמֵר לְעַבְדּוֹ — *One who instructed his slave* to arrange a *pesach* offering for him, without specifying whether he wanted a lamb or a kid. Since he did not specify, we assume that he depends completely on the slave's discretion (*Gem.*).

If the slave had one of each slaughtered, the master is considered registered on the one slaughtered first, and the second offering is burned (*Rashi*). The *Gemara* explains that this last case refers specifically to a king who, because of the abundance of food available to him, is assumed not to have any fixed preferences about the kind of meat he wants for the *pesach*. Ordinary people, who are assumed to have preferences, would have both offerings judged invalid, since a person cannot be registered on two offerings, nor can he designate his choice retroactively [אֵין בְּרֵירָה].

יִשְׁחט טָלֶה וּגְדִי וְיֹאמַר — *Let him slaughter a lamb and a kid and stipulate* that whichever his master had previously ordered be for

טָלֶה אָמַר לִי רַבִּי, טָלֶה שֶׁלּוֹ וּגְדִי שֶׁלִּי." שָׁכַח רַבּוֹ מָה אָמַר לוֹ, שְׁנֵיהֶם יֵצְאוּ
לְבֵית הַשְּׂרֵפָה, וּפְטוּרִין מִלַּעֲשׂוֹת פֶּסַח שֵׁנִי.

[ג] הָאוֹמֵר לְבָנָיו: "הֲרֵינִי שׁוֹחֵט אֶת הַפֶּסַח עַל מִי שֶׁיַּעֲלֶה מִכֶּם לִירוּשָׁלַיִם,"
כֵּיוָן שֶׁהִכְנִיס הָרִאשׁוֹן רֹאשׁוֹ וְרֻבּוֹ, זָכָה בְחֶלְקוֹ, וּמְזַכֶּה אֶת אֶחָיו עִמּוֹ.
לְעוֹלָם נִמְנִין עָלָיו עַד שֶׁיְּהֵא בוֹ כַזַּיִת לְכָל אֶחָד וְאֶחָד. נִמְנִין וּמוֹשְׁכִין אֶת
יְדֵיהֶן מִמֶּנּוּ עַד שֶׁיִּשָּׁחֵט. רַבִּי שִׁמְעוֹן אוֹמֵר: עַד שֶׁיִּזְרֹק עָלָיו אֶת הַדָּם.

[ד] הַמַּמְנֶה עִמּוֹ אֲחֵרִים בְּחֶלְקוֹ, רַשָּׁאִין בְּנֵי חֲבוּרָה לִתֵּן לוֹ אֶת שֶׁלּוֹ, וְהוּא
אוֹכֵל מִשֶּׁלּוֹ וְהֵן אוֹכְלִין מִשֶּׁלָּהֶן.

[ה] זָב שֶׁרָאָה שְׁתֵּי רְאִיּוֹת, שׁוֹחֲטִין עָלָיו בַּשְּׁבִיעִי. רָאָה שָׁלֹשׁ, שׁוֹחֲטִין עָלָיו
בַּשְּׁמִינִי שֶׁלּוֹ.

שׁוֹמֶרֶת יוֹם כְּנֶגֶד יוֹם, שׁוֹחֲטִין עָלֶיהָ בַּשֵּׁנִי שֶׁלָּהּ. רָאֲתָה שְׁנֵי יָמִים, שׁוֹחֲטִין
עָלֶיהָ בַּשְּׁלִישִׁי.

וְהַזָּבָה, שׁוֹחֲטִין עָלֶיהָ בַּשְּׁמִינִי.

[ו] הָאוֹנֵן, וְהַמְפַקֵּחַ אֶת הַגַּל; וְכֵן מִי שֶׁהִבְטִיחוּהוּ לְהוֹצִיאוֹ מִבֵּית הָאֲסוּרִים,
וְהַחוֹלֶה וְהַזָּקֵן שֶׁהֵן יְכוֹלִין לֶאֱכוֹל כְּזַיִת, שׁוֹחֲטִין עֲלֵיהֶן. עַל כֻּלָּן
אֵין שׁוֹחֲטִין עֲלֵיהֶן בִּפְנֵי עַצְמָן, שֶׁמָּא יָבִיאוּ אֶת הַפֶּסַח לִידֵי פְסוּל.

---

him and the remaining one for the slave. Retroactive selection [בְּרִירָה] is of no concern here, because no new choice will be made by anyone after the slaughter. The master has *already* made his choice; it is merely the slave who does not know. [This course, however, is not as simple as it seems because it involves the problem of a slave owning property independently of his master. See the full *Yad Avraham* comm. p. 159.]

שָׁכַח רַבּוֹ ... — *[If]* [by the time the slave returns] *his master* also cannot recall his instructions, both offerings are dispensed to the 'place of burning' to be destroyed, because it cannot be determined which offering is the master's and which the slave's. Eating of either offering, therefore, runs the risk of transgressing the prohibition against eating of a *pesach* without registration. However, if the master still remembered his instructions at the time these offerings were made [and only forgot them later], each was *offered* as a valid *pesach*, and both master and slave are exempt from participating in the *pesach sheni* [for those who did not offer a *pesach* on Nissan 14] (*Gem.*).

3. הָאוֹמֵר לְבָנָיו — *[If]* one says to his sons. The father leaves for Jerusalem to perform the sacrifice in the afternoon and allows the children to arrive after the service, in time to eat from the offering at night. To speed them on their way he offers to slaughter the *pesach for* the one to reach Jerusalem first; he will be given a single large portion [and the other brothers will have to receive their portions from him]. However, the father had actually registered all his sons on this offering. The mishnah

teaches that this statement is meant merely as a spur and not to void the original registration (*Gem.*).

רַבִּי שִׁמְעוֹן אוֹמֵר — *R' Shimon* permits withdrawal even after the slaughter, as long as the offering's blood has not been thrown [which renders the offering valid]. He concurs, however, that registration must take place before the slaughter.

4. הַמַּמְנֶה עִמּוֹ אֲחֵרִים בְּחֶלְקוֹ — *[If]* one registers others upon his portion of the *pesach* without consulting the rest of the group, the original members may claim that they do not wish to spend their meal with strangers (*Gem.*). They may therefore give him his portion (e.g., his tenth) and tell him to eat separately with those he registered. Separating presents no problems, because the *pesach* may be eaten in two groups [see 7:13] (*Rav*).

5. זָב — *A zav.* A man who experiences spontaneous seminal emissions (differing somewhat from ordinary seminal emissions in their texture and color) is rendered *tamei*. If he experiences one discharge, he may immerse in a *mikveh* immediately and be rid of his *tumah* at nightfall. If he experiences two discharges in one day or on two consecutive days, he is classified a *zav* and must observe seven consecutive 'clean' days (i.e. free of discharges) and immerse himself in a spring of running water [מַעְיָן] on the seventh day before becoming *tahor* on the evening of the eighth. Thus, if his seventh day falls on Erev Pesach, and he has already immersed himself, they may offer his *pesach* in the Temple, because he will be fit to eat it that night (*Rav*).

However, a man who experienced three discharges on one,

a lamb, let the lamb be his and the kid mine. [If] his master [also] forgot what he had specified, both are dispensed to the place of burning, and both are exempt from participating in [the] pesach sheni.

[3] *[If] one says to his sons: 'I will slaughter the pesach for the first among you to reach Jerusalem,' as soon as the first one enters [the city] with his head and the greater part of his body, he acquires his portion and acquires his brothers' [portions] for them.*

Registration for a [pesach offering] may continue for as long as there is [at least] an olive's volume for each [registrant]. People may register or withdraw from it until it is slaughtered. R' Shimon says: Until the blood is thrown for it.

[4] *[If] one registers others upon his portion [of the pesach], the [other] members of the company are permitted to [separate and] give him his [portion], and he eats his and they eat theirs.*

[5] *A zav who experienced two discharges may have his [pesach] offering slaughtered on the seventh [day]. [If] he experienced three, they may slaughter for him on his eighth [day].*

A woman who observes a day against a day may have her offering slaughtered on her second [day]. [If] she experienced discharges for two days, they may slaughter for her on the third [day]. A zavah may have her offering slaughtered on the eighth [day].

[6] *They may slaughter [the pesach] for an onain, and [a rescuer] who clears a pile of rubble; likewise for one who they have promised to release from prison, and a sick or aged person able to eat the volume of an olive. [However,] they may not slaughter for any of these alone, because they cause the pesach offering to become invalid.*

YAD AVRAHAM

two, or three consecutive days does not become *tahor* until he offers a pair of bird sacrifices on the eighth day, after completing the previous procedure. Thus, only if his *eighth* day is on Erev Pesach may they offer the *pesach* sacrifice for him, provided the *zav* offerings have already been brought to the Temple.

שׁוֹמֶרֶת יוֹם כְּנֶגֶד יוֹם — *A woman who observes a day against a day.* When a woman menstruates she becomes a *niddah* for seven days. This is followed by an eleven-day period during which she may become a *zavah* by menstruating again, as follows: If she menstruates on one day during these eleven, she must make sure that the next day is free from discharge and immerse herself before sundown; she is then totally *tahor* (purified) at nightfall. She is known as *one who observes a day* [free from discharge] *against a day* [of discharge]. Similarly, if she experiences two discharges on two consecutive days, she observes the third day free of discharge, then immerses and is *tahor* by evening. Therefore, should this second or third day fall on Erev Pesach and she has already immersed herself in a *mikveh*, they may slaughter a *pesach* for her since she will be fit to eat it that night (*Rav*).

If, however, she menstruates on three consecutive days in this eleven-day period, she is a זָבָה גְדוֹלָה, *major zavah* [in contrast to the previous cases of a *minor zavah*]. She must now observe seven consecutive days free from discharge and may immerse

herself in a *mikveh* on the seventh day. However, she must also offer sacrifices on the eighth day. Thus her *pesach* sacrifice may be offered only on her eighth clean day, provided she has brought her *zavah* sacrifices. [The above is the Scriptural law. Rabbinically, a woman who menstruates even one day requires seven clean days before she may purify herself in a *mikveh* and resume marital relations with her husband.]

6. הָאוֹנֵן — *An onain* is a person newly in mourning for the death of his father, mother, brother, sister, son, daughter, or spouse, on the day of their death. The Torah prohibits him from partaking of sacrifices until nightfall of that day. Thus, his *pesach* may be slaughtered that afternoon.

וְהַמְפַקֵּחַ אֶת הַגַּל — *[A rescuer] who clears a pile of rubble* from a collapsed building to see if anyone is trapped inside. Although he may find the victim dead and be contaminated by the body and thus forbidden to eat the *pesach* offering, the offering is slaughtered on his behalf. Since the victim's fate is not known, the searcher must be assumed to retain his uncontaminated status [חֶזְקַת טַהֲרָה] (*Rav*).

אֵין שׁוֹחֲטִין עֲלֵיהֶן בִּפְנֵי עַצְמָן — *They may not slaughter for any of these alone,* because they may in the end not be able to partake of the *pesach* and cause it to be invalidated for lack of anyone to eat it. The grief-stricken mourners may touch the corpse and become *tamei*, the rescuer may find the victim dead and become *tamei*, the prisoner may remain incarcerated, and the

לְפִיכָךְ, אִם אֵרַע בָּהֶן פְּסוּל, פְּטוּרִין מִלַּעֲשׂוֹת פֶּסַח שֵׁנִי; חוּץ מִן הַמְפַקֵּחַ בַּגַּל, שֶׁהוּא טָמֵא מִתְּחִלָּתוֹ.

[ז] אֵין שׁוֹחֲטִין אֶת הַפֶּסַח עַל הַיָּחִיד: דִּבְרֵי רַבִּי יְהוּדָה. וְרַבִּי יוֹסֵי מַתִּיר. אֲפִלּוּ חֲבוּרָה שֶׁל מֵאָה שֶׁאֵין יְכוֹלִין לֶאֱכוֹל כְּזַיִת, אֵין שׁוֹחֲטִין עֲלֵיהֶן. וְאֵין עוֹשִׂין חֲבוּרַת נָשִׁים, וַעֲבָדִים, וּקְטַנִּים.

[ח] אוֹנֵן טוֹבֵל וְאוֹכֵל אֶת פִּסְחוֹ לָעֶרֶב, אֲבָל לֹא בַקֳּדָשִׁים. הַשּׁוֹמֵעַ עַל מֵתוֹ, וְהַמְלַקֵּט לוֹ עֲצָמוֹת, טוֹבֵל וְאוֹכֵל בַּקֳּדָשִׁים. גֵּר שֶׁנִּתְגַּיֵּר בְּעֶרֶב פֶּסַח — בֵּית שַׁמַּאי אוֹמְרִים: טוֹבֵל וְאוֹכֵל אֶת פִּסְחוֹ לָעֶרֶב. וּבֵית הִלֵּל אוֹמְרִים: הַפּוֹרֵשׁ מִן הָעָרְלָה כְּפוֹרֵשׁ מִן הַקֶּבֶר.

פרק תשיעי

[א] **מִי** שֶׁהָיָה טָמֵא אוֹ בְדֶרֶךְ רְחוֹקָה, וְלֹא עָשָׂה אֶת הָרִאשׁוֹן, יַעֲשֶׂה אֶת הַשֵּׁנִי. שָׁגַג אוֹ נֶאֱנַס, וְלֹא עָשָׂה אֶת הָרִאשׁוֹן, יַעֲשֶׂה אֶת הַשֵּׁנִי. אִם כֵּן, לָמָּה נֶאֱמַר "טָמֵא" אוֹ שֶׁהָיָה "בְדֶרֶךְ רְחוֹקָה"? — שֶׁאֵלּוּ פְּטוּרִין מֵהִכָּרֵת, וְאֵלּוּ חַיָּבִין בְּהִכָּרֵת.

[ב] אֵיזוֹ הִיא "דֶּרֶךְ רְחוֹקָה"? מִן הַמּוֹדִיעִים וְלַחוּץ, וּכְמִדָּתָהּ לְכָל רוּחַ; דִּבְרֵי רַבִּי עֲקִיבָא. רַבִּי אֱלִיעֶזֶר אוֹמֵר: מֵאִסְקֻפַּת הָעֲזָרָה וְלַחוּץ. אָמַר רַבִּי יוֹסֵי: לְפִיכָךְ נָקוּד עַל ה' — לוֹמַר, לֹא מִפְּנֵי שֶׁרְחוֹקָה וַדַּאי, אֶלָּא מֵאִסְקֻפַּת הָעֲזָרָה וְלַחוּץ.

יד אברהם

sick or elderly may find it difficult to consume an adequate portion of meat. Thus, they must also register on this offering people not burdened with these problems, so that even if these prove unable to eat, the offering will not be disqualified. [A *pesach* is valid if it was slaughtered both for those fit to eat and those unable to do so (5:3).]

לְפִיכָךְ . . . פְּטוּרִין מִלַּעֲשׂוֹת פֶּסַח שֵׁנִי — *Therefore . . . they are exempt from participating in the pesach sheni.* Since they were considered fit to eat the offering at the time it was slaughtered and its blood was thrown, the sacrificial service was valid and they have discharged their obligation even if they are not in the end able to eat (see 7:4). The exception to this is the one clearing rubble, if a corpse was, in fact, discovered. In this case he became *tamei* when he started to clear the ruin, before the service took place, because a corpse contaminates even one who passes over it without touching it (*Rav*).

7. וְאֵין עוֹשִׂין חֲבוּרַת . . . — *A group may not be formed* [solely] of women, slaves and minors because heathen slaves generally had low morals and this could lead to licentiousness. However, a group may be comprised exclusively of women or of slaves.

8. אוֹנֵן טוֹבֵל וְאוֹכֵל — *An onain immerses* [himself in a *mikveh*] and *eats* his *pesach* offering in the evening because Biblical law forbids mourners to eat offerings only on the day of death. The Rabbinic law prohibiting the following night was lifted for the

sake of the *pesach*. However, he must first immerse himself in a *mikveh* because of a Rabbinic rule requiring immersion for anyone who has been prohibited to partake of offerings (*Rashi*). He may not, however, eat the other offerings that night, because that is a *mitzvah* not subject to *kares* and it does not merit a waiver of a Rabbinic prohibition (*Rambam*).

הַשּׁוֹמֵעַ עַל מֵתוֹ . . . — *One who hears about the death of his relative* after the day of death is an *onain* only by Rabbinic decree. Similarly, one who has arranged for the bones of a close relative to be exhumed from a temporary grave (e.g., one belonging to someone else) or for reburial near his parents or in *Eretz Yisrael* (see *Y.D.* 363:1), is Rabbinically obliged to observe a period of mourning until nightfall on the day of the reburial. The night after these mourning periods is not under this ban, and he may thus eat even from the other offerings as well.

בֵּית שַׁמַּאי אוֹמְרִים — *Beis Shammai say* that he may offer his *pesach* on the very day of his conversion as long as he undergoes an additional immersion (similar to the immersion required of a mourner), and eat the *pesach* that night.

וּבֵית הִלֵּל אוֹמְרִים — *But Beis Hillel* liken a convert to one who has been contaminated by a grave, requiring a seven-day purification process, including sprinkling with the water containing the ashes of the *parah adumah*. While Beis Hillel agree that the

Therefore, if any disqualification befalls them, they are exempt from participating in the pesach sheni; except for the rescuer clearing rubble, for he was [found to be] contaminated retroactively.

[7] *A pesach offering may not be slaughtered for an individual; [these are] the words of R' Yehudah. R' Yose permits [this]. [However,] we may not slaughter even for a group [consisting of] a hundred if they are unable to eat the volume of an olive. A group may not be formed [solely] of women, slaves and minors.*

[8] *An onain immerses and eats his pesach offering in the evening, but not [the other] offerings. One who hears about the death of his relative, or one who has arranged for the bones [of a close relative] to be gathered on his behalf, immerses [himself] and may eat offerings.*

[If] someone converted on Erev Pesach — Beis Shammai say: He immerses [himself] and eats his pesach offering in the evening. But Beis Hillel say: One who separates [himself] from an uncircumcised state is like one who separates himself from the grave.

CHAPTER NINE

[1] **מִי** *One who was contaminated with tumah or was on a distant journey, and [therefore] had not made [his offering] on the First [Pesach], makes [it] on the Second [Pesach]. [If] he erred or was prevented [by circumstances], and did not make [his offering] on the First [Pesach], he makes [his offering] on the Second. If so, why does [the verse] say: 'One who was contaminated or was on a distant journey' (Num. 9:10)? Because these are exempt from kares, but those are liable to kares.*

[2] *What is [considered] a 'distant journey'? From Modi'in and beyond, or a like distance in any direction; [these are] the words of R' Akiva. R' Eliezer says: From the threshold of the Temple Courtyard and beyond. Said R' Yose: Therefore, there is a dot over the letter ה — as if to say, not because it is literally distant, but rather from the threshold of the Temple Courtyard and beyond.*

YAD AVRAHAM

proselyte does not truly have corpse *tumah*, because the Torah subjects only Jews to such *tumah*, they maintain, however, that the Rabbis decreed a seven-day purification for the newly converted [and thus unlearned] proselyte, to forestall the possibility of his assuming that contact with corpses does not prevent someone from offering the *pesach* [not realizing that this was only because he was still a gentile at the time].

CHAPTER NINE

1. Although the time for the *pesach's* offering is the fourteenth of Nissan, the Torah provided a make-up date on the fourteenth of Iyar (a month after the first Pesach) for those who missed the primary date. The alternate date is called *Pesach Sheni*, the Second Pesach.

שָׁגַג — *[If] he erred* and forgot that it was Erev Pesach or that one is obligated to bring a *pesach* offering at that time.

יַעֲשֶׂה אֶת הַשֵּׁנִי — *He makes [his offering] on the Second.* The provision for offering on the Second Pesach is for anyone who neglected to bring his *pesach* offering on the first, for whatever reason, even one who willfully neglected to offer on the First Pesach (*Gem.*).

שֶׁאֵלּוּ פְּטוּרִין מֵהִכָּרֵת — *Because these* [two cases] *are exempt from*

[the punishment of] *kares*, even if they willfully (בְּמֵזִיד) neglect to offer their offering on the Second Pesach. Since the Torah *exempts* them from making an offering on the First Pesach, their obligation to make one on the Second Pesach is a new one, for which the Torah nowhere assigns a penalty of *kares*. However, those who omit the offering on the First Pesach for other reasons have violated a *kares*-bearing requirement and merely have an opportunity of making it up on the Second Pesach. If they willfully ignore this obligation, the *kares* penalty takes effect (*Gem.*).

2. מִן הַמּוֹדִיעִים — *From Modi'in,* which was about fifteen *mil* from Jerusalem (a *mil* is 2000 cubits). This is the distance one can walk at a normal pace from noontime to sunset on Erev Pesach. This is regarded as far away because had he left at noon when the *pesach* service was about to begin, he would not have reached Jerusalem in time to offer a *pesach* (*Rashi*).

רַבִּי אֱלִיעֶזֶר אוֹמֵר — *R' Eliezer says* that even if he was in Jerusalem, but was prevented by uncontrollable circumstances (e.g. illness) from reaching the Temple Courtyard in time, he is considered to have been far away. R' Akiva, however, classifies this as אוֹנֶס, *accidental delay* (*Rav*).

לְפִיכָךְ נָקוּד עַל ה׳ — *Therefore, there is a dot over the letter 'hei' of*

[ג] מַה בֵּין פֶּסַח הָרִאשׁוֹן לַשֵּׁנִי? הָרִאשׁוֹן אָסוּר בְּבַל יֵרָאֶה וּבַל יִמָּצֵא, וְהַשֵּׁנִי, מַצָּה וְחָמֵץ עִמּוֹ בַּבָּיִת; הָרִאשׁוֹן טָעוּן הַלֵּל בַּאֲכִילָתוֹ, וְהַשֵּׁנִי אֵינוֹ טָעוּן הַלֵּל בַּאֲכִילָתוֹ.

זֶה וָזֶה טְעוּנִין הַלֵּל בַּעֲשִׂיָּתָן; וְנֶאֱכָלִין צָלִי, עַל מַצָּה וּמְרוֹרִים; וְדוֹחִין אֶת הַשַּׁבָּת.

[ד] הַפֶּסַח שֶׁבָּא בְטֻמְאָה, לֹא יֹאכְלוּ מִמֶּנּוּ זָבִין וְזָבוֹת נִדּוֹת וְיוֹלְדוֹת; וְאִם אָכְלוּ, פְּטוּרִים מִכָּרֵת. רַבִּי אֱלִיעֶזֶר פּוֹטֵר אַף עַל בִּיאַת מִקְדָּשׁ.

[ה] מַה בֵּין פֶּסַח מִצְרַיִם לְפֶסַח דּוֹרוֹת? פֶּסַח מִצְרַיִם מִקָּחוֹ מִבֶּעָשׂוֹר, וְטָעוּן הַזָּאָה בַאֲגֻדַּת אֵזוֹב עַל הַמַּשְׁקוֹף וְעַל שְׁתֵּי הַמְּזוּזוֹת, וְנֶאֱכָל בְּחִפָּזוֹן, בְּלַיְלָה אֶחָד. וּפֶסַח דּוֹרוֹת נוֹהֵג כָּל שִׁבְעָה.

[ו] אָמַר רַבִּי יְהוֹשֻׁעַ: "שָׁמַעְתִּי שֶׁתְּמוּרַת הַפֶּסַח קְרֵבָה, וּתְמוּרַת הַפֶּסַח אֵינָהּ קְרֵבָה, וְאֵין לִי לְפָרֵשׁ." אָמַר רַבִּי עֲקִיבָא: "אֲנִי אֲפָרֵשׁ": הַפֶּסַח שֶׁנִּמְצָא קֹדֶם שְׁחִיטַת הַפֶּסַח, יִרְעֶה עַד שֶׁיִּסְתָּאֵב, וְיִמָּכֵר, וְיִקַּח בְּדָמָיו שְׁלָמִים. וְכֵן תְּמוּרָתוֹ. אַחַר שְׁחִיטַת הַפֶּסַח, קָרֵב שְׁלָמִים, וְכֵן תְּמוּרָתוֹ.

[ז] הַמַּפְרִישׁ נְקֵבָה לְפִסְחוֹ, אוֹ זָכָר בֶּן שְׁתֵּי שָׁנִים, יִרְעֶה עַד שֶׁיִּסְתָּאֵב, וְיִמָּכֵר, וְיִפְּלוּ דָמָיו לִנְדָבָה. הַמַּפְרִישׁ פִּסְחוֹ וָמֵת, לֹא יְבִיאֶנּוּ בְנוֹ אַחֲרָיו לְשֵׁם פֶּסַח, אֶלָּא לְשֵׁם שְׁלָמִים.

יד אברהם

the word רְחוֹקָה, *distant*. In the Torah scroll a dot is placed above certain letters indicating a hidden meaning. R' Yose expounds that the significance of this is to teach that *distant* refers to anyone who is removed from the Temple, no matter what the distance.

3. וְהַשֵּׁנִי . . . — *At the Second* [*Pesach*] there is no prohibition to possess *chametz*, even at the time of the *pesach's* offering.

הָרִאשׁוֹן טָעוּן הַלֵּל — *The First* [Pesach] *requires the recitation of Hallel* at the Seder, but the Second does not. Nor is the *Haggadah* recited at the Second Pesach (*Sfas Emes*).

4. הַפֶּסַח שֶׁבָּא בְטֻמְאָה — *A pesach offered in a state of tumah-contamination* occurs when the majority of the nation is *tamei* on Nissan 14 (see 7:4). This dispensation is granted by the Torah only for corpse-related *tumah*. Other forms of *tumah* require the affected person or community to wait for the Second Pesach (*Gem.*). Thus, even when it is offered in *tumah,* it may not be eaten by other classes of contaminated people such as *zavim, zavos* [plural of *zav, zavah* (see 8:5)], *niddos* and women who have just given birth. [Such a woman has the status of a *niddah* for a period of one week after the birth of a son and two weeks for a daughter, after which she can purify herself through immersion in a *mikveh*. However, she may not eat the offerings until she brings her birth offerings, which she cannot do before forty days after the birth of a son, or eighty days after a daughter.] Moreover, people *tamei* for these reasons are not counted to-

wards the majority necessary to permit this offering. If they do eat, though, they are exempt from *kares*, because this penalty applies only to offerings meant to be eaten by those who are *tahor*.

5. פֶּסַח מִצְרַיִם — *The Pesach* [celebrated] *in Egypt* on the eve of the Exodus was subject to special rules that applied only that year. Conversely, *chametz* was forbidden that first year for only one day (Nissan 15) rather than the usual seven.

6. The Torah prohibits substituting for a sacrifice, even a choicer animal (*Lev.* 27:10). Should a person designate a substitute, it does not remove the sanctity of the first animal, but it *does* serve to consecrate the second animal, with the result that both animals are sacred. This substitute is called a *temurah*.

שָׁמַעְתִּי . . . וְאֵין לִי לְפָרֵשׁ — *I have heard . . . but I cannot explain* [*it*]. R' Yehoshua had heard two seemingly contradictory traditions regarding the *temurah*-substitute of a *pesach*, and was at a loss to resolve it. Generally, a *pesach* offering that went unused is transformed into a *shelamim* (5:4). Since the *temurah* of any offering assumes the status of that sacrifice, the *temurah* of an unused *pesach* should also be offered as a *shelamim*. One tradition indeed said that this was so, but a second tradition said that it could not be offered but must be left until it develops a blemish, when it is sold, and a *shelamim* is bought with the money (*Rav*).

הַפֶּסַח שֶׁנִּמְצָא — [*If*] *the* [*original*] *pesach* offering was lost and

[3] *What are the differences between the First Pesach and the Second? The First [Pesach] is subject to the prohibition of 'It shall not be seen and it shall not be found' (Ex. 12:19), whereas at the Second [Pesach both] matzah and chametz [may be] with him in the house; the First requires the recitation of Hallel at [the pesach's] eating, but the Second does not require Hallel at its eating. Both [however] require the recitation of Hallel when they are offered; [both] are eaten roasted, together with matzah and bitter herbs; and [both] override the Sabbath.*

[4] *A pesach offered in a state of tumah-contamination may not be eaten by zavin, zavos, niddos, or women who have just given birth; but if they did eat, they are exempt from [the penalty of] kares. R' Eliezer exempts [them] even [from the kares due] for entering the Temple.*

[5] *What are the differences between the pesach in Egypt and the pesach of [succeeding] generations? The purchase of the Egyptian pesach [offering] was on the tenth [of Nissan], it required the sprinkling [of its blood] with a bundle of hyssop upon the lintel and upon the two doorposts, and it was eaten in haste during one night. The pesach of [succeeding] generations is observed all seven days.*

[6] *Said R' Yehoshua: I have heard that the substitute of a pesach is offered, and that the substitute of a pesach is not offered, but I cannot explain [it]. Said R' Akiva: I will explain: [If] the [original] pesach offering was [lost and then] found before a [replacement] pesach was slaughtered, it must be left to pasture until it develops a blemish, after which it is sold, and a shelamim offering is bought with its proceeds. The same is for its substitute. [But if it was found] after a [replacement] pesach was slaughtered, it is offered as a shelamim offering, as is its substitute.*

[7] *[If] someone designates a female [animal] for his pesach offering, or a male in its second year, it must be left to pasture until it develops a blemish, [then] be sold, and its money [placed] in a donative offering [chest].*

[If] a person designated his pesach offering and [then] died, his son who inherits it may not bring it as a pesach offering, but rather as a peace offering.

YAD AVRAHAM

another one was designated, but the original was then found before the time of slaughter, two animals are now available for sacrifice as a *pesach*. If the original *pesach* is bypassed in favor of the replacement, the original can no longer be offered as a *shelamim* because it had been explicitly rejected [נִדְחָה], and a rejected sacrifice cannot become qualified again. Thus, it must be left to develop a blemish that disqualifies it as an offering, after which it may be redeemed. The money from the sale assumes the *shelamim* sanctity and is used to purchase a replacement. This animal assumes the money's sanctity and is then offered as a *shelamim*.

וְכֵן תְּמוּרָתוֹ — *The same is for its substitute.* If the owner made a *temurah* substitution for the 'rejected' original *pesach* while it was awaiting a blemish and redemption, the *temurah*-substitute assumes the same level of holiness. Thus, it too must be put out to pasture, etc., and its redemption funds used to purchase a *shelamim* (*Rav*).

אַחַר שְׁחִיטַת הַפֶּסַח — *[If] the lost pesach [was found] after a [replacement] pesach was slaughtered,* then it was not rejected,

but merely unavailable. Thus, the recovered *pesach* itself may be offered as a *shelamim* and there is no need to wait for a blemish and sell it. In this case, its *temurah* is also slaughtered as a *shelamim*. Since the original *pesach* is acceptable as a *shelamim*, so is its *temurah*-substitute.

7. הַמַּפְרִישׁ נְקֵבָה . . . — *[If] someone designates a female [animal]* . . . Neither a female nor a second-year lamb are fit for a *pesach* offering, which must be a male in its first year.

לִנְדָבָה — *In* one of the six chests in the Temple marked נְדָבָה, *donative offering* (Shekalim 6:5). These are used for extra communal *olah* offerings (*Rav*). [This is the reading of our editions of the Mishnah. However, most *Rishonim* had the reading *he brings from its money shelamim-offerings*. Thus the rule here is the same as in mishnah 6, which states that a substitute of a *pesach* that cannot itself be offered becomes a *shelamim-offering*.]

הַמַּפְרִישׁ פִּסְחוֹ וָמֵת — *[If] a person designated a pesach offering* for himself, with no partners, *and [then] died,* so that it is left without anyone registered to eat it, it is invalid (5:3). His heir may

[ח] הַפֶּסַח שֶׁנִּתְעָרֵב בִּזְבָחִים, כֻּלָּן יִרְעוּ עַד שֶׁיִּסְתָּאֲבוּ, וְיִמָּכְרוּ; וְהָבִיא בִּדְמֵי הַיָּפֶה שֶׁבָּהֶן מִמִּין זֶה, וּבִדְמֵי הַיָּפֶה שֶׁבָּהֶן מִמִּין זֶה, וְיַפְסִיד הַמּוֹתָר מִבֵּיתוֹ. נִתְעָרֵב בִּבְכוֹרוֹת – רַבִּי שִׁמְעוֹן אוֹמֵר: אִם חֲבוּרַת כֹּהֲנִים, יֹאכֵלוּ.

[ט] חֲבוּרָה שֶׁאָבְדָה פִּסְחָהּ, וְאָמְרָה לְאֶחָד: „צֵא וּבַקֵּשׁ וּשְׁחֹט עָלֵינוּ," וְהָלַךְ וּמָצָא וְשָׁחַט, וְהֵם לָקְחוּ וְשָׁחֲטוּ – אִם שֶׁלּוֹ נִשְׁחַט רִאשׁוֹן, הוּא אוֹכֵל מִשֶּׁלּוֹ, וְהֵם אוֹכְלִים עִמּוֹ מִשֶּׁלּוֹ; וְאִם שֶׁלָּהֶן נִשְׁחַט רִאשׁוֹן, הֵם אוֹכְלִין מִשֶּׁלָּהֶן, וְהוּא אוֹכֵל מִשֶּׁלּוֹ. וְאִם אֵינוּ יָדוּעַ אֵיזֶה מֵהֶן נִשְׁחַט רִאשׁוֹן, אוֹ שֶׁשָּׁחֲטוּ שְׁנֵיהֶן כְּאֶחָד – הוּא אוֹכֵל מִשֶּׁלּוֹ, וְהֵם אֵינָם אוֹכְלִים עִמּוֹ, וְשֶׁלָּהֶן יֵצֵא לְבֵית הַשְּׂרֵפָה; וּפְטוּרִין מִלַּעֲשׂוֹת פֶּסַח שֵׁנִי.

אָמַר לָהֶן: „אִם אֵחַרְתִּי, צְאוּ וְשַׁחֲטוּ עָלַי," הָלַךְ וּמָצָא וְשָׁחַט, וְהֵן לָקְחוּ וְשָׁחֲטוּ – אִם שֶׁלָּהֶן נִשְׁחַט רִאשׁוֹן, הֵן אוֹכְלִין מִשֶּׁלָּהֶן, וְהוּא אוֹכֵל עִמָּהֶן; וְאִם שֶׁלּוֹ נִשְׁחַט רִאשׁוֹן, הוּא אוֹכֵל מִשֶּׁלּוֹ, וְהֵן אוֹכְלִין מִשֶּׁלָּהֶן. וְאִם אֵינוּ יָדוּעַ אֵיזֶה מֵהֶם נִשְׁחַט רִאשׁוֹן, אוֹ שֶׁשָּׁחֲטוּ שְׁנֵיהֶם כְּאֶחָד – הֵן אוֹכְלִין מִשֶּׁלָּהֶן, וְהוּא אֵינוּ אוֹכֵל עִמָּהֶן, וְשֶׁלּוֹ יֵצֵא לְבֵית הַשְּׂרֵפָה; וּפָטוּר מִלַּעֲשׂוֹת פֶּסַח שֵׁנִי.

אָמַר לָהֶן וְאָמְרוּ לוֹ, אוֹכְלִין כֻּלָּם מִן הָרִאשׁוֹן. וְאִם אֵין יָדוּעַ אֵיזֶה מֵהֶן נִשְׁחַט רִאשׁוֹן, שְׁנֵיהֶן יוֹצְאִין לְבֵית הַשְּׂרֵפָה. לֹא אָמַר לָהֶן וְלֹא אָמְרוּ לוֹ, אֵינָן אַחֲרָאִין זֶה לָזֶה.

[י] שְׁתֵּי חֲבוּרוֹת שֶׁנִּתְעָרְבוּ פִּסְחֵיהֶן, אֵלּוּ מוֹשְׁכִין לָהֶן אֶחָד, וְאֵלּוּ מוֹשְׁכִין לָהֶן אֶחָד, אֶחָד מֵאֵלּוּ בָּא לוֹ אֵצֶל אֵלּוּ, וְאֶחָד מֵאֵלּוּ בָּא לוֹ אֵצֶל אֵלּוּ,

---

יד אברהם

therefore not use it as his *pesach*. [Although people may register on an offering until its slaughter (8:3), this is so only if there is no instant when the *pesach* is completely ownerless.] It is thus like an unused *pesach*, which becomes a *shelamim* (m. 6).

8. הַפֶּסַח שֶׁנִּתְעָרֵב — *[If] a pesach offering became mixed* with other types of offerings (e.g. a *shelamim* and an *olah*) and it is not known which is which, none of them can be offered, since they are each governed by different rules. They must be left to become disqualified by a blemish, after which they are redeemed and their money is used to purchase replacements. If each of these animals fetches a different price, however, the money from the redemption sale is also subject to uncertainty, because each animal's money must be used to purchase its type of offering. Since it is not known which type of offering was the most expensive, the only way to remove all the doubts is to buy three replacements *each* worth as much as the most expensive of the original three offerings. For example, if one lamb was worth a *sela* and the other two half a *sela* each, three lambs worth at least a *sela* each must be purchased, one for each of the three types of offerings (*Rav*). The additional expense this involves must be borne by the owner.

בִּבְכוֹרוֹת — *With firstborn offerings.* The blood *avodah* is the same

for both types of sacrifices (*Zevachim* 5:8), and the confusion thus poses no problems regarding the service. However, there are differences regarding their consumption: *Bechoros* may be eaten only by *Kohanim* and members of their households, for up to two days and a night. The *pesach* may be eaten by any registrants, but only till midnight following the sacrifice. Accordingly, if the *pesach* was owned by a group of *Kohanim*, R' Shimon permits both animals to be slaughtered and eaten on *pesach* night, since regardless of which animal is which, they may be eaten by these people on this night. The Sages, however, disagree because they contend that it is forbidden to create a condition that will require an offering to be consumed in a period of time shorter than that allowed by the Torah, since that may unnecessarily result in the meat becoming *nosar* (leftover) and forbidden (*Gem.*).

9. ... אִם שֶׁלּוֹ נִשְׁחַט רִאשׁוֹן — *If his* [i.e. the lost and recovered *pesach*] *was slaughtered first,* they all eat from that offering. Since they appointed him to act as their agent to slaughter the first animal, they were all registered on his offering at the time of its slaughter, and could not be numbered on another *pesach*. Accordingly, the second animal was slaughtered with no one eligible to eat it and it must therefore be burned. However, if

[8] *[If] a pesach offering became mixed with [other] offerings [and it cannot be identified], they must all be left to pasture until they develop blemishes, after which they are sold; he must then bring one of each type of offering equal in value to the most expensive of them, and bear the added cost from his own purse. [If] the pesach became confused with firstborn offerings — R' Shimon says: If the group is composed of Kohanim, they may be eaten.*

[9] *A group that lost its pesach offering and said to one [of their company], 'Go out, seek [it] and slaughter [it] for us,' and he went, found [it] and slaughtered [it], while they bought and slaughtered [another] — if his was slaughtered first, he eats of his and they eat of his with him; but if theirs was slaughtered first, they eat of theirs and he eats of his. If it is not known which was slaughtered first, or if both were slaughtered at the same time — he eats of his, but they do not eat with him, and theirs must be burned; nevertheless, they are exempt from offering the pesach sheni.*

[If] he said to them, 'If I am delayed, go and slaughter for me,' and he went, found [it] and slaughtered [it], while they bought and slaughtered [another] — if theirs was slaughtered first, they eat of theirs and he eats with them; but if his was slaughtered first, he eats of his and they eat of theirs. If it is not known which was slaughtered first, or if both were slaughtered at the same time — they eat of theirs, but he does not eat with them, and his is burned; nevertheless, he is exempt from offering the pesach sheni.

[If] he said to them and they said to him, all [of them] eat of the first. But if it is not known which was slaughtered first, both are burned. [If] he said nothing to them and they said nothing to him, they are not responsible for each other.

[10] *[If] the pesach offering of two groups were confused, each take one for themselves, [then] a member of each group comes to the other group, and*

YAD AVRAHAM

theirs was slaughtered first, they have, in effect, withdrawn their registration from the first (lost) offering prior to its slaughter (8:4) and transferred it to the second one. Therefore, they eat of the second offering, while he alone eats from the original offering, since he never registered for the second one.

If it is not known which was slaughtered first, he eats from the original offering [since this is what he does regardless], while they may not eat from either one since it cannot be determined which is theirs. The second offering is therefore burned. Nevertheless, they are exempt from offering on the Second Pesach because that is only for those who had not offered on the First Pesach. In our situation, however, they *did* offer one of the two sacrifices; it is only their inability to identity which Pesach is theirs that bars them from eating, and this does not nullify their fulfillment of the *mitzvah* [אֲכִילָה לֹא מְעַכְּבָא] (*Rav*).

אָמַר לָהֶן — *[If] he said to them.* This case is the reverse of the previous one. The searcher told the others to slaughter for him if he did not return on time; they, however, did not instruct him to slaughter for them. Thus, he is registered on their *pesach* as well as the lost one. However, when they purchased the second offering, they effectively withdrew from the first offering. [In the absence of any instruction to their agent to the contrary, purchase alone effects withdrawal.]

אָמַר לָהֶן וְאָמְרוּ לוֹ — *[If] he said to them,* 'If I am delayed, slaughter for me,' *and they said to him,* 'Go out, seek, and slaughter for us,' they must all eat from the first *pesach* slaughtered, since each is an agent for the other (*Rav*). Therefore, if it is not known which offering was slaughtered first, none of them may eat from either of them. Nevertheless, they are all exempt from offering on the Second Pesach (*Rav*).

10. שְׁתֵּי חֲבוּרוֹת שֶׁנִּתְעָרְבוּ פִּסְחֵיהֶן . . . — *[If] the pesach offerings of two groups were confused* before their slaughter, when people may still withdraw and re-register on another *pesach* (8:3). Thus, it is possible to rectify the situation by having each group take one of the offerings, withdraw from the other [in case it was theirs], and register on the one they have now taken. However, this course may not be taken by *all* members of the group because this would leave the *pesach* momentarily ownerless, which would invalidate it (see comm. m. 7). Thus, we must insure that at least one of the original members remains registered on each offering, which is accomplished by removing one member of each group and joining him to the other. Using the mishnah's stipulation, it emerges that if each group actually receives its original lamb, only the new member has withdrawn from his lamb and re-registered on the other. If the lamb they now receive should turn out not to be their original lamb, that

וְכָךְ הֵם אוֹמְרִים: "אִם שֶׁלָּנוּ הוּא הַפֶּסַח הַזֶּה, יָדֶיךָ מְשׁוּכוֹת מִשֶּׁלָּךְ וְנִמְנֵיתָ עַל שֶׁלָּנוּ. וְאִם שֶׁלָּךְ הוּא הַפֶּסַח הַזֶּה, יָדֵינוּ מְשׁוּכוֹת מִשֶּׁלָּנוּ וְנִמְנֵינוּ עַל שֶׁלָּךְ." וְכֵן, חָמֵשׁ חֲבוּרוֹת שֶׁל חֲמִשָּׁה וְשֶׁל עֲשָׂרָה עֲשָׂרָה, מוֹשְׁכִין לָהֶן אֶחָד מִכָּל חֲבוּרָה וַחֲבוּרָה, וְכֵן הֵם אוֹמְרִים.

[יא] שְׁנַיִם שֶׁנִּתְעָרְבוּ פִּסְחֵיהֶם, זֶה מוֹשֵׁךְ לוֹ אֶחָד וְזֶה מוֹשֵׁךְ לוֹ אֶחָד; זֶה מְמַנֶּה עִמּוֹ אֶחָד מִן הַשּׁוּק, וְזֶה מְמַנֶּה עִמּוֹ אֶחָד מִן הַשּׁוּק. זֶה בָּא אֵצֶל זֶה, וְזֶה בָּא אֵצֶל זֶה, וְכָךְ הֵם אוֹמְרִים: "אִם שֶׁלִּי הוּא פֶּסַח זֶה, יָדֶיךָ מְשׁוּכוֹת מִשֶּׁלָּךְ וְנִמְנֵיתָ עַל שֶׁלִּי; וְאִם שֶׁלָּךְ הוּא פֶּסַח זֶה, יָדַי מְשׁוּכוֹת מִשֶּׁלִּי וְנִמְנֵיתִי עַל שֶׁלָּךְ."

פרק עשירי

[א] עַרְבֵי פְּסָחִים סָמוּךְ לַמִּנְחָה, לֹא יֹאכַל אָדָם עַד שֶׁתֶּחְשַׁךְ. וַאֲפִלּוּ עָנִי שֶׁבְּיִשְׂרָאֵל לֹא יֹאכַל עַד שֶׁיָּסֵב. וְלֹא יִפְחֲתוּ לוֹ מֵאַרְבָּעָה כוֹסוֹת שֶׁל יַיִן, וַאֲפִלּוּ מִן הַתַּמְחוּי.

[ב] מָזְגוּ לוֹ כוֹס רִאשׁוֹן. בֵּית שַׁמַּאי אוֹמְרִים: מְבָרֵךְ עַל הַיּוֹם, וְאַחַר כָּךְ מְבָרֵךְ עַל הַיַּיִן. וּבֵית הִלֵּל אוֹמְרִים: מְבָרֵךְ עַל הַיַּיִן, וְאַחַר כָּךְ מְבָרֵךְ עַל הַיּוֹם.

[ג] הֵבִיאוּ לְפָנָיו; מְטַבֵּל בַּחֲזֶרֶת עַד שֶׁמַּגִּיעַ לְפַרְפֶּרֶת הַפַּת. הֵבִיאוּ לְפָנָיו מַצָּה וַחֲזֶרֶת וַחֲרֹסֶת וּשְׁנֵי תַבְשִׁילִין, אַף עַל פִּי שֶׁאֵין חֲרֹסֶת מִצְוָה. רַבִּי

יד אברהם

lamb has not been left ownerless because the one member of the original company who transferred to the other group is still with it (*Rav*).

מוֹשְׁכִין לָהֶן אֶחָד מִכָּל חֲבוּרָה וַחֲבוּרָה . . . — *They take to themselves one person from each group*. For example, if there were five groups of five members each, five new groups are formed, each comprised of one member from each of the original groups, thereby ensuring that at least one of the original owners retained his original registration. Four of the new group say to the fifth member: If the *pesach* we have chosen was originally yours, four of us have withdrawn from our four respective offerings and register upon yours. Then the fifth member [to whom this declaration had been directed] joins with three of the other members and forms a new foursome (e.g., members 1, 2, 3, 5) who will now direct this formula to another member (e.g., member 4). So they continue until each member has had this declaration made to himself by the other four. This must be repeated in all the groups (*Rav*).

11. שְׁנַיִם שֶׁנִּתְעָרְבוּ פִּסְחֵיהֶם — *[If] the pesach offerings of two [individuals] were confused*. Reuven and Shimon had each designated an animal for his *pesach*, and had not yet registered a group upon it. The animals' identity then became confused before the slaughter. To rectify the situation [and keep each one valid as a *pesach*], each must register another person on his original *pesach*, whichever it happens to be, and take one animal [e.g. Reuven, A; Shimon, B]. In this manner they will be

able to switch registrations without leaving either offering ownerless even momentarily. For example, Reuven added Levi to his original *pesach*, while Shimon added Yehudah. Reuven then goes to the animal B, now held by Shimon and Yehudah, and tells Yehudah, 'If this *pesach* taken by Shimon is actually mine, then Shimon had no power to register you on *this* animal, and you are [really] registered on the other one. Therefore, I ask you to withdraw from that animal and register with me on this one. On the other hand, if this is truly Shimon's animal, you [Yehudah] *are* registered on it, and I [Reuven] withdraw from my original animal and register on this one with you.' Shimon then makes the same declaration to Levi in regard to the animal A. Accordingly, regardless of which animal originally belonged to whom, Reuven is now a partner with Yehudah in animal B, while Shimon and Levi are partners in A.

CHAPTER TEN

1. This final chapter of *Pesachim* deals with the Seder ritual. In the Temple era this included eating the *pesach* offering at the end of the meal. The Seder [literally *order*] assures the fulfillment of the many Biblical and Rabbinical *mitzvos* of the evening.

סָמוּךְ לַמִּנְחָה — *Close to the Minchah [period]*, from approximately 3 P.M. until it becomes dark one may not eat so that he will have a good appetite for the matzah. It is a הִדּוּר מִצְוָה, *enhancement of the mitzvah*, that it be done with gusto (*Gem.*). [However, one may eat small amounts of vegetables and fruits if he does not

[324] מ
שניות פסחים

they declare the following: 'If this pesach is ours, [then] you are withdrawn from your own [pesach] and are registered on ours. But if this pesach is yours, then we withdraw from ours and register on yours.' Similarly, if there were five groups [whose offerings were confused], each comprising five or ten [members], they take to themselves one person from each group and declare the same.

[11] *[If] the pesach offerings of two [individuals] were confused, each takes one [of them] for himself, and each registers some stranger with him. [Then] each goes to the other's [pesach] and says thus: 'If this pesach offering is mine, [then] you are withdrawn from yours and are registered upon mine; and if that pesach offering is yours, I am withdrawn from mine and am registered upon yours.'*

CHAPTER TEN

[1] **עַרְבֵי** *On the eve of Passover close to the Minchah [period], a person may not eat until it becomes dark. Even the poorest man in Israel may not eat unless he reclines. And they [the administrators of the charities] must provide him with not less than four cups of wine, even though he is supported from the [charity] plate.*

[2] *They pour the first cup [of wine] for him. Beis Shammai say: He recites the benediction regarding the day and then the benediction over the wine. But Beis Hillel say: He [first] recites the benediction over the wine and then the benediction regarding the day.*

[3] *They [then] bring [vegetables] before him; he eats dipped lettuce before he reaches the course secondary to the matzah. They bring matzah, lettuce, charoses, and two cooked dishes before him; although the charoses is not a mitzvah. R'*

YAD AVRAHAM

gorge himself (ibid.).]

עַד שֶׁיָּסֵב — *Unless he reclines.* Reclining during a meal was regarded as the mark of a free man, and the Seder celebration requires that one's action conform to the habits of the liberated. Therefore, even a person who does not customarily recline must do so while eating the matzah and drinking the four cups at the Seder, even if he must recline on a hard bench (see *O. Ch.* 472:2).

מֵאַרְבָּעָה כּוֹסוֹת שֶׁל יַיִן — *Than four cups of wine,* although this is a Rabbinic *mitzvah.* It goes without saying that the charities must provide the poor with matzah and food.

וַאֲפִלּוּ מִן הַתַּמְחוּי — *Even though he is* [from among the poorest of the poor, who are] *supported from the [charity] plate,* i.e., the food collected every day to be distributed that evening to the neediest.

2. כּוֹס רִאשׁוֹן — *The first cup* over which *Kiddush* is said. This contains two blessings, one for the wine [בּוֹרֵא פְּרִי הַגָּפֶן], and a second for the festival day: מְקַדֵּשׁ יִשְׂרָאֵל וְהַזְּמַנִּים. Beis Shammai reason that the benediction regarding the day be said first because the holiness of the festival began at nightfall, long before the wine is brought for *Kiddush.* In addition, the sanctity of the day is the reason that *Kiddush* is recited over wine. However, Beis Hillel reason the reverse, because if one has no wine (or bread), *Kiddush* is not recited. Moreover, the benediction over wine is more frequently used than *Kiddush,* which gives it precedence (*Gem.*).

3. מְטַבֵּל בַּחֲזֶרֶת — *He eats dipped lettuce,* i.e., the *karpas* dipped in salt water (*Rashbam*). The vegetable need not be lettuce; the mishnah states lettuce to teach that if he uses lettuce, he has not

fulfilled his obligation to eat *maror* (see 2:6). Why is it necessary to eat vegetables at this point? So that the children will [be provoked to] ask (*Gem.*).

עַד שֶׁמַּגִּיעַ לְפַרְפֶּרֶת הַפַּת — *Before he reaches the course secondary to the matzah,* i.e., the part of the meal not eaten with the matzah, but after it; in this case, *maror.* Thus, the mishnah teaches that eating dipped lettuce takes place before the eating of *maror.*

הֵבִיאוּ לְפָנָיו . . . — *They bring . . . before him . . .* The entire table, ostensibly containing all the essentials of the meal, had been before him previously (with the lettuce). *Tosafos* explain that after the dipped lettuce had been eaten, the table with the foodstuffs on it was removed in order to draw the children's attention and cause them to ask why. The matzah and bitter herbs must now be returned so that the *Haggadah* may be said over them (see mishnah 5).

וַחֲזֶרֶת — *Lettuce,* for the *mitzvah* of *maror,* bitter herbs. This is the first choice among the five vegetables mentioned as valid (2:6).

וַחֲרֹסֶת — *And charoses* as a dipping sauce for the *maror,* although it is not a required *mitzvah.* Rav describes *charoses* as made from figs, nuts, and many types of fruit, especially apples. These ingredients are pounded to a pulp, and [fruit] vinegar is added. Thin spice fibers, e.g., cinnamon, are placed upon it, to resemble the straw which was mixed into the mortar in Egypt. The *charoses* should have a thick texture as a remembrance of the טִיט, *mortar,* made by the Jews in Egypt (*Gem.*). See *Rama, O. Ch.* 473:6. R' Eliezer bar R' Tzadok maintains that using *charoses* is a *mitzvah* because of its symbolism. The apple tree was instrumental in the Jewish nation's fertility in Egypt (*Shir*

אֱלִיעֶזֶר בְּרַבִּי צָדוֹק אוֹמֵר: מִצְוָה. וּבַמִּקְדָּשׁ הָיוּ מְבִיאִין לְפָנָיו גּוּפוֹ שֶׁל פֶּסַח.

[ד] מָזְגוּ לוֹ כוֹס שֵׁנִי; וְכָאן הַבֵּן שׁוֹאֵל אָבִיו. וְאִם אֵין דַּעַת בַּבֵּן, אָבִיו מְלַמְּדוֹ: "מַה נִּשְׁתַּנָּה הַלַּיְלָה הַזֶּה מִכָּל הַלֵּילוֹת? שֶׁבְּכָל הַלֵּילוֹת אָנוּ אוֹכְלִין חָמֵץ וּמַצָּה, הַלַּיְלָה הַזֶּה כֻּלּוֹ מַצָּה. שֶׁבְּכָל הַלֵּילוֹת אָנוּ אוֹכְלִין שְׁאָר יְרָקוֹת, הַלַּיְלָה הַזֶּה מָרוֹר. שֶׁבְּכָל הַלֵּילוֹת אָנוּ אוֹכְלִין בָּשָׂר צָלִי שָׁלוּק וּמְבֻשָּׁל, הַלַּיְלָה הַזֶּה כֻּלּוֹ צָלִי. שֶׁבְּכָל הַלֵּילוֹת אָנוּ מַטְבִּילִין פַּעַם אַחַת, הַלַּיְלָה הַזֶּה שְׁתֵּי פְעָמִים." וּלְפִי דַעְתּוֹ שֶׁל בֵּן אָבִיו מְלַמְּדוֹ. מַתְחִיל בִּגְנוּת וּמְסַיֵּם בְּשֶׁבַח. וְדוֹרֵשׁ מֵ"אֲרַמִּי אֹבֵד אָבִי" עַד שֶׁיִּגְמֹר כָּל הַפָּרָשָׁה כֻּלָּהּ.

[ה] רַבָּן גַּמְלִיאֵל הָיָה אוֹמֵר: כָּל שֶׁלֹּא אָמַר שְׁלֹשָׁה דְבָרִים אֵלּוּ בַּפֶּסַח, לֹא יָצָא יְדֵי חוֹבָתוֹ. וְאֵלּוּ הֵן: פֶּסַח, מַצָּה, וּמָרוֹר. פֶּסַח — עַל שׁוּם שֶׁפָּסַח הַמָּקוֹם עַל בָּתֵּי אֲבוֹתֵינוּ בְּמִצְרָיִם. מַצָּה — עַל שׁוּם שֶׁנִּגְאֲלוּ אֲבוֹתֵינוּ בְּמִצְרָיִם. מָרוֹר — עַל שׁוּם שֶׁמֵּרְרוּ הַמִּצְרִיִּים אֶת חַיֵּי אֲבוֹתֵינוּ בְּמִצְרָיִם.

בְּכָל דּוֹר וָדוֹר חַיָּב אָדָם לִרְאוֹת אֶת עַצְמוֹ כְּאִלּוּ הוּא יָצָא מִמִּצְרַיִם — שֶׁנֶּאֱמַר: "וְהִגַּדְתָּ לְבִנְךָ בַּיּוֹם הַהוּא לֵאמֹר, בַּעֲבוּר זֶה עָשָׂה ה' לִי בְּצֵאתִי מִמִּצְרָיִם." לְפִיכָךְ אֲנַחְנוּ חַיָּבִין לְהוֹדוֹת, לְהַלֵּל, לְשַׁבֵּחַ, לְפָאֵר, לְרוֹמֵם, לְהַדֵּר, לְבָרֵךְ, לְעַלֵּה, וּלְקַלֵּס לְמִי שֶׁעָשָׂה לַאֲבוֹתֵינוּ וְלָנוּ אֶת כָּל הַנִּסִּים הָאֵלּוּ: הוֹצִיאָנוּ מֵעַבְדוּת לְחֵרוּת, מִיָּגוֹן לְשִׂמְחָה, וּמֵאֵבֶל לְיוֹם טוֹב, וּמֵאֲפֵלָה לְאוֹר גָּדוֹל, וּמִשִּׁעְבּוּד לִגְאֻלָּה! וְנֹאמַר לְפָנָיו: "הַלְלוּיָהּ!"

[ו] עַד הֵיכָן הוּא אוֹמֵר? בֵּית שַׁמַּאי אוֹמְרִים: עַד "אֵם הַבָּנִים שְׂמֵחָה." וּבֵית הִלֵּל אוֹמְרִים: עַד "חַלָּמִישׁ לְמַעְיְנוֹ מָיִם." וְחוֹתֵם בִּגְאֻלָּה." רַבִּי

יד אברהם

HaShirim 8:5, Sotah 11b), and the charoses also symbolizes the mortar produced by the slave labor of the Jews in Egypt (Gem.). The halachah follows this view (O. Ch. 475:1).

וּשְׁנֵי תַבְשִׁילִין — And two cooked dishes, to commemorate the pesach and chagigah sacrifices (6:3-4) (Gem.). It is customary nowadays to take a roasted shank bone and a boiled egg (O. Ch. 473:4). The roasted shank bone may not be eaten, for it is forbidden to eat roasted meat at the Seder in the absence of a pesach offering (4:4).

4. מָזְגוּ לוֹ כוֹס שֵׁנִי — They pour a second cup [of wine] for him prior to beginning the Haggadah, to arouse the child's curiosity (Rashi).

וְכָאן הַבֵּן שׁוֹאֵל אָבִיו — And at this point the son asks of his father the Four Questions. Even if the son is intelligent enough to formulate his own questions, there is an obligation to ask the four listed here.

הַלַּיְלָה הַזֶּה מָרוֹר — But on this night [we eat] bitter herbs; but we do not say כֻּלּוֹ מָרוֹר, only bitter herbs, for we do eat other vegetables, e.g., karpas for the first dipping.

הַלַּיְלָה הַזֶּה כֻּלּוֹ צָלִי — But on this night [we eat the meat] only

roasted. This question was posed only when the Temple stood. In our days the question about reclining is substituted for it. The mishnah follows the view that the chagigah eaten with the Pesach must also be roasted. Therefore, it is correct to say only (כֻּלּוֹ) roasted.

אָנוּ מַטְבִּילִין פַּעַם אַחַת — We might eat dipped vegetables once. The Gemara emends the text to read, אֵין אָנוּ מַטְבִּילִין אֲפִלּוּ פַּעַם אַחַת, We do not dip [greens] even one time, i.e., it is not customary to eat even one course of greens before the meal.

דַעְתּוֹ שֶׁל בֵּן — The son's [level of] intelligence. The father's response should be geared to the mental level of the child.

מַתְחִיל בִּגְנוּת... — He begins [the Haggadah] with a narrative of Israel's shameful origins. The Gemara presents two views about this: Rav says it refers to the passage עֲבָדִים הָיִינוּ, We were slaves to Pharaoh in Egypt; Shmuel says it is מִתְּחִלָּה עוֹבְדֵי עֲבוֹדָה זָרָה הָיוּ אֲבוֹתֵינוּ, In the beginning our ancestors were idol worshipers . . . Our version of the Haggadah includes both views.

וּמְסַיֵּם בְּשֶׁבַח — And concludes with a recital of the glory with which God has blessed us; for He brought us close to His service, and took our ancestors from Egypt.

Eliezer bar R' Tzadok says: [The dipping is] a mitzvah. In the Temple they would [also] bring the body of the pesach [offering] before him.

[4] *They pour a second cup [of wine] for him; and at this point the son asks of his father. If the son lacks [sufficient] understanding, his father instructs him [to ask]: 'Why is this night different from all [other] nights? On all [other] nights we may eat either chametz or matzah, but on this night only matzah. On all [other] nights we eat other greens, but on this night [we eat] bitter herbs. On all [other] nights we eat meat roasted, stewed, or cooked, but on this night [we eat the meat] only roasted. On all [other] nights we might eat dipped vegetables once, but on this night [we must do so] twice.' The father instructs the son according to [the] son's [level of] intelligence. He begins [the Haggadah] with [a recitation of our national] disgrace and concludes with the glory; and he expounds [the passage of], 'The Aramean sought to destroy my father,' until he concludes the entire passage [relating to the Exodus] (Deut. 26:5-8).*

[5] *Rabban Gamliel used to say: Whoever has not explained [the reasons for] these three things at the Pesach [Seder] has not fulfilled his obligation. They are: the pesach [offering], the matzah, and the maror. The pesach [is offered] — because the Omnipresent One passed over the houses of our ancestors in Egypt. Matzah [is eaten] — because our ancestors were redeemed in Egypt. Maror [is eaten] — because the Egyptians embittered the lives of our ancestors in Egypt.*

In every generation a man must regard himself as if he himself had gone out of Egypt — for it is said (Ex. 13:8): 'And you shall tell your son on that day saying, for the sake of this Hashem did for me when I went out of Egypt.' Therefore we are obliged to give thanks, praise, laud, glorify, exalt, honor, bless, extol, and shower acclaim upon Him Who performed all these miracles for our ancestors and for us: He brought us forth from slavery to freedom, from sorrow to joy, from mourning to festivity, from darkness to great light, and from servitude to redemption! So let us say before Him: Halleluyah!

[6] *How far does one recite [the Hallel]? Beis Shammai say: Until [the verse], 'A joyful mother of children' (Psalms 113:8). But Beis Hillel say: Until [the verse], 'The flint into a spring of water' (Psalms 114:8). He concludes [the Haggadah recital] with [a*

YAD AVRAHAM

וְדוֹרֵשׁ . . . — *And he expounds . . .* The *Haggadah's* method takes the form of citing one complete verse from this passage and then giving the midrashic exposition of it phrase by phrase. The next verse is then recited and expounded phrase by phrase, and so on until the portion is concluded.

5. לֹא יָצָא יְדֵי חוֹבָתוֹ — *Has not fulfilled his obligation* of Haggadah in an ideal manner; however, the basic obligation has been discharged without the explanation (*Ran*). Others suggest that without the explanation, one has not [fully] fulfilled even his obligation to eat them.

מַצָּה – עַל שׁוּם שֶׁנִּגְאֲלוּ אֲבוֹתֵינוּ בְּמִצְרַיִם — *Matzah [is eaten] — because our ancestors were redeemed in Egypt* and our ancestors had no time to leaven their dough before they left Egypt (*Haggadah*).

כְּאִלּוּ הוּא יָצָא מִמִּצְרַיִם — *As if he himself had gone out of Egypt*, i.e., as if he was redeemed this very night (*Rambam*).

וְנֹאמַר לְפָנָיו ,,הַלְלוּיָהּ״ — *So let us say before Him: 'Halleluyah!'* 'Who instituted this *Hallel*? The prophets among them [i.e., the Jews departing from Egypt] instituted that Israel should recite *Hallel* for every festival and at every misfortune — may it not come upon them! — from which they are redeemed, as thanks for their redemption' (*Gem.*).

6. עַד הֵיכָן הוּא אוֹמֵר — *How far does one recite [the Hallel]* before the meal? *Hallel* is cut short before the meal to help finish the *Haggadah* quicker, so that the children will not fall asleep before eating matzah (*Gem.*). Thus, only the section alluding to the Exodus is attached to the *Haggadah*; the rest, which alludes to the future redemption, is left for after the meal (*Tos. Yom Tov*). *Maharal* explains that the purpose of dividing the *Hallel* is to demonstrate that the praises are being said in conjunction with the feast of redemption. Indeed, by this insertion the Sages symbolized that the very feast of Pesach is a form of praise. Beis

טַרְפוֹן אוֹמֵר: ,,אֲשֶׁר גְּאָלָנוּ וְגָאַל אֶת אֲבוֹתֵינוּ מִמִּצְרַיִם,'' וְלֹא הָיָה חוֹתֵם. רַבִּי עֲקִיבָא אוֹמֵר: ,,כֵּן ה' אֱלֹהֵינוּ וֵאלֹהֵי אֲבוֹתֵינוּ יַגִּיעֵנוּ לְמוֹעֲדִים וְלִרְגָלִים אֲחֵרִים, הַבָּאִים לִקְרָאתֵנוּ לְשָׁלוֹם, שְׂמֵחִים בְּבִנְיַן עִירֶךְ וְשָׂשִׂים בַּעֲבוֹדָתֶךָ. וְנֹאכַל שָׁם מִן הַזְּבָחִים וּמִן הַפְּסָחִים,'' כו' עַד ,,בָּרוּךְ אַתָּה ה', גָּאַל יִשְׂרָאֵל.''

[ז] מָזְגוּ לוֹ כוֹס שְׁלִישִׁי, מְבָרֵךְ עַל מְזוֹנוֹ; רְבִיעִי, גּוֹמֵר עָלָיו אֶת הַהַלֵּל, וְאוֹמֵר עָלָיו בִּרְכַּת הַשִּׁיר. בֵּין הַכּוֹסוֹת הַלָּלוּ, אִם רוֹצֶה לִשְׁתּוֹת יִשְׁתֶּה; בֵּין שְׁלִישִׁי לִרְבִיעִי לֹא יִשְׁתֶּה.

[ח] וְאֵין מַפְטִירִין אַחַר הַפֶּסַח אֲפִיקוֹמָן. יָשְׁנוּ מִקְצָתָן, יֹאכֵלוּ; כֻּלָּן, לֹא יֹאכֵלוּ. רַבִּי יוֹסֵי אוֹמֵר: נִתְנַמְנְמוּ, יֹאכֵלוּ; נִרְדְּמוּ, לֹא יֹאכֵלוּ.

[ט] הַפֶּסַח אַחַר חֲצוֹת מְטַמֵּא אֶת הַיָּדַיִם. הַפִּגּוּל וְהַנּוֹתָר מְטַמְּאִין אֶת הַיָּדַיִם.

בֵּרַךְ בִּרְכַּת הַפֶּסַח, פָּטַר אֶת שֶׁל זֶבַח; בֵּרַךְ אֶת שֶׁל זֶבַח, לֹא פָטַר אֶת שֶׁל פֶּסַח; דִּבְרֵי רַבִּי יִשְׁמָעֵאל. רַבִּי עֲקִיבָא אוֹמֵר: לֹא זוֹ פוֹטֶרֶת זוֹ, וְלֹא זוֹ פוֹטֶרֶת זוֹ.

יד אברהם

Shammai break the recitation of the *Hallel* before the second paragraph because the redemption described in it did not occur until midnight — when the firstborns died — and it behooves us to recite this as near to midnight as possible, i.e., after the meal. Beis Hillel include the second paragraph because this section of the Seder concludes by blessing God for redeeming Israel, and it would be incongruous to say this without mentioning its climactic event, the portion of *Hallel* that speaks of the Splitting of the Sea and the drowning of the Egyptian army.

רַבִּי טַרְפוֹן אוֹמֵר . . . — *R' Tarfon* gives an abbreviated text for this blessing and therefore rules there is no need to summarize it with a final blessing [as one would a lengthy blessing]. R' Akiva adopts R' Tarfon's text for the beginning of the blessing, but adds to it. Since this makes for a lengthy blessing, it requires a brief concluding blessing to summarize its major point (*Rav*).

7. מְבָרֵךְ עַל מְזוֹנוֹ — *He recites the benediction for his food*, i.e., the *Bircas HaMazon* that is recited after meals.

גּוֹמֵר עָלָיו אֶת הַהַלֵּל — *He completes the Hallel over* the fourth cup, having already recited one or two chapters of it before the meal (mishnah 6). After the completion of the regular *Hallel*, one should recite the הַלֵּל הַגָּדוֹל, *Great Hallel*, the title given to *Psalm* 136. That psalm is composed of twenty-six verses describing God's goodness, each of which ends with the refrain כִּי לְעוֹלָם חַסְדּוֹ, *for His kindness endures forever.*

בִּרְכַּת הַשִּׁיר — The 'Blessing of the Song.' R' Yehudah says it is יְהַלְלוּךָ, the blessing with which *Hallel* always concludes. R' Yochanan says it is נִשְׁמַת כָּל חַי, the long and beautiful song of praise — concluding with the blessing יִשְׁתַּבַּח, with which the first section of the morning service is concluded on the Sabbath and festivals. There are three customs regarding the exact

order of the praises and the concluding blessing; see *O. Ch.* 480.

בֵּין הַכּוֹסוֹת הַלָּלוּ . . . — *Between these cups*, i.e., between the first two cups and the last two cups, one may drink additional wine, if he wishes, but not between the third and fourth [cups], because he might become drunk and be unable to finish the *Haggadah*. However, we do not fear that drunkenness will result from drinking during the feast because wine does not have so intoxicating an effect when it is taken with food (*Rav*). However, there is a difference of opinion whether drinking is permitted between the first two cups as well (see *O. Ch.* 473:3).

8. וְאֵין מַפְטִירִין — *One may not conclude.* After eating the *pesach*, one may not conclude the meal by having dessert. This is a Rabbinical decree enacted so that 'the taste of the *pesach* and matzah remain in his mouth' (*Rambam*). As used in our mishnah, the word *afikoman* refers to desserts. Today it is applied to the final portion of matzah eaten in place of the *pesach* offering. The reason for this is that just as one does not eat an [*afikoman*] dessert after the meat of the *pesach*, so too, in the absence of the sacrifice, one does not conclude the Seder with desert. Since the Sages ordained that the Seder meal must be concluded with the final portion of matzah, it came to be called *afikoman*, dessert.

יָשְׁנוּ מִקְצָתָן . . . — *If some of the [party] fell asleep . . .* The mishnah (7:13) taught earlier that is forbidden for members of a group to eat their *pesach* offering in one location and finish it in another. Our mishnah teaches that under certain circumstances, the Rabbis decreed that the group is considered to have ceased to exist as a unit. For its members to reconstitute themselves even in the same place is forbidden Rabbinically, because it appears

blessing about] redemption. R' Tarfon says [its text is]: 'Who redeemed us and redeemed our ancestors from Egypt,' and he does not conclude [with a final blessing]. R' Akiva says [its text is]: '. . . so may HASHEM our God, and God of our ancestors, bring us to future festivals and pilgrimages, which approach us, in peace, gladdened in the rebuilding of Your city and joyful at Your service. May we eat there of the offerings and Pesach sacrifices. . .' until [the blessing], 'Blessed are You HASHEM Who has redeemed Israel.'

[7] *They pour a third cup [of wine] for him, [and] he recites the benediction for his food; a fourth [cup, and] he completes the Hallel over it, and recites the 'Blessing of the Song' over it. Between these cups, one may drink if he wishes; [but] one may not drink between the third and fourth cups.*

[8] *One may not conclude after the pesach with dessert. If some of the [party] fell asleep, they may [still] eat [the pesach]; if all [of them fell asleep], they may not eat. R' Yose says: If they dozed, they may eat; [but] if they fell into a deep sleep, they may not eat.*

[9] *After midnight, the pesach offering contaminates the hands. Piggul and leftover [sacrificial meat] contaminate the hands.*
Reciting the benediction over the pesach offering exempts the [chagigah] offering [as well; but] reciting the [chagigah] offering's [benediction] does not exempt that of the pesach offering; [these are] the words of R' Yishmael. R' Akiva says: Neither one exempts the other.

YAD AVRAHAM

similar to a case of the same group moving elsewhere to continue its eating. The Rabbis considered sleep equivalent to having concluded the meal and left the place, because when someone sleeps he cannot be considered as yet intending to resume the meal. If the meal is subsequently resumed, it is viewed as a different meal, and it is thus akin to a *pesach* eaten in two places. However, as long as at least some members of the group remained awake, the group is not viewed as having dissolved, and they may *all* still eat the *pesach,* even those who slept (*Rav*). This rule applies today to the *afikoman* matzah, which may not be eaten if the entire group has fallen asleep (*O.Ch.* 478:2), nor in two places (*Rama*).

נִתְנַמְנְמוּ, יאכֵלוּ — *If they* [merely] *dozed, they may eat.* The *Gemara* defines dozing as 'sleeping yet not sleeping, awake yet not awake, e.g., if someone calls him he answers, yet he cannot respond coherently; however, if he is reminded [of something] he recalls.'

9. הַפֶּסַח אַחַר חֲצוֹת — *After midnight, the pesach offering . . .* Like all other offerings on the last night allotted for their consumption, the *pesach* offering may be eaten only until midnight. However, our mishnah follows the view of R' Elazar ben Azaryah, that *the pesach differs from other offerings.* While they are prohibited only Rabbinically in the second half of the night — 'to keep a man distant from transgression' (*Berachos* 1:1) — the *pesach's* permissible term of eating expires at midnight by *Biblical* law. Consequently, at midnight, it is not only forbidden for consumption, it becomes נוֹתָר, *leftover.* The Rabbis decreed *tumah*-contamination upon the hands of any-

one touching leftover sacrificial meat. For other offerings this contamination applies only in the morning, when they become leftover.

However, in R' Akiva's view the *pesach* does not differ from other offerings; it, too, may be eaten until dawn under Biblical law, and is prohibited at midnight only Rabbinically. *Rambam* rules according to R' Akiva, while *Tosafos* adopt R' Elazar ben Azaryah's view. This disagreement has implications for current practice because the *afikoman* commemorates the *pesach* and is subject to the same laws. Similarly, the *mitzvah* of matzah is subject to the same time limitations (*Gem.*). Furthermore, even in R' Akiva's view one should ideally eat the matzah before midnight 'in order to keep distance from a transgression' (*Rosh*). *Shulchan Aruch* (477:1) rules that even the *afikoman* should be eaten before midnight. If one did not eat even the first portion of matzah before midnight, there is a question whether he may recite the blessing for the *mitzvah* of matzah (see *Mishnah Berurah*).

הַפִּגוּל — *Piggul* is a term denoting a sacrifice disqualified during the performance of the blood service by the offerer's intent for the meat to be eaten or for the sacrificial parts to be burned on the Altar after the time allotted by the Torah. Consumption of *piggul* meat is forbidden under penalty of *kares* and the Rabbis decreed *tumah* of the hands for touching it, as they did for leftover.

בֵּרַךְ בִּרְכַּת הַפֶּסַח . . . — *Reciting the benediction over the pesach offering . . .* Before partaking of the *pesach,* one recites a blessing, as for most *mitzvos.* This blessing also exempts the blessing that would otherwise be said for the *chagigah* brought in conjunction with the *pesach* (6:4). [Although nothing may be eaten after the *pesach* at the conclusion of the meal (m. 8), *Tzlach* demonstrates from *Rambam* that the *pesach* was eaten twice, once at the *beginning* of the meal immediately after matzah and *maror* (when the blessing was recited over it), and at least an olive's volume of *pesach* meat again at the end of the meal.]

However, reciting the *chagigah's* benediction does not exempt the *pesach,* because *the pesach* is not included in the term *offering* used in that blessing. R' Yishmael's view is that unlike other offerings, the *pesach* has its blood poured onto the wall of the Altar rather than thrown against it. Therefore, it is not included under the term זֶבַח, *offering,* and the blessing, *to eat the offering,* cannot exempt it. The term *pesach* can include the *chagigah,* however, because in R' Yishmael's view, even offerings whose blood should be thrown are valid if their blood was poured in the fashion of the *pesach.* R' Akiva holds that other offerings are *not* valid if their blood is poured upon the Altar and they therefore cannot be included in the term *pesach,* just as the *pesach* cannot be included under the term 'offering' (*Gem.*).

This volume is part of
THE ARTSCROLLSERIES®
an ongoing project of
translations, commentaries and expositions
on Scripture, Mishnah, Talmud, Halachah,
liturgy, history, the classic Rabbinic writings,
biographies, and thought.

For a brochure of current publications
visit your local Hebrew bookseller
or contact the publisher:

Mesorah Publications, ltd

4401 Second Avenue
Brooklyn, New York 11232
(718) 921-9000